REA's Books Are T...
They have rescued lots of grades and more!

(a sample of the <u>hundreds of letters</u> REA receives each year)

"Your books are great! They are very helpful, and have upped my grade in every class. Thank you for such a great product."
Student, Seattle, WA

"Your book has really helped me sharpen my skills and improve my weak areas. Definitely will buy more."
Student, Buffalo, NY

"Compared to the other books that my fellow students had, your book was the most useful in helping me get a great score."
Student, North Hollywood, CA

"I really appreciate the help from your excellent book. Please keep up your great work."
Student, Albuquerque, NM

"Your book was such a better value and was so much more complete than anything your competition has produced (and I have them all)!"
Teacher, Virginia Beach, VA

(more on next page)

(continued from previous page)

"Your books have saved my GPA, and quite possibly my sanity. My course grade is now an 'A', and I couldn't be happier."
Student, Winchester, IN

"These books are the best review books on the market. They are fantastic!"
Student, New Orleans, LA

"Your book was responsible for my success on the exam... I will look for REA the next time I need help."
Student, Chesterfield, MO

"I think it is the greatest study guide I have ever used!"
Student, Anchorage, AK

"I encourage others to buy REA because of their superiority. Please continue to produce the best quality books on the market."
Student, San Jose, CA

"Just a short note to say thanks for the great support your book gave me in helping me pass the test... I'm on my way to a B.S. degree because of you!"
Student, Orlando, FL

All You Need to Know!

MUSIC DICTIONARY

Louis C. Elson
Professor of Music Theory

and the staff of
Research & Education Association
Carl Fuchs, Chief Editor

Research & Education Association
61 Ethel Road West
Piscataway, New Jersey 08854

Dr. M. Fogiel, Director

SUPER REVIEW®
MUSIC DICTIONARY

Copyright © 2002 by Research & Education Association. All rights reserved. No part of this book may be reproduced in any form without permission of the publisher.

Printed in the United States of America

Library of Congress Control Number 2001091878

International Standard Book Number 0-87891-407-2

SUPER REVIEW is a registered trademark of
Research & Education Association, Piscataway, New Jersey 08854

WHAT THIS Super Review WILL DO FOR YOU

This **Super Review** lists the important terms used in music with their pronunciations and concise definitions. Where compound terms are not given, the words should be looked up separately.

Among the outstanding features of this **Super Review** are:

- The Italian music terminology. A number of Italian words are quite similar to their English equivalents and they can be therefore easily translated.

- The rules for pronouncing each language.

- English phonetic spelling is provided to aid in pronouncing foreign words, as well as the names of chief composers, singers, pianists, and conductors, for example.

- Illustrations are included wherever they can be helpful in contributing to the understanding of the terms.

- A list of popular errors and doubtful terms in music.

Dr. Max Fogiel, Director
Carl Fuchs, Chief Editor

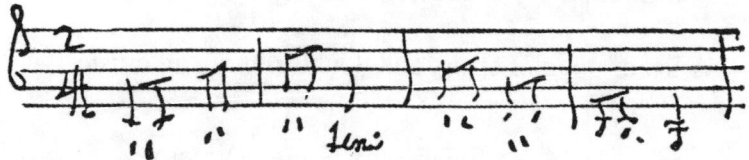

Franz Joseph Haydn

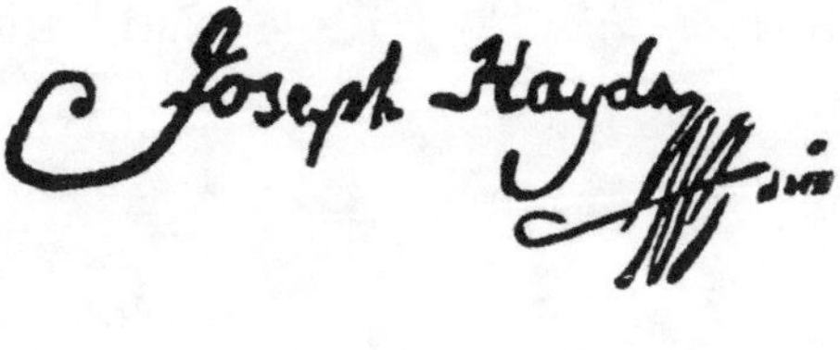

Contents

Section	Page
What This Super Review Will Do For You	v
Rules for the Pronunciation of German, Italian, and French	ix
Popular Errors and Doubtful Terms Found in Music	xii
The Music Dictionary	1
A List of Prominent Foreign Composers, Artists, etc.	291
A Short Vocabulary of English Musical Terms of Tempo or Expression, with their Italian Equivalents	302

Schubert's Monument

RULES FOR THE PRONUNCIATION OF GERMAN, ITALIAN, AND FRENCH

GERMAN

VOWELS

A has the sound of ä as in *far*.
Au is like ou in *house*.
Ai occurs but rarely, and has the sound of ī as in *pine*.
Ae or **ä** when long is like ā in *mate*; when short it is like ĕ in *met*.
Aeu or **äu** is like oy in *boy*.
E has (1) the sound of ĕ as in *help*, and (2) the sound of ā in *hate*.
Ei has always the sound of ī in *pine*.
Eu is like oi in *loiter*.
I has the sound of ĭ as in *pin*.
Ie takes the sound of ē as in *tree*.
O has (1) a long sound as in *tone*, and (2) a short sound as in *loss*.
Oe or **ö** has a sound somewhat like e in *err*, pronounced with lips held close together.
U has the sound of oo as in *moon*.
Ue or **ü** has the sound of the French ü.
Y is used only in foreign words, where it does not differ from i.

CONSONANTS

B and **d** are pronounced as in English.
C is only used in foreign words. Before e, i, and y it is pronounced like ts; before other vowels and consonants it is like k.
Ch has nothing corresponding to it in English, though the Scotch word *Loch* gives it exactly. It is a guttural aspirate, bearing the same relation to k as th does to t. At the beginning of words ch is like k.
Chs is pronounced like ks or x.

F, l, m, p, t, and **x** are the same as in English.
G has the hard sound as in *got*. In some parts of Germany the unaccented, final *ig* is softened into something like *ikh*.
H at the beginning of words is aspirated; between two vowels the aspiration is very weak, and before a consonant or at the end of words it is mute; but in this case it makes the preceding vowel long.
J is equivalent to the English y in *yet*, and is always followed by a vowel.
K is like the English k, but is never mute before n.
Ng sounds like ng in length; but in compound words where the first ends in n and the last begins with g, they are separated.
Q is always joined with u, and together they are pronounced like *kw*.
Ph has the sound of f.
Pf unites the two letters in one sound uttered with compressed lips.
R has a stronger sound than in English, and is the same at the beginning, middle, or end of a word.
S is like the English s. It is sounded at the end of words, and between two vowels it frequently takes the sound of z.
Sch is like the English sh in *ship*.
Th takes always the sound of t; h being silent. It has never the sound of th in *thee*.
Tz intensifies the sound of z.
V is pronounced like f.
W answers to the English v.
Z is pronounced like ts in *nets*.

In the German words defined and pro-

RULES FOR PRONUNCIATION

nounced in this work, the accented syllable, in words of two or more will be in Italics.

ITALIAN

VOWELS

A is always like ä in *father*.

E has (1) the sound of ĕ in *pen*, and (2) the sound of ā in *fate*.

I is pronounced like ē in *me*.

J is always a vowel, and at the beginning of a syllable is like y in *you*. At the end of a word it is like ē in *be*.

O has the sound (1) of ō in *tone;* and (2) that of ŏ in *not*.

U has always the sound of oo in *cool*.

CONSONANTS

B, d, f, l, n, p, q, v, are the same as in English.

C, before a, o, and u, has the sound of k; before e, i, and y it has the sound of tsh, or that of ch in the word *cheek*. When doubled (cc) and followed by e, i, or y, the first is pronounced like t, and the second takes its usual sound.

Ch, before e or i, has the sound of k.

G before a, o, or u, is hard as in *go;* before e or i, it has the sound of j or soft g as in *gem*. When doubled and followed by e or i, it has the sound of dj ; or like dg in *lodge*.

Gh, followed by e or i, is pronounced like g in *go*.

Gl, followed by i preceding another vowel, is pronounced like lli in *million*.

Gn, followed by a, e, i, o, or u, is like ni in the English word minion.

Gua, gue, gui, are pronounced gwä, gwā, gwē.

Gia, gio, giu, are pronounced djiä, djiō, djioo, in one syllable, giving the i a very faint sound.

S has (1) the soft sound as in *sis*, and (2) the hard sound as in *ease;* usually the latter when occurring between two vowels.

Sc, before e or i, is like sh in *shall;* before a, o, or u, it has the sound of sk.

Sch is always like sk, or sch in *school*.

Scia, scio, sciu, are pronounced shä, shō, shoo.

R, at the beginning of words, is like the English; but at the end of words or syllables, or when combined with another consonant, it should have a rolling sound.

W and x are not found in Italian, except in foreign words.

Z has usually the sound of ts; it is sometimes pronounced like dz.

Italian words are pronounced exactly as written, there being no silent letter except h. The vowels always preserve their proper sounds, forming no dipthongs and being uninfluenced by the consonants with which they may be combined.

In words of two or more syllables there is usually a slight emphasis placed on the penult, or ante-penult, but rarely on the last syllable.

FRENCH

VOWELS

A has two sounds ; ä as in *mass* and ă as in *bar*.

Ai is like ā in *fate*.

Au is similar to o in English.

E is (1) like ĕ in *met;* (2) like ā in fate; (3) similar to ŭ in *bud*. It is frequently silent at the end of words.

Ei is nearly like ā in *fate*.

Eu resembles e in *err*.

I has the sound (1) of ĭ in *pin* (2) of ē in *me*.

Ia has nearly the sound of ia in *medial*.

Ie is like ee in *bee*.

O is pronounced like ŏ in *rob;* and like ō in *rope*.

U has no equivalent in English, but resembles the sound of e in *dew*. By prolonging the sound of *e*, taking care not to introduce the sound of *w*, we get an approximate sound of the French *u*, or ü as it will be marked in this work.

Y, when initial, or coming between two consonants, or standing as a syllable by itself, is the same as the French *i;* but between two vowels it is equivalent to double i (ii), the first forming a dipthong with the preceding one, and the second with the one following.

M and n, when not nasal, have the same sound as in English; if preceded by a vowel in the same syllable, they are always nasal unless immediately followed by a vowel in the next syllable.

Am, an, em, en, are pronounced somewhat like *änh*.

x

RULES FOR PRONUNCIATION

Im, in, aim, ain, eim, ein, are pronounced like *ănh*.

Om and **on,** are like *ŏnh*.

Um and **un** are pronounced like *ŭnh*.

P is generally the same as in English. It is sometimes silent; and always when at the end of a word.

Q is usually followed by u, in which case they are together sounded like the letter k.

R is given more roughly than in English. It is often silent when preceded by the vowel *e*.

S has generally the same sound as in English; between two vowels it has generally the same sound as in the English word *rose*.

CONSONANTS

Final consonants are frequently silent.

B, at the beginning and in the middle of words, is the same as in English.

C has (1) the sound of k before a, o, or u; (2) when written with the cedilla, or before e, or i, it has the sound of s. C final is sounded, unless preceded by n, and has the sound of k.

Ch is pronounced like sh in *she*. In words derived from the Greek ch is pronounced like *k*.

D is the same as in English. It is often silent at the end of words.

F is like the English; when final it is usually sounded.

G before a, o, or u, is hard, as in *go ;* but before e, i, or y, it has the sound of z in the English word *azure*. In the combination gue, or gui, the u is silent, but the g takes its hard sound.

Gn is pronounced like ni in *union*.

H is mute or slightly aspirated.

J is pronounced like z in *azure.*

K has the same sound as in English.

L has the same sound as in English, and ll the liquid sound as in *million.*

Sc is the same as in English. S final is generally silent.

T has its hard English sound, but in tial, tiel, and tion, it has the sound of s.

Th is always the same as t alone. T final is usually silent.

V is like the English, only a little softer.

W is found only in foreign words, and is pronounced like *v.*

X, initial, is pronounced like gz; it occurs but in few words.

Ex, at the beginning of words, is sounded like egz. In other places, and between two vowels, it is pronounced like ks.

Z is like z in *zone.*

Final consonants, which would otherwise be silent, are frequently sounded by carrying them over to the next word when commencing with a vowel.

VOWEL SOUNDS AS USED IN PRONUNCIATION

ä as in *ah;* ā as in *hate;* ă as in *at;* ē as in *tree;* ĕ as in *eh;* ī as in *bine;* ĭ as in *pin;* ō as in *tone;* ô as in *dove;* ŏ as in *not;* ŭ as in *up;* ü the French sound of *u.*

POPULAR ERRORS AND DOUBTFUL TERMS FOUND IN MUSIC

Andantino. This word is generally used by musicians in the opposite sense from its Italian meaning. While its strict meaning is *slower* than "Andante," of which word it is the diminutive, it is now commonly used to indicate a tempo *less slow* than "Andante"; a rate of movement between "Andante" and "Allegretto."

Appoggiatura. Although the English use the term *short appoggiatura* for the short grace note, it is generally called "acciaccatura" in Italy. See *Appoggiatura* and *Acciaccatura*.

Arsis and Thesis. These terms are not used by musicians in the manner that they are employed in poetic scansion. See both words.

Bar. The vertical lines drawn across the staff to mark the metrical units of the music are called *bars*, and the units between these bars are called *measures*. The terms are not properly interchangeable, though often carelessly used as if they were synonymous. The *bar* is the line itself, the *measure* the space between the bars.

Bar-line. A barbarism that has arisen from the mistaken but frequent use of *bar* for *measure*.

Catgut. No musical strings are made of catgut, although always called so. Guitar, Violin, and Harp strings are made of the intestines of sheep, lamb, or goat. See *Gut*.

Clarinet. The spelling of this word as "Clarionet" is obsolete. It is spelled "Clarinette" or, more frequently, "Clarinet."

Common Time. A rather faulty term for $\frac{4}{4}$ rhythm (or measure). There is a widespread error regarding the sign ₵ which is *not* a "C" standing for "Common Time." See the article on *Time*.

Concerto. May be pronounced either as an Italian word (kontschairto) or as an English noun. "Soprano," "Scherzo," "Concerto," and numerous other musical words in constant use have become Anglicized in the course of time.

Concert Pitch. This is *not* the pitch used in our chief concerts. It is a very doubtful term. See *Pitch*.

Étude. This word is not pronounced "Etood" but "Ay-tüde, French *ü*, for since the English "Study" is its equivalent, it has not been adopted into our language.

Fantasia. The word is not pronounced "Fan-*tas*-ia" but "Fanta-*si*-a."

Flats and Sharps. These are used independently of the strict rules by almost all composers. Wherever a note is at all doubtful, the composer has a right to make its meaning sure by adding an accidental, even in defiance of the book rules.

Long Slurs. These are not amenable to any rules, almost every composer being a law unto himself in their employment in piano music. In vocal and violin music they are generally uniform, and have a more intelligible meaning. See *Slurs*.

M. M. This means "Maëlzel's Metronome" and *not* "Metronome Mark"

Mordent. Used in different senses by different teachers. See *Mordent*.

Obbligato. This word should *not* be spelled "obligato."

Piano. Although some modern dictionaries give only "pianoforte" as the noun, the word "piano" (as well as "pianist") has been sanctioned by usage.

Pitch. It is desirable *not* to write one-lined C as "C¹," but as c̄, or c′, and to be careful in every use of numerals

xii

POPULAR ERRORS AND DOUBTFUL TERMS FOUND IN MUSIC

in designating pitch, for the scientific usage of the numerals, found in every work on Acoustics, is different from the above, and endless confusion may result. See *Tablature*.

Portamento. It is unfortunate that this word means one thing to the pianist and a totally different one to the vocalist and violinist. See *Portamento*.

Sextolet. This group is very frequently found, even in the works of the great masters (Beethoven, Mozart, etc.) where two triplets are required. It is the most vague of the artificial groups. See NOTES.

Swell Mark. The mark <code>< ></code> is sometimes found on a single chord in piano music. It is here misemployed as an accent. In vocal exercises the swell is sometimes found in the *first lesson*. It ought not to be taught until the pupil has obtained good control of the breath, — after some months of practice.

Symphony. It was only after the advent of Haydn that this word began to mean a sonata for full orchestra. Before that time it meant a prelude, postlude, or interlude, or any short instrumental work. In an old English dictionary (Grassineau, 1740) we read: "Some there are who restrain Symphony to the sole music of instruments: In this sense they say that the *Recitatives* of such an Opera were intolerable, but the *Symphonies* excellent." In the earliest dictionary of Musical Terms in the English language (Brotherton, London, 1724), we find the word defined,— "*Symphony*, by which is to be understood Airs in two, three, and four Parts, for Instruments of any kind; or the Instrumental Parts of Songs, Motets, Operas, or Concertos, are so-called." It was in this sense that Handel used the word in his "Pastoral Symphony," in "The Messiah," and Bach gave forth his Three-voiced Inventions first, under the title of *Symphonies*. It may also be stated that the Italian word "Sinfonia" is often mispronounced "Sin-*fo*-nia." It should be "Sinfo-*ni*-a."

Tie. There are many teachers who regard the following  (with a dot over the second note) as a *tie*, and sound a single note only; but the consensus of opinion is that it is to be regarded as a *short slur*, and the second note is to be struck. Some teachers make a distinction between cases where the dot is *over* or *under* the slur, striking the second note in the latter case only.

Time. The misuse of this word is so universal that it may be accepted as correct by general usage. Yet it is to be desired that there should be one word for the speed of the composition and another for its rhythm. See *Time*, *Rhythm*, and *Metre*.

Turns. Turns are very often printed *over* short dotted notes when intended to be played *after*. See *Turn*.

Violoncello. This word should never be spelled or pronounced "Violincello." See *Violoncello*.

Waltz Rhythm. Although this is almost always written ¾, its actual pulsation is generally ⅜, two measures forming the measure unit.

ADDENDA

Accidentals. There is an old rule that if the last note of a measure is marked with an accidental, and the first note of the next measure is of the same pitch, this latter note is also affected by the accidental; this rule is obsolete and should never be taught. The effect of the accidental *ends* at the *bar* unless the note is *tied* into the next measure

Cello

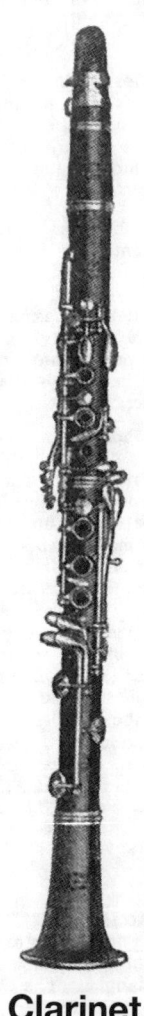

Clarinet

THE MUSIC DICTIONARY

A. 1. The alphabetical name given, in the United States and England, to the sixth tone of the diatonic major scale of C; in France and Italy called *La*.
2. Upon string instruments, the name of the string which, with the open tone, gives the sixth of the natural scale. In tuning, this string is usually first brought to the requisite pitch, and from it the others are then regulated; it is the first (smallest) string of the violoncello, the second of the violin, etc.
3. The first note of the natural minor scale the relative of C major, which, as the older scale, begins on the first letter of the alphabet. See *C*.
4. The note from which the orchestra is tuned, usually sounded by the oboe. See *Oboe*.

A. (It.) (äh.) By, for, to, at, in, etc.

Ab (Ger.) Off. Used in organ music to signify the discontinuance of certain stops.

A balláta (It.) (ä bäl-*lä*-tä.) In the style of a dance. See *ballata*.

Abandon (Fr.) (ä-bänh-dŏnh.) Without restraint; with self-abandon; with ease.

A battúta (It.) (ä bät-*too*-tä.) As beaten; strictly in time.

Abat-voix (Fr.) (ä-ba-vwä.) A voice reflector.

Abbacchiato (It.) (äb-bä-kē-ä-to.) With a dejected, melancholy expression.

Abbadare (It.) (äb-bä-dä-rē.) Take care; pay attention.

Abbandonási (It.) (äb-bän-dō-*nä*-zē.) Without restraint: with passionate expression.

Abbandonataménte (It.) (äb-bän-dō-nä-tä-*men*-tē.) Vehemently; violently.

Abbandóne (It.) (äb-bän-*dō*-nĕ.) Making the time subservient to the expression; despondingly; with self-abandonment.

Abbandonevolménte (It.) (äb-bän-dŏ-nĕ-vōl-*men*-tē.) Violently; vehemently; without restraint as to time.

Abbandóno (It.) (äb-bän-*dō*-nō.) With passionate expression; with abandon.

Abbassaménto di mano (It.) (äb-bäs-sä-*men*-tō dē mä-nō.) The down-beat, or descent of the hand in beating time.

Abbassaménto di vóce (It.) (äb-bäs-sä-*men*-tō dē vō-tshĕ.) Diminishing or lowering of the voice.

Abbelláre (It.) (äb-bĕl-*lä*-rē.) To embellish with ornaments.

Abbelliménti (It.) (äb-bĕl-lē-*men*-tē.) Ornaments introduced to embellish a plain melody.

Abbelliménto (It.) (äb-bĕl-lē-*men*-tō.) A grace note or ornament.

Abbellire (It.) (äb-bĕl-lēe-rē.) To embellish with ornaments.

Abbellitúra (It.) (äb-bĕl-lē-*too*-rä.) An ornament, embellishment.

Abbellitúre (It.) (äb-bĕl-lē-*too*-rē.) Ornaments; embellishments.

Abblasen (Ger.) (äb-blä-z'n.) To sound or flourish the trumpet; to sound the retreat.

Abbreviaménti (It.) (äb-brā-vē-ä-*men*-tē.) Abbreviations in musical notation.

Abbreviáre (It.) (äb-bre-vē-*ä*-rē.) To abbreviate or shorten the labor of notation.

Abbreviation marks. 1. Oblique strokes which distinguish the *eighth*, *sixteenth*, or *thirty-second* notes, when applied to the stem of the *quarter* or *half-note*, signify as many repetitions of the shorter note thus indicated as are equal to the longer note represented. Thus:

ABBREVIATIONS

2. A diagonal stroke with a dot each side signifies a repetition of the preceding measure.

3. When the long notes are subdivided, the oblique strokes, distinguishing *eighth*, *sixteenth* notes, etc., are sometimes employed to denote a repetition of such short notes: Thus, ⸺ ⸺ ⸺ indicate a repetition of eighths, sixteenths, thirty-seconds, respectively.

4. A short horizontal line, a row of dots, or a waving line is used to express the repetition, or a continuation of the influence, of the preceding character. Thus:

mi—sol—do

5. Figures when placed upon the staff, or over a measure in which rests are written, serve to indicate the number of whole rests or measures of silence. See *Rests*.

6. Groups of notes are sometimes abbreviated as follows:

7. The word "Simili," or "Segue" is sometimes used to continue a group in the same manner as the printed model.

8. The sign called "the direct" (𝄪) means to continue in the same manner, and at the same time indicates the first note of each succeeding group, as:

9. "Come Sopra" is sometimes used as an abbreviation, meaning to play the same notes as the part written above.

10. On concert programs certain abbreviations serve to identify an old work, composed before the opus-number was regularly used. These marks are often met with in connection with Mozart and Haydn compositions. Thus *P.* means Peters edition; *B. & H*, Breitkopf & Haertel; *K*, Köchel's catalog of Mozart's works. *B. & H.* 10 — No. 10 Breitkopf & Haertel's edition; *K. 8*, No. 8 in Köchel's catalog.

11. Abbreviations for divisions of musical form (generally used in sonatas) are derived from the German. They are Hs. (Hauptsatz) chief theme; Ss. (Seitensatz) subordinate theme; Zws. (Zwischensatz) intermediate theme; Schls. (Schlusssatz) closing theme; Rg. (Rückgang) returning passage; Ug. (Uebergang) transition; D (Durchführung) or Ds. (Durchführungssatz) development; Ms. (Mittelsatz) middle part; and Anh. (Anhang) Coda.

12. Abbreviations of Hymn Metres are as follows: L.M., Long Metre; C.M., Common Metre; S.M., Short Metre; L.P.M., Long Particular Metre; C. P.M., Common Particular Metre; S.P.M., Short Particular Metre; L. M.D., Long Metre Double; C.M.D., Common Metre Double; S.M.D., Short Metre Double; H.M., Hallelujah Metre. Numerals are also used, as 7s, meaning seven syllables to a line; 8s & 7s, meaning that the lines alternate eight and seven syllables; P. M., Particular Metre.

The following are some of the abbreviations found in modern music:

ă as in *ah*; ā as in *hate*; ă as in *at*; ē as in *tree*; ĕ as in *eh*; ī as in *pine*; ĭ as in *pin*;

ABBREVIATIONS

LIST OF GENERALLY USED ABBREVIATIONS

accel.	accelerando
accomp.	accompaniment
Adg° or Ad°	Adagio
ad lib. or ad libit.	ad libitum
Aevia	Alleluia
affett°	affettuoso
affrett°	affrettando
ag° or agit	agitato
All°	Allegro
Allgett°	Allegretto
all' ott.	all' ottava
al seg.	al segno
And^no	Andantino
And^te	Andante
Anim°	animato
arc.	arcato, or coll' arco
arp°	arpeggio
a t. or a tem.	a tempo
B. C. or Bass Con.	basso continuo
Bl.	Bläser
Br.	Bratschen
Brill.	brillante
c. a.	coll' arco
cad.	cadenza
cal.	calando
calm.	calmato
cant.	canto
cantab.	cantabile
C.B.	contra basso or col basso
c.B.	col Basso
Cb.	Contrabässe
c.d.	colla destra
c.f.	canto fermo
cello	violoncello
cemb.	cembalo
Ch.	choir organ
Clar.	clarinet
Clar°	clarino
col c.	col canto
coll' ott.	coll' ottava
c. 8va	coll' ottava
con espr.	con espressione
cont.	contano
Cor.	corno
c.p.	colla parte
cresc.	crescendo
c.s.	colla sinistra
c s. or co. so.	come sopra
C^to	concerto
c. voc.	colla voce
d.	destra, droite
D.C.	da capo
D.C.S.R.	da capo senza replica, or senza ripetizione
Dec.	decani
decresc.	decrescendo
dest.	destra
Diap.	diapasons
dim.	diminuendo
div.	divisi
dol.	dolce
dolciss.	dolcissimo
dopp. ped.	doppio pedale
D.S.	dal segno
esp. or espres.	espressivo
f.	forte
Fag.	fagotto
ff.	fortissimo
fff.	fortississimo
Fl.	flauto
F.O.	full organ
fp.	forte piano
fz. or forz.	forzato
G.	gauche
G.O.	great organ
Graz°	grazioso
Haut.	hautboy
Hlzbl.	Holzbläser
Hr. or Hrn.	Hörner
Intro.	Introduction
K.F.	Kleine Flöte
L.	Left
leg.	legato, leger
legg.	leggiero
l.h.	left hand, linke Hand
lusing.	lusingando
M.	manual
Magg.	Maggiore
manc.	mancando
marc.	marcato
m.d.	mano destra, or main droite
men.	meno
mez.	mezzo
mf.	mezzo forte
m.g.	main gauche
M.M.	Maëlzel's Metronome
mod. or modto	moderato
mor.	morendo
mp.	mezzo piano
MS.	manuscript
m.s.	mano sinistra
Mus. Bac. or Mus. B.	Bachelor of Music
Mus. Doc. or Mus. D.	Doctor of Music
m.v.	mezza voce
Ob.	oboe
Obb.	obbligato
Org.	organ
Ott., O^va, or 8va	ottava
p.	piano
p.a.p.	poco a poco

ŏ as in *tone*; ŏ as in *dove*; ŏ as in *not*; ŭ as in *up*; ü the French sound of *u*.

3

Abbreviation	Meaning
Ped.	pedal
Perd.	Perdendosi
P. F.	Più forte
Piang.	Piangendo
Pianiss.	Pianissimo
Pizz.	Pizzicato
PP.	Pianissimo
PPP.	Pianississimo
I^{ma}	Prima (volta)
I^{mo}	Primo
Q^{tte}	Quartet / Quintet
Rall.	Rallentando
Recit., or Rec.	Recitative
Rf., rfz., or rinf.	Rinforzando
R. H.	Right Hand, Rechte Hand
Ritar.	Ritardando
Riten., or Rit.	Ritenuto
S.	Senza
:§:	A Sign
Scherz.	Scherzando
2da	Seconda (volta)
2do	Secondo
Seg.	Segue
Sem. / Semp.	Sempre
7^{tt}	Septet
6^{tt}	Sestet
Sfz.	Sforzando
Sinf.	Sinfonia
Smorz.	Smorzando
S.R.	Senza ripetizione
S. S. / S. sord.	Senza sordini
Sos. / Sos^t.	Sostenuto
Spir.	Spiritoso
Stacc.	Staccato
St. Diap.	Stopped Diapason
String.	Stringendo
Sw.	Swell Organ
Sym.	Symphony
T.	Tenor, tutti, tempo
T. C.	Tre corde
Tem.	Tempo
Tem. I^o	Tempo primo
Ten.	Tenuto
Timb.	Timballes
Timp.	Timpani
Tr.	Trillo
Trem.	Tremolando
Tromb.	Trombi
Tromb.	Tromboni
T. S.	Tasto solo
U.	Una
U. C.	Una corda
Unis.	Unisoni
V.	Voce
V.	Volti
Va.	Viola
Var.	Variation
Vcllo.	Violoncello
Viv.	Vivace
Vo. / Vno. / $Viol^o$.	Violino
V.S.	Volti subito
V^{ni}	Violini

See also, *Trill, Signs, Rests,* and *Repeats.*

Abcidiren (Ger.) (äb-si-dir-'n.) A series of exercises in which the names of the notes are used instead of words.

Abellare (It.) (ä-bĕl-lä-rĕ.) To decorate, ornament, or embellish.

Abellimento (It.) (ä-bĕl-lē-men-tō.) A decoration, ornament, or embellishment.

Abendglocke (Ger.) (*ah*-bĕnd-*glŏk*-ĕ. Evening bell; curfew.

Abendlied (Ger.) (*ah*-bĕnd-leed.) Evening song or hymn.

Abendmusik (Ger.) (ä-bĕnd-moo-*zĭk*.) Evening or night music; serenade.

Abendständchen (Ger.) (ä-bĕnd-*stend*-schen.) A serenade.

Abgehen (Ger.) (*äb*-gā-ĕn.) To go off; to make an exit; to retire.

Abgestossen (Ger.) (*äb*-ghĕ-stōs-s'n.) Detached, struck off, staccato.

Ab initio (Lat.) (ăb ĭn-ē-shĭ-ō.) An obsolete term, of the same signification as *Da Capo.*

Abkürzen (Ger.) (*äb*-kiert-sen). To abridge, to abbreviate.

Abkürzung (Ger.) (*äb*-kiert-soong.) Abridgement, abbreviation.

Abnehmend (Ger.) (*äb*-nay-mend.) Diminishing.

Abrégé (Fr.) (ah-brayz-hay.) Abridgment; also, the trackers in an organ.

Abréger (Fr.) (ah-brayz-hay.) To curtail, to abridge.

Abruptio (Lat.) (*äb*-*rŭp*-shĭ-ō.) Breaking off; a sudden pause.

Absatz (Ger.) (*äb*-sätz.) A section or passage of music, usually consisting of four measures; also, a pause or stop; a cadence.

Absetzen (Ger.) (*äb*-sĕt-s'n.) A style of performance similar to *staccato.*

ä as in *ah;* ā as in *hate;* ă as in *at;* ē as in *tree;* ĕ as in *eh;* ī as in *pine;* ĭ as in *pin;*

ABSPIELEN — ACCENTOR

Abspielen (Ger.) (*äb*-speelen.) To perform on an instrument; to play a tune; to finish playing.

Absteigende Tonarten (Ger.) (*äb*-stygĕn-dĕ *tō*-när-t'n.) Descending scales or keys.

Abstossen (Ger.) (*äb*-stos-s'n.) Similar in manner of performance to staccato.

Abwechselnd (Ger.) (*äb*-veck-s'lnd.) Alternating, changing. In organ playing, alternately; in choir singing, antiphonally; in dance music, change of movements.

Académie de Musique (Fr.) An academy of music, consisting of professors and scholars; a society for promoting musical culture.

Académie spirituelle (Fr.) (äk-ä-dā-mē spĭ-rē-too-āl.) A performance or concert of sacred music.

A cappélla (It.) (ä käp-*pel*-lä.) In the church or chapel style, that is, vocal music, unaccompanied. So-called because the music of the Sistine chapel at Rome was purely vocal. Almost all of the old Masses, motetts, and madrigals were "a cappella."

A cappríccio (It.) (ä käp-*prit*-shē-ō.) In a capricious style; according to the taste of the performer.

Acathistus (Gr.) (äk-ä-*thĭs*-tŭs.) A hymn of praise sung in the ancient Greek church in honor of the Virgin.

Accadémia (It.) (äk-kä-*dāy*-mē-ä.) An academy; the word also means a concert.

Accarezzévole (It.) (äk-kä-rĕt-*zeh*-vō-lĕ.) Blandishing; in a persuasive and caressing manner.

Accarezzevolménte (It.) (äk-kä-rĕt-*zĕh*-vōl-*men*-tĕ.) Caressingly, coaxingly.

Accel. (It.) (ät-tshĕl.) An abbreviation of Accelerando.

Acceldo. An abbreviation of Accelerando.

Accelerándo (It.) (ät-tshĕl-er-*rän*-dō.) Accelerating the time; gradually increasing the velocity of the movement.

Acceleráto (It.) (ät-tshĕl-ä-*räh*-to.) Accelerated; increased rapidity.

Accent. A stress or emphasis upon a certain note or passage to mark its position in the measure, or its relative importance in regard to the composition. Accent is the force given to certain notes or chords greater than that upon the surrounding notes or chords. It can be either natural or artificial. The natural accent is indicated only by the rhythm-mark, since the succession of natural accents constitutes the rhythm. Yet not all of the natural accents are alike in stress. The primary accent, which falls upon the first beat of the measure in all rhythms, is called *Thesis* by musicians, although the term is not used with etymological correctness (see *Thesis* and *Arsis*). If there is a secondary accent in the measure, as the third beat in ¾ rhythm, or the fourth beat in ⁶⁄₈ rhythm, it is called *Arsis*. In some rhythms these are not clearly indicated by the figures attached. Thus, in many a ¾ and ⅜ rhythm the first measure presents *Thesis*, and the second measure *Arsis*, thus making (especially in waltz rhythms) a sextuple rhythm out of what appears to be triple. Artificial accents generally interrupt the rhythm and require especial signs. In piano music these represent two opposite styles of touch, — the pressure and the percussive stroke. In general music they can be classed as either explosive or resonant (without explosive character). The pressing, or resonant accents are chiefly represented by the following signs, — *Rf*, *Rfz* (see *Rinforzando*), *tenuto* (–) *marcato* (–⋅) and *Portamento* (♩♩♩) although the last is decidedly misleading in its application. (See *Portamento*.) The percussive, or explosive accents have the following signs : ∧ ≻ which have practically the same significance, unless used side by side, when the first is made the stronger; *sf.* or *sfz*. (See *Sforzando*) and *fz* (see *Forzando*). The staccato mark (see *staccato*) is sometimes used merely as an accent mark (percussive) as may be seen in the closing theme of Beethoven's "Sonate Pathétique," first movement, and in much other modern music.

Accénto (It.) (ät-*tshen*-tō.) Accent or emphasis laid upon certain notes.

Accentor (It.) (ät-*tshen*-tŏr.) An old term, signifying the performer who took the principal part in a duet, trio, etc.

ō as in *tone*; ŏ as in *dove*; ŏ as in *not*; ŭ as in *up*; ü the French sound of *u*.

5

ACCENT, ORATORICAL   ACCOMPANIMENT

Accent, oratorical. The emphasis dictated by feeling, giving the music its varying expression.

Accénti (It.) (ät-*tshen*-tee.) } Accents.
Accent (Fr.) (äk-sänh.)

Accentuáre (It.) (ät-tshĕn-too-*ä*-rĕ.) To accentuate; to mark with an accent.

Accentuato (It.) (ät-tshĕn-too-*ä*-to.) Distinctly and strongly accented.

Accentuiren (Ger.) (äk-tsĕn-too-eer'n.) To accent.

Accentus (Lat.) (ăk-*sĕn*-tŭs.) Accent.

Accentus Ecclesiastici (Lat.) The precentor's chant, almost entirely upon one tone. These chants were formerly of seven kinds, viz.: the immutabilis, medius, gravis, acutus, moderatus, interrogatus, and finalis.

Accessory notes. Those notes situated one degree above, and one degree below the principal note of a turn. The upper note of a trill is also called the accessory or auxiliary note.

Accessory tones. Harmonics. Tones faintly heard when the principal tone dies away.

Accessory voices. Accompanying voices.

Acciaccare. (It.) (ät-tshē-äk-*kä*-rĕ.) A brusque and unexpected way of striking a chord.

Acciaccáto (It.) (ät-tshē-äk-*kä*-tō.) Brusquely, forcibly.

Acciaccatúra (It.) (ät-tshē-äk-kä-*too*-rä.) A very short grace note; an accessory note placed before the principal note, the accent being on the principal note. The short grace note, or acciaccatura, or short appoggiatura, as it is variously called, receives as little time value as possible, and no accent. If a note is written to be played simultaneously with its principal note, that note should be struck with the grace note; the following examples may explain this:

Occasionally there may be deviations from this rule, but they are rare. As there are many misprints made in the notation of grace notes, it will be well to remember that the long grace note (appoggiatura) is yearning and tender in effect, while the short grace note is bright and crisp, with the single exception of sometimes imitating a sob in mournful or plaintive music. See *Appoggiatura.*

Accidentals. Occasional sharps, flats, or naturals placed before notes in the course of a piece. The composer may place an accidental before *any* note whose meaning may be considered doubtful. See *Chromatic Signs.*

Accidénti (It.) (ät-tshē-*den*-tē.) } Accidentals.
Accidents (Fr.) (ăk-si-dänh.)

Accidental chords. Chords containing one or more notes foreign to its proper harmony.

Accidental chromatics. Chromatics incidentally employed.

Accompaniment. (Ger. *Begleitung*, Fr. *Accompagnement*; It. *Accompagnamento.*) The accessory parts which support the principal part or parts of a composition. The principal parts may be either vocal or instrumental. The accompaniment is almost always instrumental. An accompaniment may be intended to assist the singer, to assure correct intonation, or it may be composed to enhance the musical beauty of the work. A necessary accompaniment is called *obbligáto.* Some accompaniments, marked *ad libitum*, can be omitted at the will of the performer or conductor.

Additional Accompaniments are parts added to a composition by an editor. These are sometimes very necessary. Some of the instruments, for which Bach and Handel wrote, are now obsolete, and their place must be filled by other instruments added by a modern hand. Neither of these two composers used the clarinette, which was very primitive in their day, and all clarinette parts in their works have been added since their time. Some of their scores were left in a mere outline state, so that the filling in of additional parts became a necessity. The writing of additional accompaniments began as early as the time of Mozart.

Accompaniment of the scale. The har-

ă as in *ah* ; ā as in *hate* ; ă as in *at* ; ē as in *tree* ; ĕ as in *eh* ; ī as in *pine* ; ĭ as in *pin* :

Mendelssohn in his twelfth year

Mendelssohn's Birthplace

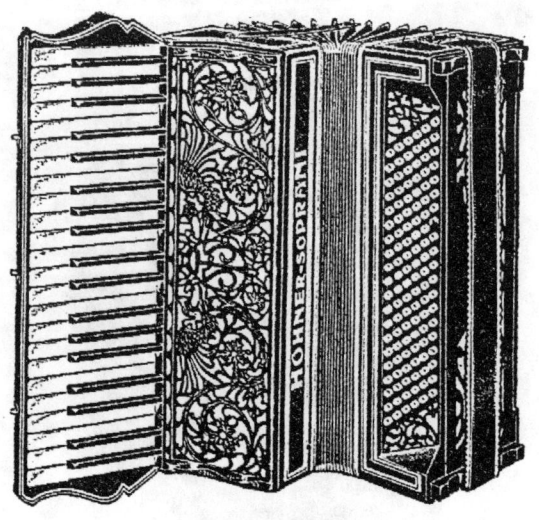

Accordion

Alto Clarinet

mony assigned to the series of notes forming the diatonic scale, ascending and descending.

Accomp. Oblto. An abbreviation of accompaniment obbligato.

Accopiáto (It.) (äk-kō-pē-*ä*-tō.) Bound, tied, joined together.

Accorciare (It.) (äk-kŏr-tshē-*ä*-rĕ.) To contract; to abridge.

Accorciatura (It.) (äk-kŏr-tshē-ä-*too*-rä.) Abridgment.

Accord (Fr.) (äk-kŏr.) A chord; a concord; consonance.

Accordamento (It.) (äk-kŏr-dä-*men*-tō.) Consonance, unison, harmony of parts.

Accordándo (It.) (äk-kŏr-*dän*-dō.) Tuning.

Accordant (Fr.) (äk-kŏr-dänh.) In concord; in unison.

Accordáre (It.) (äk-kŏr-*dä*-rĕ.) To tune; to agree in sound.

Accordáto (It.) (äk-kŏr-*dä*-tō.) In harmony; in tune.

Accordatóre (It.) (äk-kŏr-dä-*tō*-rĕ.) One who tunes instruments.

Accordatúra (It.) (äk-kŏr-dä-*too*-rä.) Concord, harmony. Also, the set of notes to which the open strings of an instrument are tuned.

Accordeon. An instrument held in the hands, the tones of which are produced by a current of air from a bellows acting on free metallic reeds.

Accorder (Fr.) (äk-kŏr-dā.) To tune an instrument; to sing or play in tune.

Accordeur (Fr.) (äk-kŏr-*dŭr*.) One who tunes an instrument.

According. An harmonious blending of different parts.

Accordion (Fr.) (äk-kŏr-dĭ-ŏnh.) An accordeon.

Accordiren (Ger.) (äk-kōr-*dē*-r'n.) To accord.

Accórdo (It.) (äk-*kŏr*-dō.) A chord, a concord, a consonance.

Accórdo consono (It.) (äk-*kŏr*-dō *kŏn*-sō-nō.) A concord.

Accórdo díssono (It.) (äk-*kŏr*-dō *dees*-sō-nō.) A discord.

Accordoir (Fr.) (äk-kŏr-*dwä*.) A tuning key, tuning hammer, an organ tuning-horn.

Accrescéndo (It.) (äk-krĕ-*shen*-dō.) Increasing; augmenting in tone and power.

Accrescere (It.) (äk-krĕ-*shai*-rĕ.) To increase; to augment;

Accrescimento (It.) (äk-krĕ-shē-*men*-tō.) Increase, augmentation of sound.

Accresciúto (It.) (äk-kre-shĕ-*oo*-tō.) Increased, augmented.

A Cemb. An abbreviation of A Cembalo.

A Cémbalo (It.) (ä tshem-bä-lō.) For the harpsichord.

Achromatic music. Simple music in which modulations seldom occur and few accidental flats and sharps are used.

Acht (Ger.) (äkht.) Eight.

Achtel (Ger.) (*äkh*-t'l.) Eighth, an eighth note.

Achtelnote (Ger.) (*ähk*-t'l-*nōt*-ē.) An eighth note.

Achtelpause (Ger.) (*äkh*-t'l-*pow*-sĕ.) An eighth rest.

Achtstimmig (Ger.) (*äkht*-stĭm-mĭg.) For eight voices.

A cinque (It.) (ä-*chink*-quĕ.) For five voices or instruments.

Acoustics (Ger. *Akustik*; It. *Acustica*; Fr. *Acoustique.*) The science of sound; the science treating of the laws of sound. A few facts connected with musical acoustics may be here stated as briefly as possible: All sound is vibration. Sounds produced by musical instruments or by voices are vibrations of air. Irregular or abrupt vibrations produce noise. Regular and continued vibrations produce tone. The piano or violin string vibrating imparts its pulsations to the air. The speed of sound through the air is about 1,100 feet per second. It takes about five seconds for sound to travel a mile through the air. Sound travels quicker in warm, damp air, slower in cold, dry air, but tone is clearer and more beautiful in cold, dry air because the atmosphere is more elastic, the particles lying further apart, and vibrating more freely. Pitch is merely rate of vibration. The higher the tone the quicker the vibrations. The proportion of rapidity in different musical intervals was known in ancient Greece, possibly, even in Egypt. If musical intervals are tuned according to the laws of nature, in two

---

ō as in *tone*; ŏ as in *dove*; ŏ as in *not*; ŭ as in *up*; ü the French sound of *u*.

tones an octave apart, the lower one will vibrate one-half as quickly as the upper one. If they are a perfect fifth apart, the lower one will vibrate two-thirds as quickly as the upper one, in a perfect fourth, three-quarters, etc. Most of our musical intervals, however, deviate more or less from the proportions indicated by nature. (See *Tempered Scale*.) The human brain cannot perceive tone at a slower rate than 16 vibrations per second. Most human brains cease to hear tone before it reaches 38,000 vibrations per second. The latter figure would represent a tone four octaves above the highest E-flat of the pianoforte. The total compass of pitch possible to an acute mind would be about eleven octaves and a minor third. The deepest tone audible is sub-contra C, produced by an open pipe 32 feet long, or a stopped pipe 16 feet long, upon the organ. The quality of musical tones depends upon the blending of faint, high tones, called overtones, or harmonics, with the chief tone heard. These harmonics are always present when we hear a musical tone. They occur in a regular order, but with varying degrees of intensity. They form a chord (called the Chord of Nature) above every tone that is sounded. Their full significance was first thoroughly explained by Helmholtz, although their presence had been noted almost three centuries ago. They are formed by the regular subdivisions of the sound-wave into halves, thirds, quarters, and other aliquot parts, sounding the octave, twelfth, fifteenth, etc., of the fundamental tone. When these over-tones are in good proportion, the lower ones full-toned and the upper ones faint, but clear, the result is a rich and pleasing tone. When the upper ones are too strong the result is a twangy, penetrating and irritating tone, like that of the harmonica, or of a worn-out piano. When all the overtones are faint, the result is a dull, or lifeless, or muddy tone, such as is given by the stopped diapason of the organ. Without the overtones, all musical tones would have precisely the same quality, no matter what instrument they were sounded on. We can alter the proportion of the overtones and make a tone brighter or duller on a string instrument by striking, plucking, or bowing at different points. The nearer the center the point of contact the hollower the tone; the nearer the end of the string, the brighter. A conical pipe or tube gives all the overtones clearly, and hence has a brighter tone than a cylindrical one, which gives fewer overtones. See also, *Pitch, Tempered Scale, Harmonics*. Books recommended upon this topic are Blaserna's "Sound and Music," Zahm's "Sound and Music," Pole's "Philosophy of Music," the "Student's Helmholtz," Tyndall's "On Sound."

Action. The mechanism attached to the keys of piano or organ; also, the mechanism attached to the pedals of a harp, which changes the pitch of the strings by shortening them; also, the mechanism attached to the pedals of an organ. See *Piano, Organ*.

Acuta (Lat.) (ah-*koot*-a.) A mixture stop in the organ.

Acute. High, in reference to pitch.

Acutus (Lat.) 1. Sharp, acute. 2. The name of one of the parts of Catholic ritual song.

Adagietto (It.) (ah-dah-*jiet*to.) 1. A short *adagio*. 2. A movement somewhat less slow than *adagio*.

Adagio (It.) (ah-*dah*-jio.) Slow. This term indicates a movement quicker than *largo* and slower than *andante*.

Adagio assai (It.) (assigh.) } Very slow.
Adagio di molto (It.)

Adagissimo (It.) (ah-dah-*jiss*-see-moh.) Extremely slow.

Addolorato (It.) (ah-doh-lo-*rah*-toh.) Sorrowful.

A demi jeu (Fr.) With half the power of the instrument.

A demi voix (Fr.) (a-demmy vwah.) At half voice; whispered.

A deux (Fr.) (ä-düh.) For two instruments or voices. This expression is also used for *à deux temps*.

A deux mains (Fr.) (ä-düh mänh.) For two hands.

Adiratamėnte (It.) (ä-di-rä-tä-*men*-tĕ.) } Angrily, sternly.
Adiráto (It.) (äd-*i-rä*-tō.)

ą as in *ah* ; ā as in *hate* ; ă as in *at* ; ē as in *tree* ; ĕ as in *eh* ; ī as in *pine* ; ĭ as in *pin* ;

8

A DIRITTÚRA   AFFETTATAMENTE

A Dirittúra (It.) (ä-di-ri-*too*-rä.) Directly; straight.

Adjunct notes. Unaccented auxiliary notes.

Adjuvant (Ger.) (*äd*-yoo-vänt.) The deputy-master of the choristers; assistant to an organist.

Ad lib. An abbreviation of Ad libitum.

Ad libitum (Lat.) (äd-*lĭb*-i-tŭm.) At will; at pleasure; changing the time of a particular passage at the discretion of the performer; also a part that may be omitted if desired.

Adornaménte (It.) (ä-dŏr-nä-*men*-tĕ.) Gaily, neatly, elegantly.

Adornaménto (It.) (ä-dŏr-nä-*men*-tō.) An ornament; an embellishment.

A dúe, or A 2 (It.) (ä *doo*-ĕ.) For two voices or instruments; a duet.

A dúe córde (It.) (ä-doo-ĕ *kŏr*-dĕ.) Upon two strings; the soft pedal pressed half way down.

A dúe córi (It.) (ä doo-ĕ kō-ree.) For two choirs.

A dúe Soprani (It.) (ä doo-*ĕ* sō-*prä*-nee.) For two sopranos.

A dúe vóce (It.) (ä doo-ĕ *vō*-tshĕ.) For two voices.

Adoucir (Fr.) (ă-doo-sēer.) To soften; to grow more sweet.

Adulatoriamente (It.) (ä-doo-lä tŏr-ē-ä-men-tĕ.) In a caressing, flattering manner.

A dur (Ger.) (ä door.) The key of A major.

Æolian. See *Piano player*.

Æolian Harp. An instrument invented by Kircher about the middle of the seventeenth century. The tones are produced by the strings being so arranged that the air causes vibration among them when it passes through.

Æolian Lyre. The Æolian Harp.

Æolian Pianoforte. A pianoforte with an Æolian or reed instrument attached in such a way that one set of keys serves for both, or for either singly, as the performer desires.

Æolodicon (Gr.) (ē-ō *lō*-dĭ-kŏn.) A keyed instrument, the tone of which resembles that of the organ, and is produced by free reeds, which are put in vibration by means of bellows. This was the predecessor of the cabinet organ.

Æolodion (Gr.) (ē-ō-*lō*-dĭ-ŏn.) An Æolodicon.

Æolopantalon. An instrument combining the pianoforte and Ælodicon.

Æolsharfe (Ger.) (*ā*-ōls-*här*-fĕ.) An Æolian Harp.

Æolus modus. The Æolian or fifth authentic mode of the Greeks, nearly allied to the Phrygian mode. The scale is the same as the old scale of A minor without any accidentals. See *Greek modes*.

Æquisonans (Lat.) (ē-qui-*sō*-năns.) A unison of the same or like sound.

Æquisonant. A term given to unisons, and also frequently to octaves, as they seem one and the same sound.

Æquisonus. Sounding in unison; concordant.

Ærophone (*ĕ*-rō-fōn.) A French reed instrument of the melodeon class.

Æsthetics (ĕs-*thĕt*-ĭks.) The rules of good taste; the laws of the beautiful. In musical art that which relates to sentiment, expression, and the power of music over the soul.

Æusserste Stimmen (Ger. *pl.*) (oissĕrs-tĕ *stĭm*-mĕn.) The extreme parts.

Ævia (It.) (*ĕ*-vē-ä.) An abbreviation of the word Allêlùia, containing all the vowels of that word.

Affábile (It.) (äf-*fä*-bē-lĕ.) In an affable and pleasing manner.

Affabilita (It.) (äf-fä-*bē*-lē-tä.)
Affabilménte or (äf-fä-bēl-*men*-tĕ.) } With ease and elegance; with affability; in a pleasing and agreeable manner.

Affannáto (It.) (äf-fä-*nä*-tō.) Sad, distressed.

Affannóso (It.) (äf-fä-*nō*-zō.) With anxious expression.

Affectírt (Ger.) (äf-fĕk-*tirt*.) With affectation.

Affectueux (Fr.) (äf-fĕk-tü-ay.) Affectionate.

Affet. An abbreviation of Affetuoso.

Affettatamente (It.) (äf-fät-tä-tä-*men*-tĕ.) Affectedly.

ō as in *tone*; ĝ as in *dove*; ŏ as in *not*; ŭ as in *up*; ü the French sound of *u*.

Affettazione (It.) (äf-fĕt-tä-tsē-ō-nĕ.) An artificial style.

Affettivo (It.) (äf-fĕt-tē-vō.) Affecting; pathetic.

Affétto (It.) (äf-*fet*-tō.) Feeling; tenderness; pathos.

Affettuosaménte (It.) (äf-fĕt-too-ō-zä-*men*-tĕ.) With tenderness and feeling.

Affettuosissimo (It.) (äf-fĕt-too-ō-sis-sē-mō.) With utmost pathos; with most tender expression.

Affettuóso (It.) (äf-fĕt-too-ō-zō.) With tender and passionate expression

Affiocamento (It.) (äf-fē-ō-kä-*men*-tō.) Hoarseness.

Affiocato (It.) (äf-fē-ō-*kä*-tō.) Hoarse.

Afflítto (It.) (äf-*flit*-tō.) Sorrow-
Afflizióne (äf-fli-tsē-ō-nĕ.) fully; with mournful expression.

Affreto. An abbreviation of Affrettando.

Affrettándo (It.) (äf-frĕt-*tän*-dō.) Hurry-
Affrettáte (äf-frĕt-*tä*-tĕ.) ing; quickening; accelerating the time.

Affrettóso (It.) (äf-frĕt-*tō*-zō.) Quick, accelerated, hurried.

After note. A small note occurring on an unaccented part of the measure, and taking its time from the note preceding it. Written. Performed.

After notes, double. Written. Performed. Two after notes, taking their time from the preceding note.

Agévole (It.) (ä-*jeh*-vō-lĕ.)

Agevolménte (It.) (ä-*jeh*-vōl-*men*-tĕ.) Lightly; easily; with agility.

Agevolézza (It.) (ä-je-vō-*leh*-tsä.) Lightness, ease, agility.

Aggiustaménte (It.) (äd-jĕ-oos-tä-*men*-tĕ.) In strict time.

Aggiustare (It.) (äd-jĭ-oos-*tä*-rĕ.) Ad-
Aggiustato (äd-jĭ-oos-*tä*-tō.) justed, arranged, adapted.

Aggraver la fugue (Fr.) (äg-grä-vā lä füg.) To augment the subject of a fugue.

Agilita (It.) (ä-jil-ē-*tä*.) Lightness, agility.

Agilita, con. (It.) With agility; with lightness; with rapidity.

Agilménte (It.) (ä-jēl-*men*-tĕ.) Lively, gay.

Agitamento (It.) (ä-jē-tä-*men*-tō.) Agitation, restlessness, motion.

Agitáto (It.) (äj-i-*tä*-tō.) Agitated, hurried, restless.

Agitato allegro (It.) (äj-i-*tä*-tō äl-lāy-grō.) A nervous, agitated, and rapid movement.

Agitáto con passióne (It.) (äj-i-*tä*-tō kŏn päs-sē-ō-nĕ.) Passionately agitated.

Agite (Fr.) (ä-zhēt.) Agitate.

Agli (It. pl.) (äl-yee.) See *Alla*.

Agnus Dei (Lat.) (*ăg*-nŭs *dā*-ē.) Lamb of God; one of the movements in a Mass.

Agoge rhythmica (Gr.) (ä-*gō*-ghĕ rĭth-mē-kä.) Time; rhythmical division.

Agraffe. A metallic support of the string in a pianoforte, between the pin and the bridge, serving to check vibration at that part.

A grand chœur (Fr.) (kür.) For the entire chorus.

A grand orchestre (Fr.) (ŏr-kĕstr). For the full or complete orchestra.

Agréménts (Fr. pl.) (ä-grāy-mänh.) Embellishments, ornaments. Usually applied in Harpsichord or Spinet music.

Ai (It.) (ä-ē.) To the; in the style of.

Aigre (Fr.) (ägr.) Harsh, sharp.

Aigrement (Fr.) (ägr-mănh.) Sharply, harshly.

Aigu (Fr.) (ä-gü.) Acute, high, sharp, shrill.

A in alt. The A placed upon the first upper added line.

A in altissimo. An octave above A in Alt.

Air. A short song, melody, or tune, with or without words. The upper voice in a harmonized composition.

Air à boire (Fr.) (är-ä-bwär.) A drinking song.

Air à reprises (Fr.) (är ä rĕh-prēz.) A catch.

Air détaché (Fr.) (är dā-tä-shā.) A single air or melody extracted from an opera or larger work.

Air Écossais (Fr.) (e-cōs-sāy.) A Scotch air.

Air Irlandais (Fr.) (är ēr-länh-dāy.) Irish air.

ă as in *ah*; ā as in *hate*; ă as in *at*; ē as in *tree*; ĕ as in *eh*; ī as in *pine*; ĭ as in *pin*;

Air Italien (Fr.) (ār ĭ-tăl-ĭ-änh.) An Italian air.
Airs Français (Fr.) (fränh-sāy.) French airs.
Airs Russes (Fr.) (rüs.) Russian airs.
Airs tendres (tänh-dr.) Amatory airs; love songs.
Air varié (Fr.) (vä-rĭ-āy.) Air with variations; an air embellished and ornamented.
Ais (Ger.) (ah-*iss*.) The note A sharp.
Aisé (Fr.) (ā-zāy.) Glad, joyful; also, easy, facile, convenient.
Aisément (Fr.) (āy-zā-mänh.) Easily, freely.
Ajouté (Fr.) (āsz-*hoot*-ay.) Added.
Ajoutez (Fr.) (āsz-*hoot*-ay.) Add. Used in organ-music.
Akkord (Ger.) (äk-*kōrd*.) See *Accord*.
Akromatisch (Ger.) (äk-rō-*mä*-tĭsh.) See *Achromatic*.
Akustik (Ger.) (ä-*koos*-tĭk.) See *Acoustics*.
Al (It.) (äl.) To the; in the style of.
Alberti Bass. A species of bass, the chords of which are taken in arpeggios of a particular kind;
ex., [music notation] etc. It was so called because first used by Domenico Alberti, who died in 1739.
Album leaf (Ger. *Albumblatt*.) A short and simple piece, such as might be written in an autograph album.
Alcuna licenza, con (It.) (al-koo-na lē-*tschĕn*-tsä kŏn.) With a little license.
Al fíne (It.) (äl fēe-nĕ.) To the end.
Al fíne, e pói la códa (äl fēe-nĕ ā pō-ē lä *kō*-dä.) After playing to where the Fine is marked, go on to the coda.
Aliquot tones. Accessory or secondary sounds; the overtones or harmonics. See *Acoustics*.
A l'Italienne (Fr.) (ä lĭ-täl-ē-änh.) In the Italian style.
Al riverso (It.) (äl rē-*vär*-sō.) } By
Al rovescio (It.) (äl rō-*vä*-shē-o.) } contrary motion, that is, answering an ascending interval by one descending a like distance.

Al (It.) (äl.) ⎫
All' (It.) (äl.) ⎪
Alla (It.) (äl-lä.) ⎬ To the; in the style
Alle (It.) (äl-lĕ.) ⎪ or manner of.
Agli (It.) (äl-yēe.) ⎪
Allo (It.) (äl-lō.) ⎭
Alla Bréve (It.) (äl-lä brăvĕ.) This was originally 4/2 rhythm, so called from the fact that one *breve*, or double-whole-note filled each measure. To-day the term is more generally applied to 2/2 rhythm, marked ₵.
Alla cáccia (It.) (*äl*-la *kät*-tshē-ä.) In the style of hunting music.
Alla cámera (It.) (*äl*-lä *kä*-mĕ-rä.) In the style of chamber music.
Alla Cappélla (It.) (*äl*-lä käp-*pel*lä.) In the church or sacred style; derived from Alla Bréve style, the bar being sub-divided, also unaccompanied vocal music. See *Alla Bréve*.
Alla dirítta (It.) (*äl*-lä dē-*ri*-tä.) In direct ascending or descending style. With the right hand.
Alla Francése (It.) (*äl*-lä frän-tshāy-zĕ.) ⎫
Alla Franzése (It.) (*äl*-lä frän-tsāy-zĕ.) ⎬
In the French style.
Allargando (It.) (ah-lahr-*gan*-doh.) Growing broader, *i.e.*, louder and slower.
Alle (It.) (äl-lĕ.) To the; in the style of.
Alle (Ger.) (*äl*-lĕ.) All: alle Instrumente, all the instruments; the whole orchestra.
Allegraménte (It.) (äl-lĕ-grä-*men*-tĕ.) ⎫
Allégrement (Fr.) (äl-lā-grĕ-mänh.) ⎬
Gaily, joyfully, quickly.
Allegrante (It.) (äl-lĕ-*grän*-tĕ.) Joyous, mirthful.
Allegrettíno (It.) (äl-lĕ-grĕt-*tēe*-nō.) A diminutive of Allegrétto and rather slower. A short Allegretto movement.
Allegrétto (It.) (äl-lĕ-*gret*-tō.) Rather light and cheerful but not as quick as Allégro.
Allegrétto Scherzándo (It.) (äl-lĕ-grĕt-tō skĕr-*tsän*-dō.) Moderately playful and lively.
Allegrézza (It.) (äl-lĕ-*gret*-zä.) } Joy,
Allegría (It.) (äl-lĕ-*grēe*-ä.) } gladness, cheerfulness, gaiety.
Allegrézza, con (It.) With cheerfulness, joy, animation.

ō as in *tone*; ô as in *dove*; ŏ as in *not*; ŭ as in *up*; ü the French sound of *u*.

Allegrissimaménte (It.) (äl-lĕ-griss-i-mah-*men*-tĕ.) Very joyfully; with great animation.

Allegríssimo (It.) (äl-lā-*gris*-si-mō.) Extremely quick and lively; the superlative of Allégro.

Allégro (Fr. and It.) (äl-*lāy*-grō.) Quick, lively; a rapid, vivacious movement, the opposite to the pathetic, but it is frequently modified by the addition of other words that change its expression: as,

Allégro agitato (It.) (äl-*lāy*-grō äj-ē-*tä*-tō.) Quick, with anxiety and agitation.

Allégro appassionato (It.) (äl-*lāy*-grō äp-päs-si-ō-*nä*-tō.) Passionately quick.

Allégro assái (It.) (äl-*lā*-grō äs-*sä*-ē.) Very quick.

Allégro brillante (It.) (bril-*län*-tĕ.) Requiring a brilliant style of execution.

Allégro cómodo (It.) (*kō*-mō-dō.) With a convenient degree of quickness.

Allégro con brío (It.) (kŏn *brē*-ō.) Quick, with brilliancy.

Allégro con fuóco. (It.) (äl-*lā*-grō kŏn foo-*ō*-kō.) Quick, with fire and animation.

Allégro con moto (It.) Quick, with more than the usual degree of movement.

Allégro con spírito (It.) (äl-*lā*-grō kŏn *spi*-rē-tō.) Quick, with much spirit.

Allégro di bravúra (It.) (äl-*lā*-grō dē brä-*voo*-rä.) Quick, with brilliant and spirited execution.

Allégro di molto (It.) (äl-*lā*-grō di *mōl*-tō.) Exceedingly quick and animated.

Allégro furioso (It.) (äl-*lā*-grō foo-rē-*ō*-zō.) Quick, with fury and impetuosity.

Allégro giústo (It.) (äl-*lā*-grō joos-tō.) Quick, with exactness; in steady and precise time. An Allegro Moderato.

Allégro ma grazioso (It.) (äl-*lā*-grō mä grä-tse-*ō*-zō.) Quick, but gracefully.

Allégro ma non présto (It.) (äl-*lā*-grō mä nŏn *pres*-tō.) Quick, but not so fast as Presto.

Allégro ma non tánto (It.) (äl-*lā*-grō mä nŏn tän-tō.) Quick, but not too fast.

Allégro ma non tróppo (It.) (äl-*lā*-grō mä nŏn *trop*-pō.) Quick and lively, but not too fast.

Allégro moderáto (It.) (äl-*lā*-grō mŏd-ĕ-*rä*-tō.) Moderately quick.

Allégro mólto (It.) (äl-*lā*-grō *mōl*-tō.) Very quick and animated.

Allégro non molto (It.) (äl-*lā*-grō nŏn *mōl*-tō.) Not very fast.

Allégro non tánto (It.) (äl-*lā*-grō nŏn *tän*-tō.) Quick, but not too fast.

Allégro non tróppo (It.) (nōn-*trŏp*-po.) Not too fast.

Allégro risolúto (It.) (ri-zō-*loo*-tō.) Quick, with vigor and decision.

Allégro velóce (It.) (vĕ-*lō*-tshĕ.) Quick, with velocity.

Allégro viváce (It.) (vi-*vä*-tshĕ.) With vivacity; very rapidly.

Allégro vívo (It.) (*vēe*-vō.) With life and rapidity.

Allein (Ger.) (äl-*lihn*.) Alone, single.

Alléluia (Fr.) (äl-lĕ-*loo*-yä.) Praise the Lord; Hallelujah.

Allelujah (Heb.) (äl-lĕ-loo-yä.) An ascription of praise; Hallelujah.

Allemande (Fr.) (*äll*-mänhd.) A lively German dance in ¾ and also in ¾ rhythm; also a slow dance or melody in ¼ rhythm. The first dance movement in the old suite.

Allentaménto (It.) (äl-lĕn-tä-*men*-tō.) } Relaxation; giving way;
Allentáto (It.) (äl-lĕn-*tä*-tō.) } slackening of the time.

Allentándo (It.) (äl-lĕn-*tän*-dō.) Decreasing the time.

Alle Saiten (Ger.) (alleh *sigh*-ten.) Tutte Corde. Release the soft pedal.

All' Espagnuóla (It.) (äl-lĕs-pän-yoo-*ō*-lä.) In the Spanish style.

Allied tones. Accessory tones.

Alliévo (It.) (äl-lē-*ā*-vō.) A scholar; a pupil.

All' improvíso (It.) (äl-l'ēm-prō-*vē*-zō.) } Without previous study; extemporaneously.
All' improvísta (It.) (äl-l'ēm-prō-*ves*-tä.) }

All' Inglése (It.) (äl-l'-ēn-*glāy*-zĕ.) In the English style.

All' Italiána (It.) (äl-l'-ē-tä-lē-*ä*-nē.) In the Italian style.

Allmählich (Ger.) (äl-*mä*-līkh.) Little by little.

Al' lóco (It.) (äl-*lō*-kō.) To the previous place.

ä as in *ah*; ā as in *hate*; ă as in *at*; ē as in *tree*; ĕ as in *eh*; ī as in *pine*; ĭ as in *pin*;

12

ALL' ONGARESE — ALTO

All' Ongaráese (It.) (äl ōn-gä-*räy*-zĕ.) In the Hungarian style.

Allonger (Fr.) (äl-lŏnh-zhāy.) To lengthen, prolong, delay.

Allonger l'archet (Fr.) (äl-lŏnh-zhā l-är-shay.) To lengthen or prolong the stroke of the bow in violin music.

Allontandosi (It.) (äl-ōn-*tän*-dō-zĕ.) Gradually disappearing in the distance; further and further away.

All' ottáva (It.) (äl ŏt-*tä*-vä.) In the octave; meaning that one part must play an octave above or below another. It is frequently met with in scores and orchestra parts.

All' ottáva alta (It.) (äl ōt-tä-vä äl-tä.) In the octave above.

All' ottáva bassa (It.) (äl ōt-tä-vä bäs-sä.) In the octave below.

All' unísono (It.) (äl oo-nē-*so*-nō.) In unison: a succession of unisons or octaves.

All' 8va. An abbreviation of All' ottáva.

Almain.
Alman. } An Allemande.
Almand.

Alma Redemptoris (Lat.) (äl-mä rĕ-dĕm-tō-rís.) A hymn to the Virgin.

Almehs (Tur.) (äl-mäs.) Turkish singing and dancing girls.

Alpenhorn (Ger.) (*äl*-p'n-hōrn.) The Alpine, or cowhorn.

Al piacére (It.) (äl pē-ä-*tschai*-rĕ.) At pleasure. See *A piacére*.

Al più (It.) (äl pē-oo.) The most.

Alpine Horn. A great tube of firwood used by the Alpine shepherds for conveying sounds a long distance.

Al rigóre di tempo (It.) (äl rĭ-*gō*-rĕ di-*tĕm*-pö.) In very rigorous and strict time.

Al rigóre del tempo (It.) (äl ri-*gō*-rĕ dĕl *tĕm*-pō.) In very rigorous and strict time.

Al riverso (It.) (äl rē-*vair*-sō.)

Al Rovescio (al Ro-*vesch*-eeo.) In reverse motion; in contrary motion; answering an ascending interval by a descending one, or a descending by an ascending one.

À la Russe (Fr.) (ä lä rüss.) In the Russian style.

Al Seg. An abbreviation of Al Segno.

Al Segno (It.) (äl *sen*-yō.) To the sign; meaning that the performer must return to the sign 𝄋 in a previous part of the piece and play from that place to the word Fine, or the mark 𝄌 over a double bar.

Alt (It.) (ält.) High. This term is applied to the notes which lie between F on the fifth line of treble staff and G on the fourth added line above. Notes above this are called "in altissimo"; the German name for alto. The name is also applied to alto instruments of different families, as alt-clarinet, alt-horn, etc.

Al Tedésco (It.) (äl tĕ-des-kō.) In the German style.

Altera prima donna (It.) (äl-tĕ-rä *prē*-mä *dŏn*-nä.) One of two principal female singers.

Alteratio (Lat.) (äl-tĕ-rä-shĭ-o.)
Alteráto (It.) (äl-tĕ-*rä*-tō.) } Changed, augmented. Chromatic alteration.
Altéré (Fr.) (äl-tĕ-*rä*.)

Alternaménte (It.) (äl-tĕr-nä-*men*-tĕ.) Alternating; by turns.

Alternándo (It.) (äl-tĕr-*nän*-dō.) See *Alternaménte*.

Alternativo (It.) (äl-tĕr-nä-*tee*-vō.) Alternating one movement with another.

Altgeige (Ger.) (*ält*-ghī-ghĕ.) The viola.

Alti (It.) (*äl*-tee.) High; the plural of Alto.

Altieraménte (It.) (äl-tē-ĕr-ä-*men*-tĕ.) With grandeur; haughtily.

Altisonante (It.) (äl-tē-zō-*nän*-tĕ.) Loud, sounding.

Altísono (It.) (äl-*tē*-sō-nō.) Sonorous.

Altissimo (It.) (äl-*tis*-sē-mō.) The highest; extremely high as to pitch. It is applied to notes above.

Altist. An alto singer.

Altitonans (Lat.) (äl-tĭ-*tō*-năns.) The alto, or highest part under the treble; used in choral music in the sixteenth century.

Alto (It.) (*äl*-tō.) High. In vocal music the highest male voice, some-

---

ō as in *tone*; o as in *dove*; ŏ as in *not*; ŭ as in *up*; ü the French sound of *u*.

times called the counter tenor. In *mixed chorus* it is the part next below the soprano sung by low female voices. In French *hauteontre*, in German *Alt*. There is practically no distinction made between alto and contralto, although *formerly* the latter meant the deeper alto voice. Ordinary alto compass is A high head voice in men. The word *alto* means high, and the part was originally sung by either high tenors or boys' voices. The viola is sometimes called the *Alto*.

Alto clef. The C clef on the third line of the staff.

Alto Flauto (It.) (äl-tō flä-*oo*-tō.) An alto flute, used in bands.

Alt' ottáva (It.) (äl-t' ōt-tä-vä.) The same notes an octave higher.

Alto primo (It.) (äl-tō *prē*-mō.) The highest alto.

Alto secondo (It.) (äl-tō sĕ-*kōn*-dō.) The lowest alto.

Alto tenore (It.) (äl-tō tĕn-*ō*-rĕ.) The highest tenor.

Alto Trombone. See *Trombone*.

Alto Vióla (It.) (äl-tō vē-o-lä.) The viola or tenor violin.

Alto Violino (It.) (äl-tō vē-o-lē-nō.) Small tenor violin on which the alto may be played.

Altposaune. Alto Trombone.

Altra (It.) (*äl*-trä.) } Other, another.
Altro (It.) (*äl*-trō.) }

Altri (It.) (*äl*-trēe.) Others.

Altro modo (It.) (äl-trō *mō*-dō.) Another mode or manner.

Altsänger (Ger.) (*ält*-seng-ĕr.) Alto singer, counter tenor singer.

Altschlüssel (Ger.) (*ält*-shlüs-s'l.) The alto clef; the C clef on the third line.

Altus (Lat.) (*ăl*-tŭs.) The alto or counter tenor.

Altviole (Ger.) (*ält*-fī-*ō*-lĕ.) The viola or tenor violin.

Altzeichen (Ger.) (*ält*-tsī-k'n.) See *Altschlüssel*.

Alzaménto (It.) (äl-tsä-*men*-tō.) An elevating of the voice; lifting up.

Alzaménto di máno (It.) (äl-tsä-*men*-tō dē *mä*-nō) To elevate the hand in beating time.

Alzaménto di voce (It.) (äl-tsä-*men*-tō dē *vō*-tshĕ.) Elevation of the voice.

Alzándo (It.) (äl-*tsän*-dō.) Raising; lifting up.

Amábile (It.) (ä-*mä*-bē-lĕ.) Amiable, gentle, graceful.

Amabilitá (It.) (ä-*mä*-bi-li-tä.) Tenderness, amiability.

Amabilitá, con. With amiability.

Amabilménte (It.) (ä-mä-bēl-*men*-tĕ.) Amiably, gently.

Amarévole (It.) (ä-mär-*ĕ*-vō-lĕ.) Bitterly. Sometimes mistaken for Amorevole, which means lovingly.

Amarézza (It.) (ä-mä-*ret*-zä.) Bitterness, sadness.

Amarézza, con (It.) With bitterness; with sorrow.

Amarissimaménte (It.) (ä-mä-rēs-sē-mä-*men*-tĕ.) } Very bitterly; in a very mournful, sad, and afflicted manner.
Amarissimo (It.) (ä-mä-ris-sē-mō.) }

Amáro (It.) (ä-*mä*-rō.) Grief, bitterness, affliction.

Amateur (Fr.) (ăm-ä-*tŭr*.) One who has taste and proficiency in an art, but does not practice it as a profession. A lover of any art.

Amati. A name applied to violins made by the family of Amati, in Italy, in the middle of the seventeenth century. They are smaller than the ordinary violin, and distinguished for their peculiar sweetness of tone.

Ambrosian Chant. A series of sacred melodies or chants collected and introduced into the church by St. Ambrose, Bishop of Milan, in the fourth century, and supposed to have been borrowed from the ancient Greek music. It was founded upon four authentic modes or scales, *i.e.*

It was entirely diatonic, without accidentals of any sort.

Ambrosianus Cantus (Lat.) (ăm-brō-sĭ-ä-nŭs *kăn*-tŭs.) Ambrosian chant.

Ambrosian Hymn. The "Te Deum" is so-called because it is supposed to have been written by St. Ambrose.

Ambulant (Fr.) (änh-bü-länh.) Wandering; an itinerant musician.

Âme (Fr.) (äm.) The sound-post of a violin, viola, etc.

Amen (Heb.) (*ä*-měn.) So be it. A word used as a termination to psalms, hymns, and other sacred music. It is sometimes set as a chorus by itself, in which case it is always contrapuntal, and very frequently a fugue.

American fingering. That style of fingering in which the sign × is used to indicate the thumb in piano playing, in distinction from the German or foreign fingering, in which the thumb is called the first finger. This did not have its origin in America, but in Germany and England. See *English Fingering*, and *Fingering*.

American organ. A variety of the harmonium which differs from the European harmonium in the arrangement of the bellows, and in producing varieties of expression; a reed organ.

A mézza aria (It.) (ä *met*-sä *ä*-rē-ä.) An air partly in the style of a recitative; between speaking and singing.

A mézza vóce (It.) (ä *met*-sä vō-shě.)
A mezza di vóce (It.) (ä *met*-sä dē vō-tshě.) } In a soft subdued tone; with half the power of the voice. The term is also applied to instrumental music.

A mézza manico (It.) (ä *met*-sä mä-*nē*-kō.) In violin playing, the placing the hand near the middle of the neck.

Ammaestratore (It.) (äm-mä-ĕs-trä-*tō*-rě.) An instructor.

Ammaestratrice (It.) (äm-mä-ĕs-trä-*trē*-tshě.) An instructress.

Ammodulato (It.) (äm-mō-doo-*lä*-tō.) Tuned.

A moll (Ger.) (ä mŏll.) The key of A minor.

À monocorde (Fr.) (ä mŏnh-ō-kŏrd.) On one string only.

Amóre (It.) (ä-*mō*-rě) Tenderness, affection, love.

Amóre, con. (It.) With tenderness and affection.

Amorévole (It.) (ä-mō-*re*-vō-lě.) Tenderly, gently, lovingly.

Amorévolménte (It.) (ä-mō-re-vŏl-*men*-tě.) With extreme tenderness.

A morésco (It.) (ä mō-*res*-kō.) In the Moorish style; in the style of a morésco or Moorish dance.

Amorosaménte (It.) (ä-mō-rō-zä-*men*-tě.) In a tender and affectionate style.

Amoróso (It.) (ä-mō-*rō*-zō.) See *Amorosaménte*.

Amousikos (Gr.) (ă-*moo*-sĭ-kōs). Unmusical; a term used by the ancient Greeks implying a deficiency in the organs of sound or want of cultivation.

Amphibrach (Gr.) (*ăm*-fĭ-bräk.) A musical foot, comprising one short, one long and one short note or syllable, accented and marked thus, ᴗ — ᴗ.

Amphimacer (Gr.) (*ăm*-fĭ-mä-sěr.) A musical foot, comprising one long, one short and one long note, or syllable, accented and marked thus, — ᴗ —.

Amphion (Gr.) (*ăm*-fĭ-ŏn.) An ancient Greek musician. He played upon the lyre.

Ampollosaménte (It.) (äm-pŏl-lō-zä-*men*-tě.)
Ampollóso (It.) (äm-pŏl-*lō*-zō.) } In a bombastic and pompous manner.

Ampoulé (Fr.) (ämh-poo-lā.) High flown; bombastic.

Amusement (Fr.) (ä-müz-mänh.) A light and pleasing composition called in Italian *Divertimento*.

An (*Ger.*) (äln.) On; To; organ music, draw, or add.

Anabasis (Gr.) (ä-*nä*-bă-sĭs.) A succession of ascending tones.

Anacamptos (Gr.) (ăn-ä-*kămp*-tŏs.) A course of retrograde or reflected notes; notes proceeding downwards or from acute to grave.

Anacreontic (Gr.) (ăn-ăk-rě-*ŏn*-tĭk.) In the Bacchanalian or drinking style.

Anakara (It.) (ăn-ä-*kä*-rä.) The ancient kettle drum.

Anakarista (It.) (ăn-ä-kä-rēs-tä.) A tympanist, or kettle-drum player.

Análisi (It.) (ä-*nä*-l -zē.)
Analyse (Fr.) (ăn-ä-lēz.) } An analysis.

ō as in *tone*; ô as in *dove*; ŏ as in *not*; ŭ as in *up*; ü the French sound of *u*.

ANALYZATION   ANFANG

Analyzation. The resolution of a musical composition into the elements which compose it for the sake of ascertaining its construction.

Ananes (Gr.) (ä-nä-nēs.) The modes or tones of the ancient Greek church.

Anapest (Gr.) (ăn-ä-pĕst.) A musical foot, containing two short notes or syllables, and a long one, accented and marked thus, ⌣ ⌣ —.

Anapesto (Spa.) (än-ä-pĕs-tō.) An anapest.

Anarmonia. Dissonance, false harmony.

Anche (Fr.) (änhsh.) The reed of the oboe, bassoon, clarinet, etc.; also the various reed stops in an organ.

Anche d'orgue (Fr.) (änhsh d'örg.) A reed stop of an organ.

Ancher (Fr.) (ähn-shā.) To put a reed to a musical instrument.

Ancia (It.) (än-tshē-ä.) See *Anche*.

Ancient modes. The modes or scales of the ancient Greeks and Romans.

Ancient signatures. Old signatures in which the last sharp or flat was suppressed and used as an accidental note when required.

Ancilla (Gr.) (ăn-sĕl-lä.) Shields, by the beating of which the ancient Greeks marked the measure of their music on festive occasions.

Ancóra (It.) (än-kō-rä.) Once more; repeat again; also, yet, still, etc.

Ancór più mósso (It.) (än-kōr pē-oo mōs-sō.) Still more motion, quicker.

Andacht (Ger.) (än-däkht.) Devotion.

Andächtig (Ger.) (än-däkh-tĭg.) Devotional.

Andaménto (It.) (än-dä-men-to.) A rather slow movement; also an accessory idea or episode introduced into a fugue to produce variety; in the style of an Andante.

Andante (It.) (än-dän-tĕ.) A movement in moderate time but flowing easily, gracefully. Andante literally means "going." In the 18th century it was often used as meaning "steadily," "distinctly." At present it often indicates a degree of expression and tenderness as well as a moderately slow tempo. This term is often modified both as to time and style by the addition of other words; as,

Andánte affettuóso (It.) (än-dän-tĕ äf-fĕt-too ō-zō.) Moderately, and with much pathos.

Andánte amabile (It.) (än-dän-tĕ ä-mä-bi-lĕ.) An andante expressive of affection.

Andánte cantábile (It.) (än-dän-tĕ cän-tä-bi-lĕ.) Slowly, and in a singing and melodious style.

Andánte con móto (It.) (än-dän-tĕ kŏn mō-tō.) Moving easily, with motion or agitation.

Andánte grazióso (It.) (än-dän-tĕ grä-tsē-ō-zō.) Moderately slow in time, and in graceful, easy style.

Andánte largo (It.) (än-dän-tĕ lär-gō.) Slow, distinct, and broadly.

Andánte maestóso (It.) (än-dän-tĕ mä-ĕs-tō-zō.) Moving rather slowly and in majestic style.

Andánte ma non troppo (It.) (än-dän-tĕ mä nŏn trŏp-pō.) Not too slow.

Andánte non troppo. Moving slowly but not too much so.

Andánte pastoråle (It.) (än-dän-tĕ päs-to rah-lĕ.) Moderately slow and in simple pastoral style.

Andánte più tosto allegretto (It.) (än-dän-tĕ pē-oo tŏs-tō äl-lĕ-gret-tō.) Andante, or somewhat allegretto.

Andánte quasi allegretto (It.) An andante nearly as rapid as allegretto.

Andánte sostenuto (It.) (sŏs-tĕn-oo-tō.) Very smooth and sustained.

Andanteménte (It.) (än-dän-tĕ-men-tĕ.) See *Andante*.

Andantíno (It.) (än-dän-tēe-nō.) A little slower than Andante is the literal meaning of Andantino, but it has become a doubtful term, and is generally used as meaning *quicker* than Andante. See *Popular Errors* in introduction.

Andare (It.) (ähn-däh-rĕ.) To go; go on.

Anelanteménte (It.)(än-ĕ-län-tĕ-men-tĕ.) Ardently.

Anelánza (It.) (än-ĕ-län-tsä.) } Shortness
Anélito (It.) (än-ĕ-lē-tō.) } of breath.

Anemochord. A species of Æolian Harp.

Anemometer. A wind gauge, or machine for measuring the wind in an organ.

Anfang (Ger.) (än-fäng.) Beginning, commencement.

ă as in *ah* ; ā as in *hate* ; ă as in *at* ; ē as in *tree* ; ĕ as in *eh* ; ī as in *pine* ; ĭ as in *pin* ;

Anfänger (Ger.) (*än*-fĕng-ĕr.) A beginner.

Anfangsgründe (Ger.) (*än*-fängs-*grün*-dĕ.) Rudiments, elements, principles.

Anfangsritornell (Ger.) (*än*-fängs-rē-tōr-*nĕl.*) Introductory accompaniment to an air.

Anfibraco (Spa.) (än-fē-*brä*-kō.) See *Amphibrach.*

Anfiteátro (It.) (än-fē-tĕ-*ä*-trō.) See *Amphitheatre.*

Anführer (Ger.) (*än*-fee-rĕr.) A conductor, director, leader.

Angeben (Ger.) (*än*-gāy-b'n.) To give a sound; to utter a tone; *den Ton angeben,* to give the pitch.

Angelica (Ger.) (än-*jä*-lĭ-kä.) } An organ stop;
Angélique (Fr.) (änh-zhá-lĕk.) } also an Angelot.

Angelot. An old musical instrument somewhat similar to the lute.

Angelus. A prayer to the Virgin, instituted by Pope Urban II, beginning "Angelus Domini." It is offered at morning, noon, and evening, at the sound of a bell which is also called "The Angelus."

Angemessen (Ger.) (*än*-ghĕ-*mĕs*-s'n.) Conformable, suitable, fit.

Angenehm (Ger.) (*än*-ghĕn-ām.) Agreeable, pleasing, sweet.

Anglaise (Fr.) (änh-glāz.) } In the English style; a
Anglico (It.) (*än*-gli-kō.) } tune adapted for an English air or country dance. It has been used by Bach in his French Suites. It somewhat resembles the Hornpipe.

Angóre (It.)(än-*gō*-rĕ.) Distress, anguish, passion, grief.

Angoscévole (It.) (än-gŏs-*tsheh*-vō-lĕ.) Sad, sorrowful.

Angóscia (It.) (än-*gōs*-tshē-ä.) }
Angosciaménte (It.) (än-gōs-tshē-ä-*men*-tĕ.) Anxiety, anguish, grief.

Angosciosaménte (It.) (än-gŏs-tshē-ō-zä-*men*-tĕ.) Apprehensively, anxiously, with anguish.

Angoscióso (It.) (än-gŏs-tshē-*ō*-zō.) Afflicted, distressed.

Ängstlich (Ger.) (*engst*-līkh.) Uneasy, timid, anxious.

Anhaltende Cadenz (Ger.) (*än*-häl-tĕn-dĕ kä-*dĕnts.*) A pedal note or organ point; a protracted cadence.

Anhang (Ger.) (*än*-häng.) A coda; a postscript; an appendix.

Anhänglich (Ger.) (*än*-häng-līkh.) Attached.

Anima (It.) (*än*-ē-mä.) Soul, feeling, animated, lively.

Anima, con. (It.) With life and animation. It can also be applied as meaning "soulful"; thus Chopin uses "Lento e con anima," as "slow and with soul."

Animas (Spa.) (än-ē-*mäs.*) The ringing of a bell in the Roman Catholic church for prayers for souls in purgatory.

Animáto (It.) (än-ē-*mä*-to.) Animated; with life and spirit.

Animazióne (It.) (än-ē-mä-tsē-*ō*-nĕ.) Animation.

Animé (Fr.) (änh-ē-meh.) } Animated,
Animo (It.) (än-ē-mō.) } lively, spirited.

Animo, con. (It.) With boldness.

Animo corde (Lat.) (*än*-è-mō kŏr-dĕ.) An instrument invented in 1789, by Jacob Schnell, of Paris, The tone is produced by wind passing over the strings.

Animosaménte (It.) (än-ē-mō-zä-*men*-tĕ.) Boldly, resolutely.

Anímosissimaménte (It.) (än-ē-mō-zĭs-sē-mä-*men*-tĕ.) Exceedingly bold and resolute.

Animosissimo (It.) (än-ē-mō-*zĭs*-sē-mō.) Exceedingly bold and resolute.

Animóso (It.) (än-ē-*mō*-zō.) In an animated manner; lively, energetic.

Aniversario (Spa.) (än-ē-vĕr-*sä*-rĭ-ō.) A Mass celebrated on the anniversary of a person's death.

Anklang (Ger.) (*än*-kläng.) Accord, harmony, sympathy.

Anklingeln (Ger.) (*än*-klĭng-ĕln.) To ring a bell.

Anklingen (Ger.) (*än*-klĭng-ĕn.) To accord in sound; to be in time.

Anlage (Ger.) (*än*-lä-ghĕ.) The plan or outline of a composition.

Anlaufen (Ger.) (*än*-lou-f'n.) To increase in sound; to swell.

Anleitung (Ger.) (*än*-lī-toong.) An introduction; a preface, guidance, instruction.

Anmuth (Ger.) (*än*-moot.) Sweetness, grace.

Anmuthig (Ger.) (*än*-moo-tĭg.) Agreeable, sweet, pleasant.

Anomalies. False scales or intervals which are found in keyed instruments; they are so-called because incapable of being perfectly tempered.

Anomalous chord. A chord whose intervals are sometimes greater and sometimes less; a chord containing an interval which the tempering of the scale has rendered very sharp or flat.

Anomalous triads. See *Altered Triads.*

Annoner (Fr.) (än-nŏnh-nā.) To hesitate, blunder, or stammer.

Anpfeifen (Ger.) (*än*-pfī-f'n.) To whistle at; to hiss at.

Ansatz (Ger.) (*än*-säts.) The embouchure of a wind instrument; the setting of the lips of a wind instrument player; the attack of a vocal phrase.

Anschlag (Ger.) (*än*-shläg.) A stroke; the percussion of a chord; the striking of a chord or key; the touch in piano playing; a double grace note.

Ansingen (Ger.) (*än*-sĭng-ĕn.) To welcome with a song.

Ansprache (Ger.) (*än*-sprä-khĕ.) Intonation.

Ansprechen (Ger.) (*än*-sprĕ-kh'n.) To sound; to emit, or give forth a sound.

Anstimmen (Ger.) (*än*-stĭm-měn.) To strike up; to begin to sing; to tune.

Anstimmung (Ger.) (*än*-stĭm-moong.) Intonation, tuning.

Answer (Lat. *Comés;* Ger. *Gefährte;* Fr. *Response;* It. *Riposta.*) The response to the subject of a fugue, given by the second voice, either above or below.

Antecedent (ăn-tĕ-sē-děnt.) The subject of a fugue or of a canon; the first phrase of a musical period.

Ante-chapel. That portion of the chapel leading to the choir.

Antanzen (Ger.) (*än*-tän-ts'n.) To begin to dance.

Anth. An abbreviation of anthem.

Anthem. A vocal composition, the words of which are usually selected from the Bible, used in church either with or without organ accompaniment See *Stainer & Barrett.*

Anthem, choral. An anthem in a slow, measured style, after the manner of a choral.

Anthem, full. An anthem consisting wholly of chorus.

Anthem, solo. An anthem consisting of solos and choruses.

Anthologue (Gr.) (*ăn*-thō-lŏg.) A collection of choice pieces.

Anthologium (Gr.) (*ăn*-thō-*lŏg*-I-ŭm.) See *Antiphonarium.*

Anthropoglossa (Gr.) (ăn-thrō-pō-*glŏs*-sä.) The vox humana; an organ stop somewhat resembling the human voice.

Antibacchius (*ăn*-tĭ-*băk*-kī-ŭs.) A musical foot of three syllables, the first two long or accented and the last short or unaccented, thus, — — ᴗ.

Antica (It.) (än-*tē*-kä.) Ancient.

Anticipaménto (It.) (än-tē-tshē-pä-*men*-tō.) Anticipation.

Anticipation. The taking of a note or chord before its natural and expected place, as the starred notes below:

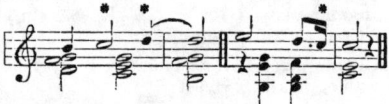

Anticipazione (It.) (än-tē-tshē-pä-zē-ō-nĕ.) See *Anticipation.*

Antico (It.) (än-*tē*-kō.) Ancient.

Antico all' (It.) (än-*tē*-kō äll'.) In the ancient style.

Antienne (Fr.) (ähn-tyĕn.) An anthem.

Antifona (It.) (än-tē-fō-nä.) An anthem.

Antifonario (It.) (än-tē-fō-*nä*-rē-ō.) A book of anthems; an anthem singer.

Antifonero (Spa.) (än-tē-fō-*nä*-rō.) A precentor.

Antiphon. The chant or alternate singing between two choirs in churches and cathedrals; responsive chanting.

Antiphona (Gr.) (än-*tē*-fō-nä.) An anthem.

Antiphonaire (Fr.) (änh-tē-fō-*näir*.) A book of anthems, responses, etc.

Antiphonarium (Gr.) (*ăn*-tĭ-fō-*nä*-rĭ-ŭm.) The collection of Antiphons

ă as in *ah*; ā as in *hate*; ă as in *at*; ē as in *tree*; ĕ as in *eh*; ī as in *pine*; ĭ as in *pin*;

used in the Catholic church; they are sung responsively by the priest and congregation.

Antiphonary. Book of anthems, responses, etc., in the Catholic church.

Antiphone (Gr.) (*ăn*-tĕ-fō-ne.) The response made by one part of the choir to another, or by the congregation to the priest in the Roman Catholic service; also, alternate singing.

Antiphon. Alternate singing or chanting in choirs. See *Antiphone*.

Antiphony. The response of one choir to another when an anthem or psalm is sung by two choirs; alternate singing or chanting.

Antistrophe. } The second couplet of
Antistrophy. } each period in the ancient Greek odes sung in parts; that part of a song or dance which was performed by turning from left to right, in opposition to the *strophe* which turns from right to left.

Antithesis. In fugues, this term is applied to the *answer;* it generally signifies contrast.

Antönen (Ger.) (*än*-tā-nĕn.) To begin to sound; to intone.

Antrommeln (Ger.) (*än*-trōm-mĕln.) To begin to drum.

Antrompeten (Ger.) (*än*-trōm-*pā*-t'n.) To publish by sound of trumpet.

Antwort (Ger.) (*ahn*-tvohrt.) Answer.

Anwachsend (Ger.) (*än*-väkh-sĕnd.) Swelling, increasing.

A otto voci (It.) (ä *ŏt*-tō *vō*-tshē.) For eight voices.

A parte (It.) (ä pär-tĕ.) On the side of; aside.

A parte equale (It.) (ä pär-tĕ ā-*quäh*-lĕ.) A term applied to a musical performance where the voices or instruments sustain an equally prominent part; where two or more performers sustain parts of equal difficulty.

A passo a passo (It.) (ä päs-sō ä päs-sō.) Step by step; regularly.

Apérto (It.) (ä-*pair*-tō.) Open; in pianoforte music it signifies that the damper or open pedal is to be pressed down; clear, distinct; (organ) open pipe.

Apertus (Lat.) (ä-*pĕr*-tŭs.) Open; as, open diapason, open canon, etc.

Aphonie (Fr.) (ă-fō-*nee*.) Aphony; want of voice.

Aphonous. Being destitute of voice.

Aphony (*af*-ō-ny.) Dumbness; loss of voice.

A piacere (It.) (ä pē-ä-*tshair*-rĕ.) At pleasure.

A piaciménto (It.) (pē-ä-tshē-*men*-tō.) At the pleasure or taste of the performer.

Apieni (It.) (ä-pē-*ăy*-nē.) Sounds which are one or more octaves apart, but not discordant.

A piena orchestra (It.) (ä pē-*ăy*-nä ŏr-*kes*-trä.) For full orchestra.

Aplomb (Fr.) (ä-plŏnh.) Firm, in exact time, steadiness, coolness.

A póco (It.) (ä *pō*-kō.) By degrees gradually.

A póco a póco (It.) (ä *pō*-kō ä *pō*-kō.) By little and little.

A póco più lénto (It.) (ä *pō*-kō pē-oo *len*-tō.) A little slower.

A póco più mósso (It.) (ä *pō*-kō pē-oo mōs-sō.) A little quicker.

Apollo. In ancient mythology, the god of music, and said to be the inventor of the lyre.

Apollonicon. A large organ, invented in 1817, with immense self-acting machinery which brought the whole power of the instrument into operation at once, producing the effect of a full orchestra. It had five keyboards, and could be played upon by five performers at the same time.

Apotome (Gr.) (*ăp*-ō-tōme.) That portion of a major tone that remains after deducting from it an interval less by a comma than a major semitone.

Apotome major (Gr.) An enharmonic interval.

Apotome minor (Gr.) An interval smaller than the Apotome Major.

Appassionaménte (It.) (äp-päs-sē-ō-nä-tä-*men*-tĕ.)

Appassionaménto (It.) (äp-päs-sē-ō-nä-tä-*men*-tō.)

Appassionáto (It.) (äp-päs-sē-ō-*nä*-tō.) Passionately; with intense emotion and feeling.

ō as in *tone*; ô as in *dove*; ŏ as in *not*; ŭ as in *up*; ü the French sound of *u*.

19

APPEL

Appel (Fr.) (ăp-pāl.) Military signal to fall in; assembly.

Appenáto (It.) (äp-pĕ-*nä*-tō.) Grieved, distressed; an expression of suffering and melancholy.

Applaudissement (Fr.) (ăp-plō-dĕss-mŏnh.)
Applaúso (It.) (äp-plō-oo-zō.)
Applause.

Applikatur (Ger.) (äp-plĭ-kä-*toor*.) The art of fingering.

Appoggiándo (It.) (äp-pōd-jē-*än*-do.)
Appoggiáto (It.) (äp-pōd-jē-*ä*-tō.)
Leaning upon; dwelt upon; drawn out.

Appoggiatura (It.) (äp-pŏd-jē-ä-*too*-rä.) Leaning note; grace note; note of embellishment. See below.

Appoggiatura, compound. An appoggiatura consisting of two or more grace notes or notes of embellishment.

Appoggiatura, inferior. An appoggiatura situated one degree below its principal note.

Appoggiatura, superior. An appoggiatura situated one degree above its principal note.

The word "Appoggiare," to lean against, accurately describes the character of this long grace-note. It is one of the most charming embellishments of song and of instrumental music. The cause of writing so long and accented a note as a grace note, lies in the fact that the appoggiatura is almost always extraneous to the melody and to the harmony. As there are many misprints made in this connection it will be well for the musician to remember that the character of the appoggiatura is almost always yearning, sorrowful or tender. It has become customary, in recent days, to write the appoggiatura out in full notation. This obviates many mistakes, but it does not always present the character of the progression. Before an even note the appoggiatura generally receives its face value, *i. e.* one half the value of the note which follows. Before a dotted note it receives more than its face value, *i. e.* it should be given two-thirds of the value of the following note.

APPRESTÁRE

If the next note is of the same pitch as the principal note of the appoggiatura, the grace note receives the entire value of its principal note, but is carried to the next note with a strong portamento.

This occurs chiefly in vocal music.

An old rule chiefly used in Italy gave to the appoggiatura its face value even when this was less than half the value of the principal note. Thus:

But this rule is seldom applied nowadays. The appoggiatura effects in many of the works of the old masters have been changed into full notation by modern editors.

It will be noticed that in all cases the appoggiatura is to receive at least half of the length of the note as well as the accent. The principal note (the note following the grace note) is to be made light and short. It will not be wrong sometimes to increase the value of the appoggiatura and decrease the principal note proportionately. The appoggiatura is sometimes called the long grace-note. Some dictionaries (Grove and others) call the short grace-note "appoggiatura" also; for the use of the *short* appoggiatura see *Acciaccatura*. Confusion can here be avoided by using the English equivalents — "*Long grace-note*" and "*Short grace-note*." Authorities to be consulted on this subject are Stainer and Barrett, and Dannreuther's "Musical Ornamentation."

Apprestáre (It.) (äp-prĕs-*tä*-rĕ.) To

ä as in *ah*; ā as in *hate*; ă as in *at*; ē as in *tree*; ĕ as in *eh*; ī as in *pine*; ĭ as in *pin*

20

prepare, or put in a condition to be played.

À première vue (Fr.) (ä prĕm-Ī̆-ār vü.) } At first sight.
A príma vista (It.) (ä *pree*-mä vēz-tä.) }

Âpre (Fr.) (äpr.) Harsh.

Âprement (Fr.) (äpr-mŏnh.) Harshly.

Âpreté (Fr.) (äp-rĕ-tä.) Harshness.

A púnta d'arco (It.) (ä poon-tä d'är-kō.) With the point of the bow.

A púnto (It.) (ä *poon*-tō.) Punctually, exactly, correctly.

À quatre mains (Fr.) (ä kătr-mănh.) } For four hands.
A quáttro máni (It.) (ä *quät*-trō *mä*-ni.) }

For two performers on one pianoforte.

A quáttro, or a 4 (It.) For four voices or instruments; a quartette.

A quáttro parti (It.) (ä *quät*-trō pär-tē.). In four parts.

À quatre voix (Fr.) (ä kătr vwä.) } For four voices.
A quáttro vóci (It.) (ä *quät*-trō vō-tshee.) }

À quatre seuls (Fr.) (ä kătr sŭl.) } For four solo
A quáttro sóli (It.) (ä *quät*-trō sō-lē.) }

voices or instruments.

Arabesque or Arabesk, an ornament, or an embellished work. From the Moorish architecture which was much ornamented.

Arbitrii (Lat.) (ä-*bĭt*-rĭ-ē.) Certain points or embellishments which a singer introduces or improvises at pleasure while singing an aria or tune.

Abítrio (It.) (är-*bē*-tre-ō.) At the will or pleasure of the performer.

Arc (It.) (ärk.) The bow; an abbreviation of Arco.

Arcata (It.) (är-*kä*-tä.) Manner of bowing.

Arcáto (It.) (är-*kä*-tō.) Bowed; played with the bow.

Arch. A curve formerly placed over a bass note to show that it was accompanied by the imperfect fifth.

Arch-chanter. The leader of the chants; the chief chanter.

Arche (Ger.) (*är*-khĕ.) The sounding board of an organ.

Archeggiaménto (It.) (är-kād-jē-ä-*men*-tō.) The management of the bow in playing the violin, etc.

Archeggiare (It.) (är-kād-jē-*ä*-rĕ.) To use the bow; to fiddle.

Archet (Fr.) (är-shāy.) } A violin bow
Archettino (It.) (är-kĕt-*tē*-nō.) }

Archétto (It.) (är-*kĕt*-tō.) } A little bow.
Archicéllo (It.) (är-kē-*tshĕl*-lō.) }

Archiluth (Fr.) (är-shē-lüt.) } See Archlute.
Arciliúto (It.) (är-tshēl-*yoo*-tō.) }

Archlute. A theorbo or lute with two nuts and sets of strings, one for the bass. The strings of the theorbo were single, but in the bass strings were doubled with an octave, and the small strings with a unison.

Arco (It.) (*är*-kō.) The bow.

Ardénte (It.) (är-*den*-tĕ.) With fire glowing, vehement.

Ardenteménte (It.) (är-dĕn-tĕ-*men*-tĕ.) Ardently, vehemently.

Ardentíssimo (It.) (är-dĕn-*tis*-sē-mō.) Very ardently.

Arditaménte (It.) (är-di-tä-*men*-tĕ.) Boldly; with ardor.

Arditezza (It.) (är-di-*tet*-sä.) Boldness.

Ardíto (It.) (är-*dē*-to.) Bold; with energy.

Ardíto di molto (It.) (är-*dē*-tō dē *mōl*-tō.) Passionately; with much force.

Ardóre (It.) (ahr-*dor*-eh.) *Con Ardore* with ardor and warmth.

Aretinian syllables. The syllables ut, re, me, fa, sol, la, introduced by Guido d'Arezzo for his system of hexachords or six notes: these syllables to occur in consecutive notes of the scale, in an ancient hymn to St. John.

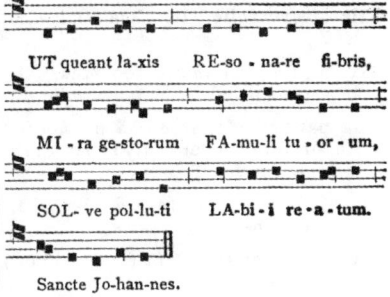

UT queant la-xis RE-so-na-re fi-bris,

MI-ra ge-sto-rum FA-mu-li tu-or-um,

SOL-ve pol-lu-ti LA-bi-i re-a-tum.

Sancte Jo-han-nes.

ō as in *tone;* ô as in *dove;* ŏ as in *not;* ŭ as in *up;* ü the French sound of *u.*

21

Argentin (Fr.) (är-zhän-tănh.) Silver toned.

Arghool (Tur.) (är-gool.) A musical instrument of the Turks, of the flute species.

Aria (It.) (ä-rē-ä.) An air; a song; a tune; sung by a single voice either with or without an accompaniment. The aria first developed into shape in the early operas. Cavalli, Cesti and D. Scarlatti may be regarded as the founders of the *Da Capo Aria* in three large divisions. Div. I was generally brilliant and powerful. Div. II of *Cantabile* character in contrast of style and key. After this there came a literal repeat of Div. I. " He was Despised " is an example of this aria. When the repeat of Div. I was varied, a better form resulted. See " Rejoice Greatly " for this varied return. Sometimes the aria was in two contrasted divisions without return, as in " I know that my Redeemer liveth." Modern composers sometimes use an abbreviated return of first division, as, for example, Mendelssohn in " Oh God, have mercy," or in " It is enough."

Aria bûffa (It.) (ä-rē-ä *boof-*fä.) A comic or humorous air.

Aria cantábile (It.) (ä-rē-ä-kän-*ta*-bē-lĕ.) An air in a graceful and melodious style.

Aria concertáta (It.) (ä-rē-ä kŏn-tshĕr-*ta*-tä.) An air with orchestral accompaniments in a Concertánte style; a concerted air.

Aria d'abilitá (It.) (ä-rē-ä d'ä-bēl-lē-*ta*.) A difficult air requiring great skill and musical ability in the singer.

Aria di bravúra (It.) (ä-rē-ä dē brä-*voo*-rä.) A florid air in bold, marked style and permitting great freedom of execution.

Aria di cantábile (It.) See *Aria Cantábile*.

Aria fugáta (It.) (ä-rē-ä foo-*ga*-tä.) An air accompanied in the fugue style.

Aria parlánte (It.) (ä-rē-ä pär-*län*-tĕ.) An air in the declamatory style; a recitative *a tempo*.

Aria tedésca (It.) (ä-rē-ä tĕ-*das*-kä.) An air in the German style.

Aria und chor (Ger.) (ä-rĭ-ä oond kōr.) Air and chorus.

Arie (It. pl.) (ä-rē-ĕ.) } Airs or
Arien (Ger. pl.) (ä-rĭ-ĕn.) } songs.

Arie aggiúnte (It.) (ä-rē-ĕ äd-jē-*oon*-tĕ.) Airs added to or introduced into an opera, or other large work.

Ariétta (It.) (ä-rē-*et*-tä.) } A short air or
Ariette (Fr.) (ä-rē-ĕt.) } melody.

Ariétta alla Veneziána (It.) (ä-rē-*at*-tä äl-lä vĕn-ä-tsē-ä-nä.) A short air in the style of the Venetian Barcarolles.

Ariettina (It.) (ä-rē-ĕt-*te*-nä.) A very short air or melody.

A rigore del tempo (It.) (ä rē-*go*-rĕ dĕl *tĕm*-pō.) In strict time.

Arigot (Fr.) (ä-rē-gō.) A fife.

Ariosa (It.) (ä-rē-*o*-zä.) In the movement of an aria or tune.

Arióse cantáte (It. pl.) (ä-rē-*o*-zĕ kän-*ta*-tĕ.) Airs in a style between a song and recitative, introducing frequent changes in time and manner.

Arióso (It.) (ä-rē-*o*-zō) Melodious, graceful; a short piece in the style of an aria, but less symmetrical in construction. Sometimes containing some recitative effects. " Behold and See " in *The Messiah* is an example of the latter.

Arm. A small piece of iron at the end of the roller of an organ.

Armer la clef (Fr.) (är-mā lä klā.) The signature; or, the flats and sharps placed immediately after the clef.

Armoneggiáre (It.) (är-mŏ-nĕd-jē-*a*-rĕ.) To sound in harmony.

Armonía (It.) (är-mō-*ne*-ä.) Harmony, concord.

Armoniáco (It.) (är-mō-nē-*a*-kō.) Harmonized.

Armoniále (It.) (är-mō-nē-*a*-lĕ.) Harmonious, concordant.

Armoniáto (It.) (är-mō-nē-*a*-tō.) See *Armoniáco*.

Armónica (It.) (är-*mo*-nē-kä.) The earliest form of the accordion; a collection of musical glasses, so arranged as to produce musical effects.

Armonica, guida (It.) (är-*mo*-nē-kä gwē-dä.) A guide to harmony.

Armonici (It.) (är-mō-*ne*-tshee.) Harmonics.

ă as in *ah*; ā as in *hate*; ă as in *at*; ē as in *tree*; ĕ as in *eh*; ī as in *pine*; ĭ as in *pin*;

ARMONICO   ARSIS

Armónico (It.) (är-*mō*-nē-kō.) Harmonious.

Armoniosaménte (It.) (är-*mō*-nē-ō-zä-*men*-tĕ.) Harmoniously.

Armonióso (It.) (är-mō-nē-*ō*-zō.) Concordant, harmonious.

Armonísta (It.) (är-mō-*nēs*-tä.) One who is acquainted with the principles of harmony.

Armonizzamento (It.) (är-mō-nēt-zä-*men*-tō.) Agreement, concord.

Armonizzánte (It.) (är-mō-nēt-*tsän*-tĕ.) That is harmonious; musical.

Armonizzáre (It.) (är-mō-nēt-*tsä*-rĕ.) To harmonize; to make harmony.

Arm viol. The viola, called by the Italians, Viola di Braccio, because it rested on the arm.

A rovescio (It.) (ä-rō-*vā*-shē-ō.) Reversed; in an opposite direction; responding to rising intervals by falling ones, and vice versa.

Arpa (It.) (*är*-pä.) }
Arpa (Sp.) (*är*-pä.) } The harp.

Arpa d' Eolo (It.) (*är*-pä d' ā-*ō*-lō.) An Æolian harp.

Arpa dóppia (It.) (*är*-pä *dōp*-pē-ä.) The double action harp; it meant formerly a harp with two strings to each note.

Arpa eolica (It.) (är-pä ā-*ō*-lē-kä.) Æolian harp or lyre.

Arpanétta (It.) (är-pä-*nāt*-tä.) }
Arpinélla (It.) (är-pē-*nel*-lä.) } A small harp or lute.

Arpeg. An abbreviation of Arpeggio.

Arpègement (Fr.) (är-pezh-mänh.) An arpeggio.

Arpegger (Fr.) (är-pĕ-zhā.) To play arpeggios.

Arpeggi (It.) (är-*pĕd*-jē.) Arpeggios.

Arpeggiaménto (It.) (är-päd-jē-ä-*men*-tō.) In the style of the harp; arpeggio.

Arpeggiándo (It.) (är--ped-jē-*än*-dō.) }
Arpeggiáto (It.) (är-ped-jē-*ä*-tō.) } Music played arpeggio, in imitation of the harp; harping, harp music.

Arpeggiáre (It.) (är-ped-jē *ä*-rĕ.) To play upon the harp.

Arpeggiatúra (It.) (är-ped-jē-ä-*too*-rä.)

Playing arpeggio, or in the style of the harp.

Arpéggio (It.) (är-ped-jē-ō.) Playing the notes of a chord quickly one after another in the harp style, thus: In pianoforte music a waved line is written beside a chord intended to be played *arpeggio*: The first of these means arpeggio both hands together, but the second signifies to arpeggio from the lowest to the highest note. An arpeggioed chord is generally written and played as follows:

The arpeggio should begin at the rhythmic value of the chord, whether it is indicated by the sign or by small notes, as the effect of a chord is weakened by being begun before its time, as is the bad habit of many inexperienced players.

Arpeggio accompaniment. An accompaniment which consists chiefly of chords played in arpeggio style.

Arpicórdo (It.) (är-pē-*kōr*-dō.) A Harpsichord.

Arp'o. An abbreviation of Arpeggio and Arpeggiato.

Arr. }
Arrang. } Abbreviations of *arrangement*.

Arrangement. The selection and adaptation of a composition or parts of a composition to instruments for which it was not originally designed, or for some other use for which it was not at first written.

Arranger (Fr.) (ăr-ränh-zhā.) } To ar-
Arrangiren (Ger.) (är-ränh-*zhē*-r'n.) } range music.
See *Arrangement*.

Ars canendi (Lat.) (ärs kä-*nĕn*-dē.) The art of singing with taste and expression.

Ars componentis (Lat.) (ärs *kŏm*-pō-*nĕn*-tīs.) The art of composing.

Arsis (Gr.) (*är*-sĭs.) The upstroke of

ō as in *tone*; ô as in *dove*; ŏ as in *not*; ŭ as in *up*; ü the French sound of *u*.

the hand in beating time. The light accent of the measure. Not employed by musicians in the same sense that it is used in poetry. See *Accent*.

Ars musica (Lat.) (ärs *mū*-sĭ-kä.) The art of music.

Art (Ger.) (ärt.) Species, kind, quality. As "Auf Russische Art," in Russian style.

Art de l'archet (Fr.) (ärt düh l'ar-shā.) The art of bowing.

Articoláre (It.) (är-tē-kō-lä-rĕ.) }
Articuler (Fr.) (är-tē-kü-lā.) } To pronounce the words distinctly; to articulate each note.

Articulate. To utter distinct separate tones; to sing with a distinct and clear enunciation.

Articulation. A distinct and clear utterance; a clear and exact rendering of every syllable and tone.

Articoláto (It.) (är-tē-kō-*lä*-tō.) Articulated; distinctly enunciated.

Articolazíone (It.) (är-tē-kō-*lä*-tsē-*ō*-nĕ.) Exact and distinct pronunciation.

Artificial. Not natural; a term applied to notes or chords when chromatics are introduced.

Artikuliren (Ger.) (är-tĭk-oo-*lē*-r'n.) To articulate.

Artísta (It.) (är-*tis*-tä.) }
Artiste (Fr.) (är-*tēst*.) } An artist; one who excels in the composition or performance of music.

Arzillo (It.) (är-*tsēl*-lō.) Lively, sprightly.

As (Ger.) (äs.) The note A flat.

Ascoltatore (It.) (äs-kŏl-tä-*tō*-rĕ.) An auditor; a hearer.

Asculæ (Gr.) (äs-*koo*-lē.) A name given by the ancients to performers on the organ.

As dur (Ger.) (äs door.) The key of A♭ major.

Asheor (Heb.) (ä-shĕ-ōr.) A ten-stringed instrument of the Hebrews. The Azor.

As moll (Ger.) (äs-mōll.) The key of A♭ minor.

Asperges me (Lat.) (äs-*pĕr*-gĕs mā.) The opening of the Mass in the Catholic service. Not a number of the musical Mass itself, but sung during the purification of the altar at the beginning of the service.

Aspiráre (It.) (äs-pē-*rä*-rĕ.) To breathe loudly; to use too much breath in singing.

Asprézza (It.) (äs-*prād*-sä.) Roughness, dryness, harshness.

Assái (It.) (äs-*sä*-ē.) Very, extremely; in a high degree, as Allégro Assái, very quick.

Assai più (It.) (äs-*sä*-ē pēe-oo.) Much more.

Assemblage (Fr.) (äs-sanh-bläzh.) Double tongueing on the flute; executing rapid passages on wind instruments.

Assez (Fr.) (äs-sāy.) Enough, sufficiently.

Assez lent (Fr.) (äs-say länh.) Quite slowly.

Assolúto (It.) (äs-sō-*loo*-tō.) Absolute, free; alone, one voice. Also applied to artists as "prima donna assoluta," the chief *prima donna*.

Assonant. Having a resemblance or agreement of sounds.

Assonánte (It.) (äs-sō-*nän*-tĕ.) Harmonious, consonant.

Assonanz (Ger.) (äs-sō-*nän*-ts.) }
Assonánza (It.) (äs-sō-*nän*-tsä.) } Similarity, or consonance of tone.

Assourdir (Fr.) (äs-soor-*dēr*.) To muffle to deafen; to stun.

A súo arbítrio (It.) (ä swō är-*bē*-trē-ō.) }
A súo béne plácito (It.) (ä swō bā-nĕ *plä*-tshēe-tō.) }
A súo cómodo (It.) (ä swō *kō*-mō-dō.) }
At pleasure; at will; at the inclination or discretion of the performer; synonymous with ad libitum.

A súo luógo (It.) (ä swō loo-*ō*-gō.) Synonymous with Loco.

Asymphonie (Ger.) (ä-sĭm-fō-*nēe*.) Dissonance.

À table sec (Fr.) (ä täbl sĕk.) }
À table sèche (Fr.) (ä täbl säsh.) } The practice of vocal exercises unaccompanied by an instrument.

A tém (It.) }
A temp (It.) } Abbreviations of A Tempo.

A témpo (It.) (ä tĕm-pō.) In time; a term used to denote that after some

ă as in *ah*; ā as in *hate*; ă as in *at*; ē as in *tree*; ĕ as in *eh*; ī as in *pine*; ĭ as in *pin*;

deviation or relaxation of the time, the performers must return to the original movement.

A témpo dell' allegro (It.) (ä těm-pō děll' äl-lā-gro.) In allegro time.

A tempo cómodo (It.) (ä těm-po kō-mŏ-dō.) In convenient time; an easy, moderate time.

A tempo di gavótta (It.) (ä těm-pō dē gä-*vōt*-tä.) In the time of a gavot; moderately quick.

A tempo giústo (It.) (ä těm-pō *joos*-tō.) In just, strict, exact time. Sometimes employed after Tempo Rubato — irregular time.

A tempo ordinário (It.) (ä těm-pō ŏr-dē-nä-rē-ō.) In ordinary, moderate time.

A tempo primo (It.) (ä täm-pō prē-mō.) In the time first given.

A tempo rubáto (It.) (ä těm-pō roo-*bä*-tō.) Irregular time; deviation in time so as to give more expression, but so that the time of each measure is not altered on the whole.

Athem (Ger.) (*ä*-těm.) Breath, breathing, respiration.

Athemholen (Ger.) (*ä*-těm-*hō*-l'n.) To breathe; to respire.

Athemlos (Ger.) (*a*-těm-los.) Breathlessly.

Athmen (Ger.) (*ät*-měn.) To blow softly.

Athemzug (Ger.) (*ä*-těm-tsoog.) Act of respiration; breathing.

À ton basse (Fr.) (*ä* tōnh bäss.) In a low tone of voice.

A tre, or a 3 (It.) (ä tray.) For three voices or instruments; a Trio or Terzétto.

A tre córde (It.) (ä trāy-*kōr*-dě.) For three strings; with three strings; without the soft pedal. See *Pedals*.

A tre máni (It.) (ä trāy *mä*-nē.) For three hands.

A tre parti (It.) (ä trāy *pär*-tē.) In three parts.

A tre soli (It.) (ä trāy *sō*-lē.) For three solo voices.

A tre soprani (It.) (ä trāy sō-*prä*-nē.) For three soprano voices.

A tre voci (It.) (ä trāy *vō*-tshē.) For three voices.

À trois mains (Fr.) (ä trwäh mänh.) For three hands.

À trois, or a 3 (Fr.) (ä trwäh.) For three voices or instruments.

À trois parties (Fr.) (ä trwäh pär-tē.) In three parts.

À trois voix (Fr.) (ä träwh vwäh.) For three voices.

Attable (Fr.) (ät-*täbl*.) A kind of Moorish drum.

Attácca (It.) (ät-*täk*-kä.) Go on. Begin the next.

Attácca súbito (It.) (ät-*täk*-kä *soo*-bē-tō.) Attack or commence the next movement immediately.

Attacca l'allegro (It.) (ät-*täk*-kä l' äl-*lä* grō.) Commence the allegro immediately.

Attaccáre (It.) (ät-täk-*kä*-rě.) ⎫ To attack or
Attaquer (Fr.) (ät-täk-ā.) ⎭ commence the performance.

Attack. The method or clearness of beginning a phrase. The term is applied to solo or concerted music, either vocal or instrumental.

Attacco (It.) (ah-*tahk*-cō.) A short, decisive subject, or passage, in fugal work.

Attastáre (It.) (ät-täs-tä-rě.) To touch; to strike.

Attendant keys. Those scales having most sounds in common with the scale of any given key; the relative keys. In C major the attendant keys are: its relative minor A, the dominant G, and its relative minor E, the sub-dominant F, and its relative minor D.

Attillatamente (It.) (ät-tēl-lä-tä-*men*-tě.) With affection.

ŏ as in *tone*; ǫ as in *dove*; ŏ as in *not*; ŭ as in *up*; ü the French sound of *u*.

25

ATTO   AUGMENTED UNISON

Atto (It.) (*ät*-tō.) An act of an opera or play.

Atto di cadenza (It.) (*ät*-tō dē kä-*den*-tsa.) The point in a piece where a cadence may be introduced.

Atto primo (It.) (*ät*-tō *prē*-mō.) The first act.

Attóre (It.) (ät-*tō*-rĕ.) An actor or singer in an opera or play.

Attóri (It.) (ät-*tō*-rē.) The principal actors or singers in an opera.

Atto secóndo (It.) (*ät*-tō sĕ-*kōn*-dō.) The second act.

Atto terzo (It.) (ät-tō tĕr-tsō.) The third act.

Aubade (Fr.) (ō-*bad*.) Morning music; a morning concert in the open air. The opposite of a serenade. Schubert's setting of Shakespeare's "Hark, Hark the Lark" is an aubade. A morning concert by a military band.

Au commencement (Fr.) (ō cŏm-mänhs-mänh.) At the beginning.

Audáce (It.) (ä-oo-*dä*-tshĕ.) Bold, spirited, audacious.

Auf (Ger.) (ouf.) On, upon, in, at, etc.

Auf blasen (Ger.) (*ouf*-blä-z'n.) To sound a wind instrument.

Auf dem Oberwerk (Ger.) (ouf dĕm *ō*-bĕr-vārk.) Upon the *upper-work* or highest row of keys in organ playing.

Aúffassung (Ger.) (*ouf*-fas-soong.) The interpretation or conception of a work.

Aufführung (Ger.) (*ouf*-fear-roong.) Performance.

Aufgeregt (Ger.) (*ouf*-gĕ-raygt.) With agitation; excitedly.

Aufgeweckt (Ger.) (*ouf*-ghĕ-vĕkt.) Lively, sprightly, cheerful, wide awake.

Aufgewecktheit (Ger.) (*ouf*-ghĕ-*vĕkt* hīt.) Liveliness, cheerfulness.

Aufhalten (Ger.) (*ouf*-häl-t'n.) To stop; to retard; to keep back.

Aufhaltung (Ger.) (*ouf*-häl-toong.) Keeping back; a suspension.

Auflage (Ger.) (*ouf*-lä-ghĕ.) Edition.

Auflösung (Ger.) (*ouf*-lô-zoong.) The resolution of a discord.

Auflösungs zeichen. The cancel or natural.

Aufpfeifen (Ger.) (*ouf*-pfī-f'n.) To play on a pipe, fife, or flute.

Aufs (Ger.) (*oufs*.) To the; on the.

Aufschlag (Ger.) (*ouf*-shläg.) Up-beat; the arsis; the unaccented part of a bar.

Aufschallen (Ger.) (*ouf*-shäl-l'n.) To sound loudly.

Aufschnitt (Ger.) (*ouf*-schnit.) The mouth of an organ pipe.

Aufsingen (Ger.) (*ouf*-sïng-ĕn.) To sing to; to awaken by singing.

Aufspielen (Ger.) (*ouf*-spē-l'n.) To play upon; to play for the dance.

Aufsteigende Tonarten (Ger. pl.) (*ouf*-stī-ghĕn-dĕ *tōn*-är-t'n.) Ascending scales or keys.

Aufstrich (Ger.) (*ouf*-strĭkh.) An up-bow.

Auftakt (Ger.) (*ouf*-täkt.) The arsis; the up-beat.

Augmentatio (Lat.) (aug-mĕn-*tä*-shĭ-ō.) Augmentation.

Augmentation. In counterpoint this signifies that the notes of the subject are repeated or imitated with notes of more than their original value.

Augmenté (Fr.) (ōg-mänh-*tā*.) Augmented.

Augmentazione (It.) (oug-mĕn-tä-tsē-*ō*-nĕ.) Increase.

Augmented. An epithet applied to such intervals as are more than a major or perfect.

Augmented fifth. An interval containing four whole tones or steps.

Augmented fourth. An interval containing three whole tones or steps.

Augmented intervals. Those which include a semitone A perfect fifth. Augmented fifth. more than major or perfect intervals; as,

Augmented octave. An interval containing a semitone more than an octave.

Augmented second. An interval containing one whole and one semitone equal to three half steps.

Augmented sixth. An interval containing four whole tones or steps and one semitone or half step.

Augmented unison. A semitone, or half step with both notes written on the same degree as,

---

ă as in *ah*; ā as in *hate*; ă as in *at*; ē as in *tree*; ĕ as in *eh*; ī as in *pine*; ĭ as in *pin*,

26

AUGMÉNTO

Augménto (It.) (oug-*měn*-to.) Augmentation.

Auletes (Gr.) (ou-*lē*-tēs.) A flute player; a piper.

Au lever du rideau (Fr.) (ō lĕ-vä dü rē-do.) At the rising of the curtain.

Aulo (It.) (ou-lō.) } A species of ancient flute.
Aulos (Gr.) (*ou*-lŏs.) }

Aulodia (It.) (ou-*lō*-dĭ-ä.) Singing accompanied by the flute.

Augmentazióne (It.) (ou-měn-tä-tsē-*ō*-nĕ.) Augmentation.

A úna córda (It.) (ä *oo*-nä *kōr*-dä.) The soft pedal, in piano playing; one string.

Aus (Ger.) (ous.) From; out of.

Ausarbeitung (Ger.) (*ous*-är-bī-toong.) The last finish or elaboration of a composition.

Ausblänken (Ger.) (*ous*-blän-k'n.) To play the closing chords of a piece on a wind instrument.

Ausblasen (Ger.) (*ous*-blä-z'n.) To blow out; to publish by sound of trumpet.

Ausdehnung (Ger.) (*ous*-dā-noong.) Expansion, extension, development.

Ausdruck (Ger.) (*ous*-drook.) Expression.

Ausdrucksvoll (Ger.) (*ous*-drooks-fŏll.) Expressive.

Ausführung (Ger.) (*ous*-fear-roong.) Performance; the working out of a subject in composition; the exposition.

Ausfüllung (Ger.) (*ous*-fül-loong.) The filling up; the middle parts.

Ausgabe (Ger.) (*ous*-gä-bĕ.) Edition.

Ausgang (Ger.) (*ous*-gäng.) Going out; exit; conclusion.

Ausgehalten (Ger.) (*ous*-ghĕ-häl-t'n.) Sostenuto.

Ausgelassen (Ger.) (*ous*-ghĕ-*läs*-s'n.) Wild, ungovernable, with abandon.

Ausgelassenheit (Ger.) (*ous*-ghĕ-*läs*-s'n-hīt.) Extravagance; with wild abandon.

Aushalten (Ger.) (*ous*-häl-t'n.) To hold on; to sustain a note.

Aushaltung (Ger.) (*ous*-häl-toong.) The sustaining of a note.

Aushaltungszeichen (Ger.) (*ous*-häl-toongs-*tsī*-kh'n.) A pause (⌢).

Auslauten (Ger.) (*ous*-lou-t'n.) To emit a sound.

AUXILIARY NOTES

Ausklingen (Ger.) (*ous*-klĭng-ĕn.) To cease sounding.

Aussingen (Ger.) (*ous*-sĭng-ĕn.) To sing out; to sing to the end.

Ausweichen (Ger.) (*ous*-vī-kh'n.) To make a transition from one key to another; to modulate.

Ausweichung (Ger.) (*ous*-vī-khoong.) A transient modulation or change of key.

Auténtico (It.) (ou-*tän*-tē-kō.) Authentic.

Auteur (Fr.) (ō-tŭr.) An author; a composer.

Authentic. A name given to those church modes whose melody was confined within the limits of the tonic, or final, and its octave.

Authentic cadence. The old name for a perfect cadence; the harmony of the dominant followed by that of the tonic, or the progression of the dominant to the tonic.

Authentic keys. Among the ancient Greeks, those keys whose tones extended from the tonic to the fifth and octave above.

Authentic modes are those ecclesiastical modes or tones (scales) which are composed of a fifth and a fourth (for instance, $\widehat{d\,e\,f\,g}\,\widehat{a\,b\,c\,d}$), and have their final on the first degree of the scale. The *Plagal* modes, which were constructed on the authentic modes, are composed of a fourth and a fifth (for instance, $\widehat{a\,b\,c\,d}\,\widehat{e\,f\,g\,a}$), and have their final on the fourth degree of the scale.

Authentic part of the Scale, in Counterpoint and Fugue, is that which lies between a note and its Dominant, whilst that which lies between the Dominant and the tonic above it is termed Plagal. The terms are used chiefly in connection with Subject and Answer.

Authentique (Fr.) (ō-těn-těk.) Authentic.

Autóre (It.) (ou-tō-rĕ.) An author; a composer.

Auxiliary notes. Notes standing on the next degree above or below an essential note; the harmony remaining stationary and not moving from one essential note to another. If occurring below the essential note of the melody, they are a semitone below, but if above

ō as in *tone*; ô as in *dove*; ŏ as in *not*; ŭ as in *up*; ü the French sound of *u*.

27

they may be either a tone or a semitone distant from the principal note. The following, from Rossini's overture to "William Tell," shows the auxiliary note above the principal:

Auxiliary scales. This name is sometimes given to the *relative* or *attendant* keys.

Avant-dernier (Fr.) (ä-vänh děr-nē-ā.) The penultimate; the last but one.

Avant-scène (Fr.) (ä-vänh sān.) Before the opening of the opera or scene.

Ave (Lat.) (a-vĕ.) Hail.

Avec (Fr.) (ä-vĕk.) With.

Avec allégresse (Fr.) (ä-vĕk ăl-lĕ-grĕs.) Lively, sprightly.

Avec âme (Fr.) (ä-vĕk äm.) With feeling or grace.

Avec douleur (Fr.) (ä-vĕk doo-lŭr.) With grief; with sadness.

Avec feu (Fr.) (ä-vĕk fü.) With fire.

Avec force (Fr.) (ä-vĕk fōrss.) With power.

Avec goût (Fr.) (ä-vĕk goo.) With taste.

Avec grande expression (Fr.) (ä-vĕk granh dĕx-prā-sĭ-ŏnh.) With great expression.

Avec le chant (Fr.) The same as *Col Canto*.

Avec lenteur (Fr.) (ä-vĕk länh-tür.) With slowness; lingering.

Avec les pieds (Fr.) (ä-vĕk lĕ pĕ-ā.) With the feet, in organ playing.

Avec liaison (Fr.) (ä-vĕk lĭ-ā-sŏnh.) With smoothness.

Avec mouvement (Fr.) (ä-vĕk moov-mŏnh.) With movement.

Ave Maria (Lat.) (*ä-vĕ* mä-*rēe*-ä.) Hail Mary. A hymn or prayer to the Virgin Mary. See Luke I, 42, for the origin of the words.

Ave Maris Stella. A hymn of the Catholic Church, the words meaning, "Hail, Star of the Sea."

Ave regina (Lat.) (*ä-vĕ* rĕ-*gē*-nä.) Vesper hymn to the Virgin, sung from the Purification till Easter.

A vicénda (It.) (ä vē-*tshen*-dä.) Alternately; by turns.

A vide (Fr.) (ä vēd.) Open.

A vísta (It.) (ä *vēs*-tä.) At sight.

A vóce sóla (It.) (ä *vö*-tshĕ *sō*-lä.) For one voice alone.

À voix forte (Fr.) (ä vwä fŏrt.) With a loud voice.

À volonté (Fr.) (ä vō-lŏnh-tā.) At will, at pleasure.

À vue (Fr.) (ä vü.) At sight.

Azióne sacra (It.) (ä-tsē-*ō*-nĕ *sä*-krä.) An Oratorio; a sacred musical drama.

B

B. The seventh note in the scale of C. It is called *Si* in France and Italy, and *H* in Germany. The Germans use the letter B to designate B flat. As the flat came from the letter B the Germans still call flats "B's." See *Flat, Sharp, Natural, Cancel*.

Babillage (Fr.) (*bä*-biy-ähg.) Playful chatter.

Bacchanale (Ger.) (bach-ah-*nah*-leh.) } Drinking songs

Bacchanalian songs, songs pertaining to drinking and revelry.

Bacchius (Gr.) (*băk*-kĭ-ūs.) A musical foot, consisting of one short, unaccented, and two long, accented notes or syllables marked ◡ — —.

Bacchuslied (Ger.) (*bäkh*-oos-lēd.) A Bacchanalian song.

Bachelor of Music. The first musical degree taken at the universities.

ä as in *ah* ; ā as in *hate* ; ă as in *at* ; ē as in *tree* ; ĕ as in *eh* ; ī as in *pine* ; ĭ as in *pin*;

BADINAGE

Badinage (Fr.) (bä-dĭ-*näzh*.) Playfulness, sportiveness.

Bagatelle (Fr.) (băg-ä-*tĕl*.) A trifle; a toy; a short, easy piece of music.

Bagpipes. A favorite Scotch instrument, one of whose pipes is a *drone*, producing always the same sound, which serves as a perpetual bass for every tune. It is a very ancient instrument, and in one form or another has been in general use, not only in England and Scotland, but many European countries.

Baguette (Fr.) (bä-*ghĕt*.) A drumstick.

Baguettes de tambour (Fr.) (bä-ghĕt dŭh täm-boor.) Drumsticks.

Baisser (Fr.) (bās-sā.) To lower or flatten the tone or pitch.

Baisser le rideau (Fr.) (bās-sā lŭh rē-dō.) To drop the curtain.

Balalaika (Rus.) (bä-lä-*lā*-kä.) A rude instrument of the Russians, with three strings.

Bälgetreter (Ger.) (*băl*-ghĕ-trĕt-ēr.) Organ blower or bellows treader in old German organs.

Balgzug (Ger.) (*bälg*-tsoog.) In an organ; the bellows stop.

Balancé (Fr.) (bă-länh-*sā*.) A step or figure in dancing.

Balancement (Fr.) (băl-*änhs*-mänh.) Quivering motion; a tremolo.

Balcken (Ger.) (*băl*-k'n.) The bass bar placed under the fourth string of a violin.

Baldaménte (It.) (bäl-dä-*men*-tĕ.) Boldly.

Baldánza (It.) (bäl-*den*-tsä.) } Audacity,
Baldézza (It.) (bäl-*det*-sä.) } boldness.

Balken (Ger.) (*băl*-k'n.) See *Balcken*.

Ballábile (It.) (bäl-*lä*-bēe-lĕ.) In the style of a dance.

Ballad. A short, simple song of natural construction, usually in the narrative or descriptive form. It formerly had a wider signification and was applied to music set to romance or historical poem, and also to a light kind of music used both in singing and dancing. The word "Ballad" means, now, any unvaried simple song, each verse being sung to the same melody, or any song which is narrative in character. Loewe's ballads illustrate the latter class. See Chappell's "National English Airs," "Old English Ditties," etc.

BALLI UNGARÉSI

Ballade (Ger.) (bäl-*lä*-dé.) } A dance; dancing; also a
Balláta (It.) (bäl-lä-tä.) } Ballad.

Balladendichter (Ger.) (bäl-*läd'n*-dĭkh-tĕr.) A ballad writer.

Balladensänger (Ger.) (bäl-*läd'n*-säng-ĕr.) A ballad singer.

Ballad opera. Light opera; an opera in which ballads and dances predominate.

Balladry. The subject or style of ballads.

Balláre (It.) (bä-lä-rĕ.) To dance.

Ballatélla (It.) (bäl-lä-*tel*-lä.) } A short
Ballatétta (It.) (bäl-lä-*tet*-tä.) } Balläta.

Ballatóre (It.) (bäl-lä-*tō*-rĕ.) A dancer; a male dancer.

Ballatríce (It.) (bäl-lä-*trēe*-tshĕ.) A female dancer.

Ballamatia (It.) (bäl-lĕ-*mä*-tē-ä.) } Songs or melodies
Ballistia (It.) (bäl-*lēs*-tē-ä.) } in the dance style.

Ballerína (It.) (bäl-lĕ-*rēe*-nä.) A dancing mistress; a female dancer.

Balleríno (It.) (bäl-lĕ-*rēe*-nō.) A dancing master; a male dancer.

Ballet (Fr.) (bă-lā.) } A theatrical representation
Balléto (It.) (bäl-*lĕt*-tŏ.) } of some story by means of dances or pantomimic action, accompanied with music. In the sixteenth century the term *ballet*, *ballad*, or *ballette* was applied to a light kind of music which was both sung and danced. A madrigalian part-song with a "Fa-la" chorus.

Ballet master. The person who superintends the rehearsals of the ballet, and who frequently invents the plot and its details.

Ballette. A ballet.

Balletti (I.) (bäl-*lăt*-tē.) Dance airs.

Bálli (It. pl.) (*bäl*-lē.) Dances.

Bálli Inglési (It. pl.) (*băl*-lē ēn-glä-zē.) English country dances.

Bálli Ungarési (It. pl.) (*băl*-lē oon-gä-*rā*-zē.) Hungarian dances in ¾ time, generally syncopated, or accented or the weak part of the bar.

ŏ as in *tone*; ô as in *dove*; ŏ as in *not*; ŭ as in *up*; ü the French sound of *u*.

Bállo (It.) (*bäl*-lŏ.) A dance or dance tune.

Ballónchio (It.) (bäl-*lōn*-kē-ō.) An Italian country dance.

Ballonzáre (It.) (bäl-lōn-tsä-rĕ.) To dance furiously.

Band. A number of instrumental performers playing together.

Band (Ger.) (Bähnd.) A volume.

Bánda (It.) (*bän*-dä.) A band. The brass band of an opera orchestra.

Band, brass. A band where only brass instruments are played.

Band, full. Where all the instruments proper to a band are employed.

Band, marine. A band located in a garrison or employed on ships of war.

Band master. The leader or conductor of a band, generally military.

Bandola (Spa.) (bän-*dō*-lä.) An instrument resembling a lute.

Bandóra (It.) (bän-*dō*-rä.)
Bandóre (It.) (bän-*dō*-rĕ.) } An ancient stringed instrument of the lute or zither species.

Band, reed. A band with only reed instruments.

Band, regimental. A band belonging to a regiment; a military band.

Band, string. A band with only stringed instruments; the stringed instruments of the regular orchestra.

Bandurría (Spa.) (bän-*door*-rē-ä.) A species of Spanish guitar; a *Bandóra*.

Banjo. An African-derived stringed instrument with a drum-head sounding-board. The banjo is generally strung with four strings, so arranged that they may be *stopped* in the ordinary way, together with an octave string which is rarely stopped. The tuning, which may be in any key, is generally as follows:—

Octave string.

The tuning varies, however, and also the number of strings.

Bänkelsänger (Ger.) (bän-k'l-säng-ĕr.) A ballad singer.

Bar. Lines drawn perpendicularly across the staff to divide it into measures; the term is also applied to each of these measures by European usage, but strictly the bar is the line itself, not the measure it defines. The bar came into use in music after 1600.

Barbiton (Gr.) (*bär*-bĭ-tón.) A name formerly applied to the lyre.

Barbitos (Lat.) (*băr*-bĭ-tŏs.) An ancient instrument of the lyre species.

Barcaróla (It.) (bär-kä-*rō*-lä.) } A song
Barcarolle (Fr.) (bär-kä-*rōl*.) } or air sung by the Venetian *gondoliêrs*, or boatmen, while following their avocations; it is generally in 6/8 time.

Barcaruola (It.) (*bär*-kä-roo-*ō*-lä.) The song of the gondolier.

Bard. A poet and singer among the ancient Celts. The bard was a person of great importance and received great attention from high and low.

Bardo (It.) (*bär*-dō.) A bard among the ancient Celts.

Bardóne (It.) (bär-*dō*-nĕ.) See *Bourdon*.

Bar, dotted double. A double bar with dots preceding it, shows that the music before it is to be repeated; the dots after the double bar show that the following music is to be repeated. Dots each side of the double bar show that both the preceding and following music are to be repeated.

Bar, double. Heavy lines drawn across the staff to divide off different parts of the movement or show the end of the piece.

Bardus (Cel.) (*bär*-dŭs.) A singer.

Bari. An abbreviation of Baritone.

Bari-basso. A deep baritone voice.

Bariolage (Fr.) (băr-ĭ-ō-läzh.) A passage for the violin, etc., in which the open strings are more especially used; a Cadenza; a Medley.

Baripicni (Gr.) (bä-rĭ-*pĕk*-nē.) A term applied by the ancient Greeks to low tones in general.

Baripicni suoni (It.) (bä-rē-*pĕk*-nē *swō*-nē.) Fixed sounds.

Bari-tenor. The deeper sort of tenor voice.

Bariton-clef. The F clef, placed upon the third line; now obsolete.

Bariton (Fr.) (bä-rĭ-*tŏnh*.) }
Baritono (It.) (bär-rē-*tō*-nō.) } A male voice intermediate
Baritone. }

ā as in *ah*; ā as in *hate*; ă as in *at*; ē as in *tree*; ĕ as in *eh*; ī as in *pine*; ĭ as in *pin*;

30

Baritone

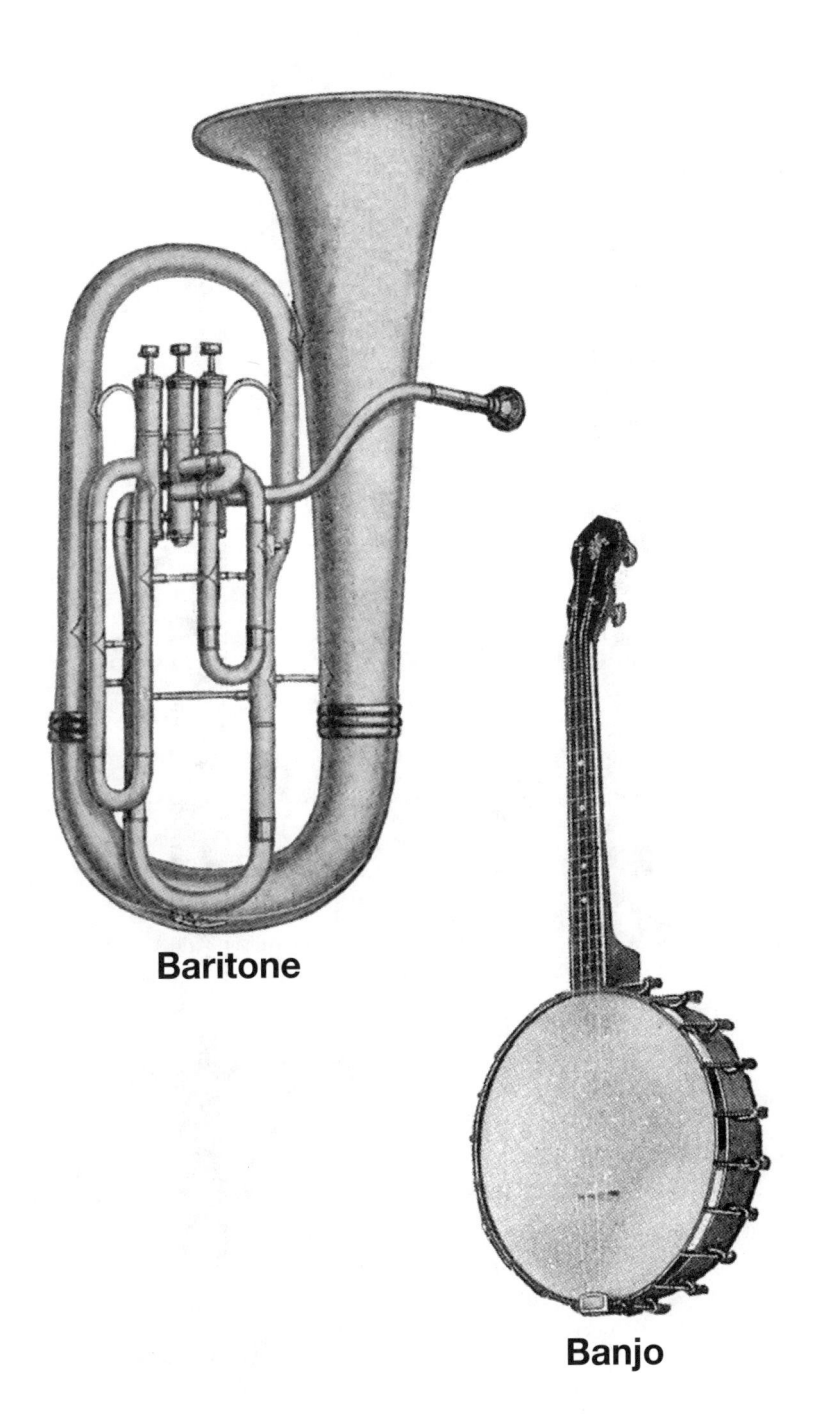

Banjo

Bass Clarinet

Bassoon

BARITONO　　　　　　　　　　　　　　　　BASSET HORN

in respect to pitch between the bass and tenor, the compass usually extending from: the Euphonium is also called "Baritone."

Baritono (It.) (bä-rē-*tō*-nō.) Baritone.
Barócco (It.) (bä-*rōk*-kō.) ⎫ A term applied to music
Baroque (Fr.) (bä-*rōk*.) ⎭ in which the harmony is confused and abounding in unnatural modulations; eccentric; bizarre.
Bärpfeife (Ger.) (*bär*-pfī-fĕ.) Bear pipe; an obsolete reed stop of soft intonation.
Barquarde (Fr.) (bär-*kärd*.) An obsolete term for *barcarolle*.
Barr*ȝ*ȝe (Fr.) (bär-*räzh*.) See *Barrĕ*.
Barre (Fr.) (bär.) A bar, in music.
Barré (Fr.) (băr-*rā*.) In guitar playing, a temporary nut formed by placing the forefinger of the left hand across some of the strings.
Barre de luth (Fr.) (bär dŭh lüt.) The bridge of the lute.
Barre de ʌnesure (Fr.) (bär dŭh mĕ-zür.) A bar-line.
Barre de répétition (Fr.) (bär dŭh rā-pā-tē-sĭ-ŏnh.) A dotted double bar; also a thick line used as an abbreviation to mark the repetition of a group of notes.
Barrel. The body of a bell.
Barrel chime. The cylindrical portion of the mechanism sometimes used for the purpose of ringing a chime of bells.
Barrel organ. An organ, the tones of which are produced by the revolution of a cylinder. The tunes are produced by an arrangement of pins and staples with which the cylinder is studded. See *Orchestrion*.
Barrer. The act of employing the forefinger of the left hand as a nut in guitar playing.
Barrer, great. The act of pressing all the strings of the guitar at the same time, with the forefinger of the left hand.
Barrer, small. The act of pressing two or three strings of a guitar with the forefinger of the left hand.
Barrure (Fr.) (băr-*rür*.) The bar of a lute, etc.

Baryton (Fr.) (bä-rĭ-*tŏnh*.) A kind of bass viol, now obsolete. A euphonium.
Barytone. See *Baritone*.
Bas (Fr.) (bäh.) Low.
Bas dessus (Fr.) (bäh däs-sü.) A mezzo soprano.
Base. ⎫ The lowest or deepest male
Bass. ⎭ voice; the lowest part in a musical composition. See *Voice*.
Basílica (It.) (bä-*zēl*-ē-kä.) A cathedral
Bássa (It.) (*bäs*-sä.) Low, deep; 8va bássa; play the notes an octave lower.
Bass Alberti. A bass formed by taking the notes of chords in arpeggios.
Bássa, ottáva (It.) (*bäs*-sä ōt-*tä*-vä.) Play the passage an octave lower than written.
Bass beam. The small beam inside the viol, nearly under the bass string.
Bass clef. The base or F clef, placed upon the fourth line. See *Clefs*.
Bass, continued. Bass continued through the whole piece; the figured bass. Basso continuo.
Bass cornet. An ancient instrument consisting of a tube four or five feet long, of conical shape.
Bass, double. The double bass viol; the contra bass.
Bass drone. The monotonous bass produced by the large tube of the bagpipe.
Basse (Fr.) (bäss.) The bass part.
Basse chantante (Fr.) (bäss shänh-tänht.) Lyric bass; a bass voice of baritone quality.
Basse chiffrée (Fr.) (bäss shēf-frā.) A figured bass.
Basse continue (Fr.) (bäss kŏnh-tēn-ü.) Thorough bass.
Basse contre (Fr.) (bäss kŏntr.) Bass counter; double bass; also, the deep bass voice called by the Italians *básso profóndo*.
Basse figurée (Fr.) (bäss fē-gü-rā.) The figured bass.
Basse fondamentale (Fr.) (bäss fŏnh-dä-mänh-täl.) The fundamental bass.
Basse taille (Fr.) (bäss tä-yŭh.) Baritone voice of bass quality.
Basset horn. (It. *Corno di Bassetto*.) A transposing instrument of the clarinet order, of a beautiful, soft, and rich

ŏ as in *tone*; ô as in *dove*; ŏ as in *not*; ŭ as in *up*; ü the French sound of *u*.

31

quality. In form like a long clarinet, with a curved and bell-shaped metal end. The compass is as follows:

It sounds a fifth deeper than written. Mozart used it prominently.

Bassétto (It.) (bäs-*set*-tō.) The little bass; also, an obsolete instrument with four strings; also, a 4-foot reed organ stop of bright tone.

Bass, figured. A bass figured, or accompanied by numerals, denoting the harmony to be played by the other parts of the composition.

Bass, first. High bass.

Bass-flöte (Ger.) (bäss flō-tĕ.) } An old
Bass-flute. } instrument of the bassoon species; also, the name of an organ stop of 8-foot tone.

Bass, fundamental. The bass which contains the roots of the chords only.

Bass-geige (Ger.) (*bäss* ghī-ghĕ.) Bassviol; the contra-basso.

Bass, given. A bass to which harmony is to be placed.

Bass, ground. A bass consisting of a few notes or bars containing a subject of its own, repeated throughout the movement, and each time accompanied by a new or varied melody.

Bass, high. A baritone; a voice midway between bass and tenor.

Bass horn. An instrument resembling the serpent, formerly much used in bands; it was of wood, with a brass bell

Bassist (Ger.) (bäs-*sis*.) } A bass singer.
Bassista (It.) (bäs-*sis*-tä.) }

Bass low. Second bass.

Básso (It.) (*bäs*-sō.) The bass part; the contra-bass; an 8-foot organ stop.

Básso, búffo (It.) (*bäs*-sō *boof*-fō.) A humorous bass; a musical comedian of bass register.

Básso cantánte (It.) (*bäs*-sō kän-*tän*-tĕ.) A bass voice of baritone quality; a lyric bass.

Básso comico (It.) (*bäs*-sō kō-mē-kō.) A comic bass singer in an opera.

Básso concertánte (It.) (*bäs* sō kŏn-tshĕr *tän*-tĕ.) The principal bass; also, the lighter and more delicate parts performed by the violoncello or bassoon.

Básso continuo (It.) (*bäs*-sō kŏn-*tē*-noo-ō.) The continued bass; a bass that is figured to indicate the harmony.

Básso contra (It.) (*bäs*-sō *kŏn*-trä.) A double bass viol; the lowest part of a musical composition.

Básso d'accompagnamento (It.) (*bäs*-sō d'äk-kŏm-pän-yä-*men*-tō.) An accompanying bass.

Básso figurato (It.) (*bäs*-sō fē-goo-*rä*-tō.) The figured bass.

Básso fondamentále (It.) (*bäs*-sō fŏn-dä-men-*tä*-lĕ.) The fundamental bass.

Básso numeráto (It.) (*bäs*-sō noo-mĕ-*rä*-tō.) Figured bass.

Básso ostináto (It.) (*bäs*-sō ōs-tē-*nä*-tō.) A ground bass; a single bass figure constantly repeated.

Básso primo (It.) (*bäs*-sō *prē*-mo.) The first bass.

Básso recitante (It.) (*bäs*-sō rä-tshĕ-*tän*-tĕ.) Bass of the small chorus.

Básso ripiéno (It.) (*bäs*-sō rē-pē-*ä*-nō.) A bass part only intended to be played in the full or tutti passages.

Básso secondo (It.) (*bäs*-sō sĕ-*kŏn*-dō.) The second bass.

Básso tenuto (It.) (*bäs*-sō tĕ-*noo*-tō.) Continued bass.

Básso violino (It.) (*bäs*-sō vē-ō-*lee*-nō.) A small bass viol.

Bass F Schüssel (Ger.) (bäss, or F *shüls*-s'l.) The bass, or F clef.

Basson (Fr.) (bäs-*sŏnh*.) Bassoon.

Bassoon (Ger. *Fagott*, It. *Faggotto*.) A double reed wind-instrument of deep pitch, with a compass of about three octaves from low B flat. It is of

the oboe family, but has not the pastoral character of the oboe. The bassoon ordinarily forms the bass or deepest tone among wood wind-instruments, and is capable of excellent independent effects. It is often used for comical or grotesque effects as, for example, in Beethoven's " Pastoral Symphony," and in the overture to " Midsummer Night's Dream," by

ä as in *ah*; ā as in *hate*; ă as in *at*; ē as in *tree*; ĕ as in *eh*; ī as in *pine*; ĭ as in *pin*;

BASSOONIST   BATTRE LA MESURE

Mendelssohn. It is customary to write for the Bassoon in the Bass clef, and as the instrument is usually employed in pairs, one stave serves for the two parts. The tenor clef is often employed for the higher notes of the register of the Bassoon.

Bassoonist. A performer on the bassoon.

Basson quinte (Fr.) (*bäs*-sŏnh kănht.) A small bassoon, of the same written compass as the ordinary bassoon, but the tones are a fifth higher.

Bassoon stop. A reed stop in the organ which imitates the tones of the bassoon.

Bass-pfeife (Ger.) (*bäss* pfī-fĕ.) Basspipe.

Bass-posaune (Ger.) (bäss pŏ-zou-nĕ.) Bass trombone.

Bass, radical. The fundamental bass.

Bass-saite (Ger.) (bäss *sī*-tĕ.) Bass string.

Bass-schlüssel (Ger.) (bäss shlüs-s'l.) The bass clef.

Bass staff. The staff marked with the bass clef.

Bass-stimme (Ger.) (bäss stĭm-mĕ.) Bass voice; bass part.

Bass string. The string of any instrument upon which the lowest note is sounded.

Bass, sub. The lowest notes of an organ; the ground bass.

Bass, thorough. The art of writing out harmony for different parts or voices through the bass alone, it being the only part given. It is a species of musical short-hand which was much employed in the 18th century when it was often customary to write only the bass notes of the accompaniment of a song or recitative; it is thus found in some editions of Bach's "Passion Music." To-day it is chiefly used for the study of chord progressions in musical theory.

Bass trombone. A trombone having a compass from the great C to the one lined e, and noted in the bass clef. See *Trombone*.

Bass tuba (Lat.) (bäss tū-bä.) A brass instrument; a deep Saxhorn. It has the following compass:

Bass viol. An old name for the viol da gámba, now often given to the violoncello.

Bass viol, double. The contra-bass.

Bass voice. The lowest or deepest of male voices. See *Voice*.

Bass-zeichen (Ger.) (bäs tsī-k'n.) The bass clef.

Básta (It.) (*bäs*-tä.)   } Enough,
Bastánte (It.) (bäs-*tän*-tĕ.) } sufficient; proceed no further unless directed by the conductor.

Batócchio (It.) (bät-*tōk*-kē-ō.) } The
Battáglio (It.) (bät-*täl*-yē-ō.) } tongue
Battant (Fr.) (băt-*tänh*.) } of a bell

Bâton (Fr.) (Bahtong.) A conductor's stick.

Battement (Fr.) (băt-*mŏnh*.)   } An
Battiménto (It.) (bät-tē-*men*-tō.) } ornament in singing, the opposite of a cadence;

is called a *cadence*, whereas the following is a *battement*.

Báttere (It.) (bät-*tā*-rĕ.) The down stroke in beating time.

Báttere a ricolta (It.) (bät-*tā*-rĕ ä rē-*kōl*-tä.) To beat a retreat.

Batterie (Fr.) (băt-trē.) The roll of the drum; also, a particular way of playing the guitar by striking the strings instead of pulling them; broken-chord figures; the drums, cymbals, etc., of an orchestra.

Battitúra (It.) (bät-tē-*too*-rä.) The act of beating time.

Battre (Fr.) (băttr.) To beat.

Battre la caisse (Fr.) (bătr lä kăss.) }
Battre le tambour (Fr.) (bătr lüh } tămboor.) }
To beat the drums.

Battre la mesure (Fr.) (bătr lä mā-sür.) To beat time; to mark the time

ŏ as in *tone*; ô as in *dove*; ŏ as in *not*; ŭ as in *up*; ü the French sound of *u*.

BATTÍST BEL CANTO

by beating with the hand or with a stick.

Battísta (It.) (bàt-tēs-ta.) Time or measure; the accented part of a bar.

Battuta (It.) (Bä-*too*-täh.) A beat; a measure or bar; *A Battuta*, in strict time.

Bau (Ger.) (bou.) The structure, the fabric, the construction of musical instruments.

Bäuerisch (Ger.) (*boy*-ĕr-ĭsh.) Rustic; coarse.

Bauernflöte (Ger.) (*bou*-ĕrn-flāt-ĕ.) Rustic flute; a stopped register in an organ.

Bauernlied (Ger.) (*bou*-ĕrn-lēd.) A peasant's ballad.

Baxoncillo (Spa.) An organ stop like an open diapason.

B. C. Basso continuo.

B cancellatum (Lat.) The cancelled B. The note B♭ as altered by means of a ♮ or ♯ in old music. Up to the middle of the eighteenth century the ♯, when following a flat, frequently had the same meaning as the ♮ as now used.

B du- (Ger.) (Bā door.) The key of B flat major.

B durum (Lat.) (B *dū*-rŭm.) B *hard* or B major. See *Flat*.

Bearbeitet (Ger.) (bĕ-*är*-bī-tĕt.) Arranged; adapted.

Bearbeitung (Ger.) (bĕ-*är*-bī-toong.) Adaptation.

Bearing notes. In tuning instruments those erroneous or falsely-tempered fifths on which "the wolf" is said to be thrown.

Beat. The rise or fall of the hand or *bâton* in marking the divisions of time in music; an important musical embellishment, consisting of the principal note and the note *below* it, resembling a short trill; a throbbing which is heard when two tones are slightly out of unison.

Beat, down. The falling of the hand in beating time.

Beating time. Marking the division of the bar by means of the hand, foot, or bâton.

Beat, up. The elevation of the hand in beating time.

Beben (Ger.) (*bāy*-b'n.) To tremble; to shake; to vibrate.

Bebende Stimme (Ger.) (*bā*-bĕn-de stĭm-mĕ.) A trembling voice.

Bebung (Ger.) (*bāy*-boong.) A shaking; a vibration; a German organ stop; a tremulous tone produced upon the clavichord by varying the pressure of the finger upon the key.

Bec (Fr.) (bĕk.) The mouth-piece of a clarinet.

Bécarre (Fr.) (bā-kăr.) The mark called a natural (♮).

Bécco (It.) (bĕ-kō.) The mouth-piece of a clarinet, flageolet, etc.

Becken (Ger.) (bĕk'n.) Cymbals.

Beckenschläger (Ger.) (*bĕk'n*-shlāg-ĕr.) A cymbal player.

Bedon (Fr.) (bĕ-*dŏnh*.) An old name for a tabret, or drum.

Be (Ger.) (bā.) Flat, b flat.

Beffroi (Fr.) (bĕf-*frwä*.) The frame that supports the bell in a belfry; a belfry.

Begeisterung (Ger.) (bĕ-*ghīs*-tĕ-roong.) Inspiration, animation, enthusiasm.

Begl. An abbreviation of *Begleitung*

Begleiten (Ger.) (bĕ-*glī*-t'n) To ac company.

Begleitende Stimmen (Ger. pl.) (bĕ-*glī*-tĕn-dĕ *stĭm*-mĕn.) The accompanying parts.

Begleiter (Ger.) (bĕ-*glī*-tĕr.) An accompanist.

Begleitung (Ger.) (bĕ-*glī*-toong.) An accompaniment.

Beharrlich (Ger.) (bĕ-*här*-llkh.) Perseveringly.

Beherzt (Ger.) (bĕ-*härtst*.) Courageous.

Beinahe (Ger.) (bī-*nä*-ĕ.) Almost.

Beisp. An abbreviation of *beispiel*.

Beispi·l (Ger.) (*bī*-spēl.) Example

Beitöne (Ger.) (*bī*-tā-nĕ.) Accessory tones.

Beizeichen (Ger.) (*bī*-tsī-kh'n.) An accidental.

Bel canto (It.) (bell-*kahn*-to) Literally, "beautiful song." In one sense

BELFRY

it can be applied to all good singing, but, practically, it means a tender, pure, and sympathetic legato, the opposite of bravura singing.

Belfry. A tower in which a bell or bells are hung.

Belieben (Ger.) (bĕ-*lē*-b'n.) Pleasure; at pleasure.

Beliebig (Ger.) (bĕ-*lēe*-bĭg.) At one's liking, or pleasure.

Béliere (Fr.) (bā-lǐ-*ār*) The tongue of a bell.

Bell. 1. A vessel or hollow body of cast metal, used for making sounds. It consists of a barrel or hollow body enlarged or expanded at one end, an ear or cannon by which it is hung to a beam, and a clapper inside. 2. A hollow body of metal perforated, and containing a solid ball to give sounds when shaken. 3. The wide circular opening at the end of a trumpet, horn, and similar instruments.

Bellézza (It.) (bĕl-*lāt*-sä.) Beauty of tone and expression.

Bellézza della vóce (It.) (bĕl-*let*-sä dĕl-lä *vō*-tshĕ.) Beauty or sweetness of voice.

Bell gamba. A gamba stop in an organ; the top of each pipe spreading out like a bell.

Bell Harp. 1. An old instrument, probably the lyra or cithera of the Ancients. 2. A stringed instrument, so named from its being swung like a bell when played.

Bellicosaménte (It.) (bĕl-lē-kō-zä-*men*-tĕ.) } In a
Bellicóso (It.) (bĕl-lē-*kō*-zō.) } martial and warlike style.

Bellicum (Lat.) (*bĕl*-lǐ-kum.) The sound of a trumpet calling to battle.

Bell, Mass. A small bell used in the Roman Catholic service to call attention to the more solemn parts of the Mass.

Bell metronome. A metronome with a small bell that strikes at the beginning of each bar. See *Metronome*.

Bellows. A pneumatic appendage for supplying organ pipes with air.

Bellows, exhaust. A kind of bellows used on organs and other reed instruments; the air, when the chamber is exhausted, being drawn *in* through the reeds.

BENEDICTUS

Bellows, panting. A style of bellows designed to prevent all jerkings, and to produce a regular flow of wind in the pipes of an organ.

Bell-ringers. Performers who, with bells of different sizes, ranging from smallest to largest, are able to produce pleasing music.

Bells. Bells both small and large are freqently used in orchestral works. The small chime of bells is called *Glockenspiel* (which see). Large bells have been used by Meyerbeer, "Huguenots"; Wagner, "Parsifal"; Tchaikovsky, "1812 Overture," etc. See Prout's "The Orchestra," and A. Elson's "Orchestral Instruments and Their Use."

Bell sacring. A small bell used in the Roman Catholic Church. See *Bell, Mass*.

Bell scale. A diapason with which bell founders measure the size, thickness, weight, and tone of their bells.

Bell, vesper. The sounding of a bell about sunset, in Roman Catholic countries, calling the people to vespers, the evening service of the church.

Belly. The sound-board of an instrument; that part over which the strings are distended.

Bemerkbar (Ger.) (bĕ-*mairk*-bär.) Observable, marked; to be played in a prominent manner.

Bémol (Fr.) (be-mŏl.) } The mark called a *flat* (♭).
Bemólle (It.) (be-*mōl*-lĕ.) }

Bemol, double. B double flat.

Bemolisée (Fr.) (bĕ-mō-lǐ-*zā*.) A note preceded by a flat.

Bémoliser (Fr.) (bĕ-mō-lǐ-*zā*.) } To flatten
Bemollizzare (It.) (bā-*mōl*-lĕt-sä-rĕ.) } notes; to lower the pitch by putting a flat before them.

Bén (It.) (bān.) } Well, good.
Béne (It.) *bā*-nĕ.) }

Benedicite (Lat.) (bĕn-ĕ-*dē*-sĭ-tĕ.) A canticle used at morning prayer, in the church, after the first lesson.

Benedictus (Lat.) (bĕn-ĕ-*dĭk*-tŭs.) One of the movements in a Mass.

ȯ as in *tone;* ȏ as in *dove;* ŏ as in *not;* ŭ as in *up;* ü the French sound of *u*.

BENE PLACITO

Béne plácito (It.)(*bā*-nĕ *plä*-tshē-tō.) At will; at pleasure; at liberty to retard the time and ornament the passage.

Ben marcáto (It.) (bĕn mär-*kä*-tō.)

Bené marcáto (It.) (bā-nĕ mär-*kä*-to.) Well marked in a distinct and strongly accented manner.

Ben marcato il cánto (It.) (ben mär-*kä*-tō ēl *kän*-tō.) Accent the melody strongly.

Ben moderáto (It.) (bān mŏd-ĕ-*rä*-tō.) Very moderate time.

Ben pronunciato (It.) (bān prō-noon-tshē-*ä*-tō

Ben pronunziato (It.) (bān prō-noon-tsē-*ä*-tō.) Pronounced clearly and distinctly.

Ben tenuto (It.) (bān tĕ-noo-tō.) Held on; fully sustained.

Be quadro (It.) (bāy *quä*-drō.) The mark called a natural (♮).
Béquarré (Fr.) (bāy-*kär*-rā.)

Bequem (Ger.) (bĕ-*quãm*.) Convenient.

Berceuse (Fr.) (bār-*sãys*.) A cradle song; a lullaby.

Bergamásca (It.) (bĕr-gä-mäs-kä.) A kind of rustic dance.

Bergeret (bĕr-jĕ-*rĕ*.) An old term signifying a rustic song or dance.

Bergomask. A rustic dance. See *Bergamásca*. Used in Shakespeare's "Midsummer Night's Dream."

Bergreigen (Ger.) (*bĕrg*-rī-ghĕn.) Alpine melody.

Berlingozza (It.) (bĕr-lēn-*gōt*-sä.) A country dance.

Berloque (Fr.) (bĕr-*lōk*.) In military service the drum calling to meals.

Bes (Ger.) (bĕs.) The note B double flat, B♭♭, also called *Doppel B*, or *bb*.

Besaiten (Ger.) (bĕ-*sī*-t'n.) To string an instrument.

Beschleunigend (Ger.) (bĕ-*shloi*-nĕ-gĕnd.) Hastening.

Beschreibung (Ger.) (bĕ-*shrī*-boong.) A description.

Befiedern (Ger.) (bĕ-*fē*-dĕrn.) To quill a harpsichord.

Besingen (Ger.) (bĕ-*sĭng*-ĕn.) To sing; to celebrate in song.

Bestimmt (Ger.) (bĕs-*tĭmt*.) Distinct.

Bestimmtheit (Ger.) (bĕs-*tĭmt*-hīt.) With decision; certainty.

Betglocke (Ger.) (*bait*-glŏk-ĕ.) Prayer bell.

Betónend (Ger.) (bĕ-*tō*-nĕnd.) Accented.
Betont (Ger.) (bĕ-*tōnt*.)

Betónung (Ger.) (bĕ-*tō*-noong.) Accentuation.

Betrübniss (Ger.) (bĕ-*trüb*-nĭss.) Grief, sadness.

Betrübt (Ger.) (bĕ-*trübt*.) Afflicted, grieved.

Bewegung (Ger.) (bĕ-*vā*-goong.) Motion, movement.

Beweglich (Ger.) (bĕ-*vā*-glīkh.) Movable.

Bewegt (Ger.) (bĕ-*vāgt*.) Moved; rather fast.

Beyspiel (Ger.) (*bī*-spēl.) An example. See *Beispiel*.

Bezeichnung (Ger.) (bĕ-*tsīkh*-noong.) Mark, accentuation.

Bezifferte Bass (Ger.) (bĕr-*tsĭf*-fĕr-tĕ bäss.) The figured bass.

B flat. The flat seventh of the key of C.

Bhát. (bät.) The Hindu name for a *bard*.

Bianca (It.) (bē-*än*-kä.) A minim or half note, from the word "white."

Bichord (Lat.) (*bē*-kŏrd.) A term applied to instruments that have two strings to each note.

Bichordon (Lat.) (bĭ-*kŏr*-dŏn.) An instrument with only two strings.

Bicinium (Lat.) (bĭ-*sĭn*-ĭ-ŭm.) A composition in two parts; a duet, or two part song.

Bifara (Lat.) (bĭ-*fär*-ä.) An organ stop each pipe having two mouths, causing gentle waves or undulations.

Bimólle (It.) (bēm-*mōl*-lĕ.) The mark called a flat (♭).

B in alt (It.) (bē ĭn ält.) The third note in the alt octave.

B in altissimo (It.) (bē ĭn äl-*tēs*-sē mō.) The octave above *B in alt*.

Binary. Two-fold. Binary form,—a form of two divisions, periods, or sections.

ā as in *ah*; ā as in *hate*; ă as in *at*; ē as in *tree*; ĕ as in *eh*; ī as in *pine*; ĭ as in *pin*;

Binary measure. Two beats to a measure.
Bind. A tie uniting two notes on the same degree of the staff. See *Tie*.
Binde (Ger.) (*bēn*-dĕ.) A tie or bind.
Binding notes. Notes held together by the tie or bind.
Bindung (Ger.) (*bĭn*-doong.) Connection.
Bindungszeichen (Ger.) (*bĭn*-doongs-tsī-kh'n.) A tie or bind.
Binotonus (Lat.) (bĭ-nō-*tō*-nŭs.) Consisting of two notes.
Biquadro (It.) (bē-*quä*-drō.) A natural (♮).
Bird organ. A small organ used in teaching birds to sing.
Birn (Ger.) (bĭrn.) That part of the clarinet, basset horn, etc., into which the mouth-piece is inserted; a socket.
Bis (Lat.) (bĭs.) Twice; indicating that the passage marked is to be repeated. It is seldom written for a long repetition. It is placed under or over a slur, *e.g.:*

It is often used to indicate the repeat of words in a song; it is used by the French in the sense of *encore* in applauding a performance; it may mean a subdivision of some section or number of a musical work, as 1 *bis*, 2 *bis*, etc.
Bischero (It.) (*bĭs*-kair-oh.) The peg, or pin, with which the strings of an instrument are secured.
Biscroma (It.) (bis-krōm-a.) } A 16th
Biscrome (Fr.) (bis-krōm.) } note, ♬.
Bisdiapason. The interval of a double octave, or fifteenth.
Bissex. A kind of guitar with twelve strings (Ger. *Zwölfsaiter*), invented by Vanhecke in 1770. Of the twelve strings, six were over the finger-board, six below (to resound in sympathy with the others), hence the name *twice-six*. Its compass was three and a half octaves.
Bitterkeit (Ger.) (*bĭt*-tĕr-kīt.) Bitterness.
Bizzarraménte (It.) (bit-sär-rä-*men*-tĕ.) Oddly; in a whimsical style.
Bizzarría (It.) (bĭt-sär-*rēe*-ä.) Written in a capricious, fantastic style; sudden, unexpected modulations.
Bizzáro (It.) (bĭt-*sär*-rō.) Whimsical, odd, fantastical.
Blanche (Fr.) (blänsh.) A half-note.
Blanche pointée (Fr.) (blänsh pwänh-*tā*.) A dotted half-note.
Blasebalg (Ger.) (*blä*-zĕ-bälg.) The bellows of an organ.
Blasegeräth (Ger.) (*blä*-zĕ-ghĕ-*rät*.) A wind instrument.
Blasehorn (Ger.) (*blä*-zĕ-hŏrn.) Bugle horn; hunter's horn.
Blase-instrument (Ger.) (*blä*-zĕ in-stroo-*mĕnt*.) A wind instrument.
Blase-musik (Ger.) (*blä*-zĕ moo-*zēk*.) Music for wind instruments.
Blasen (Ger.) (*blä*-z'n.) To blow; to sound.
Bläser (Ger.) (*blä*-z'r.) A blower; an instrument for blowing.
Blast. The sudden blowing of a trumpet or other instrument of a similar character.
Blatt (Ger.) (bläht.) A reed of a wind instrument; *Doppel-blatt*, a double reed.
Blech-instrumente (Ger.)(blĕkh-ĭn-stroo-*mĕn*-tĕ.) The brass instruments, as trumpets, trombones, etc.
Blockflöte (Ger.) (*blŏk*-flô-tĕ.) An organ stop, composed of large scale-pipes, the tone of which is full and broad.
Blower, organ. One who works the bellows of an organ.
Bluette (Fr.) (blü-*ĕt*.) A short, brilliant piece. The word means a spark, or a flash.
B-mol (Fr.) (bāy-mōl.) The character called a flat (♭). See *Bé mol*.
B moll (Ger.) (bāy mōl.) The key of B-flat minor.
Boans (Lat.) (*bō*-äns.) Echoing, resounding.
Board, finger. The key-board of a pianoforte, organ, or similar instrument; that part of a stringed instrument which the fingers press in playing.
Board, fret. That part of a guitar or similar instrument on which the frets are placed.
Board, key. The rows of keys of a pianoforte, organ, or similar instrument. See *Finger board*.

ō as in *tone ;* ô as in *dove ;* ŏ as in *not ;* ŭ as in *up ;* ü the French sound of *u*.

37

Board, sound. In the organ a broad, shallow box, extending almost the whole width of the instrument and divided into as many grooves as there are keys, and upon which are placed the rows of pipes forming the stops; a thin board designed to intensify the vibration of tone in musical instruments.

Board, sounding. See *Sound board*.

Boat songs. Gondolier songs. Barcarolles.

Bobiation (bō-bĭ-*ā*-shŭn.) ⎱ Solfégg adapted to the syllables of the Flemish or Belgian language.
Bocedisation (bō-sē-dĭ-*sā*-shŭn.) ⎰

Bocal (Fr.) (bō-käl.) ⎱ The mouth-piece of a horn, trumpet, trombone, and similar instruments.
Bóccá (It.) (*bōk*-kä.) ⎰

Bocca chiusa (It.) (Bōk·kä ke-*oo*-zä.) With closed mouth. Humming.

Bócca ridente (It.) (*bōk*-kä rĭ-*děn*-tĕ.) *Smiling mouth.* A term in singing, applied to a peculiar opening of the mouth approaching to a smile, believed to be conducive to the producing of a pure tone.

Bocchino (It.) (bōk-*kē*-nō.) Mouth-piece of a horn or other wind instrument.

Bociaccia (It.) (bōt-tshē-ät-tshē-ä.) A loud, strong voice.

Bocciuola (It.) (bōt-tshē-*oo*-ō-ä.) A small mouth-piece.

Bocinilla. A small speaking trumpet.

Bockpfeife (Ger.) (*bŏk*-pfī-fĕ.) A bag-pipe.

Bockstriller (Ger.) (*bŏks*-trĭl-lĕr.) A bad trill; with false intonation.

Boden (Ger.) (*bō*-d'n.) The back of a violin, viola, etc.

Body. The resonance box of a string instrument. That part of a wind instrument which remains after the removal of mouth-piece, crooks, and bell. The tube of an organ-pipe above its mouth.

Boehm Flute (bôhm.) An instrument with the holes arranged in their natural order, and with keys, by means of which the fingers are enabled to act with greater facility. Invented by Boehm. See *Flute*.

Bogen (Ger.) (*bō*-g'n.) The bow of a violin, etc.; a slur or tie.

Bogenführung (Ger.) (*bō*-g'n-fü-roong.) The management of the bow; the act of bowing.

Bogen-instrument (Ger.) (*bō*-g'n in-stroo-*měnt.*) A bow instrument; an instrument played with a bow.

Bogenstrich (Ger.) (*bō*-g'n-strĭkh.) A stroke of the bow.

Boléro (Spa.) (bō-*lā*-ro.) A lively Spanish dance, in ¾ time, with castanets. It is much like the Andalusian cachucha. It is accompanied by castanets with a rhythm as follows:

alternating with the melody-rhythm; and the performer assumes, in the course of the dance, all the various feelings supposed to be excited by love, from the greatest shyness to the highest ecstasy, singing as he dances.

Bombarde (Fr.) (bŏnh-*bärd*.) ⎱ A powerful reed stop in an organ of 16-foot scale; also an old wind instrument of the oboe species.
Bombárdo (It.) bŏm-*bär*-dō.) ⎰

Bombardon (Ger.) (*bŏm*-bär-dŏn.) A large bass wind instrument of brass, with valves something like the ophicleide. The bass of the Saxhorn family.

Bombilatus (Lat.) (bŏm-bĭ-*lā*-tŭs.) To make a humming noise.

Bombix (Gr.) (*bŏm*-bĭx.) An ancient Greek instrument, formed of a long reed and tube.

Bon (Fr.) (bong.) Good.

Bonang (Jav.) (bō-*năng*.) A Javenese instrument, consisting of a series of gongs placed in two lines on a frame.

Bones. A name sometimes given to castanets; castanets made of bone; also four slips of bone or wood, held between the fingers and rattled together in certain folk songs and dances.

Bon temps de la mesure (Fr.) (bŏnh tŏnh d lä mĕ-*sür*.) The accented parts of a measure.

Book, choral. A collection of choral melodies.

ă as in *ah*; ā as in *hate*; ă as in *at*; ē as in *tree*; ĕ as in *eh*; ī as in *pine*; ĭ as in *pin*;

Book, Mass. The Missal, the Roman Catholic service book.

Boot. The foot of a reed pipe.

Boquilla (Spa.) (bō-*kĕl*-yä.) Mouthpiece of a wind instrument.

Bordóne (It.) (bŏr-dō-nĕ.)
Bourdon (Fr.) (boor-dŏnh.) } An organ stop, the pipes of which are stopped or covered, and produce the 16-foot, and sometimes the 32-foot tone; also a drone bass.

Bordun. See *Bourdon.*

Bordone, falso (It.) (bŏr-dō-nĕ fäl-zō.) A term formerly used for harmony having a drone bass, or one of the other parts continuing in the same pitch.

Bordun-flöte (Ger.) (*bŏr*-doon *flō*-tĕ.) An organ stop. See *Bordóne.*

Bouche (Fr.) (Boosh.) The mouth.

Bouche fermée (Boosh fairmay.) With closed mouth; humming; "Bocca Chiusa."

Bouchée (Fr.) (Booshay.) Applied to wind-instruments this means muted; applied to organ pipes it means stopped.

Bourdon de cornemuse (Fr.) (boor-dŏnh dŭh kŏrn-mūz.) The drone of a bagpipe.

Bourdon de musette (Fr.) (boor-dŏnh dŭh mū-zĕt.) The drone of a small bagpipe.

Borée (Fr.) (bō-rā.) A dance introduced from Biscay.

Botto (It.) (bŏt-tō.) The tolling of a bell.

Boudoir piano (boo-dwär.) An upright piano.

Bouffe (Fr.) (boof.) A buffoon. *Opera Bouffe*, a burlesque comic opera.

Bourdon de l'orgue (Fr.) (boor-dŏnh dŭh l'ŏrg.) The drone of an organ.

Bourdonnement (Fr.) (boor-dŏnh-mŏnh.) Humming, singing.

Bourrée (Fr.) (boor-rā.) An old French dance said to have come from Auvergne, but others claim it to be a Spanish dance coming from Biscay, where it is still in use. The Bourrée is to be found in the Suites of Bach and of other old masters. It is very rapid and hearty, generally in $\frac{2}{4}$ or in $\frac{4}{4}$

time. It generally begins on the fourth quarter of the measure.

Boutade (Fr.) (boo-*täd.*) An impromptu ballet in a fanciful, capricious style.

Bow. An instrument of wood and horsehair, employed to set the strings of the violin, etc., in vibration. The bow, originally curved, as its name implies, has been subject to many changes of shape from time to time, from a large curve to an almost flat form. The bow is not found in connection with the ancient stringed instruments of Rome, Egypt or Greece. It is probable that it was first used in ancient India and China. The bow remained a very primitive affair until, in the 17th century, violin playing began to be cultivated. Towards the end of the 18th century François Tourte brought the bow to perfection. He was the inventor of the present shape. The present length of the bow is from 27 to 30 inches. The stick is of pernambuco or cheaper materials. The 120 to 150 horsehairs in the bow are drawn to proper tension by the nut, which is attached to a screw and can be readily tightened or loosened. The nut is usually made of ebony.

Bow, contrary. A reversed stroke of the bow.

Bow hair. Hair used in making the bows of violins, violoncellos, etc.; it is usually horsehair, which is best suited to cause friction by its dentiform protuberances. It wears smooth by usage, and requires renewal at intervals.

Bow hand. The right hand; the hand which holds the bow.

Bow harpsichord. An instrument invented at Königsberg by Garbrecht.

Bowing. The art of using the bow playing with the bow. "The bowing" also refers to the marks used to guide the player, as ⊓ a downstroke, ∧ an upstroke, etc. All notes under a slur are to be played in one stroke of the bow.

Bow instruments. All instruments whose tones are produced by the bow.

Box, music. A small box producing tunes by the revolution of a cylinder, moved by a spring, in which steel pins are fixed that touch steel points at such

ŏ as in *tone*; ô as in *dove*; ŏ as in *not*; ŭ as in *up*; ü the French sound of *u*

BOYAUDIER / BRELOQUE

intervals as to produce the variations of a tune.

Boyaudier (Fr.) (bŏ-yō-dí-â.) A maker of violin strings from Boyau, gut, *i.e.*, a gut-string.

Boy-choir. A choir of boys, from eight to fourteen years of age. Such organizations are confined mostly to Episcopal and Catholic churches.

B quadratum (Lat.) (b quăd-*rä*-tŭm.) } An old name
B quadrum (Lat.) (b *quăd*-rŭm.) for the natural, ♮; formerly, this was applied to the note B.

B-quarre (Fr.) (bā-kär.) See *Béquarre*.

Brabançonne. The Belgium national hymn.

Brace. A character curved or straight used to connect together the different staves; the leather slide which tightens or loosens the cords of a drum.

Branle (Fr.) (bränhl.) A lively old dance in ¾ time; a species of "follow my leader," in which all the motions of the leading couple were imitated.

Bransle (Fr.) (bränhsl.) The Branle.

Bransle double (bränhsl doo-bl.) A dance in a quicker time than the Bransle.

Bransle simple (Fr.) See *Branle*.

Brass band. A number of performers whose instruments are exclusively brass. The brass band differs from the full military band in having no reed instruments.

Brass wind. The term applied to the horns, trumpets, trombones, and tuba of an orchestra.

Bratsche (Ger.) (*brä*-tshĕ.) The viola or tenor violin. From *Braccio* (It.) the arm, since the instrument was held on the arm. See *Viola*.

Bratschen (Ger.) (*brä*-tshĕn.) Violas.

Bratschenspieler (Ger.) (*brä*-tchĕn-*spēe*-lĕr.) Violist: one who plays on the viola.

Bratschenstimme (Ger.) (*brä*-tchĕn-*stǐm*-mĕ.) The viol part of any composition.

Braul. See *Brawl*.

Braut-lied (Ger.) (*brout*-lēd.) A bridal hymn; a wedding song.

Braut-messe (Ger.) (*brout*-mĕs-sĕ.) Music before the wedding ceremony; the ceremony itself.

Bráva (It. fm.) (*brä*-vä.) } An exclamation of approval often
Brávi (It. pl.) (*bräv*-ē.)
Bravo (It. mas.) (*brä*-vō.) used in theatres; excellent, very good, etc. It is held by some philologists that as "Bravo!" is an *exclamation* its form should not change, but remain *bravo* under all circumstances. Nevertheless "bravo" is usually applied to a male, "brava" to a female artist, and "bravi" to two or more.

Bravíssima (It. fem.) (brä-*vēs*-sē-mä.) } Exceedingly good;
Bravíssimi (It. pl.) (brä-*vēs*-sē-mē.) exceedingly well done.
Bravissimo (It. mas.) (brä-*vēs*-sē-mo.) The application as above.

Bravour-arie (Ger.) (brä-*voor*-ä-rē-ĕ.) An *aria di bravúra*. A vocal solo full of technical display.

Bravúra (It.) (brä-*voo*-rä.) Spirit; skill; requiring great dexterity and skill in execution.

Bravúra, con. (It.) (brä-*voo*-rä kŏn.) With spirit and boldness of execution.

Brawl. } 1. A shaking, or swinging motion.
Brawle. 2. An old round dance in which the performers joined hands in a circle; the old English balls were usually opened with it. The Branle.

Break. 1. The point of change in the quality of tenor, soprano, and alto voices. A genuine bass voice has no break. The lower range is called *voce di petto*, or chest voice; the upper, *voce di testa*, or head voice; and the place of junction is called the *break*. A properly-cultivated voice should have the break so under control, that the unison of the two qualities should be imperceptible. 2. In the clarinet the break in the tone of the instrument occurs between B flat and B natural.

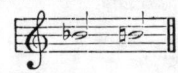

3. An imperfectly-formed tone on horn, trumpet or clarinet.

Breit (Ger.) (brīt.) Broad.

Breloque (Fr.) (brĕ-*lōk*.) In military service the call of a drum for meals.

ă as in *ah*; ā as in *hate*; ă as in *at*; ē as in *tree*; ĕ as in *eh*; ī as in *pine*; ĭ as in *pin*;

Brett-geige (Ger.) (brĕt-ghī-ghĕ.) A small pocket fiddle; a kit.

Bréve (It.) (ĕrā-vĕ.) 1. Short; formerly the Breve was the shortest note. The notes then used were the Large, the Long, and the Breve. The Breve is now the longest note; it is equal to two *semibreves* or whole notes. 2. A Double whole note (𝄺) or (𝄻). See *Notes* and *Notation*.

Bréve alla (It.) (brā-vĕ äl-lä.) A term to indicate a 2/2 time; formerly it meant 4/2 (a breve) to each measure.

Breve rest. A rest equal in duration to a Breve or Double whole note.

Breviario (It.) (brĕv-ē-ä-rē-ō.) A breviary.

Breviary. A book containing the matins, lauds, and vespers of the Catholic church.

Brevis (Lat.) (brā-vĭs.) A breve.

Bridge. That part of a stringed instrument that supports the strings.

Bridge, bass. The bass beam; the small beam inside a viol nearly under the bass.

Brill. An abbreviation of Brillánte.

Brilláante (It.) (brēl-*län-tĕ*.) Bright,
Brillante (Fr.) (brē-*yänht*.) sparkling, brilliant.

Brindisi (It.) (*brin*-dizzy.) A drinking song.

Brío (It.) (*brēe*-ō.) Vigor, animation, spirit.

Brióso (It.) (brēe-ō-zō.) Lively; vigorous; with spirit.

Brisé (Fr.) (brē-*zāy*.) Split; broken into an *arpéggio*.

Broderies (Fr.) (brō-dĕ-rē.) Ornaments, embellishments.

Broken cadence. See *Interrupted Cadence*.

Broken chords. Chords whose notes are not taken simultaneously, but in a broken and interrupted manner.

Broken Octaves. Octaves in which the notes are played separately, as

B rotundum (Lat.) (B rō-*tŭn*-dŭm.) The character called a flat, ♭; formerly this was applied only to the note B.

Bruit (Fr.) (brü-*ē*.) Noise, rattle, clatter.

Brúmmen (Gr.) (*broom*-mĕn.) To hum; to growl.

Brúmmton (Ger.) (*broom*-tōn.) A humming sound; a drone bass.

Brunette (Fr.) (brü-nĕt.) A love song; usually of a pastoral, rustic character.

Bruscaménte (It.) (broos-kä-*men*-tĕ.) Abruptly, coarsely.

Brusquement (Fr.) (brüsk-mŏnh.) Brusque, rough, rude.

B sharp. The sharp seventh of the diatonic scale of C; in keyed instruments the same as C natural.

Búccina (It.) (*boot*-tshē-nä.) An ancient instrument of the trumpet species.

Buccinal (Lat.) (*bŭk*-sĭ-näl.) Sounding like a horn or trumpet.

Buccinateur (Fr.) (bük-sĭ-nä-*tŭr*.) A trumpeter.

Buccinum (Lat.) (*buk*-sĭ-nŭm.) A trumpet.

Buccólica (It.) (book-*kō*-lē-kä.) Pastoral
Bucolic (Lat.) (bū-*kŏl*-ĭk.) songs or
Bucólique (Fr.) (bü-kŏl-*ēk*.) verses.

Bucolica (Lat.) (bū-*kŏl* ĭ kä.) In the pastoral style.

Búffa (It.) (*boof*-fä.) Comic; humor-
Búffo (It.) (*boof*-fō.) ous; in the comic style; also a singer who takes comic parts in the opera.

Búffa caricáta (It.) (*boof*-fä kär-ē-*kä*-tä.) A comic
Búffo caricáto (It.) (*boof*-fō kar-ē-*kä*-tō.) character in opera.

Buffet d'orgue (Fr.) (büf-fĕ d' ōrg.) An organ case.

Búffo burlesco (It.) (*boof*-fō boor-*lĕs*-kô.) A buffo singer and caricaturist.

Buffóne (It.) (boof-*fō*-rˣ) Comic singer in an opera.

Buffonescaménte (It.) (boof-fō-nĕs-kä-*men*-tĕ.) In a burlesque and comical manner.

Buffo, opera (It.) (*boof*-fō ō-pĕ-rä.) A comic opera; a burletta.

Bugle. 1. A hunting horn. 2. An instrument of copper or brass, similar to the cornet, but higher and more piercing. There are different kinds; one furnished with keys; another kind with pistons or cylinders; and some natural tubes without keys. The last, much used for cavalry and infantry calls, generally gives the following harmonics:

and excellent players can produce the fundamental (small *c*) and one or two higher tones, than above given.

Bugle horn. A hunting horn.

Büh′nenweihfestspiel (Ger.) (*Bēe*-nen-ɑ-*fĕst*-spēel.) "Stage-consecrating festival play"; the title bestowed by Wagner on *Parsifal*.

Buon (It.) (bwōn.) Good.

Buonaccórdo (It.) (bwōn-näk-*kŏr*-dō.) An instrument resembling a pianoforte, but smaller, to accommodate children.

Buóna nota (It.) (bwō-nä nō-tä.) Accented note.

Buón gusto (It.) (bwōn goos-tō.) Good taste; refinement of style.

Burden. A regular return of a theme or phrase in a song, at the close of each verse; the drone of a bagpipe.

Burla (It.) (*boor*-lä.)
Burlándo (It.) (boor-*län*-dō.)
Burléscó (It.) (boor-*lĕs*-kō.)
Burlescaménte (It.) (boor-lĕs-kä-*mĕn*-tĕ.) Facetious, droll, comical; in a playful manner.

Burlétta (It.) (boor-*lĕt*-tä.) A comic operetta; a light musical and dramatic piece, somewhat in the nature of the English farce.

Burrasca (It.) (boor-*räs*-kä.) A composition descriptive of a tempest.

Burthen. See *Burden.*

Busaun (Ger.) (boo-*soun*.) A reed-stop in an organ, generally of 16-foot tone and on the pedal.

Busna (It.) (boos-nä.) A species of trumpet.

Buxum (Lat.) (*bŭx*-ŭm.) A pipe.

Buxus (Lat.) (*bŭx*-ŭs.) A pipe with two rows of holes.

Buzain (Ger.) (boo-tsīn.) See *Busaun*.

Button. A small round piece of leather in an organ, which, when screwed on the tapped wire of a tracker, prevents it from jumping out of place. The keys of the first-made accordions. The knob at the base of the violin.

C

C. The first note of the natural scale. The note *Ut* of the Guidonian System. (See *Aretinian Syllables*.) The note from which pianos and organs are tuned. It would be impossible to tune the orchestra from this note since the violin has no C string. There are therefore two different tuning-forks used, an A fork for orchestra and a C fork for piano and organ. Sometimes students are puzzled why the natural scale should begin on C instead of with A, the first letter of the alphabet. Although the origin of the letter system is involved in some obscurity, and letters have been applied to musical tones even in ancient Greek times, yet the answer to the above may be found in the fact that the minor scale was more used in ancient times than the major — and the natural minor scale begins with A.

C is called *Ut* in France and *Do* in Italy. It is an error to suppose that the sign ₵ is C as an abbreviation for "Common Time." The sign came from a broken circle, used in the middle ages and called the *Imperfectum*. See *Time*.

C The lowest note on the manuals of an organ, and called an 8-foot note, that being the length of the open pipe required to produce it.

C C. This note is an octave below C, and requires a 16-foot pipe.

C C C. A note an octave below C C; it requires a 32-foot pipe.

C with *one stroke*; one-lined C ; c̄. The German method of indicating middle C. The six notes above it are marked in the same manner.

C with *two strokes*; two-lined C ; c̿; an octave above C with one stroke.

C with *three strokes*; three-lined C ; c̿̄; an octave above C with two strokes.

N.B. It is an error to write the above

ä as in *ah*; ā as in *hate*; ă as in *at*; ē as in *tree*; ĕ as in *eh*; ī as in *pine*; ĭ as in *pin*;

as C^1, C^2, or C^3; these mean notes of a deeper pitch. See *Tablature.*

C. A. The initials of *Col Arco;* sometimes used in abbreviation.

Cabalétta (It.) (kä-bä-*lĕt*-tä.) A simple melody of a pleasing and attractive character; an operatic air like the rondo in form; a cavaletta. The word means "a little horse," and the cabaletta was probably so-called from its trotting accompaniment, generally in triplets.

Cabinet d'orgue (Fr.) (kăb-ĭ-nā d'ōrg.) The case or cabinet in which the keys of an organ are sometimes placed.

Cabinet pianoforte. An upright pianoforte.

Cabiscola. The ancient name of the leader of the choristers in a church.

Cáccia (It.) (*kät*-tshē-ä.)

Cáccia, alla (It.) (*kät*-tshē-ä *äl*-lä.) In the hunting style.

Cachúcha (Spa.) (kä-*tchoo*-tchä.) A popular Spanish dance in triple time, very similar to the Bolero.

Cacofonío (It.) (kä-kō-fō-*nē*-ä.) } Want
Cacophonie (Fr.) (kăk-ō-fō-*nē*.) } of harmony, cacophony.

Cacofónico (It.) (kä-kō-*fō*-nē-kō.) Cacophonous, discordant.

Cacophony (kă-*kŏf*-ŏ-ny.) A combination of discordant sounds, false intonation, bad tones.

Cad. An abbreviation of *Cadenza.*

Cadence (Fr.) (kă-dänhs.) A shake or trill; also a close in harmony.

Cadence. 1. A close in melody or harmony, dividing it into numbers or periods, or bringing it to a final termination. 2. An ornamental passage. See below and also *Cadenza.*

Cadence, authentic. A perfect or final cadence; the harmony of the dominant followed by that of the tonic or the progression of the dominant to the tonic.

Cadence, church. The plagal cadence.

Cadence, complete. A full cadence; when the final sound of a verse in a chant is on the key-note.

Cadence, deceptive. When the dominant chord resolves into another harmony instead of the tonic.

Cadence, demi. A half cadence.

Cadence, false. A deceptive or interrupted cadence.

Cadence, Greek. Plagal cadence.

Cadence, half. A cadence that is imperfect; a half-close on the dominant.

Cadence imperfaite (Fr.) (ănh-pĕr-fā.) An imperfect cadence.

Cadence, imperfect. When the dominant harmony is preceded by the common chord of the tonic; a half cadence.

Cadence interrompue (Fr.) (änh-tĕr-rŏnh-pü.) An interrupted cadence.

Cadence, interrupted. Similar to the perfect cadence, except that in place of the final tonic harmony some other chord is introduced; a false, or deceptive cadence.

Cadence, irregular. See *Imperfect Cadence.*

Cadence marks. Short lines placed perpendicularly to indicate the cadence notes in chanting.

Cadence parfaite (Fr.) (pär-fāt.) A perfect cadence.

Cadence, perfect. Where the dominant passes into the harmony of the tonic.

Cadence, plagal. When tonic harmony is preceded by subdominant.

Cadence, radical. The cadence resulting when the basses of both chords are the roots of their respective triads.

Cadence rompue (Fr.) (rŏnh-pü.) A broken or interrupted cadence.

Cadence, suspended. Where the cadence passes through several modulations from the dominant to the tonic chord.

ŏ as in *tone;* ô as in *dove;* ŏ as in *not;* ŭ as in *up;* ü the French sound of *u.*

43

CADENCIA   CALMÁTO

rupted, False or Deceptive Cadences.

VI   V   IV   V   VI

V   II# V   IVb³
Plagal Cadences.

IV   I   IVb³   I

Cadencia (Spa.) (kä-*athn*-thē-ä.) ⎱ Ca-
Cadens (Lat.) (*kä*-děns.) ⎰ dence.
Cadenz (Ger.) (kä-*děnts*.) ⎱ A ca-
Cadénza (It.) (kä-*den*-tsä.) ⎰ dence; an ornamental passage introduced near the close of a song or solo, either by the composer or extemporaneously by the performer. In the concerto, however, the cadenza reaches its largest form, being sometimes a dozen pages in length. It is generally not printed in the composition, but published separately, even when written by the composer of the work itself. It is often composed by the artist who performs the concerto. It is a brilliant technical display, developing themes of the composition. It is introduced in the coda of the first and last movement of a concerto, its place being signified by a hold ⌒ placed over a dominant chord, or a $\frac{6}{4}$ chord of the tonic. Beethoven, in his last piano concerto, declined to allow a solo cadenza, and Brahms and other modern composers have sometimes receded from it.

Cadenza d'ingánno (It.) (kä-*den*-tsä dēn-gän-nō.) An interrupted or deceptive cadence.

Cadenza fiorita (It.) (kä-*den*-tsä fē-ō-rē-tä.) An ornate, florid cadence with graces and embellishments.

Cadenza sfuggíta (It.) (kä-*den*-tsä sfoog-ghē-tä.) An avoided or broken cadence.

Cadénza sospésa (It.) (kä-*den*-tsä sŏs-*pay*-zä.) A suspended cadence.
Cahier de chant (Fr.) (kä-ĭ-ā dŭh shänh.) A singing book.
Cahier de musique (Fr.) (kä-ĭ-ā dŭh mü-zēk.) A music book.
Caisse (Fr.) (käss.) A drum.
Caisse grosse (Fr.) (kasse gross.) The bass drum.
Caisse roulante (Fr.) (käss roo-länht.) The side drum.
Caisses claires (Fr.) (käss klair.) The drums.
Cal. An abbreviation of *Calando*.
Calamo (Spa.) (kä-*lä*-mō.) A kind of flute.
Calamus pastoralis (Lat.) (kă-*lä*-mŭs păs-tō-*rä*-lĭs.) A reed or pipe used by shepherds.
Caland (It.) (kä-*länd*.) ⎱ Gradually
Calándo (It.) (kä-*län*-dō.) ⎰ diminishing the tone and retarding the time; becoming softer and slower by degrees.
Calándo nella forza (kä-*län*-dō něl-lä *fŏr*-tsä.) A decrease in the power or strength of a tone.
Calascione (It.) (kä-lä-shē-*ō*-ně.) A species of guitar.
Calathumpian music. A discordant combination of sounds. A vulgar and grotesque performance upon instruments unmusical and out of tune.
Caláta (It.) (kä-*lä*-tä.) An Italian dance in $\frac{2}{4}$ time.
Calcándo (It.) (käl-*kän*-dō.) Pressing forward and hurrying the time.
Calcant (Ger.) (käl-känt.) The bellows treader, in old German organs.
Call. The beat of a drum.
Call, adjutant's. A drum-beat directing the band and field music to take the right of the line.
Calliope (käl-*lēe*-ŏ-pě.) 1. In pagan mythology the muse that presided over eloquence and heroic poetry. 2. An instrument formed of metal pipes, with keys like an organ; they are placed on steam engines sometimes, and the tones are produced by currents of steam instead of air.
Cálma (It.) (*käl*-mä.) ⎱ Calmness,
Calmáte (It.) (käl-*mä*-tě.) ⎰ tranquility,
Calmáto (It.) (käl-*mä*-tō.) ⎰ repose.

ä as in *ah*; ā as in *hate*; ă as in *at*; ē as in *tree*; ě as in *eh*; ī as in *pine*; ĭ as in *pin*;

44

Calo. An abbreviation of *Calándo.*

Calóre (It.) (kä-*lō*-rĕ.) Warmth, animation.

Caloróso (It.) (käl-ō-*rō*-zo.) Animation and warmth.

Cambiáre (It.) (käm-bē-*ä*-rĕ.) To change; to alter.

Camena (Lat.) (kă-*mä*-nä.) } The muse.
Camoena (Lat.) (kă-*mö*-nä.) }

Cámera (It.) (*kä*-mĕ-rä.) Chamber; a term applied to music composed for private performance or small concerts.

Cámera musica (It.) (kä-mĕ-rä *moo*-zē-kä.) Chamber music.

Caminándo (It.) (kä-mi-*nän*-dō.) Flowing; with easy and gentle progression.

Campána (It.) (käm-*pä*-nä.) A bell.

Campanélla (It.) (käm-pä-*nĕl*-lä.) } A
Campanéllo (It.) (käm-pä-*nĕl*-lō.) } little bell.

Campanellíno (It.) (käm-pä-nĕl-*lee*-nō.) A very little bell.

Campaneta (Spa.) (käm-pä-*ne*-tä.) A small bell.

Campanétta (It.) (käm-pä-*net*-tä.) A set of bells tuned diatonically, and played with keys like a pianoforte.

Campanile (It.) (käm-pä-*nee*-lĕ.) A belfry.

Campanésta (It.) (käm-pä-*nes*-tä.) A player upon the *campanetta.*

Campanologist (käm-pä-*nŏl*-ō-jĭst.) An artistic bell ringer.

Campanology (käm-pä-*nŏl*-ō-gy.) The art of ringing bells.

Campanóne (It.) (käm-pän-*nō*-nĕ.) A great bell.

Canarder (Fr.) (kă-när-*dā*.) To imitate the tones of a duck.

Canarie (Fr.) (kă-nä-*rē*.)   ) An old
Canaries (Eng.) (kă-*nā*-rĕs.) } dance, in
Canário (It.) (kä-*nä*-rē-ō.)) lively $\frac{3}{4}$ or $\frac{6}{8}$, and sometimes $\frac{12}{8}$ time, of two strains. It derives its name from the Canary Islands, whence it is supposed to have come.

Cancelling sign. A natural (♮), employed to remove the effect of a previous flat or sharp.

Cancion (Spa.) (kän-thē-*ōn*.) A song; words set to music.

Cancrizans (It.) (kän-*krē*-tsäns.))
Cancrizante (It.) (kän-krē-*tsän*-tĕ.) } Retrograde movement; going backward; crab-like.

Canon. The strictest form of contrapuntal composition, in which each voice imitates exactly the melody sung or played by the first voice. The word is derived from "Canone," a rule or law. Canon was the earliest form of skilful composition. The oldest existing contrapuntal work of merit is a canon entitled, "Sumer is icumen in," which is for four voices, and is supposed to have been composed about A.D. 1200. Canon may be defined as the strict imitation of a melody throughout. The imitating voice, or voices, may enter above or below the subject, or sometimes upon the same degree. In the last case, the canon is called a Round. The imitation may enter at any interval, from a second, above or below, to a double octave, or fifteenth. Thus, "A canon at the fifth," would be imitated at the fifth, above or below. The imitation may enter at any time-distance after the first voice has begun, yet it ought not to come many measures after, since in such a case it would be difficult to follow the imitation. A single measure, or two measures, is best, since if such an even distance is taken the imitation preserves the same rhythmic construction of measures as the subject. Most canons are two-voiced (consisting of subject and imitation) at the octave (above or below), and are at one or two measures time-distance. The subject of the canon is sometimes called Antecedent, and the imitation Consequent. The canon was called "Fugue," by the oldest contrapuntists. When more than one voice is used in imitation, it is sometimes best to use different intervals for the imitations; one voice imitating at the octave, another at the fifth, etc. A double canon is two canons going on simultaneously, and consequently has at least four voices. See the Requiem at the close of Schumann's "Manfred," for a short example of double canon; also Bach's organ prelude on "In dulci jubilo." See also Richter, Chadwick, Jadassohn, Goetschius, works or Counterpoint.

ō as in *tone*; ŏ as in *dove*; ô as in *not*; ŭ as in *up*; ü the French sound of *u*.

Cánone (It.) (*kä*-nō-ně.) } A canon.
Canónico (It.) (kä-*nŏn*-ē-kō.) }

Cánone al sospíro (It.) (*kä*-nō-ně äl sŏs-*pē*-rō.) A canon whose different parts commence at the distance of one beat from each other.

Cánone apérto (It.) (*kä*-nō-ně ä-*pair*-tō.) An *open canon*; a canon of which the solution or development is given.

Canon, augmented. A canon in which the imitation reproduces the subject, or melody, in notes of a larger denomination. For an example of a canon that is both augmented and diminished. See Bach's organ prelude on "Ach Gott und Herr."

Cánone cancrizans. A crab canon. A canon in which the imitating voice reproduces the subject played through backwards. Also *Canone per Recte et Retro*, a canon making the same melody whether played through forwards or backwards, the last half reversing the first half. See the Fugue in Beethoven's "Sonata in B♭, Op. 106."

Cánone chiúso (It.) (*kä*-nō-ně kē-*oo*-zō.) A *close* or *hidden* canon, the solution or development of which must be discovered; an enigmatical canon.

Cánone sciólto (It.) (*kä*-nō-ně shē-*ōl*-tō.) A free canon, not in the strict style.

Canon, free. A canon not in strict conformity to the rules, the melody of the first part not being followed throughout.

Canon, hidden. A close canon. See *Cánone Chiúso*.

Canon, infinite. A canon, the end of which leads to the beginning; a perpetual canon.

Canon, inverted. A canon in which the imitating voice repeats the subject upside down, — *in motu contrario*, — ascending intervals being imitated by descending ones, etc.

Canon, mixed. A canon of several voices, beginning at different intervals.

Canon perpetuus (Lat.) (*kăn*-ŏn pĕr-pĕt-ū-ŭs.) See *Canon, infinite*.

Canon, strict. A canon in which the rules of this form of composition are strictly followed.

Canonical hours. The 7 canonical hours of the Catholic Church are the established times for daily prayer; called *matins, prime, terce, sext, nones, vespers*, and *complin*. Those from prime to nones are named after the hours of the day, prime (the first hour) being at or about 6 A.M., terce (the third) at 9, sext (the sixth) at noon, and nones (the ninth) at 3 P.M.

Canonical Mass. A Mass in which the musical numbers are in strict ritualistic or canonical order.

Cantab. An abbreviation of *cantabile*.

Cantábile (It.) (kän-*tä*-bi-lĕ.) That can be sung; in a melodious, singing, and graceful style, full of expression.

Cantábile ad libitum (It.) (kän-*tä*-bē-lĕ äd lē-bē-tŭm.) In singing style; at pleasure.

Cantando (It.) (kän-*tän*-dōh.) In a singing style; *cantabile*.

Cantáre (It.) (kän-*tä*-rě.) To sing; to celebrate; to praise.

Cantáre a ária (It.) (kän-*tä*-rē ä ä-*rē*-ä.) To sing without confining one's self strictly to the music as written.

Cantáre a libro (It.) (kän-tä-rĕ ä lē-brō.) To sing from notes.

Cantáre a orécchio (It.) (kän-tä-rĕ ä ō-*re*-kē-o.) To sing by ear, without a knowledge of musical notation; singing by rote.

Cantáre di maniéra (It.) (kän-tä-rĕ dē mä-nē-*di*-rä.) To sing in a correct style, with grace and expression.

Cantáre manieráta (It.) (kän-tä-rĕ mä-nēe-ĕ-*rä*-tä.) To sing with too many embellishments, without taste or judgment.

Cantáta (It.) (kän-*tä*-tä.) } A poem set
Cantate (Fr.) (känh-*tät*.) } to music; a
Cantate (Ger.) (kän-*tä*-tĕ.) } vocal composition of several movements, comprising airs and recitatives; a short oratorio or operetta without action. A cantata consisted originally of a mixture of recitative and melody, and was given to a single voice, but the introduction of choruses altered the first character of the cantata, and gave rise to some confusion in the manner of describing it. Therefore it has been variously defined. A cantata is now generally understood to be a short work somewhat like the oratorio, but without characters. But the word is still used

CANTÁTA AMOROSE — CANTO FERMO

in many different senses by different composers. Examples: Bennett's "Woman of Samaria"; Haydn's "Seasons," etc.

Cantáta amorose (It.) (kän-tä-tä ä-mò-rō-zĕ.) A cantata having love for its subject.

Cantatílla (It.) (kän-tä-*til*-lä.) ⎫
Cantatille (Fr.) (känh-tä-*til*.) ⎬ A short cantata;
Cantatína (It.) (kän-tä-*tee*-nä.) ⎭ an air preceded by a recitative.

Cantatorium (Lat.) (kăn-tä-*tō*-rĭ-ŭm.) The book from which the priests in the Roman Catholic service chant or recite the responses.

Cantatríce (It.) (kän-tä-*trē*-tshĕ.) A female singer.

Cantatrice buffa (It.) (kän-tä-*trēe*-tshĕ *boof*-fä.) A female burlesque singer; a woman who sings in comic opera.

Cantellerándo (It.) (kän-täl-lĕ-rän-dō.) Singing with a subdued voice; murmuring, trilling.

Canterelláre (It.) (kän-tä-rĕl-lä-re.) To chant or sing.

Canteríno (It.) (kän-tĕ-rē-nō.) A singer; a chanter.

Cántica (It.) (kän-tē-kä.) ⎫
Canticæ (Lat.) (*kăn*-tĭ-sē.) ⎬ Canticles;
Cántici (It. pl.) (kän-tē-tshē.) ⎪ the ancient *lau-*
Cantico (Spa.) (kän-*tē*-kō.) ⎭ *di*, or sacred songs of the Roman Catholic Church.

Cánti carnascialéschi (It.) (*kän*-tē cär-näs-tshē-ä-les-kē.)

Cánti charneváli (It.) (*kän*-tē kär-nĕ-*vä*-lē.) Songs of the *carnival* week.

Canticchiáre (It.) (kän-ti-kē-*ä*-rĕ.) To sing; to hum.

Canticle. 1. A sacred hymn or song. One of the non-metrical hymns of praise and jubilation in the Bible. 2. The Evangelical canticles (*Cantica majora*) of both the Catholic and Anglican Church are taken from the Gospels. The word is applied to certain detached psalms and hymns used in the service of the Anglican Church, such as the *Venite exultemus, Te Deum laudamus, Benedicite omnia opera, Benedictus, Jubilate Deo, Magnificat, Cantate Domino, Nunc dimittis. Deus miserea-*

tur, and the verses used instead of the Venite on Easter-day.

Cantico (It.) (kän-tē-kō.) ⎫ A canticle.
Canticum (Lat.) (*kăn*-tĭ-kŭm.) ⎭

Cantillate (*kăn*-tĭl-lāte.) To chant; to recite with musical tones.

Cantillation. A chanting; a recitation with musical modulations; a combination of speaking with music.

Cantillatio (Lat.) (kăn-tĭl-*lä*-shĭ-ō.) A singing style of declamation.

Cantiléna (It.) (kän-tĭ-*lāy*-nä.) The melody, air, or principal part in any composition; generally the highest vocal part; it is also applied to any light and simple song, or in instrumental music a piece of song-like character. It sometimes indicates a smooth, *cantabile* style of playing.

Cantilene (It.) (kän-tē-*lāy*-nĕ.) A *cantiléna.*

Cantinela (Spa.) (kän-tē-*na*-lä.) A ballad.

Cantíno (It.) (kän-*tē*-nō.) The smallest string of the violin, guitar, etc.; also, called *chanterelle.*

Cantio (Lat.) (*kăn*-tĭ-ō.) A song.

Cantion. A song or number of verses.

Cantiones sacræ (Lat.) (kăn-shĭ-*ō*-nēs sä-krä.) Sacred songs.

Cantique (Fr.) (kähn-*tēek.*) A canticle or hymn of praise.

Cantique des Cantiques (Fr.) Solomon's song.

Cantiuncula (Lat.) (kăn-tĭ-*ŭn*-kŭ-lä.) A ballad; a catch.

Cánto (It.) (*kän*-tō.) 1. Song, air, melody; the highest vocal part in choral music. 2. A part or division of a poem.

Cánto armónico (It.) (*kän*-tō är-*mō*-ni-kō.) A part-song for two, three, or more voices.

Cánto clef. The C clef when placed on the first line. The Soprano clef.

Cánto concertante (It.) (*kän*-tō kŏn-tshär-*tän*-tĕ.) The treble of the principal concerting parts.

Cánto férmo (It.) (*kän*-tō *fäir*-mō.) 1. A chant or melody. 2. Choral singing in unison on a plain melody. 3. Any subject consisting of a few long, plain notes, given as a theme for counterpoint; also, *Cantus firmus.*

ŏ as in *tone;* ô as in *dove;* ŏ as in *not;* ŭ as in *up;* ü the French sound of *u.*

47

CÁNTO FIGURÁTO   CANZÓNE

Cánto figuráto (It.) (*kän*-tō fi-goo-rä-tō.) A figured melody.

Cánto fioritto (It.) (*kän*-tō fē-ō-*rēt*-tō.) A song in which many ornaments are introduced.

Cánto funébre (It.) (*kän*-tō foo-*nāy*-brĕ.) A funeral song.

Cánto Gregoriáno (It.) (*kän*-tō grĕ-gō-rē-*ä*-nō.) The Gregorian chant.

Cánto Ilánо (Spa.) (*kän*-tō *lyä*-nō.) The plain chant or song.

Cánto necessário (It.) (*kän*-tō nĕ-tshĕs-*sä*-rē-o.) A term indicating those parts that are to sing through the whole piece.

Cánto pláno (It.) (*kän*-tō plä-nō.) The plain chant or song.

Cánto prímo (It.) (*kän*-tō prē-mō.) The first treble or soprano.

Cantór (It.) (kän-*tór*.) A singer; a chanter.

Cantor (Lat.) (*kăn*-tŏr.)
Cantor choralis (Lat.) (*kăn*-tŏr kō-rä-līs.)
A *precentor*; a leader of the choir.

Cantorate (It.) (kän-tō-*rä*-tĕ.) A leading singer of a choir.

Cantóre (It.) (kän-tō-rĕ.) A singer; a chanter; a poet.

Cánto recitatívo (It.) (kän-tō rä-tshē-tä-*tē*-vō.) Recitative; declamatory singing.

Cantoren (Ger.) (kän-*tö*-r'n.) Chanters; a choir of singers.

Cantoria (It.) (kän-*tö*-rē-ä.)   A sing-
Cantoria (Spa.) (kän-*tō*-rē-ä.)   ing gallery; a musical canto ; singing.

Cantor figuralis (Lat.) (*kăn*-tŏr fīg-ū-*rä*-līs.) Oratorio singer; conductor of the choir.

Cantor in choro (Lat.) (*kán*-tŏr ĭn kō-rō.) A chorister.

Canto ripieno (It.) (*kän*-tō rē-pē-*āy*-nō.) The treble of the grand chorus; the part that sings or plays only in the grand chorus.

Cantoris (Lat.) (kän-*tō*-ris.) A term used in cathedral music to indicate the passages intended to be sung by those singers who are placed on that side of the choir where the *cantor* or *precentor* sits. This is usually on the left-hand side on entering the choir from the nave. See *Decani*.

Cánto rivoltato (It.) (*kän*-tō rē-vōl-*tä*-tō.) The treble changed.

Cánto secondo (It.) (*kän*-tō sĕ-*kōn*-dō.) The second treble.

Cantríce (It.) (kän-*trē*-tshĕ.)   A female
Cantrix (Lat.) (*kăn*-trĭx.)   singer; a songstress.

Cantus (Lat.) (*kăn*-tŭs.) A song; a melody; also, the treble or soprano part. Canto.

Cantus ambrosianus (Lat.) (*kăn*-tŭs ăm-brō-sĭ-*ä*-nŭs.) The four chants or melodies, introduced into the church by St. Ambrose, Bishop of Milan, in the fourth century, and which are supposed to be derived from the ancient Greek modes. See *Ambrosian chant*.

Cantus durus (Lat.) (*kăn*-tŭs *dū*-rŭs.) A song written in major key; also, old music which modulated into a key having one or more sharps in its scale. Such keys were at one period strictly proscribed by church musicians.

Cantus ecclesiasticus (Lat.) (*kăn*-tŭs ĕk-klä-sĭ-*ăs*-tĭ-kŭs.) Sacred song; ecclesiastical or church music; plain song.

Cantus figuratus (Lat.) (*kăn*-tŭs fīg-ū-*rä*-tŭs.) Embellished or figurative chants or melodies.

Cantus firmus (Lat.) (*kăn*-tŭs *fĭr*-mŭs.) The plain song or chant. See *cánto fĕrmo*.

Cantus Gregorianus (Lat.) (*kăn*-tŭs Grĕ-gō-rĭ-*ä*-nŭs.) Those four modes introduced into the church by St. Gregory, and which, with the Ambrosian chants, formed a series of eight *modes* or *tones*, as they were called. See *Gregorian chant*.

Cantus mensurabilis (Lat.) (*kăn*-tŭs mĕn-sŭr-*ä*-bĭ-lĭs.) A regular or measured melody.

Cantus mollis (Lat.) (*kăn*-tŭs *mŏl*-lĭs.) A song written in the minor key.

Canzóna (It.) (kän-*tsō*-nä.)   1. Song;
Canzóne (It.) (kän-*tsō*-nĕ.)   ballad; canzonet. 2. A graceful and somewhat elaborate air in two or three strains or divisions. 3. An air in two or three parts with passages of fugue and imitation, somewhat similar to the madrigal.

ă as in *ah*; ā as in *hate*; ă as in *at*; ē as in *tree*, ĕ as in *eh*; ī as in *pine*; ĭ as in *pin*;

CANZONÁCCEA   CARILLON A CLAVIER

Canzonáccia (It.) (kän-tsō-*nät*-tshē-ä.) A low, trivial song; a poor canzone.

Canzoncína (It.) (kän-tsōn-*tshēe*-nä.) A short *canzóne*.

Canzóne sácra (It.) (kän-*tsō*-ně *sä*-krä.) A sacred song.

Canzonet. A short song in one, two, or three parts.

Canzonétta (It.) (kän-*tsō-net*-tä.) A short *canzóne*. A little song.

Canzoniére (It.) (kän-tsō-nē-*ä*-rě.) A song book.

Canzonina (It.) (kän-tsō-*nēe*-nä.)
Canzonuccia (It.) (kän-tso-*noot*-tshē-ä.)
A *canzonet*; a little song.

Capelle (Ger.) (kä-*pěl*-lě.) A chapel; a musical band. See *Kapelle*.

Capell-meister (Ger.) (kä-*pět*-mīs-ter.) The director, composer, or master of the music in a choir or orchestra. See *Kapell-meister*.

Capilla (Spa.) (kä-*pēl*-yä.) A band of chapel musicians.

Capiscol (Spa.) (kä-pēs-*kōl*.)
Capiscolus (Lat.) (kä-pǐs-*kō*-lǔs.)
The *chanter* or *precentor* of a choir.

Capo (It.) (*kä*-pō.) The head or beginning; the top.

Capodastro (It.) (kä-pō-*däs*-trō.) See *Capotásto*.

Cápo d' inestrumenti (It.) (*kä*-pō d' ēn-ěs-stroo-*men*-tē.) The leader or director of the instrumental performers.

Capolavoro (It.) (*käh*-pōh-lä-*vōh*-rōh.) A masterpiece.

Cápo d' opera (It.) (*kä*-pō d' *ō*-pě-rä.) The masterpiece of a composer.

Cápo d' orchestra (It.) (*kä*-pō d' ǒr-*kěs*-trä.) The leader of the orchestra.

Capona (Spa.) (kä-*pō*-nä.) A Spanish dance.

Capotásto (It.) (kä-pō-*täs*-tō.) 1. The nut or upper part of the finger board of a violin, violoncello, etc. 2. A piece of wood or ivory used by guitar players to form a temporary nut upon the finger board, to raise the pitch of all the strings simultaneously.

Capo violino (It.) (*kä*-pō vē-ō-*lēe*-nō.) The first violin.

Cappélla (It.) (käp-*pel*-lä.) 1. A chapel or church. 2. A band of musicians that sing or play in a church, or in private employ. 3. An orchestra.

Cappélla alla (It.) (käp-*pel*-lä äl-lä.) In the church style; vocal chorus work without any accompaniment. Also, *A Cappella*.

Cappélla música (It.) (käp-*pel*-lä moo-zē-kä.) Chapel or church music.

Capricciétto (It.) (kä-prēt-shē-*ět*-tō.) A short *capríccio*.

Capríccio (It.) (kä-*prēt*-shē-ō.) A fanciful and irregular species of composition; a species of *fantasia*; in a capricious and free style.

Capricciosaménte (It.) (kä-prēt-shē-ō-zä-*men*-tě.) Capriciously.

Capriccióso (It.) (kä-prēt-shē-*ō*-zō.) In a fanciful and capricious style.

Caprice (Fr.) (kǎ-*prēs*.) A caprice. See *Capríccio*.

Capricieusement (Fr.) (kǎ-prē-*süs*-mǒnh.) Capriciously.

Capricieux (Fr.) (kǎ-prē-sü.) In a fanciful and capricious style.

Car (It.) An abbreviation of Carta.

Caractères de musique (Fr.) (kär-äk-*tār* dǔh mü-*zēek*.) A term applied to musical signs; all the marks or symbols belonging to musical notation.

Caramillo (Spa.) (kär-ä-*měl*-yō.) A flageolet; a small flute.

Caráttere (It.) (kä-*rät*-tāi-rě.) Character, quality, degree.

Caráttere, mezzo (It.) (kä-*rät*-tāi-rě, mět-sō.) A term applied to music of moderate difficulty. A song with few embellishments.

Caressant (Fr.) (kä-rěs-*sänh*.) Caressing, tenderly.

Carezzándo (It.) (kä-rět-*tsän*-dō.)
Carezzovole (It.) (kä-rät-sǒ-*vō*-lě.)
In a caressing and tender manner.

Caricáto (It.) (kä-rē-*kä*-tō.) Exaggerated, caricature.

Caricatura (It.) (kä-rē-kä-*too*-rä.) A caricature; an exaggerated representation.

Carillon (Fr.) (kǎ-rē-yǒnh.) Chime. See *Carillons*.

Carillon à clavier (Fr.) (kǎ-rē-yǒnh ä klǎv-ī-ā.) A set of keys and pedals acting upon the bells.

ō as in *tone*; ô as in *dove*; ǒ as in *not*; ǔ as in *up*; ü the French sound of *u*.

Carillonment (Fr.) (kă-rē-yŏnh-mänh.) Chiming.

Carillonner (Fr.) (kă-rē-yō-*nā*.) To chime or ring bells.

Carillonneur (Fr.) (kă-rē-yo-*nŭr*.) A player or ringer of bells or *carillons*.

Carillons (Fr. pl.) (kă-rē-*yŏnh*.) 1. Chimes; a peal or set of bells, upon which tunes are played by the machinery of a clock, or by means of keys, like those of a piano. 2. Short simple airs adapted to such bells. 3. A mixture stop in an organ, to imitate a peal of bells.

Carita (It.) (kä-*rē*-tä.) Tenderness, feeling.

Carita con (It.) (kä-*rē*-tä kŏn.) With tenderness.

Carmagnole (Fr.) (kä-măn-*yōl*.) A dance accompanied by singing, named from Carmagnola in Piedmont. Many of the wildest excesses of the French Reign of Terror were associated with this dance. The song commenced with "Madame Véto avait promis," and each verse ended with the burden "Dansons la Carmagnole, vive le son du canon." "Madame Véto" was the opprobrious nickname given by the mob to the unfortunate Marie Antoinette. See Elson's "Our National Music."

Carmen (Ger.) (*kär*-měn.) } A tune; a
Carmen (Lat.) (*kär*-měn.) } song; a poem.

Carmen natalitium (Lat.) (*kär*-měn nä-tä-*lē*-shĭ-ŭm.) A carol on the Nativity.

Carol. 1. A song. 2. A song of joy and exultation; a song of devotion. 3. Old ballads sung at Christmas and Easter.

Carola (It.) (kä-*rō*-lä.) A ballad; a dance with singing. The carol was originally a song combined with dancing.

Carolare (It.) (kä-rō-*lä*-rě.) To sing in a warbling manner; to carol.

Caroletta (It.) (kä-rō-*lĕt*-tä.) A little dance.

Carolle (Fr.) (kä-*rōl*.) A carol.

Carrée (Fr.) (*kar*-ray.) A double whole note 𝄻 .

Carrure des phrases (Fr.) (kär-rür dě fräz.) The quadrature or balancing of the phrases.

Cart. (It.) An abbreviation of *Carta*.

Carta (It.) (kär-tä.) A page; a folio.

Case, organ. The frame or outside of an organ.

Cássa (It.) (*käs*-sä.) A large drum.

Cássa grande (It.) (*käs*-sä *grän*-dĕ.) The bass drum in military music.

Castagnet. Castanet.

Castagnétta (It.) (käs-tän-*yĕt*-tä.)
Castagnettes (Fr.) (käs-tänh-*yĕt*.)
Castagnole (Spa.) (käs-tän-*yō*-lĕ.)
Castanétas (Spa.) (käs-tän-yä-*täs*.)
} Clappers; castanets, used in dancing. See *Castanets*.

Castanets. Clappers used to accompany dancing; an instrument of music formed of small concave shells of ivory, or hard wood, shaped like spoons. Castanets are used by dancers in Spain and other southern countries to mark the rhythm of the *boléro*, cachucha, etc. The name comes from "Castagna," a chestnut, from their resemblance to the large chestnuts of France and Italy.

Castanheta (Por.) (käs-tän-ā-tä.) }
Castanuélas (Spa.) (käs-tän-yoo-*ā*-läs.) } Castanets.

Castráto (It.) (käs-*trä*-tō.) A male singer with a soprano voice; a eunuch.

Catacoustics (kät-ă-*koos*-tĭks.) }
Cataphonics (kät-ă-*fŏn*-ĭks.) } That part of acoustics that treats of reflected sounds.

Catalectic. Pertaining to metrical composition or to measure. Lacking part of a final foot. Thus, the last line of the following is catalectic—
 "In the cross of Christ I glory
 Tow'ring o'er the rocks of time."
 — ‿ — ‿ — ‿ — ‿
 — ‿ — ‿ — ‿

Catalectic verses. Verses that want either feet or syllables.

Catch. A humorous composition for three or four voices, supposed to be of English invention and dating back to the Tudors. The parts are so contrived that the singers catch up each other's words, thus giving them a different sense from that of the original reading. The oldest catches were

George Friedrich Handel

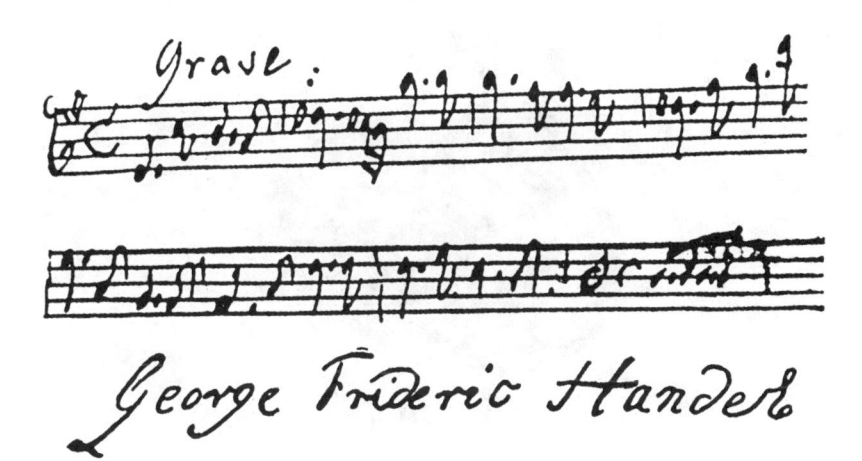

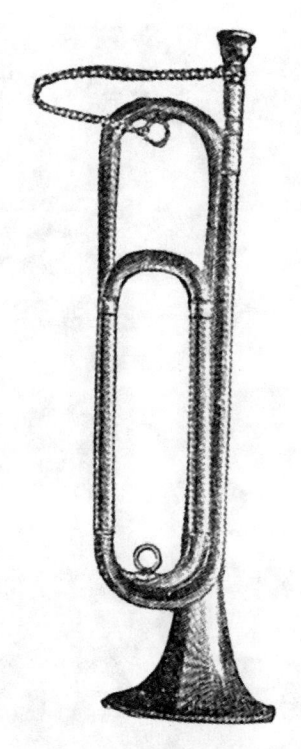

Bugle

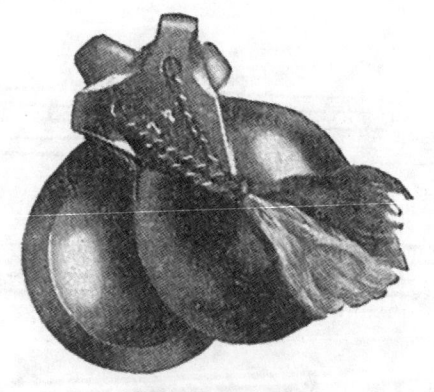

Castanets

rounds. The catch is finely alluded to by Shakespeare in "Twelfth Night," and was extremely popular in the reign of Charles II.

Caténa di trílli (It.) (kä-tā́-nä dē trĭl-lē) A chain, or succession of trills.

Catgut. A small string for violins and other instruments of a similar kind, made of the intestines of sheep, lambs, or goats.

Cathédrale (Fr.) (kăt-ā-drāl.) } A cathe-
Cattedrále (It.) (kät-tĕ-drä-lē.) } dral.

Catling. A lute string.

Cattivo (It.) (kät-tēe-vō.) Bad, unfit.

Cattivo tempo (It.) (kät-tēe-vō tĕm-pō.) A part of a measure where it is not proper to end a cadence, place a long syllable, etc. The arsis.

Cauda (Lat.) (kau-dä.) Coda.

Cavalletta (It.) (kä-väl-lĕt́-tä.) } A caba-
Cavalletto (It.) (kä-väl-lĕt́-tō.) } létta.

Cavalquet (Fr.) (käv-ăl-kā́.) Trumpet signal for the cavalry.

Cavata (It.) (kä-vā́-tä.) A small song, sometimes preceded by a recitative; a cavatina.

Cavatína (It.) (kä-vä-tēe-nä.) } An air of
Cavatine (Fr.) (käv-ä-tēen.) } one strain only. Shorter than an aria, which it sometimes precedes, and generally of simple and expressive character.

C. B. The initials of *col basso* and *contra basso*.

C barré (Fr.) (bär-rā.) } The character
C barred. } ₵ used to indicate *álla bréve* or *álla cappélla* or 2/2 time.

C clef. It is called the C clef, because, on whatever line it is placed, it gives to the notes on that line the name and pitch of *middle* C. Is used for Tenor, Sop., and Alt. See *Clef*.

C dur (Ger.) (tsā door.) The key of C major.

Cebell. The name of an old air in common time, characterized by a quick and sudden alternation of high and low notes.

Célébrer (Fr.) (sā-lĕ-brā́.) To celebrate; to extol; to praise.

Célere (It.) (tshā́-lĕ-rĕ.) Quick; rapid; with velocity.

Celeritá (It.) (tshā-lā-rē-tä.) } Celerity,
Célérité (Fr.) (sā-lā-rē-tä.) } velocity, rapidity

Céleste (Fr.) (sā-lĕ́st.) Celestial, heavenly; *voix celeste*, a sweet-toned organ stop.

Celestial music. Among the ancients the harmony of sounds supposed to result from the movements of the planets.

Celestína (It.) (tshā-lĕs-tē-nä.) An organ stop of small 4-foot scale, producing a very delicate and subdued tone.

'Célli (It.) (*tshĕl*-lē.) An abbreviation of *violoncélli*.

'Céllist (It.) (*tshĕl*-lēst.) An abbreviation of *violoncellist*.

'Céllo (It.) (*tshĕl*-lō.) An abbreviation of *violoncello*.

Cemb. An abbreviation of *Cémbalo*.

Cembalísta (It.) (tshĕm-bä-lēz-tä.) A player on the harpsichord; also, a player on the cymbals.

Cémbalo (It.) (*tshĕm*-bä-lō.) } A harpsi-
Cémbolo (It.) (*tshĕm*-bō-lō.) } chord; also the name for a cymbal.

Cenobites. Monks of a religious order who live in a convent and perform the services of the choir.

Cento (Lat.) (sĕn-tō.) The title of a poem made up of various verses of another poem. A composition formed by verses and passages from other authors and disposed in a new order.

Centone (Lat.) (sĕn-tō-nĕ.) A cento, or medley of different tunes or melodies.

Cercár la nóta (It.) (tshĕr-kär lä nō-tä.) To seek or feel for the note; a gliding from one note to another, in singing, by anticipating the proper time of the second note.

Cerdana (Spa.) (thär-dä-nä.) A dance in Catalonia.

Cervalet. An ancient wind instrument resembling in tone the bassoon.

Ces (Ger.) (tsĕs.) The note C flat.

Ces dur (tsĕs dōor.) The key of C flat major.

C. Espr. An abbreviation of Con Espressione.

Cesure (Fr.) (sĕ-sür.) } 1. A pause
Cesura (It.) (tshĕ-soo-rä.) } in verse, so
Cesura (Lat.) (sē-sū-rä.) } introduced

CESURA   **CHANGEABLE**

as to aid the recital and make the versification more melodious. 2. A break or section in rhythm. 3. The rhythmic termination of any passage consisting of more than one musical foot. 4. The last accented note of a phrase, section, or period.

Cesura. } **Cesure.** } A pause in verse introduced to aid the recital and render the versification more melodious.

Cétera (It.) (*tshā*-tĕ-rä.) A cittern; a guitar.

Cetêránte (It.) (tshā-tĕ-*rän*-tĕ.) A player upon the cittern or guitar.

Ceteráre (It.) (tshā-tĕ-*rä*-rĕ.) To play upon the cittern or guitar.

Ceteratojo (It.) (tshā-tĕ-rä-*tō*-yō.) A song accompanied upon the cittern.

Ceteratóre (It.) (tshā-tĕ-rä-*tō*-rĕ.) } **Ceterista** (It.) (tshā-tĕ-*rēs*-tä.) } A player upon the cittern or guitar.

Ceterizzare (It.) (tshā-tĕ-rēt-*zä*-rĕ.) To sing with or play upon the cittern.

Cetra (It.) (*tshā*-trä.) A small harp; a zither.

Cetrarciéro (It.) (tshĕt-rär-tshē-*ä*-rō.) A harp with the bow and lyre.

Cetráre (It.) (tshĕt-*rä*-rĕ.) See *Ceterāre*.

Ch. An abbreviation of *choir* and *chorus*.

Chacóna (Spa.) (tshä-*kō*-nä.) } **Chaconne** (Fr.) (shä-*kŏnh*.) } A graceful, slow Spanish movement in ¾ time, and composed upon a ground bass. It is generally in the major key, and the first and third beats of each bar are strongly accented. Bach's Chaconne with variations, for violin alone, is one of the most famous specimens of this old dance.

Chacoon. A dance like a saraband. See *Chacóna*.

Chair organ. Found in old organ music. See *choir organ*.

Chal. An abbreviation of *Chalumeau*.

Chalil (Heb.) (kä-*lēl*.) An old Hebrew instrument similar to a pipe or flute.

Chalmey. See *Chalumeau*.

Chalotte. A tube of brass made to receive the reed of an organ pipe.

Chalmeau (Fr.) (shäl-*mō*.) } **Chalumeau** (Fr.) (shäl-ü-*mō*.) } The lowest register of

the clarinet and the basset-horn is called the *chalumeau*, from the obsolete instrument *shawm*, *schalmey*, precursor of the oboe and clarinet. In clarinet music "chalumeau" is used to indicate an octave lower than written.

Chamade (Fr.) (shä-*mäd*.) Beat of drum declaring a surrender or parley.

Chamber band. A company of musicians whose performances are confined to chamber music.

Chamber music. Music composed for private performance or for small concerts; such as instrumental duets, trios, quartets, etc. The term is less frequently applied to vocal music. In a broad sense "chamber music" is *any* music suited to a room, or small hall, as distinct from music for a large auditorium, as church, operatic, or symphonic music. Practically, the term is most frequently applied to concerted pieces of instrumental music in the sonata form, as string quartets, quintets, etc.

Chamber voice. A voice especially suited to the execution of parlor music.

Chamber Organ. A cabinet organ.

Changeable. A term applied to chants which may be sung either in the major or minor mode of the key or tonic in which they are written.

ă as in *a*ʰ; ā as in *hate*; ă as in *at*; ē as in *tree*; ĕ as in *eh*; ī as in *pine*; ĭ as in *pin*;

Change, enharmonic. A passage where the notation is changed, but the same keys of the instrument are employed.

Changer de jeu (Fr.) (shänh-zhā dŭh zhü.) To change the stops or registers in an organ.

Changes. The various alternations and different passages produced by a peal of bells.

Changing notes. A term applied by some theorists to passing notes or discords, which occur on the *accented* parts of a bar.

Chans. An abbreviation of *Chanson*.

Chanson (Fr.) (shänh-sŏnh.) A song.

Chanson bachique (Fr.) (shänh-sŏnh băk-ĕk.) A drinking song.

Chanson des rues (Fr.) (shänh-sŏnh dĕ rü.) A street song; a vaudeville.

Chansonner (Fr.) (shăh-sŏnh-nā.) To make songs.

Chansonnette (Fr.) (shänh-sŏnh-nĕt.) A little or short song, or canzonet.

Chansonnier (Fr.) (shănh-sŏnh-nĭ-ā.) A maker of songs or ballads.

Chansons de geste (Fr.) (shănh-sŏnh dŭh zhĕst.) The romances formerly sung by the wandering minstrels of the middle ages.

Chant. 1. A simple melody, generally harmonized in four parts, to which lyrical portions of the Scriptures are set, part of the words being recited *ad libitum*, and part sung in strict time. A Gregorian chant consists of five parts: the intonation; the first reciting note or dominant; the mediation; the second reciting note or dominant; the cadence. The Gregorian chant is the one chiefly used in the Catholic and Anglican service. See Helmore's "Plain Song." 2. To recite musically; to sing.

Chant. (Fr.) (shänh.) The voice part; a song or melody; singing.

Chant, Ambrosian. The chant introduced by St. Ambrose into the church at Milan, in the fourth century. See *Ambrosian chant*.

Chant amoureux (Fr.) (shänh ämoo-rüh.) A love song; an amorous ditty.

Chantant (Fr.) (shänh-tänh.) Adapted to singing; in a melodious and singing style.

Chantante (Fr.) (shänh-tänht.) Singing.

Chantante, basse (Fr.) (shänh-tänht bäss.) Lyric bass.

Chant d' église (Fr.) (shänh d' ĕ-glēez.) Church singing.

Chant de noël (Fr.) (shänh dŭh nō-āl.) A Christmas carol.

Chant des oiseaux (Fr.) (shänh dĕ swä-zō.) Singing of the birds.

Chant de triomphe (Fr.) (shänh dŭh trē-ŏnhf.) A triumphal song; a song of victory.

Chant, double. A chant extending through two verses of a psalm. It would have four reciting-notes and four cadences.

Chant du soir (Fr.) (shänh dü swär.) Evening chant.

Chantée (Fr.) (shän-tāy.) Sung.

Chanter. 1. One who chants. 2. The pipe that sounds the treble or tenor in a bagpipe.

Chanter (Fr.) (shänh-*tāy*.) To sing; to celebrate; to praise.

Chanter à livre ouvert (Fr.) (shänh-*tā* ă lēvr oo-*vār*.) To sing at sight.

Chanter à pleine voix (Fr.) (shänh-*tā* ä plān vwä.) To sing in full voice.

Chanter, arch. The chief chanter; the leader of the chants.

Chanterelle (Fr.) (shänh-tĕ-rāl.) Treble string; the *E* string of the violin. The highest string of any instrument of the violin or lute family.

Chanter en choeur (Fr.) (shänh-tā änh kür.) To sing in chorus.

Chanteur (Fr.) (shänh-tūr.) A singer.

Chanteur des rues (Fr.) (shänh-tŭr dĕ rü.) A street singer.

Chanterie (Fr.) (shänh-trē.) } Institu-
Chantry. } tions established and endowed for the purpose of singing the souls of the founders out of purgatory. A church or chapel endowed with revenue for the purpose

of saying Mass daily for the souls of the donors.

Chanteuse (Fr.) (shänh-*tüs*.) A female vocalist.

Chant funèbre (Fr.) (shänh fü-*nābr*.) Dirge; a funeral song.

Chant, Gregorian. See *Gregorian Chant*.

Chant lugubre (Fr.) (shänh lü-*gübr*.) A dismal, doleful song.

Chant, Lydian. A melody in a tender style, sung in a languid and melancholy manner.

Chant, plain. A single chant, seldom extending beyond the limits of an octave, or through more than one verse of a psalm.

Chant, Roman. The Gregorian chant.

Chantry priests. Priests selected to sing in the chantry.

Chant sacre (Fr.) (shänh säkr.) Sacred music.

Chant, single. A simple harmonized melody, extending only through one verse of a psalm.

Chantonner (Fr.) (shänh-tŏnh-*nā*.) To hum a tune.

Chapeau chinois (Fr.) (shă-*pō* shĕ-*nwä*.) A crescent or set of small bells used in military music.

Chapel, ante. That portion of the chapel leading to the choir.

Chapelle (Fr.) (shăp-*ĕl*.) A chapel. See *Cappélla*.

Chapier (Fr.) (shä-pĭ-*ā*) A cope bearer; a singer in his cope

Characteristic chord. The leading or principal chord.

Characteristic note. A leading note.

Characters. A general name for musical signs.

Charfreitag (Ger.) (kär-*frī*-täg.) Good Friday. Thus Wagner's *Charfreitag's Zauber* means the magic or enchantment of Good Friday.

Charivari (Fr.) (shä-rī-vä-rē.) Noisy music made with tin dishes, horns, bells, etc.; clatter; a mock serenade. See *Calathumpian music*.

Chasse (Fr.) (shäss.) Hunting; in the hunting style.

Chatsoteroth (Heb.) (kăt-*sō*-tĕ-rŏth.)
Catzozerath (Heb.) (kăt-zō-*zĕ*-räth.) The silver trumpet of the ancient Hebrews.

Chaunt. See *Chant*.

Che (It.) (kā.) Then, that, which.

Chef (Fr.) (shā.) Leader, chief.

Chef-d'attaque (Fr.) (shā d'ät-tăk.) The leader, or principal first violin performer; also, the leader of the chorus. The head of the first violins of an orchestra (chef d'attaque) is the most important person in the orchestra. He is the conductor's lieutenant, a subconductor, who should be able to fill the conductor's place when required.

Chef d'œuvre (Fr.) (shā d'oovr.) A masterpiece; the principal or most important composition of an author. See *Capolavoro*.

Chef-d'orchestre (Fr.) (shā d'ŏr-kästr.) The conductor of an orchestra.

Cherubical hymn. A hymn of great importance in the early Christian Church; the Trisagion.

Chest of viols. An old expression applied to a set of viols, two of which were basses, two tenors and two trebles, each with six strings.

Chest tones. } The lowest register of
Chest voice. } the voice.

Chest, wind. A reservoir in an organ for holding the air, which is conveyed from thence into the pipes by means of the bellows.

Chevalet (Fr.) (shĕv-ă-*lāy*.) The bridge of a violin, viola, etc.

Cheville (Fr.) (shĕ-*vil*.) The peg of a violin, viola, etc.

Chevrotement (Fr.) (shĕ-vrŏt-mŏnh.) A tremor or shake in singing.

Chevroter (Fr.) (shĕ-vrō-*tāy*.) To sing with a trembling voice; to make a bad or false shake.

Chiamare (It.) (kē-ä-*mä*-rĕ.) To chime.

Chiára (It.) (kē-*ä*-rä.) } Clear; brilliant; pure as
Chiáro (It.) (kē-*ä*-rō.) } to tone.

Chiaraménte (It.) (kē-ä-rä-*män*-tĕ.) Clearly, brightly, purely.

Chiarentana (It.) (kē-ä-rĕn-*täh*-nä.) An Italian country dance.

ä as in *ah* ; ā as in *hate* ; ă as in *at* ; ē as in *tree* ; ĕ as in *eh* ; ī as in *pine* ; ĭ as in *pin*;

CHIAREZZA

Chiarézza (It.) (kē-ä-*ret*-sä.) Clearness, neatness, purity.

Chiarína (It.) (kē-ä-*rēe*-nä.) A clarion.

Chiaroscuro (It.) (kē-ä-*rŏs*-koo-rō.) Light and shade; the modifications of piano and forte.

Chiavette (It.) (kee-a-*vĕt*-tĕh.) Transposing clefs. See *Clefs*.

Chiáve (It.) (kē-ä-vĕ). A clef, or key.

Chiáve maestro (It.) (kē-ä-vĕ mä-*ăs*-trō.) The fundamental key or note.

Chiésa (It.) (kē-*ā*-zä.) A church. Applied to various musical works, as *Sonata da Chiesa*, a sacred sonata; *Concerto da Chiesa*, a sacred concerto, etc. *Da Chiesa* signifies in church style.

Chiffres (Fr.) (shēfr.) Figures used in Harmony and Thorough Bass.

Chifla (Spa.) (*tshē*-flä.)
Chifladera (Spa.) (tshē-*flä*-dĕ-rä.) } A whistle.

Chifladura (Spa.) (shē-flä-*doo*-rä.) Whistling.

Chiflar (Spa.) (tshĕ-*flär*.) To whistle.

Chime. A set of bells tuned to a musical scale; the sound of bells in harmony; a correspondence of sound.

Chime barrel. The cylindrical portion of the mechanism sometimes used for ringing a chime of bells.

Chimney. In an organ, a small tube passing through the cap of a stopped pipe.

Chinese flute. An instrument used by the Chinese, made of bamboo.

Chinese musical scale. A scale consisting of five notes without semitones, the music being written on five lines in perpendicular columns, and the elevation and depression of tones indicated by distinctive names. Our diatonic scale, with the fourth and seventh notes omitted, would represent the chief Chinese scale or mode. The hymn, "There is a Happy Land," and the Scottish tunes, "Auld Lang Syne," and "Bonnie Doon" are in this scale. See *Scale*.

Chinnor (Heb.) (kĕn-nōr.)
Chinor (Heb.) (kē-nōr.) } An instrument of the harp or psaltery species, supposed to have been used by the ancient Hebrews.

CHOIR ORGAN

Chirogymnast (Gr.) (*kē*-rō-*ghĭm*-năst.)
Chirogymnaste (It.) (*kē*-rō-gĭm-*näs*-tĕ.) } A cross-bar or board on which are placed various mechanical contrivances for exercising the fingers of a pianist.

Chiroplast (Gr.) (*kĭ*-rō-pläst.) A small machine invented by Logier, to keep the hands and fingers of young pianoforte players in the right position.

Chitarone (It.) (kē-tä-*rō*-nĕ.) A large or double guitar.

Chitárra (It.) (kē-*tär*-rä.) A guitar; a cithara.

Chittárra coll' arco (It.) (kē-*tär*-rä kŏll' är-kō.) A species of guitar played with a bow like a violin.

Chitarriglia (It.) (kē-tär-*rēl*-yä.) A small guitar.

Chittarrína (It.) (kēt-tär-*rē*-na.)
Chittarríno (It.) (kēt-tär-*rē*-nō.) } The small Neapolitan guitar.

Chitarrista (It.) (kēt-är-*rēs*-tä.) One who plays on the guitar.

Chiucchiurlája (It.) (kē-oot-kä-oor-*lä*-yä.) A buzzing or humming sound.

Chiudéndo (It.) (kē-oo-*dăn*-dō.) Closing; ending with.

Chiudéndo col aria (It.) (kē-oo-*dăn*-dō kŏl ä-rē-ä.) Ending with the air.

Chiudéndo col ritornello (It.) (kē-oo-*dăn*-do kŏl rē-tōr-*năl*-lō) Ending with the postlude.

Chiuso (It.) (ki-*oo*-zo.) Close; hidden; *Bocca chiuso*, with closed mouth; humming.

Cho. Abbreviation of *Chorus*.

Choeur (Fr.) (kur.) The choir or chorus.

Choice notes. Notes placed on different degrees in same measure in a solo, either of which may be sung.

Choir. 1. That part of a cathedral or church set apart for the singers. 2. The singers themselves taken collectively.

Choir, boy. A choir formed of boys from eight to fourteen years of age. These choirs are confined mostly to the Episcopal and Catholic Church.

Choir, grand. In organ playing; the union of all the reed stops.

Choir organ. In a large organ, the lowest row of keys is generally the

ŏ as in *tone*; ô as in *dove*; ŏ as in *not*; ŭ as in *up*; ü the French sound of *u*

55

choir organ, which contains some of the softer and more delicate stops, and is used for accompanying solos, duets, etc. It derived its name from its use in accompanying the vocal choir in the chief parts of the choral service. A good choir organ should have a sufficient number of reed and string-toned stops to give variety both in accompaniment and in solo work. The choir-organ is often enclosed in a swell-box to admit of shading. See Hopkins and Rimbault — "The Organ."

Choir, trombone. Among the Moravians a number of trombone-players, whose duty it is to announce from the steeple of the church the death of one of the members, and assist at the funeral solemnities.

Chor (Ger.) (kōr.) Choir; chorus; choir of a church

Choragus (Lat.) (kŏ-rā-gŭs.) The leader of the ancient dramatic chorus.

Choral. Belonging to the choir; full, or for many voices.

Choral (Ger.) (kō-räl.) Psalm or hymn tune; choral song or tune.

Choral anthem. An anthem in a simple, measured style in the manner of a choral.

Choral book. A collection of choral melodies either with or without a prescribed harmonic accompaniment.

Choral-buch (Ger.) (kō-räl-bookh.) Choral book; a book of hymn tunes.

Chorale (Ger. *pl.*) (kō-rā-lĕ.) Hymn tunes of the early German Protestant church.

Choraleon (Pol.) (kō-rä-lĕ-ŏn.) An instrument invented at Warsaw, of similar construction to an organ.

Choral hymn. A hymn to be sung by a chorus.

Choralist. Chorister, choir singer.

Choraliter (Ger.) (kō-räl-ĭ-tĕr.) ⎫ In the
Choralmässig (Ger.) (kō-räl- ⎬ style
 mäs-sĭg.) ⎭ or
measure of a psalm tune or choral.

Chor-amt (Ger.) (kŏr-ämt.) Cathedral service, choral service.

Chord. The union of two or more sounds heard at the same time. Chords are often indicated by figures attached to their bass notes, and are classified as follows:

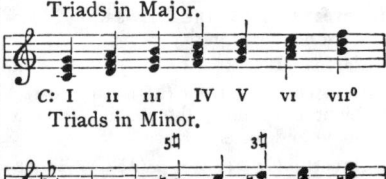

Triads in Major.

C: I II III IV V VI VII⁰

Triads in Minor.

c: I II⁰ III' IV V VI VII⁰

Chords of the Seventh in Major.

C: I₇ II₇ III₇ IV₇ V₇ VI₇ VII⁰₇

Chords of the Seventh in Minor.

c: I₇ II⁰₇ III'₇ IV₇ V₇ VI₇ VII⁰₇

Chords of the Ninth.

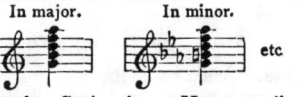

In major.   In minor.   etc

Consult Stainer's "Harmony," or York's "Harmony Simplified."

Chorda (Lat.) (kŏr-dä.) A string of a musical instrument.

Chorda characteristica (Lat.) (kŏr-dä kăr-äk-tĕr-ĭs-tĭ-kä.) The leading, or characteristic note or tone.

Chord, accidental. A chord produced either by anticipation or suspension.

Chordæ vocales (Lat.) (kŏr-dē vō-kä-lēs.) Vocal chords.

Chord, anomalous. A chord in which one or more of the intervals are greater or less than of those of the fundamental chord.

Chord a vido (It.) (kŏrd ä vē-dō.) A name formerly given to a sound drawn from the open string of a violin, violincello, or similar instrument.

Chord, characteristic. The principal chord; the leading chord.

Chord, chromatic. A chord that contains one or more chromatic signs.

Chord, common. A chord consisting of a fundamental note together with its third and fifth.

ă as in *ah*; ā as in *hate*; ă as in *at*; ē as in *tree*; ĕ as in *eh*; ī as in *pine*; ĭ as in *pin*;

Chord, dominant. 1. A chord that is found on the dominant of the key in which the music is written. 2. The *leading* or *characteristic* chord.

Chorda, dominant septima. The dominant chord of the seventh.

Chordaulodian. ⎱ The name given to a
Chordomelodion. ⎰ musical instrument resembling a large barrel organ, self-acting. It was invented by Kaufman of Dresden.

Chor-dienst (Ger.) (*kōr*-dēnst.) Choir or choral service.

Chordometer. An instrument for measuring strings.

Chord fundamental. A chord consisting of the fundamental tone with its third and fifth and its inversions.

Chord, imperfect, common. A chord founded on the leading tone. It has a *minor third* and *diminished fifth*.

Chord, inverted. A chord whose lowest tone is not the fundamental but the third, fifth, or seventh from the lowest or bass note.

Chord Inversions

Chord, leading. The *dominant* chord.

Chord, nona. Chord of the *Ninth*.

Chord of Nature. See *Acoustics* and *Harmonics*.

Chord of the eleventh. A chord founded on the chord of the ninth by adding the interval of the eleventh.

Chord of the fifth and sixth. (6–5.) The first inversion of the chord of the seventh, formed by taking the third of the original chord for the bass, and consisting of that together with its *third, fifth*, and *sixth*.

Chord of the fourth and sixth. (6–4.) The second inversion of the common chord. Also called chord of the sixfour.

Chord of the ninth. (9.) A chord consisting of a third, fifth, seventh, and ninth with its root.

Chord of the second and fourth. (4–2.) The third inversion of the *seventh*.

Chord of the seventh. (7.) A chord consisting of the root together with the third, fifth, and seventh.

Chord of the sixth. (6.) The first inversion of the common chord.

Chord of the third, fourth, and sixth. (6–4–3.) The second inversion of the chord of the *seventh*.

Chord of the thirteenth. Founded on the chord of the ninth by adding the eleventh and the thirteenth.

Chords, derivative. Chords derived from the fundamental chords.

Chords, diminished. Chords with less than *perfect* intervals.

Chords, imperfect. Those which do not contain all the intervals belonging to them.

Chords, relative. Chords which by reason of affinity admit of an easy and natural transition from one to the other. Chords which possess many notes in common.

Chord, transient. A chord in which, in order to smooth the transition from one chord to another, notes are introduced which do not form any component part of the fundamental harmony.

Chöre (Ger. pl.) (*kai*-rĕh.) Choirs, choruses.

Chorea (Lat.) (*kō*-rĕ-ä.) A dance in a ring.

Choriambus. A musical foot, accented thus, — ◡ ◡ —, two short syllables between two long ones.

Chorist (Ger.) (kō-rĭst.) ⎱ A chorister; a
Choriste (Fr.) (kō-rēst.) ⎰ choral singer.

Chorister. A leader of a choir; a singer.

Chorknabe (Ger.) (*kōr*-knä-bĕ.) Singing boy.

Chor-regent (Ger.) (*kōr*-rĕ-*ghĕnt.*) Leader or director of the choristers.

Chor-sänger (Ger.) (*kōr*-sāng-ĕr.)
Chor-schüler (Ger.) (kōr-*shü*-lĕr.) A chorister; a choral singer; a member of the choir.

Chor-ton (Ger.) (*kōr*-tōn.) *Choral-tone;* the usual pitch or intonation of the organ, and therefore of the choir. A choral tune.

Chorus. 1. A company of singers; a composition intended to be sung by a number of voices. 2. Among the ancient Greeks the chorus was a band of singers and dancers who assisted at the performance of their dramas. 3. A refrain.

Chorus, cyclic (*sĕ*-klĭk.) The chorus among the ancient Athenians which performed at some of their dramatic representations, dancing in a circle around the altar of Bacchus.

Chorus-tone. See *Chor-ton.*

Christe eleison (Gr.) (krĭs-tĕ ā-lī-sŏn.) O Christ, have mercy; a part of the Kyrie or first movement in a Mass.

Christmas carols. Light songs, or ballads, commemorating the birth of Christ, sung during the Christmas holidays.

Christmesse (Ger.) (*krĭst*-mĕs-sĕ.)
Christmette (Ger.) (*krĭst*-mĕt-tĕ.)
Christmas matins.

Chroma (Gr.) (*krō*-mä.) The chromatic signs; a *sharp* ♯, or *flat* ♭. In ancient music the eighth note was called Chroma.

Chroma diesis (Gr.) (*krō*-mä dī-*ä*-sĭs.) A semitone, or half tone.

Chroma duplex. The *double-sharp,* marked by the sign ✕, ✇. In ancient music a sixteenth note.

Chromameter (krō-mä-mĕ-ter.) A tuning fork.

Chromatic. Proceeding by semitones. Any music or chord containing notes not belonging to the diatonic scale.

Chromatic depression. The lowering a note by a semitone.

Chromatic elevation. The elevation of a note by a semitone.

Chromatic Fugue. A fugue in which the subject has many chromatic intervals.

Chromatic horn. The French horn with values, or keys.

Chromatic instruments. All instruments upon which chromatic tones and melodies can be produced.

Chromatic keyboard. An attachment applied to the ordinary keys of a piano, for the purpose of enabling players of moderate skill to execute with greater facility the simple chromatic scale, chromatic runs, cadenzas, etc.

Chromatic keys. 1. The black keys of a pianoforte. 2. Every key in the scale of which one or more chromatic tones occur.

Chromatic melody. A melody the tones of which move by chromatic intervals.

Chromatic scale. A scale which divides every whole tone of the diatone scale, and consists of twelve semitones or half-steps in an octave.

Chromatic signature. The flats or sharps placed after the clef at the beginning of the staff.

Chromatic signs. Accidentals; sharps, flats, and naturals. The chromatic signs used in modern music are the sharp (♯), the flat (♭), the natural (♮), the double sharp (✕), and the double flat (♭♭). The natural, or cancel, can annul the effect of a double sharp or a double flat, but if we desire a note to be flatted, after using a double flat, we must write (♮♭), and if sharped after a double sharp, (♮♯). The chromatics are also called "accidentals." The flat was the first of these signs in music, and was used to indicate the position of a single note — B — which was sometimes sounded as B, and often "softened" into B flat. This was about A.D. 1000, when the letter notation was in use, and ran (for the scale of C) as follows: c, d, e, f, g, a, b, ♭, c. The round b, called *b rotundum,* was b-flat, the square b (♮), called *b quadratum,* was b-natural. In Germany, the note b-flat is still called B, and as the square b (♮) was mistaken for an h (of the German print), it was called "H" and is called so to-day, a clerical error that has been perpetuated nearly a thousand years. After some time the

ă as in *ah*; ā as in *hate*; ă as in *at*; ē as in *tree*; ĕ as in *eh*; ī as in *pine*; ĭ as in *pin*;

two *b's* were used as chromatic signs. The sharp came in later and was originally a St. Andrew's cross (♯). Double sharps and double flats only came into free use in music after Bach, with his "Well-tempered Clavichord" (Part I, 1722; Part II, 1742), had brought in the use of all the keys in modulation and composition. In the music of the seventeenth century, the effect of a flat was generally annulled, not by a natural, or cancel, but by a *sharp*, and *each* accidental was written as it occurred. Today the effect of the accidental extends through the measure, on all subsequent notes of the same pitch, but it is often allowed to apply to the same note an octave higher or lower, if written on the same staff. There are many redundant and unnecessary chromatic signs employed in music, for this rule is followed by almost every composer — *If a note can for any reason be considered doubtful, make its meaning sure by using an accidental!* — See Elson's "Theory of Music."

Chromatics, accidental. Chromatics employed in preparing the leading note of the minor scale; chromatics incidentally employed.

Chromatic tuning fork. A tuning fork sounding all the tones and semitones of the octave.

Chromatique (Fr.) (krō-măt-*ēk*.) } Chro-
Chromatisch (Ger.) (krō-*măt*-ĭsh.) } matic; moving by semitones.

Chromatiquement (Fr.) (krō-măt-*ēk*-mönh.) Chromatically.

Chromatisches Klanggeschlecht (Ger.) (krō-*măt*-ĭ-shĕs kläng-ghĕ-*shlĕkht*.) The chromatic genus or mode.

Chromatische Tonleiter (Ger.) (krō-*măt*-ĭ-shĕ *tōn*-lī-tĕr.) The chromatic scale.

Chronometer (Gr.) (krō-*nŏm*-ĕ-tĕr.) The name given to any machine for measuring time.

Chronometer, Weber. An invention of Godfrey Weber, and of Étienne Loulié, before the existence of the metronome, and simpler in construction, consisting of a cord marked with fifty-five inch spaces and having a weight attached to its lower end. The degree of motion is varied by the length of the cord.

Chrotta (It.) (*krŏt*-tä.) The primitive fiddle, differing from the modern in the absence of a neck; the *crowle*.

Church cadence. Another name for the *Plagal Cadence*.

Church modes. See *Gregorian modes*.

Ciaccóna (It.) (tshēe-ä-*kō*-nä.) } A slow
Ciaccónne (It.) (tshēe-ä-*kōn*-nĕ.) } Spanish dance generally constructed on a ground bass. See *Chaconne*.

Cimbalí (It. pl.) (tshim-*bä*-lē.) } Cym-
Cimballes (Fr. pl.) (sĭmbäl.) } bals; military instruments used to mark the time.

Cimbalello (Spa.) (thĕm-bä-*lä*-yō.) A small bell.

Cimbalo (Spa.) (thĕm-*bä*-lō.) A cymbal.

Cimbel (Ger.) (*tsĭm*-bĕl.) A mixture stop of acute tone.

Cimbal-stern (Ger.) (*tsĭm*-bĕl stärn.) *Cymbal star.* An organ stop consisting of five bells, and composed of circular pieces of metal cut in the form of a star, and placed at the top of the instrument in front.

C in alt. The fourth note of the *alt* octave.

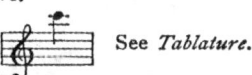

See *Tablature*.

C in altissimo. The octave above C in alt; the fourth note in altissimo.

Cinelle (Tur.) } A cymbal; a Turkish
Cinellen (Tur.) } musical instrument.

Cinelli (It.) (tschĭ-*nel*-lee.) Cymbals.

Cink (Ger.) (tsĭnk.) A small reed stop in an organ.

Cinq (Fr.) (sănhk.) } Five; the
Cinque (It.) (*tshēn*-quĕ.) } fifth voice or part in a quintet.

Ciphering (*sī*-fĕr-ĭng.) The sounding of the pipes of the organ when the keys are not touched.

Circular Canon. A canon which modulates through the twelve major keys.

Circle of fifths. A method of modulation, from dominant to dominant, which conveys us round through all the scales back to the point from which we started.

Circle of keys. } See *Keys*.
Circle of scales. }

ō as in *tone*; ŏ as in *dove*; ö as in *not*; ŭ as in *up*; ü the French sound of *u*.

Circular scale. The row of tuning pins and the wrest-plank of a piano made in a curved form.

Cis (Ger.) (tsĭs.) The note C♯.

Cis-cis (Ger.) (tsĭs-tsĭs.) The note C double sharp, C𝄪.

Cis-dur (Ger.) (tsĭs-*door*.) The key of C♯ major.

Cis moll (Ger.) (tsĭs mōll.) The key of C♯ minor.

Cistella (Lat.) (sĭs-*těl*-lä.) A small chest or box, triangular in shape, and strung with wires which are struck with little rods. See *Dulcimer*.

Cistre (Fr.) (sēstr.) A cithern, a small harp.

Cistrum. See *Cittern*.

Cítara (It.) (*tshē*-tä-rä.) A cittern, a guitar.

Cithar (Dan.) (*tsĭth*-ăr.) A cittern.

Cithara (Lat.) (*sĭth*-ă-ră.) ⎫ The lute;
Cithara (Spa.) (*thĕt*-ä-rä.) ⎭ an old instrument of the guitar kind.

Cithára hispánica (Spa.) (*thĕt*-ä-rä hĭs-*pän*-ĭ-kä.) The Spanish guitar.

Citharista (Lat.) (*sĭth*-ä-*rĭs*-tă.) A player upon the harp.

Cither. ⎫
Cithera. ⎪ An old instrument of the lute or guitar species; the
Cithern. ⎬ oldest on record had three strings, which were afterward increased to eight,
Cittern. ⎪
Cythorn. ⎭
nine, and up to twenty-four. The *cither* was very popular in the sixteenth century. The cittern and guitar seem to be derived from the same Greek word. The cither is strung with wire and played with a plectrum.

Citole (Lat.) (sĭt-*ō*-lĕ.) An old instrument of the dulcimer species, and probably synonymous with it.

Civettería (It.) (tshē-vĕt-*tā*-re-ä.) Coquetry; in a coquettish manner.

Clair (Fr.) (klār.) Clear, shrill, loud.

Clairçylindre (klār-sĭ-lănhdr.) An instrument invented by Chladni, in 1787, for the purpose of experimenting in acoustics.

Clairon (Fr.) (klä-rŏnh.) Trumpet; also the name of a reed stop in the organ. A clarion.

Clam. In bell ringing, to unite sounds on the peal.

Clamour. In bell ringing, a rapid multiplication of strokes.

Clamoroso (Spa.) (klä-mō-*rō*-zō.) Plaintive sounds.

Clang. A sharp, shrill noise.

Clangor tubarum (Lat.) (*klăn*-gŏr tū-*bă*-rŭm.) A military trumpet used by the ancient Romans, consisting of a large tube of bronze surrounded by seven smaller tubes, all terminating in one point, or a single mouth-piece.

Clang-tint. The color or quality of any musical sound, and therefore its emotional character. The clang-tint depends upon the power of the overtones. See *Acoustics*.

Clan marches. These are composed for the Scotch bagpipe, with a strong accent and marked rhythm.

Clapper. The tongue of a bell.

Claquebois (Fr.) (klăk-bwä.) The Xylophone.

Clar. An abbreviation of *Clarinet*.

Ciara voce (Lat.) (*klä*-rä vō-sĕ.) A clear, loud voice.

Clarabella (Lat.) (*klä*-rä-*běl*-lä.) An organ stop of eight-foot scale, with a soft fluty tone; the pipes are of wood and not stopped.

Caribel-flute. An organ stop of the flute species, of four-foot tone.

Clarichord. See *Clavichord*.

Clarichorde (Fr.) (klăr-ĭ-*kŏrd*.) The clarichord or clavichord.

Clarim (Por.) (klä-*rĕm*.) ⎫
Clarin (Spa.) (klä-*rēn*.) ⎬ A clarion.

Clarin (Ger.) (klä-*rēn*.) A clarion; also the name of a four-foot reed stop in German organs.

Clarinero (Spa.) (klä-rĕ-*nā*-rō.) A trumpeter.

Clarinet (also Clarinette.) A rich and full-toned wind instrument of wood, with a single reed mouth-piece. It is one of the most important wood wind instruments. It is said to have been invented about 1700, by J. C. Denner, of Nuremberg. It consists of a cylindrical tube, with finger-holes and keys, which terminates in a bell, and has a beak-like mouth-piece. Its extreme

---

ă as in *ah*; ā as in *hate*; ă as in *at*; ē as in *tree*; ĕ as in *eh*; ī as in *pine*; ĭ as in *pin*;

compass is ♪ There are clarinets of different pitch; those commonly used in the orchestra are the clarinets in C, in B♭, and in A. The clarinets in E♭, or A♭, are rarely used except in military bands. All clarinets, the one in C excepted, are transposing instruments; they do not sound the notes which are written. The B♭ clarinet sounds a tone lower, and the A clarinet a minor third lower. Music for the clarinet is written in the G clef. Besides the above-mentioned clarinets, there is a bass clarinet (see *Clarinet, Bass.*) The lowest register of the clarinet is hollow-toned and spectral. It is called "Chalumeau." The middle register is much like the human voice. The highest notes are very acute and fierce. The B-flat clarinet has the best quality of tone. See A. Elson's "Orchestral Instruments and their Use," and Prout's "The Orchestra."

Clarinet, bass. A clarinet whose tones are an octave deeper than those of the C or B-flat clarinet.

Clarinette (Fr.) (klär-ĭ-năt.) The clarinet; also the name of an organ stop.

Clarinettísta (It.) (klä-rē-nĕt-*tēs*-tä.)
Clarinettiste (Fr.) (klăr-ĭ-nĕt-*tēst*.)
A performer upon the clarinet.

Clarinétto (It.) (klä-rē-*nĕt*-tō.) A clarinet.

Clarinétto secondo (It.) (klä-rē-*nĕt*-tō sĕ-*kōn*-dō.) The second clarinet.

Claríno (It.) (klä-*rēe*-nô.) } A small or octave trumpet;
Clarion. also the name of a 4-foot organ reed stop tuned an octave above the trumpet stop. The term is also used to indicate the trumpet parts in a full score.

Clarion harmonique (Fr.) (klä-rĭ-ŏnh hăr-mŏnh-*nēk*.) An organ reed stop.

Clarionet. A wind instrument of the single reed species, of a full, rich tone; also an organ reed stop of 8-foot scale and soft quality of tone. See *Clarinet*.

Clarionet-flute. An organ stop of a similar kind to the stopped diapason.

Clarone (It.) (klä-*r-ō*nĕ.) A clarinet.

Clarté de voix (Fr.) (klär-tā dŭh vwä.) Clearness of voice.

Classical music. Standard music, music of first rank, written by composers of the highest order. Music whose form and style has been accepted as suitable for a model to composers.

Clause. A *phrase*.

Clausel (Ger.) (*klou*-z'l.) } A close; a
Clausula (Lat.) (*klau*-sŭ-lä.) } cadence; a concluding musical phrase.

Clausula affinalis (Lat.) (*klau*-sŭ-lä ăf-fĭ-*nä*-lĭs.) A cadence in a key nearly related to the original key of the piece.

Clausula dissecta (Lat.) (*klau*-sŭ-lä dĭs-*sĕk*-tä.) A half cadence.

Clausula dominans (Lat.) (*klau*-sŭ-lä *dŏm*-ĭ-năns.) A cadence on the dominant.

Clausula falsa (Lat.) (*klau*-sŭ-lä *făl*-sä). A false or deceptive cadence.

Clausula finalis (Lat.) (*klau*-sŭ-lä fĭ-*nä*-lĭs.)
Clausula primaria (Lat.) (*klau*-sŭ-lä prĭ-*mä*-rĭ-ä.)
Clausula principalis (Lat.) (*klau*-sŭ-lä prĭn-sĭ-*pä*-lis.)
A final cadence or close in the original key.

Clausula peregrina (Lat.) (*klau*-sŭ-lä pĕr-ĕ-*grē*-nä.) A cadence in a key whose fundamental tone is not in the principal key.

Clausus (Lat.) (*klaw*-sŭs.) A close canon.

Clav. An abbreviation of Clavecembalo, Clavichord, and Clavecin.

Clave (Lat.) (*klä*-vĕ.) A key; a clef.

Clavecin (Fr.) (klăv-ĕ-sănh.) The harpsichord, or the spinte.

Clavecin acoustique (Fr.) (klăv-ĕ-sănh ä-kooz-*tēk*.) An instrument of the harpsichord or pianoforte class.

Clavecin harmonieux (Fr.) (klăv-ĕ-sănh hăr-mō-nĭ-ŭh.) An old instrument of the harpsichord or pianoforte class.

Claveciniste (Fr.) (klä-vĕ-sănh-*ēst*.) A harpsichord player, or maker.

Claveoline (Fr.) (*klăv*-ĭ-ō-*lēn*.) An instrument of the harpsichord or pianoforte class.

Claves (Lat.) (*klä*-vēs.) A word formerly used for clefs.

Claves signatæ (Lat.) A term applied by Guido to colored lines used before the invention of clefs, to mark the situation of the notes.

Claviatur (Ger.) (klä-vēe-äh *toor.*) The keyboard.

Clavicémbalo (It.) (klä-vē-*tshām*-bä-lō.)
Clavicembalum (Lat.) (*klä*-vĭ-sĕm-*bä*-lŭm.) The harpsichord.

Clavichord. A small, keyed instrument, like the spinet, and the forerunner of the pianoforte. The tone of the clavichord was agreeable and impressive, but very weak. Its mechanism pushed a sharp edge, like the point of a chisel, against the wire, and this point remained, pressing the wire while the key was held, forming a bridge. It may be well, in playing clavichord music, to remember that the clavichord could *shade* and play very expressively, which the spinet and harpsichord could not. See Weitzmann's "History of Pianoforte Music."

Clavichordium (Lat.) (klăv-ē-*kŏr*-dĭ-ŭm.) See *Clavichord.*

Clavicytherium (Lat.) (*klăv*-ĭ-sĕ-*thē*-rĭ-ŭm.) A species of upright harpsichord, said to have been originally in the form of a harp or lyre. It was invented in the thirteenth century and was the earliest approach to the modern pianoforte.

Clavicylinder. An instrument exhibited in Paris in 1806. It consisted of a series of cylinders which were operated upon by bows set in motion by a crank, and brought in contact with the cylinders by means of the keys of a fingerboard. It was the invention of Chladni.

Clavier (Fr.) (klä-*vēer.*) The keys or key-board of pianoforte, organ, etc. The German name for spinets, harpsichords and clavichords. At present the Germans call the piano "Clavier" or "Klavier."

Clavier (Ger.) (klä-*fēer.*)

Clavier-auszug (Ger.) (klä-*fēer* oustsoog.) An arrangement of a full score for the use of piano players.

Clavier-drath (Ger.) (klä-*fēer* drät.) Wire for the pianoforte, etc.

Clavier-lehrer (Ger.) (klä-*fēer* lā-rĕr.) A pianoforte teacher.

Clavieren (Ger. pl.) (klăf-*ēe*-rĕn.) The keys. See *Clavier.*

Clavierschule (Ger.) (klăf-*ēer-shoo*-lĕ.) A pianoforte instruction book.

Clavierspieler (Ger.) (klăf-*ēer-spēe*-lĕr.) A pianoforte player.

Clavierstimmer (Ger.) (klăf-*ēer-stĭm*-mĕr.) A pianoforte tuner.

Clavierübung (Ger.) (klăf-*ēer-ü*-boong.) Exercises for the piano.

Clavierunterricht (Ger.) (klăf-*ēer-oon*-tĕr-rĭkht.) Lessons or instruction on the pianoforte.

Clavis (Lat.) (*klä*-vĭs.)
Clavis (Ger.) (*klä*-fĭs.) } A key; a clef.

Clear-flute. An organ stop of four-foot scale, the tone of which is very clear and full.

Clé (Fr.) (klā.)
Clef } A key; a character used to determine the name and pitch of the notes on the staff to which it is prefixed. The clefs began in music about A. D. 900. There were then no notes, but certain characters called neumes, without definite pitch, indicating the rise and fall of the voice and its general progression. Through these a red line was drawn and marked "F." The F clef was thus the earliest clef. Soon after (before 1000), another line, generally green, was drawn above it and marked "C." Originally all the clefs were letters, and all were movable. The following are used in music to-day:— The G clef, placing $\bar{g}$ on the second line, thus ; the bass, or F clef, placing f on the fourth line, thus ; these two are now fixed, immovable clefs. The c clef, which fixes the position of middle c, or $\bar{c}$, is a movable clef, and is used to-day, as follows:

Soprano clef

Alto clef

Tenor clef

ä as in *ah*; ā as in *hate*; ă as in *at*; ē as in *tree*; ĕ as in *eh*; ī as in *pine*; ĭ as in *pin*;

and often in America

The object of such a moveable clef is to avoid leger lines above or below the staff. The c clef is sometimes varied in shape, as or . In old music the following are sometimes found:—Mezzo soprano clef

French violin clef and the baritone clef

The following is a recent use of the tenor clef: and signifies that the notes are to be played an octave lower than in the G clef. In Italy this clef is at present written , a tenor and G clef combined. See Elson's "Realm of Music," article on "The Rise of Notation."

Clef, alto. The C clef on the third line of the staff.

Clef, baritone. The F clef when placed on the third line.

Clef, bass. The character at the beginning of the staff, where the lower or bass notes are written, and serving to indicate the pitch and name of those notes. The F clef.

Clef, C. So called because it gives its name to the notes placed on the same line with itself.

Clef d'accordeur (Fr.) (klā d'ăk-kŏr-dŭr.) A tuning hammer.

Clef de fa (Fr.) (klā dŭh fā.) The F, or bass clef.

Clef descant. The treble or soprano clef.

Clef d'ut (Fr.) (klā d'oot.) The C clef.

Clef, F. The bass clef.

Clef, French Treble. The G clef on the bottom line of the staff; formerly much used in French music for the violin, flute, etc.

Clef, German soprano. The C clef placed on the first line of the staff for soprano.

Clef, mean. The tenor clef

Clef, mezzo-soprano. The C clef when placed on the second line of the staff.

Clef, sol (Fr.) (klā sōl.) The G, or treble clef.

Clef, soprano. The C clef placed on the first line.

Clef, tenor. See *Mean clef.* The C clef when on the fourth line of the staff.

Clef, treble. The G clef; soprano clef.

Cloche (Fr.) (klōsh.) A bell.

Cloche de l'élévation (Fr.) (klōsh dŭh l'ĕl-ĕ-vä-sĭ-ŏnh.) Saint's bell, rung at *elevation* in Mass.

Cloche funèbre (Fr.) (klōsh fü-nābr.) Funeral bell.

Cloche mortuaire (Fr.) (klōsh mŏr-tŭ-är.) The passing, funeral bell.

Clocher (Fr.) (klō-shā.) A belfry.

Cloche sourde (Fr.) (klōsh soord.) A muffled bell.

Clochette (Fr.) (klō-*shĕt*.) A little bell a hand bell.

Clocks, musical. Clocks containing an arrangement similar to a barrel organ, moved by weights and springs and producing various tunes.

Close. A cadence; the end of a piece or passage.

Close harmony. Harmony in which the notes or parts are kept as close together as possible.

C. O. An abbreviation of *choir organ.*

Co (It.) (kō.)
Coi (It.) (kō-ēe.) } With, with the.
Col (It.) (kŏl.)

Cocchina (It.) (kŏt-*kĕ*-nä.) An Italian country dance

Códa (It.) (*kō*-dä.) The *end;* a few bars added to the end of a piece of music to make a more effective termination. From the Latin "Cauda"—a tail. The coda, originally a few added chords after the completion of the musical form, was developed by some of the great masters, especially by Beethoven,

ō as in *tone*; ô as in *dove*; ŏ as in *not*; ŭ as in *up*; ü the French sound of *u*.

CÓDA BRILLANTE — CÓME PRIMA

into a great summing-up of the movement or composition; a climax of the entire work. The final episode of a fugue is called *Coda*.

Códa brillante (It.) (*kō*-dä brēl-*län*-tĕ.) A brilliant termination.

Codétta (It.) (kō-*det*-tä.) A short coda or passage added to a piece; a connecting passage in a fugue.

Codon. A bell.

Coffre (Fr.) (kōfr.) The frame of a lute, guitar, etc.

Cogli (It.) (*kōl*-yēe.) With the.

Cogli stromenti (It. pl.) *kōl*-yēe strō-*men*-tē.) With the instruments.

Cognoscente (It.) (kōn-yō-*shen*-tĕ.) One well versed in music; a *connoisseur*.

Coi bassi (It.) (kō-ēe bäs-sē.) With the basses.

Coi fagotti (It.) (kō-ēe fä-gōt-tē.) With the bassoons.

Colachon (Fr.) (kō-lä-shŏnh.) An Italian instrument, much like a lute, but with a longer neck.

Col árco (It.) (kōl-*är*-kō.) *With the bow;* see *Coll 'árco.*

Col basso (It.) (kōl *bäs*-so.) With the bass.

Col C. An abbreviation of *Col Canto.*

Col cánto (It.) (kōl *kän*-tō.) With the melody or voices; see *Colla Voce.*

Coll (It.) (kōl.) ⎫
Colla (It.) (kōl-lä). ⎬ With the.
Collo (It.) (kōl-lō.) ⎭

Colla déstra (It.) (kōl-lä des-trä.) With the right hand.

Colla mássima discrezione (It.) (kōl-lä *mäs*-sē-mä dēz-krä-tsē-*ō*-nĕ.) With the greatest discretion.

Colla párte (It.) (kōl-lä *pär*-tĕ.) *With the part;* indicating that the time is to be accommodated to the solo singer or player.

Colla púnta d'arco (It.) (kōl-lä poon-tä d'är-kō.) With the point or tip of the bow.

Colla sinístra (It.) (kōl-lä sĭ-*nis*-trä.) With the left hand.

Colla vóce (It.) (kōl-lä *vō*-tshĕ.) *With the voice;* implying that the accompanist must accommodate and take the time from the singer.

Coll' árco (It.) (kōl- l'är-kō.) *With the bow* the notes are to be played with the bow, and not *pizzicáto.*

Col' legno (It.) (kōl *län*-yō.) *With the bow stick.*

Col légno dell' arco (It.) (kōl län-yō dĕll'är-kō.) With the bow stick; strike the strings with the wooden side of the bow.

Colle parti (It.) (kōl-lĕ *pär*-tē.) With the principal parts.

Colle trombe (It.) (kōl-lĕ *trōm*-bĕ.) With the trumpets.

Collinet. Flageolet.

Coll' ottava (It.) (kōl-l' ōt-tä-vä.) With the octave. Add the octave to the printed note.

Colofane (Fr.) (kōl-ŏ-fäne.) ⎫
Colofónia (It.) (kōl-ō-fō-nē-ä.) ⎪
Colophane (Fr.) (kōl-ō-fäne.) ⎬
Colophon (Fr.) (kōl-ō-fŏnh.) ⎪
Colophonium (Ger.) (kŏ-lō-*fō*-nĭ-oom.) ⎪
Colophony (Eng.) ⎭
Resin; used for the hair in the bow of a violin, etc., to enable the horsehair to get a better hold upon the strings.

Coloratúra (It.) (kō-lō-rä-*too*-rä.) ⎫
Colorature (It.)) (kō-lō-rä-*too*-rĕ.) ⎬
Coloraturen (Ger.) (kō-lō-rä-*too*-rĕn.) ⎭
Ornamental passages, roulades, embellishments, etc., in vocal music.

Col violini (It.) (*kōl* vē-ō-*lē*-nē.) With the violins.

Combination pedals. See *Composition Pedals.*

Cóme (It.) (*kō*-mĕ.) As, like, the same as.

Comédie (Fr.) (kŏm-ā-dē.) Comedy, play.

Comédien (Fr.) (kŏm-ā-dĭ-*ănh*.) ⎫
Comediante (Spa.) (kō-mä-dē-*än*-tĕ.) ⎬
A comedian; an actor.

Comédienne (Fr.) (kŏm-ā-dĭ-*ănh*.) An actress.

Comedy, lyric. A comedy specially adapted for singing.

Cóme il primo tempo (It.) (kō-mĕ ĭl prē-mō tĕm-pō.) In the same time as the first.

Cóme prima (It.) (kō-mĕ prē-mä.) As before; as at first.

ă as in *ah*; ā as in *hate*; ă as in *at*; ē as in *tree*; ĕ as in *eh*; ī as in *pine*; ĭ as in *pin*

Comes (Lat.) (*kō-mĕs.*) A *companion*; this term was used by old theorists to indicate the *answer*, in a fugue or the imitation in a canon.

Cóme sópra (It.) (kō-mĕ sō-prä.) *As above; as before*; indicating the repetition of a previous or similar passage.

Cóme sta (It.) (kō-mĕ stä.) *As it stands*; perform exactly as written.

Cóme témpo del téma (It.) (kō-mĕ tĕm-pō dĕl tāy-mä.) In the same time as that of the theme.

Cómico (It.) (*kō-mē-kō.*)) Comic; also a
Comique (Fr.) (kŏm-ēek.)) comic actor, and a writer of comedies.

Cominciáre (It.) (kō-min-tshē-ä-rĕ.) To begin.

Cominciáta (It.) (kō-min-tshē-ä-tä.) The beginning; the commencement.

Comiquement (Fr.) (kŏm-ēek-mänh.) Comically; jocosely.

Cómma (It.) (*kōm*-mä.) The smallest of all the sensible intervals of tone, and used in treating or analyzing musical sounds. As an illustration, the difference between D♯ and E♭ as played upon the violin by the best performers. A *tone* is divided into *nine* almost imperceptible intervals, called *commas*, five of which constitute the major semitone, and four the minor semitone. The comma is therefore the small interval between a major and a minor tone, that is, between a tone whose ratio is 8 : 9, and one whose ratio is 9 : 10. The ratio of a comma is therefore 80 : 81. A Pythagorean comma is the difference between the note produced by taking 7 octaves upwards and 12 fifths. The sign of a comma (,) is often used as a breathing mark in vocal music.

Commencer (Fr.) (kŏm-mänh-sā.) To begin; to commence.

Commodamente (It.) (kŏm-mō-dä-*men*-tĕ.) With ease and quietude.

Commodo (It.) (*kŏm*-mō-dō.) Quietly, easily, composedly.

Common chord. A chord consisting of a bass note with its third and fifth, to which its octave is usually added.

Common hallelujah metre. A stanza of six lines of iambic measure, the syllables of each being in number and order as follows : 8, 6, 8, 6, 8, 8.

Common measure. That measure which has an even number of parts in a bar; ¼ rhythm, sometimes marked [𝄴]

Common metre. A verse or stanza of four lines in iambic measure, the syllables of each being in number and order, thus : 8, 6, 8, 6.

Common particular metre. A stanza of six lines in iambic measure, the number and order of syllables as follows : 8, 8, 6, 8, 8, 6.

Common time. That time which has an even number of parts in a bar; *common measure*; ¼ rhythm, sometimes also ⅔.

Common time, compound. Sextuple time, or 12/8 time.

Common time, half. A measure containing only two quarter notes or their equivalents.

Common turn. A turn consisting of the *principal* note, the note *above* it and the note *below* it.

Comodaménte (It.) (kŏ-mō-dä-*men*-tĕ.)) Conven-
Cómodo (It.) (*kō*-mō-dō.)) iently, easily, quietly; with composure.

Comparsés (Fr.) (kŏnh-pär-sā.) Supernumeraries; persons who appear upon the stage to swell the numbers without taking active part.

Compass. The range of notes or sounds of which any voice or instrument is capable.

Compensation mixture. An organ mixture stop, in the pedals, and intended to assist the intonation of the pedal pipes.

Compiacévole (It.) (kŏm-pē-ä-*tshe*-vō-lĕ.)) Agreeable,
Compiacimento (It.) (kŏm-pē-ä-tshē-*men*-tō.)) pleasing, attractive.

Compiacevolmente (It.) (kŏm-pē-ä-tshĕ-vōl-*men*-tĕ.) In a pleasant and agreeable style.

Compiéta (It.) (kŏm-pē-ā-tä.) Complin; evening prayers.

Complaint (Fr.) (kŏm-plänht.) A religious ballad.

o as in *tone*; ō as in *dove*; ŏ as in *not*; ŭ as in *up*; ü the French sound of *u*.

65

Complement. That quantity which is wanting to any interval to fill up an octave.

Complementary part. That part which is added to the subject and countersubject of a fugue.

Complete cadence. A full cadence.

Complin (Lat.) (*kŏm*-plĭn.) The latest evening service of the Catholic church.

Compónere (It.) (kŏm-*pōn*-nā-rĕ.) ⎫
Componiren (Ger.) (kŏm-pō-*nee*-r'n.) ⎬ To compose music.
Compórre (It.) (kŏm-*pōr*-rĕ.) ⎭

Componitóre (It.) (kŏm-pō-nē-tō-rĕ.) ⎫ A composer; an author.
Componista (It.) (kŏm-pō-*nis*-tä.) ⎭

Composer (Fr.) (kōnh-pō-zā.) To compose music.

Composite intervals. Those intervals which consist of two or more semitones.

Compositeur (Fr.) (kŏm-pŏs-ĭ-tŭr.) ⎫
Compositóre (It.) (kŏm-pŏs-ē-*tō*-rĕ.) ⎬ A composer of music.
Componist (Ger.) (kŏm-pō-*nĭst*.) ⎭

Composition. Any musical production; the art of inventing or composing music, according to the rules of harmony.

Composition, free. That which deviates somewhat from the rules of composition.

Composition pedals. Pedals connected with a system of mechanism for arranging the stops of an organ.

Composition, strict. A composition that adheres rigidly to the rules of art.

Compositor, music. A person who sets music type.

Compositúra (It.) (kŏm-pŏs-ē-*too*-rä.) ⎫
Composizióne (It.) (kŏm-pŏs-ē-tsē-*ō*-nĕ.) ⎬ A composition, or musical work.

Composizióne di tavolíno (It.) (kŏm-pŏs-ē-tsē-*ō*-nĕ dē täv-ō-lē-nō.) Table music; music sung at table, as glees, catches, rounds.

Composso (It.) (kŏm-*pōs*-sō.) ⎫ Composed;
Compósto (It.) (kŏm-*pōs*-tō.) ⎭ set to music.

Compound appoggiatura. An appoggiatura consisting of two or more small notes.

Compound harmony. Simple harmony with an octave added.

Compound intervals. Those which exceed the extent of an octave; as a ninth, tenth, etc.

Compound stops. Where three or more organ stops are arranged so that by pressing down one key, they all sound at once.

Compound times. Those which include or exceed *six* parts in a measure, and contain *two*, or more, principal accents, as, $\frac{6}{4}$, $\frac{6}{8}$, $\frac{9}{4}$, $\frac{9}{8}$, $\frac{12}{8}$. See *Rhythm*, and *Time*.

Compressed harmony. See *Close Harmony*.

Con (It.) (kŏn.) With.

Con abbandóno (It.) (kŏn ä-bän-*dō*-nō.) With passion; with ardent feeling.

Con affétto (It.) (kŏn äf-*fet*-tō.) ⎫ In an
Con affezióne (It.) (kŏn äf-fe-tsē-*ō*-nĕ.) ⎬ affectionate manner; with warmth. ⎭

Con afflizióne (It.) (kŏn äf-fli-tsē-*ō*-nĕ.) With affliction; mournfully.

Con agilitá (It.) (kŏn ä-jil-ē-tä.) With agility; neatly.

Con agitazióne (It.) (kŏn äj-ē-tä-tsi-*ō*-nĕ.) With agitation; hurriedly.

Con alcúna licenza (It.) (kŏn äl-*koo*-nä-lē-*tshen*-tsä.) With a certain degree of license as regards time and expression or construction.

Con allégrezza (It.) (kŏn-äl-lĕ-*gret*-sä.) With lightness; cheerfully.

Con alterézza (It.) (kŏn äl-tĕ-*ret*-sä.) With an elevated and sublime expression.

Con amabilitá (It.) (kŏn ä-mä-bēl-ē-tä.) With gentleness and grace.

Con amarézza (It.) (kŏn ä-mä-*ret*-sä.) With affliction; with bitterness.

Con amóre (It.) (kŏn ä-*mō*-rĕ.) With tenderness and affection.

Con anima (It.) (kŏn *än*-ē-mä.) ⎫ With
Con animo (It.) (kŏn än-ē-mō.) ⎬ animation and boldness.

Con animazióne (It.) (kŏn är-ē-mä-tsē-*ō*-nē.) With animation; decision; boldness.

ä as in *ah*; ā as in *hate*; ă as in *at*; ē as in *tree*; ĕ as in *eh*; ī as in *pine*; ĭ as in *pin*

CON AUDACE

Con audáce (It.) (kŏn ou-*dä*-tshĕ.) With boldness; audacity.

Con bellézza (It.) (kŏn bĕl-*let*-zä.) With beauty of tone and expression.

Con bizarria (It.) (kŏn bē-*tsär*-rē-ä.) Capriciously; at the fancy of the player or composer.

Con bravura (It.) (kŏn brä-*voo*-rä.) With dash, with boldness.

Con brío (It.) (kŏn *brēe-ō*.) With life; spirit; brilliancy.

Con brío ed animáto (It.) (kŏn *brēe*-ō ed än-ē-*mä*-to.) With brilliancy and animation.

Con calma (It.) (kŏn-*käl*-mä.) With calmness and tranquillity.

Con calóre (It.) (kŏn kä-*lō*-rĕ.) With warmth; with fire.

Con carita (It.) (kŏn kä-*rē*-tä.) With tenderness.

Con celerita (It.) (kŏn tshe-*lĕr*-ē-tä.) With celerity; with rapidity.

Concénto (It.) (kŏn-*tshĕn*-to.) Concord; agreement; harmony of voices and instruments.

Concentual. Harmonious.

Concentus (Lat.) (kŏn-*sĕn*-tŭs.) Harmonious blending of sounds; concord.

Concert. 1. A performance in public of practical musicians, either vocal or instrumental, or both. 2. Harmony, unison; (Ger.) a concerto. *Concert Spirituel* (Fr.) a sacred concert.

Concertant (Fr.) (kŏnh-sĕr-*tänh*.) Performer in a concert; a musician.

Concertánte (It.) (kŏn-tshĕr-*tän*-tĕ.) 1. A piece in which each part is alternately principal and subordinate, as in a *dúo concertánte*. 2. A concerto for two or more instruments, with accompaniments for a full band. 3. A female concert singer.

Concertata messa (It.) (kŏn-tshĕr-*tä*-tä *mĕs*-sä.) A concerted Mass.

Concertate madrigali (It.) (kŏn-tshĕr-*tä*-tē mäd-rē-*gä*-lē.) Accompanied madrigals.

Concertato (It.) (kŏn-tshĕr-*tä*-tō.) Concerted. See also *Concertánte*.

Concerted music. Music in which several voices or instruments are heard at the same time; in opposition to *sólo* music.

CONCERTO

Concert-grand pianoforte. The largest grand pianoforte.

Concertina (It.) (kŏn-tshĕr-*tēe*-nä.) A small instrument, hexagonal in shape, held in the hands. The sounds are produced by pressing the fingers upon the keys, which are placed upon each side of the instrument, and working the bellows at the same time, to produce the requisite supply of wind to the reeds. It is an improved accordion.

Concertíno (It.) (kŏn-tshĕr-*tēe*-nō.) 1. A short concerto. 2. A principal part in a concerto, or other full orchestral piece. 3. The principal instrument in a concert.

Concertiren (Ger.) (kŏn-tsĕr-*tēe*-r'n.) To accord; to agree in sound; also a soli movement where each instrument or voice has in its turn the principal part.

Concert-meister (Ger.) (kŏn-*tsĕrt mīs*-tĕr.) The chief violinist of the orchestra. He is leader of the violins, and next in importance to the conductor himself. See *Chef d'Attaque*.

Concerto (It.) (kon-*tschair*-to); (Ger.) Konzert (kont-*sairt*). Also pronounced as an English word — concerto. Originally the term was applied loosely to almost any kind of concerted music. Viadana used the term for motets with organ, in 1602. The real inventor of the concerto, as an instrumental concerted form, was Torelli, who, in 1686, wrote concerted works for two violins and basso. The form was developed along the lines of the old sonata, by Corelli, Geminiani and Vivaldi. The old concerto, in the time of Bach and Handel, were much like an orchestral suite, and the form was much freer than it became later. With Mozart the concerto took the classical sonata-form, although it is still the freest presentation of this classical form of music. The central idea of the concerto is the display of a solo instrument, or sometimes more than one. There are concertos for almost every instrument, but the piano concerto is the most successful and the most numerous. Among masterpieces in this form one may mention the "Emperor" and the fourth concerto, by Beethoven; the two piano concertos, by Brahms; the two by Liszt (rather rhapsodies than

---

ō as in *tone*; ŏ as in *dove*; ŏ as in *not*; ŭ as in *up*; ü the French sound of *u*.

67

CONCÉRTO A SOLÒ CON DIVOZIÓNE

concertos); the A minor, by Schumann; the great violin concerto, by Beethoven; the violin concerto, by Brahms; etc. There is a concerto for harp and flute by Mozart, and one for violin, violoncello and piano by Beethoven, illustrating the use of two or more instruments simultaneously. There are even concertos for the kettle-drums! While the concerto is intended to display the solo instrument, it should still give an orchestral impression. The last concertos by Beethoven, and all of those by Brahms, are symphonic in their effect, although giving great difficulties to the solo artist. The two concertos (*concerti* is the Italian plural) by Chopin, spite of their great beauties, have the fault of being too entirely piano compositions. Sometimes the concerto movements are continuous. The regular number of movements is, however, three, the minuet or scherzo of the full sonata form being omitted. See also *Cadenza*. Reference works: Prout's "Musical Forms," Mathew's "Primer of Musical Forms," Elson's "Theory of Music," Grove's "Dictionary."

Concérto a solo. A concerto written for the purpose of displaying the powers of a particular instrument without accompaniment.

Concérto di chiesa (It.) (kŏn-*tshĕr*-tō dē kē-ā-za.) A concert of church music.

Concérto doppio (It.) (kŏn-*tshĕr*-tō dŏp-pē-ō.) A concerto for two or more instruments.

Concérto grande (Fr.) (kŏn-*tshĕr*-tō gränd.) } A grand or-
Concérto grósso (It.) (kŏn-*tshĕr*-tō grōs-sō.) } chestral composition for many instruments, with two or three especially prominent.

Concérto spirituále (It.) (kŏn-*tshĕr*-tō spē-rē-too-äl-ĕ.) A miscellaneous concert consisting chiefly of sacred or classical music.

Concertone (It.) (kŏn-tshĕr-tō-nĕ.) A *concertánte*.

Concert pitch. The pitch adopted by different manufacturers of musical instruments as best suited to display them. It is a dubious and vague standard, but almost always means a very high pitch. In America it has been displaced by the "International Pitch." See *Pitch*.

Concert-saal (Ger.) (kŏn-*tsĕrt* säl.) Concert hall.

Concert-spieler (Ger.) (kŏn-*tsĕrt* spē-lĕr.) A solo player; concerto player.

Concert spirituel (Fr.) (kŏn-*tsĕrt* spē-rē-too-*ăl*.) See *Concérto Spirituále*.

Concert-stück (Ger.) (kŏn-*tsĕrt* stük.) A concert-piece; a concerto.

Con civettería (It.) (kŏn tshē-vĕt-*air*-rē-ä.) With coquetry; in a coquettish manner.

Conclusione (It.) (kŏn-kloo-zē-ō-nĕ.) The conclusion, or winding up.

Con cómodo (It.) (kŏn *kō*-mō-dō.) With ease; in convenient time.

Concord. A harmonious combination of sounds; the opposite to a *discord*.

Concordabilis (Lat.) (kŏn-kŏr-*dä*-bĕ-lĭs.) Easily, according, harmonizing.

Concordant. Agreeing, correspondent, harmonious.

Concordante (It.) (kŏn-kŏr-*dän*-tĕ.) Concordant.

Concordanten (Ger.) (kŏn-kŏr-*dän*-t'n.) Those sounds which, in combination, produce a concord.

Concordánza (It.) (kŏn-kŏr-*dän*-tsä.) }
Concorde (Fr.) (kŏn-kŏrd.) } Concord; harmony.
Concordia (It.) (kŏn-*kŏr*-dē-ä.) }

Concords, perfect. The perfect fourth, fifth and eighth.

Con delicatézza (It.) (kŏn dĕl-ē-kä-*tet*-sä.) With delicacy and sweetness.

Con desidério (It.) (kŏn dā-zē-*dă*-rē-ō.) With desire and ardent longing.

Con devozióne (It.) (kŏn de-vō-tsē-ō-nĕ.) With devotion; devoutly.

Con diligenza (It.) (kŏn di-lē-*jĕn*-tsä.) With care and diligence.

Con discrezióne (It.) (kŏn dēs-kre-tsē-ō-nĕ.) With discretion; at the discretion of the performer.

Con disperazióne (It.) (kŏn dis-pĕ-rä-tsē-ō-nĕ.) With despair; violence of expression.

Con divozióne (It.) (kŏn di-vō-tsē-ō-

ă as in *ah*; ā as in *hate*; ă as in *at*; ē as in *tree*; ĕ as in *eh*; ī as in *pine*; ĭ as in *pin*;

68

ně.) With religious feeling; in a devotional manner.

Con dólce maniéra (It.) (kŏn dŏl-tshĕ mä-nē-á-rä.)
Con dolcézza (It.) (kŏn dŏl-*tsche*-tsä.) In a simple, delicate manner; with softness, sweetness, delicacy.

Con dolóre (It.) (kŏn dō-*lō*-rĕ.) Mournfully; with grief and pathos.

Conductor. A director or leader of an orchestra or chorus. The earliest conductors were found among the Assyrians, to regulate the rhythm of the songs or dances. They conducted with two sticks, one of which they beat against the other, and so marked the time or accent. Among the Greeks the Coryphœus led the dance and chorus, and in everything requiring united action, by his beating of time, by stamping with a leaden shoe, held his forces together. In the middle ages the conductor led with a long staff, with which he beat the ground, and occasionally the musicians. The word, in connection with music, has several applications. It generally signifies one who directs with a bâton the performance of a band of players. It is also applied to one who accompanies vocal or instrumental pieces on the pianoforte. A conductor, as an independent time-beater, was not known until the end of the eighteenth century. The player who sat at the harpsichord gave the time to the leader of the band, who, directing his subordinates, was called conductor. The art of conducting is comparatively young. The bâton was not used until after 1800. Weber and Spohr were among the very first conductors to use it. Mendelssohn and Berlioz were probably the first great conductors in the modern sense. The conductor is far more than a mere drill-master. He is the poet of the orchestra. It is his conception of the work that is produced; he plays upon his orchestra as an organist upon his manuals and pedals. The art of conducting is far more advanced at present than it has ever been in musical history. It is not necessary that the conductor should be a composer; spite of the fact that some composers have been famous as conductors, the composer is apt to become wedded to some particular school, and to be but a poor conductor of any other *genre*. One extremely fine conductor, Hans Richter, determined to give up composition when he entered on his career as a conductor, and without having a low opinion of his creative talent, we must hold the decision to have been a wise one, for the interpretative faculty would have conflicted with the creative. The conductor of the modern orchestra has a manifold task. First of all comes the technical drill, which is the most wearing of all. The ruling of a band of sensitive musicians is, in itself, not an easy matter. To repress an enthusiastic cellist and cause him to subordinate his phrases to a viola passage which he considers of minor importance, or to subdue an over-zealous trombonist, is not a trifling thing to do. But before even this is done the conductor's work has begun, and he has carefully studied the score that he may have a clear idea of what he intends to do. The discipline of an orchestra should be as rigid as that of a military company. The ideal conductor must not only feel the emotion of a work, but he must be able to express it to his men, by words at rehearsal, by gesture at the concert. The beating of the time is very important, as an indecisive beat will cause the attacks to be irregular. Many composers sin in this respect and cannot conduct their own works with nearly as good results as are achieved by the trained conductor. The signaling of the different entrances of the instruments is another task of the conductor; if the kettle-drums have had fifty-seven measures rest, they should count them, and know exactly when they are to resume playing, but, as a matter of fact, they often rest with calm tranquillity on the shoulders of the conductor, and rely on him to give them the signal to play the first note of their phrase. These are a few of the chief duties of a modern orchestral conductor; to those who imagine that to shake a stick rhythmically over an orchestra is to lead it, they may seem exaggerated, but they are rather under than over-stated. See Schroeder's "Handbook of Conducting," Wagner's "On Conducting."

ō as in *tone*; ŏ as in *dove*; ŏ as in *not*; ŭ as in *up*; ü the French sound of *u*.

Con duólo (It.) (kŏn doo-ō-lō.) Mournfully; with grief.
Conduttóre (It.) (kŏn-doot-tō-rĕ.) A conductor.
Con elegánza (It.) (kŏn ā-lĕ-gàn-tsä.) With elegance.
Con elevatezza (It.) (kŏn ĕ-lĕ-vä-tet-sä.)
Con elevazióne (It.) (kŏn ĕ-lĕ-vä-tse-ō-nĕ.)
With elevation of style; with dignity.
Con energía (It.) (kŏn ā-nĕr-jē-ä.) With energy and emphasis.
Con entusiásmo (It.) (kŏn ĕn-too-zē-às-mō.) With enthusiasm.
Con equalianza (It.) (kŏn ā-quä-lē-än-tsä.) With smoothness and equality.
Con e senza stromenti (It.) (kŏn ā sĕn-tsä strō-mĕn-tē.) With and without instruments.
Con e senza violini (It.) (kŏn ā sĕn-tsa vē-ō-lē-nē.) With and without violins.
Con esp. An abbreviation of *Con*
Con espres. *Espressione*.
Con espressióne (It.) (kŏn ĕs-prĕs-sē-ō-nĕ.) With expression.
Con facilitá (It.) (kŏn fä-tshi-lē-tä.) With facility and ease.
Con fermézza (It.) (kŏn fĕr-met-sä.) With firmness.
Con festivitá (It.) (kŏn fĕs-ti-vē-tä.) With festive gayety.
Con fidúcia (It.) (kŏn fē-doo-tshē-ä.) With hope; with confidence.
Con fierézza (It.) (kŏn fē-ĕ-ret-sä.) With fire; proudly.
Conflation. The act of blowing two or more instruments together.
Con flessibilitá (It.) (kŏn flĕs-sē-bi-lē-tä.) With freedom; flexible.
Con forza (It.) (kŏn fōr-tsä.) With force; with vehemence.
Con freddezza (It.) (kŏn frĕd-det-tsä.) With coldness and apathy.
Con frétta (It.)(kŏn fret-tä.) Hurriedly, with an increase of time.
Con fuóco (It.) (kŏn foo-ō-kō.) With fire and passion.
Con fúria (It.) (kŏn foo-rē-ä.) With
Con fúróre (It.) (kŏn foo-rō-rĕ.) fury; rage; vehemence.

Con gárbo (It.) (kŏn gär-bō.) With elegance.
Con gentilézza (It.) (kŏn jĕn-tē-let-tsä.) With grace and elegance.
Con giustezza (It.) (kŏn doos-tet-tsä.) With justness and precision.
Con gli (It. pl.) (kön glē.) With the.
Con gli stromenti (It.) (kŏn lyee strō-men-tē.) With the instruments.
Con gradazione (It.) (kŏn grä-dä-tsē-ō-nĕ.) With gradual increase and decrease.
Con gránde espressióne (It.) (kŏn grän-de ĕs-prĕs-sē-ō-nĕ.) With much expression.
Con grandézza (It.) (kŏn grän-det-tsä.) With dignity and grandeur.
Con gravita (It.) (kŏn grä-vi-tä.) With gravity.
Con grázia (It.) (kŏn grä-tsē-ä.) With grace and elegance.
Con gústo (It.) (kŏn goos-tō.) With taste.
Con ímpeto (It.) (kŏn ĕm-pe-tō.)
Con impetuosita (It.) (kŏn ĕm-pĕ-too-ō-sē-tà.)
With impetuosity and vehemence.
Con indifferénza (It.) (kon in-dēf-fĕ-ren-tsä.) In an easy and indifferent manner.
Con innocénza (It.) (kŏn ēn-nō-tshen-tsä.) In a simple, artless style.
Con intimíssimo sentiménto (It.) (kŏn ēn-tē-mēs-sē-mō sĕn-tē-men-tō.) With very much feeling; with great expression.
Con intrepidézza (It.) (kŏn ēn-trĕ-pē-det-tsä.) With intrepidity, boldly.
Con ira (It.) (kŏn ē-rä.) With anger.
Con isdegno (It.) (kŏn ēs-dāin-yō.) With anger; angrily.
Con ismania (It.) (kŏn ēs-mä-nē-ä.) In a frenzied style.
Con istrepito (It.) (kŏn ēs-trä-pē-tō.) With noise and bluster.
Conjoint degrees. Two notes which immediately follow each other in the order of the scale.
Conjoint tetrachords. Two tetrachords or fourths of which the highest note of one is the lowest of the other.
Conjunct (Lat.) (kŏn-jŭnkt.) A term applied by the ancient Greeks to tetrachords, or fourths, when the highest

ă as in *ah*; ā as in *hate*; ă as in *at*; ē as in *tree*; ĕ as in *eh*; ī as in *pine*; ĭ as in *pin*;

70

CONJUNCT DEGREE   CONSECUTIVE FIFTHS

note of the lower tetrachord was also the lowest note of the tetrachord next above it.

Conjunct degree. A degree in which two notes form the interval of a second.

Conjunct succession. Where a succession of tones proceed regularly upward or downward through several degrees.

Con leggerézza (It.) (kŏn lĕd-jē-*ret*-tsä.)
Con leggierezza (It.) (kŏn lĕd-jē-ĕ-*ret*-tsä.)
With lightness and delicacy.

Con lenézza (It.) (kŏn lĕ-*net*-tsä.) With mildness; sweetness.

Con lentézza (It.) (kŏn lĕn-*ted*-tsä.) With slowness; lingering.

Con maesta (It.) (kŏn mä-ĕs-*tä*.) With majesty and grandeur.

Con malanconia (It.) (kŏn mä-län-*kō*-nē-ä.)
Con malenconía (It.) (kŏn mä-lĕn-*kō*-nē-ä.)
Con malinconía (It.) (kŏn mä-lēn-*kō*-nē-ä.) With an expression of melancholy and sadness.

Con máno déstra (It.) (kŏn *mä*-nō *dĕs*-trä.)
Con máno drítta (It.) (kŏn *mä*-nō *drēt*-tä.) With the right hand.

Con máno sinístra (It.) (kŏn *mä*-nō si-*nis*-trä.) With the left hand.

Con mistério (It.) (kŏn mēz-*tā*-rē-ō.) With mystery; with an air of mystery.

Con moderazióne (It.) (kŏn mŏd-ĕ-rä-tsē-ō-nĕ.) With a moderate degree of quickness.

Con mólto caráttére (It.) (kŏn *mōl*-tō kär-*ät*-tĕ-rĕ.) With much character and emphasis.

Con mólto espressióne (It.) (kŏn *mōl*-tō ĕs-prĕs-sē-ō-nĕ.) With much expression.

Con mólto passióne (It.) (kŏn *mōl*-tō päs-sē-ō-nĕ.) With much passion and feeling.

Con mólto sentiménto (It.) (kŏn *mōl*-tō sĕn-tē-*men*-tō.) With much feeling or sentiment.

Con morbidézza (It.) (kŏn mŏr-bē-*det*-tsä.) With excess of feeling or morbidly.

Con móto (It.) (kŏn *mō*-tō.) With motion; not dragging.

Connecting note. A note held in common by two successive chords.

Con negligénza (It.) (kŏn nāl-yē-*jen*-tsä.) In a negligent manner; without restraint.

Con nobilita (It.) (kŏn nō-*bē*-lē-tä.) With nobility.

Connaisseur (Fr.) (kŏn-nā-sür.)
Connoisseur (Fr.) (kŏn-wä-*sür*.) One skilled in any art; in music; a composition and performance.

Con osservánza (It.) (kŏn ŏs-sĕr *an*-zä.) With great care and exactness in regard to time and expression.

Con ottáva (It.) (kŏn ŏt-*tä*-vä.)
Con 8va. With the octave; to be played in octaves.

Con passióne (It.) (kŏn päs-sē-*ō*-nĕ.) In an impassioned manner; with great emotion.

Con piacevolézza (It.) (kŏn pē-ä-tshĕv-o-*let*-tsä.) With pleasing and graceful expression.

Con più moto (It.) (kŏn pē-oo mō-tō.) With increased motion.

Con precipitazióne (It.) (kŏn prĕ-tshē-pē-tä-tsē-*ō*-nĕ.) With precipitation; in a hurried manner.

Con precisióne (It.) (kŏn-prĕ-tshē-zē-*ō*-nĕ.) With exactness and precision.

Con prestézza (It.) (kŏn prĕs-*ted*-tsä.) With precision and exactness.

Con rábbia (It.) (kŏn *räb*-bē-ä.) With rage; with fury.

Con rapiditá (It.) (kŏn rä-pi-dē-*tä*.) With rapidity.

Con réplica (It.) (kŏn *re*-plē-kä.) With repetition.

Con risoluzióne (It.) (kŏn rĕ-zō-loo-tsē-*ō*-nĕ.) With firmness and resolution.

Con scioltezza (It.) (kŏn shē-ōl-*ted*-tsä.) Freely; dashingly.

Con sdégno (It.) (kŏn *sdān*-yŏ.) With wrath; in an angry and scornful manner.

Consecutive. A term applied to two or more similar intervals or chords, immediately following one another.

Consecutive fifths. Two or more perfect fifths, immediately following one another in similar motion. Consecutive fifths are disagreeable to the ear and forbidden by the laws of harmony,

ŏ as in *tone*; ŏ as in *dove*; ŏ as in *not*; ŭ as in *up*; ü the French sound of *u*.

although much used by the modern composer.

Consecutive intervals. Where two parallel parts or voices of a score proceed in succession by similar motion.

Consecutive octaves. Two parts moving in octaves with each other.

Consecutives covered. Passages in which consecutive fifths may be imagined, though they do not really exist; as, where a third or a sixth moves to a fifth.

Con semplicitá (It.) (kŏn sĕm-plē-tshē-tä.) With simplicity.

Con sensibilitá (It.) (kŏn sĕn-sē-bē-lē-*tä*.) With sensibility and feeling.

Con sentiménto (It.) (kŏn sĕn-tē-*men*-tō.) With feeling and sentiment.

Consequent (Lat.) (kŏn-sĕ-quĕnt.) The **Consequente** (It.) (kŏn-sĕ-*quen*-tĕ.) answer in a fugue, or of a point of imitation. A musical phrase following a similar one. In musical periods the antecedent and consequent are two balancing divisions, like two rhyming lines, in a verse or couplet. In simple music, there is a close resemblance to poetic construction, and the two divisions cap each other as follows:

Antecedent.   CARL PREYER.

Consequent.

In more developed music, while the antecedent is most frequently 4 or 8 measures long and is treated simply and clearly, the consequent may be extended to any length and is sometimes treated far more freely than the antecedent phrase. See *Form*.

Conservatoire (Fr.) (kŏn-sĕr-vä-*twär*.)
Conservatória (It.) (kŏn-sĕr-vä-*tō*-rĕ-ä.)
Conservatório (It.) (kŏn-sĕr-vä-*tō* rē-ō.)
Conservatorium (Ger.) (kŏn-sĕr-fä-*to*-rĭ-ŭm.)
Conservatory. A school or academy of music, in which every branch of musical art is taught.

Con severita (It.) (kŏn sĕ-*vĕr*-ē-tä.) With strict and severe style.

Consolante (It.) (kŏn-sō-*län*-tĕ.) In a cheering and consoling manner.

Consolataménte (It.) (kŏn-sō-lä-tä-*men*-tĕ.) Quietly, cheerfully.

Console. The keyboard, pedals, stops, of an organ, etc. The portion of the instrument at which the organist sits in playing.

Con solennita (It.) (kŏn sō-lĕn-nē-*tä*.) With solemnity.

Con sómma espressione (It.) (kŏn *sŏm*-mä ĕs prĕs-sē-*ō*-nĕ.) With the utmost expression.

Consonance. An accord of sounds agreeable and satisfactory to the ear; the opposite to a discord or dissonance.

Consonance, perfect. A consonance in which the interval is invariable; octaves, fifths and fourths, are called *perfect* consonances.

Consonances, imperfect. The major and minor thirds and sixes.

Consonant. Accordant, harmonious.

Consonante (It.) (kŏn-sō-nän-tĕ.) Harmonious, consonant.

ä as in *ah* ; ā as in *hate* ; ă as in *at* ; ē as in *tree* ; ĕ as in *eh* ; ī as in *pine* ; ĭ as in *pin*:

Consonantaménte (It.) (kŏn-sō-nän-tä-*men*-tĕ.) Consonant.

Consonantia (Lat) (kŏn-sō-*năn*-shī-ä.) Accord; agreement of voices.

Consonant sixths The major and minor sixths.

Consonant thirds. The major and minor thirds.

Consonanz (Ger.) (kŏn-sō-*nänts*.) } A consonance;

Consonánza (It.) (kŏn-sō-*nän*-tsä.) } a concord.

Consonáre (It.) (kŏn-sō-*nä*-rĕ.) To tune in unison with another.

Consoniren (Ger.) (kŏn-sō-*nē*-r'n.) To harmonize; to agree in sound.

Con sonoritá (It.) (kŏn sō-nō-rē-tä.) With a sonorous, vibrating kind of tone.

Con sordíni (It. pl.) (kŏn sōr-*dē*-nē.) With *mutes*, in violin playing; in pianoforte music, *with dampers*, indicating that the dampers are not to be raised by the pedal; the damper pedal *not* to be used.

Con sordíno (It.) (kŏn sor-*dē*-nō.) *With the mute;* meaning that a mute or damper is to be affixed to the bridge of the violin, viola, etc.

Con spírito (It.) (kŏn *spi*-rē-tō.) With spirit, life, energy.

Con strépito (It.) (kŏn *stre*-pē-tō.) In a boisterous manner; with impetuosity.

Con stroménti (It. pl.) (kŏn strō-*men*-tē.) } With the instru-

Con struménti (It. pl.) (kŏn stroo-*men*-tē.) } ments; meaning that the orchestra and voices are together.

Con suavézza (It.) (kŏn swä-*vet*-tsä.) } With sweet-

Con suavitá (It.) (kŏn swä-*vĕ-tä*.) } ness and delicacy.

Cont. An abbreviation of *Contano.*

Contadína (It.) (kŏn-tä-*dē*-nä.) A country dance.

Contadinésco (It.) (kŏn-tä-dē-*nes*-kō.) Rustic; in a rural style.

Contano (It.) (kŏn-*tä*-nō.) To count or rest; a term applied to certain parts not played for the time being, while the other parts move on.

Con tenerézza (It.) (kŏn tĕ-nĕ-*ret*-tsä.) With tenderness.

Con tepiditá (It.) (kŏn tĕ-pē-dē-*tä*.) With coldness and indifference.

Con timedézza (It.) (kŏn tē-mĕ-*det*-tsä.) With timidity.

Con tínto (It.) (kŏn *tin*-tō.) With various shades of expression.

Continuáto (It.) (kŏn-tē-noo-*ä*-tō.) Continued; held on; sustained.

Continued bass. See *Básso Contínuo.*

Continued harmony. A harmony that does not change, though the bass varies.

Continued rest. A rest continuing through several successive measures, the number of measures being indicated by a figure over a whole rest. Sometimes such a long rest is indicated by a figure marked in the staff, thus: The broad line written across one or more spaces (called the *bâton*), is also sometimes used, thus, etc. In such a case the rest would have the same value even if the figure was omitted; but in practical usage the figure is always present.

Continuo (It.) (kŏn-*tē*-noo-ō.) Without cessation.

Contra (It.) (*kŏn*-trä.) Low, under.

Contrabássist. A double bass player.

Cóntra-bass (It.) (*kŏn*-trä-bäs.) } The double bass; the

Cóntra-basso (It.) (*kŏn*-trä-bäs-sō.) } deepest-toned stringed in-

Contra-bass viol. strument of the bow species. The strings are usually tuned a fourth apart to the following notes when three strings are employed: with the addition of the lower E: when there are four strings. The compass generally written for the instrument

---

ō as in *tone ;* ô as in *dove ;* ɷ as in *not ;* ŭ as in *up ;* ü the French sound of *u.*

extends to the upper F: The contra-bass sounds an octave lower than written. The orchestral contra-basses have four strings (very rarely five), but the solo instruments sometimes have three. The contra-bass is the deepest regular instrument of the orchestra.

Contra-bassoon. The contra-bassoon, or double bassoon, is the deepest instrument of the bassoon family. It has a double-reed mouth-piece, and its tone is powerful and solemn. Its compass is written: but it sounds an octave deeper. It is the deepest instrument that is ever used in the orchestra. It is found only in large scores and in great orchestras. See A. Elson's "Orchestral Instruments and Their Use" and Prout's "The Orchestra."

Contraction. When two parts in a fugue compress the subject, counter-subject, or an intervening subject.

Contraddánza (It.) (kŏn-träd-dän-tsä.) A country dance.

Cóntra fagótto (It.) (*kŏn*-trä-fä-*gŏt*-tō.) The contra-bassoon; also, the name of an organ-stop of 16 or 32-foot scale.

Contr' alti (kŏn-*träl*-tē.) The higher male voices; usually called countertones.

Contrálto (It.) (kŏn-*träl*-tō.) The deepest species of female voice. It is often used as synonymous with alto. See *Alto*.

Con tranquillézza (It.) (kŏn trän-quēl-*lĕt*-tsä.)
Con tranquillita (It.) (kŏn trän-quēl-lē-*tä*.) } With tranquillity; with calmness.

Contra-posaune (Ger.) (*kŏn*-trä-pō-*zou*-ně.) Bass trombone; a 16 or 32-foot reed-stop in an organ.

Contrappuntísta (It.) (kŏn-träp-poon-*tēz*-tä.) One skilled in counterpoint.

Contrappúnto (It.) (kŏn-träp-*poon*-tō.) Counterpoint.

Contrappúnto dóppio (It.) (kŏn-träp-*poon*-tō *dŏp*-pē-ō.) Double counterpoint.

Contrappúnto dóppio alla duodécima (It.) (kŏn-träp-*poon*-tō *dŏp*-pē-ō *äl*-lä doo-o-*dä*-tshe-mä.) Double counterpoint in the twelfth.

Contrappúnto sciolto (It.) (kŏn-träp-*poon*-tō shē-*ŏl*-tō.) A free counterpoint.

Contrappúnto sópra il soggétto (It.) (kŏn-träp-*poon*-tō *sō*-prä ēl sōd-*jet*-tō.) Counterpoint *above* the subject.

Contrappúnto sotto il soggétto (It.) (kŏn-träp-*poon*-tō *sōt*-tō ēl sōd-*jet*-tō.) Counterpoint *below* the subject.

Contrappúnto syncopato (It.) (kŏn-träp-*poon*-tō sēn-kō-*pä*-tō.) The syncopation of one part for the purpose of producing discord.

Contrapunkt (Ger.) (kŏn-trä-poonkt.) Counterpoint.

Contrapunctum floridum (Lat.) (kŏn-trä-*pŭnk*-tum *flō*-rĭ-dŭm.) Ornamental counterpoint.

Contrapuntal. Relating to counterpoint

Contrapuntist. } One skilled in counterpoint.
Contrapuntista (It.) (kŏn-trä-poon-*tēz*-tä.)

Contrapuntus simplex (Lat.) (kŏn-trä-pŭn-tūs sĭm-plĕx.) Simple counterpoint.

Contrário (It.) (kŏn-*trä*-rē-o.) Contrary; in an opposite direction.

Contrary bow. A reversed stroke of the bow.

Contrary motion. Motion in an opposite direction to some other part; one rising as the other falls.

Contrassoggetto (It.) (kŏn-träs-sōd-*jĕt*-tō.) The counter subject of a fugue.

Con traspórto (It.) (kŏn träs-*pōr*-tō.) With anger, excitement, passion.

Contra-tenor. See *Counter Tenor*.

Centratöne (Ger.) (*kŏn*-trä tô-ně.) A term applied to the deeper tones of the bass voice.

Contre. See *Contra*.

Cóntra violóne (It.) (kŏn-trä vē-ō-*lō*-ně.) } The double bass.
Contre-basse (Fr.) (kŏntr-bäss.)

Contredance (Fr.) (kŏntr-dähns.) A country dance; a dance in which the parties engaged stand in two opposite ranks. See *Country Dance*.

Contre partie (Fr.) (kŏntr pär-tē.) The second part.

ă as in *ah*; ā as in *hate*; ă as in *at*; ē as in *tree*; ĕ as in *eh*; ī as in *pine*; ĭ as in *pin*;

Contrepoint (Fr.) (kŏntr-pwänh.) Counterpoint.

Contre-sujet (Fr.) (kŏntr-sü-zhā.) The counter-subject, or second subject in a fugue.

Con tristézza (It.) (kŏn trēz-tāt-tsä.) With sadness; with heaviness.

Contro (It.) (kŏn-trō.) Counter, low.

Contro basso (It.) (kŏn-trō bäs-sō.) Properly written, *Contra Basso*. A double-bass viol; the lowest part of a musical composition.

Contro fagotto. See *Contra Fagotto*.

Controviolone. See *Contraviolone*.

Con tútta fórza (It.) (kŏn toot-tä-főr-tsä.)
Con tútta la fórza (It.) (kŏn toot-tä lä főr-tsä.) With all possible force; with the whole power; as loud as possible.

Con un díto (It.) (kŏn oon dē-tō.) With one finger.

Con variazone (It.) (kŏn vä-rē-ä-tsē-ō-nĕ.) With variations.

Con veeménza (It.) (kŏn vā-ĕ-*men*-tsä.) With vehemence; force.

Con velocita (It.) (kŏn vĕ-lō-tshē-*tä*.) With velocity.

Conversio (Lat.) (kŏn-*vĕr*-sĭ-ō.) Inversion in counterpoint.

Con vigóre (It.) (kŏn vi-*gō*-rĕ.) With vigor, sprightliness, strength.

Con violénza (It.) (kŏn vē-ō-len-tsä.) With violence.

Con vivacitá (It.) (kŏn vē-vä-tshē-*tä*.)
Con vivézza (It.) (kŏn vē-*vet*-tsä.) With liveliness; vivacity; animation.

Con volubilitá (It.) (kŏn vō-loo-bē-lē-*tä*.) With volubility; with fluency, and freedom of performance.

Con zélo (It.) (kŏn *tsā*-lō.) With zeal.

Con 8va. An abbreviation of Con Ottava.

Con 8va ad libitum. With octaves at pleasure.

Copérto (It.) (kŏ-*pär*-tō.) Covered, muffled.

Coppel-flöte (Ger.) (*kŏp*-p'l *flŏ*-tĕ.) Coupling flute; an organ stop of the clarabella, or stopped diapason species, in tended to be used in combination with some other stop.

Cópula (It.) (*kō*-poo-lä.)
Copule (Fr.) (kŏ-*pül*.) A *coupler*; an arrangement by which two rows of keys can be connected together, or the keys connected with the pedals; a codetta; a connecting phrase in a fugue.

Copyright. The exclusive right of an author or his representative to print, publish, or sell his work during a specified term of years.

Cor. An abbreviation of *Cornet*.

Cor (Fr.) (kŏr.) A horn; commonly called the French horn.

Coràle (It.) (kō-*rä*-lĕ.) Choral; the plain chant.

Coranach (Gaelic.) A funeral song or dirge.

Cor Anglais (Fr.) (kōr änh-glās.) *English horn;* the tenor oboe; also a reed stop in an organ. The compass of the English horn is written about the same as that of the oboe, but it sounds a fifth deeper than notated. Its music is written in the treble clef. See A. Elson's "Orchestral Instruments," Prout's "Orchestra," etc.

Coránte (It.) (kō-*rän*-tĕ.)
Corànto (It.) (kō-*rän*-to.) A dance in ¾ or ¾ time. See *Courante*.

Córda (It.) (*kŏr*-dä.) A string; *úna córda*, one string.

Cordatúra (It.) (kŏr-dä-*too*-rä.) The scale or series of notes to which the strings of any instrument are tuned.

Corde (Fr.) (kŏrd.) A string.

Corde à boyau (Fr.) (kŏrd ä bwä-yō.) Catgut; strings for the violin, harp, etc.

Corde à jour (Fr.) (kŏrd ä zhoor.)
Corde à vide (Fr.) (kŏrd ä vēd.) An open string on the violin, viola, etc.

Cor de chasse (Fr.) (kŏr dŭh shäss.) The hunting horn; the French horn.

Corde de luth (Fr.) (kŏrd dŭh-loot.) A lute string.

Cor de postillon (Fr.) (kŏr dŭh pŏs-tē-yŏnh.) Postillion's horn.

Cor de signal (Fr.) (kŏr dŭh sēn-yăl.) a bugle.

Cor de vaches (Fr.) (kŏr dŭh väsh.) The cowboy's horn.

ō as in *tone;* ŏ as in *dove;* ŏ as in *not;* ŭ as in *up;* ü the French sound of *u.*

Cordiéra (It.) (kŏr-dē-*ā*-rä.) The tail piece of a violin, viola, etc.

Coregrafía (It.) (kō-rĕ-*grä*-fē-ä.) The method of describing the figures of a dance.

Coriambus (Ger.) (ko-rē-*ăm*-bŭs.) In ancient poetry, a foot consisting of four syllables, the first and last long and the others short: — ⌣ ⌣ —

Córica (It.) (*kō*-rē-kä.) } Choral.
Córico (It.) (*kō*-rē-kō.)

Coriféo (It.) (kō-rē-fā-ō.) The leader of the dances in a ballet.

Corimagístro (It.) (kō-rēm-ä-*jĕs*-trō.) The leader of a choir.

Coriphæus (Gr.) (kō-*rĭf*-ē-ŭs.) A leader, chief, head of a chorus, which, in ancient times, combined singing and dancing. See *Coriféo*.

Corista (It.) (kō-*rēs*-tä.) A chorister.

Cormorne. A soft-toned horn; also a reed-stop in English organs. See *Cremóna*.

Cornamúsa (It.) (kŏr-nä-*moo*-zä.) A species of bagpipe.

Cornamute. A wind instrument; a species of bagpipe.

Corne (Fr.) (kŏrn.) A horn.

Corne de chasse (Fr.) (kŏrn dŭh shäss.) See *Cor de Chasse*.

Cornemuse (Fr.) (kŏrn-ŭh-müz.) See *Cornamúsa*.

Corner (Fr.) (kŏr-nā.) To sound a horn, or cornet.

Cornet. The name of an organ-stop consisting of several ranks of pipes. Also, a small horn, of the nature of a trumpet, used in brass bands. The cornet, in the time of Shakespeare, was a rough-toned instrument, like the old serpent, but smaller. The cornet, with keys, is an invention of the early part of the nineteenth century. The cornets most used in military bands are in B flat, and sound a whole tone deeper than written. These are best in flat keys, but, by the addition of an extra crook, which can be thrown open at will, the pitch is lowered a semi-tone and the instrument plays easily in the sharp keys. There is also a smaller cornet in E flat, which sounds a minor third higher than written, and has a very bright and incisive tone. The cornet in C (non-transposing) is little used. The full name of this instrument is *Cornet a pistons*, and it is always supplied with keys which make the instrument capable of producing the chromatic scale. Without touching these keys the cornet can produce the following tones, which are the harmonic series of this fundamental

See *Harmonics*. Some soloists can produce the fundamental and lower it chromatically by means of the keys, this set of tones being called the "pedal tones." There are also skillful performers who can play higher tones than we have given in the above series. The ordinary compass used in modern works would be about

sounding one tone deeper upon the B-flat cornet. See Prout's "Orchestra," or A. Elson's "Orchestral Instruments."

Corneta (Spa.) (kŏr-nā-*tä*.) Cornet; a French horn.

Corneta } A name sometimes applied
Cornetto } to a reed-stop in an organ of 16-foot scale.

Cornet a bouquin (Fr.) (kŏr-nĕt ä boo-*känh*.) Cornet; bugle horn.

Cornet a pistons (Fr.) (kŏr-nĕt ä pēs-tŏnh.) A species of trumpet, but shorter and wider, with valves or pistons to produce the semi-tones. See *Cornet*.

Cornet dreifach (Ger.) (kŏr-*nĕt drī*-fäkh.) Cornet with three ranks in German organs.

Cornete (Spa.) (kŏr-*nā*-tĕ.) }
Cornett (Ger.) (kŏr-*nĕt*.) } A cornet.
Cornétta (It.) (kŏr-*net*-ä.) }

Cornetica (Spa.) (kŏr-*nā*-tē-kä.) } A
Cornettino (It.) (kŏr-nāt-*tēe*-nō.) } small cornet.

Cornétto (It.) (kŏr-*net*-tō.) A cornet.

Cornet stop. An organ-stop, consisting of from three to five pipes to each note

Corni (It. pl.) (kŏr-nēe.) The horns.

Cornicello (It.) (kŏr-nē-*tshel*-lō.) A small horn or cornet

Cornist. ⎱ A performer on the cornet or horn.
Corneter. ⎰

Corniste (Fr.) (kŏr-*nist.*) A player upon the horn

Cornmuse. A Cornish pipe, similar to a bagpipe

Córno (It.) (kŏr-nō.) A horn.

Córno alto (It.) (*kŏr*-nō *äl*-tō.) A horn of a high pitch.

Córno básso (It.) (*kŏr*-nō *bäs*-sō.) A bass horn; a horn of a low pitch.

Córno cromático (It.) (*kŏr*-nō krō-*mä*-tē-kō.) The chromatic horn.

Córno di bassétto (It.) (*kŏr*-nō dē bäs-*set*-tō.) 1. The basset horn. A species of clarinet a fifth lower than the C clarinet. 2. A delicate-toned organ-stop (reed) of 8-foot scale.

Córno di cáccia (It.) (*kŏr*-nō dē *kät*-tshē-ä.) The hunting or French horn.

Córno dólce (It.) (*kŏr*-nō *dŏl*-tshĕ.) Soft horn; an organ-stop, occurring both in the manuals and pedals.

Córno flute. An organ-stop of 8 foot scale; of soft, agreeable tone.

Córno in Bbásso (It.) A low B-flat horn.

Córno Inglése (It.) (*kŏr*-nō In-glā-zĕ.) The English horn.

Cornopean. An organ reed-stop of 8-foot scale; also, a wind-instrument of the trumpet species.

Córno prímo (It.) (*kŏr*-nō *prē*-mō.) The first horn.

Córno quarto (It.) (*kŏr*-nō quär-tō.) The fourth horn.

Córno secóndo (It.) (kŏr-nō sĕ-*kŏn*-dō.) The second horn.

Córno ventíle (It.) (kŏr-nō vĕn-*tē*-lĕ.) ⎫ Chromatic horn with valves or keys for producing the semi-tones.
Cór omnitonique (Fr.) (kŏr-ŏnh-nĭt-ō-*nēk*.) ⎬
⎭

Córo (It.) (*kō*-rō.) A choir; a chorus; a piece for many voices.

Coróna (It.) (kō-*rō*-nä.) ⎫ A pause or hold,
Coronata (It.) (ko-rō-*nä*-tä.) ⎬
Couronne (Fr.) (k⌒o-*ronn*.) ⎭

Coronach (kō-rō-näk.) Funeral hymn.

Coro prímo (It.) (kō-rō *prē*-mō.) The first chorus.

Corps (Fr.) (kōr.) 1. The body of a musical instrument. 2. A band of musicians.

Corps de ballet (Fr.) (kōr dŭh băl-lā.) A general name for the performers in a ballet.

Corps de voíx (Fr.) (kōr dŭh vwä.) Body or fulness of tone.

Corrénte (It.) (kōr-*ren*-tĕ.) An old dance tune in triple time. See *Coránto*.

Corrépétiteur (Fr.) (kŏr-rā-pā-tĭ-*tür*.) ⎫
Corripetitore (It.) (kŏr-rē-pā-tē-*tō*-rĕ.) ⎬
A musician who instructs the chorus singers of the opera.

Corybant (Gr.) (*kŏ*-rĭ-bănt.) A priest of Cybele, whose rites were celebrated with dances to the sound of the drum and cymbal.

Coryphæus (Gr.) (kō-*rĭf*-ē-ŭs.) The conductor of the chorus. See *Corifeo*.

Coryphée (Fr.) (kō-rĭ-fā.) The leader or chief of the group of dancers in a *ballet*.

Cosaque (Fr.) (kō-săk.) A Cossack dance.

Cotil. An abbreviation of *cotillon*.

Cotillon (Fr.) (kō-tē-yŏnh.) A lively dance, similar to the "German"; a quadrille.

Couac (Fr.) (quăk.) The quacking sound produced by bad playing of oboe or clarinet

Couched harp. The original name of the spinet.

Coulé (Fr.) (koo-*lāy*.) A group of two notes, connected by a slur.

Couler (Fr.) (koo-*lāy*.) To slide; to slur.

Counter. A name given to a part sung or played against another, as *counter tenor*.

Counter-bass. A second bass.

Counter-dance. See *Contredanse*.

Counter-fugue. A fugue in which the subjects move in contrary directions.

ŏ as in *tone*; ô as in *dove*; ŏ as in *not*; ŭ as in *up*; ü the French sound of *u*.

77

Counterpoint. *Point against point.* The art of adding one or more parts to a given theme or subject. Before the invention of notes, the various sounds were expressed by *points.* Counterpoint is the support of melody by melody instead of by chords (harmony). Hauptmann expressed the difference between counterpoint and harmony by calling the latter "vertical," and the former "horizontal music."

Counterpoint, double. A counterpart that admits of an inversion of two parts

Counterpoint, equal. Where the notes are of equal duration.

Counterpoint, quadruple. Counterpoint in four parts, all of which can invert above or below each other, in twenty-four different positions.

Counterpoint, single. Where the parts are not invertible.

Counterpoint, triple. A counterpoint in three parts, all of which can be inverted, making six possible positions.

Counter-subject. The second division in a fugue, coming against the answer in the second voice.

Counter-tenor. High tenor; the highest male voice. It is generally *a falsetto.*

Counter-tenor clef. The C clef, when placed on the third line.

Counter theme. See *Counter-subject.*

Country Dance. *Contre-danse* (Fr.) *Contradanza* (It.) A rustic dance, of English origin, in which performers were arranged face to face, "one set against another," and performed certain prescribed figures. The old method of dancing the "country dance" was to place the ladies and the gentlemen in two parallel lines, the former on the left, the latter on the right, facing their partners. Various figures were then executed to sprightly music, each figure occupying the time of four or eight measures.

Coup d'Archet (Fr.) (koo dar-*shay.*) A stroke of the bow.

Coup de baguette (Fr.) (koo dŭh bă-gwĕt.) Beat of the drum.

Coup de cloche (Fr.) (koo dŭh klōsh.) Stroke of the clock.

Couper le sujet (Fr.) (koo-pā lŭh soo-jā.)

To curtail or contract the subject or theme

Coupler. See *Cópula.*

Couplet (Fr) (koo-plā.) } A stanza, or
Couplet. } verse; two lines of poetry forming complete sense.

Coups d'archet (Fr.) (koo d'är-shā.) Strokes of the bow; ways or methods of bowing.

Courante (Fr.) (koo-ränht.) *Running;* an old dance in triple time; the second number in the old Suites des Danses. It is in rapid *tempo.*

C. P. Abbreviation of *Colla Parte.*

Cr. }
Cres. } Abbreviations of Crescendo.
Cresc. }

Cracovienne (Fr.) (kră-*kō*-vē *ĕnn.*) A Polish dance in $\frac{2}{4}$ (sometimes erroneously given as $\frac{3}{4}$) rhythm.

Cravicembalo (It.) (krä-vē-tshĕm-*bä*-lō.) A general name for all instruments of the harpsichord species. Also *Clavicembalo* and *Gravicembalo.*

Credo (Lat.) *(krāy*-dō.) *I believe;* one of the principal movements of the Mass. The Creed.

Crembala. An ancient instrument, resembling the castanets.

Cremóna (It.) (krĕ-*mō*-nä.) An organ-stop; the name of a superior make of violins. As Amati, Guarnerius, Stradivarius, and other great violin makers lived in the city of Cremona, in northern Italy, the name "Cremona" is given to their instruments. See Stoeving's "The Violin."

Cremorn. A reed-stop organ of 8-foot scale.

Cres. al fortissimo. Increasing to very loud.

Crescéndo (It.) (krĕ-*shen*-dō.) A word denoting an increasing power of tone; it is often indicated by the sign, ⎯⎯⎯.

Crescéndo al diminuendo (It.) (krŏ-*shen*-dō äl dē-mēn-oo-ĕn-dō.)

Crescéndo e diminuendo (It.) (krĕ-*shen*-dō ā dē-min-oo-ĕn-dō.)

Crescéndo pói diminuendo (It.) (krĕ-*shen*-dō pō-ē dē-mēn-oo-én-dō.)

ă as in *zh* ; ā as in *hate* ; ă as in *at* ; ē as in *tree* ; ĕ as in *eh* ; ī as in *pine* ; ĭ as in *pin* ;

Increase and then diminish the tone; indicated often by the sign, ⋖⋗

Crescéndo al fortissimo (It.) (krĕ-*shen*-dō äl fōr-*tĕs*-sē-mō.) Increase the tone until the greatest degree of power is obtained.

Crescéndo póco a póco (It.) (krĕ-*shen*-dō pō-kō ä pō-kō.) Increasing the tone by little and little.

Crescendo-zug (Ger.) (krĕ-shĕn-dō-tsoog.) The swell-box in the organ.

Crescent. A Turkish instrument made of small bells hung on an inverted crescent.

Cres. dim. An abbreviation of Crescéndo e Diminuéndo.

Cres. e legato (It.) Crescéndo and *legato.*

Criard (Fr.) (krē-är.) Bawling; shouting; relating to the quality of the tone of the voice.

Crier (Fr.) (krē-ā.) To bawl; to shriek; to sing badly.

Croche (Fr.) (krōsh.) An eighth note.

Croche, double (Fr.) (krōsh doobl.) A sixteenth note.

Croche pointée (Fr.) (krōsh pwän-tā.) A dotted eighth note.

Croche quadruple (Fr.) (krōsh quä-drü-pl.) A sixty-fourth note.

Croche triple (Fr.) (krōsh trēpl.) A thirty-second note, thus,

Crochet (Fr.) (krō-shā.) The *hook* of a quaver, semi-quaver, etc.

Crotchet. The quarter note.

Crotchet rest. A rest equal in duration to a quarter note. It was formerly written ⌐, but the close resemblance to the eighth rest has led to its change into ⌠ or ⌡

Croma (It.) (*krō*-ma.) An eighth note.

Cromática (It.) (krō-*mä*-tē-kä.) ⎱ Cromático (It.) (krō-*mä*-tē-kō.) ⎰ matic, referring to intervals and scales.

Crom-horn (Ger.) (*krŏm*-hŏrn.) A reed-stop in an organ. Also *Krum-horn.*

Cromorna-stop. (krŏ-mōr-nä.) ⎱ The **Cromorne** (Fr.) (krō-mōrn.) ⎰ name of a reed-stop in an organ.

Crooks. Small curved tubes to be added to horns, trumpets, etc., to change their pitch, and adapt them to the key of the piece in which they are to be used

Crotale (Fr.) (krō-*täl*.) ⎫ An an-
Crótalo (It.) (*krō*-tä-lō.) ⎬ cient
Crotalum (Gr.) (krō-*tä*-lŭm. ⎭ musical instrument, used by the priests of Cybele. From the reference made to it by different authors, it seems to have been a small cymbal or a species of castanet.

Crotales. Little bells.

Crowd. An old name for the violin See *Crwth.*

Crowth. The English name of the *Crwth.*

Crucifixus (Lat.) (krū-sĭ-fĭx-ŭs.) Part of the *Credo* in a Mass.

Cruth. See *Crwth.*

Crwth (Welsh.) (krŭth.) An old Welsh instrument, having six strings, resembling the violin. By some the *Crwth* is held to be the progenitor of the violin.

C. S. The initials of *Con Sordino.*

Csardas (Hun.) (tsär-dăs.) Hungarian dance.

C Schlüssel (Ger.) (*tsā* shlü-s'l.) The C clef.

Cto. Abbreviation of *Concerto.*

Cue. *The tail; the end of a thing.* The last words of an actor on a stage, serving as an intimation to the one who follows, when to speak and what to say. In concerted music the "cue" is certain small notes giving a prominent phrase of the music to serve as guide for the entrance of the player or singer after a long rest; for example:

Cuivre (Fr.) (queevr.) Meaning "cop-

ō as in *tone ;* ô as in *dove ;* ŏ as in *not ;* ŭ as in *up ;* ü the French sound of *u.*

79

per"; applied to the brass wind-instruments of an orchestra.

Cum cantu (Lat.) (kŭm *kăn*-tū.) *With song; with singing.*

Cum Sancto Spiritu (Lat.) (kŭm *sănk*-tō spĭr-ĭ-tū.) Part of the *Gloria* in a Mass.

Cupo (It.) (koo-pō.) Dark, obscure.

Custo (It.) (koos-to.) } *A direct w*. A
Custos (Lat.) (*kŭs*-tŏs.) } mark sometimes placed at the end of a staff, or of a figure, to indicate the note next following.

Cycle forms, or Cyclical forms. Such forms in music as are made up of several complete forms, movements, or compositions placed in contrast with each other. The Sonata, Symphony, Suite, String Quartet, etc., are examples.

Cymbales (Fr.) (sähn-bäl.) } Circular
Cymbals. } metal-plates used in bands, usually in combination with the great drum; they are clashed together, producing a ringing, brilliant effect. They originally came from Turkey.

Cymbalum (Lat.) (sĭm-*bä*-lŭm.) The cymbal.

Cymbale (Fr.) (sähn-bäl.) } A mixture
Cymbel (Ger.) (*tsĭm*-b'l.) } organ-stop of a very acute quality of tone.

Cypher system. An old system of musical notation, in which the notes were represented by numerals.

Cytara. The cithara.

Cyter (Dan.) (sü-tĕr.) A cithern or cithera.

Cythorn (sĭth-ŏrn.) A cithorn or cithera.

Czardas. See *Csardas*.

D

D. The second note in the diatonic scale of C; the syllable *re* is applied to this note. The major scale with two sharps in its signature. Abbreviation for "Da" or "Dal," as *D. S.* — "Dal Segno;" *D. C.* — "Da Capo."

Da (It.) (dä.) By, from, for, through, etc.

Da bállo (It.) (dä *bäl*-lō.) In the style of a dance; like a dance.

Da cámera (It.) (dä *kä*-mĕ-rä.) For the chamber; in the style of chamber music.

Da cappélla (It.) (dä käp-*pel*-lä.) For the church; in the style of church or chapel music.

Da cápo (It.) (dä *kä*-pō.) *From the beginning;* an expression placed at the end of a movement to indicate that the performer must return to the first strain. In such a case the repeats indicated by dots are generally not made after *D. C.*

Da cápo al fíne (It.) (dä *kä*-pō äl *fee*-nĕ.) Return to the beginning and conclude with the word *Fine*.

Da cápo, sin' al fíne (It.) (dä *kä*-pō sēn äl *fee*-nĕ.) Return to the beginning and conclude with the word *Fine*.

Da capo e pói la códa (It.) (dä *kä*-pō ā *pō*-ē lä *kō*-dä.) Begin again and then play to the *Códa*.

Da capo sin' al ségno (It.) (dä *kä*-pō sin äl *sän*-yō.) Return to the beginning and play to the sign ⊕, after which play the *coda*.

D' accord (Fr.) (d' ăk-*kŏrd*.) } In
D' accordo (It.) (d' äk-kŏr-dō.) } tune; in concord; in harmony.

Da chiésa (It.) (dä kē-*ä*-zä.) For the church.

Dactilo (Spa.) (däk-*tē*-lō.) A dactyl.

Dactyl (Lat.) (*dăk*-tĭl.) A metrical foot, consisting of one long syllable followed by two short ones, marked thus, — ‿ ‿.

Dactylion (Gr.) (dăk-*tĭl*-ĭ-ŏn.) A machine invented by Henri Herz, for strengthening the fingers and rendering them independent of each other in pianoforte playing.

Dactylus (Lat.) (*dăk*-tĭl-ŭs.) See *Dactyl*.

Daddy-mammy. A term used to indicate the double strokes of a roll (marked *tr*) on the snare-drum.

Daktylus (Gr.) (*dăk*-tĭl-oos.) A *dactyl*.

Dal (It.) (däl.)
Dall' (It.) (däll'.)
Dalla (It.) (*däl*-lä.) } From the; by
Dalle (It.) (*däl*-lĕ.) } the; of the; etc
Dallo (It.) (*däl*-lō.)

Da lontáno (It.) (dä lŏn-*tä*-nō.) *At a distance;* the music is to sound as if far away.

Dal ségno (It.) (däl sän-yō.) *From the*

ă as in *ah*; ā as in *hate*; ă as in *at*; ē as in *tree*; ĕ as in *eh*; ī as in *pine*; ĭ as in *pin*;

Felix Mendelssohn Bartholdy

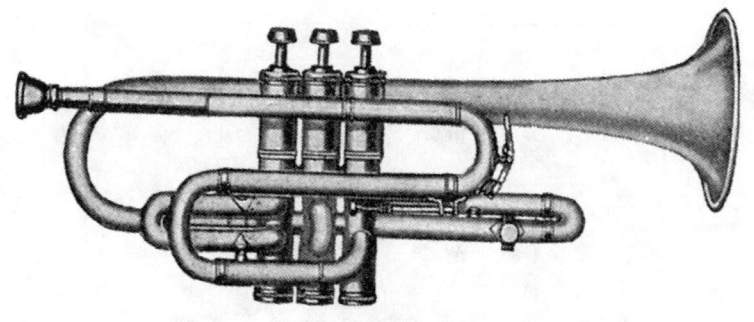

Coronet

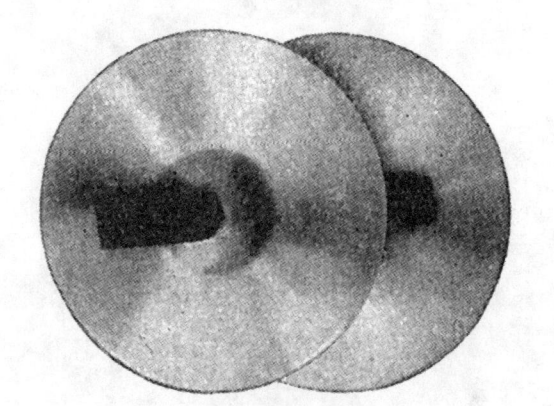

Cymbals

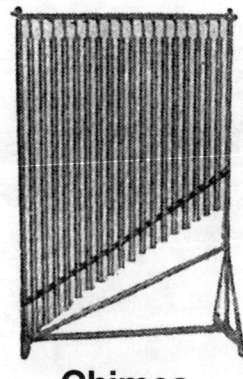

Chimes

sign :𝄋:. A mark directing a repetition from the sign.

Dal ségno alla fíne (It.) (däl *sen*-yo ä-lä *fee*-ně.) From the sign to the end.

Dal teatro (It.) (däl tě-*ä*-trō.) In the style of theatre music.

Damenisation. *Solfeggi*, to which are adapted the syllables, da, me, ni, po, tu, la, be. The system was invented by Graun, and the syllables do not indicate any scale degree, but are merely intended to advance the student in vocal pronunciation.

Damper pedal. That pedal in a pianoforte which raises the dampers from the strings and allows them to vibrate freely. Its use is indicated by the abbreviation *ped.* See *Pedal.*

Dampers. A portion of the movable mechanism of the pianoforte covered with felt, and, by means of a pedal, brought in contact with the wires in order to stop their vibration and prevent a confusion of sounds. The mute of any brass instrument.

Dämpfen (Ger.) (*däm*-pfěn.) To muffle, or deaden the tone of an instrument.

Dämpfer (Ger.) (*däm*-pfěr.) A mute, or damper, used to deaden the tone of a violin, or other similar instrument.

Dämpfung (Ger.) (*däm*-pfoong.) Damping; smothering the tone.

Dance, country. A quadrille; any lively, pointed melody suitable for dancing.

Dance, morrice. ⎫
Dance, morris. ⎬ A dance in imitation
Dance, morriske. ⎭ of the Moors, usually performed by young men dressed in loose frocks, adorned with bells and ribbons, and accompanied by castanets, tambours, etc.

Dances. Certain tunes composed especially for dancing.

Danklied (Ger.) (*dänk*-lēd.) A thanksgiving song.

Danse (Fr.) (dänhs.) A dance tune.

Danser (Fr.) (danh-*sāy*.) To dance.

Danseur (Fr.) (dänh-*sür*.) A male dancer.

Danseuse (Fr.) (dänh-*süs*.) A female dancer.

Danse, contre (Fr.) (dänhs kŏntr.) A country dance; a quadrille.

Danse de matelot (Fr.) (dänhs dŭh mät-ä-lō.) A dance resembling the hornpipe. A sailor's dance.

Dánza (It.) (*dän*-tsä.) ⎫
Danza (Spa.) (*dän*-thä.) ⎬ A dance.

Danzánte (It.) (dän-*tsän*-tě.) A dancer.

Danzáre (It.) (dän *tsä*-rě.) To dance.

Danzatore (It.) (dän-tsä-*tō*-rě.) A male dancer.

Danzatríce (It.) (dän-tsä-*trēe*-tshě.) A female dancer.

Danzétta (It.) (dän-tset-tä.) A little dance; a short dance.

Da príma (It.) (dä *prēe*-mä.) At first, from the beginning.

Dar la voce (It.) (där lä vō-tshě.) To strike or give the key-note.

Darm-saite (Ger.) (*därm*-sī-tě.) A gut-string; cat-gut.

Darm-saiten (Ger. pl.) (*därm*-sī-t'n.) Gut-strings used for the harp, violin, guitar, etc.

Darsteller (Ger.) (*där*-stěl-lěr.) A performer.

Da schérzo (It.) (dä *skärt*-sō.) In a lively, playful manner.

Da teátro (It.) (dä tě-*ä*-trō.) For the theatre; music composed for the theatre.

Dáttilo (It.) (*dät*-tē-lō.) A dactyl.

Dauer (Ger.) (*dou*-ěr.) The length or duration of notes.

Daum (Ger.) (doum.) ⎫
Daumen (Ger.) (*dou*-měň.) ⎬ The thumb.

Daumenklapper (Ger.) (*dou*-měn-kläp-pěr.) Castanet, snapper.

D. C. The initials of *Da Capo.*

D dur (Ger.) (dä-door.) D major; the key of D major.

Débander (Fr.) (dě-bǎn-dä.) To unbrace a drum.

Débile (It.) (*de*-bē-lē.) ⎫
Débole (It.) (*de*-bō-lě.) ⎬ Weak, feeble, faint.

Début (Fr.) (*dā*-bü.) First appearance; the first public performance.

Débutant (Fr.) (*dā*-bü-tǎnh.) ⎫
Débutante (Fr.) (*dā*-bü-tǎnht.) ⎬ A singer or performer who appears for the first time before the public.

Débuter (Fr.) (*dā*-bü-tä.) To begin; to play first.

ŏ as in *tone* ; ô as in *dove* ; ŏ as in *not*; ŭ as in *up*; ü the French sound of *u*.

Decameróne (It.) (děk-ä-mě-*rō*-ně.) A period of ten days; a collection of ten musical pieces.

Decani (Lat. pl.) (dĕ-*kä*-nē.) In cathedral music this term implies that the passages thus marked must be taken by the singers on the side of the choir where the *Dean* usually sits.

Decanto (Lat.) (dĕ-*kăn*-tō.) To sing; to chant.

Decastich. A poem consisting of ten lines.

Deceptive cadence. A cadence which, instead of closing upon the tonic, or a chord bearing a close relation to it, takes the ear wholly by surprise, and terminates with a chord foreign to the harmony of the tonic.

Deceptive modulation. A modulation by which the ear is deceived and led into unexpected harmony.

Décidé (Fr.) (dĕ-sē-dā.)
Décidément (Fr.) (dĕ-sē-dā-mänh.) } With decision; with resolution.

Decima (Lat.) (*děs*-ĭ-mä.) A *tenth*; an interval of ten degrees in the scale; also the name of an organ-stop sounding the tenth.

Decima acuta (Lat.) (*děs*-ĭ-mä ă-*kū*-tä.) Tenth above.

Decima gravis (Lat.) (*děs*-ĭ-mä *grä*-vĭs.) Tenth below.

Decima quarta (Lat.) (*děs*-ĭ-mä *quär*-tä.) The interval of a fourteenth.

Decima quinta (Lat.) (*děs*ĭ-mä quĭn-tä.) The interval of a fifteenth.

Decima tertia (Lat.) (*děs*-ĭ-mä *těr*-shĭ-ä.) The interval of a thirteenth.

Décime (Fr.) (dā-sēm.) A tenth. See *Decima.*

Decimole. A group of ten notes of artificial value, equal to eight of the natural notes of the same denomination. See *Note, Notation.*

Décisif (Fr.) (dā-sē-sĭf.) Decisive, clear, firm.

Decisióne (It.) (dā-tshē-zē-*ō*-nĕ.) Decision, firmness.

Décisivement (Fr.) (dā-sē-zēv-mänh.) Decisively.

Decisívo (It.) (dā-tshē-*zē*-vō.)
Decíso (It.) (dā-*tshē*-zō.) } In a bold and decided manner.

Decke (Ger.) (*děk*-ĕ.) The sound board of a violin, violoncello, etc.; also the cover or top in those organ-stops which are *covered* or *stopped.*

Declamándo (It.) (děk-lä-*män*-dō.) With declamatory expression.

Declamátio (It.) (děk-lä-*mä*-tē-ō.) Declamation, recitative.

Declamation. Dramatic singing; the art of rendering words set to music in a correct and effective style.

Declamazióne (It.) (děk-lä-mä-tsē-*ō*-nē.) Declamation.

Décomposé (Fr.) (dā-kŏm-pō-zā.) Incoherent, unconnected.

Décoration (Fr.) (dā-kō-rä-sĭ-ŏnh.) Used by some French theorists to indicate the *signature.*

Decorative notes. Notes of embellishment, appoggiaturas, etc.

Decr.
Decres. } Abbreviations of *decrescendo.*

Decrescéndo (It.) (de-krĕ-*shen*-dō.) Gradually diminishing in power of tone

Decrescéndo sin al pianissimo (It.) (de-krĕ-*shen*-dō sĕn äl pē-än-*ĕs*-si-mō.) Diminishing to the softest possible sound.

Dedicáto. (It.) (děd-ē-kä-tō.)
Dédié (Fr.) (dā-dĭ-ā.) } Dedicated.

Defettiva quinta (It.) (dā-fĕt-*tē*-vä *quĕn*-tä.) A defective or false fifth.

Deficiéndo (It.) (dā-fē-tshē-*än*-dō.) Dying away.

Degli (It.) (dāl-yē.) Of the.

Degré (Fr.) (dĕ-*grä*.) A degree of the staff.

Degree. The step between two notes; each line and space of the staff.

Degree, conjunct. A degree in which two notes form the interval of a second.

Degree, disjunct. A degree in which two notes form a third or any greater interval.

Degree, half. A semi-tone.

Dehnen (Ger.) (*day*-nen.) To extend, or prolong.

ă as in *ah*; ā as in *hate*; ă as in *at*; ē as in *tree*; ĕ as in *eh*; ī as in *pine*; ĭ as in *pin*;

Del (It.) (dĕl.) Of the.

Délassement (Fr.) (dā-läss-mänh) An easy and agreeable composition

Deliberataménte (It.) (dĕ-lē-bĕ-rä-tä-*men*-tĕ.)

Deliberáto (It.) (dĕ-lē-bā-*rä*-tō.) Deliberately.

Delicataménte (It.) (dĕl-ē-kä-tä-*men*-tĕ) Delicately, smoothly.

Délicatesse (Fr.) (dā-lē-kä-tĕss)
Delicatézza (It.) (dĕl-ē-kä-*tet*-zä) Delicacy; refined execution.

Delicatissimaménte (It.) (dĕl-ē-kä-tēs-sē-mä-*men*-tĕ.)
Delicatíssimo (It.) (dĕl-ē-kä-*tis*-sē-mō) With extreme delicacy.

Delicato (It.) (dĕl-ē-*kä*-tō.) Delicately, smoothly.

Delírio (It.) (dĕ-*lēe*-rē-ō.) Frenzy, excitement.

Delivery. The act of controlling the respiration and using the vocal organs so as to produce a good tone.

Deliziosamente (It.) (dĕ-lēt-sē-ō-zä-*men*-tĕ.) Deliciously, sweetly.

Dell' (It.) (dĕll.)
Della (It.) (*dĕl*-lä.)
Delle (It.) (*dĕl*-lĕ.) Of the, by the, etc.
Dello (It.) (*dĕl*-lō.)

Dem (Ger.) (dĕm.) To the.

Démancher (Fr.) (dā-mänh-shāy.) To change or alter the position of the hand; to shift on the violin, etc.; to cross hands on the pianoforte, making the left hand play the part of the right, and *vice versa*.

Demande (Fr.) (dĕ-*mänhd*.) The question, or proposition of a fugue; called also, *dux*, or leading subject.

Demi (Fr.) (dĕ-*mē*.) Half.

Demi-baton (Fr.) (dĕ-*mē bä*-tŏnh.) A double whole-rest.

Demi-cadence (Fr.) (dĕ-*mē* kä-*dänhs*.) A half-cadence, or cadence on the dominant.

Demi-croche (Fr.) (dĕ-*mē* krōsh.) An eighth note.

Demi-jeu (Fr.) (dĕ-*mē* jhü.) Same as *mézzo fórte*.

Demi-mesure (Fr.) (dē-*mē* mĕ-*zür*.) A half-rest.
Demi-pause (Fr.) (dĕ-*mē*-pōz.)

Demi-quart de soupir (Fr.) (dĕ-*mē* kär dŭh soo-*pēr*) A 32d rest.

Demi-semiquaver. A 32d note or thus

Demi-semiquaver rest. A mark of silence, equal in duration to a demi-semiquaver, made thus

Demi-soupir (Fr) (dĕ-*mē* soo-pēer.) An eighth rest.

Demiton (Fr.) (dĕ-*mē*-tŏnh.)
Demitone (Fr.) (dĕ-*mē*-tōn.) An interval of a half-tone.

Demoiselle (Fr.) (*dem*-wa-sel.) A coupler in the organ.

De plus en plus vite (Fr.) (dŭh plü-zänh plü-vēet.) More and more quickly.

Depressio (It.) (dĕ-*präs*-sē-ō.) The fall of the hand in beating time.

Depression. The lowering of a tone.

Depression, chromatic. The depression of a tone by a chromatic sign.

De profundis (Lat.) (dĕ prō-*fŭn*-dĭs.) One of the seven penitential psalms.

Dérivé (Fr.) (dĕ-rē-vā.) Derivative.

Derivative chords. Chords derived from others by inversion.

Des (Ger.) (dĕs.) The note D flat.

Désaccordé (Fr.) (dāz-ăk-kŏr-dā.) Untuned; put out of tune.

Désaccorder (Fr.) (dāz-ăk-kör-dā.) To untune; to put out of tune.

Descant, Discantus (Lat.) 1. The addition of a part or parts to a tenor or subject. This art, the forerunner of modern counterpoint and harmony, grew out of the still earlier art of diaphony or the organum. In the latter the parts ran in parallel motion, generally in consecutive fifths or fourths, but in descant, oblique and contrary motion of parts began to appear as early as the eleventh or twelfth century. 2. *Descant* or *discant* is the treble or soprano voice. The highest part in the old contrapuntal works, as the old rhyme may show:

" Ye little youths and maidens neat,
We want your voices, high and sweet.
Your study to the Discant bring,
The only part that you should sing."

See *Voice* and *Soprano*.

ō as in *tone*; ō as in *dove*; ŏ as in *not*; ŭ as in *up*; ü the French sound of *u*.

83

Descant clef. The treble or soprano clef.

Descant, double. An arrangement of the parts of a composition that admits of the treble, or any high part, being converted into the bass, and *vice versa*.

Descant, figured. A form of descant consisting of a free and florid melody.

Descant, plain. Simple counterpoint.

Descendant (Fr.) (dĕ-sänh-dänh.) Descending.

Descendere (It.) (dĕ-shĕn-dā-rĕ.) } To descend.
Descendre (Fr.) (dĕ-sänhdr.)

Descendre d'un ton (Fr.) (dĕ-sänhdr d'ŭnh tŏnh.) To sing a note lower.

Des dur (Gr.) (dĕs-door.) D flat major.

Desinvolturáto (It.) (dā-zēn-vŏl-too-*rä*-tō.) See *Disinvolturato*.

Des moll (Ger.) (dĕs mŏll.) The key of D flat minor.

Desperazióne (It.) (dĕs-pĕ-rä-tsē-*ō*-nĕ.) See *Disperazione*.

Dessauer Marsch (Ger.) (*dĕs*-sou-ĕr märsh.) A famous instrumental march; one of the national airs of Germany.

Dessin (Fr.) (dĕs-*sänh*.) The design or sketch of a composition.

Dessiner (Fr.) (dĕs-sĭ-nā.) To make the sketch or design of a composition.

Dessus (Fr.) (dĕs-sü.) The treble, soprano, or upper part.

Desterita (It.) (däs-tĕr-ē-tä.) Dexterity.

Désto (It.) (des-tō.) Brisk, sprightly.

Déstra (It.) (des-trä.) *Right; déstra máno*, the right hand.

Détaché (Fr.) (dā-tä-shāy.) Detached, staccato.

Determinatíssimo (It.) (dā-tĕr-mē-nä-*tēs*-sē-mō.) Very determined; very resolutely.

Determináto (It.) (dā-tĕr-mē-*nä*-tō.) Determined, resolute.

Determinazióne (It.) (dā-tĕr-mē-nä-tsē-ō-nĕ.) Determination, resolution.

Détonnation (Fr.) (dā-tŏnh-*nä*-sē-ŏnh.) False intonation.

Détonner (Fr.) (dā-tŏnh-*nā*.) To sing or play out of tune.

Détto (It.) (*dăt*-tō.) The same.

Deutlich (Ger.) (*doit*-lĭkh.) Distinctly.

Deutsch (Ger.) (Doytsch.) German.

Deutsche Flöte (Ger.) (*doit*-shĕ *flŏ*-tĕ.) A German flute.

Deux (Fr.) (dü.) Two.

Deux fois (Fr.) (dü fwä.) Twice.

Deuxième (Fr.) (dü-zĭ-*ăm*.) Second.

Deuxième position (Fr.) (dü-zĭ-*ăm* pō-*zĕ*-sĭ-onh.) The second position of the hand or fingers in playing the violin, etc.

Development. The elaboration of a theme by making new combinations of its figures and phrases. It forms a most important part in symphony and sonata. See *Durchführung*.

Devóto (It.) (dā-*vō*-tō.) Devout, religious.

Devozióne (It.) (dā-vō-tsē-ō-nĕ.) Devotion; religious feeling.

Dextra (Lat.) (*dĕx*-trä.) } The right hand.
Dextre (Fr.) (dĕxtr.)

Di (It.) (dē.) Of, with, for, from, to.

Dia (Gr.) (dĭ-ä.) Through, throughout.

Diaconicon (Gr.) (dĭ-ä-*kŏn*-ĭ-kŏn.) The set of collects chanted in the service of the Greek church.

Diagramma (Gr.) (dē-ä-*grăm*-mä.) The ancient Greek scale or system of sounds.

Dialogue. A composition in which two parts or voices respond alternately to each other.

Diálogo (It.) (dē-ä-*lō*-gō.) } A dialogue.
Dialogue (Fr.) (dē-ä-*lŏg*.)

Diap. An abbreviation of *diapason*.

Diapase (Gr.) (dē-ă-*pä*-sĕ.) Diapason.

Diapason (Lat.) (dē-ă-*pä*-sŏn.) } 1. *The whole*
Diapason (Eng.) (dĭ-ă-*pā*-sŏn.) *octave*. 2. Among musical instrument makers, a rule or scale by which they adjust the pipes of organs, the holes of flutes, etc., in order to give the proper proportion for expressing the tones and semi-tones. 3. The two foundation stops in an organ (sometimes called *Principal*) — the open diapason and the stopped diapason. Open diapasons on the manuals are nearly always of metal, but on the pedals are often of wood. Stopped diapasons were formerly, in most cases, of wood, but now are frequently made of metal. When two or more open diapasons are on the same manual, they are of different

scales. 4. Fixed pitch; *normal diapason;* a recognized standard of pitch. See *Pitch*.

Diapason, bis. Twice through the octave; a double octave.

Diapason cum diapente (Gr.) An *octave* and *fifth;* the interval of a twelfth.

Diapason cum diatessaron (Gr.) An *octave and fourth;* the interval of an *eleventh.*

Diapason, open. An organ-stop, the pipes of which are open at the top, and generally made of metal.

Diapason, stopped. An organ-stop having its pipes closed at their upper end with a wooden plug.

Diapente (Gr.) (dē-ă-*pĕn*-tĕ.) A perfect *fifth;* also an organ-stop.

Diapente col ditono (Gr.) (dē-ă-*pĕn*-tĕ kŏl dĭ-*tō*-nō.) A major seventh.

Diapente col semiditono (Gr.) (dē-ă-*pĕn*-tĕ kŏl sĕm-ĭ-dĭ-*tō*-nō.) A minor seventh.

Diapentisare (Gr.) (dē-ä-pĕn-tĭ-*sä*-rĕ.) To *descant*, or modulate in fifths.

Diaphonie (dē-*ăf*-ō-nē.) Clear; transparent; two sounds heard together.
Diaphony (dē-*ăf*-ō-ny.)

Diaphonics (Gr.) (dē-ă-*fŏn*-ĭks.) The science of refracted sounds.

Diatessaron (Gr.) (dē-ä-*tĕs*-sä-rŏn.) A perfect fourth.

Diatoni (Lat. pl.) (dē-ä-tō-nĭ.) The natural or diatonic series of notes; the diatonic scale.

Diatonic (Gr.) (dē-ä-*tŏn*-ĭk.) *Naturally;* proceeding in the order of the degrees of the natural scale, including tones and semi-tones.

Diatonic flute. A flute capable of producing the various shades or differences of pitch of the major and minor scales.

Diatonic melody. A melody in which no tones foreign to the key are used.

Diatónico (It.) (dē-ä-*tŏn*-ē-kō.)
Diatonique (Fr.) (dē-ä-tŏnh-*nēk*.) } Diatonic.
Diatonisch (Ger.) (dĭ-ä-*tōn*-ĭsh.)

Diatonic scale. The different gradations of tone of the scale or gamut arranged in proper order in conformity to some particular key.

Diatonic scale, major. Where the semi-tones fall between the third and fourth and seventh and eighth, both in ascending and descending.

Diatonic scale, minor. That in which the semi-tones occur between the second and third and seventh and eighth ascending, and between the fifth and sixth and second and third descending. See *Scale*.

Diatoniquement (Fr.) (dē-ä-tŏnh-*nēk*-mänh.) Diatonically.

Di chiáro (It.) (dēe-kē-*ä*-rō.) Clearly.

Dichord (Ger.) (dĭ-kŏrd.) Two-stringed lyre. See *Bichord*.

Dichten (Ger.) (*dĭhk*-t'n.) To compose metrically.

Dichter (Ger.) (*dĭhk*-tĕr.) A poet; a minstrel.

Di cólto (It.) (dē *kōl*-tō.) At once; instantly; suddenly.

Didactic. That which is calculated to instruct.

Didactic exercises. Scale exercises and compositions designed to give a correct knowledge of musical execution.

Diesáre (It.) (dē-ä-*zä*-rĕ.) } To raise the
Diéser (Fr.) (dĭ-*ăy*-zä.) } pitch of a note, either at the signature or in the course of a composition by means of a sharp.

Dièse (Fr.) (dĭ-āz.) A sharp (♯).

Dièse, double (Fr.) (dĭ-āz doobl.) A double sharp (𝄪).

Diesi (Spa.) (dĭ-ā-zē.) The smallest division of a tone.

Dies iræ (Lat.) (dĭ-āz ē-rā.) A principal movement in a requiem.

Diésis (Gr. and It.) (dē-*ăy*-sĭs.) } The
Diésis (Fr.) (dĭ-*ăy*-sĭs.) } Pythagorean semi-tone (later *Limma*), which is the difference between a fourth and two whole tones = 256:243.2. In modern theory, the difference between an octave and three major thirds, the modern *enharmonic diesis* (128 : 125). In modern music it means a *sharp*. See Pole's *Philosophy of Music*.

Diesis chromatica (Gr.) (dĭ-*ă*-sĭs krō-*măt*-ĭ-kä.) The third part or fraction of a whole tone.

Diesis enharmonica (Gr.) (dĭ-*ă*-sĭs ĕn-här-*mŏn*-ĭ-kä.) A quarter-tone. As an illustration, the difference between G♯

ō as in *tone;* ô as in *dove;* ŏ as in *not;* ŭ as in *up;* ü the French sound of *u*.

85

and A♭, or between D♯ and E♭, on the violin.

Diesis magna (Gr.) (dĭ-*ā*-sĭs *măg*-nä.) A semi-tone.

Dies, music. Steel punches for the purpose of stamping music-plates.

Difficile (It.) (dēf-*fē*-tshē-lĕ.) Difficult.

Di gala (It.) (dē gä-lä.) Merrily, cheerfully.

Digital exercises. Exercises for strengthening the fingers and rendering them independent of each other.

Digitórium. A small portable apparatus for exercising the fingers, resembling a diminutive piano in shape, and having five keys set on strong springs; sometimes called *Dumb Piano.*

Dignitá (It.) (dēn-yē-*tā*.) ⎫
Dignitáde (It.) (dēn-yē-*tä*-dĕ.) ⎬ Dignity, grandeur, greatness.
Dignitáte (It.) (dēn-yē-*tä*-tĕ.) ⎭

Di Grádo (It.) (dē *grä*-dō.) By *degrees;* step by step; in opposition to *di salto.*

Di grádo ascendente (It.) (dē *grä*-dō ä-shĕn-*den*-tĕ.) A series of notes of regular ascent.

Di grádo descendente (It.) (dē *grä*-dō dä-shĕn-*den*-tĕ.) A series of notes descending regularly.

Digressing. Moving from one key into another to return to the first.

Digressione (It.) (dē-grĕs-sē-*ō*-nĕ.) A deviation from the regular course of a piece.

Diiambus (dē-ĭ-*ăm*-bŭs.) A metrical foot consisting of two iambic feet.

Di leggiére (It.) (dē lĕd-jē-*ai*-rĕ.) ⎫
⎬ Easily, lightly.
Di leggiéro (It.) (dē lĕd-jē-*ai*-rō.) ⎭

Dilettant (Ger.) (dē-lĕ-*tänh*.) ⎫ A lover
Dilettánte (It.) (dē-lĕt-*tänh*-tĕ.) ⎬ of art; an amateur who composes or performs without making music a profession.

Dilettosamente (It.) (dē-lĕt-tō-zä-*men*-tĕ.) Agreeably, pleasantly.

Diligénza, con (It.) (dē-lē-*jen*-tsä kŏn.) In a diligent and careful manner.

Diludium (Lat.) (dĭ-*lū*-dĭ-ŭm.) An interlude.

Diluéndo (It.) (dē-lōo-*en*-dō.) Diminishing; a gradual dying away of the tone until it is extinct.

Di ⅃. ⎫
⎬ Abbreviations of *diminuéndo.*
Dimin. ⎭

Dimeter. A poetic measure of four feet; a series of two meters.

Diminished. This word is applied to intervals or chords, which are less than minor or perfect intervals.

Diminished chords. Chords that have a diminished interval between their highest and lowest notes.

Diminished fifth. An interval containing two whole tones and two semi-tones.

Diminished fourth. One whole tone and two semi-tones.

Diminished imitation. A style of imitation in which the answer is given in notes of less value than that of the subject.

Diminished intervals. Those which are one semi-tone less than minor or perfect intervals.

Diminished octave. One semi-tone less than a full octave.

Diminished seventh. One semi-tone less than a minor seventh.

Diminished sixth. One semi-tone less than a minor sixth.

Diminished third. One semi-tone less than a minor third.

Diminished triad. A chord composed of the minor third, and the diminished or imperfect fifth.

Diminué (Fr.) (dĭ-mēn-oo-ay.) Diminished. See *Diminuíto.*

Diminuéndo (It.) (dē-mē-noo-*en*-dō.) Diminishing gradually the intensity or power of the tone.

Diminuer (Fr.) (dĭ-mē-noo-ā.) To diminish.

Diminuíto (It.) (dē-mĭ-noo-*ē*-tō.) ⎫ Diminished, lessened, in speaking of intervals or chords.
Diminuto (Lat.) (dē-mē-*noo*-tō.) ⎬
⎭

Diminutio (Lat.) (dĭm-ĭ-*nū*-shĭ-ō.) Diminution.

Diminution. In counterpoint this means the imitation of a given subject or theme, in notes of shorter length or

ä as in *ah*; ā as in *hate*; ă as in *at*; ē as in *tree*; ĕ as in *eh*; ī as in *pine*; ĭ as in *pin*;

duration; in opposition to *augmentation*.

Diminuzióne (It.) (dē-mē-noo-tsē-ō-nĕ.) Diminution.

Di molto (It.) (dē mōl-tō.) *Very much;* an expression which serves to augment the meaning of the word to which it is applied.

D in alt (It.) The fifth note in alt.

D in altissimo (It.) The fifth note in altissimo.

D'inganno (It.) (d'ēn-gän-nō.) An unexpected ending.

Di nuóvo (It.) (dē noo-ō-vō.) Anew; once more; again.

Dioxia. A perfect fifth; the fifth tone or sound.

Diphonium. A vocal duet.

Di pósta (It.) (dē pōs-tä.) At once.

Di quieto (It.) (dē quē-ä-tō.) Quietly.

Direct. A mark sometimes placed at the end of a staff; a phrase or figure to indicate the note next following (𝐰)

Directeur (Fr.) (dĭ-rĕk-tŭr.) The director or conductor of a musical performance.

Direct intervals. Intervals reckoned from their fundamental tones upward, on which any kind of harmony may be produced.

Direct motion. Similar or parallel motion; the parts rising or falling in the same direction.

Dirge. A musical composition, either vocal or instrumental, designed to be performed at a funeral, or in commemoration of the dead.

Diritta (It.) (dē-rēt-tä.) Direct; straight on, in ascending or descending intervals.

Dirizzatóre (It.) (dē-rēt-tsä-tō-rĕ.) A director.

Dis (Ger.) (dēs.) The note D ♯.

Disaccentáto (It.) (dēz-ät-tshĕn-tä-tō.) Unaccented.

Di salto (It.) (dē-säl-tō.) By *leaps* or by *skips;* in opposition to *di grádo*.

Disarmonichíssimo (It.) (dēz-är-mō-ni-kĭs-si-mō.) Extremely discordant.

Disarmónico (It.) (dēz-är-mō-nē-kō.) Inharmonious, discordant.

Discant. The upper part. See also *Descant*.

Discant-schlüssel (Ger.) (dĭz-känt-shlü-s'l.) The soprano clef; the C clef placed upon the first line—the note upon that line being called C.

Discantist (Ger.) (dĭs-kän tĭst.) Treble, or soprano singer.

Discant-saite (Ger.) (dĭs känt sī tĕ.) Treble string.

Discant-sänger (Ger.) (dĭs-känt-säng-ĕr.) Treble, or soprano singer.

Discantus (Lat.) (dĭs-kän tŭs.) Descant.

Discendere (It.) (dē-shän-dā-rĕ.) To descend.

Disciólto (It.) (di-shē-ōl-tō.) Skilful, dexterous.

Disconcórdia (It.) (dis-kŏn-kōr-dē-ä.) Discord.

Discord. A dissonant or inharmonious combination of sounds. In strict harmony it requires to be resolved or proceed to a concord in order to satisfy the ear.

Discordánte (It.) (dis-kōr-dän-tĕ) Discordant.

Discordanteménte (It.) (dis-kōr-dän-tĕ-men-tĕ.) Discordantly.

Discordánza (It.) (dis-kōr-dän-tsä.) Discord.

Discordare (It.) (dis-kōr-dä-rĕ.) ⎫ To be
Discorder (Fr.) (dis-kōr-dä.) ⎭ out of tune.

Discorde (Fr.) (dĭs-kŏrd.) ⎫ Dis-
Discordia (Lat.) (dĭs-kŏr-dĭ-ä.) ⎭ cord.

Discord, prepared. Where the ear has been prepared for the discordant note in a previous concord.

Discréto (It.) (dis-krä-to.) Discreetly.

Discrezióne (It.) (dis-krät-tsē-ō-nĕ.) Discretion, judgment, moderation.

Dis-diapason (Gr.) (dēz-dē-ă-pă-sŏn.) A double octave; an interval of two octaves; a fifteenth.

Dis-dis (Ger.) (diss-diss.) D 𝄪, also called *disis*.

ȏ as in *tone;* ô as in *dove;* ŏ as in *not;* ŭ as in *up;* ü the French sound of *u*.

DISINVÓLTO

Disinvólto (It.) (diz-ēn-*vōl*-tō.)
Disinvolturáto (It.) (diz-ēn-vŏl-too-*rä*-tō.)
Offhand; bold; not forced; naturally.

Disjunct. A term applied by the Greeks to those tetrachords where the lowest sound of the upper one was one degree higher than the acutest sound of the one immediately beneath it.

Disjunct degree. Where two notes form the interval of a third or any greater interval.

Disjunct succession. A succession of sounds passing from one degree to another, without touching the intermediate degrees.

Dis moll (Ger.) (dĭs mōl.) The key of D ♯ minor.

Disonare (It.) (dez-ō-*nä*-rĕ.) To sound discordantly.

Di soppiano (It.) (dē sōp-pē-ä-nō.) Low; with a low voice.

Di sopra (It.) (dē sō-prä.) Above.

Disperáto (It.) (dēz-pĕ-*rä*-tō.) With desperation.

Disperazióne (It.) (dēz-pĕ-rät-sē-*ō*-nĕ.) Despair, desperation.

Dispersed harmony. Harmony in which the notes forming the various chords are separated from each other by wide intervals.

Dispondee. In Greek and Latin poetry, a double spondee, comprising four long syllables.

Disposition. The arrangement of the stops in an organ, disposing them according to power, quality of tone, etc.

Dissonance. A discord; an interval or chord displeasing to the ear and requiring to be followed by another in which the dissonant note is resolved.

Dissonant. An inharmonious combination of sounds.

Dissonant chords. All the chords except the perfect concord and its derivatives.

Dissonant (Fr.) (dis-sō-nänh.)
Dissonánte (It.) (dis-sō-nän-tĕ.)
Dissonant; out of tune; discordant.

Dissónant sixths. The diminished and superfluous sixths.

DITONUS

Dissonanz (Ger.) (dĭs-sō-*nänts*.)
Dissonánza (It.) (dis-sō-*nän*-tsä.)
Dissonance, discord.

Dissonáre (It.) (dis-sō-*nä*-rĕ.) To sound out of tune.
Dissoner (Fr.) (dis-sō-*nā*.)

Distance. The interval between any two sounds differing in pitch.

Distánza (It.) (dēz-*tän*-tsä.) Distance; space between.

Distich. A couplet; a couple of verses, or poetic lines, making complete sense. See *Couplet*.

Distínto (It.) (dēs-*tēn*-tō.) Clear; distinct.

Distique (Fr.) (dĭs-*tēk*.) A distich.

Distonáre (It.) (dis-tō-*nä*-rĕ.) To be out of tune.

Distoniren (Ger.) (dĭs-tō-*nē*-r'n.) To get out of tune; to produce discord either in singing or playing.

Dital. A key which on being pressed raises the pitch of the guitar string a semi-tone.

Di testa (It.) (dē *tes*-tä.) Of the head; in speaking of the voice.

Dithyrambe (Fr.) (dē-tĭ-*rähmb*.)
Dithyrambe (Ger.) (dē-tĭ-*räm*-bĕ.)
A song or ode sung in ancient times in honor of Bacchus; a wild rhapsodical composition.

Dithyrambic (Gr.) (dē-thĭ-*răm*-bĭk.) A song in honor of Bacchus; any poem written in a wild rhapsodical manner.

Dithyrambique (Fr.) (de-tĭ-ränh-*bēk*.)
Dithyrambisch (Ger.) (dē-tĭ-*räm*-bĭsh.)
Dithyrambic.

Dithyrambus (dĭ-thĭ-*răm*-būs.) See *Dithyrambe*.

Ditirámbica (It.) (dē-te-*räm*-bē-kä.)
Ditirámbico (It.) (dē-tē-*räm*-bē-kō.)
Dithyrambic.

Ditirámbo (It.) (dē-tē-*räm*-bo.) See *Dithyrambe*.

Díto (It.) (*dē*-tō.) The finger.

Diton (Fr.) (dē-tŏnh.)
Ditone (Gr.) (dē-tōn.)
Dítono (It.) (dē-tō-nō.)
Ditonus (Lat.) (dĭ-*tō*-nŭs.)
Of two parts or tones; a major third or interval of two whole tones. A Pythagorean major third of two greater

ä as in *ah*; ā as in *hate*; ă as in *at*; ē as in *tree*; ĕ as in *eh*; ī as in *pine*; ĭ as in *pin*;

88

DITROCHEE — DOLCÉZZA

whole tones (81 : 64); wider by a comma than a true major third (5 : 4).

Ditrochee. A double trochee; a foot made up of two trochees.

Ditty. A song; a little poem to be sung.

Divertiménto (It.) (dē-věr-tē-*men*-tō.) A short, light composition, written in a pleasing and familiar style; a series of airs and dances introduced between the acts or at the conclusion of an opera; also, an instrumental composition like the suite, of several short movements in contrast.

Divertissement (Fr.) (dee-ver-*tiss*-mänh.) See *Divertimento*.

Divided accompaniment. A form of accompaniment in which the intervals are taken by both hands.

Divísi (It.) (di-vē-zē.) Divided, separated. In orchestral parts this word implies that one-half the performers must play the upper notes and the others the lower notes. The term has a similar meaning when it occurs in vocal music.

Division. A series of notes sung to one syllable. Formerly this word implied a sort of variation upon a given subject. The performance of this style of music is called *running* a division:

HANDEL.

To ev - er last - - - - - - - - ing.

Division (Fr.) (dĭ-vē-zē-ŏnh.) A double bar.

Division du temps (Fr.) (dĭ-vē-zē-ŏnh dü tänh.) Time-table.

Division marks. Figures with a curved line above them, showing the number of equal parts into which the notes are divided, ⌒3, ⌒5, ⌒7, ⌒9, etc.

Divotaménte (It.) (dē-vō-tä-*men*-tĕ.)
Divóto (It.) (dē-vō-to.) Devoutly; in a solemn style.

Divozione (It.) (dē-vot-tsē-ō-ně.) Devotion; religious feeling.

Dixième (Fr.) (dēz-ĭ-*ām*.) The *tenth*, or octave to the third.

D. M. The initals of *Destra Máno*, generally written M. D.

D moll (Ger.) (dā-mŏll.) The key of D minor.

Do (It.) (dō.) A syllable applied to the first note of a scale in solfaing. In the "fixed Do" system, Do is always C, but in the "movable Do," it always represents the key-note, whether that note is C or not. In the "tonic-sol-fa" system it is movable and is spelt "Doh." See *Tonic Sol-fa*, and *Aretinian Syllables*.

Doctor of music. The highest musical degree conferred by the universities. This degree is not conferred in Germany. See *Grove's Dictionary*, article "Degrees in Music."

Dodedachordon (Gr.) (dō-děd-ä-*kŏr*-dŏn.) The twelve ancient modes.

Dóglia (It.) (*dōl*-yē-ä.) Grief, affliction, sadness.

Doigt (Fr.))dwä.) Finger.

Doigté (Fr.) (dwä-tāy.) Fingered.

Doigter (Fr.) (dwä-tāy.) To finger; the art of fingering any instrument.

Doigts fixes (Fr.) (dwä fēk-sě.) Fixed fingers.

Dol. An abbreviation of *dolce*.

Dolcan. An organ-stop of 8-foot scale the pipes of which are of larger diameter at the top than at the bottom. The dulciana.

Dólce (It.) (*dōl*-tshě.) Sweetly, softly, delicately.

Dólce con gústo (It.) (*dōl*-tshě kŏn *goos*-tō.) Softly; sweetly; with taste and expression.

Dólce e cantabile (It.) (*dōl*-tshě ā kän-*tĭ* bě-lě.) Sweet; soft; in singing style.

Dólce e lusingándo (It.) (*dōl*-tshě ā loc sēn-*gän*-dō.) In a soft and insinuating style.

Dólce maniéra (It.) (*dōl*-tshě mä-nē-*ā*-rä.) A delicate and expressive manner of delivery.

Dolceménte (It.) (dōl-tshě-*men*-tě.) Sweetly, gently, softly.

Dolcézza (It.) (dōl-*tshet*-zä.) Sweetness; softness of tone.

ō as in *tone*; ŏ as in *dove*; ŏ as in *not*; ŭ as in *up*; ü the French sound of *u*.

DOLCIÁNO

DORIC MODE

Dolciáno (It.) (dōl-tshē-ä́-nō.) ⎱ A small
Dolcíno (It.) (dōl-*tshē*-nō.) ⎰ bassoon, formerly much used as a tenor to the oboe. A reed-stop (8 or 16-foot tone) in the organ.

Dolcimello (It.) (dōl-tshē-*mel*-lō.) A dulcimer.

Dolciss. An abbreviation of *dolcissimo*.

Dolcissimo (It.) (dōl-*tshis*-sē-mō.) With extreme sweetness and delicacy.

Dolent (Fr.) (dō-länh.) ⎱ Sorrowful,
Dolénte (It.) (dō-*len*-tĕ.) ⎰ mournful, pathetic.

Dolenteménte (It.) (dō-lān-tĕ-*men*-tĕ.) Sorrowfully, mournfully.

Dolentíssimo (It.) (dō-len-*tēs*-sē-mō.) With extreme sadness; with very pathetic and mournful expression.

Dolóre (It.) (dō-*lō*-rĕ.) Grief, sorrow.

Dolorosaménte (It.) (dō-lō-rō-zä-*men*-tĕ.) ⎫
Doloróso (It.) (dō-lō-*rō*-zō.) ⎭ Dolorously, sorrowfully, sadly.

Dom (Ger.) (dōm.) A cathedral.

Dom-chor (Ger.) (*dōm*-kōr.) The cathedral choir.

Dominant. The name applied by theorists to the *fifth* note of the scale.

Dominant chord. A chord found on the dominant or *fifth* note of the scale and introducing a perfect cadence.

Dominante (Fr.) (dŏm-ĭ-nänht.) ⎱ The
Dominante (Ger.) (dŏm-ĭ-*nän*-tĕ.) ⎰ dominant.

Dominant harmony. Harmony on the dominant or *fifth* of the key.

Dominant section. A section terminating on the common chord of the dominant.

Domine salvum fac (Lat.) (dō-mĭ-nĕ *săl*-vŭm făk.) A prayer for the reigning sovereign, sung after Mass.

Dominicali psalmi (Lat.) (dō-mĭ-nē-*kä*-lē săl-mē.) Certain psalms of the Roman Catholic Church, sung in the vespers.

Dom-kirche (Ger.) (*dōm kēr*-khĕ.) A cathedral.

Dona nóbis pacem (Lat.) (dō-nä *nō*-bĭs pä-sĕm.) The concluding movement of the Mass.

Dónna (It.) (*dōn*-nä.) Lady; applied to the principal female singers in an opera.

Dónne (It. pl.) (*dōn*-nĕ.) Ladies. See *Dónna*.

Dópo (It.) (*dō*-pō.) After.

Doppel (Ger.) (*dŏp*-p'l.) Double.

Doppel-be (Ger.) (*dŏp*-p'l bā.) A double flat (♭♭); lowering a note two semitones.

Doppel-flöte (Ger.) (*dŏp*-p'l *flŏ*-tĕ.) *Double flute;* a stop in an organ the pipes of which have two mouths. It is of 8-foot tone.

Doppel-fuge (Ger.) (*dŏp*-p'l *foo*-ghe.) Double fugue.

Doppelgeige (Ger.) (*dŏp*-p'l *ghī*-ghĕ.) An organ-stop. See *Viola d'Amour*.

Doppelgriffe (Ger.) (*dŏp*-p'l-*grĭf*-fĕ.) Double-stop on the violin, etc.

Doppelkreuz (Ger.) (*dŏp*-p'l-kroitz.) A double sharp ⨯ or ×, raising a note two semitones.

Doppelschlag (Ger.) (*dŏp*-p'l-shläg.) A turn.

Doppelschritt (Ger.) (*dŏp*-p'l-shrit.) A quick march.

Doppelt (Ger.) (*dŏp*-p'lt.) Double.

Doppelten Noten (Ger.) (*dŏp*-p'l-tĕn *nō*-t'n.) Double notes.

Doppelzunge (Ger.) (*dŏp*-p'l *tsoon*-ge.) Double-tongueing on flutes and brass wind-instruments.

Doppia lyra (It.) (*dŏp*-pē-ä *lē*-rä.) A double lyre.

Dóppio (It.) (*dōp*-pē-ō.) Double; two-fold; sometimes indicating that octaves are to be played.

Dóppio moviménto (It.) (*dōp*-pē-ō mō-vĕ-mĕn-tō.) Double-movement, or time, that is, *twice as fast*.

Dóppio pedále (It.) (*dōp*-pē-ō pĕ-*dä*-lĕ.) Playing a bass passage on the organ with the pedals moving in octaves, etc.; that is, using both feet at the same time.

Dóppio tempo (It.) (*dōp*-pē-ō *tĕm*-pō.) Double-time; *as fast again.*

Dorian (Gr.) (dō-rĭ-ăn) ⎱ The name of
Dorien (Fr.) (dō-rĭ-änh.) ⎰ one of the ancient modes or scales.

Doric mode. The first of the authentic Greek modes.

ă as in *ah*; ā as in *hate*; ă as in *at*; ē as in *tree*; ĕ as in *eh*; ī as in *pine*; ĭ as in *pin*;

90

Dossologia (It.) (dŏs-sō-*lō*-jē-ä.) Doxology.

Dot. A mark, which when placed *after* a note increases its duration one-half. When the dot is placed *over* a note it signifies that the note is to be played *staccáto*.

Dot, double. Two dots placed after a note to increase its duration three-fourths of its original value.

Dots. When placed at the side of a bar, or double bar, they show that the music on that side is to be repeated.

Dotted double bar. A double bar with dots preceding it, indicates that the preceding strain is to be repeated; when the dots are *after* the double bar, it shows that the following strain is to be repeated. A double bar with dots both sides indicates that both the preceding and following strains are to be repeated.

Double (Fr.) (*doo*-bl.) The old name for a *variation*; used by Handel, Scarlatti, etc.

Double A, or AA. In England, the term *double* is applied to all those bass notes from G to F inclusive.

Double-action harp. A harp with pedals, by which each string can be raised two semi-tones.

Double after-note. Two after-notes taking their time from the previous note.

Written   Played

Double appoggiatura. A union of two short grace-notes.

Double bar. Two thick strokes drawn down through the staff, to divide one strain or movement from another.

Double-bass. The largest and deepest toned of all bow-instruments. See *Contra-bass*.

Double-bassoon. A large bassoon the sounds of which are an octave deeper than the bassoon; also, a 16 or 32-foot organ-reed stop, of smaller scale and softer tone than the double trumpet.

Double bémol (Fr.) (bā-mōl.) Double-flat.

Double chant. A simple harmonized melody in four strains or phrases, and extending to *two* verses of a psalm or canticle.

Double chorde (Fr.) (doobl kŏrd.) Playing one and the same note, on the violin, upon two strings at once.

Double counterpoint. A counterpoint which admits of the parts being inverted.

Double croche (Fr.) (doobl krōsh.) *Double-hooked;* a sixteenth note.

Doubled. A term applied when one of the notes of a chord is repeated in a different part of the same chord.

Double-demisemiquaver. A note equal in duration to one-half of a demisemiquaver; a sixty-fourth note. It is written thus:

Double-descant. Where the treble or any high part can be converted into the bass, and *vice versa*.

Double diapason. An organ-stop tuned an octave below the diapasons. It is called a 16-foot stop on the manuals; on the pedals it is a 32-foot stop.

Double dièse (Fr.) (doobl dīäz.) A double sharp ✕.

Doubled letters. Capital letters doubled, indicating that the tone is an octave lower than where the letters stand single.

Double flat. A character (♭♭) which, placed before a note, signifies that it is lowered two semi-tones.

Double flute. A flute so constructed that two tones may be produced from it at the same time; a stop in an organ See *Doppel Flöte*.

Double fugue. A fugue on two subjects.

Double G. Contra G; the lowest G on the pianoforte. In England the term *double* is applied to all those bass notes from G to F inclusive:

Double hautboy. A 16-foot reed-organ stop of small scale.

Double lyre. The *Lyria Doppia*; an old instrument of the viol kind.

Double note. A breve; a note twice the length of a whole note.

Double octave. An interval of two octaves; a fifteenth.

ŏ as in *tone*; ô as in *dove*; ŏ as in *not*; ŭ as in *up*; ü the French sound of *u*.

91

Double quartet. A composition written for eight instruments or voices.

Double reed. The mouth-piece of the hautboy, bassoon, etc., formed of two pieces of cane joined together.

Doubles. An old term for variations. See *Double*.

Double sharp. A character which, when placed before a note, raises that note two semi-tones. It is usually written as follows : ⨯ or x.

Double sonata. A sonata composed for two instruments concertante; as, the pianoforte and violoncello.

Double-stopped diapason. An organ-stop of 16-foot tone on the manuals ; the pipes are stopped or covered at the top.

Double-stopping. The stopping of two strings simultaneously with the fingers in violin playing. The practice was first suggested by John Francis Henry Biber, in 1681.

Double suspension. A suspension that retards two notes and requires a double preparation and resolution.

Double tierce. An organ-stop tuned a tenth above the diapasons, or a major third above the principal.

Double-time. A time in which every measure is composed in two equal parts. It is marked by letting the hand fall and rise alternately.

Double-tongueing. A method of articulating quick notes used by flute players, and on brass instruments. The tongue is moved in quick alternation from the upper front teeth to the hard palate and back, producing a rapid staccato.

Double trill. Two trills played simultaneously.

Double triplet. The union of two triplets ; thus, a double triplet is often erroneously written as a sextolet. See *Notes, Grouping, Sextolet*.

Double trumpet. An organ-stop of 16-foot scale; sometimes the lowest octave of pipes is omitted, and it is then called the *Tenoroon* trumpet.

Double twelfth. An organ-stop, sounding the fifth above the foundation-stops; it is generally composed of stopped pipes.

Doublette (Fr.) (doob-*lĕt*.) A compound organ-stop, consisting of two ranks, generally a twelfth and fifteenth.

Doucement (Fr.) (*doos*-mänh.) Sweetly, softly, pleasingly.

Douleur (Fr.) (doo-*lŭr*.) Grief, sorrow, pathos.

Douloureusement (Fr.) (doo-loor-üs-mänh.) Plaintively, sorrowfully.

Douloureux (Fr.) (doo-loor-üh.) Sorrowful, tender, plaintive.

Doux (Fr.) (dooz.) Sweet, soft, gentle.

Douzième (Fr.) (doo-zhǐ-*ăm*.) A twelfth.

Down beat. The falling of the hand or baton in beating or marking time.

Down bow sign. A sign used in violin music indicating that the bow is to be drawn down; thus, ⊓.

Doxologia (Lat.) (dŏx-ō-*lō*-jǐ-ä.) } Dox-
Doxologie (Fr.) (dŏx-*ŏl*-ō-zhē.) } ology.

Doxology. A form of praise sung in divine service, usually at the close of a prayer, psalm, or hymn; the Gloria Patri, used at the end of the psalms in the Christian Church ; also any metrical form of the same.

Draht-saite (Ger.) (*drät-sī*-tĕ.) Music wire; wire string.

Dramatic. A term applied to music written for the stage and to instrumental music that conveys a definite story or picture; program music.

Dramaticamente (It.) (drä-mä-tē-kä-mĕn-tĕ.)
Dramatiquemente (Fr.) (drä-mä-tēk-mänht.)
Dramatically.

Dramatique (Fr.) (drä-mä-*tēk*.) } Dra-
Dramatisch (Ger.) (drä-*mä*-tǐsh.) } matic.

Dramatis personæ (Lat.) (*dra*-mă-tǐs pĕr-*sō*-nē.) The characters of an opera or play.

Drame (Fr.) (dräm.) } A drama.
Drámma (It.) (*dräm*-mä.) }

Drámma lírico (It.) (drä-mä-*lī*-rē-kō.) }
Drámma per musica (It.) (drä-mä pär *moo*-zē-kä.) }
An opera or musical drama.

Drammaticaménte (It.) (dräm-mä-tē-cä-*men*-tĕ.) Dramatically; in a declamatory style.

Drammático (It.) (dräm-*mä*-tē-kō.) Dramatic.

Draw-stops. In an organ, stops placed on each side of the rows of keys by moving which the player opens or closes the stops within the organ.

Dreh-orgel (Gr.) (*drā*-ōrg'l.) Barrel organ.

Dreher (Ger.) (*drā*-ĕr.) A slow waltz, or German dance.

Drei (Ger.) (drī.) Three.

Dreifach (Ger.) (*drī*-fäkh.) Three-fold, triple.

Dreigesang (Ger.) (*drī*-ghĕ-*säng*.) For three voices; a trio.

Dreiklang (Ger.) (*drī*-kläng.) A triad; a chord of three sounds.

Dreimal (Ger.) (*drī*-mäl.) Thrice.

Dreisang (Ger.) (*drī*-säng.) }
Dreispiel (Ger.) (*drī*-spēl.) } A trio.

Dreist (Ger.) (drīst.) Brave, bold, confident.

Dreistigkeit (Ger.) (*drīs*-tĭg-kīt.) Boldness, confidence, resolution.

Dreistimmig (Ger.) (*drīs*-tĭm-mĭg.) Three-voiced.

Dringend (Ger.) (*drĭng*-ĕnd.) Pressing.

Drítta (It.) (*drĭt*-tä.) } Right; *máno*
Drítto (It.) (*drĭt*-tō.) } *drítta*, the right hand.

Drítte (Ger.) (*drĭt*-tĕ.) Third.

Driving notes. An old term applied to a passage consisting of long notes placed between shorter notes in the same measure and accented contrary to the usual and natural flow of the rhythm; a syncopation.

Drohne (Ger.) (*drō*-nĕ.) A heavy tone; a drone.

Droite (Fr.) (drwät.) Right; *main droite*, the right hand.

Drone. The largest of the three tubes of the bagpipe. It only sounds one deep note, which answers as a perpetual bass to every tune. *Drone-oass*, a bass on the tonic, or tonic and dominant, which is persistent throughout a movement or piece, as in the *Musette*.

Drönen (Ger.) (*drö*-nĕn.) To give a low, dull sound; to drone.

Drum. An instrument of percussion formed of a cylinder made of thin wood or metal, over each end of which is drawn a skin, tightened by means of cords. There are three kinds of drums; 1. The bass drum, held laterally and played with a stuffed knob drumstick. 2. The side-drum having two heads, the upper one only being played upon by two sticks of wood, the lower head has occasionally strings of catgut stretched over its surface, and then it is called a *snare-drum*. 3. The kettledrum, always employed in pairs.

Drum, bass. A large drum used in military bands.

Drum, kettle. A bass drum of a cup-like shape, over the top of which the parchment head is stretched. These drums are used in pairs, one being tuned to the key-note and the other generally to the fifth of the key. The compass of the larger kettle-drum, called the G drum, is between And of the smaller, or C drum, between so that the two drums overlap each other in compass by a tone. The tuning is effected by tightening or loosening the head or skin by means of a ring of metal moved by screws turned by a key. Many devices have been invented by which the tuning can be rapidly effected by a single screw. Such improved kettledrums are called *machine drums*. In the modern orchestra three kettledrums are often used. It must be borne in mind that the kettledrums give definite pitch, which the other drums do not. See Prout's "The Orchestra," or Arthur Elson's "Orchestral Instruments." The different names for the drums in orchestral scores are: 1. the side-drum or military drum (Ger. *Trommel;* Fr. *Tambour Militaire;* It. *Tambura;*) 2. The bass drum, or long drum (Ger. *Grosse Trommel;* Fr. *Grosse Caisse;* It. *Gran Cassa*, or *Gran Tamburo;*) 3. The kettledrum (Ger. *Pauken;* Fr. *Timbales;* It. *Timpani.*)

Drum, snare. The small drum, so called on account of having strings of twisted hide or catgut, drawn over its lower head, and to distinguish it from the bass drum; the side-drum.

Drum, side. The common drum, the snare-drum.

D. S. The initials of *Dal Segno*.

ŏ as in *tone;* ô as in *dove;* ŏ as in *not;* ŭ as in *up;* ü the French sound of *u.*

Dudelkasten (Ger.) (*doo*-d'l-käs-t'n.) Barrel organ; a hurdy-gurdy.

Dudelkastensack (Ger.) (*doo*-d'l-käst'n-säk.) A bagpipe, a cornemuse; a hornpipe.

Dudeln (Ger.) (*doo*-d'ln.) To play on the bagpipe; also a contemptuous term for playing badly on the flute, etc.

Dudelsack (Ger.) (*doo*-d'le-sakh.) The bagpipe.

Dúe (It.) (doo-ĕ.) Two; in two parts.

Dúe clarini (It.) (doo-ĕ klä-*rē*-nē.) Two trumpets.

Dúe córde (It.) (doo-ĕ *kōr*-dĕ.) Two strings. See *A due Corde*.

Dúe córi (It.) (doo-ĕ *kō*-rē.) Two choirs or choruses.

Dúe pedáli (It.) (doo-ĕ pĕ-*dä*-lē.) The two pedals are to be used.

Duet. A composition for two voices or instruments.

Duett (Ger.) (doo-ĕt.) A duet.

Duette (Ger. pl.) (doo-*ĕt*-tĕ.) } Duets.
Duetti (It. pl.) (doo-ĕt-tē.) }

Duettíno (It.) (doo-ĕt-*tēe*-nō.) A short and easy duet.

Duétto (It.) (doo-*et*-tō.) A duet.

Dúe volte (It.) (*doo*-ĕ *vōl*-tĕ.) Twice.

Dulcian (Fr.) (dül-sē-änh.) A small bassoon; an organ-stop. See *Dolciáno*.

Dulciana-stop. An 8-foot organ-stop of a soft and sweet quality of tone.

Dulciana principal. A 4-foot organ-stop of delicate tone.

Dulcimer. An instrument usually of a triangular shape, the strings of which are struck with little rods held in each hand. The name of an ancient Hebrew instrument, the qualities of which we are ignorant, but probably of the wind species.

Dumb piano. An instrument like a small piano in form, having a key-board of narrow compass, but neither hammers nor strings; intended for silent finger practice, *i.e.*, merely for increasing the mechanical dexterity of the fingers.

Dumka (Bohem.) (*doom*-kah.) A dirge, an elegy, or a funeral song. It has been introduced into the symphony by Dvorák. It possibly gave rise to the early English slow dance called the *dump* or *dumpe*, and mentioned by Shakespeare.

Dump or Dumpe. The name of an old dance in slow time with a peculiar rhythm. It is doubtful whether it was entirely "dull and heavy," or merely the slowness of the measure that made the title of the dance synonymous with wearisomeness, whence the saying — "In the Dumps." The dumpe was usually in $\frac{4}{4}$ rhythm. See Elson's "Shakespeare in Music."

Dumpf (Ger) (doompf.) } Of a dull,
Dumpfig (Ger.) (*doomp*-fīg.) } hollow, muffled sound.

Dumpfigkeit (Ger.) (*doomp*-fīg-kīt.) Hollowness; dullness of sound.

Dúo (It.) (*doo*-ō.) Two; in two parts; a composition for two voices or instruments; a duet.

Duo concertante (It.) (*doo*-ō kŏn-tshĕr-tän-tĕ.) A duo in which each part is alternately principal and subordinate.

Duodécima (It.) (doo-ō-*de*-tshē-mä.) }
Duodécimo (It.) (doo-ō-*de*-tshē-mō.) }
The twelfth; the twelfth note from the tonic; the name is also applied to an organ-stop tuned a twelfth above the diapasons.

Duodecima acuta (Lat.) (dū-ō-*dĕs*-ē-mä ă-*kū*-tä.) A twelfth above.

Duodecima gravi (Lat.) (dū-ō-*dĕs*-ē-mä *grä*-vē.) A twelfth below.

Duodecimóle (It.) (doo-ō-dĕ-tshē-*mō*-lĕ.) A musical figure formed by a group of twelve notes.

Dúodene. A 12-tone group applied to the solution and correction of problems in temperament and harmony. A *duodénal* is the symbol of the root-tone of a duodene. See Stainer & Barrett's Dictionary, and Ellis' translation of Helmholtz's "Sensations of Tone."

Duodrámma (It.) (doo-ō-*dräm*-mä.) A kind of melodrama in which only two persons act and sing.

Duólo (It.) (*dwō*-lō.) Sorrow, sadness, grief.

Duómo (It.) (*dwō*-mō.) A cathedral.

Dupla (Lat.) (doo-plä.) Double.

Duple time. Double time.

Duplex longa (Lat.) (dū-plĕx *lŏn*-gä.)

ā as in *ah* · ă as in *hate*; ă as in *at*; ē as in *tree*; ĕ as in *eh*; ī as in *pine*; ĭ as in *pin*;

Maxima, one of the notes in the old system of music 𝄺.

Duplication. Doubling; where one or more of the intervals of a chord are repeated in different parts.

Duplo (It.) (doo-plō.) Double.

Dur (Ger.) (door.) *Major*, in speaking of keys and modes; as C *dur*, C *major*.

Dur (Fr.) (dür.) Hard; harsh of tone.

Durale (It.) (doo-rä-lĕ.) Hard, harsh, sharp.

Duraménte(It.)(doo-rä-*men* tĕ) Harshly; roughly; also meaning that the passage is to be played in a firm, bold style and strongly accented.

Durchcomponiren (Ger.) (*doorkh*-kōm-pō-*nē*-r'n.) To set a song, through all its stanzas, to music, without repetitions of the same tune to each verse; the art-song form.

Durchdringend (Ger.) (doorkh-*drĭng*-ĕnd.) Penetrating, piercing.

Durchführung (Ger.) (*doorkh*-fü-roong.) Development. The term means "carrying-out," and is applied to the working-out of figures in a sonata-allegro form. It forms one of the chief divisions in a sonata. It is the chief intellectual point of classical music.

Durchgang (Ger., *doorch*-gang; Lat., *transitus*.) The "passage" or progression of one principal tone to another through a tone or tones foreign to the harmony or key... *Durchgangston*, passing-tone; changing-tone.

Durchgängig (Ger.) (*doorkh*-gäng-ĭg.) }
Durchgänglich (Ger.) (*doorkh*-gäng-likh.) }
Throughout.

Durchgehend (Ger.) (*doorkh*-gä-ĕnd.) Passing; transient; passing through, as *Durchgehender Akkord*, passing-chord; *durchgehende Stimmen*, complete organ-stops; *i.e.*, extending through the manual.

Durchschallen (Ger.) (doorkh-*shäl*-l'n.) To sound through; to penetrate with sound.

Durchschlagend (Ger.) (*doorkh*-shlä-gĕnd.) A term applied to some organ-stops, indicating that they extend through the whole compass of the manual; it also signifies a *free reed*-stop.

Durchspielen (Ger.) (*doorkh*-spē-l'n.) To play to the end.

Durchtrillen (Ger.) (*doorkh*-trĭl-l'n.) To trill from beginning to end.

Durée (Fr.) (dü-*rā*.) Length; duration of notes.

Durement (Fr.) (dür-mänh.) Hard, harsh.

Dureté (Fr.) (dü-rĕ-*tā*.) See *Duráte*.

Durézza (It.) (doo-*ret*-zä.) Hardness· harshness of tone or expression.

Dúro (It.) (*doo*-ro.) Rude, harsh.

Düster (Ger.) (düs-tĕr.) Gloomy.

Dux (Lat.) (dŭx.) *Leader; guide;* the subject, or leading phrase of a fugue.

Dynamics. This term in music has reference to expression and the different degrees of power to be applied to notes.

E

E called in France and Italy *mi;* the third note of the scale of C.

E. Ed (It.) *And.*

E. The smallest and most acute string on the violin and guitar.

Ear. A "musical ear" consists in the power of appreciating and distinguishing aerial vibrations both simple and compound, just as "the good eye for color" consists in the power of appreciating and distinguishing the simple and compound vibrations of light. See *Stainer & Barrett;* Blaserna's "Sound and Music"; Tyndall "On Sound."

Ebollimento or **Ebollizione** (It.) (eh-bol-litz-ee-*o*-neh.) Boiling over; sudden expression of passion.

Eccheggiánte (It.) (ĕk-kĕd-jē-*än*-tĕ.) Resounding; echoing.

Eccheggiáre (It.) (ĕk-kĕd-jē-*ä*-rĕ.) To resound; to echo.

Ecclésia (It.) (ĕk-*klā*-zē ä.) Church.

Ecclesiastical. A term applied to all music written for the church.

Ecclesiastical modes. See *Church Modes.*

Ecclesiastico stilo (It.) (ĕk-klā-zē-*äs*-tē-kō stē-lō.) In the church or ecclesiastical style

Echeggiare (It.) (ĕ-kĕd-jē-*ä*-rĕ.) To echo; to resound.

Échelle (Fr.) (āshĕll.) The scale, or gamut.

ŏ as in *tone*; ô as in *dove*; ŏ as in *not*; ŭ aꞋ in *up*; ü the French sound of *u.*

Échelle chromatique (Fr.) (e-shĕll krō-mät-*eek.*) The chromatic scale.

Échelle diatonique (Fr.) (e-shĕll dī-ä-tŏnh-*eek.*) The diatonic scale.

Échelon (Fr.) (āsh-ĕ-lŏnh.) (Step, or degree of the scale.

Écho (Fr.) (ā-kō.) 1. In music, this term means a repetition, or imitation of a previous passage, with much less force than the original passage. In old organ music the use of this term signified that a passage so marked was to be played upon the echo-organ, a set of pipes enclosed in a box, by which a soft and distant effect was produced, incapable, however, of so great expression as that obtained by the use of the *swell*, which is an improvement upon the echo-organ. 2. Echo-stop on a harpsichord was a contrivance for obtaining a soft and distant effect.

Echo cornet. An organ-stop, the pipes of which are of small scale, with a light, delicate tone. It is usually placed in the swell.

Echometre. An instrument for measuring the powers of echoes and other sounds.

Echometry. The art of measuring the duration of sounds.

Éclat (Fr.) (ā-*klä.*) With dash; brilliancy; an outburst.

Éclatante (Fr.) (ā-klä-*tänht.*) Piercing, loud.

Éclisses (Fr.) (ā-klēss.) The sides or hoops of a violin, guitar, etc.

Ecloga (Spa.) (ĕk-*lō*-ga.) ⎫ An eclogue,
Eclogue (Gr.) (ĕk-lōg.) ⎭ selection, choice.

Eclogue or Eglogue (from Greek, to select.) A pastoral; a poem, or song, in which shepherds and shepherdesses are the actors.

Eco (It.) (*ā*-kō.) An echo; the repetition of a previous passage in a softer tone.

École (Fr.) (ā-kōl.) A school; a method or course of instruction; a style formed by some eminent artist.

École de chant (Fr.) (ā-kōl dŭh shänh.) A singing-school.

Écolier (Fr.) (ā-kō-lĭ-ā.) A pupil.

Écossais (Fr.) (ā-kŏs-*sā.*) ⎫ Scotch; a
Écossaise (Fr.) (ā-kŏs-*sāz.*) ⎭ dance, tune,

or air, in the Scotch style. A contradance of lively tempo in $\frac{2}{4}$ rhythm.

Ecossäse (Ger.) (ā-kŏs-*sā*-zē.) See *Ecossaise*.

Ed (It.) (ād.) And.

Edel (Ger.) (āy-del). Noble and distinguished.

E dur (Ger.) (ā door.) The key of E major.

Effet (Fr.) (ĕf-fā.) ⎫ Effect; the effect
Effétto (It.)(ĕf-*fet*-to.) ⎭ of music upon an audience.

Également (Fr.) (ā-gäl-mänh.) Equally, evenly, smoothly.

Égalité (Fr.) (ā-gäl-ĭ-*tā.*) Equality, evenness.

Église (Fr.) (ā-*glēz.*) Church.

Egloga (It.) (*ăl*-yō-gä.) ⎫ An eclogue;
Églogue (Fr.) (ā-*glōg.*) ⎭ a pastoral poem.

Eguagliánza (It.) (ā-gwäl-yē-*änt*-sä.) Equality, evenness.

Eguále (It.) (ā-*gwä*-lĕ.) Equal; even; alike; also applied to a composition for several voices or instruments of one kind, as, male voices only, female voices only, trombones only.

Egualézza (It.) (ā-gwä-*let*-zä.) Equality, evenness.

Egualménte (It.) (ā-gwäl-*men*-tĕ.) Equally, evenly, alike.

Eighth. An octave.

Eilen (Ger.) (*ī*-len.) To hasten; accelerate; go faster ... *Eilend*, hastening; *accelerando, stringendo* ... *Eilig*, hasty; in a hurried style; rapid; swift.

Ein (Ger.) (īn.) ⎫
Eine (Ger.) (*ī*-nĕ.) ⎭ A, an, one.

Einblasen (Ger.) (*īn*-blä-z'n.) To blow into.

Einen (Ger.) (*ī*-nĕn.) A, one.

Einfach (Ger.) (*īn*-fäkh.) Simple, plain, ornamented.

Einfacher choral (Ger.) (*īn*-fäkh-ĕr kō-*räl.*) Plain choral, without variation or ornament.

Eingang (Ger.) (*īn*-gäng.) Introduction, preface, prelude.

Eingang der Messe (Ger.) (*īn*-gäng dĕr *mĕs*-sĕ.) The entrance or beginning of a Mass; the introit.

ă as in *ah*: ā as in *hate*; ă as in *at*; ē as in *tree*; ĕ as in *eh*; ī as in *pine*; ĭ as in *pin*;

96

Eingangs-schlüssel (Ger.) (*īn*-gängs-shlüs-s'l.) Introductory key.

Eingestrichen (Ger.) (*īn*-ghĕ-strĭ-kh'n.) Note of the treble marked with *one stroke*. This refers to the octave from middle C to the B above.

Eingestrichene Octave (Gr.) (*īn*-ghĕ-strĭ-kh'n-ĕ ŏk-*tä*-fĕ.) The notes from middle C to the B above, both inclusive:

Einglied (Ger.) (*eyn*-glēd.) *One-linked* or *one chord*, in speaking of sequences.

Einhällig (Ger.) (*eyn*-hāl-līg.) Unison, harmonious.

Einhalt (Ger.) (*eyn*-hält.) A pause.

Einhalten (Ger.) (*eyn*-häl-t'n.) To pause.

Einhauchen (Ger.) (*eyn*-hou-kh'n.) To breathe into.

Einheit (Ger.) (*eyn*-hīt.) Unity.

Einhelfen (Ger.) (*eyn*-hĕl-f'n.) To prompt.

Einhelfer (Ger.) (*eyn*-hĕl-fĕr.) Prompter.

Einigen (Ger.) (*eyn*-ni-ghĕn.) Some, any.

Einigkeit (Ger.) (*eyn*-nig-kīt.) Concord, harmony, unity.

Einklang (Ger.) (*eyn*-klăng.) Consonance, harmony.

Einklingen (Ger.) (*eyn*-klĭng-ĕn.) To accord.

Einlage (Ger.) (*eyn*-lohge.) An inserted piece; an interpolation.

Einlaut (Ger.) (*eyn*-lout.) Monotonous.

Einleitung (Ger.) (*eyn*-lī-toong.) Introduction, prelude.

Einleitungs-satz (Ger.) (*eyn*-lī-toongs-sätz.)

Einleitungs-spiel (Ger.) (*eyn*-lī-toongs-spēl.)
Introductory movement; overture, prelude.

Einmal (Ger.) (*eyn*-mäl.) Once.

Einmüthigkeit (Ger.) (*eyn*-mü-tig-kīt.) Concord, unanimity.

Einsang (Ger.) (*eyn*-säng.) A solo.

Einschlafen (Ger.) (*eyn*-shlä-f'n.) To die away; to slacken the time and diminish the tone; to fall asleep.

Einschmeichelnd (Ger.) (*eyn*-shmī-khĕlnd.) Flattering, insinuating.

Einschnitt (Ger.) (*eyn*-shnĭt.) A phrase, or incomplete musical sentence.

Einstimmen (Ger.) (*eyn*-stĭm-m'n.) To agree in tune; to be concordant; to join in.

Eistimmener Gesang (Ger.) (*eyn*-stĭm-mĕ-nĕr ghĕ-*säng*.) A solo.

Einstimmigkeit (Ger.) (*eyn*-stĭm-mĭg-kīt.) A concord, agreement.

Eintönig (Ger.) (*eyn*-tô-nĭg.) Monotonous.

Eintracht (Ger.) (*eyn*-träkht.) Concord, unity.

Einträchtig (Ger.) (*eyn*-trĕkh-tĭg.) Concordant, harmonious.

Einträchtigkeit (Ger.) (*eyn*-trĕkh-tĭg-kīt.) Concordance, harmony.

Eintretend (Ger.) (*eyn*-trä-tĕnd.) Entering, beginning.

Eintritt (Ger.) (*eyn*-trĭt.) Entrance, entry, beginning.

Eis (Ger.) (īs.) The note E sharp.

Eisis. E double sharp.

Eisteddfod (Welsh.) A bardic congress; an assemblage of bards.

Ela. The name originally given to the highest note in the scale of Guido.

Electric piano. A piano invented in 1851, the wires of which were vibrated by electromagnetism. Another version of the electric piano is said of by Baker's Dictionary: "It was invented in 1891 by Dr. Eisenmann, of Berlin. Over each unison of strings an electromagnet is fixed; on closing the circuit (by depressing a digital) each magnet attracts its strings, and (the magnetic action being duly controlled and limited by a set of microphones) causes their continuous vibration. Tone (of the improved instrument) full, sweet, capable of the most various dynamic shading, timbre like that of the string orchestra; the ordinary hammer-action may be employed alone, or in combination with the above. A peculiar (sustaining) pedal-mechanism permits a given tone, a full chord, or any harmony, to sound on as long as desired, even after lifting the fingers. Newer electric pianos abound, most notably the Rhodes and the Wurlitzer.

ŏ as in *tone*; ô as in *dove*; ŏ as in *not*; ŭ as in *up*; ü the French sound of *u*

Élégamment (Fr.) (ĕl-ā-găm-mähn.) }
Elegantemènte (It.) (ĕl-ā gän-tĕ-*men*-tĕ.) Elegantly, gracefully.

Elegánte (It.) (ĕl-ā-*gän*-tĕ.) Elegant, graceful.

Elegánza (It.) (ĕl-ā-*gän*-tsä.) Elegance, grace.

Elegía (It.) (ĕl-ā-jē-ä.) An elegy, or monody; music of a mournful or funereal character.

Elegiac. Plaintive, mournful, sorrowful.

Elegiáco (It.) (ĕl-ā-jē-*ä*-kō.) }
Élégiaque (Fr.) (ĕl-ā-zhĭ-*ăk*.) } Mournful, plaintive, elegiac.

Élégie (Fr.) (ĕl-ā-zhē.) An elegy.

Elegy. A mournful or plaintive poem, or a funeral song.

Elementary music. Exercises and studies specially adapted to beginners in the study of music.

Élémens (Fr.) (ĕl-ā-mänh.) }
Eleménti (It.) (ĕl-ĕ-*men*-tĕ.) } The rudiments, or elements, of musical science.

Elements. The first or constituent principles or parts of anything; the principles or rudiments of musical science.

Eleutheria (Gr.) (ĕ-lū-*thā*-rĭ-ä.) A festival of liberty; a song or hymn of liberty.

Elevaménto (It.) (ĕl-ĕ-vä-*men*-tō.) }
Elevatezza (It.) (ĕl-ĕ-vä-*tet*-zä.) } Grandeur; sublimity; loftiness of expression.

Elevatio (Lat.) (ele-*vah*-teeo.) The upbeat; the arsis; also the *elevation*.

Elevation. A motet or organ piece played or sung, in the Catholic service during the elevation of the Host, in the Mass.

Eleváto (It.) (ĕl-ĕ-*vä*-tō.) Elevated, exalted, sublime.

Elevazióne (It.) (ĕl-ĕ-vä-tsē-*ō*-nĕ.) Elevation, grandeur.

Élève (Fr.) (ā-*lāv*.) A pupil.

Eleventh. An interval comprising an octave and a fourth.

Élever (Fr.) (ā-lĕ-vā.) To raise or lift up the hand in beating time.

Elf (Ger.) (ĕlf.) Eleven.

Elfte (Ger.) (*ĕlf*-tĕ.) Eleventh.

Éloge (Fr.) (ā-*lōzh*.) }
Elogio (Spa.) (ā-*lō*-hĭ ō.) } Praise, eulogy.

Elogy. See *Eulogy*.

Embellir (Fr.) (änh-bĕl-*lēr*.) To embellish; to adorn; to ornament.

Embellissement (Fr.) (änh-bĕl-lēss-mŏnh.) Embellishment.

Embellishments. Ornament, decoration, notes added for the purpose of heightening the effect of a piece. See *Trill, Turn, Mordent, Appoggiatura, Acciacatura, Grace-notes.*

Embouchure (Fr.) (änh-boo shoor.) The mouth-piece of a flute, oboe, horn, or other wind-instrument; that part to which the lips are applied to produce the sound. It also refers to the position which the mouth must assume in playing the instrument. Also called *Lip.*

Émérite (Fr.) (ĕ-mār-ēt.) Said of a professor who has honorably retired from the duties of his profession.

Émettre (Fr.) (ĕ-*metr*.) To utter sounds.

E moll (Ger.) (ā mōll.) The key of E minor.

Emozióne (It.) (ĕm-ōt-sē-*ō*-nĕ.) Emotion, agitation.

Empâter les sons (Fr.)(änh-pă-tā lĕ sŏnh.) To sing or play in a masterly manner, without defects or imperfections. To produce a very smooth legato.

Empfindsam (Ger.) (ĕm-*pfĭnd*-säm.) Sensitive, sentimental.

Empfindung (Ger.) (ĕmp-*fĭn*-doong.) Emotion, passion, feeling.

Emphase (Ger.) (ĕm-*fä*-zĕ.) Emphasis.

Emphatique (Fr.) (änh-fä-*tĕk*.) }
Emphatisch (Ger.) (ĕm-*fä*-tĭsh.) } Emphatical.

Emphatiquement (Fr.) (änh-fä-*tĕk*-mänh.) Emphatically.

Emphasis. Particular stress or accent on any note, indicated thus: > ∧ fz., sf., etc.

Emphasize. To sing with marked accent.

Empito (It.) (ĕm-*pē*-tō.) Impetuosity.

Empituosaménte (It.) (ĕm-pē-twō-zä-*men*-tĕ.) Impetuously.

Emplumer (Fr.) (änh-plü-mā.) To *pen*, or put quills into the *jacks* of a spinet, etc.

ä as in *ah*; ā as in *hate*; ă as in *at*; ē as in *tree*; ĕ as in *eh*; ī as in *pine*; ĭ as in *pin;*

Franz Peter Schubert

Das Wandern.

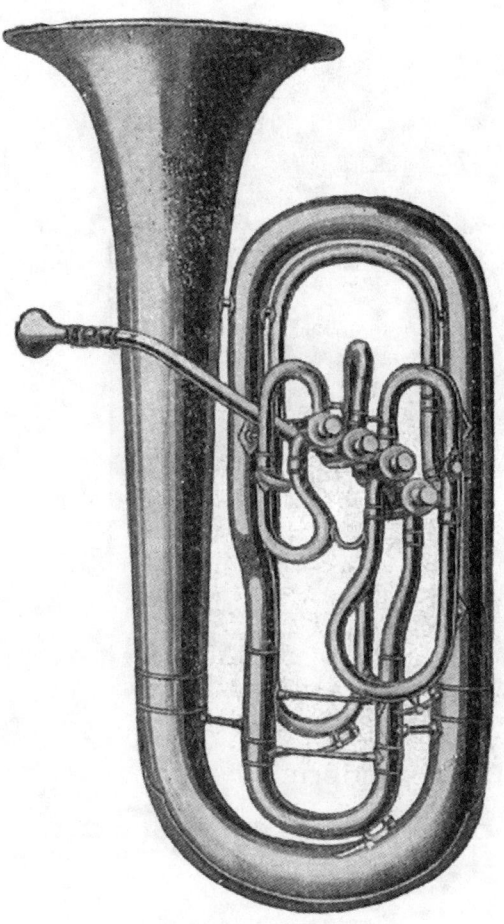

Euphonium

English Horn

Emporté (Fr.) (änh-pŏr-tā.) Passionate; hurried; carried away.

Emportement (Fr.) (änh-pŏrt-mänh.) Passion, transport.

Empressé (Fr.) (änh-prĕs-sā.) In haste, eager, hurried.

Empressement (Fr.) (änh-prĕss-mänh.) Eagerness, zeal.

En (Fr.) (änh.) In.

En accélérant (Fr.) (änh năk-sā-lā-ränh.) Accelerating.

En chantant (Fr.) (änh shänh-tänh.) In a singing style.

En chœur (Fr.) (änh kür.) In a chorus.

Encore (Fr. *ong-cor*; It. *Ancora*.) Again; a demand for the reappearance of a performer; the piece sung or played on the reappearance of the performer.

Ende (Ger.) (*ĕnd*-ĕ.) End; conclusion; concluding piece.

En descendant (Fr.) (änh dĕ-sänh-*dänh*.) In descending.

En diminuant la force (Fr.) (änh dĭ-mēn-oo-änh lä fōrs.) Diminishing the force of the tone.

Energeticaménte (It.) (ĕn-ĕr-jā-tē-kä-*men*-tĕ.) Energetically, forcibly.

Energético (It.) (ĕn-ĕr-*jā*-tē-kō.) Energetic; with emphasis.

Energía (It.) (ĕn-ĕr-jē ä.) } Energy,
Énergie (Fr.) (ĕn-ĕr-zhē.) } force, emphasis.

Energicaménte (It.) (ĕn-ĕr-jē-kä-*men*-tĕ.) Energetically, forcibly.

Enérgico (It.) (ĕn-*är*-jē-kō.) Energetic, vigorous, forcible.

Énergique (Fr.) (ĕn-ĕr-*zhēk*.) } Ener-
Energisch (Ger.) (en-*är*-ghĭsh.) } getic; with emphasis.

Énergiquement (Fr.) (ĕn-ĕr-zhēk-mänh.) Energetically, forcibly.

Enfant de chœur (Fr.) (änh-fänh dūh kür.) Singing boy.

Enfasi (It.) (ĕn-fä zē.) Emphasis; earnestness.

Enfaticaménte (It.) (ĕn-fä-tē-kä-*men*-tĕ.) Emphatically.

Enfático (It.) (ĕn-*fä*-tē-kō.) Emphatical; with earnestness.

Enfiataménte (It.) (ĕn-fē-ä-tä-*men*-tĕ.) Proudly, pompously.

Enfler (Fr.) (änh-*flā*.) To swell; to increase the tone.

Enge (Ger.) (ĕng-ĕ.) Close, condensed, compressed; this term is applied to the *stretto* in a fugue. In speaking of organ-pipes, it means narrow, straight.

Enge Harmonie (Ger.) (ĕng-ĕ här-mō-*nē*.) Contracted, or close harmony, the intervals or sounds being close together.

English fingering. In pianoforte music the use of a sign (×) to designate the thumb, in distinction from the German fingering, where the thumb is designated as the first finger. It is often erroneously called *American* fingering. In 1571, according to Ammerbach's "Orgel oder Instrument Tablatur," the fingers were marked "0, 1, 2, 3, 4," in Germany, and this continued for more than a century. At that period England often marked the fingers, " 1, 2, 3, 4, 5," so that the German fingering really began in England, and the English fingering" in Germany. The "English fingering" of the present was chiefly established by Clementi and Dussek, in the last part of the eighteenth century. See *Fingering*.

English horn. A species of oboe, a fifth lower than the instrument usually designated by that name. It sounds a fifth lower than its notation, and, since in such a case the scale of C sounds the F scale, it is said to stand in the key of F. Its tone-color is melancholy and tender, and it is also used by modern composers to represent a shepherd's pipe. Wagner, Schumann, Rossini, etc., have thus employed it. It is a double-reed instrument. See *Cor Anglais*.

Enguichure (Fr.) (änh-ghē-*shūr*.) The mouth-piece of a trumpet.

Enharmonic (Ger.) (ĕn-här-*mōn*-ĭk.) One of the ancient scales or modes, proceeding by quarter-tones. On the pianoforte these cannot be expressed; but on the violin, cello, etc., they may be described as something like the difference between G♯ and A♭, or between D♯ and E♭, etc. In modern music it also means such a change in the nature of an interval or chord, as can be effected by merely altering the notation of one or more notes, thus:

ō as in *tone*; ô as in *dove*; ŏ as in *not*; ŭ as in *up*; ü the French sound of *u*.

ENHARMONIC CHANGE — ENTRÁRE

Enharmonic change. A passage in which the notation is changed, but the same keys of the instrument are employed:

[musical notation] etc.

Enharmonic diesis (Lat.) (ĕn-här-*mōn*-ĭk dĭ-*ā*-sĭs.) The difference between the greater and lesser semi-tone; the least sensible interval in music.

Enharmonic genus. A style of melody constructed from a scale of tones nominally about one-fourth as far from each other as those of the common diatonic scale.

Enharmonic intervals. Such as have only a nominal difference; for instance, the minor third C, E♭, and the extreme second, C, D♯; or, the augmented fifth, C, G♯, and the minor sixth, C, A♭, etc.

Enharmonic keys. They include (in the pianoforte) the same notes, and have the same scales, but under different names; for instance, the scales of F♯ and G♭: — B and C♭: — D♯ and E♭: — E♯ and F, etc.

Enharmonic modulation. A modulation produced by altering the notation of one or more intervals belonging to some chord, and thus changing the key into which the chord would naturally have resolved.

Enharmonic organ. An organ in which the octave, instead of being limited to a division of twelve intervals, contains from seventeen to twenty-four. An organ giving the propositions of intervals demanded by nature and not the compromise pitch known as "Equal Temperament." Such an organ was recently invented by a Japanese gentleman named Tanaka.

Enharmonic relation. The relation existing between two chromatics, when, by the elevation of one and depression of the other, they are united into one.

Enharmonic scale. A scale proceeding by quarter-tones.

Enharmonicus (Lat.) (ĕn-här-*mōn*-i-kŭs.) ⎫
Enharmonique (Fr.) (änh-när-mŏnh-*ēk*.) ⎬ Enharmonic.
Enharmonisch (Ger.) (ĕn-här-*mōn*-ish.) ⎭

Enjoué (Fr.) (änh-zhoo-ā.) Cheerful, gay.
Enjouement (Fr.) (änh-zhoo-mönh.) Cheerfulness, gaiety.
Enlever (Fr.) (änh-lĕ-vā.) To lift up the hand in beating time.
En mesure (Fr.) (änh me-süre.) In time; *a tempo.*
Énoncer (Fr.) (ā-nŏhn-sā.) To enunciate; to proclaim.
Énonciation (Fr.) (ā-nŏnh-sē-*ä*-sē-ŏnh.) Enunciation, declaration.
En passant (Fr.) (änh păs-sänh.) In passing; by the way.
En ralentissant (Fr.) (änh răl-länh-tēs-sänh.) Slackening the time.
En rondeau (Fr.) (änh rŏnh-*dō*.) In the style of *a rondeau.*
Enseignement (Fr.) (änh-sān-mänh.) Instructions.
Enseigner (Fr.) (änh-sān-yā.) To instruct; to teach.
Ensemble (Fr.) (änh-*sänh*-bl.) *Together; the whole;* applied to concerted music when the whole is given with perfect smoothness of style. It means precision of attack; unity of shading. A *morceau d'ensemble* is a composition for two or more parts, more especially quintets, sextets, septets, etc., in an opera, oratorio, or similar work.
Entgegen (Ger.) (ĕnt-*gā*-gh'n.) ⎫ Contrary;
Entgegengesetzt (Ger.) (ĕnt-*gā*-g'n-ghĕ-*sĕtzt*.) ⎬ opposite, speaking of motion.
Enthousiasme (Fr.) (änh-too-zē-äsm.) ⎫
Enthusiasmus (Ger.) (ĕn-too-zē-*äz*-moos.) ⎬
Enthusiasm.
Enthusiastisch (Ger.) (ĕn-too-zē-*äs*-tĭsh.) Enthusiastically.
Entoner (Fr.) (änh-tŏ-nā.) ⎱ To begin
Entonner (Fr.) (ähn-tŏnh-nā.) ⎰ to chant; to begin to sing; to intone.
Entr' acte (Fr.) (änh-tr' äkt.) Between the acts; music played between the acts of a drama.
Entránte (It.) (ĕn-trän-tĕ.) ⎫ An entrance;
Entráta (It.) (ĕn-*trä*-tä.) ⎬ trance;
Entráda (It.) (ĕn-*trä*-dä.) ⎭ introduction; prelude.
Entráre (It.) (ĕn-*trä*-rĕ.) To enter; to begin.

ă as in *ah*; ā as in *hate*; ă as in *at*; ē as in *tree*; ĕ as in *eh*; ī as in *pine*; ĭ as in *pin*:

100

Entrée (Fr.) (änh-*trā*.) Entry, entrance, beginning.

Entremets (Fr.) (änh-trĕ-mā.) Movements introduced for the sake of variety. Short allegorical or dramatic musical scenes.

Entries. Name formerly given to operatic scenes, burlettas, etc.

Entscheidung (Ger.) (ĕnt-*shī*-doong.) Decision, determination.

Entschieden (Ger.) (ĕnt-*shēe*-d'n.) Decided; in a determined manner.

Entschlafen (Ger.) (ĕnt-*shlä*-f'n.) To die away; to diminish.

Entschliessung (Ger.) (ĕnt-*shlēes*-soong.) Resolution, determination.

Entschlossen (Ger.) (ĕnt-*shlōs*-s'n.) Determined, resolute.

Entschlossenheit (Ger.) (ĕnt-*shlōs*-s'n-hīt.) Resoluteness, firmness.

Entschluss (Ger.) (ĕnt-*shlooss*.) Resolution.

Entusiasmo (It.) (ĕn too-zē-äs-mō.) Enthusiasm.

Entwurf (Ger.) (ĕnt-*woorf*.) Sketch; outline of a composition.

Enunciáre (It.) (ā-noon-tshē-*ä*-rĕ.) To enunciate; to declare; to proclaim.

Enunciatíva (It.) (ā-noon-tshē-ä-*tē*-vä.) Enunciation, declaration.

Enunciáto (It.) (ā-noon-tshē-*ä*-tō.) Enunciated, proclaimed.

Enunciazione (It.) (ā-noon-tshē-ät-sē-*ō*-nĕ.) Enunciation, declaration.

Eólia (It.) (ā-*ō*-lē-ä.) } One of the
Eolian (Gr.) (ĕ-*ō*li-ăn.) } most ancient
Eolien (Fr.) (ā-ō-lē-änh.) } modes. See *Greek Modes*.

Eolique (Fr.) (ā-ō-*lēk*.) Eolic. See *Eolian*.

Eoli harpe (Fr.) (ā-ō-lē härp.) The Æolian harp.

Epic. A poem in the heroic, narrative style.

Epicaménte (It.) (ĕp-ē-kä-*men*-tĕ.) In the epic style.

Epicédio (It.) (ĕp-ē-*tshā*-dē-ō.) } An elegy,
Epicedion (Gr.) (ĕp-ĭ-*sā*-dĭ-ŏn.) } dirge, funeral song, or ode.

Epico (It.) (ĕp-ē-kō.) Epic, heroic.

Epilogue. A speech or short poem addressed to the spectators by one of the actors, after the conclusion of the play. A concluding piece.

Episode. An incidental narrative or digression. A portion of a composition not founded upon the principal subject or theme. An accessory part of a composition, as contrasted with the themes and their development. An intermediate division. The parts of a fugue that intervene between the repetitions of the main theme.

Episodicaménte (It.) (ĕp-ē-sō-dē-kä-*men*-tĕ.) In the manner of an episode.

Episódico (It.) (ĕp-ē-*sō*-dē-kō.) Episodic, digressive.

Episódio (It.) (ĕp-ē-*sō*-dē-ō.) Episode, digression.

Episodisch (Ger.) (ĕp-ĭ-*sō*-dĭsh.) In the manner of an episode.

Epistrophe (Ger.) (ĕp-ĭ-*strō*-fĕ.) A repetition of the concluding melody.

Epitalámio (It.) (ĕp-ē-tä-*lä*-mē-ō.) } Epithalamium.

Epithalme (Fr.) (ĕp-ĭ-tăl-mĕ.) }

Epithalamion (Gr.) (ĕp-ĭ-thă-*lä*-mĭ-ŏn.) } A marriage song;
Epithalamium (Gr.) (ĕp-ĭ-thă-lä-mĭ-ŭm.) } a nuptial
Epithalamium (*Eng.*) }
Epithalamy (*Eng.*) } song, or ode.

Epitonium (Lat.) (ĕp-ĭ-*tō*-nĭ-ŭm.) A tuning hammer; a peg or pin to which the strings of an instrument are fastened.

Epitrite (Gr.) (ĕp-ĭ-*trī*-tĕ.) A metrical foot consisting of three long syllables and one short.

Epode (Gr.) (ĕp-*ō*-dĕ.) Conclusion of a chorus; a short lyric poem.

Epode. In lyric poetry, the third or last part of the ode; that which follows the strophe and anti-strophe. The word is now used for any little verse or verses, that follow one or more great ones; thus, a pentameter after a hexameter is an epode.

E pói (It.) (ā pō-ē.) And then.

E pói la coda (It.) (ā pō-ē lä kō-dä.) And then the coda.

Epopee (Gr.) (ĕp-ō-pā.) An epic poem.

Epopeja (It.) (ĕp-ō-*pā*-yä.) } An
Epopeya (Spa.) (ĕp-ō-pā-yä.) } epic or heroic poem.

Epos (Gr.) (ĕp-*ōz*.)

ŏ as in *tone*; ô as in *dove*; ŏ as in *not*; ŭ as in *up*; ü the French sound of *u*.

101

Equábile (It.) (ĕ-quä-bē-lĕ.) Equal, alike, uniform.

Equabilménte (It.) (ĕ-quä-bēl-men-tĕ.) Equally, smoothly, evenly.

Equal counterpoint. A composition in two, three, four, or more parts, consisting of notes of equal duration.

Equal temperament. That equalization, or tempering of the different sounds of an octave which renders them all of an equal degree of purity; the imperfection being divided among the whole. The division of the octave into *twelve equal semi-tones*. See *Temperament*.

Equal voices. Compositions in which either all male or all female voices are employed.

Equisonant. Of the same or like sound; a unison. In guitar music the term is used to express the different ways of stopping the same note.

Equísono (It.) (ā-quē-zō-nō.) Having the same sound.

Erhaben (Ger.) (er-hä-b'n.) Elevated; sublime; in a lofty and exalted style.

Erheben (Ger.) (er-hā-b'n.) To raise; to elevate; to lift up the hand in beating time.

Erhebung (Ger.) (er-hā-boong.) Elevation; raising the hand in beating time.

Erhöhen (Ger.) (er-hŏ-ĕn.) See *Erheben*.

Erhöhung (Ger.) (er-hŏ-oong.) See *Erhebung*.

Erhöhungs-zeichen (Ger.) (ĕr-hŏ-oongs-tsī-kh'n.) An expression for raising a note a semi-tone.

Erklingen (Ger.) (er-klĭng-ĕn.) To ring; to resound.

Erlehren (Ger.) (er-lā-r'n.) To acquire by teaching.

Ermattet (Ger.) (er-maht-tet.) Wearied, exhausted.

Ermunterung (Ger.) (er-moon-tĕ-roong.) Animation, excitement.

Erniedrigung (Ger.) (er-nē-drĭ-goong.) The depression of a note by means of a flat or natural.

Erniedrigungs-zeichen (Ger.) (er-nēd-rĭ-goongs-tsī-kh'n.) A flat, or other sign for lowering a note a semi-tone.

Ernst (Ger.) (ārnst.) } Earnest;
Ernsthaft (Ger.) (ārnst-häft.) } serious; in a grave and earnest style.

Ernsthaftigkeit (Ger.) (ārnst-häf-tĭg-kīt.) Earnestness, seriousness.

Ernstlich (Ger.) (ārnst-līkh.) Earnest, serious, grave.

Ernstlichkeit (Ger.) (ārnst-līkh-kīt.) Earnestness.

Erntelied (Ger.) (ārn-tĕ-lēd.) Harvest song.

Eröffnung (Ger.) (er-ŏf-noong.) Opening, beginning.

Eröffnungs-stück (Ger.) (er-ŏf-noongs-stük.) Overture; prelude; opening piece.

Eroico (Gr.) (ĕr-ō-ĭ-kō.) Heroic.

Erotic (ĕr-ŏt-ĭk.) An amorous composition, or poem.

Erotical (ĕr-ŏt-ĭ-kăl.) Pertaining to love.

Erótica (It.) (ĕr-ō-tē-kä.) Love songs; amatory ditties.

Erotic songs. Love songs.

Erst (Ger.) (ārst.) First.

Erstemal (Ger.) (ārs-tĕ-mäl.) First time.

Ersterben (Ger.) (er-ster-b'n.) To die away.

Ertönen (Ger.) (er-tŏ-nĕn.) To sound; to resound.

Erweckung (Ger.) (er-vĕk-oong.) Animation, excitement.

Erweitert (Ger.) (er-vī-tĕrt.) Expanded, developed, extended.

Erzähler (Ger.) (ert-szā-ler.) The *Narrator* or *Evangelist* in a Passion Play or Passion Music.

Es (Ger.) The note E flat.

Esátta (It.) (ĕz-ät-tä.) Exact, strict.

Esátta intonazióne (It.) (ĕz-ät-tä in-tō-nät-sē-ō-nĕ.) Exact intonation.

Es dur (Ger.) (āz door.) The key of E flat major.

Esecutóre (It.) (ĕz-ā-koo-tō-rĕ.) A performer.

Esecuzióne (It.) (ĕz-ā-koot-sē-ō-nĕ.) Execution; facility of performance.

Esecutríce (It.) (ĕz-ā-koo-tree-tshĕ.) A female performer.

Eseguire (It.) (ĕz-ā-gwē-rĕ.) To execute, or perform, either vocally or on an instrument.

Esémpio (It.) (ĕz-em-pē-ō.) Example.

Esercízio (It.) (ĕz-ār-tshĕt-sē-ō.) An exercise; a study.

ä as in *ah*; ā as in *hate* ă as in *at*; ē as in *tree*; ĕ as in *eh*; ī as in *pine*; ĭ as in *pin*;

ESERCIZI ETUI

Esercizi (It. pl.) (ĕz-ār-*tshĕt*-sē.) } Exercises.
Esercizj (It. pl.) (ĕz-ār-*tshĕt*-sē.) }
Es es (Ger.) (āz āz.) The note E doubleflat (E♭♭).
Esitaménto (It.) (ĕz-ē-tä-*men*-tō.) } Hesitation.
Esitazióne (It.) (ĕz-ē-tät-sē-ō-nĕ.) }
Es moll (Ger.) (āz mōll.) The key of E flat minor.
Esonáre (It.) (ĕz-ŏr-*nä*-rĕ.) To adorn; to embellish.
Espace (Fr.) (ĕs-*päs*.) A space; the interval between two lines of the staff.
Espagnol (Fr.) (ĕs-păn-*yōl*.) } Spanish; in the Spanish style.
Espagnuólo (It.) (ĕs-pän-yoo-ō-lō.) }
Espagnuola, all' (It.) (ĕs-pän-yoo-ō-lä.) In the Spanish style.
Espansione (It.) (*ĕs*-pän-sē-ō-nĕ.) With breadth; expansion.
Espirándo (It.) (ĕs-pe-*rän*-dō.) Breathing deeply; gasping.
Espr. } Abbreviations of *Espressivo*.
Espress. }
Espressióne (It.) (ĕs-pres-sē-ō-nĕ.) Expression, feeling.
Espressívo (It.) (ĕs-pres-*sēe*-vō.) Expressive; to be played or sung with expression.
Esquisse (Fr.) (ess-*quisse*.) A sketch.
Essai (Fr.) (ĕs-*sā*.) An essay; a trial.
Essential harmonies. The three harmonies of the key; tonic, dominant, and subdominant.
Essential notes. The real, component notes of a chord; in contradistinction to all merely accidental, passing, or ornamental notes.
Essential seventh. The dominant seventh.
Essodio (It.) (ĕs-*sō*-dē-ō.) Interlude.
Estemporále (It.) (ĕs-tĕm-pō-*rä*-lĕ.) }
Estemporáneo (It.) (ĕs-tām-pō-*rä*-nē-ō.) } Extemporaneous.
Estinguéndo (It.) (ĕs-tēn-*guen*-dō.) }
Estínte (It.) (ĕs-*tēn*-tĕ.) }
Estínto (It.) (ĕs-*tēn*-tō.) }
Becoming extinct; dying away in time and strength of tone; extinguished.
Estravagánte (It.) (ĕs-träv-ä-*gän*-tĕ.) }
Estravagánza (It.) (ĕs-träv-ä-*gänt* sä.) }
Extravagant; a fanciful and extravagant work.

Estremaménte (It.) (ĕs-trā-mä-*men*-tĕ.) Extremely.
Estrinienda (It.) (ĕs-trē-nē-*en*-dä.) A close, binding style of performance; extremely *legáto*.
Estrinciendo (It.) (ĕs-trēn-tshē-*en*-dō.) Playing a passage with force and precision.
Estro (It.) (*es*-trō.) Elegance and grace.
Estro poético (It.) (*es*-trō pō-*ä*-tē-kō.) Poetic inspiration; imaginative power in a composer.
Esultazióne (It.) (ĕs-ool-tät-sē-ō-nĕ.) Exultation.
Et (Lat. and Fr.) (ĕt.) And.
Éteinte (Fr.) (ē-tănht.) See *Estínte*.
Étendre (Fr.) (ē-tänhdr.) To extend; to spread.
Étendue (Fr.) (ĕ-tänh-dü.) The extent or compass of an instrument or voice.
Et incarnatus (Lat.) (ĕt ĭn-kār-*nä*-tüs.) A portion of the Credo, in the Mass.
Étouffé (Fr.) (ā-toof-fā.) Stifled; smothered; a word used in harp-playing to signify a deadening of the tones with the hand; in pianoforte music it means an exceedingly soft style of playing.
Étouffer (Fr.) (ā-toof-fā.) To stifle; to deaden the tone.
Étouffoirs (Fr. pl.) (ā-too-fwär.) The dampers.
Et resurrexit (Lat.) (ĕt rĕs-ŭr-*ĕx*-ĭt.) A brilliant part of the Credo, in the Mass.
Etta (It.) (ĕt-tä.) } Little; an Italian final diminutive; as *Trombétta*, a little trumpet, *Adagietto*, a little adagio.
Etto (It.) (ĕt-tō.) }
Ettachordo (It.) (ĕt-tä-*kŏr*-dō.) Instruments having seven strings; a scale of seven notes; a heptachord; the interval of the seventh. Also *eptacordo*.
Étude (Fr.) (ā-*tüd*.) A study; an exercise. An étude usually furnishes technical difficulties of some description. *Etude de concert* is a very difficult study for concert performance. Chopin's *Etudes* are among the most famous.
Étudier (Fr.) (ā-tü-dē-ā.) To study; to practice.
Étui (Fr.) (ā-twē.) A case for an instrument.

ŏ as in *tone*; ô as in *dove*; ŏ as in *not*; ŭ as in *up*; ü the French sound of *u*.

103

Et vitam (Lat.) (ĕt-*vēe*-tăm.) A part of the Credo, in the Mass.

Etwas (Ger.) (*ĕt*-väs.) Some; somewhat; a little.

Etwas langsamer (Ger.) (*ĕt*-väs *läng*-sä-mĕr.) A little slower.

Eufonía (It.) (yoo-fō-nē-ä.) } Euphony;
Eufonía (Spa.) (yoo-*fō*-nē-ä.) } an agreeable sound.

Eufónico (It.) (yoo-*fō*-nē-kō.) Harmonious; well-sounding.

Euharmonic. Producing harmony or concordant sounds.

Euharmonic organ. An organ containing three or four times the usual number of distinct sounds within the compass of an octave, furnishing the precise intervals for every key. The name is not to be confounded with *enharmonic*.

Euphone (Fr.) (üh-fōn.) A reed-stop in an organ of 16-foot scale.

Euphonie (Fr.) (üh-fō-*nē*.) } Euphony;
Euphonie (Ger.) (oi-fō-*nē*.) } sweetness of tone; sounds agreeable to the ear.

Euphonious (yū-*fō*-nĭ-ŭs.) Smooth and melodious.

Euphonique (Fr.) (üh-fō-*nēk*.) Euphonious.

Euphonism (*yū*-fō-nĭsm.) An agreeable combination of sounds.

Euphonium. A bass wind-instrument of modern invention, used in military bands. The bass saxhorn.

Euphony. Agreeable sound; an easy, smooth enunciation of sounds.

Euterpe (yū-*tĕr*-pĕ.) The seventh muse, celebrated for the sweetness of her singing.

Eutimía (It.) (yoo-tē-mē-ä.) Alacrity, vivacity.

Eveillé (Fr.) (ā-vā-yā.) Lively, gay, sprightly.

Eviráti (It.) (ĕv-ē-*rä*-tē.) Men with soprano voices among the Italians, who formerly took the treble parts in the church and theatre. They are now nearly, if not quite, extinct. *Castrati*.

Evolutio (Lat.) (ĕv-ō-*lū*-shĭ-ō.) Inversion of the parts in double counterpoint.

Evovæ. The vowels of Sec*u*l*o*rum am*e*n, the last two words in the Gloria Patri. In Gregorian music, the trope closing the Lesser Doxology; in a wider sense, any trope. Also *Euouæ*.

Exaltation (Fr.) (ĕx-ăl-tä-sē-ŏnh.) In an exalted, dignified mannner.

Exécutant (Fr.) (ĕx-ā-koo-tänh.) A performer, either vocal or instrumental.

Exécuter (Fr.) (ĕx-ā-koo-tä.) To perform; to execute.

Execution. Dexterity and skill, either vocal or instrumental; agility in performance.

Exemple (Fr.) (ĕx-*änh*-pl.) Example.

Exequiæ (Lat.) (ĕx-*ā*-quĭ-ē.) Dirge.

Exequien (Ger.) (ĕx-*ā*-quē-ĕn.) Masses for the dead.

Exercice (Fr.) (ĕx-ĕr-*sĕss*.) Exercise.

Exercice de l'archet (Fr.) (ĕx-ĕr-*sĕss* dŭh l'är-shā.) Practice of the bow in violin playing.

Exerciren (Ger.) (ĕx-är-*tsē*-r'n.) To practice.

Exercise. A musical composition calculated to improve the technique of the performer. Exercises for the purpose of imparting instruction in musical execution.

Exercises, digital. Exercises for the purpose of acquiring an independent action of the fingers.

Exercitium (Ger.) (ĕx-ĕr-*tsĭt*-sē-oom.) An exercise.

Exercitien (Ger. pl.) (ĕx-ĕr-*tsĭt*-sē-ĕn.) Exercises.

Exercizi (It. pl.) (ĕx-är-*tshēt*-sē.) See *Eserciẓi*.

Exit (Lat.) (*ĕx*-ĭt.) A word set in the margin of operas or plays, to mark the time when the actor is to leave the stage.

Explosive tone. A tone produced by sounding a note suddenly and with great emphasis and suddenly diminishing; indicated thus, > ∧, or Sf.

Expressif (Fr.) (ĕx-präs-*sĕf*.) Expressive.

Expressio (Lat.) (ĕx-*prĕss*-ĭ-ō.) Indicates that the passage is to be executed with expression.

Expression. That quality in a composition or performance which appeals to our feelings, taste or judgment displayed in rendering a composition and

ă as in *ah*; ā as in *hate*; ă as in *at*; ē as in *tree*; ĕ as in *eh*; ī as in *pine*; ĭ as in *pin*;

imparting to it the sentiment of the author. *Expression marks* are signs, words or phrases, written against the music to direct the performer in giving its proper expression.

Expressivo (It.) (ĕx-prās-sĕ-vō.) See *Espressivo*.

Extempore (Lat.) (ĕx-*tĕm*-pŏ-rĕ.) Unpremeditated, improvised.

Extemporize. To perform extemporaneously; without premeditation; to improvise.

Extended harmony. See *Dispensed Harmony*.

Extended phrase. Whenever, by repeating one of the feet, or by any other variation of the melody, three measures are employed instead of two, the phrase is termed *extended*, or irregular.

Extended section. A section containing from five to eight bars.

Extension pedal. The loud pedal of a pianoforte.

Extraneous. Foreign; far-fetched; belonging to a remote key.

Extraneous modulation. A modulation into some remote key, far distant from the original key and its relatives.

Extravagánza (It.) (ĕx-träv-ä-*gänt*-sä.) An extravagant and eccentric composition.

Extreme. A term referring to the most distant parts, as the treble and bass. Relating also to intervals in an augmented state; as *extreme sharp sixth*, etc. The extreme sixth is resolved as follows in minor:

Ex. 1.   Ex. 2.

Ex. 3.

or it can resolve into major as follows:

The first form is called the *Italian Sixth*, the second the *French Sixth*, and the last the *German Sixth*.

F

F. The fourth note in the diatonic scale of C. It was the note first used as a clef sign to give definite pitch to the mediæval notation (Neumes) because " small f " was a good medium note in the baritone voice in the chants, which were therefore almost always composed around this note. F is also the abbreviation of *Forte;* ff, *fortissimo;* fff, *fortississimo;* ffff is rarely used.

Fa. The name applied to F in France and Italy; the fourth of the syllables used in solfeggio. In the "fixed do" system it is always F; in the "movable do" it is the fourth note of *any* diatonic scale. In "tonic sol-fa" it is spelled "Fah."

Fabliau (Fr.) (*fab*-lioh.) A versified tale or romance of the *trouvères*, in vogue chiefly during the twelfth and thirteenth centuries; a fable.

Faburden, Falsobordone (It.) *Faux-bourdon* (Fr.) 1. One of the early systems of harmonizing a given portion of plain song, or a *canto fermo*. As the word implies, *to faburden* signified originally to hold a *drone*. It afterwards became the primitive harmonization of a *cantus firmus* by adding the third and the sixth above, and progressing in parallel motion throughout, only the first and last chords having key-note, fifth, and octave. 2. Later, the setting of a simple (note against note) counterpoint to the *cantus firmus*, the strict parallel motion of parts now being no longer retained.

Façade d'orgue (Fr.) (fă-*säd* d'ŏrg.) The front of an organ-case.

Facciata (It.) (fät-tshē-ä-tä.) Page, folio.

Fach (Ger.) (fäkh.) Ranks; thus, *fünffach*, five *ranks*.

Fácile (Fr.) (fä-*sēl*.)
Facile (It.) (fa-shē-lĕ.) } Light, easy.

Facilita (It.) (fä-*tshēl*-ē-tä.) } Facility;
Facilité (Fr.) (fä-sēl-ĭ-tā.) } an easier arrangement or adaptation. Sometimes in a difficult passage in a musical work an easier method of execution is printed above or below the passage, and marked *Facilita*, or *Ossia* (*Also*).

Facilement (Fr.) (fä-sēl-mänh.) } Easily;
Facilménte (It.) (fä-tshēl-*men*-tĕ.) } with facility.

Fackel-tanz (Ger.) (fäk-'l-tänts.) Dance with torches.

Facteur de pianos (Fr.) (fäk-*tŭr* dŭh pǐ-ä-nō.) A piano-maker.

Facteur d'orgue (Fr.) (fäk-*tŭr* d'ŏrg.) An organ-maker.

Facture (Fr.) (fäk-tür.) The composition, or workmanship, of a piece of music. The scale of organ-pipes.

Facture d'orgues (Fr.) (fäk-tür d'ŏrg.) Dimensions or scale of the pipes of an organ.

Fa dièse (Fr.) (fä dĭ-āz.) The key of F ♯.

Fa dièse majeur (Fr.) (fä dĭ-*āz* mä-*zhŭr*.) The key of F ♯ major.

Fa dièse mineur (Fr.) (fä dĭ-*āz* mǐ-*nŭr*.) The key of F ♯ minor.

Faggiólo (It.) (fäd-jē-*ō*-lō.) The flageolet.

Fagott (Ger.) (fä-*gŏtt*.) A bassoon.

Fagottíno (It.) (fä-gŏt-*tēe*-nō.) A small bassoon.

Fagottist (Ger.) (fä-gŏt-*tĭst*.) } A performer
Fagottísta (It.) (fä-gŏt-*tēes*-tä.) } on the bassoon.

Fagótto (It.) (fä-*gōt*-tō.) A bassoon; also an organ-stop.

Fagótto contra (It.) (fä-gŏt-tō kŏn-trä.) A large bassoon an octave lower than the common bassoon; the contra-bassoon.

Fagóttone (It.) (fä-gŏt-*tō*-nĕ.) A large bassoon an octave lower than the *fagótto*; the contra-bassoon.

Fahnen-marsch (Ger.) (fä-nĕn-märsh.) The march or tune that is played when the colors are lodged.

Faible (Fr.) (*fā*-bl.) Weak, feeble, thin.

Faiblement (Fr.) (fāy-bl-mänh.) Feebly, weakly.

Faire (Fr.) (fār.) To do; to execute.

Fa-las. Short songs with the syllables *fa la* at the end of each line or strain. Morley (c. 1580), who composed some, speaks of them as being a kind of *ballet*. The *fa las* of Hilton (c. 1600) are held in highest estimation for the freedom of their construction and the beauty of their melodies. Morley's " Now is the Month of Maying " is an excellent example of a *Fa la*.

Fall. A cadence. Shakespeare uses the term in " Twelfth Night."

Falsa (It.) (*fäl*-sä.) } False, wrong,
Falsch (Ger.) (fälsh.) } inharmonious.

Falsa musica (Lat.), called also *musica ficta*. False or feigned music was that in which notes were altered by the use of accidentals.

False. Those intonations of the voice that do not truly express the intended intervals are called *false*, as well as all ill-adjusted combinations. The term *false* is applied in music to any violation of acknowledged or long-established rules, or to anything imperfect or incorrect.

False accent. When the accent is removed from the first beat of the bar to the second or fourth, it is called *false* accent.

False cadence. An imperfect or interrupted cadence. See *Deceptive Cadence*.

False chords. An epithet applied by theorists to certain chords, because they do not contain *all* the intervals appertaining to those chords in their perfect state.

False fifth. An old term for an imperfect or diminished fifth; a fifth containing only *six* semi-tones, as C, G♭.

False harmony. Harmony contrary to established rules.

False intonation. Incorrect intonation; where the voice does not express the intended or correct intervals.

False relation. When a note which has occurred in one chord, is found chromatically altered in the followed chord, but in a *different part*.

False triad. The diminished triad, formerly so-called on account of its having a false fifth.

Falsett (Ger.) (fäl-*sĕt*.)
Falsétto (It.) (fäl-*set*-tō.) } Falsetto.

Falsette. } The male head-voice as dis-
Falsetto. } tinguished from the chest-voice. A singer who sings soprano or alto parts with such a voice. *Falsetti* must not be confounded with *castrati*. A false or artificial voice; that part of a person's voice that lies above its natural compass.

Falso (It.) (*fäl*-sō.) False.

Fálso bordóne (It.) (*fäl*-sō bŏr-dō-ně.) A term formerly applied to such counterpoint as had a drone bass, or some part constantly moving in the interval with it. See *Faburden*.

Fa majeure (Fr.) (fä mă-*zhŭr*.) } The
Fa majore (Fr.) (fä mă-*zhŏr*.) } key of F major.

Fa mineur (Fr.) (fä mĭ-*nŭr*.) Key of F minor.

Fanático (It.) (fä-*nä*-tē-kō.) A fanatic or passionate admirer.

Fancies. An old name for little lively airs or tunes.

Fandángo (Spa.) (fän-*dän*-gō.) A dance much used in Spain, in ¾ or ⅜ time, generally accompanied with castanets and having a strong emphasis upon the second beat of each bar.

Fandanguéro (Spa.) (fän-dän-*gwä*-rō.) One who is skilful in dancing the fandango.

Fanfare (Fr.) (fänh-fär.) A short, lively, loud and warlike piece of music, composed for trumpets and kettledrums. Also short, lively pieces performed on hunting-horns in the chase. A flourish of trumpets.

Fantaisie (Fr.) (făn-tä-*zee*.) } Fancy,
Fantasía (It.) (făn-tä-*zee*-ä.) } imagina-
Fantasie (Ger.) (făn-tä-*zee*.) } tion, caprice; a species of music in which the composer yields to his imagination and gives free scope to his ideas, without regard to those restrictions by which other productions are regulated. A free fantasie follows the exposition of themes in the sonata-allegro of symphony or sonata. This is called the *Development*. The word "Fanta*si*-a" is often mispronounced "Fant*a*sia."

Fantasiosaménte (It.) (fän-tä-zē-ō-zä-men-tĕ.) Fantastically, critically.

Fantasióso (It.) (fän-tä-zē-*ō*-zō.) Fantastic, capricious.

Fantasiren (Ger.) (fän-tä-*zee*-r'n.) To improvise; to play extemporaneously.

Fantasticaménte (It.) (fän-täs-tē-kä men-tĕ.) In a fantastic style.

Fantástico (It.) (fän-*täs*-tē-kō.) } Fan-
Fantastique (Fr.) (fän-täs-*teek*.) } tasti
Fantastisch (Ger.) (făn-*täs*-tish.) } cal; whimsical; capricious in relation to style, form, modulation, etc.

Farandole (Fr.) (fä-ränh-*dōl*.) } A
Farandoule (Fr.) (fä-ränh-*dool*.) } lively dance in ⅜ or ¼ time, peculiar to Provence. See Bizet's "Suite Arlesienne."

Fársa (It.) (*fär*-sä.) } Farce.
Farsa (Spa.) (*fär*-sä.) }

Fársa in música (It.) (*fär*-sä ēn moo-zē-kä.) Musical farce; a species of little comic opera, in one act.

Fáscie (It. pl.) (*fäs*-tshē-ĕ.) The sides or hoops of a violin, viola, etc.

Fastosaménte (It.) (fäs-tō-zä-*men*-tĕ.) Pompously, proudly.

Fastóso (It.) (fäs-*tō*-zō.) Proudly; stately; in a lofty and pompous style.

Faucette (Fr.) (fō-*sĕt*.) } Falsetto.
Fausset (Fr.) (fō-*sā*.) }

Faux (Fr.) (fō.) False; out of tune.

Faux accord (Fr.) (fō zăh-*kŏrd*.) A dissonance.

Faux bourdon (Fr.) (fō boor-dŏnh.) See *Faburden*.

F clef. The bass clef; a character placed on the fourth line of the staff so that the two dots are in the third and fourth spaces. See *Clefs*.

F dur (Ger.) (f door.) The key of F major.

Feathering. A term sometimes applied to a particularly delicate and lightly detached manner of bowing certain rapid passages on the violin.

Feeders. Small bellows sometimes employed to supply the large bellows of an organ with wind.

Feier (Ger.) (*fī*-ĕr.) Festival, celebration.

Feier-gesang (Ger.) (*fī*-ĕr-ghĕ-*säng*.) Solemn hymn; anthem.

Feierlich (Ger.) (*fī*-ĕr-lĭkh.) Solemn, festive.

Feierlichkeit (Ger.) (*fī*-ĕr-lĭkh-kīt.) Solemnity, pomp.

Feigned voice. A *falsétto* voice.

Feinte. An old name for a semi-tone; an accidental.

Feld-musik (Ger.) (*fĕld*-moo-zĭk.) Military music.

Feldrohr (Ger.) (*fĕld*-rōr.) A rural pipe.

Feldton (Ger.) (*fĕld*-tōn.) The tone or key-note of the trumpet and other military wind-instruments.

Feld-trompete (Ger.) (fĕld-trōm-*pā*-tĕ.) Military trumpet.

Férma (It.) (*fär*-mä.) Firm, resolute, steady.

Fermaménte (It.) (fär-mä-*men*-tĕ.) Firmly, steadily.

Fermáta (It.) (fär-*mä*-tä.) } A pause
Fermate (Ger.) (fär-*mä*-tĕ.) } or hold marked thus, ⁀. The fermata has been used in music for four centuries. Its length varies with the character of the music. When found over a long note it is not necessary to double the value of that note, but when found over a sixteenth 𝄐 it may more than double the value. Its length can be varied by the words, *lunga* (long), *piccola* (a little), G. P. (*grosse pause*, great pause), and other signs. Over a double bar it usually signifies the end of the composition..

Fermáte (It.) (fär-*mä*-tĕ.) } Firmly,
Fermáto (It.) (fär-*mä*-tō.) } steadily, resolutely.

Fermement (Fr.) (fär-mĕ-mänh.) Firmly, resolutely.

Fermeté (Fr.) (fär-mĕ-*tā*.) } Firmness,
Fermézza (It.) (fär-*māt*-zä.) } resolution.

Férmo (It.) (*fär*-mō.) Firm, resolute.

Fern-werk (Ger.) (*fairn*-värk.) Distant, or remote work; a term applied to the "echo" in German organs.

Feróce (It.) (fā-*rō*-tshĕ.) }
Feroceménte (It.) (fā-rō-tshĕ-*men*-tĕ.) } Fierce; with an expression of ferocity.

Ferocita (It.) (fā-rō-tshē-*tä*.) Fierceness, roughness.

Fertig (Ger.) (*fĕr*-tĭg.) Quick, nimble, dexterous.

Fertigkeit (Ger.) (*fĕr*-tĭg-kīt.) Quickness, dexterity.

Fervemment (Fr.) (fär-vä-mänh.) Fervently, vehemently.

Fervénte (It.) (fär-*ven*-tĕ.) Fervent, vehement.

Ferventeménte (It.) (fär-vän-tĕ-*men*-tĕ.) }
Fervidaménte (It.) (fär-vē-dä-*men*-tĕ.) } Fervently, vehemently.

Férvido (It.) (*fär*-vē-dō.) Fervent, vehement.

Fes (Ger.) (fĕs.) The note F flat.

Fest (Ger.) A festival; firm; steady. *Musik-fest*, a musical festival.

Festigkeit (Ger.) (*fĕs*-tĭg-kīt.) Firmness, steadiness.

Festiglich (Ger.) (*fĕs*-tĭg-lĭkh.) Firmly, steadily.

Festivaménte (It.) (fĕs-tē-vä-*men*-tĕ.) Gayly, brilliantly.

Festivita (It.) (fĕs-tē-vē-*tä*.) Festivity, gayetv.

Festívo (It.) (fes-*tē*-vō.) Merry, cheerful, gay.

Festlich (Ger.) (*fĕst*-lĭkh.) Festive, solemn.

Festlichkeit (Ger.) (*fĕst*-lĭkh-kīt.) Festivity, solemnity.

Festlied (Ger.) (*fĕst*-lēd.) A festive song.

Festóso (It.) (fes-*tō*-zō.) Merry, cheerful, gay.

Fest-ouvertüre (Ger.) (fest-ō-ver-*türe*.) Festival overture; an overture in a vigorous, brilliant style.

Festzeit (Ger.) (*fĕst*-tsīt.) Festival.

Feuer (Ger.) (*foi*-ĕr.) Fire, ardor, passion.

Feuille (Fr.) A leaf; *feuilles volantes*, flying leaves.

Feuillet (Fr.) (*fāy*-āy.) A leaf, leaflet. *Feuillet d'album*, album-leaf.

ă as in *ah*; ā as in *hate*; ă as in *at*; ē as in *tree*; ĕ as in *eh*; ī as in *pine*; ĭ as in *pin*;

108

FEURIG   FIGURES OF DIMINUTION

Feurig (Ger.) (*foi-*rĭg.) Fiery, ardent, passionate.

F holes. The sound holes on a violin are so called because of their resemblance to an *f*.

Fiácca (It.) (fē-*äk*-kä.) ⎱ Feeble, weak,
Fiácco (It.) (fē-*äk*-kō.) ⎰ languishing.

Fiásco (It.) (fē-*äs*-kō.) The technical term for a failure; a complete breakdown in a musical performance.

Fiáto (It.) (fē-*ä*-tō.) The breath; the voice.

Fiddle-stick. A violin bow.

Fidicula (Lat.) (fē-dĭ-koo-lä.) A small lute, or guitar.

Fiducia (It.) (fē-*doo*-tshē-ä.) Confidence.

Fiedel (Ger.) (*fee*-d'l.) A fiddle; a violin. *Strohfiedel*, a xylophone.

Fiel. An old name for the fiddle or violin.

Field music. Music for military instruments; martial music.

Fieraménte (It.) (fē-ĕr-ä-*men*-tĕ.) Proudly, vehemently, boldly.

Fière (Fr.) (fī-ār.) Proud, lofty, fierce.

Fièrement (Fr.) (fī-ār-mänh.) In a fierce manner.

Fieramente assai (It.) (fē-ā-rä-*men*-tĕ äs-*sä*-ĕ.) Very bold and energetic.

Fiéro (It.) (fē-*ä*-rō.) Bold, energetic, proudly.

Fierté (Fr.) (fēr-tā.) Fierceness, boldness.

Fife. A small, shrill-toned instrument, used only in martial music together with drums. An octave cross-flute with six holes and without keys (thus differing from the *piccolo*); compass about ⟶. An organ-stop of 2-foot pitch; a piccolo-stop.

Fifre (Fr.) (fēfr.) A fife; also a fifer; the name is also applied to one of the stops in a harmonium.

Fifteenth. An interval of two octaves; also the name of an organ-stop, tuned two octaves above the diapasons, and therefore of 2-foot pitch.

Fifth. A distance comprising four diatonic intervals; that is, three tones and a semi-tone. (Ger., *Quinte;* Fr., *Quinte;* It., *Quinta.*)

Fifth, augmented. An interval containing four whole tones. Also called *Sharp Fifth*.

Fifth, diminished. An interval containing two whole tones and two semi-tones.

Fifth, perfect. An interval containing three whole tones and one semi-tone.

Fifths, consecutive. Two or more perfect fifths immediately following one another in two parallel parts of the score.

Figur (Ger.) (fĭ-*goor.*) A musical figure, phrase, or idea.

Figura (It.) (fē-goo-*rä.*) Note employed as an ornament.

Figural-gesang (Ger.) (fĭ-goo-*räl*-ghĕ-*säng.*) Varied and ornamented chant, as opposed to plain chant.

Figural-gesänge (Ger. pl.) (fĭ-goo-*räl*-ghĕ-*säng*-ĕ.)

Figurantes (Fr.) (fē-gü-*ränht.*) Those dancers in a ballet who do not dance singly, but in groups, and many together. In the drama, people who figure without having anything to say.

Figuration. An ornamental treatment of a passage; a mixture of concords and discords.

Figuration, harmonic. The progression of a chord from one tone to another of the same chord, and similarly through successive different chords.

Figuráto (It.) (fē-goo-*rä*-tō.) ⎱ Figured,
Figuré (Fr.) (fĭ-gü-*rā.*) ⎰ florid, embellished.

Figured. Free, florid; a term applied to an air which, instead of moving note by note with the bass, consists of a free and florid melody. It also means indicated or noted by figures.

Figured bass. A bass with figures placed over or under the notes to indicate the harmony. See *Thorough Bass*.

Figured harmony. Where one or more of the parts of a composition move during the continuance of a chord, through certain notes which do not form any of the constituent parts of that chord.

Figures. Numerical characters written upon the staff, usually in the form of a fraction, to denote the measure.

Figures of diminution. Numerical char-

ŏ as in *tone;* ŏ as in *dove;* ŏ as in *not;* ŭ as in *up;* ü the French sound of *u.*

109

acters which change the time of the notes over which they are placed, one-third of their relative length. The notes with a figure three are called *triplets*. See *Grouping*.

Filár la vóce (It.) (fē-lär lä *vō*-tshĕ.) To spin out; to prolong the tone; gradually augmenting and diminishing the sound of the voice.

Filarmónico (It.) (fē-lär-*mō*-nē-kō.) Philharmonic, music-loving.

Filer (Fr.) (fĭ-lā.) To spin; to draw out.

Filer le son (Fr.) (fĭ-lā lŭh sŏnh.) See *Filár la Voce*.

Fileur (Fr.) (fĭ-lŭr.) A spinner; fem., *Fileuse*.

Filum (Lat.) (fē-lŭm.) A name formerly given to the *stem* of a note.

Fin (Fr.) (fănh.) The end.

Fin al (It.) (fēn äl.) End at; play as far as.

Final An old application given to the last sound of a verse in a chant which, if complete, is on the key-note of the chant; if incomplete, on some other note in the scale of that key.

Final close. Final cadence.

Finále (It.) (fi-*nä*-lĕ.) Final; concluding; the last piece of any act of an opera or of a concert; or, the last movement of a sonata or symphony, etc.

F in alt. The seventh above G in alt; the seventh note in alt.

F in altissimo. The octave above F in alt; the seventh note in altissimo.

Fín a qui (It.) (fĭn ä qui.) To this place.

Fíne (It.) (*feen*-ay.) The end; the termination.

Fine del aria (It.) (*fi*-nĕ dĕl ä-rē-ä.) The end of the air.

Fine del atto (It.) (*fi*-nĕ dĕl *ät*-tō.) The end of the act.

Finement (Fr.) (făh-mänh.) Finely, acutely.

Finger-board. That part of a stringed instrument on which the fingers press; the key-board or manual of a pianoforte, organ, etc.

Fingered. A term applied to piano music, signifying that figures or other characters are applied to the notes to show the method of fingering.

Fingering. The method of applying the fingers to the keys, strings, or holes, of different instruments. The figures which are written in music to show the performer which finger to use in sounding a note. The art of fingering is comparatively modern in music. The system of marking numerals to guide the player began with violin music. As the violinist does not use the thumb, this system (the oldest of all) numbered the fingers, 1, 2, 3, 4. When this was transferred to the piano key-board (or harpsichord, clavichord, and spinet), the same figures were used, as the thumb was very rarely upon the key-board in the seventeenth century. The thumb was sometimes used in left-hand passages before it was allowed in right-hand work. When the thumb was applied, the figure o was used to designate it. Therefore the earliest fingering ran, o, 1, 2, 3, 4. This was used in Germany as early as 1571. But the "o" was apt sometimes to be mistaken for a whole note, therefore in England it was soon changed to a sign like the following — ↶ — afterwards written x. (See *English Fingering*.) In Germany, as early as the time of Bach, the figures were used as they are to-day — 1, 2, 3, 4, 5. There was very little attempt at any system of fingering upon the spinet or harpsichord, for those instruments gave a continual staccato and could not shade. Therefore, almost any fingers were used, at the will of the performer. We copy the following from a volume of fingered pieces published in England one hundred and fifty years ago:

and

Probably the earliest practical system of fingering came in with the works of

ă as in *ah*; ā as in *hate*; ă as in *at*; ē as in *tree*; ĕ as in *eh*; ī as in *pine*; ĭ as in *pin*;

J. S. Bach. He introduced the thumb freely, and used the fingers in a much more modern style than his predecessors. He did not, however, publish any system of fingering, but contented himself with teaching the system to his sons and other pupils. In Philipp Em. Bach's "Versuch uber die wahre Art das Klavier zu Spielen" (1753), this system was first published. Nevertheless, there was published, in England, a work on the same subject, which antedates Bach's book. This is entitled "Pasquali's Art of Fingering, for the Harpsichord." In this (which has the numeration 0, 1, 2, 3, 4), the thumb is as freely used as in modern music. The Italian masters undoubtedly aided the advance in fingering, some of them before the time of Philipp Em. Bach. It will be seen from the above that the so-called "American fingering" began in Germany, took root in England, and was probably the earliest numeration of the fingers. See *English Fingering.* Also consult Naylor's "An Elizabethan Virginal Book."

Fingering, American. The use of the sign (x) to indicate the thumb in pianoforte playing, in distinction from the German or foreign fingering, in which the thumb is called the first finger.

Fingering, foreign. ⎫ A method of fin-
Fingering, German. ⎬ gering piano music which designates the thumb as the first finger.

Fingering, scale. The system of scale fingering at present in use is found in the works of Philipp Em. Bach. Yet the principle of it is to be found in some earlier Italian works. In the old spinet and harpsichord works, and in an old organ-book of 1571, the scale was fingered (German fingering) as follows, 2, 3, 2, 3, 2, 3, 2, 3—and in some later methods — 2, 3, 4, 2, 3, 4, 2, 3. The earliest valuable system of scale fingering gave the rule to pass the thumb under on the first white key after a black one, which is the basis of our scale fingering to-day. This would present such fingerings as follows (Pasquali's "Art of Fingering"):

But in the right hand, the fingering very nearly followed our present system. In modern scale fingering a few notable theories may be mentioned. A few German pedagogues attempted strongly to change the accustomed fingering so that the thumbs shall always fall together, in both hands. This would never be quite accepted as an advantageous change. As an advanced study, in difficult fingering many great teachers, Rosenthal among others, apply the fingering of the C scale to many other scales. To play the scale of D flat with the C scale fingering is a task of some difficulty. Some teachers are in favor of ending each scale exercise with a slow trill on the last two notes. This counteracts the chief defect of scale practice. In scale work the fingers 1, 2, and 3, have the most work allotted to them; the fourth finger is less used, and the fifth least of all. See Stainer & Barrett, and Grove's Dictionary.

Fingern (Ger.) (*fĭng*-ĕrn.) To play; to finger.

Finger-leiter (Ger.) (*fĭng*-ĕr-*lī*-tĕr.) Finger-guides.

Finger-satz (Ger.) (*fĭng*-ĕr-sätz.) Fingering.

Finiménto (It.) (fē-nē-*men*-tō.) Conclusion, end.

Finíta (It.) (fē-*nē*-tä.) ⎫ Finished, ended,
Finíto (It.) (fē-*nē*-tō.) ⎭ concluded.

Finite canon. A canon which is not repeated.

Fino al (It.) (fē-nō äl.) Play as far as; stop at; end at. Also *Fino.*

Fín qui (It.) (fēn quē.) To this place.

Fint (It.) ⎫ Feigned, false, interrupted,
Finto (It.) ⎭ in respect to cadences; a feint, or deceptive close.

Fióca (It.) (fē-*ō*-kä.) ⎫ Hoarse, faint,
Fióco (It.) (fē-*ō*-kō.) ⎭ feeble.

Fiochézza (It.) (fē-ō-*kāt*-zä.) Hoarseness.

Fioreggiánte (It.) (fē-ō-rĕd-jē-*än*-tĕ.) Too ornate; decorated with roulades, cadences, etc.

Fiorétti (It.) (fē-ō-*ret*-tē.) Little graces or ornaments in vocal music.

FIORISCÉNTE   FLAT SEVENTH

Fioriscénte (It.) (fē-ō-rē-*shen*-tĕ.) }
Fioríto (It.) (fē-ō-*rēe*-tō.)   }
Florid; abounding with ornaments.

Fiorita cadenza (It.) (fē-ō-*rēe*-tä kä-*dent*-sä.) A cadenza whose last note but one is divided into many notes.

Fioritezza (It.) (fē-ō-rē-*tet*-sä.) Embellishment; a florid style of performance.

Fioritúre (It.) (fē-ō-rē-*too*-rĕ.) }
Fioritúri (It.) (fē-ō-rē-*too*-rĕ.) } Literally, *little flowers*; graces and embellishments in singing.

First. A word applied to the upper part of a duet, trio, quartet, or any other composition, vocal or instrumental; such parts generally express the air. In piano duets the first part is marked *Primo*. The first string of an instrument is its highest one.

First bass. High bass.

First inversion. A term applied to a chord when the bass takes the third.

First soprano. The high soprano.

First tenor. The high tenor.

Fis (Ger.) (fĭs.) The note F sharp. *Fis-is*, F double sharp.

Fischiare (It.) (fē-skē-*ä*-rĕ.) To whistle; to hiss.

Fis dur (Ger.) (fĭs door.) The key of F ♯, major.

Fis moll (Ger.) (*fĭs* mōll.) The key of F ♯, minor.

Fistel (Ger.) (*fĭs*-t'l.) Feigned voice; falsetto.

Fistola (It.) (*fĭs*-tō-lä.)   } A reed; a pipe.
Fistula (Lat.)(*fĭs*-tū-lä.) }

Fistula Germanica (Lat.) (*fĭs*-tū-lä gĕr-*män*-ĭ-kä.) German flute.

Fistula panis (Lat.) (*fĭs*-tū-lä *pä*-nĭs.) The Pandean pipes; wind-instruments of the ancients.

Fistula pastoralis (Lat.) (*fĭs*-tū-lä păs-tō-*rä*-lĭs.) The Pandean pipes; wind-instruments of the ancients.

Fistulator (Lat.) (*fĭs*-tū-*lä*-tŏr.) } A
Fistulatóre (It.)(*fĕs*-too-lä-tō-rĕ.) } piper; a player on a flute or flageolet.

Fistuliren (Ger.) (fĭs-too-*lēr'n*.) To sing in a falsetto voice.

Fithel. The old English name for the fiddle.

Fixed syllables. Vocal syllables which do not change with the change of key. The Italians and French use fixed syllables. The *fixed-Do* system is that in which the tone C, and all its chromatic derivatives (C ♯, C ×, and C ♭, C ♭♭) are called *Do*, D and its derivatives *Re*, etc., in whatever key or harmony they may appear.

Flach-flöte (Ger.) (fläkh *flō*-tĕ.) Shallow flute; flageolet; also an organ-stop of rather thin tone.

Flageolet (Fr.) (flä-zhĕ-ō-*lä*.)   } A small
Flageolet (Ger.) (flä-ghē-ō-*lĕt*.) } pipe or flute, resembling a straight flute, the notes of which are exceedingly clear and shrill. It is generally made of box or other hard wood, but sometimes of ivory. The flageolet is not used in the orchestra, its tones being too rough and shrill. Its compass is *8va*. Also an organ-stop of 2-foot scale and wood pipes.

Flageolet, double. A flageolet having two tubes.

Flageolet tones. Tones produced on instruments of the violin species by drawing the bow very lightly and merely touching the strings with the fingers. See *Harmonics*.

Flagiolétta (It.) (flä-jē-ō-*let*-tä.) See *Flageolet*.

Flat (Ger., *Be*; Fr., *Bémol*; It., *Bemolle*.) The sign ♭, which lowers the pitch of the note following it by a semi-tone. It came originally from the letter *b*, as its shape and its foreign names indicate. See *Chromatic Signs*.

Flat, double. A character composed of two flats which lowers a note two semi-tones, (♭♭).

Flat eighth, extreme. The octave diminished by the chromatic semi-tone.

Flat, fifth. An interval consisting of five degrees and containing two tones and two semi-tones. The diminished fifth.

Flat fourth, extreme. The perfect fourth diminished by a chromatic semi-tone.

Flat seventh. The minor seventh containing four tones and two diatonic semi-tones.

ă as in *ah;* ā as in *hate;* ă as in *at;* ē as in *tree;* ĕ as in *eh;* ī as in *pine;* ĭ as in *pin;*

FLATTER LA CORDE — FLUGBLATT

Flatter la corde (Fr.) (flăt-*lă* lä kŏrd.) To play the violin, etc., in a soft, expressive manner. Literally to "caress the string."

Flautándo (It.) (flä-oo-*tăn*-dō.) ⎫
Flautáto (It.) (flä-oo-*tä*-tō.) ⎭ *Flute like tone;* that quality of tone obtained by drawing the bow smoothly and gently across the strings over that end of the finger-board nearest the bridge.

Flautína (It.) (flä-oo-*tēe*-nä.) ⎫
Flautíno (It.) (flä-oo-*tēe*-nō.) ⎭ A small flute; an octave flute; a piccolo.

Flautísta (It.) (flä-oo-*tēes*-tä.) A performer on the flute.

Flauti unisoni (It.) (flä-oo-tē oo-nē-*sō*-nē.) The flutes in unison.

Fláuto (It.) (flä-*oo*-tō.) A flute.

Fláuto a becco (It.) (flä-oo-tō ä *bek*-kō.) A beaked flute; a flute having a mouth-piece like a flageolet. A straight flute called by Shakespeare "The Recorders."

Fláuto amábile (It.) (flä-oo-tō ä-*mä*-bēe-lĕ.) The name of an organ-stop of soft and delicate tone.

Fláuto amoróso (It.) (flä-oo-tō ä-mŏ-*rō*-zō.) A 4-foot organ-stop of delicate tone.

Fláuto di Pan (It.) (flä-oo-tō dē pän.) *Pan's flute;* an organ-stop of small size.

Fláuto dolce (It.) (flä-oo-tō *dŏl*-tshĕ.) An organ-stop of soft, agreeble tone.

Fláuto doris (It.) (flä-oo-tō *dō*-rēs.) ⎫
Fláuto douce (It.) (flä-oo-tō *doo*-tshĕ.) ⎭
See *Fláuto Dolce* and *Flûte Douce.*

Fláuto e violino (It.) (flä-oo-tō ā vē-ō-*lē*-nō.) Flute and violin.

Fláuto gráve (It.) (flä-oo-tō *grä*-vĕ.) An organ-stop of 8-foot tone.

Flautóne (It.) (flä-oo-*tō*-nĕ.) The bass flute, not in use; also a 16-foot pedal-stop in an organ, of soft tone.

Fláuto o violino (It.) (flä-oo-tō o vē-ō *lē*-nō.) Flute or violin.

Fláuto píccolo (It.) (flä-oo-tō *pĭk*-kō-lō.) An octave flute; a small flute of very shrill tone. See *Piccolo.*

Fláuto tacere (It.) (flä-oo-tō tä-*tshe*-rĕ.) The flute is not to play.

Fláuto tedesco (It.) (flä-oo-tō tĕ-des-kō.) A German flute.

Fláuto transverso (It.) (flä-oo-tō träns-*vāir*-sō.) ⎫
Fláuto travérso (It.) (flä-oo-tō trä-*vāir*-sō.) ⎭
The flute; the *transverse flute,* thus named because it is held *across,* and blown at the side, contrary to the *flûte a bec;* it is also often called the *German flute.* The name is also applied to an organ-stop.

Flébile (It.) (*flā*-bē-lĕ.) Mournful, sad, doleful.

Flebilménte (It.) (flā-bēl-*men*-tĕ.) Mournfully, dolefully.

Flessíbile (It.) (flĕs-*sēe*-bē-lĕ.) Flexible; pliant.

Flessibilita (It.) (flĕs-si-bē-lē-tä.) Flexibility.

F-löcher (Ger.) (ĕf *lŏkh*-ĕr.) The F holes or sound holes of a violin, etc.

Florid. Ornamental, figured, embellished.

Florid counterpoint. Free counterpoint.

Flöten (Ger.) (*flŏ*-t'n.) To play upon the flute.

Flöten-begleitung (Ger.) (*flŏ*-t'n bĕ-*glī*-toong.) Flute accompaniment.

Flöten-bläser (Ger.) (*flŏ*-t'n *blā*-z'r.) Flute player.

Flöten-duo (Ger.) (*flŏ*-t'n *doo*-ō.) Flute duet.

Flötenspieler (Ger.) (*flŏ*-'n-*spē*-lĕr.) A flute player.

Flötenstimme (Ger.) (*flŏ*-t'n-*stĭm*-mĕ.) A soft, sweet voice; the part for the flute.

Flötenzug (Ger.) (*flŏ*-t'n tsoog.) A flute-stop in an organ.

Flötist (Ger.) (flŏ-*tĭst*.) A flute player.

Flourish. An appellation sometimes given to the decorative notes which a performer adds to a passage, with the double view of heightening the effect and showing his own dexterity and skill. A fanfare of trumpets or brass instruments.

Flüchtig (Ger.) (*flükh*-tĭg.) Lightly, nimbly.

Flüchtigkeit (Ger.) (*flükh*-tĭg-kīt.) Lightness, fleetness.

Flugblatt (Ger.) (*floog*-blät.) A fugitive piece.

ŏ as in *tone;* ô as in *dove;* ŏ as in *not;* ŭ as in *up;* ü the French sound of *u.*

113

Flügel (Ger.) (*flü-g'l.*) A grand piano, so-called because it is shaped like a "wing," or "flügel."

Flügelhorn. A bugle, or a valve horn.

Fluit (Dut.) (floit.) } A flute.
Fluta (Lat.) (*floo*-tä.) }

Flute. A common and well-known wind-instrument. It was once made of wood, now usually made of metal, consisting of a tube closed at one end and being furnished with holes and keys at its side for producing various pitches. It is also called *Traverse flute, German flute,* and *D flute.* It was greatly improved by Theobald Boehm about 1834, and flutes with his system of keys attached are also called *Boehm flutes* or *concert flutes.* The usual compass of the flute is: although the instrument may, exceptionally, have an added semi-tone above and below. It is generally a non-transposing instrument, although transposing flutes are sometimes used in military bands. The *piccolo* or octave flute sounds an octave higher than the ordinary flute. Consult Prout's "Orchestra," and A. Elson's "Orchestral Instruments and their Use."

Flute. An organ-stop of the diapason species, the tone of which resembles that of the flute.

Flûte à bec (Fr.) (floot ä běk.) *Flute with a beak;* the old English flute, with a lip or *beak;* it was blown at the end. The *Recorders* used in England in the Elizabethan era.

Flûte allemande (Fr.) (floot äl-mänhd.) The German flute.

Flute, ancient. An instrument which had some sort of a mouth-piece and was double as well as single. It also frequently was composed of two tubes both played together. It is probable that the Ancients possessed oboes and bassoons calling them all by the name *Aulia* or *Tibia* which we translate *Flutes.*

Flute, Boehm (bôm.) An instrument invented by M. Boehm, of Germany, in 1834. It differs from the common flute in having the size and location of the holes arranged in their natural order with keys.

Flûte conique (Fr.) (floot kŏn-ēk.) Conical flute; an organ-stop.

Flûte d'allemande (Fr.) (floot d'äl-mänhd.) A German flute.

Flûte d'amour (Fr.) (floot d'ä-moor.) A flute, the compass of which is a minor third below that of the German flute; the name is also applied to an organ-stop of 8 or 4-foot scale.

Flûte douce (Fr.) (floot dooss.) *Soft flute;* the *flûte à bec;* there were four kinds, the treble, alto, tenor, and bass.

Flûtée (Fr.) (floo-tā.) Soft, sweet.

Flute, German. See *Flute.*

Flûte, harmonique (Fr.) (floot härmŏnhn ēk.) See *Harmonic Flute.*

Flute, octave. A flute the tones of which range an octave higher than the regular flute; the piccolo.

Flûte octaviante (Fr.) (floot ŏk-tä-vǐänht.) Octave flute; an organ-stop.

Flûte, ouverte (Fr.) (floot oo-vär.) An organ-stop of the diapason species.

Flute, pastoral. } A flute shorter
Flute, sheperd's. } than the transverse flute, and blown through a lip-piece at the end.

Flûter (Fr.) (floo-tā.) To play the flute.

Flute, transverse. The German flute.

Flûte traversière (Fr.) (floot trăv-ĕr-sǐär.) The transverse or German flute.

Flute-work. In the organ, the *flute-work* includes all flue-stops not belonging to the *principal-work* and *gedact-work,* as well as various modifications of these two groups.

Flutist. } A flute player.
Flûtiste (Fr.) (floo-tēst.) }

Fluttuan. An organ-stop with a tone resembling a horn.

Flying cadence. See *False Cadence.*

F moll (Ger.) (ĕf mŏll.) The key of F minor.

Fóco (It.) (fō-kō.) Fire, ardor, passion. Also *Fuoco.*

Focosaménte (It.) (fō-kō-zä-men-tĕ.) Ardently, vehemently.

Focosíssimo (It.) (fō-kō-*zēe*-sē-mō.) Very ardently; with a great deal of passion.

Focóso (It.) (fō-*kō*-zō.) Fiery, passionate.

ă as in *ah;* ā as in *hate;* ă as in *at;* ē as in *tree;* ĕ as in *eh;* ī as in *pine;* ĭ as in *pin*

Robert Schumann

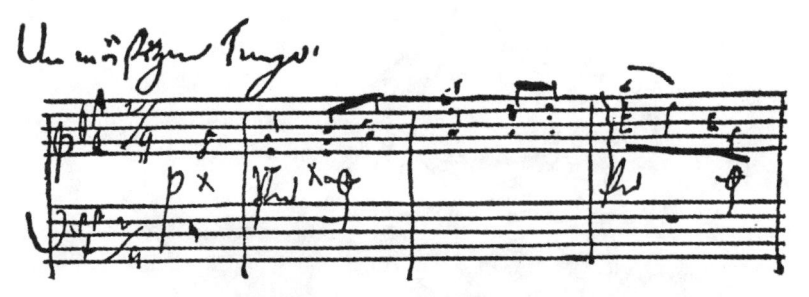

"Ländliches Lied" from No. 20, Album for the Young

Flute

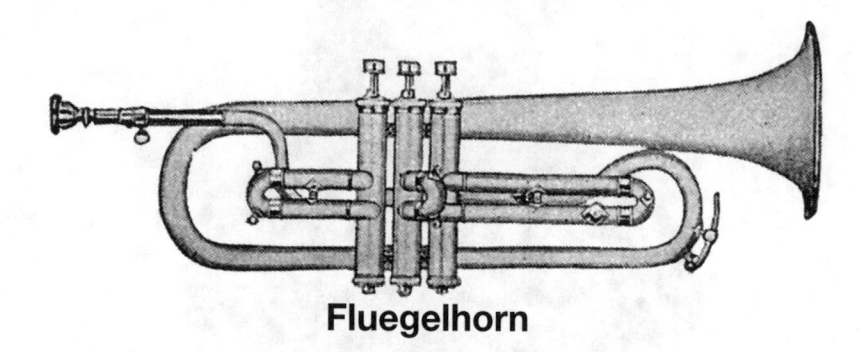

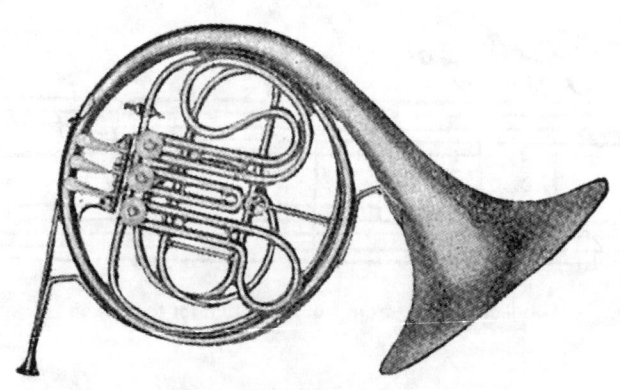

Fluegelhorn

French Horn

Fogliétto (It.) (fōl-yē-*et*-tō.) Copy of the first violin part, in which the *sólo* passages of the other instruments, the voice parts, and the cues for the entrance of different instruments, are indicated for the use of the leader.

Fois (Fr.) (fwä.) Time.

Fois, deuxième (Fr.) (fwä dü-zĭ-ām.) The second time.

Fois, première (Fr.) (fwä prĕm-ĭ-ār.) The first time.

Folâtre (Fr.) (fō-*lätr*.) Frolicsome, wild, playful.

Folio, music. A case for holding loose sheets of music; a wrapper used in a music-store for the convenience of classifying the music.

Fondamentále (It.) (fŏn-dä-měn-*tä*-lĕ.)
Fondamentale (Fr.) (fŏnh-dä-mänh-*täl*.)
} Fundamental; fundamental bass.

Fondaménto (It.) (fŏn-dä-*men*-tō.) The fundamental bass; the roots of the harmony.

Fond d'orgue (Fr.) (fŏnh d'ŏrg.) The most important stop in an organ, called in England the "open diapason, 8-foot scale." In Germany this is called the "8-foot principal."

Foot. 1. A certain number of syllables constituting a distinct metrical element in a verse. In very old English music it was a kind of drone accompaniment to a song which was sustained by another singer. 2. That part of an organ-pipe below the mouth. 3. The unit of measure in organ-pipes. An open-pipe 8-foot long sounds, and if a series of organ-pipes begin with this tone given by such a pipe, we call the series "8-foot tone." Any stop sounding its actual pitch (as a piano-key would do), is called "8-foot." If sounding an octave higher, "4-foot," two octaves higher, "2-foot," an octave lower "16-foot," etc. The sound-waves of being eight feet long, of the octave lower sixteen feet, the octave higher four feet, etc. See Pole's "Philosophy of Music," and Zahm's "Sound and Music."

Fork, tuning. A small steel instrument with two tines and a handle, used for ascertaining the pitch of any given tone. Tuning-forks were invented by John Shore, a sergeant trumpeter in the English army, in 1711. The early forks were always dated, which helps us greatly in ascertaining the ancient pitches. Tuning-forks generally sound a or a^3, for orchestral purposes and c or c^4 for tuning pianos and organs. Inventions have been made by which the pitch of the tuning-fork can be changed to any note.

Forlána (It.) (fŏr-*lä*-nä.)
Forlane (Fr.) (fŏr-*län*.)
} A lively Venetian dance in 6/8 time, used by the gondoliers. It is introduced in Ponchielli's "La Gioconda."

Form. Although modern music has become very vague in its shapes and frequently eludes analysis, yet there is in most music a definite architecture that can be studied as readily as the shape of a building. "Architecture is frozen music," and the converse of this proposition is also true, for every classical work and almost every bit of folk-song has a clear and recognizable shape. Musical form generally possesses two elements — contrast and symmetry. In a simple period there are two divisions in contrast and balance, See *Antecedent* and *Consequent*. This in itself makes a complete shape, as follows:

ŏ as in *tone*; ô as in *dove*; ŏ as in *not*; ŭ as in *up*; ü the French sound of *u*.

Starting from this as a unit, we can build a larger form by balancing two such periods against each other, ending the first in any key, but returning to the tonic key at the end of the second period. "Annie Laurie" is an example of the form of two periods. Another principle now comes into play, as the forms grow larger. This is *to end as we began*, thus bringing symmetry more strongly to the foreground. This can be attained even in the form of two periods by causing the consequent of the second period to repeat (with alterations) the antecedent phrase of the first period. "The Blue Bells of Scotland," "The Last Rose of Summer," "Auld Lang Syne," "Drink to Me Only with thine Eyes," "The Old Folks at Home," and a host of folk-songs are built upon this model. The principle of ending as we began is carried still further in the form of three divisions in which the entire first period returns.

In this form of three divisions the second division may be a symmetrical period, a countertheme, or it may be a free interlude without a cadence (as above) — an episode. In the return of the first period (the third division), the antecedent is usually presented exact, or nearly so, but the consequen may be freely altered and even a new consequent may appear. Without dwelling upon the variants of this three-division form which is very freely used in drawing-room music (see Mendelssohn's "Songs without Words" for many examples) we pass to a still larger form of three divisions. The forms above described are generally called "Song-forms." By placing two of these complete song-forms in contrast with each other, in a single composition, we obtain a larger form which we call "Minuet-form" or "Song-form with Trio." The shape of this is as follows: Part I. A complete song-form of two or three divisions. Part II. Another complete song-form of from one to three divisions. This is called the *Trio*, from the fact that in the eighteenth century the contrasting piece was generally in three-part harmony. It is most frequently in the subdominant key. Part III. A return of Part I, either complete or its first period only. If the abbreviated form is used the trio should be larger than a single period. See Chopin's "Polonaise in A," for full form. Another form, a simple "second rondo," although sometimes called a "five-part song-form," is made as follows: Div. 1. A period. Div. 2. Another period, in contrast. Div. 3. The first period again. Div. 4. A second contrasted period, different from Div. 2. Div. 5. A return of the first period, once more. Schumann made a still larger form from this by having each of the above divisions complete song-forms, thus making a song-form with two trios. Larger forms still were evolved from the cycle-forms (which see) of the seventeenth and eighteenth centuries. In these, the Suite, Partita, etc., several different movements were placed in contrast with each other. See *Suite, Sonata, Symphony.* Consult Parry's "The Evolution of the Art of Music," Goetschius' "Lessons in Music Form," and Elson's "Theory of Music," for fuller details.

Fórte (It.) (*fōr*-tĕ.) Loud, strong.
Fortement (Fr.) (*fōrt*-mänh.) ⎫
Forteménte (It.) (fōr-tĕ-*men*-tĕ.) ⎬ Loudly, powerfully, vigorously.
Forte mezzo (It.) (fōr-tĕ mā-zō.) With medium power.
Fortézza (It.) (fōr-*tet*-zä.) Force, power, strength.
Fórte-piáno (It.) (fōr-te-pē-*ä*-nō.) ⎫
Forte-piano (Fr.)(fōrt pĭ-*ä*-nō.) ⎬ The piano.
Forte-piano (Ger.) (*fōr*-té pĭ-*ä*-nō.) ⎭
Fórte possíbile (It.) (*fōr*-tĕ pŏs-*sē*-bē-lĕ.) As loud as possible.
Fortiss. An abbreviation of *Fortissimo.*
Fortíssimo (It.) (fōr-*tēs*-sē-mō.) Very loud.
Fortíssimo quanto possíbile (It.) (fōr-*tēs*-sē-mō quän-tō pŏs-*sē*-bē-lĕ.) As loud as possible.
Fortsetzung (Ger.) (*fōrt*-sĕt-soong.) A continuation.
Fortsingen (Ger.) (*fōrt*-sĭng-ĕn.) To continue singing.

Fórza (It.) (*fōrt*-sä) Force, strength, power.
Forzándo (It.) (fōr-*tsän*-dō.) ⎫ Forced;
Forzáto (It.) (fōr-*tsä*-tō.) ⎬ laying a stress upon one note or chord; sometimes marked ∧ >.
Forzare (It.) (fōr-*tsä*-rĕ.) To strengthen; to force.
Fourchette tonique (Fr.) (foor-shĕt tŏnh-ēk.) A tuning-fork.
Fourth. A distance comprising three diatonic intervals; that is, two tones and a half.
Fourth, augmented. An interval containing three whole tones.
Fourth flute. A flute sounding a fourth higher than the concert flute.
Fourth, perfect. An interval containing two whole tones and a semi-tone.
Française (Fr.) (fränh-*sāyz.*) A graceful dance in ¾ time.
Française (Fr.) (fränh-*sāis.*) ⎫ French;
Franzése (It.) (frän-*tsā*-zĕ.) ⎬ in the French style.
Französisch (Ger.) (fränt-*sŏ*-zĭsh.) ⎭
Franchézza (It.) (frän-*ket*-zä.) Freedom, confidence, boldness.
Frappé (Fr.) (frăp-pā.) *Stamping, striking;* a particular manner of beating time or striking notes with force.
Frapper (Fr.) (frăp-pā.) To beat the time; to strike.
Frási (It.) (*frä*-zē.) Phrases; short musical passages.
Frauenchor (Ger.) A female chorus.
Frauenstimme (Ger.) (frow-ĕn-stĭm-mĕ.) A female voice.
Freddamente (It.) (fred-de-*men*-tĕ.) Coldly; without animation.
Freddézza (It.) (frĕd-*de*-tsä.) Coldness, frigidity.
Fréddo (It.) (*fred*-dō.) Cold; devoid of sentiment.
Fredon (Fr.) (fre-dŏnh.) Trilling; a flourish, or other extemporaneous ornament.
Fredonner (Fr.) (fre-dŏnh-nā.) To trill; to shake; also, to hum; to sing low.
Free composition. In a free style; a composition not in strict accordance with the rules of musical art.

ō as in *tone*; ŏ as in *dove*; ŏ as in *not*; ŭ as in *up*; ü the French sound of *u*.

Free reed. A reed-stop in an organ, in which the tongue by a rapid vibratory motion to and fro produces the sound. The tone of a *free* reed is smooth and free from rattling, but not usually so strong as that of the *striking* reed.

Fregiáre (It.) (frä-jē-ä-rĕ.) To adorn; to embellish.

Fregiáto (It.) (fre-jē-ä-tō.) Embellished, ornamented.

Fregiatúra (It.) (fre-jē-ä-tōo-rä.) An ornament; an embellishment.

Frei (Ger.) (frī.) Free; unrestrained as to style.

Freie Schreibart (Ger.) (*frī*-ĕ *shrīb*-ärt.) Free style of composition.

Frémissement (Fr.) (*frā*-mēss-mänh.) Humming; singing in a low voice; a murmur.

French horn. See *Horn*.

French sixth. One form of an augmented sixth; a chord composed of a major third, extreme fourth, and extreme sixth. See *Extreme*.

French treble clef. The G clef on the lowest line of the staff, formerly much used in French music for violin, flute, etc. See *Clef*.

Frenetico (It.) (frĕ-*nĕt*-ē-kō.) Frenzied.

Frescaménte (It.) (frĕs-kä-*men*-tĕ)
Frésco (It.) (*frĕs*-kō.)
Freshly, vigorously, lively.

Frétta (It.) (*fret*-tä.) Increasing the time; accelerating the movement.

Frets. Short pieces of wire, wood, or ivory, fixed on the finger-board of guitars, etc., which, as the strings are brought in contact with them by the pressure of the fingers, serve to vary and determine the pitch of the tone.

Freude (Ger.) (*froy*-dĕ.) Joy, rejoicing.

Freuden-gesang (Ger.) (*froy*-d'n gĕ-*säng*.) A song of joy.

Freudig (Ger.) (*froy*-dĭg.) Joyfully.

Freudigkeit (Ger.)(*froy*-dĭg-kīt.) Joyfulness, joyousness.

Friedens-marsch (Ger.) (*frē*-d'ns märsh.) A march in honor of peace.

Frisch (Ger.) (frĭsh.) Freshly, briskly, lively.

Frívolo (It.) (*frē*-vō-lō.) Frivolous; trifling, trashy.

Frohgesang (Ger.) (*frō*-ghĕ-*säng*.) A joyous song.

Fröhlich (Ger.) (*frŏ*-līkh.) Joyous, gay.

Fröhlichkeit (Ger.) (*frŏ*-līkh-kīt.) Joyfulness, gayety.

Frohnamt (Ger.) (*frōn*-ämt.) High Mass.

Frosch (Ger.) (frōsh.) The lower part or nut of a violin bow.

Fróttola (It.) (*frōt*-tō-lä.) A ballad; a song.

Frühlingslied (Ger.) (*frü*-lĭngs-lēd.) Spring song.

Frühmesse (Ger.) (*frü*-mĕs-sĕ.) Matins; early Mass.

F-schlüssel (Ger.) (ĕf-*shlüs*-s'l.) The F or bass clef.

Fúga (It.) (*foo*-gä.) A *flight*; a chase. See *Fugue*.

Fúga authentica (Lat.) (*fū*-gä aw-*thĕn*-tĭ-kä.) A fugue with an *authentic* theme or subject.

Fúga canonica (Lat.) (*fū*-gä kä-*nŏn*-ĭ-kä.) A canon.

Fúga contraria (Lat.) (*fū*-gä kŏn-*trä*-rĭ-a.) A fugue in which the answer is generally *inverted*.

Fúga doppia (It.) (foo-gä *dōp*-pē-ä.) A double fugue.

Fúga irregularis (Lat.) (fū-gä ĭr-rĕg-ū-*lä*-rĭs.) An irregular fugue.

Fúga libera (Lat.) (fū-gä *lĭb*-ĕ-rä.) A free fugue.

Fúga mixta (Lat.) (fū-gä *mĭx*-tä.) A mixed fugue.

Fúga obbligata (Lat.) (fū-gä ŏb-lĭ-gä-tä.) A strict fugue.

Fúga plagale (It.) (*foo*-gä plä-*gä*-lĕ.) A fugue with a *plagal* theme or subject.

Fúga propria (Lat.) (fū-gä *prō* prĭ-ä.) A regular fugue strictly according to rule.

Fugara (Lat.) (fū-*gä*-rä.) An organ-stop of the gamba species.

Fúga ricercáta (It.) (*foo*-gä rē-tshär-*kä*-tä.) A fugue with many contrapuntal devices.

Fúga sciólta (It.) (*foo*-gä shē-*ōl*-tä.)
Fúga soluta (Lat.) (*fū*-gä sŏ-*lū*-tä.)
A free fugue.

ä as in *ah*; ā as in *hate*; ă as in *at*; ē as in *tree*; ĕ as in *eh*; ī as in *pine*; ĭ as in *pin*;

Fugáto (It.) (foo-*gä*-tō.) In the style of a fugue.

Fuge (Ger.) (*foo*-ghĕ.) }
Fugha (It.) (*foo*-gä.) } A fugue.

Fughétta (It.) (foo-*get*-tä.) A short fugue.

Fughetten (Ger.) (foo-*ghĕt*-t'n.) Fugues.

Fugirtes (Ger.) (foo-*gēer*-tĕs.) } In the
Fugirt (Ger.) (foo-*gēert*.) } fugue style; *fugirt* is also applied to the ranks of a mixture-stop in an organ.

Fugitive pieces. Ephemeral, compositions.

Fugue (fūg.) A term derived from the Latin word *fuga*, a flight. It is a composition in the strict style, in which a subject is proposed by one part and answered by other parts, according to certain rules. The old canons were called *fugues*. Fugues can be classified as follows: 1. According to the number of voices appearing, as "a two-voiced fugue," "a three-voiced fugue," etc. 2. According to the number of subjects; a fugue with one subject is a "single fugue," one with two subjects is a "double fugue," etc. 3. According to the exactness of the answer; an answer that exactly imitates the subject on the degree of the dominant, constitutes a "real fugue," while an answer which has some alterations from the subject, in order to keep it in the "tone" or key of the composition, constitutes a tonal fugue. 4. According to the modulations and scale-form of the composition; a fugue which keeps within the diatonic progressions is called a "diatonic fugue," while one which has chromatic progressions in its subject and answer is a "chromatic fugue." There are also fugues written in the old Greek scales (similar to the Gregorian tones) and these are called by the names of these scales as a "doric fugue," etc. 5. According to the style of the answer, which may be inverted or augmented, producing an inverted or augmented fugue. Finally, a fugue may be strict or free, according to the style of its treatment. Fugues differ very greatly in their construction, but in one point they are all alike; every fugue is a contrapuntal development of the subject which is announced quite alone at the beginning. Most fugues use more than this material; they develop the entire *exposition*. This exposition is made up of: 1st. The subject, which is a figure or phrase, *not* a complete melody. 2d. The answer, which is the subject reproduced on the degree of the dominant, either above or below. 3d. The counter-subject, which is a contrasted phrase, accompanying the subject or the answer, from the entrance of the second voice. One shape of four-voiced expositions in a strict fugue may be presented as follows:

Soprano	———	———	———	Answer.
Alto	———	———	Subject	{ Counter-subject.
Tenor	———	Answer	{ Counter-subject	Free part.
Bass	Subject	{ Counter-subject	Free part	Free part.

But there are many more free than the above. The moment that the exposition is ended (there is no pause) the voices go on to treatment of the matter presented. Every device of counterpoint is used, so that the fugue becomes the most intellectual composition in music. Episodes may occur, in which we find interesting derivations from figures of the first part; *strettos* may be found in which the subject and answer overlap each other, as in a *canon*. The normal fugue is made of an alternation of *strettos* (strict) and *episodes* (free). In Bach's "Well-tempered Clavichord," Vol. II, No. 9, there is an example of this. No. 5, in the same volume, is another. Sometimes the fugue does not attempt stretto work at all, but is made (a free fugue) of episodes. See No. 12 of the same volume. Sometimes a fugue can be made wholly of strettos without episodes, as in the same work, Vol. I, No. 1. Sometimes the strettos become absolute canons, as in Vol. II, No. 7 (Mozart's favorite fugue): but whichever mode of treatment is followed, the body of the fugue is logically derived from the exposition, there are no full cadences, no complete melodies, and no repetitions of any divisions. An organ-point is given in some fugues near the end, and the last division is an episode which is called *The Coda*. In some fugues the counter-subject is regularly worked up with the subject and answer. See *Well-tempered Clavichord*, Vol. II,

No. 9, for example of this. In others, there is no regular recurring counter-subject. See VOL. II, No. 7, for this. Some fugues are chiefly developed by double or triple counterpoint (see VOL. I, Nos. 2, 3, and 10, for this) not relying upon strettos in any degree. A stretto driven through all the voices at regular time-distance and intervals, forming a short canon, is called a *Stretto Maestrale*, or *Masterly Stretto*. See VOL. II, No. 5, in the final stretto, for an example of this. The double fugue is two fugues going on at the same time; that is, it presents two subjects and two answers, worked up simultaneously. For examples of this, see the "Kyrie Eleison" of Mozart's Requiem or the finale of the second part of Haydn's "Creation." For further details regarding fugues see Prout's "Fugue" and "Fugal Analysis," Higg's "Primer of Fugue," and Boekelman's colored edition of "Bach's Fugues."

Fugue, counter. A fugue in which the subjects move in contrary directions.

Fugue, double. A fugue on two subjects.

Fugue renversée (Fr.) (füg ränh-věr-sā.) A fugue, the answer in which is made in contrary motion to that of the subject.

Fugue, simple. A fugue containing but a single subject.

Fugue, strict. A fugue in which the fugal form and its laws are strictly observed.

Führer (Ger.) (*füh*-rěr.) Conductor, director; also the subject or leading theme in a fugue.

Full. For all the voices of instruments.

Full anthem. An anthem in four or more parts, without verses or solo passages; to be sung by the whole choir in chorus.

Full band. A band in which all the instruments are employed.

Full cadence. See *Perfect Cadence.*

Füll-flöte (Ger.) (*fül* flô-tě.) *Filling-flute;* a stopped organ-register of 4-foot tone.

Full orchestra. An orchestra in which all the orchestral stringed and wind instruments are employed.

Full organ. An organ with all its registers or stops in use.

Full score. A complete score of all the parts of a composition, vocal or instrumental, or both combined, written on separate staves placed under each other.

Full service. A service for the whole choir in chorus.

Fundamental. An epithet applied to a chord when its lowest note is that from which the chord is derived.

Fundamental bass. The name given to any bass note when accompanied with the chord derived from that note.

Fundamental chord. A chord whose lowest note is that from which the chord is derived.

Fundamental note. The note on which the chord is constructed.

Fundamental tones. The tonic, dominant, and subdominant of any scale or key.

Funèbre (Fr.) (fü-*nābr*.) ⎫
Funeràle (It.) (foo-ně-*rä*-lě.) ⎬ Funereal, mournful.
Funéreo (It.) (foo-*nā*-rě-ō.) ⎭

Funestamente (It.) (foo-něs-tä-*men*-tě.) Mournfully.

Fünf (Ger.) (fünf.) Five.

Fünf-fach (Ger.) (*fünf* fäkh.) *Five-fold;* five ranks; speaking of organ-pipes.

Fünf-stimmig (Ger.) (*fünf* stĭm-mĭg.) For five voices.

Funzióne (It.) (foont-sē-*ō*-ně.) Function, or ceremony in a church.

Funzióni (It. pl.) (foont-sē-*ō*-nē.) Oratorios, Masses, and other sacred musical performances in the Roman Catholic Church.

Fuóco (It.) (foo-*ō*-kō.) Fire, energy, passion.

Fuocóso (It.) (foo-ō-*kō*-zō.) Fiery, ardent, impetuous.

Für (Ger.) (für.) For.

Für das ganze Werk (Ger.) (für däs *gänt*-sě värk.) ⎫
Für das volle Werk (Ger.) (für däs *fōl*-lě värk.) ⎬
For the full organ.

Für die linke Hand allein (Ger.) (für dě

ä as in *ah;* ā as in *hate;* ă as in *at;* ē as in *tree;* ĕ as in *eh;* ī as in *pine;* ĭ as in *pin;*

līn-kĕ händ äl-*līn*.) For the left hand alone.

Für die rechte Hand allein (Ger.) (für dē rĕkh-tĕ händ äl-*līn*.) For the right hand alone.

Fureur (Fr.) (fü-*rŭr*.) } Fury, passion,
Fúria (It.) (*foo*-rē-ä.) } rage.

Furibóndo (It.) (foo-rē-*bŏn*-dō.) Furious; mad; extreme vehemence.

Furie (Fr.) (fü-rē.) Fury, passion.

Furieusement (Fr.) (fü-riüz-mänh.)
Furiosaménte (It.) (foo-rē-ō-zä-*men*-tĕ.)
Furiously, madly.

Furiosíssimo (It.) (foo-rē-ō-*sēs*-sē-mō.) Very furiously.

Furióso (It.) (foo-rē-*ō*-zō.) Furious, vehement, mad.

Furlándo (It.) (foor-*län*-dō.) } The for-
Furláno (It.) (foor-*lä*-nō.) } lana; the gondolier's dance in Venice.

Furniture stop. An organ-stop consisting of several ranks of pipes, of very acute pitch. A mixture-stop.

Furóre (It.) (foo-*rō*-rĕ.) Fury, rage, passion.

Fusa (Lat.) (*fū*-sä.) An eighth note.

Fusée (Fr.) (fü-*zā*.) A very rapid roulade or passage; a skip, etc.

Fusella (Lat.) (fū-*sĕl*-lä.) Name formally applied to the demisemiquaver.

Fuss (Ger.) (foos.) Foot; the lower part of an organ-pipe.

Füsse (Ger. pl.) (*füs*-sĕ.) Feet.

Füssig (Ger.) (*füs*-sĭg.) Footed; 8-füssig, of 8-foot pitch.

Fusston (Ger.) (*foos*-tōn.) The *tone*, or *pitch*; as 8-*Fusston*, a pipe of 8-foot tone.

Fz. An abbreviation of *Forzando*.

G

G. The fifth note of the normal scale of C, called *Sol*. The lowest or fourth string of a violin, the third of the viola and violoncello. The key-note of the major scale, having one sharp in the signature. The letter-name of the treble clef.

G (Fr.) (*abb.* for *gauche*.) *Left*; as, *m.g.*, with the left hand.

Gagliárda (It.) (gäl-yē-*är*-dä.) A *galliard*.

Gagliardaménte (It.) (gäl-yē-är-dä-*men*-tĕ.) Briskly, gayly.

Gagliárdo (It.) (gäl-yē-*är*-dō.) Brisk, merry, gay.

Gai (Fr.) (gā.) Gay, merry.

Gaiement (Fr.) (gā-mänh.) } Merrily,
Gaiment (Fr.) (gā-mänh.) } lively, gay.

Gaillarde (Fr.) (gā-*yärd*.) Merry, brisk; also a *galliard*.

Gaillardement (Fr.) (gā-*yärd*-mänh.) Merrily, briskly.

Gaio (It.) (gä-ē-ō.) With gayety and cheerfulness.

Gája (It.) (gä-*yä*.) } Gay, merry, lively.
Gájo (It.) (gä-yō.) }

Gajamente (It.) (gä-yä-*men*-tĕ.) Gayly, cheerfully.

Galánte (It.) (gä-*län*-tĕ.) }
Galantemént (It.) (gä-län-tĕ-*men*-tĕ.) }
Gallantly, boldly.

Galanterie-fuge (Ger.) (gä-län-tĕ-*rēe* foo-gĕ.) A fugue in the free style.

Galanterien (Ger. pl.) (gä-län-tĕ-*rēe*-ĕn.) The ornaments, turns, trills, etc., with which the old harpsichord music was embellished.

Galanterie-stücke (Ger. pl.) (gä-län-tĕ-*rēe*-stü-kĕ.) Pieces in the free ornamental style.

Galliard. A lively old dance in triple time, formerly very popular. It was possibly the parent of the minuet, but was much quicker than that dance.

Galop (Fr.) (*găl*-ō.) A quick dance, generally in ¾ time.

Galopade (Fr.) (găl-ō-*päd*.) }
Galopp (Ger.) (găl-*ŏp*.) } A *galop*.
Galóppo (It.) (gä-*lŏp*-pō.) }

Gamba (It.) (gäm-bä.) The *viol di gámba*. See that term.

Gamba-bass. A 16-foot organ-stop, on the pedals.

Gámba major. A name given to a 16-foot organ-stop or double gamba.

Gambe (Ger.) (*gäm*-bĕ.) Viol di gámba.

Gamma (It.) (*gäm*-mä.) } The gamut or
Gamme (Fr.) (gäm.) } scale.

ō as in *tone*; ô as in *dove*; ŏ as in *not*; ŭ as in *up*; ü the French sound of *u*.

121

Gamme chromatique (Fr.) (găm krō-măt-ĕk.) The chromatic scale.

Gamut. The scale of notes belonging to any key; the lines and spaces on which the notes are placed.

Gamut G. That G which is on the first line of the bass staff.

Gamut, Guido's. The table or scale introduced by Guido, and to which he applied the syllables ut, ra, mi, fa, sol, la. It consisted of twenty notes, namely, two octaves and a major sixth, the first octave distinguished by the capital letters, G, A, B, etc., the second by the small letters, g, a, b, etc., and the major sixth by double letters, gg, aa, bb, etc.

Ganascióne (It.) (gän-ä-shē-ō-nĕ.) An Italian lute.

Gang (Ger.) (gäng.) Pace; rate of movement or motion.

Ganz (Ger.) (gänts.) Whole, entire; also, all, very.

Ganz langsam (Ger.) (*gänts läng*-säm.) Very slowly.

Ganze Note (Ger.) (*gän*-tsĕ *nō*-tĕ.) A *whole note*, or semibreve.

Ganzer Ton (Ger.) (*gän*-tsĕr tōn.) A whole tone.

Ganzes Werk (Ger.) (*gän*-tsĕs värk.) The full organ.

Garbaménte (It.) (gär-bä-tä-*men*-tĕ.) Gracefully.

Garbáto (It.) (gär-*bä*-tō.) Graceful.

Gárbo (It.) (*gär*-bō.) Simplicity, grace, elegance.

Gariglione (It.) (gä-rēl-yē-ō-nĕ.) Chime; musical bells.

Garríre (It.) (gär-*rē*-rĕ.) To chirp; to warble like a bird.

Gastrollen (Ger.) (gäs-trōl-l'n.) A term applied to the rôles of a singer or actor on a starring expedition.

Gauche (Fr.) (gōzh.) Left.

Gauche, main (Fr.) (gōzh mănh.) The left hand.

Gaudénte (It.) (gow-*den*-tĕ.) Blithe, merry, sprightly.

Gaudenteménte (It.) (gow-dĕn-tĕ-*men*-tĕ.) Merrily, joyfully.

Gaudioso (It.) (gow-dē-ō-zō.) Merry, joyful.

Gavot (Eng.) (gă-*vŏt*.) } Even rhythm,
Gavótta (It.) (gä-*vōt*-tä.) } generally
Gavotte. (Fr.) (gä-vōt.) } quadruple.
The character of this dance should be genial and skipping. It should, properly, begin on the third beat, which results in a mild syncopation which is one of the charms of the gavotte. The phrases are generally short. Some gavottes have a *musette* as second part (or trio), the character of which should always be rustic. The musette has generally a drone-bass, which imitates the bagpipe.

Gazzarra (It.) (gät-zär-rä.) Rejoicings with music and cannon.

G clef. The treble clef; a character representing the letter G which invariably turns on the second line of the staff. It determines the position of one-lined G (g^3) upon the staff. See *Clef*.

G double or double G. The octave below G gamut.

G dur (Ger.) (gā door.) The key of G major.

Geberdenspiel (Ger.) (ghĕ-*bär*-d'n-spēl.) Pantomine.

Geblase (Ger.) (ghĕ-*blä*-zĕ.) Trumpeting, blowing.

Gebläse (Ger.) (ghĕ-*blā*-zĕ.) Bellows: apparatus for blowing.

Gebrochen (Ger.) (ghĕ-*brō*-kh'n.) Broken.

Gebrochene Akkorde (Ger.) (ghĕ-*brō*-kh'n-ĕ äk-*kōr*-dĕ.)
Gebróchener Accord (Ger.) (ghĕ-*brō*-kh'n-ĕr äk-*kōrd*.)
Broken chords; chords played in arpéggio.

Gebunden (Ger.) (ghĕ-*boon*-d'n.) Connected, syncopated, in regard to the style of playing or writing.

Gebundene Note (Ger.) (ghĕ-*boon*-dĕ-nĕ *nō*-tĕ.) A tied note; a note which is to be held and not repeated.

Geburts-lied (Ger.) (ghĕ-*boorts*-lēd.) Birthday song.

Gedackt (Ger.) (ghĕ-*däkht*.) } Stopped;
Gedeckt (Ger.) (ghĕ-*dĕkht*.) } in opposition to the open pipes in an organ.

Gedact. See *Gedackt*.

GEDACKT-FLÖTE   GELLENFLOTE

Gedackt-flöte (Ger.) (ghĕ-*däkht flō*-tĕ.) Stopped flute, in an organ.

Gedeckte Stimmen (Ger. pl.) (ghĕ-*dĕk*-tĕ *stĭm*-mĕn.) Stops with covered pipes, as the stopped diapason.

Gedehnt (Ger.) (ghĕ-*dānt*.) Lengthened.

Gedicht (Ger.) (ghĕ-*aĭkht*.) A poem; tale; fable.

Gefährte (Ger.) (ghĕ-*fār*-tĕ.) The answer in a fugue. Also called *Comes*.

Gefällig (Ger.) (ghĕ-*fäl*-lĭg.) Pleasingly, agreeably.

Gefühl (Ger.) (ghĕ-*fühl*.) Sentiment, expression.

Gegenbewegung (Ger.) (*gā*-g'n-bĕ-*vā*-goong.) Contrary motion.

Gegengesang (Ger.) (*gā*-g'n-ghĕ-*săng*.) Antiphony.

Gegenstimme (Ger.) (*gā*-g'n-stĭm-mĕ.) Counter-tenor, or alto part.

Gegensubject (Ger.) (*gā*-g'n-soob-jĕct.) Counter-subject, in a fugue.

Gehaucht (Ger.) (ghe-*howcht*.) Whispered; sighed out.

Gehend (Ger.) (*gā*-ĕnd.) A word referring to movement, and having the same meaning as *andánte*.

Geige (Ger.) (*ghī*-ghĕ.) The violin.

Geigen (Ger.) (*ghī*-g'n.) To play on the violin.

Geigen-blatt (Ger.) (*ghī*-g'n blät.) The finger-board of a violin.

Geigen-bogen (Ger.) (*ghī*-g'n-*bō*-g'n.) Violin-bow.

Geigen-clavicymbel. An instrument similar to a harpsichord.

Geigen-futter (Ger.) (*ghī*-g'n foot-tĕr.) Case for a violin.

Geigen-hals (Ger.) (*ghī*-g'n häls.) The neck of a violin.

Geigen-harz (Ger.) (*ghī*-g'n härts.) Spanish resin; hard resin.

Geigen-macher (*ghī*-g'n mä-khĕr.) A violin-maker.

Geigen-principal (Ger.) (*ghī*-g'n prĭn-tsĭ-*päl*.) A German organ diapason stop with a tone like that of the gamba, but fuller.

Geigen-saite (Ger.) (*ghī* g'n *say*-tĕ.) Violin-string.

Geigensattel (Ger.) (*ghī*-g'n sät-t'l.) }
Geigenseg (Ger.) (*ghī*-g'n stĕg.) { The bridge of a violin.

Geigenschule (Ger.) (*ghī*-g'n shoo-lĕ.) A violin school, or method of instruction.

Geigen-strich (Ger.) (*ghī*-g'n strīkh.) A stroke of the violin-bow.

Geigen-stück (Ger.) (*ghī*-g'n stük.) A tune for the violin.

Geigen-werk (Ger.) (*ghī*-g'n vărk.) The celestina, an organ-stop of 4-foot scale.

Geigen-wirbel (Ger.) (*ghī*-g'n vēr-b'l.) A violin-peg.

Geigen-zug (Ger.) (*ghī*-g'n tsoog.) A violin-stop.

Geiger (Ger.) (*ghī*-gher.) Violin-player.

Geistlich (Ger.) (*ghīst*-līkh.) Ecclesiastical, clerical.

Geistliche Gesänge (Ger.) (*ghīst*-līkh-ĕ gĕ-*sān*-ghĕ.) }
Geistliche Lieder (Ger.) (*ghīst*-līkh-ĕ *lē*-dĕr.) { Psalms, hymns, spiritual songs.

Geistreich (Ger.) (*ghīst*-rīkh.) } Full of
Geistvoll (Ger.) (*ghīst*-fōl.) { soul and of sentiment.

Geklingel (Ger.) (ghĕ-*klĭng*-'l.) Tinkling; ringing of a bell.

Gelassen (Ger.) (ghĕ-*läs*-s'n.) Calmly, quietly.

Gelassenheit (Ger.) (ghĕ-*läs*-'n-hīt.) Calmness, tranquility.

Geläufe (Ger.) (ghĕ-*loy*-fĕ.) } Running
Geläufen (Ger.) (ghĕ-*loy*-f'n.) { passages; scale passages; rapid movements.

Geläufig (Ger.) (ghĕ-*loy*-fĭg.) Easy, fluent, rapid.

Geläufigkeit (Ger.) (ghĕ-*loy*-fĭg-kīt.) Fluency, ease, velocity.

Geläut (Ger.) (ghĕ-*loyt*.) A peal of bells; ringing of bells.

Gelinde (Ger.) (ghĕ-*lĭn*-dĕ.) Softly, gently.

Gelindigkeit (Ger.) (ghĕ-*lĭn*-dĭg-kīt.) Softness, gentleness, sweetness.

Gellen (Ger.) (*ghĕl*-l'n.) To sound loudly.

Gellenflöte (Ger.) (*ghĕl*-l'n flō-tĕ.) Clarionet.

ō as in *tone*; ŏ as in *dove*; ŏ as in *not*; ŭ as in *up*; ü the French sound of *u*.

123

GEMACHLICH   GES

Gemachlich (Ger.) (ghĕ-*mäkh*-lĭkh.)
Gemachsam (Ger.) (ghĕ-*mäkh*-säm.)
Quietly; in a calm, slow manner.

Gemählig (Ger.) (ghĕ-*mä*-lĭg.) Gradually; by degrees.

Gemisch (Ger.) (ghĕ-*mĭsh*.) Mixed; mixture, or compound stops in an organ.

Gems-horn (Ger.) (*ghĕms* hōrn.) "Chamois-horn." In the organ, a metal flue-stop having tapering pipes of 8, 4, or 2-foot pitch on the manuals and of 16-foot pitch on the pedal, with mellow, horn-like timbre. The tone is light, but very clear.

Gems-horn-quint (Ger.) (*ghĕms*-hōrn-kwĭnt.) An organ-stop with conical pipes, sounding a fifth above the foundation stops.

Gemüth (Ger.) (ghĕ-*müt*.) Mind, soul.

Gemüthlích (Ger.) (ghĕ-*müt*-lĭkh.) Agreeable, expressive, genial.

Genera (Lat.) (*jĕn*-ĕ-rä.)
Genus (Lat.) (*jē*-nŭs.)
A term used by the Ancients to indicate the modes according to which they divided their tetrachords. The different methods of dividing the octave: when both tones and semi-tones are employed, according to the natural arrangement of the diatonic scale, it is called the *diatonic* or *natural genus*; when it is divided by semi-tones only, it is called the *chromatic* genus, and the *enharmonic* genus when quarter-tones alone are used.

General bass (Ger.) (gĕn-ĕr-*ahl* bass.) Thorough bass; figured bass.

General-pause (Ger.) (gĕn-ĕ-rahl *pow*-seh.) A general cessation or silence of all the parts.

Générateur (Fr.) (zhā-nĕ-rä-*tŭr*.) The fundamental note of the common chord.

Generator. The principal sound or sounds by which others are produced: the fundamental note of the common chord.

Génere (It.) (*je*-nĕ-rĕ.) See *Genera*.

Generoso (It.) (je-nĕ-*rō*-sō.) Noble; in a dignified manner.

Génie (Fr.) (*zhā*-nēe.)
Génis (It.) (jā-nēes.)
Genius, talent, spirit.

Genre (Fr.) (zhänhr.) Style, manner.

Genre chromatique (Fr.) (zhänhr krō-mä-*tēk*.) The chromatic genus.

Genre diatonique (Fr.) (zhänhr dĭ-ä-tŏnh-*ēk*.) The diatonic, or natural genus.

Genre enharmonique (Fr.) (zhänhr änh-här-mŏnh-*ēk*.) The enharmonic genus.

Genre expressif (Fr.) (zhänhr ĕks-prĕs-*sēf*.) The expressive style.

Gentíle (It.) (jĕn-*tē*-lĕ.) Pleasing, graceful, elegant.

Gentilézza (It.) (jĕn-tēl-*lĕt*-zä.) Grace; elegance; refinement of style.

Gentilménte (It.) (jĕn-tēl-*men*-tĕ.) Gracefully, elegantly.

Genus (Lat.) (*jā*-nŭs.) See *Genera*.

Genus chromaticum (Lat.) (*jā*-nüs krō-*mät*-ĭ-kŭm.) The chromatic genus or mode.

Genus diatonicum (Lat.) (*jā*-nŭs dĭ-ä-*tŏn*-ĭ-kŭm.) The diatonic genus or mode.

Genus enharmonicum (Lat.) (*jā*-nŭs ĕn-här-*mŏn*-ĭ-kŭm.) The enharmonic genus or mode.

Gerade Bewegung (Ger.) (ghĕ-*rä*-dĕ bĕ-*vä*-goong.) Parallel motion.

Gerade Taktart (Ger.) (ghĕ-*rä*-dĕ *täkt*-ärt.) Common time.

Geriesel (Ger.) (ghĕ-*rēe*-z'l.) A soft, murmuring sound.

German fingering. A method of fingering piano-music which designates the thumb as the first finger, in distinction from the English or American mode, which indicates the use of the thumb by a sign (x). See *Fingering*.

German flute. See *Fláuto Travérso*.

German scale. A scale of the natural notes, consisting of A, H, C, D, E, F, G, instead of A, B, C, etc., the B being always reserved to express B flat.

German sixth. A name given to a chord composed of a major third, perfect fifth, and extreme sixth, as —

German soprano clef. The C clef placed on the first line of the staff for soprano.

Ges (Ger.) (ghĕs.) The note G flat.

ă as in *ah*; ā as in *hate*; ă as in *at*; ē as in *tree*; ĕ as in *eh*; ī as in *pine*; ĭ as in *pin*;

124

GESANG GITANA

Gesang (Ger.) (ghĕ-*säng*.) Singing; the art of singing; a song; melody; air.

Gesang-buch (Ger.) (ghĕ-*säng* bookh.) Song-book, hymn-book.

Gesänge (Ger. pl.) (ghĕ-*säng*-ĕ.) Songs, hymns.

Gesangsweise (Ger.) (ghĕ-*sängs*-vī-zĕ.) In the style of a song.

Gesangverein (Ger.) (ghĕ-*sang*-fer-īn.) A singing society; a choral union.

Gesause (Ger.) (ghĕ-*sou*-zĕ.) Humming, whistling.

Geschick (Ger.) (ghĕ-*shĭk*.) Skill, dexterity.

Geschleift (Ger.) (ghĕ-*shlīft*.) Slurred, legato.

Geschwind (Ger.) (ghĕ-*shvĭnd*.) Quick, rapid.

Geschwindigkeit (Ger.) (ghĕ-*shvĭnd*-īg-kīt.) Swiftness, rapidity, speed.

Geschwindmarsch (Ger.) (ghĕ-*shvĭnd*-märsh.) A quickstep.

Ges dur (Ger.) (ghĕs door.) The key of G flat major.

Gestossen (Ger.) (ghĕ-*stōs*-s'n.) Separated, detached.

Gestrichene (Ger.) (ghĕ-*strĭ*-khĕ-nĕ.) A quaver. Also meaning *lined*, as *eingestrichene oktave*, the one-lined octave.

Getheilt (Ger.) (Gĕ-*tīlt*.) Divided, separated; *Getheilte Violinen*, violini divisi; *Getheilte Stimmen*, partial stops (organ).

Getragen (Ger.) (ghĕ-*trä*-g'n.) Well-sustained; carried.

Geübtere (Ger.) (ghĕ-*üb*-tĕ-rĕ.) Expert performers.

Gewirbel (Ger.) (ghĕ-*vĭr*-b'l.) The roll of drums.

Gewiss (Ger.) (ghĕ-*vĭss*.) Firm, resolute.

Gewissheit (Ger.) (ghĕ-*vĭss*-hīt.) Firmness, resolution.

Geziert (Ger.) (ghĕ-*tsērt*.) With affectation; embellished.

G flat. The flat seventh of A flat; the fifth flat introduced in modulating by fourths from the natural diatonic mode.

G gamut. The G on the first line of the bass staff, from the Greek *Gamma*, the lowest note of the ancient scale.

Ghiribízzi (It.) (ghĕ-rē-*bēt*-zē.) Unexpected intervals; eccentric; fantastical passages.

Ghiribizzóso (It.) (ghē-rē-bēt-*sō*-zō.) Fantastical, whimsical.

Ghironda (It.) (ghē-*rōn*-dä.) A hurdygurdy.

Giambo (It.) (jē-*äm*-bō.) Iambic.

Gicheróso (It.) (jē-kä-*rō*-zō.) Merry, playful.

Gíga (It.) (*jēe*-gä.) } A jig, or lively
Gigue (Fr.)(zhēg.) } species of dance.
Gige (Ger.) (ghēgeh.) } The name is supposed to be derived from the German word *geig*, or *geige*, meaning a fiddle, as the music is particularly adapted to instruments of that class. It is in $\frac{3}{4}$, $\frac{6}{8}$, $\frac{12}{8}$, and sometimes even $\frac{4}{8}$ rhythm. In almost every case it will be found to have a basis of rapidly-moving groups of three notes. It is the final movement of the suite, and is not unlike the modern tarantella in character, being very rapid, and possessing a rough heartiness.

G in alt. The first note in alt:

G in altissimo. The first note in altissimo; an octave above G in alt.

Giochévole (It.) (jē-ō-*kĕ*-vō-lĕ.) Merry, sportive, gay.

Giochevolménte (It.) (jē-ō-ke-vōl-*men*-tĕ.)

Giocolarménte (It.) (jē-ō-kō-lär-*men*-tĕ.)

Merrily, sportively.

Giocondaménte (It.) (jē-ō-kŏn-dä-*men*-tĕ.) Merrily, joyfully, gayly.

Giocóndo (It.) (jē-ō-*kŏn*-dō.) Cheerful, merry, gay.

Giocosaménte (It.) (jē-ō-kō-zä-*men*-tĕ.) }
Giocoso (It.) (jē-ō-*kō*-zō.) }
Humorously, sportively.

Giója (It.) (jē-*ō*-yä.) Joy, gladness.

Giojánte (It.) (jē-ō-*yän*-tĕ.) } Blithe, joy-
Giojóso (It.) (jē-ō-*yō*-zo.) } ful, gay.

Giojosaménte (It.) (jē-ō-yō-zä *men*-tĕ.) Joyfully, merrily.

Gioviále (It.) (jē-ō-vē-*ä*-lĕ.) Jovial.

Giovialita (It.) (jē-ō-vē-ä-lē-*tä*.) Joviality, gayety.

Gis (Ger.) (ghĭs.) The note G sharp.

Gis moll (Ger.) (ghĭs mōll.) The key of G ♯ minor.

Gitana (It.) (jē-*tä*-nä.) A Spanish dance.

ŏ as in *tone*; ô as in *dove*; ŏ as in *not*; ŭ as in *up*; ü the French sound of *u*.

Giubbilóso (It.) (joob-bē-*lō*-zō.) Jubilant, exulting.
Giúbilazione (It.) (joo-bē-lät-sē-*ō*-nĕ.)
Giúbilio (It.) (joo-bē-lē-ō.)
Giúbilo (It.) (*joo*-bē-lō.)
Jubilation, rejoicing.
Giucante (It.) (joo-*kän*-tĕ.) } Merry,
Giuchevole (It.) (joo-*kĕ*-vo-lĕ.) } joyful. See *Giojante*.
Giulivaménte (It.) (joo-lē-vä-*men*-tĕ.) Joyfully, lively.
Giulivíssimo (It.) (joo-lē-*vēs*-sē-mō.) Very joyful.
Giulívo (It.) (joo-*lē*-vō.) Cheerful, joyful.
Giuocante (It.) (joo-ō-*kän*-tĕ.) With sport and gayety.
Giuocóso (It.) (joo-ō-*kō*-zō.) See *Giocoso*.
Giustaménte (It.) (joos-tä-*men*-tĕ.) Justly; with precision.
Giústo (It.) (*joos*-tō.) A term signifying that the movement indicated is to be performed in an equal, steady, and exact time. *Giusto* is sometimes used to indicate moderation, as *Allegro Giusto*, a moderate allegro.
Giustezza (It.) (joos-*tet*-zä.) Precision.
Given bass. A bass given, to which the harmony is to be added.
Giving out. The prelude by which the organist announces to the congregation the tune they are to sing.
Glais (Fr.) (glä.) The passing bell.
Glais funèbre (Fr.) (glä fü-*nābr*.) A funeral knell.
Glapissant (Fr.) (*glä*-pĭs-sänh.) Shrill, squeaking.
Glasses, musical. An instrument formed of a number of glass goblets shaped like finger-glasses, tuned by filling them with more or less water, and played upon with the fingers.
Glatt (Ger.) (glät.) Smooth, even.
Glätte (Ger.) (*glāt*-tĕ.) Smoothness, evenness.
Glee. A vocal composition in three or four parts, generally consisting of more than one movement, the subject of which may be grave, tender, or gay, and bacchanalian. The glee was less intricate than the madrigal, and was frequently accompanied, while the madrigal was sung *a cappella*. It is a composition peculiar to England.
Gleek. An old Anglo Saxon word, signifying *music* or *musician*. Also *Gligg;* probably the root of the word "Glee."
Gleemen. An ancient name for minstrels.
Gleich (Ger.) (glīkh.) Equal, alike, consonant.
Gleichklang (Ger.) (*glīkh*-kläng.) Consonance of sound.
Gleichstimmig (Ger.) (*glīkh*-stĭm-mĭg.) Harmonious, accordant.
Greiten (Ger.) (*glī*-t'n.) To slide the fingers *Glissando*.
Gli (It. pl.) (lyēe.) The (masculine plural) as *gli stromenti*, the instruments.
Glide. Portamento.
Gliding. In flute playing, a sliding movement of the fingers for the purpose of blending the tones.
Glissade (Fr.) (glĭs-*säd*.) Gliding; the act of passing the fingers in a smooth, unbroken manner over the keys or strings.
Glissándo (It.) (glēs-*sän*-dō.) } Slurred;
Glissáto (It.) (glēs-*sä*-tō.) } smooth;
Glissement (Fr.) (glēs-*mŏnh*.) } in a gliding manner. Sliding the finger.
Glisser (Fr.) (glēs-*sāy*.) An embellishment which is executed by turning the nail and drawing the thumb or finger rapidly over the keyboard. *Glissando*.
Glissez le pouce (Fr.) (glēs-sāy lŭh poos.) Slide the thumb.
Glissicándo (It.) (glis-sē-*kän*-dō.) } Slurred;
Glissicáto (It.) (glis-sē-*kä*-tō.) } smooth; in a gliding manner. See also *Glisser*.
Gli stroménti (It.) (lyēe strō-*men*-tē.) The instruments.
Glitschen (Ger., (*glĭt*-shĕn.) To glide the finger. See *Glisser*.
Glöckchen (Ger.) (*glŏk*-kh'n.) A little bell.
Glocke (Ger.) (*glōk*-ĕ.) A bell.
Glockengeläute (Ger.) (*glō*-k'n-gĕ-*loy*-tĕ.) The ringing or chiming of bells.
Glockenist (Ger.) (*glōk*-ĕn-ĭst.) } Player
Glöckner (Ger.) (*glŏk*-nĕr.) } on the chimes, or bell ringer.

ä as in *ah* ; ā as in *hate* ; ă as in *at*; ē as in *tree* ; ĕ as in *eh* ; ī as in *pine* ; ĭ as in *pin;*

126

GLOCKENKLANG   GRACE-NOTE

Glockenklang (Ger.) (*glōk*-ĕn-kläng.) The sound of bells.

Glockenläuter (Ger.) (*glōk*-ĕn-*loy*-tĕr.) Bell ringer.

Glockenspiel (Ger.) (*glōk*-ĕn-spēl.) Chimes; also, a stop in imitation of bells, in German organs. This German name, signifying a chime of bells, is applied to a set of small bars of polished steel, used in the orchestra, which, on being struck with a mallet, give forth tinkling tones of definite pitch. The glockenspiel is only used in passages of extreme sweetness, and the instrument is scarcely used in symphonies at all. It is sometimes supplied with a keyboard. Examples of its use can be found in the Feuer-Zauber in Wagner's opera "Die Walküre," and in Mozart's "Magic Flute."

Gloria (Lat.) (*glō*-rī-a.) A movement in a Mass, following the Kyrie.

Glottis (Gr.) (*glŏt*-tĭs.) The narrow opening in the larynx, forming the mouth of the windpipe, which by its dilation and contraction contributes to the modulation of the voice. The name is also applied to a kind of reed used by the ancient flute-players, which they held between their lips, and blew through in performance.

Glühend (Ger.) (*glü*-ĕnd.) Ardent, glowing.

G moll (Ger.) (gā môl.) The key of G minor.

Góla (It.) (*gō*-lä.) The throat; also, a gutteral voice.

Gondellied (Ger.) (*gŏn*-d'l-lēd.) A gondolier song.

Gondolier songs. Songs composed and sung by the Venetian gondoliers, of a very graceful and pleasing style; barcarolles.

Gong. A Chinese instrument of the pulsatile kind, consisting of a large, circular plate of metal, which, when struck, produces an exceedingly loud noise, not of definite pitch. Also called *Tamtam*.

Gorghéggi (It. pl.) (gŏr-*ged*-jē.) Rapid divisions, or passages, as exercises for the voice to acquire facility.

Gorgheggiaménto (It.) (gŏr-gĕd-jē-ä-men-tō.) Trilling, quavering.

Gorgheggiáre (It.) (gŏr-ged-jē-*ä*-rĕ.) To trill, to shake.

Gorgeggio (It.) (gŏr-*ged*-jē-ō.) A trill; a shake of the voice in singing.

Goût (Fr.) (goo.) Taste, style, judgment.

Governing key. The principal key; that key in which a piece is written.

Grab-gesang (Ger.) (*gräb* gĕ-säng.) ⎱ Dirge;
Grab-lied (Ger.) (*gräb* lēed.) ⎰ funeral song.

Grace.   ⎱ Ornamental notes and em-
Grace-note. ⎰ bellishments, either written by the composer, or introduced by the performer. The principal embellishments are the *appoggiatúre*, the *turn* and the *shake*. Any note added to a composition as an embellishment. Embellishments of every kind were most copious in harpsichord, spinet, and clavichord music, as well as in violin music, in the eighteenth century. In the first-named instruments their presence was often necessary, since they served to prolong a note (by trill, turn, or mordent) which these instruments could not sustain. But what began in necessity soon became a perverted taste. Marchand, in Paris, used to boast that he could add an embellishment to every note of a composition. Bach followed Marchand's plan of ornamentation in his suites and inventions. The matter of embellishments has been a very misty one from the beginning. In studying the eighteenth century rules one finds numerous inconsistencies. Ph. Em. Bach contradicts Leopold Mozart, and Brossard and Grassineau, in their dictionaries, differ from Callcott. It is not in the province of a dictionary to enter into the polemics of this subject. The reader can find a small encyclopedia of this matter in Dannreuther's "Musical Ornamentation" (2 vols.). Many of the signs are becoming obsolete, and it has become the custom to write the notation in full, in modern editions, avoiding the signs altogether. The chief signs of embellishments used at present are the *Trill, Turn, Mordent, Appoggiatura and Acciaccatura*, which will be found defined under their respective names. A brief synopsis of graces may be thus presented:

ō as in *tone*; ô as in *dove*; ŏ as in *not*; ŭ as in *up*; ü the French sound of *u*.

GRACE-NOTE   GRACILE

Appoggiatura.   *Trill.*
Written.   tr.
Played.

Turn.   *Mordent.*   *Anschlag.*

Schleifer.   *Schneller.*

Pralltriller.

Other signs with varying nomenclature are found in Bach and his contemporaries, as follows:

Written.   Played.

When the tempo is rapid, and there is difficulty in executing the figure in full, it can be played in five notes. Example:

Written.   Played.

The inversion of this figure is signified by this sign, ⌒⌇. Example:

Written.
Played.

There are also combinations of turns and trill, represented by single signs. This sign, ⌒⌇ signifies a trill beginning and ending with a turn:

Written.
Played.

while the following, ⌇⌒ signifies a trill beginning with an inverted turn, and ending with a simple turn. Example:

Written.
Played.

If, however, either of these signs occur over a short note, where there would not be time to trill, the two turns alone can be played. Example:

Written.
Played.

Although many more signs of embellishment and grace-notes might be added to the above, these (with the turn, trill, etc.) are all that will be found in practical use to-day, and even these are rapidly disappearing from modern notation, being written out in full when required.

Gracieux (Fr.) (grä-sĭ-ŭh.) Graceful.

Grácile (It.) (grä-tshēe-lĕ.) Thin, weak, small; referring to the tone.

ä as in *ah*; ā as in *hate*; ă as in *at*; ē as in *tree*; ĕ as in *eh*; ī as in *pine*; ĭ as in *pin*;

128

Grad (Ger.) (gräd.) Steps, degree. See *Grado*.

Gradáre (It.) (grä-*dä*-rĕ.) To descend step by step.

Gradataménte (It.) (grä-dä-tä-*men*-tĕ.)

Gradation (Fr.) (grä-dä-sē-ŏhn.)

Gradazióne (It.) (grä-dä-tsē-*ō*-nĕ.) By degrees; a gradual increase, or diminution of speed, or intensity of tone.

Gradévole (It.) (grä-*de*-vō-lĕ.)

Gradevolménte (It.) (grä-dā-vōl-*men*-tĕ. Gracefully, pleasingly.

Gradíre (It.) (grä *dēe*-rĕ.) To ascend step by step.

Gradleiter (Ger.) (*gräd*-lī-tĕr.) A scale.

Grádo (It.) (*grà*-dō.) A degree, or single step on the staff; *di grádo* means that the melody moves by degrees, ascending or descending, in opposition to *di sálto*, by skips of greater intervals.

Grádo ascendénte (It.) (grä-dō ä-shĕn-den-tĕ.) An ascending degree.

Grado descendénte (It.) (grä-dō dā-shĕn-den-tĕ.) A descending degree.

Gradual. 1. That part of the Roman Catholic service that is sung between the Epistle and the Gospel, and which was anciently sung on the steps of the altar. The name comes from *Gradus*, a step. 2. A *cantatorium* (book of chants) containing the graduals, introits, and other antiphons of the Catholic Mass.

Gradualménte (It.) (grä-doo-äl-*men*-tĕ.)

Graduataménte (It.) (gräd-doo-ä-tä-*men*-tĕ.) Gradually; by degrees or steps.

Graduáre (It.) (grä-doo-*ä*-rĕ.) To divide into degrees.

Graduazióne (It.) (grä-doo-ä-tsē-*ō*-nĕ.) See *Gradazione*.

Graduellement (Fr.) (grä-*dwăl*-mänh.)

Gradweise (Ger.) (*gräd*-vī-zĕ.) Gradually; by degrees.

Grammatical accent. The common measure accent, marked by the length of the words, and a regular succession of strong and weak parts. The regular rhythmic accent.

Grán (It.) (grän.)
Gránde (It.) (grän-dĕ.) Great, grand.

Grán cássa (It.) (grän *käs*-sä.) The bass drum.

Grand-barré (Fr.) (gränh bär-*rā*.) In guitar-playing this means laying the first finger of the left hand upon all the six strings of the guitar at once.

Grand bourdon. Great or double bourdon; an organ-stop of 32-foot tone in the pedal.

Grand chantre (Fr.) (gränh shäntr.) A precentor.

Grand choir. In organ-playing, the union of all the stops of the choir-organ.

Grand cornet. This name is sometimes given to a reed-stop of 16-foot scale on the manuals of an organ.

Grande messe (Fr.) (gränhd mäss.) High Mass.

Grande mesure à deux temps (Fr.) (gränhd mä-zhür ä dü tänh.) Common time of *two beats* in a bar, marked $\frac{2}{4}$. See also *Alla Cappélla*.

Grandézza (It.) (grän-*det*-sä.) Grandeur, dignity.

Grandióso (It.) (grän-dē-ō-zō.) Grand, noble.

Grandisonánte (It.) (grän-dē-zō-*nän*-tĕ.) Very sonorous; full-sounding.

Grand jeux (Fr.) (gränh zhü.) Full organ; all the stops in organ-playing.

Grand opera. A full opera with an intricate plot and full cast of performers.

Grand orgue (Fr.) (gränh dōrg.) Great organ.

Grand pianoforte. The largest size wing-shaped piano.

Grand sonata. An extended sonata, consisting generally of four movements.

Grán gústo (It.) (grän *goos*-tō.) In a lofty, elevated manner; a full, rich, high-wrought composition.

Grán prova (It.) (grän *prō*-vä.) A full rehearsal.

Grán tambúro (It.) (grän täm-*boo*-rō.) The bass drum.

Graphophone. See *Phonograph*.

Gráppa (It.) (*gräp*-pä.) The brace, or character used to connect two or more staves.

Gratias agimus (Lat.) (*grä*-shĭ-ăs *ăj*-ĭ-mŭs.) Part of the Gloria in a Mass.

ŏ as in *tone;* ô as in *love;* ŏ as in *not;* ŭ as in *u*₁ ü the French sound of *u*.

120

Grave (It.) (*grä*-vĕ.) A slow and solemn movement; also a deep low pitch in the scale of sounds. The slowest tempo in music.

Gravecembalum (Lat.) (*grä*-vĕ-sĕm-*bä*-lŭm.) An old name for the harpsichord.

Gravement (Fr.) (gräv-mänh.) }
Graveménte (It.) (grä-vĕ-*men*-tĕ.) } With gravity; in a dignified and solemn manner.

Gravézza (It.) (grä-*ve*-tsä.) Gravity, solemnity.

Gravicémbalo (It.) (grä-vē-*tshem*-bä-lō.) }
Gravicémbolo (It.) (grä-vē-*tshem*-bō-lō.) }
An old name for the harpsichord.

Gravisonante (It.) (grä-vē-zō-*nän*-tĕ.) Loud-sounding.

Gravita (It.) (grä-vē-*tä*.) }
Gravität (Ger.) (grä-fĭ-*tät*.) } Gravity, majesty.
Gravité (Fr.) (grä-vĭ *tä*.) }

Gravity. That modification of any sound by which it becomes deep or low in respect to some other sound. The gravity of sounds depends in general on the mass, extent, and tension of the sonorous bodies. The larger and more lax the bodies, the slower will be the vibrations and the graver the sounds.

Grázia (It.) (*grä*-tsē-ä.) } Grace, elegance.
Grazie (Ger.) (*grä*-tsī-ĕ.) }

Graziosaménte (It.) (grä-tsē-ō-zä-*men*-tĕ.) Gracefully, smoothly.

Grazióso (It.) (grä tsē-*ō*-zō.) In a graceful style.

Greater sixth. A name sometimes given to the major sixth.

Greater third. A name sometimes given to the major third.

Great octave. The name given in Germany to the notes between C and B inclusive; these notes are expressed by capital letters.

Great organ. In an organ with three rows of keys, usually the middle row, so-called because containing the most important stops, and having its pipes voiced loude than those in the swell or choir organ.

Great sixth. The appellation given to the chord of the fifth and sixth when the fifth is perfect and the sixth major.

Greek modes. The ancient Greek modes or scales were twelve in number; of these, six were *authentic*, and six *plagal*. The sounds are supposed to have been somewhat similar to those in the scale of C, but with different notes of beginning and completion. The Greek systems are composed of tetrachords (series of four notes with a compass of a perfect fourth) which succeed each other in two ways — either the last note of one tetrachord coincides with the first note of the adjoining tetrachord, or an interval of tone is left between them. See Monroe, "The Modes of Ancient Greek Music," and the "Oxford History of Music," Vol. I.

Gregorian chant. A style of choral music, according to the eight celebrated church modes introduced by Pope Gregory in the sixth century.

Gregorianisch (Ger.) (grĕ-gō-rĭ-*än*-ĭsh.) Gregorian.

Gregorianischer Gesang (Ger.) (grĕ-gō-rĭ-*än*-ĭsh.) The Gregorian chant.

Gregorian modes. } Those chants or melodies used for the psalms in the Roman Catholic service, and also in many English churches. They are taken from the ancient Greek modes, and the sounds are supposed to have been somewhat similar to those in the modern or natural scale of C; but with different orders of progression. See the "Oxford History of Music," Vol. I.
Gregorian tones. }

Gregoriáno (It.) (grĕ-gō-rē-*ä*-nō.) } Gregorian.
Grégorien (Fr.) (grĕ-gō-rĭ-änh.) }

Grell (Ger.) (grĕll.) Shrill, acute.

Grellheit (Ger.) (*grĕl*-hīt.) Sharpness, shrillness.

Grelot (Fr.) (grä-lō.) A small bell.

Griffbret (Ger.) (*griff*-brĕt.) The fingerboard of a violin, violoncello, etc.

Grillig (Ger.) (*grĭl*-lĭg.) Capricious, fanciful.

Gringotter (Fr.) (grănh-gō-*tä*.) To quaver; to warble.

Grisoller (Fr.) (grĕ-zō-*lä*.) To sing like a lark.

Grob (Ger.) (grōb.) Deep, low voice, coarse, rough.

Grob-gedackt (Ger.) (*grōb* ghĕ-*däkht*.) Large stopped diapason of full tone.

ä as in *ah*; ā as in *hate*; ă as in *at*; ē as in *tree*; ĕ as in *eh*; ī as in *pine*; ĭ as in *pin*;

Groppétto (It.) (grōp-*pet*-tō.) See *Gruppétto*.

Gróppo (It.) (grōp-pō.) A group of notes; a rapid vocal passage.

Grossartig (Ger.) (*grōs*-är-tĭg.) Grand.

Grosse (Ger.) (*grōs*-sĕ.) Major, speaking of intervals; also grand in respect to style.

Grosse caisse (Fr.) (*grōs*-kāss.) The bass drum.

Grosse nazard (Ger.) (*grōs*-sĕ nä-*tsärd*.) An organ-stop, sounding a fifth above the diapasons.

Grosse Principal (Ger.) (*grōs*-sĕ prĭn-tsĭ-*päl*.) An organ-stop of 32-foot scale of the open diapason species.

Grosse Quint (Ger.) (*grōs*-sĕ quĭnt.)
Grosse Quinten-bass (Ger.) (*grōs*-sĕ *quĭn*-t'n bäss.
An organ-stop in the pedals sounding a fifth or twelfth to the great bass of 32-foot or 16-foot.

Grosse Sonate (Ger. pl.) (*grōs*-sĕ sō-*nä*-tĕ.) Grand sonata.

Grosse Tierce (Ger.) (*grōs*-sĕ *tēr*-sĕ.) *Great third* sounding stop in an organ, producing the third or tenth, above the foundation stops.

Grosse Trommel (Ger.) (*grōs*-sĕ-*trōm*-m'l.) The bass drum.

Gross-gedacht (Ger.) (*grōs* ghĕ-*däkht*.) Double-stopped diapason of 16-foot tone in an organ.

Grósso (It.) (*grōs*-sō.) Full, great, grand.

Grossvatertanz (Ger.) (*grōs*-fä-tĕr-*tänts*.) Grandfather's dance; an antiquated, old fogy dance.

Gros tambour (Fr.) (grō tänh-boor.) The great-drum.

Grottésco (It.) (grō-*tes*-kō.) Grotesque.

Ground. The name of any composition in which the bass, consisting of a few bars of independent notes, is perpetually repeated to an ever-varying melody.

Ground bass. A bass consisting of a few simple notes, intended as a theme, on which, at each repetition, a new melody is constructed.

Group. Several short notes tied together.

Grund-stimme (Ger.) (*groond* stĭm-mĕ.) The bass part.

Grund-ton (Ger.) (groond tōn.) The bass note; fundamental, or principal tone.

Gruppe (Ger.) (*groop*-pĕ.) } A group of
Grúppo (It.) (*groop*-pō.) } notes; formerly it meant a trill, shake, or turn.

Gruppetto (It.) (groo-*pet*-to.) A turn. Also, a collective term applied loosely to various "groups," or grace-notes, such as:

[musical notation] etc.

G-schlüssel (Ger.) (gä-shlüs-s'l.) The G, or treble clef.

Guarácha (Spa.) (gwär-*äk*-ä.) A Spanish dance.

Guarnerius (gwär-*nä*-rĭ-ŭs.) A make of violin highly prized, so-called from the name of the manufacturer.

Guerriéro (It.) (gwĕr-rē-*ā*-rō.) Martial, warlike.

Guída (It.) (*gwē*-dä.) *Guide:* also, the mark called a *direct*. The subject of a fugue.

Guída armónica (It.) (gwē-dä är-*mō*-nē-kä.) A guide to harmony.

Guída musica (It.) (gwē-dä moo-zē-kä.) An instruction-book in music.

Guide-main (Fr.) (ghēd mănh.) The hand-guide, an instrument invented by Kalkbrenner, for assisting young players to acquire a good position of the hands on the pianoforte.

Guidon (Fr.) (ghē-dŏnh.) The mark called a *direct*.

Guidonian hand. The figure of a left hand used by Guido and upon which was marked the names of the sounds forming his three hexachords.

Guidonian syllables. The syllables, ut re, mi, fa, sol, la, used by Guido d'Arezzo, and called the Aretinian scale. See *Aretinian*.

Guido's gamut. The table or scale introduced by Guido d'Arezzo to the notes of which he applied the syllables ut, re, mi, fa, sol, la. It consisted of twenty notes, viz., two octaves and a major sixth, the first octave being distinguished by capital letters, the second by small letters, and the sixth by double small letters. See *Gamut*.

ŏ as in *tone*; ō as in *dove*; ŏ as in *not*; ŭ as in *up*; ü the French sound of *u*.

GUIMBARDE   HALLELUJAH

Guimbarde (Fr.) (ghĕm-bärd.) A Jew's harp.

Guitar (ghĭt-är.) An instrument with six strings, the body of which is somewhat oval in form and the neck somewhat similar to the violin. The strings are tuned in fourths, with the exception of the third string which is tuned a third below the second. There are many variations: acoustic, electric, 12-string, etc. It is supposed to be of Spanish invention and is very popular in that country. The guitar is not admitted to the orchestral ranks, although Schumann at first thought of employing it as accompaniment to the "Romanza" of his D minor symphony; but finding it too light toned he substituted violins, *pizzicato*, for it This same substitution is made in a few other cases where composers have used guitar or similar instruments, as, for example, the serenade of Almaviva in Rossini's "Barber of Seville," or the serenade of Don Giovanni in Mozart's opera. In the latter case the composer used the mandolin. The guitar is generally tuned:

having six strings, and sounds an octave lower than written. Compass (in actual pitch),

Guitare (Fr.) (ghĭt-är.)
Guitárre (Spa.) (ghē-tär-rä.) } A guitar.
Guitarre (Ger.) (ghĭt-är-rĕ.)

Guitare d'amour (Fr.) (ghē tär d'ä-moor.) A modification of the German guitar.

Guitare, lyre (Fr.) (ghē-tär lērh.) A French instrument having six strings and formed somewhat like an ancient lyre.

Gunst (Ger.) (goonst.) Grace, tenderness, favor.

Gurácho (Spa.) (goo-rä-kō.) See *Guarácha*.

Gústo (It.) (goos-tō.) Taste, expression.

Gustosaménte (It.) (goos-tō-zä-*men*-tĕ.) Tastefully, expressively.

Gustóso (It.) (goos-tō-zō.) Expressive, tasteful.

G, ut. A name applied by Guido to the tone large G, because this tone was the lowest of the whole system of tones.

Gut. The gutstrings of violins, guitars, etc., are *never* made of *Catgut*, although always called so. The best are made from the entrails of young lambs, and the finest come from Rome. (Ger., *Darmseite*; Fr., *Corde a boyau*; It., *Minugia*.)

Gutdünken (Ger.) (*goot*-dün-k'n.) At pleasure; according to the taste of the performer.

Guttural. Formed in the throat · pertaining to the throat.

Gutturalmente (It.) (goot-too-räl *men* tĕ.) Gutturally.

H

H. This letter is used by the Germans for B natural, which note is called b, the French and Italians, *si*. The German "H" came from the mistake, made nine centuries ago, of reading the "square b" (♮) as "h." See *Flat*.

Habanera (Spa.) (hä-*bän*-ĕ-rä.) A slow Spanish dance in ¾ or 6/8 time.

Haber-rohr (Ger.) (*hä*-bĕr rōr. Shepherd's flute.

Hackbrett (Ger.) (*häk*-brĕt.) The dulcimer.

Halb (Ger.) (hälb.) Half.

Halb-cadence (Ger.) (hälb kä-*dĕn*-tsĕ.) Half-cadence.

Halb-note (Ger.) (hälb *nō*-tĕ.) A half-note.

Halb-ton (Ger.) (hälb tōn.) Half-tone, semi-tone.

Half-cadence. An imperfect cadence; a close on the dominant.

Half-note. A minim, ♩.

Half-rest. A pause equal in duration to a half-note.

Half-shift. The first shift on a violin; that on the fifth line.

Half-step. The smallest interval used in our musical system.

Half-tone. A semi-tone.

Hall (Ger.) (häll.) } Sound,
Halle (Ger.) (*häl*-lĕ.) } clangor, clang.

Hallelujah (Heb.) (häl-lĕ-*loo*-yäh.)

ă as in *ah*; ā as in *hate*; ă as in *at*; ē as in *tree*; ĕ as in *eh*; ī as in *pine*; ĭ as in *pin*;

Praise ye the Lord; a song of thanksgiving.

Hallelujah metre. A stanza in six lines of Iambic measure, the syllables of each being in number and order as follows: 6, 6, 6, 6, 8, 8.

Hallen (Ger.) (*hāl*-l'n.) To sound; to clang.

Halmpfeife (Ger.) (hälm-*pfī*-fĕ.) Shepherd's pipe.

Hals (Ger.) (häls.) Neck of a violin, viola, etc.

Hammer. That part of the *action* or mechanism of a pianoforte, which strikes the strings and thus produces the sound.

Hammer, tuning. An instrument by which pianos and harps are tuned, by tightening or loosening the strings.

Hanché (Fr.) (hänh-shĕ.) See *Anche.*

Hand-drum. A tambourine.

Hände (Ger.) (hān-dĕ.) Hands.

Händespiel (Ger.) (hān-dĕ-spēl.) Organ keys, manuals.

Hand-glocke (Ger.) (händ*glō*-kĕ.) Handbell.

Hand-guide. See *Guide-main.*

Hand-klapper (Ger.) (*händ kläp*-pĕr.) A castanet.

Hand-harmonica. An accordion.

Handlage (Ger.) (*händ-lä*-ghĕ.) The position of the hand.

Handleiter (Ger.) (*händ-lī*-tĕr.) Handguide. See *Guide.*

Hand organ. A portable instrument consisting of a cylinder, on which by means of wires, pins, and staples are set the tunes, the revolution of the cylinder causing the pins, etc., to act on the keys and also to give admission to the wind.

Hardiment (Fr.) (här-dĭ-mänh.) Boldly, firmly.

Harfe (Ger.) (*här*-fĕ.) A harp.

Harfen (Ger.) (*här*-f'n.) To play on the harp.

Harfener (Gr.) (*här*-f'n-ĕr.) Harp-player.

Harfenist (Ger.) (här-*f'nĭst*.) Harp-player.

Harfen-saite (Ger.) (här-f'n sī-tĕ.) Harp-string.

Harmonia (Lat.) (här-*mō*-nĭ-ä.) A daughter of Mars and Venus. Her name was first used to indicate music in general.

Harmonic. Concordant, musical.

Harmonica. A musical instrument invented by Benjamin Franklin, consisting of glasses, sometimes globular and sometimes flat. The tone is produced by rubbing the edge of the globular glasses with a moistened finger, or striking the flat ones with small hammers. The name is also applied to an organ-stop of delicate tone. *Mouth-harmonica.* See *Harmonicon.*

Harmonica-ätherisch (Ger.) (här-mō-nĭ-kä ā-tĕr-ĭsh.) A mixture stop of very delicate scale in German organs.

Harmonic figuration. Broken chords.

Harmonic flute. An open metal organ-stop, of 8 or 4-foot pitch; the pipes are of double length, that is, 16 or 8 feet, and the bodies have a hole bored in them, midway between the foot and the top; the tone is exceedingly full, fluty, and powerful.

Harmonic hand. The Guidonian hand.

Harmonichord. An instrument having the form of an upright piano, but a tone something like that of a violin, produced by the friction of a cylinder covered with leather upon the strings. It was invented in 1785, by Fr. Kaufman.

Harmonici (It. pl.) (här-mō-nē-tshē.) Harmonics in violin music.

Harmonic mark. A sign used in violin, harp music, etc., to indicate that certain passages are to be played upon such parts of the open strings as will produce the harmonic sounds, marked O.

Harmonic modulation. A change in the harmony from one key to another.

Harmonicon. A small instrument held in the hand, the sounds being produced from metal reeds, set in motion by blowing from the mouth.

Harmonics. 1. An epithet applied to those concomitant, accessory sounds accompanying a principal, and apparently simple tone. See *Acoustics.* 2. *Harmonics* is also the name given to certain tones produced on the violin, harp, and other stringed instruments, tones which have another name — *flageolet tones* — owing to

ŏ as in *tone;* ō as in *dove;* ŏ as in *not;* ŭ as in *up;* ü the French sound of *u.*

their peculiar character. By touching a vibrating string very lightly in the middle, or at a point a third, fourth, fifth, etc., of its length distant from one of its ends, it is made to vibrate in two, three, four, five, etc., divisions, and the results are notes respectively an octave, twelfth, fifteenth, seventeenth, nineteenth, etc., higher than the tone obtained from the open string. 3. The harmonics can be sounded one by one on any tube or wind-instrument under certain conditions. They are produced from the column of air by subdivision, exactly as with the string described above. Thus, a tube 8 feet in length, will sound but by forcing the column of air to divide into regular segments we can obtain the over-tones, or harmonics. The first will be produced by one-half the length of the column, and will be the octave, the second by one-third, and will be the fifth above that tone, and the column can be subdivided into fourths, fifths, sixths, etc. The series will be as follows:

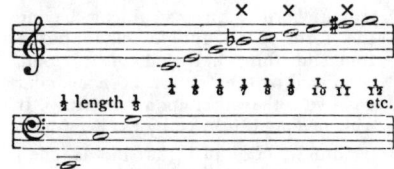

Fundamental.

And a similar series of tones will be produced from any other fundamental, *i. e.*, the octave, twelfth, fifteenth, etc. All of these over-tones are also sounding simultaneously with the fundamental tone. But these are not all exactly notated, nor can they be, in our musical system. The intervals grow closer and closer, as the column is more and more subdivided. The notes marked " x " in the above series are not exactly represented in the table. On the brass instruments, such as horns, cornets, trumpets, trombones, etc., the larger part of such a series as the above is sounded in playing.

Harmonic triad. The common chord, consisting of a fundamental note, its third and fifth.

Harmonie (Fr.) (här-mō-*nē*.) } Har-
Harmonie (Ger.) (här-mō-*nē*.) } mony.

Harmonie-musik (Ger.) (här-mō-*nē* moo-*zēk*.) Music for wind-instruments only.

Harmonie-regeln (Ger.) (här-mō-*nē* rā́-g'ln.) The rules or laws of harmony.

Harmonieusement (Fr.) (här-mō-nĭ-üs-mänh.) Harmoniously.

Harmonieux (Fr.) (här-mō-nĭ-*üh*.) Harmonious.

Harmonious. A term applicable to any two or more sounds which form a consonant or agreeable union.

Harmoniphon. A small instrument with a keyboard like a pianoforte, invented in 1837, and intended to supply the place of oboes in an orchestra. The sounds are produced from small metal tongues acted upon by a current of air through a flexible tube.

Harmonique (Fr.) (här-mō-*nēek*.) Harmonic; the relation of sounds to each other; also applied to organ pipes of double length.

Harmoniquement (Fr.) (här-mō-nēk-mänh.) Harmonically.

Harmoniren (Ger.) (här-mō-*nēe*-r'n.) To harmonize; to be in unison.

Harmonisch (Ger.) (här-*mō*-nĭsh.) Harmonious, harmonical.

Harmonium. An instrument played upon by means of keys, like a pianoforte, and furnished with bellows, the tones being produced by the vibration of metallic reeds. A cabinet-organ.

Harmonize. To combine two or more parts according to the laws of harmony.

Harmonized. A melody is said to be *harmonized* when additional parts are subjoined in order to give it more fulness.

Harmonomètre (Fr.) (här-mŏ-nō-*mātr*.) An instrument to measure the proportion of sounds, a species of monochord.

Harmony. The agreement or consonance of two or more united sounds. The art of combining sounds into chords and treating those chords according to certain rules.

Harmony, borrowed. Chords of the added ninth derived from the dominant seventh, by substituting the ninth in place of the eighth.

Harmony, close. A harmony whose

ă as in *ah*; ā as in *hate*; ă as in *at*; ē as in *tree*; ĕ as in *eh*; ī as in *pine*; ĭ as in *pin*;

tones are compact, the upper three voices lying within the compass of an octave.

Harmony, compound. Simple harmony with the harmony of another octave added.

Harmony, dispersed. A harmony in which the notes forming the different chords are separated by wide intervals.

Harmony, dominant. Harmony on the fifth of the key.

Harmony, false. A harmony contrary to the received rules.

Harmony, figured. Harmony in which, for the purpose of melody, one or more of the parts of a composition move, during the continuance of a chord, through certain notes that do not form any of the constituent parts of that chord. Harmony in which simple tones are broken up by foreign, passing tones, etc.

Harmony, natural. The harmonic triad, or common chord.

Harmony, simple. A harmony in which there is no concord to the fundamental above an octave; it is sometimes termed *close* harmony.

Harmony, suspended. One or more notes of a chord retained in the following chord.

Harp. A stringed instrument of very ancient origin, consisting of a triangular frame, having strings extended in parallel sections from the upper part to one of its sides, and played with the fingers. It had its origin in the bow of most ancient races. It was a highly developed instrument in ancient Egypt. But, in all its ancient forms, it was a diatonic instrument and could only modulate by pausing to retune the strings. Such was the instrument of the Cymric and Celtic bards. In 1758, an improvement was made by M. Simon, which altered the pitch of the strings, by wheels, with pins attached, worked by pedals. From this time the composers began to use the harp, and Mozart, Gluck, and others, employed it in their scores. But it was still far from being a thoroughly modulatory instrument. The perfection of the harp did not occur until 1810, when Sebastian Erard introduced a system of double-acting pedals by which any note could be raised either a semi-tone or a whole tone, at will. As the pedals could only raise, not lower, the pitch of any note, in order that the natural and sharp degrees of a tone could be gained in every case, and in a similar manner, it was necessary that each open wire should represent a flat note in the first place. This is done in tuning the modern harp (called the *double action* or *concert-harp*) and as there is but one key in which the notes are all flat, the harp is tuned in that key, C^b. The harp has very nearly the compass of the piano, starting with the lowest C^b of that instrument, and ending with its highest $F\sharp$. It is notated as the piano, on two staves, one treble and one bass. Its strings were originally made of catgut, but are now usually of wire. The C-strings are colored red, the F-strings blue, that the performer may readily see the position of any note. The harp sounds best in flat keys. It has usually forty-six strings. An attempt was made, though briefly, in France to do away with the pedals, and string the harp chromatically. See Flood's "Harp."

Harp, Æolian. An instrument consisting of wire or catgut drawn in parallel lines over a box of thin wood and placed so that a current of air may cause the strings to vibrate.

Harpchorde (Fr.) (härp-kŏrd.) An old French name for the harpsichord.

Harp, couched. Name originally given to the spinet.

Harp, double-action. A harp with pedals that can be used in two positions, the first, raising the instrument a half-tone, and the second a whole tone.

Harpe (Fr.) (härp.) A harp.

Harpe Eolienne (Fr.) (härp ā-ō-lǐ-ĕnn.) Æolian harp.

Harpeggiate (It.) (här-pĕd-jē-ä-tĕ.) In the style of a harp; in arpeggios.

Harpeggiato (It.) (här-pĕd-jē-ä-tō.) Causing the sounds of a chord to be played not together, but distinctly, one after another. See *Arpeggiato*.

Harpeggiren (Ger.) (här-pĕ-*ghē*-r'n.) To play arpeggios.

Harper. } A performer upon the harp.
Harpist. }

ō as in *tone*; ŏ as in *dove*; ŏ as in *not*; ŭ as in *up*; ü the French sound of *u*.

Harp, Jews'. A small instrument made of brass or steel with a flexible metal tongue, played upon by placing it between the teeth and vibrating the tongue by striking it with the finger; the action of the breath determines the power of the tone.

Harp pedal. The pedal of a pianoforte, generally called the *soft pedal*.

Harpsecol. See *Harpsichord*.

Harpsichord. An instrument much used before the invention of the pianoforte. In shape it resembled the grand pianoforte and had sometimes two rows of keys, but it was very inferior to that instrument in capacity for power and expression; the various shades of loud or soft could only be obtained by changing from one set of keys to another, or by moving certain stops as in the organ. Its wires were not struck by hammers, but plucked by quills. See *Piano*. The compass was about four octaves, but sometimes more.

Harpsichord, double. A harpsichord with two keyboards, one for loud and one for soft effects.

Harpsichord, single. A harpsichord with one keyboard.

Harpsichord, viol. An old French instrument resembling a viol, played with a wheel.

Harpsichord, vis-a-vis. A harpsichord arranged for two performers at the same time. A double harpsichord.

Harp, single-action. A harp whose pedals can be used in one position only raising the sounds of the instrument a half-tone.

Harp style. In the arpeggio style.

Harte (Ger.) (*här*-tĕ.) Major, in respect to intervals and scales.

Hart-klingend (Ger.) (*härt klĭng*-ĕnd.) Hard-sounding; harsh.

Hâte (Fr.) (hät.) Haste, speed.

Haupt (Ger.) (houpt.) Head, principal.

Haupt-kirche (Ger.) (*houpt* kĭr-khĕ.) Cathedral.

Haupt-manual (Ger.) (*houpt* mä-noo-äl.) The great or principal manual; the great organ.

Haupt-note (Ger.) (*houpt no*-tĕ.) The principal note in a shake or turn.

Haupt-periode (Ger.) (*houpt* pĕ-rĭ-ō-dĕ.) Capital period; the principal period in a musical phrase.

Haupt-satz (Ger.) (*houpt* sätz.) Principal theme, or subject; the *motive*, or leading idea.

Haupt-schluss (Ger.) (*houpt* shloos.) A final cadence.

Haupt-tonart (Ger.) (*houpt* tō-närt.) The principal key of a composition.

Haupt-stimme (Ger.) (*houpt stĭm*-mĕ.) Principal voice; principal part.

Haupt-ton (Ger.) (*houpt* tōn.) Fundamental, or principal tone; the tonic.

Haupt-werk (Ger.) (*houpt*-värk.) Chief work, or manual; the great organ.

Hausse (Fr.) (hōss.) The nut of a bow.

Hausser (Fr.) (hŏs-*sā*.) To raise, or sharpen the pitch.

Haut (Fr.) (hō.) Acute, high, shrill.

Hautb. An abbreviation of hautboy.

Hautbois (Fr.) (hō-bwä.) The *oboè* or hautboy.

Haute-contre (Fr.) (hōt-kōntr.) High or counter-tenor.

Haute-dessus (Fr.) (hōt-dĕs-sü.) High treble; first treble.

Hautement (Fr.) (hōt-mänh.) Haughtily; in dignified manner.

Haute-taille (Fr.) (hōt *tā*-yŭh.) High tenor.

H dur (Ger.) (hä door.) B major.

Head. That part of a note which determines its position on the staff and to which the stem is joined.

Head-tones. Tones produced by the upper register of the voice.

Head-voice. The upper or highest register of the voice; the falsetto in men's voices.

Hebdomadary. A member of a convent whose weekly turn it is to officiate in the choir, rehearse the anthems, prayers, etc.

Heftig (Ger.) (*hĕf*-tĭg.) Vehement, boisterous.

Heftigkeit (Ger.) (*hĕf*-tĭg-kīt.) Vehemence, impetuosity.

Heiss (Ger.) (hīss.) Hot, ardent.

Heiter (Ger.) (*hī*-tĕr.) Genial, bright.

Helden-lied (Ger.) (*hĕl*-d'n-lēd.) Heroic song.

ă as in *ah*; ā as in *hate*; ă as in *at*; ē as in *tree*; ĕ as in *eh*; ī as in *pine*; ĭ as in *pin*.

Guitar

Harp

Frederic Chopin

From Prelude in E Minor, Op. 28, No. 4

Heldenmüthig (Ger.) (hĕl-d'n-*mü*-tīg.) Heroic.

Helikon (Gr.) (*hĕl*-ĭ-kŏn.)
Helicon (Eng.) (hĕl-ĭ-kŏn.) } 1. The name of an ancient instrument said to be invented by Ptolemy, for demonstrating, or measuring consonances. 2. The bass tuba is so-called when made in a circular form to carry on the shoulder in marching.

Hell (Ger.) (hĕl.) Clear, bright.

Helle Stimme (Ger.) (*hĕl*-lĕ *stĭm*-mĕ.) A clear voice.

Hemi (Gr.) (*hā*-mĭ.) Half.

Hemidemisemiquaver. A sixty-fourth note.

Hemidemisemiquaver rest. A sixty-fourth rest.

Hemiditonos (Gr.) (hĕm-ĭ-dē-*tō*-nŏs.) Lessor or minor third.

Hemiphrase. A half-phrase.

Hemistich. Half a poetic verse, or a verse not completed.

Hemitone. A half-tone, called now a *semi-tone.*

Hemitonium (Gr.) (hā-mĭ-*tō*-nĭ-ŭm.) A semi-tone or half-tone.

Heptachord. A scale or system of seven sounds. In ancient poetry verses sung or played on seven chords or different notes; a lyre or cithera having seven strings.

Herabstrich (Ger.) (hār-*äb*-strĭkh.) A down-bow.

Heraufgehen (Ger.) (hār-*ouf*-gā'n.) To ascend.

Herstrich (Ger.) (*hair*-strĭch.) Down-bow on the 'cello and double-bass.

Herunterstrich (Ger.) (hār-*oon*-tĕr-strikh.) Down-bow on the violin, etc.

Hervorgehoben (Ger.) (hār-*fōr*-ghĕ-hō-b'n.)
Hervorhebend (Ger.) (hār-*fōr*-hā-bĕnd.)
Hervortretend (Ger.) (hār-*fōr*-trĕ-tĕnd.) } Prominently and distinctly.

Herzlich (Ger.) (*hĕrts*-līkh.) Tenderly, delicately.

Hexachord (Ger.) (*hĕx*-ă-kŏrd.) A scale or system of six sounds; an interval of a sixth; a lyre having six strings.

Hexachordon (Gr.) (hĕx-ă-*kŏr*-dŏn.) A major sixth.

Hexachorde (Fr.) (hĕx-ă-*kŏrd*.) A *hexa-chord.* See that word.

Hexameron (Gr.) (hĕx-*ăm*-ĕ-rŏn.) Set of six musical pieces or songs.

Hexameter. In ancient poetry, a verse of six feet, the first four of which may be either dactyls or spondees, the fifth always a dactyl and the sixth a spondee, or a trochee.

Hexaphonic. Composed of six voices.

Hexastich (Gr.) (hĕx-*ăs*-tĭch.) A poem of six verses.

Hiatus (Lat.) (hĭ-*ă*-tŭs.) A gap; imperfect harmony.

Hidden. A term applied to octaves and fifths when the harmony moves in such a manner that consecutive octaves and fifths may be imagined, although they do not really occur; two voices in parallel motion taking a fifth or octave.

Hidden consecutives. Such as occur in passing by parallel motion from an imperfect to a perfect concord.

Hief-horn (Ger.) (*hēf*-hōrn). Bugle-horn; hunting-horn. Also *Hifthorn.*

Hief (Ger.) (hēf.)
Hief-stoss (Ger.) (*hēf* stōss.) } Sound given by the bugle or hunting-horn.

Hierophon (Gr.) (*hē*-rō-fŏn.) A singer of sacred music.

High. Acute in pitch; speaking of sounds.

High bass. A voice between bass and tenor; a baritone.

Higher rhythm. A rhythmical form which is larger than a single measure.

High Mass. The Mass celebrated in the Roman Catholic churches by the singing of the choristers, distinguishing it from the low Mass in which the prayers are read without singing.

High soprano. The first soprano.

High-tenor. Counter-tenor voice; the highest male voice.

Hilfs (Ger.) Auxiliary; *Hilfslinie,* leger-line; *Hilfsnote,* auxiliary note; *Hilfsstimme,* mutation-stop (often *Hülfs*).

Hinaufstrich (Ger.) (hĭn-*ouf*-strĭkh.)
Hinstrich (Ger.) (*hĭn*-strĭkh.) } An up-bow.

Hinchar (Spa.) (hēn-*kär*.) To fill a musical instrument with air.

ō as in *tone;* ŏ as in *dove;* ŏ as in *not;* ŭ as in *up;* ü the French sound of *u.*

Hirten-flöte (Ger.) (*hĭr*-t'n flō-tĕ.) Shepherd's flute.

Hirten-gedicht (Ger.) (*hĭr*-t'n ghĕ-*dĭkht*.) Pastoral poem; idyl.

Hirten-lied (Ger.) (*hĭr*-t'n lēd.) A pastoral song.

Hirten-pfeife (Ger.) (*hĭr*-t'n-*pfī*-fĕ.) Rural pipe; pastoral pipe.

Hirtlich (Ger.) (*hĭrt*-lĭkh.) Pastoral, rural.

His (Ger.) (hĭs.) The note B sharp.

H moll (Ger.) (hä mōl.) The key of B minor.

Hoboe (Ger.) (*hō*-bō-ĕ.) } Oboè, hautboy.
Hoboy (Ger.) (hō-boy.)

Hoboen (Ger. pl.) (*hō*-bō-ĕn.) Oboès, hautboys.

Hoboist (Ger.) (hō-bō-*ĭst*.) Oboe-player.

Hoch (Ger.) (hōkh.) High.

Hoch-amt (Ger.) (bōkh-ämt.) High Mass.

Hochfeierlich (Ger.) (*hōkh-fī*-ĕr-likh.) Exceedingly solemn.

Hoch-gesang (Ger.) (*hōkh*-ghĕ-*zäng*.) Ode, hymn.

Hoch-messe (Ger.) (*hōkh mĕs*-sĕ.) High Mass.

Hochmuth (Ger.) (*hōkh*-moot.) Dignity, elevation, pride.

Höchsten (Ger.) (*hŏkh*-stĕn.) Highest.

Hochzeits-gedicht (Ger.) (*hōkh*-tsīts-ghĕ-*dĭkht*.
Hochzeits-lied (Ger.) (*hōkh*-tsīts lēd.) Epithalamium nuptial poems; wedding-song.

Hochzeits-marsch (Ger.) (*hōkh*-tsīts märsh.) Wedding march.

Hof-capelle (Ger.) (hōf kä-*pĕl*-lĕ.) Court-chapel choir, or orchestra.

Hof-concert (Ger.) (hōf kŏn-*tsĕrt*.) Court-concert.

Hof-dichter (Ger.) (hōf *dĭkh*-tĕr.) Poet laureate.

Hof-kirche (Ger.) (hōf *kĭrkh*-ĕ.) Court church.

Höflich (Ger.) (*hŏf*-lĭkh.) } In a
Höflichkeit (Ger.) (*hŏf* lĭkh-kīt.) } pleasing and polite style.

Hof-musikant (Ger.) (hōf moo-zĭ-*känt*.) Court-musician.

Hof-organist (Ger.) (*hōf* ōr-gän-*ĭst*.) Court-organist.

Hoheit (Ger.) (*hō*-hīt.) Dignity, loftiness.

Hohen (Ger.) (*hō*-ĕn.) High, upper.

Hohl-flöte (Ger.) (*hōl*-flô-tĕ.) *Hollow-toned flute*; an organ-stop producing a thick and powerful hollow tone. Each pipe has two holes in it, near the top, and opposite each other.

Hohl-quinte (Ger.) (*hōl* quĭn-tĕ.) A *quint* stop of the *hohl-flute* species, sounding a fifth higher.

Hold (Ger.) (hōld.) Pleasing, agreeable.

Hold. A character (⌒) indicating that the time of a note or rest is to be prolonged. See *Fermata*.

Holding-note. A note that is sustained or continued while the others are in motion.

Holzbläser (Ger.) (*hŏlz*-blāzer.) Players on the wood wind-instruments of an orchestra.

Holzblasinstrumente (Ger.) (*hŏlz*-blahz-in-stroo-ment-ĕ.) Wood wind-instruments, technically called *The Wood wind*.

Holz-flöte (Ger.) (*hŏlts* flô-tĕ.) *Wood flute*; an organ-stop.

Homophonie (Fr.) (hō-mō-fo-nē.) Homóphony.

Homophonous. Of the same pitch; in unison.

Homophonoi suoni (It.) (hō-mō-*fō*-nō-ē swō-nē.) Unisons.

Homophony. Unison; two or more voices singing in unison. In modern music, a style in which *one melody* or part, supported to a greater or less extent by chords (an *accompanied melody*) predominates. It is the opposite of polyphony, where different melodies are heard simultaneously.

Hook (Ger., *Fahne*; Fr., *crochet*; It., *coda uncinata*.) A stroke attached to the stems of eighth notes, sixteenth notes, etc., (♪ ♫). Also *Flag, Pennant*.

Hopser (Ger.) (*hŏp*-sĕr.) A German dance; a lively waltz.

Hops-tanz (Ger.) (*hŏps*-tänts.) Hop-dance.

Hops-walzer (Ger.) (*hŏps-väl*-tsĕr.) Quick waltzes.

ä as in *ah*; ā as in *hate*; ă as in *at*; ē as in *tree*; ĕ as in *eh*; ī as in *pine*; ĭ as in *pin*;

Horæ (Lat.) (*hō-rē.*) Hours.

Horæ Canonicæ. The canonical hours at which religious services are held, in monasteries, etc. The following is the order of the canonical hours: *Lauds*, at daybreak; *Prime*, or first hour, a later service; *Tierce*, or third hour, at 9 A. M.; *Sext*, or sixth hour at noon; *Nones*, or ninth hour, at 3 P. M.; *Vespers*, or evening service; *Compline*, or final service, at bed-time. Each of these has fixed psalms, except vespers, which has certain psalms read in course, and a canticle. The book for these offices is called the *Breviary*.

Horæ regulares (Lat.) (*hō-rē rĕg-ū-lä-rēs.*) *Hours:* chants sung at prescribed hours, in convents and monasteries.

Horizontal lines. } Used in connec-
Horizontal strokes. } tion with the figured bass, they usually show the continuation of the same harmony, the bass note being unchanged.

Horn. See *Horn, French*.

Horn, alpine. An instrument made of wood, and used to convey sounds to a great distance.

Horn, basset. An instrument resembling the clarinet, but of greater compass, embracing nearly four octaves. A species of clarinet a fifth lower than the C clarinet. Like the English horn it stands in F, that is, it sounds a perfect fifth lower than written. Its written compass is about

It has a very mournful, gloomy tone-color, which suits it well to funereal music. It plays easiest in flat keys. It was prominently used by Mozart in his great *Requiem*, and in other works.

Horn, bugle. A trumpet with keys.

Horn, chromatic. The French horn.

Horn, English. A species of oboe, a fifth lower than the ordinary oboe. It is more melancholy and also more masculine than the oboe. It has been freely used by Wagner, Berlioz, Rossini, and Schumann, to represent a shepherd's pipe. The English horn, as it sounds a fifth below the written notes, is said to stand in F, as the scale of C, written, will actually sound the scale of F. If, for example, we desired to employ the English horn in a composition in the key of E flat, we should be obliged to write it in the key of B flat, a fifth above, to attain the required sounds. The written compass of the English horn is

but the actual sounds thus represented are

(Ger., *Das Englische Horn;* Fr., *Cor Anglais;* It., *Corno Inglese.*) It probably had its origin in England from a shepherd's pipe.

Horn, French. An orchestral instrument of brass or silver, consisting of a long tube, twisted into several circular folds, and gradually increasing in diameter from the mouth-piece to the end. This instrument is most frequently called simply *the horn*. There are horns in all the different keys, but it is not necessary to make a special instrument in each key, for, by the addition of sections of tubing, called *crooks*, the horn (as also the trumpet and cornet) can be lengthened and set in another key than its natural one. The horn generally used in the orchestra is the one in F, which, in its natural state, without any added crooks, would sound a perfect fifth lower than its notation. The highest horn made is that in C-alto, which is non-transposing, sounding as written. By drawing out the mouth-piece the horn can be lowered a semitone in pitch, the C-alto horn thus becoming B-alto. All the horns but the C-alto transpose downwards. In an orchestral score the horns are generally notated in the key of C, and the B-alto sounds a semi-tone deeper than notated, the B-flat alto one tone, the A-horn a minor third, the A-flat horn a major third, etc., the deepest being the *B-flat bass* which sounds a ninth deeper than written. The horns from the C-alto down to the G-flat horn give the harmonic series (see *Harmonics*) of tones from the fundamental note to about the ninth harmonic

ŏ as in *tone;* ŏ as in *dove;* ŏ as in *not;* ŭ as in *up;* ü the French sound of *u*.

, without touching the keys. The keys by constantly lengthening the tube (see *Ventil*), add lower series to the natural tones, so that a chromatic scale can be played on the instrument. The horns from that in F, to that in B-flat basso, lose the fundamental tone of the series, but give the entire harmonic series of tones up to the fifteenth harmonic, although the tenth overtone is difficult to produce. The tone of the horn is modified by the player's right hand, which is placed in the bell of the instrument. When the hand is pressed very firmly in the tube, as if to prevent the escape of any air, a "stopped" tone is the result, and the pitch is lowered a semitone. The quality of the horn is mellow and tender, its tone-color suiting it to romantic effects, and woodland and forest pictures, but the stopped tones are the reverse of this, and are the most repulsive tone-color that can be produced in the orchestra.

Horn, Gemsen. An instrument formed of a small pipe made of the horn of the chamois or wild goat.

Horn, hunting. A bugle.

Horn, kent. A horn having six keys, four of which are used by the right hand and two by the left.

Horn, Klappen. The kent-horn.

Horn, valve. A horn in which a portion of the tube is opened or closed by the use of valves, by means of which a higher or lower pitch is obtained. See *Key.*

Hörner (Ger. pl.) (*hôr*-ner.) The horns.

Hörnerschall (Ger.) (*hôr*-nĕr-shall.) Sound of horns.

Hornpipe. An old dance in triple time, peculiar to the English nation. It is supposed to have received its name from the instrument played during its performance. Modern hornpipes are usually in common time and of a more lively character than the ancient hornpipe.

Hornquinten (Ger.) (*horn-fifths.*) The covered fifths produced by the natural tones of a pair of horns:

Hornsordin (Ger.) (horn-sŏr-dēen.) Mute for a horn.

Hosanna (Lat.) (hō-*zär*-nä.) Part of the Sanctus in a Mass.

Huchet (Fr.) (hü-shä.) A huntsman's or postman's horn.

Huer (Fr.) (hwä.) To shout.

Hüft-horn (Ger.) (*hüft*-hōrn.) Buglehorn.

Huitain (Fr.) (hwē-tănh.) A stanza of eight lines.

Hülfslinien (Ger.) (*hülfs-līn*-ĭ-ĕn.) Ledger lines.

Hülfs-note (Ger.) (*hülfs-nōt*-ĕ.) ⎫ Auxiliary
Hülfs-ton (Ger.) (*hülfs*-tōn.) ⎭ note; accessory note; a note standing one degree above, or below the principal note.

Hummel (Ger.) (*hoom*-mĕl.) ⎫
Hummelchen (Ger.) (*hoom*-mĕl-khĕn.) ⎭
A sort of bagpipe; in organs the bass drone.

Hunting-horn. A bugle; a horn used to cheer the hounds.

Hunting-song. A song written in praise of the chase.

Hurdy-gurdy. An old instrument consisting of four strings, which are acted upon by a wheel, rubbed in resin powder, which serves as a bow. Two of the strings are affected by certain keys, which stop them at different lengths and produce the *tune*, while the others act as a drone bass. This instrument was imitated by Schubert in his song, *Der Leiermann.*

Hurtig (Ger.) (*hoor*-tĭg.) Quick; swiftly; same meaning as *Allégro.*

Hurtigkeit (Ger.) (*hoor*-tĭg-kīt.) Swiftness, quickness, agility.

Hydraulicon (Ger.) (hī-*draw*-lĭ-kŏn.) An ancient instrument whose tones were produced by the action of water.

Hydraulic organ. An organ whose motive power was water, and the invention of which is of much greater antiquity than the pneumatic or wind-organ. It is supposed to have been invented by Ctesibius, a mathematician of Alexandria.

Hydraulon (Gr.) (hī-*draw*-lŏn.) ⎫ An
Hydraulus (Lat.) (hī-*draw*-lŭs.) ⎭ organ blown by the action of water.

ă as in *ah*; ā as in *hate*; ă as in *at*; ē as in *tree*; ĕ as in *eh*; ī as in *pine*; ĭ as in *pin*;

140

Hymenæa (Gr.) (hĭm-ĕn-ē-ä.) ⎫ A
Hymenäus (Ger.) (hĭm-ĕn-ä-oos.) ⎬ mar-
Hymenaion (Gr.) (hĭm-ĕn-ä-ŏn.) ⎭ riage song.
Hymeneal (hī-mē-nĕ-ăl.) ⎫ A marriage
Hymenean (hī-mē-nĕ-ăn.) ⎬ song.
Hymn. A song of praise or adoration to the Deity; a short, religious lyric poem intended to be sung in church. Anciently, a song in honor of the gods or heroes.
Hymnal. ⎫ A compilation, or collec-
Hymn-book. ⎭ tion of hymns.
Hymn, choral. A hymn to be performed by a chorus.
Hymne (Fr.) (ēmn.) ⎫ A hymn;
Hymne (Ger.) (hĭm-nĕ.) ⎭ sacred song; an anthem.
Hymne de louange (Fr.) (ēmn dŭh looänzh.) Doxology; hymn of praise.
Hymnologie (Fr.) (ēmn-nŏl-ō-jē.) Hymnology.
Hymnologist. A writer or composer of hymns.
Hymnology. The art of composing hymns.
Hymn, Orphic. A hymn pertaining to Orpheus.
Hymnus (Lat.) (hĭm-nŭs.) A hymn.
Hymnus, ambrosianus (Lat.) (hĭm-nŭs ăm-brō-zhĭ-ä-nŭs.) The Ambrosian chant.
Hymn, vesper. A hymn sung in the vesper service of the Catholic Church.
Hypate (Gr.) The first or most grave string in the lyre; the lowest of the Greek tetrachords.
Hypathoides. The lower sounds in the ancient Greek scale.
Hyper (Gr.) (hī-pĕr.) *Above.* This word in connection with the name of any mode or interval signifies that it is higher than when without it.
Hyper-diapason (Gr.) (hī-pĕr-dĭ-ä-päsŏn.) The upper octave.
Hyper-ditonos (Gr.) (hī-pĕr-dĭ-tō-nŏs.) The third above.
Hypo. *Below.* The word prefixed to the name of any ancient mode or interval, signifies that it is lower than when without it.

Hypo-Æolian (Gr.) (hī-pō-ē-ō-lĭ-ăn.) The *plagal* Æolian mode
Hypo-diapason (Gr.) (hī-pō-dē-ă-pä-sŏn.) The lower octave.
Hypo-diapente (Gr.) (hī-pō-dē-ă-pĕn-tē.) The fifth below.
Hypo-ditonos (Gr.) (hī-pō-dē-tō-nŏs.) The third below.

I

I (It.) (masculine plural.) The.
Iambic. ⎫ A poetical and musical foot,
Iambus. ⎭ consisting of one short unaccented, and one long accented note or syllable, ⌣ —.
Iambics. Certain songs or satires which are supposed to have been the precursors of the ancient comedy; they were of two kinds, one for singing and one for recitation, accompanied by instruments.
Iastian (Gr.) (ē-ăs-tĭ-ăn.) One of the ancient Greek modes; Ionian.
Ictus (Gr.) (ĭk-tŭs.) A stroke of the foot, marking the point of emphasis in music, or poetry.
Idillio (It.) (ēd-ēel-lĭ-ō.) An idyl.
Idyl. A short poem in pastoral style; an eclogue.
Idylle (Fr.) (ē-dĭll.) ⎫ An idyl.
Idylle (Ger.) (ĭd-ĭl-lĕ.) ⎭
Il (It.) (ēl.) The.
Ilarita (It.) (ē-lär-ē-tä.) Hilarity, cheerfulness, mirth.
Il basso (It.) (il bäs-sō.) The fundamental tone; the lowest note of a chord; the bass part.
Il canto (It.) (il kän-tō.) The song.
Il più (It.) (il pē-oo.) The most.
Im (Ger.) (ēm.) In the.
Imboccatúra (It.) (ēm-bōt-kä-too-rä.) Mouth-piece, *embouchure.*
Imbróglio (It.) (im-brōl-yō.) Confusion; want of distinct ideas; a mixture of rhythms.
Imitándo (It.) (im-ē-tän-dō.) Imitating.
Imitándo la voce (It.) (im-ē-tän-dō lä vo-tshē.) Imitating the inflections of the voice.
Imitatio (Lat.) (ĭm-ĭ-tä-shĭ-ō.) Imitation; in counterpoint.
Imitation (Lat., *imitatio;* Fr., *imitation;* It., *imitazione;* Ger., *Nachahmung.*)

ŏ as in *tone;* ô as in *dove;* ŏ as in *not;* ŭ as in *up;* ü the French sound of *u.*

141

The repetition of a motive, phrase, or theme proposed by one part (the *antecedent*) in another part (the *consequent*), with or without modification.

Imitation, augmented. A style of imitation in which the answer is given in notes of greater value than those of the subject.

Imitation, diminished. A style of imitation in which the answer is given in notes of less value than those of the subject.

Imitation, free. Where the order of successive notes is not strictly retained.

Imitation, in contrary motion. That in which the answers invert the subject so that the rising intervals descend, and the falling intervals ascend.

Imitation, in different divisions. That in which the subject is answered in a different division of the bar; for instance, the subject beginning on the accented division, is answered on the unaccented.

Imitation, in similar motion. Where the answer retains the same order of notes as the subject.

Imitation, retrograde. A form of imitation in which the subject is commenced backwards in the answer.

Imitative music. Music written to imitate some of the operations of nature, or art, as, the firing of cannon, the rolling of thunder, etc.

Imitato (It.) (ēm-ē-*tä*-tō.) Imitation.

Imitazióne (It.) (ēm-ē-tä-tsē-*ō*-nĕ.) Imitation; referring to counterpoint.

Immer (Ger.) (*ĭm*-mĕr.) Always, ever.

Imparfait (Fr.) (ănh-pär-*fä*.) Imperfect.

Impaziénte (It.) (im-pä-tsē-*en*-tē.) Impatient, hurried

Impazienteménte (It.) (im-pä-tsē-ĕn-tĕ-*men*-tĕ.) Impatiently, hurriedly.

Imperfect Not perfect; less than perfect in speaking of intervals and chords.

Imperfect cadence. A cadence which ends on a triad of the dominant; the preceding chord may be either that of the tonic or subdominant or in minor keys the sixth of the scale; the triad of the dominant always being *major*.

Imperfect close. Imperfect cadence.

Imperfect concords. Thirds and sixths are called imperfect concords because they are liable to change from major to minor, or the contrary, still remaining consonant.

Imperfect consonances. The major and minor third and the major and minor sixth.

Imperfect intervals. Those which include one semi-tone less than the perfect interval of the same name.

Imperfect time. (*Imperfectum*.) A term by which the Ancients designated common time, indicated by the semi-circle C.

Imperfect triad. The chord based on the seventh of the key, consisting of two minor thirds. A diminished triad.

Imperfetto (It.) (im-pĕr-*fet*-tō.) Imperfect.

Imperiosaménte (It.) (im-pā-rē-ō-zä-*men* tĕ.) Imperiously, pompously.

Imperiosita (It.) (im-pā-rē-ō-zē-*tä*.) Stateliness, pomposity.

Imperióso (It.) (im-pā-rē-*ō*-zō.) Imperious, pompous.

Imperturbábile (It.) (im-pĕr-toor-*bä*-bĕ-lĕ.) Quietly, easily, imperturbable.

Impeto (It.) (*im*-pĕ-tō.) Impetuosity, vehemence.

Impetuosaménte (It.) (im-pā-too-ō-zä-*men*-tĕ.) Impetuously.

Impetuosita (It.) (im-pā-too-ō-zē-*tä*.) Impetuosity, vehemence.

Impetuóso (It.) (im-pā-too-*ō*-zō.) Impetuous, vehement.

Imponénte (It.) (im-pō-*nen*-tĕ.) Imposingly, haughtily.

Impresário (It.) (im-prĕ-*zä*-rē-ō.) A term applied by the Italians to the manager or conductor of operas or concerts.

Imprómptu (Fr.) (ănh-*prŏmp*-tü.) An extemporaneous production.

Improperia (Lat.) (*reproaches*.) In the Roman ritual, a series of antiphons and responses forming part of the solemn service substituted, on the morning of Good Friday, for the usual daily Mass.

Improvisare (It.) (im-prō-vē-*zä*-rĕ.) To compose, or sing extemporaneously.

IMPROVISATEUR   INFURIÁTO

Improvisateur (Fr.) (ănh-prō-vē-zä-*tŭr*.)
Improvisator (Ger.) (ĭm-prō-fĭ-zä-tōr.) } An improviser.

Improvisation. The act of singing, playing, or composing music without previous preparation; extemporaneous performance.

Improvisatrice (Fr.) (ănh-prō-vē-zä-*trĕss*.) A female who plays or sings extemporaneously.

Improvise. To sing or play without premeditation.

Improviser (Fr.) (ănh-prō-vē-*zā*.) To improvise.

Improvísé (Fr.) (ănh-prō-vē-zä.) Extemporaneous.

Improvvisaménte (It.) (im-prō-vē-zä*men*-tĕ.) Extemporaneously.

Improvvisare (It.) (im-prō-vē-*zä*-rĕ.) To improvise.

Improvvisáta (It.) (im-prō-vē-*zä*-tä.) An extempore composition.

Improvvisatóre (It.) (im-prō-vēs-sä-tō-rĕ.) One who sings or declaims in verse extemporaneously.

Improvviso (It.) (im-prōv-*vē*-zō.) Extemporaneous.

Im Tact (Ger.) (ĭm *täkt*.) In time.

In (It. and Lat.) (ēn.) In, into, in the.

In alt (It.) (in ält.) Notes are said to be *in alt* when they are situated above F on the fifth line of the treble staff.

In altissimo (It.) (in äl-*tis* sē-mō.) A term applied to all notes which run higher than F above the third leger line in the treble, or F *in alt*.

Inbrunst (Ger.) (ĭn-broonst.) Fervor; ardor; warmth of passion.

Inbrünstig (Ger.) (*ĭn*-brüns-tĭg.) Ardent, fervent, passionate.

Incalzando (It.) (In-cal-*tsan*-do.) With growing warmth and fervor.

Incantation. Enchantment; a form of words pronounced or sung in connection with certain ceremonies, for the purpose of enchantment.

Incantazione (It.) (ēn-kän-tä-tsē-*ō*-nĕ.) Songs of incantation.

Incarnatus (Lat.) Part of the *Credo* of the Mass.

Inconsoláto (It.) (ēn-kŏn-sō-*lä*-tō.) In a mournful style.

Inconsonant. Discordant.

Incordaménto (It.) (ēn-kŏr-dä-*men*-tō.) Tension of the strings of an instrument.

Incordáre (It.) (in-kŏr-*dä*-rĕ.) To string an instrument.

Indecíso (It.) (in-dĕ-*tshē*-zō.) Undecided, wavering, hesitating; slight changes of time and a somewhat capricious value of the notes.

Indegnataménte (It.) (in-dān-yä-tä-*men*-tĕ.)
Indegnáto (It.) (ēn-dān-*yä*-tō.) } Angrily, furiously, passionately.

Index. A direct ₩; also the forefinger. See *Direct*.

Indications scéniques (Fr.) (ănh-dē-*kä*-sē-ŏnh sā-*nēk*.) Stage directions.

Indifferénte (It.) (in-dēf-fĕ-*ren*-tĕ.)
Indifferenteménte (It.) (in-dēf-fĕ-ren-tĕ-*men*-tĕ.) } Coldly; with indifference.

Indifferenza (It.) (in-dēf-fĕ-*ren*-tsä.) Indifference.

In distánza (It.) (in dēs-*tän*-tsä.) At a distance.

Infernále (It.) (in-fĕr-*nä*-lĕ.) Infernal, diabolic.

Infervoráto (It.) (in-fĕr-vō-*rä*-tō.) Fervent, impassioned.

Infiammataménte (It.) (in-fē-äm-mä-tä-*men*-tĕ.) Ardently, impetuously.

Infinite canon. An epithet given to those canons which are so constructed that the end leads to the beginning, and the performance may be indefinitely repeated; also called *endless* canon.

Infinito (It.) (in-fē-*nē*-tō.) Perpetual.

Inflatile. An epithet applied to wind-instruments. Inflatable.

Inflection. Any change or modification in the pitch or tone of the voice.

Infra (Lat.) (*ĭn*-frä.) Beneath.

In frétta (It.) (in *frāt*-tä.) In haste; hastily.

Infuriánte (It.) (in-foo-rē-*än*-tĕ)
Infuriáto (It.) (ĭn-foo-rē-*ä*-tō.) } Furious, raging.

ŏ as in *tone*; ô as in *dove*; ŏ as in *not*; ü as in *up*; ü the French sound of **u**.

143

Ingánni (It. pl.) (in-gän-nē.) See *Ingánno*.

Ingánno (It.) (in-gän-nō.) A *deception;* applied to a deceptive or interrupted cadence; also, to any unusual resolution of a discord, or an unexpected modulation.

Ingégno (It.) (ēn-jän-yō.) Art, skill, discretion.

Inharmonic relation. The introduction of a dissonant sound, not heard in the preceding chord.

Innario (It.) (ēn-nä-rē-ō.) Hymn-book.

Inneggiare (It.) (in-näd-jē-ä-rĕ.) To compose or sing hymns.

Inni (It. pl.) (ĭn-nē.) Hymns.

Innig (Ger.) (ĭn-nĭg.) Sincere; cordial; with depth of feeling.

Inno (It.) (in-nō.) A hymn; canticle; ode.

Innocénte (It.) (in-nō-*tshen*-tĕ.)
Innocenteménte (It.) (in-nō-tshen-tĕ-men-tĕ.) Innocently; in an artless and simple style.

Innocénza (It.) (in-nō-*tshen*-tsä.) Innocence.

Ino (It.) (ē-nō.) An Italian final diminutive. As *Scherzo, Scherzino.* The feminine is *Ina,* as *Sonata, Sonatina.*

In pálco (It.) (in *päl*-kō.) On a stage; applied to musical performances *on the stage.*

Inquiéto (It.) (in-quē-ä-tō.) Restless, uneasy, agitated.

Insegnaménto (It.) (in-sän-yä-*men*-tō.) Instruction.

Insegnatóre (It.) (in-sän-yä-*tō*-rĕ.) Teacher, instructor.

Insensíbile (It.) (in-sĕn-*sēe*-bi-lĕ.)
Insensibilménte (It.) (in-sĕn-sē-bēl-men-tĕ.) Insensibility; by small degrees; by little and little.

Instanteménte (It.) (in-stän-tĕ-*men*-tĕ.) Vehemently, urgently.

Instrument à cordes (Fr.) (änh-strü-mänh ä kŏrd.) A stringed instrument.

Instrument à l'archet (Fr.) (änh-strü-mänh ä l'är-shä.) Instrument played with a bow.

Instrumental. A term applied to music composed for or performed on instruments.

Instrumentále (It.) (ēn-stroo-mĕn-*tä*-lĕ.) Instrumental.

Instrumental score. A score in which the instrumental parts are given in full.

Instrumentare (It.) (in-stroo-mĕn-*tä*-rĕ.) To compose or arrange instrumental music.

Instrumentation. The act of writing for an orchestra, with a practical knowledge of each instrument, and of the distribution of harmony among the different instruments.

Instrument à vent (Fr.) (änh-strü-mänh ä vänh.) A wind-instrument.

Instrumentazióne (It.) (in-stroo-mĕn-tä-tsē-ō-nĕ.) Instrumentation.

Instrumentiren (Ger.) (ĭn-stroo-mĕn-tē-r'n.)
Instrumentirung (Ger.) (ĭn-stroo-mĕn-tē-roong.) Instrumentation.

Instruménto a corda (It.) (in-stroo-men-tō ä *kŏr*-dä.)
Instruménto da arco (It.) (in-stroo-men-tō dä *är*-kō.) A stringed instrument.

Instruménto da fiáto (It.) (in-stroo-*men*-tō dä fē-ä-tō.) A wind-instrument.

Instruménto da pénna (It.) (in-stroo-men-tō dä *pĕn*-nä.) *Instrument with the quill;* an old name for the spinet.

Instruménto da percotimento (It.) (in-stroo-*men*-tō dä pĕr-kō-tē-*men*-tō.) An instrument of percussion.

Instruménto da tasto (It.) (in-stroo-*men*-tō dä *täs*-tō.) A keyed instrument.

Instruments. See Classified Table on next page.

Instruments, bow. All instruments whose tones are produced by means of a bow.

Instruments, brass. Wind-instruments formed of brass and used chiefly for military purposes.

Instruments, keyed. All instruments the sounds of which are produced by the pressure of the fingers upon the keys.

Instruments, mechanical. Instruments which produce tunes by the means of some mechanical contrivance, as, crank, springs, weights, etc.

Instruments, percussive. } Instruments
Instruments, pulsatile. } whose sounds are produced by being struck.

Instruments, reed. Instruments whose tones are produced by the action of air upon reeds of metal or wood.

Instruments, stringed. Instruments whose tones are produced by striking or drawing strings or the friction of a bow.

Instruments, tubular. Instruments consisting of one or more tubes of wood or metal.

Instruments, wind. Instruments the sounds of which are produced by the breath or the wind of bellows.

A CLASSIFIED TABLE OF MUSICAL INSTRUMENTS.

String Instruments:
Percussion —
  Piano.
  Schlagzither.
Friction (Bowing) —
  Violin.
  Viola.
  Violoncello.
  Contrabass.
  Viol d'Amore
Plucking —
  Harp.
  Guitar.
  Mandolin (plectrum or pick).
  Zither.
  Banjo.

Wind-instruments of Wood:
With open mouth-piece —
  Flute.
  Piccolo.
  Fife.
Single reed —
  Clarinet.
  Bass Clarinet.
  Basset-horn.
  Pedal Clarinet.
Double Reed —
  Oboe.
  English Horn.
  Bassoon.
  Contrabassoon.

Brass Instruments:
With cup mouth-piece —
  Cornet.
  Trumpet.
  French Horn.
  Trombone (keyed).
  Trombone (slide).
  Tuba.
  Saxhorns.
  Bugle.
  Post-horn.
  Ophicleide.
With single reed —
  Saxophone.
With double reed —
  Sarussophone.

Instruments of Percussion:
With definite pitch —
  Kettle drum.
  Xylophone.
  Glockenspiel.
  Bells.
Without pitch —
  Bass-drum.
  Military Drum.
  Cymbals.
  Gong.
  Tambourine.
  Castagnettes.
  Triangle.

The organ combines most of the effects of the above-given wind-instruments, and there are also obsolete instruments, such as the clavichord, harpsichord, oboe di caccia, etc., which are not given in the above list.

Intavoláre (It.) (ēn-tä-vō-*lä*-rĕ.) To write notes; to copy music.

Intavolatúra (It.) (ēn-tä-vō-lä-*too*-rä.) Musical notation; figured bass.

In témpo (It.) (ēn-*tĕm*-pō.) In time.

Intendant (Fr.) (ănh-tänh-dänh.) } Director,
Intendénte (It.) (ēn-tĕn-*dĕn*-tĕ.) } conductor. See *Impresário*.

Interligne (Fr.) (In-ter-*leen*.) The space (between two lines) of the staff.

Interlude. A short musical representation, introduced between the acts of any drama or between the play and afterpiece; an intermediate strain or movement played between the verses of a hymn, or of a song.

ō as in *tone;* ô as in *dove;* ŏ as in *not;* ŭ as in *up;* ü the French sound of *u.*

Interludium (Lat.) (ĭn-tĕr-loo-dĭ-oom.)
Intermède (Fr.) (ănh-tĕr-mād'.)
Intermedio (It.) (ĭn-tĕr-mā-dĭ-ō.)
Intermezzo (It.) (ĭn-tĕr-mēt-sō.)
An interlude; intermediate, placed between two others; detached pieces introduced between the acts of an opera. Also a short movement in the symphony taking the place of the Scherzo. In the old Suite, the *Intermezzi* were from two to four short movements, of moderate tempo (generally minuets or gavots), placed between the sarabande and the finale, — the *gigue*.

Interval (Lat., *intervallum*; Ger., *Intervall*; Fr., *intervalle*; It., *intervallo*.) The difference in pitch between two tones. The interval is counted from the lowest note to the highest. Thus in the scale of C major the intervals would be named as follows:

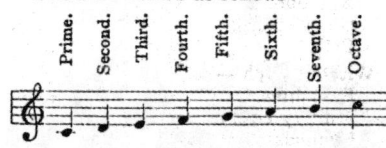

Prime. Second. Third. Fourth. Fifth. Sixth. Seventh. Octave.

In the inversion of these, the prime becomes an octave, the second a seventh, the third a sixth, etc. But the character of the interval may change in the inversion. The intervals are thus classified:

| PRIMES. Perfect. or Unison. Augmented. | SECONDS. Major. Minor. Augmented. |

THIRDS. Major. Minor. Diminished.

FOURTHS. Perfect. Augmented. Diminished.

FIFTHS. Perfect. Augmented. Diminished.

SIXTHS. Major. Minor. Augmented.

SEVENTHS. Major. Minor. Diminished.

OCTAVES. Perfect. Diminished.

It will be noticed that each *major* or *perfect* interval, when widened by a semi-tone, becomes *augmented*; that each *major* interval, contracted by a semi-tone, becomes *minor*; and that each *minor* or *perfect* interval contracted by a semi-tone, becomes *diminished*; and that in the inversion

a Perfect interval remains perfect,
a Major " becomes minor,
a Minor " " major,
an Augmented " " diminished,
a Diminished " " augmented.

Thus, if we invert the three sevenths above given they become seconds, but of the following kinds:

Minor. Major. Augmented.

Interval, augmented. An interval which is a semi-tone, or half-step, greater than a major or perfect interval.

Interval, consecutive. An interval passing in the same direction in two parallel parts.

Interval, diminished. An interval less than a perfect interval by a half-step or semi-tone.

Interval, enharmonic. An interval — which is only nominal, as from G♯ to A♭.

Interval, extreme. A larger interval than the major, or a smaller than the minor.

Intimíssimo (It.) (in-tē-*mēes*-sē-mō.) Very expressive; with great feeling.

ă as in *ah*; ā as in *hate*; ă as in *at*; ē as in *tree*; ĕ as in *eh*; ī as in *pine*; ĭ as in *pin*;

146

Intimo (It.) (*in*-tē-mō.) Inward feeling; expressive. See *Innig*.

Intonare (It.) (in-tō-*nä*-rĕ.) } To pitch the voice; to sound the key-note; to begin.
Intuonáre (It.) (in-twō-*nä*-rĕ.) }

Intonation. A word referring to the proper emission of the voice so as to produce any required note in exact tune; the act of modulating the voice. The chanting of *Plain-song*.

Intonation, false. A variation in pitch from what is understood to be the true tone.

Intonato (It.) (in-tō-*nä*-tō.) Tuned; set to music.

Intonatúra (It.) (in-tō-nä-*too*-rä.) }
Intonazione (It.) (in-tō-nä-tsē-*ō*-nĕ.) }
Intonation.

Intoniren (Ger.) (in-tō-nē-r'n.) To intone; to sound.

Intráda (It.) (in-*trä*-dä.) } A short prelude or introductory movement.
Intrade (Ger.) (ĭn-*trä*-dĕ.) }

Intrepidaménte (It.) (in-trĕ-pē-dä-*men*-tĕ.) Boldly; with intrepidity.

Intrepidezza (It.) (in-trĕ-pē-*det*-sä.) Intrepidity, boldness.

Intrépido (It.) (ēn-*trä*-pē-dō.) Intrepid, bold.

Introduciménto (It.) (ēn-trō-doo-tshē-*men*-tō.) An introduction.

Introduction. That movement in a composition, the design of which is to prepare the ear for the movements which are to follow. It may be a mere phrase, or an entire division of a work. See *Beethoven's* 1st, 2d, and 7th Symphonies.

Introductorio (It.) (ēn-trō-dook-*tō*-rē-ō.) Introductory, preliminary.

Introduzione (It.) (ēn-trō-doo-tsē-*ō*-nĕ.) An introduction.

Introit (Eng.) (ĭn-*trō*-ĭt.) }
Introit (Fr.) (ănh-trwä.) } *Entrance;*
Intróito (It.) (en-trō-*ē*-tō.) } a hymn
Introito (Spa.) (ēn-trō-*ē*-tō.) } or antiphonal
Introitus (Lat.) (ĭn-*trō-ĭ*-tŭs.) }
chant sung while the priest approaches the altar at the commencement of the Mass. In the Anglican Church, a short anthem, psalm, or hymn, sung while the minister proceeds to the table to administer the Holy Communion. Formerly, in some English cathedrals, the Sanctus was sung as an Introit.

Invention (Fr.) (ănh-vänh-sĭ-ŏnh.) An old name for a species of prelude or short fantasia: a short piece in free contrapuntal style.

Invenzione (It.) (ēn-vĕn-tsē-*ō*-nĕ.) Invention, contrivance.

Inversio (Lat.) (ĭn-*vär*-sĭ-ō.) Inversion. See that word.

Inversio cancrizans (Lat.) (ĭn-*vär*-sĭ-ō kăn-krĭ-*zäns*.) Retrograde, or *crab-like* inversion, or imitation; because it goes backwards.

Inversio in octavam acutam (Lat.) (ĭn-*vär*-sĭ-ō ĭn ŏk-*tä*-väm ä-*kū*-täm.) Inversion in the octave above, the transposition of the lower part an octave above.

Inversio in octavam gravem (Lat.) (ĭn-*vär*-sĭ-o ĭn ŏk-*tä*-väm grä-vĕm.) Inversion in the octave below; the transposition of the upper part an octave below to form the bass, while the other part remains stationary.

Inversion. A change of position with respect to intervals and chords; the lower notes being placed above, and the upper notes below. See *Interval*. A chord is inverted when the bass takes some note other than the fundamental.

Chord. Inversions. Chord. Inversions.

Inversion, first. A term given to a chord when the written bass takes the *third*.

Inversion, retrograde. An inversion made by commencing on the last note of the subject and writing it backwards to the first note.

Inversion, second. Where the bass note takes the fifth from the fundamental.

Inversion, simple. An inversion made by reversing the notes of a subject in its answer, so that the ascending notes of the original passage descend in the answer, and *vice versa*.

Inversion, strict. The same as simple inversion, yet requiring that whole tones should be answered by whole tones, semi-tones by semi-tones, etc.

ō as in *tone* · ô as in *dove;* ŏ as in *not;* ŭ as in *up;* ü the French sound of *u*.

Inversion, third. Name given to a chord when the bass takes the seventh.
Invert. To change the position either in a subject or chord.
Inverted. Changed in position.
Inverted chord. A chord whose fundamental tone is not its lowest.
Inverted turn. A turn which commences with the lowest note instead of the highest.
Invitatorio (Spa.) (ēn-vē-tä-*tō*-rĭ-ō.) Psalm or anthem sung at the beginning of the matins.
Invitatorium (Lat.) (ĭn-vĭ-tă-*tō*-rĭ-ŭm.) The name applied to the *antiphone*, or response, to the psalm " Venite Exultemus."
Invitatory. A part of the service sung in the Roman Catholic Church; a psalm or anthem sung in the morning.
Invocatis (Lat.) (ĭn-vō-*kä*-tĭs.)
Invocáto (It.) (in-vō-*kä*-tō.)
Invocazióne (It.) (in-vō-kä-tsē-*ō*-ně.)
An invocation, or prayer.
Io bacche (Lat.) (yō-bäk-kě.) A burden used in the lyric poetry of the Romans.
Ionian (Gr.) (ĭ-*ō*-nĭ-ăn.)
Ionic (Gr.) (ĭ-*ŏn*-ĭk.) modes.
} One of the ancient Greek
Ionic music. A light, airy style of music.
Io triumphe (Lat.) (yō trĭ-*ŭm*-fě.) A phrase of exultation often found in the lyric poetry of the ancient Romans.
Ira (It.) (ē-rä.) Anger, wrath.
Iráta (It.) (i-*rä*-tä.)
Iráto (It.) (i-*rä*-tō.)
Irataménte (It.) (i-rä-tä-*men*-tě.)
} Angrily, passionately.
Irlandais (Fr.) (ir-länh-*dā*.)
Irländisch (Ger.) (*ir*-län-dish.)
} An air, or dance tune, in the Irish style.
Ironicaménte (It.) (i-rŏn-ē-kä-*men*-tě.) Ironically.
Irónico (It.) (i-*rŏn*-ē-kō.) Ironical.
Irregolare (It.) (ir-rä-gō-*lä*-rě.) Irregular.
Irregular cadence. An imperfect cadence.
Irregular period. A period in which a false cadence interrupts or suspends an expected final close.
Irresolúto (It.) (ir-rě-zō-*loo*-tō.) Irresolute, wavering.
Isdegno, con (It.) (is-*dān*-yō kŏn.) With indignation.
Ismania, con (It.) (is-*mä*-nē-ä.) With wildness; with madness.
Isochronal (Gr.)
Isochronous.
} Uniform in time, performed in equal time.
Isotonic system. A system of music consisting of intervals in which each concord is tempered alike, and in which there are twelve equal semi-tones.
Istésso (It.) (is-*tes*-sō.) The same.
Istésso tempo (It.) (is-*tes*-sō těm-pō.) The same time.
Istrepito, con (It.) (is-trě-pē-tō.) With noise and bluster.
Istrumentálo (It.) (is-troo-měn-*tä*-lě.) Instrumental.
Istrumentazióne (It.) (is-troo-měn-tä-tsē-*ō*-ně.) Instrumentation.
Istruménto (It.) (is-troo-*men*-tō.) An instrument.
Italian sixth. A name sometimes given to a chord composed of a major third and an augmented sixth.
Italiáno (It.) (i-tä-lē-*ä*-nō.)
Italienisch (Ger.) (ĭt-ä-lĭ-*ān*-ĭsh.)
Italienne (Fr.) (it-ä-lē-ěnn.)
} Italian.
Ita missa est (Lat.) (ē-tä mĭs-sä ěst.) The termination of the Mass sung by the priest to Gregorian music. It means " Go, ye are dismissed," and gave the name *Míssa* or *Mass* to the entire service.

J

Jack. The quill which strikes the strings of a harpsichord, or the upright lever in piano action.
Jaeger-chor (Ger.) (*yä*-ghěr-kŏr.) Hunting-chorus.
Jagd-ruf (Ger.) (*yägd*-roof.) Sound of the bugle or hunting-horn.
Jagd-horn (Ger.) (*yägd*-hōrn.)
Jagd-zink (Ger.) (*yägd*-tsĭnk.)
} Hunting-horn, bugle-horn.
Jagd-sinfonie (Ger.) (*yägd*-sĭn-fō-*nē*.) Hunting symphony.

ă as in *ah ;* ā as in *hate ;* ă as in *at ;* ē as in *tree ;* ě as in *eh ;* ī as in *pine ;* ĭ as in *pin ;*

148

JAGD-STUCK   JUBEL-LIEB

Jagd-stück (Ger.) (*yägd*-stük.) A hunting-piece.

Jäger-chor (Ger.) (*yā*-ghĕr-kōr.) See *Jaeger-chor*.

Jäger-horn (Ger.) (*yā*-ghĕr-hŏrn.) Hunting-horn, bugle-horn.

Jaléo (Spa.) (*hä*-lā-ō.) A national Spanish dance.

Jambe (Ger.) (*yäm*-bĕ.) See *Iambus*.

Jambico (It.) (ē-*äm*-bē-kō.) } An iambic.
Jambo (It.) (ē-*äm*-bō.) }

Janko keyboard. A system of pianoforte keys invented by a Hungarian, Paul von Janko, in 1882. It is two series of keys (each key representing a step of one whole tone), set in three different positions (six ranks of keys in all), and presents the following advantages: 1. The same fingering of scales and runs in any key. 2. The widest intervals are brought within the compass of a small hand. 3. Octave passages are made especially easy. There are other advantages, but, as yet, very few prominent artists have used the ingenious invention.

Janitscharen-musik (Ger.) (yä-nĭt-shär'n-moo-zīk.) Janizary music, Turkish music. In the orchestra, music for triangle, bass-drum and cymbals.

Jarábe (Spa.) (hä-*rä*-bĕ.) A Spanish dance.

Jauchzend (Ger.) (*youkh*-tsĕnd.) Shouting, joyful.

Jeu (Fr.) (zhŭh.) Play; the style of playing on an instrument; also a register in an organ or harmonium; also *Grand jeu, plein jeu,* full organ; full power; *demi-jeu,* half-power.

Jeu céleste (Fr.) (zhŭh sā-lĕst.) The name of a soft stop in an harmonium; also an organ-stop of French invention, formed of two dulciana pipes, the pitch of one being slightly raised, giving to the tone a waving undulating character.

Jeu d'anche (Fr.) (zhŭh d'änsh.) A reed-stop in an organ.

Jeu d'anges (Fr.) (zhŭh d'änzh.) Soft stops.

Jeu d'échos (Fr.) (zhŭh d'ā-kō.) Echo stop.

Jeu de flûtes (Fr.) (zhŭh dŭh floot.) Flute stop.

Jeu d'orgues (Fr.) (zhŭh d'ŏrg.) Register, or row of pipes, in an organ.

Jeux (Fr. pl.) (zhŭh.) *Stops* or *registers,* in an organ, or harmonium.

Jeux forts (Fr.) (zhŭh fōr.) Loud stops; *forte* stops.

Jew's harp. A small instrument of brass or steel, and shaped somewhat like a *lyre* with a thin, vibrating tongue of metal: when played, it is placed between the teeth, and struck with the forefinger.

Jewstrump. A term applied by old writers to the jews-harp.

Jig. A light, brisk movement; an old species of dance in $\frac{6}{8}$ or $\frac{12}{8}$ time; the name is supposed to have been derived from *Geige*, a fiddle. See *Gigue*.

Jingles. Loose pieces of metal placed around a tambourine to increase the sound.

Jocosus (Lat.) (jō-*kō*-sŭs.) Jocose, merry, funny.

Jodeln (Ger.) (*yō*-d'ln.) A style of singing peculiar to the Tyrolese peasants, the natural voice, and the falsetto, being used alternately.

Jodler (Ger.) (*yō*-dler.) A song sung in the above manner.

Joie (Fr.) (zhwä.) Joy, gladness.

Jonglours (Fr. pl.) (zhŏnh-gloor.) } An
Jongleurs (Fr. pl.) (zhŏnh-glŭr.) } old term for the itinerant musicians of the eleventh and following centuries.

Jóta (Spa.) (hō-tä.) A Spanish national dance in triple time and rapid movement.

Jouer (Fr.) (zhoo-ā.) To play upon an instrument.

Joueur de flûte (Fr.) (zhoo-ŭr dŭh floot.) A flutist.

Joueur de musette (Fr.) (zhoo-ŭr dŭh mŭ-zĕt.) A bagpiper.

Joueur d'instrumens (Fr.) (zhoo-ŭr d'änh-strü-mänh.) A player upon musical instruments.

Jovialisch (Ger.) (yō-fĭ-*ä*-lĭsh.) Jovial, joyous, merry.

Jubel-flöte (Ger.) (*yoo*-b'l-*flō*-tĕ.) An organ-stop of the flute species.

Jubel-gesang (Ger.) (*yoo*-b'l ghĕ-*zäng*.) }
Jubel-lied (Ger.) (*yoo*-b'l-lēd.) } Song of jubilee.

ō as in *tone*; ŏ as in *dove*; ŏ as in *not*; ŭ as in *up*; ü the French sound of *u*.

Jubelnd (Ger.) (*yoo*-bĕlnd.) Rejoicing.
Jubilar (Ger.) (yoo-bĭ-*lär*.) The recipient of a jubilee; one in whose honor a public performance is given.
Jubilate. In the Anglican liturgy, the one hundredth psalm, following the second lesson in the morning service.
Jubilee. A season of great public joy and festivity. Among the Jews, every *fiftieth* year was a jubilee.
Jubilóso (It.) (yoo-bē-*lō*-zō.) Jubilant, exulting.
Just. A term applied to all consonant intervals, and to those voices, strings, and pipes that give them with exactness.
Juste (Fr.) (zhüst.) Accurate in time, tone, harmony, and execution.
Justesse (Fr.) (zhüs-*tāss*.) Exactness, correctness, or purity of intonation.
Justesse de la voix (Fr.) (zhüs-*tāss* dŭh lä vwä.) Purity of voice.
Justesse de l'oreille (Fr.) (zhüs-*tāss* dŭh l'ō-*rā*-yŭh.) Correctness of ear.
Justo, con (It.) (yoos-tō kŏn.) With exact precision.
Just relations. Relations whose extremities form consonant intervals.

K

Kalamaika (kăl-ä-*mā*-kä.) A lively Hungarian dance in ⅔ time.
Kammer (Ger.) (*käm*-mĕr.) Chamber.
Kammer-concert (Ger.) (*käm*-mĕr-kŏn-tsĕrt.) Chamber-concert.
Kammer-musik (Ger.) (*käm*-mĕr-moo-*sĭk*.) Chamber-music; music for private performance. See *Chamber-music.*
Kammer-musikus (Ger.) (*käm*-mĕr-*moo*-zĭ-koos.) Chamber-musician; member of a private band.
Kammer-sängerin (Ger.) (*käm*-mĕr-*sāng*-ĕr-ĭn.) Private singer to a prince or king; court-singer (female).
Kammer-spiel (Ger.) (*käm*-mĕr-spēl.) See *Kammer-musik.*
Kammer-styl (Ger.) (*käm*-mĕr-stēl.) Style of chamber-music, as opposed to the ecclesiastical and theatrical styles.
Kammer-ton (Ger.) (*käm*-mĕr-tōn.) The *pitch,* or lower *tuning,* of the instruments in chamber-music. Normal pitch (ā=435.)

Kanon (Ger.) (*kä*-nōn.) A canon.
Kanzel-lied (Ger.) (*kän*-tsĕl-lēd.) Hymn before the sermon.
Kapelle (Ger.) (käp-*pĕl*-lĕ.) Chapel.
Kapell-meister (Ger.) (käp-*pĕl*-mīs-tĕr.) Chapel-master; musical director.
Karfreitag (Ger.) (kär-*frī*-täg.) Good Friday.
Kathedrale (Ger.) (kät-ĕ-*drä*-lĕ.)
Kathedral-kirche (Ger.) (kät-ĕ-*dräl kĭr*-khĕ.) Cathedral.
Keck (Ger.) (kĕk.) Pert, fearless, bold.
Keckheit (Ger.) (*kĕk*-hīt.) Boldness, vigor.
Keeners. Singers engaged by the Irish, to sing lamentations over the dead.
Kehle (Ger.) (*kā*-lĕ.) The voice: the throat. *Kehlfertigkeit,* vocal skill; *Kehlkopf,* larynx; *Kehlschlag* Fr., *coup de glotte ;* sudden firm attack of a vocal tone.
Kehraus (Ger.) (*kā*-rous.) A peculiar kind of dance, practiced at the conclusion of an entertainment.
Kent bugle. A bugle having six keys, four of which are commanded by the right hand and two by the left.
Keranim (kĕ-*rä*-nĭm.) The sacred trumpet of the ancient Hebrews.
Keren (Heb.) (kĕr-ĕn.) A horn; an instrument first used by the Hebrews formed of a ram's horn, and subsequently made of metal.
Keraulophon (Ger.) (kĕ-rou-lō-fŏn.) An 8-foot organ-stop, of a reedy and pleasing quality of tone; its peculiar character being produced by a small round hole bored in the pipe near the top.
Keron-jebel (Heb.) (*kĕr*-ŏn-yä-b'l.) Jubilee-horn.
Ketten-triller (Ger.) (*kĕt*-t'n *trĭl*-lĕr.) Chain of trills.
Kettledrum. A brass drum, of a cup-like shape, over which the parchment head is stretched; used in pairs, one of which is usually tuned to the key-note, the other to the fifth of the key. See *Drum.*
Kettledrummer. A performer upon the kettledrum.
Key. The lever by which the sounds of a pianoforte, organ, or harmonium, are

ă as in *ah*; ā as in *hate*; ă as in *at*; ē as in *tree*; ĕ as in *eh*; ī as in *pine*; ĭ as in *pin*;

150

KEY

produced. Also an arrangement by which certain holes are opened and closed in flutes, oboes, and other wind-instruments. A key also means, a scale, or series of notes progressing diatonically, in a certain order of tones and semi-tones, the first note of the scale being called the *Key-note*.

The signature of these keys would be as follows:

TABLE OF KEYS IN

	ENGLISH	FRENCH	ITALIAN	GERMAN
7 Sharps	C sharp major A sharp minor	Ut dièse majeur La dièse mineur	Do diesis maggiore La diesis minore	Cis dur. Ais moll.
6 Sharps	F sharp major D sharp minor	Fa dièse majeur Ré dièse mineur	Fa diesis maggiore Re diesis minore	Fis dur. Dis moll.
5 Sharps	B major G sharp minor	Si majeur Sol dièse mineur	Si maggiore Sol diesis minore	H dur. Gis moll.
4 Sharps	E major C sharp minor	Mi majeur Ut dièse mineur	Mi maggiore Do diesis minore	E dur. Cis moll.
3 Sharps	A major F sharp minor	La majeur Fa dièse mineur	La maggiore Fa diesis minore	A dur. Fis moll.
2 Sharps	D major B minor	Ré majeur Si mineur	Re maggiore Si minore	D dur. H moll.
1 Sharp	G major E minor	Sol majeur Mi mineur	Sol maggiore Mi minore	G dur. E moll.
No Signature	C major A minor	Ut majeur La mineur	Do maggiore La minore	C dur. A moll.
1 Flat	F major D minor	Fa majeur Ré mineur	Fa maggiore Re minore	F dur. D moll.
2 Flats	B flat major G minor	Si bémol majeur Sol mineur	Si bemolle maggiore Sol minore	B dur. G moll.
3 Flats	E flat major C minor	Mi bémol majeur Ut mineur	Mi bemolle maggiore Do minore	Es dur. C moll.
4 Flats	A flat major F minor	La bémol majeur Fa mineur	La bemolle maggiore Fa minore	As dur. F moll.
5 Flats	D flat major B flat minor	Ré bémol majeur Si bémol mineur	Re bemolle maggiore Si bemolle minore	Des dur. B moll.
6 Flats	G flat major E flat minor	Sol bémol majeur Mi bémol mineur	Sol bemolle maggiore Mi bemolle minore	Ges dur Es moll.
7 Flats	C flat major A flat minor	Ut bémol majeur La bémol mineur	Do bemolle maggiore La bemolle minore	Ces dur. As moll.

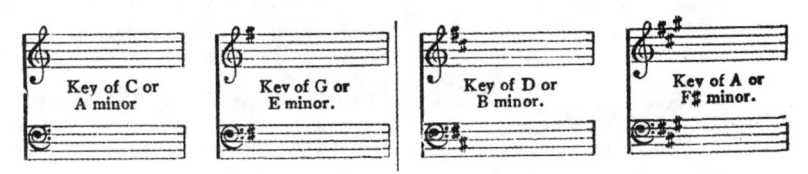

Key of C or A minor.   Key of G or E minor.   Key of D or B minor.   Key of A or F♯ minor.

ō as in *tone*; ô as in *dove*; ŏ as in *not*; ŭ as in *up*; ü the French sound of *u*.

KEY

Key of E or C♯ minor.
Key of B or G♯ minor.
Key of F♯ or D♯ minor.
Key of C♯ or A♯ minor.
Key of F or D minor.
Key of B♭ or G minor.
Key of E♭ or C minor.
Key of A♭ or F minor.
Key of D♭ or B♭ minor.
Key of G♭ or E♭ minor.
Key of C♭ or A♭ minor.

The relationship of these keys can best be illustrated by the following diagram, which is called the *Circle of the keys:*

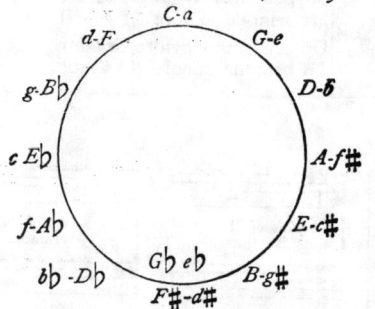

C-a
d-F / G-e
g-B♭ / D-b
c E♭ / A-f♯
f-A♭ / E-c♯
b♭ -D♭ / B-g♯
G♭ e♭
F♯-d♯

KEYS, AUTHENTIC

Keyboard. (Ger., *Klaviatur*, Fr., *Clavier*, It., *Tastatura*.) The rows of keys upon a pianoforte, organ, or similar instrument. The keyboard as at present arranged for piano, or organ, is very ancient. The principle of the present keyboard existed on the Halberstadt organ in the fourteenth century. The earliest known record of the clavichord occurs in some rules of the minnesingers, dated 1404, preserved at Vienna. The monochord is named with it, showing a differentiation of these instruments, and of them from the clavicymbalum, the keyed cymbal, cembalo (Italian), or psaltery. From this we learn that a keyboard had been thus early adapted to that favorite mediæval stringed instrument, the *cembalo* of Boccaccio, the *sautrie* of Chaucer. The oldest actually existing keyboard of the present style is on a spinet in the Paris *Conservatoire*, which is dated 1523. It is probable that the shape of the piano keyboard has not materially changed in the last five hundred years.

Key-bugle. A Kent-bugle.

Keyed. Furnished with keys.

Keyed cithara. An oblong box holding a series of strings in triangular form, struck by plectra of quill affixed to the inner ends of the keys.

Keyed harmonica. An instrument with keys, the hammers striking upon plates of glass.

Key, fundamental. The original key.

Key, governing. The principal or original key.

Key-harp. An instrument resembling a piano externally, with a similar arrangement of keys and pedals. It consists of an adjustment of tuning forks of various pitches, over cavities of sonorous metal.

Key, major. That scale or key in which the third from the tonic is major.

Key, minor. That scale or key in which the third from the tonic is minor.

Key, natural. That which has neither sharp nor flat at the signature.

Key-note. The tonic, or first note of every scale.

Keys, authentic. Keys in the ancient system of the Greeks, whose tones extend from the tonic to the fifth and octave above.

ä as in *ah*; ā as in *hate*; ă as in *at*; ē as in *tree*; ĕ as in *eh*; ī as in *pine*; ĭ as in *pin*;

152

KEYS, CHROMATIC   KLAVIATUR

Keys, chromatic. The black keys of a pianoforte; every key in whose scale one or more so-called chromatic tones occur, and in which a chromatic signature is requisite.

Keys, parallel. The major and minor of the same tonic or key-note.

Keys, pedal. That set of keys belonging to an organ which are acted upon by the feet.

Keys, plagal. In the ancient Greek system, those keys whose tones extended from the dominant or fifth upward to the octave and twelfth.

Keys, relative. Keys which only differ by having in their scales one flat or sharp more or less, or which have the same signature.

Keys, remote. Those which are at a distance from each other as the keys of one sharp and six sharps.

Key-tone. The key-note.

Key, transposed. A key removed or changed from that in which a piece was originally written.

Key, tuning. An instrument for the purpose of tightening or loosening the strings of a piano or harp. Tuning-hammer.

Kicks (Ger.) (*kix.*) A *couac* or break in the tone of an oboe or clarinet-player.

Kinnor (Heb.) (kĭn-*nōr.*) A small harp held in the hand and played upon while dancing.

Kirchen-componist (Ger.) (*kĭr*-kh'n-kŏm-pō-*nĭst.*) Composer of church music.

Kirchen-dienst (Ger.) (*kĭr*-kh'n-dēnst.) Church-service; form of prayer.

Kirchen-fest (Ger.) (*kĭr*-kh'n-fĕst.) Church festival.

Kirchen-gesang (Ger.) (*kĭr*-kh'n ghĕ-säng.)

Kirchen-lied (Ger.) (*kĭr*-kh'n-lēd.) Spiritual song, canticle, psalm, or hymn.

Kirchen-musik (Ger.) (*kĭr*-kh'n-moo-*zĭk.*) Church music.

Kirchen-sänger (Ger.) (*kĭr*-kh'n-*säng*-ĕr.) A chorister; a chanter.

Kirchen-stück (Ger.) (*kĭr*-kh'n-stük.) Church-piece, or composition.

Kirchen-styl (Ger.) (*kĭr*-kh'n-stēl.) Church style; ecclesiastical style.

Kirchen-ton (Ger.) (*kĭr*-kh'n-tōn.) Church mode, or tone.

Kirchen-tonarten (Ger. pl.) (*kĭr*-kh'n *tōn*-är-t'n.) The old church modes.

Kirchen-weise (Ger.) (*kĭr*-kh'n-*vī*-zĕ.) A church melody.

Kit. The name of a small pocket-violin used by dancing masters. Its length is about sixteen inches, and that of the bow about seventeen.

Kitar (kĭ-*tär.*) A musical instrument of the Arabs.

Kithara (Gr.) (*kĭth*-ă-rä.) A cithara.

Klage (Ger.) (*klä*-ghĕ.) Lamentation.

Klagend (Ger.) (*klä*-g'nd.) Plaintive.

Klage-gedicht (*klä*-ghĕ-gl.ĕ-*dĭkht.*)

Klage-lied (Ger.) (*klä*-ghĕ-lēd.) Elegy; mournful song; lamentation.

Klage-ton (Ger.) (*klä*-ghĕ-tŏn.) Plaintive tune, or melody.

Klang (Ger.) (*kläng.*) Sound, tune, ringing.

Klang-boden (Ger.) (kläng-bō-d'n.) Sound-board.

Klänge (Ger. pl.) (*kläng*-ĕ.) Sounds, melodies.

Klangeschlecht (Ger.) (*klän*-ghĕ-*shlĕkht.*) A genus, or mode.

Klangfarbe (Ger.) (*kläng*-fahrbeh.) Tone-color; quality of tone; clang-tint.

Klanglehre (Ger.) (*kläng*-lā-rĕ.) Acoustics.

Klangnachbildung (Ger.) (*kläng-näkh-*bĭl-doong.) Imitation of a sound.

Klappe (Ger.) (*kläp*-pĕ.) Key of any wind-instrument; a valve.

Klappen-flügelhorn (Ger.) (*kläp*-p'n-*flü*-g'l-hŏrn.) The keyed bugle.

Klappen-horn (Ger.) (*kläp*-p'n-hŏrn.) A keyed horn; a bugle.

Klapp-trompete (Ger.) (kläp-trŏm-*pā*-tĕ.) A keyed trumpet.

Klar (Ger.) (klär.) Clear, bright.

Klarheit (Ger.) (*klär*-hīt.) Clearness, plainness.

Klärlich (Ger.) (*klär*-lĭkh.) Clearly, distinctly.

Klausel (Ger.) (*klou*-zĕl.) A close; a regular section of a movement.

Klaviatur (Ger.) (klah-veeah-*toor.*) See *Keyboard*.

ō as in *tone;* ŏ as in *dove;* ŏ as in *not;* ŭ as in *up;* ü the French sound of *u.*

153

Klavier (Ger.) (klä-*fēr*.) Pianoforte, harpsichord. See *Clavier*.
Klaviermässig (Ger.)(klä-*fēer*-may-sich.) Suited to the piano.
Klavier-sonaten (Ger.) (klä-*fēr*-sō-*nä*-tĕn.) Piano sonatas.
Klavier-spieler (Ger.) (klä-*fēr-spē*-lĕr.) Piano-player.
Klein (Ger.) (klīn.) Minor; speaking of intervals.
Klein-bass (Ger.) (*klīn*-bäss.)
Klein-bass-geige (Ger.) (klīn-*bäss-ghī*-ghĕ.) Violoncello.
Kleine Alt-posaune (Ger.) (*klī*-nĕ *ält* pōs-*sou*-nĕ.) A small alto trombone.
Kleine Lieder (Ger.) (*klī*-nĕ *lē*-dĕr.) Little songs.
Kleine-gedacht (Ger.) (*klī*-nĕ-ghĕ-*däkht*.) A small covered stop in an organ; a stopped flute.
Kleinlaut (Ger.) (*klīn*-lout.) Small or low in tone, or voice; timid.
Klingbar (Ger.) (*klĭng*-bär.) Resonant, sonorous.
Klingeln (Ger.) (*klĭng*-ĕln.) To ring, or sound a small bell; to jingle.
Klingen (Ger.) (*klĭng*-'n.) } Sonorous,
Klingend (Ger.) (*klĭng*-ĕnd.) } resonant, ringing.
Kling klang (Ger.) (*klĭng* kläng.) Tinkling.
Klingspiel (Ger.) (*klĭng*-spēl.) The sound or noise of instruments.
Knabenstimme (Ger.) (*knä*-b'n-*stĭm*-mĕ.) A boy's voice; a counter tenor.
Knee-stop. A knee-lever under the manual of the reed-organ; there are three kinds, used (*a*) to control the supply of wind; (*b*) to open and shut the swell box; (*c*) to draw all the stops.
Knell. The tolling of a bell at a death or funeral.
Knie-geige (Ger.) (*knē*-ghĭ-ghĕ.) *Viol da Gámba*, violoncello.
Kollo (Jap.) (kŏl-lō.) A Japanese instrument somewhat resembling a harp.
Komisch (Ger.) (*kōm*-ĭsh.) Comical.
Komma (Gr.) (*kŏm*-mä.) } Comma; a
Komma (Ger.) (*kŏm*-mä.) } musical section or division.
Komödiant (Ger.) (kō-mô-dĭ-*änt*.) Comedian, actor, player.

Komödie (Ger.) (kō-*mô*-dĭ-ĕ.) Comedy, play.
Komponiren (Ger.) (kŏm-pō-*nēr*-'n.) To compose.
Komponist (Ger.) (kŏm-pō-*nĭst*.) A composer.
Komposition (Ger.) (kŏm-pō-zĭt-sĭ-*ōn*.) A composition.
Konzert-meister (Ger.) (kŏn-*tsĕrt*-mĭs-tĕr.) See *Concert-meister*.
Kopf-stimme (Ger.) (*köpf*-stim-mĕ.) Falsetto; head voice.
Koppel (Ger.) (*kōp*-p'l.) Coupler; coupling stop in an organ.
Koryphæus (Gr.) (kō-rĭf-*ē*-ŭs.) Chief or leader of the chorus in ancient Athens.
Kos (Hun.) (kōz.) An Hungarian dance.
Kosake (kō-sä-kĕ.) A national dance of the Cossacks.
Koto. The Japanese zither-harp, with thirteen silk strings stretched over an arching oblong soundboard, each having a separate movable bridge, by adjusting which the string can be tuned. Compass about two octaves.
Krächzen (Ger.) (*krākh*-ts'n.) To sing with a croaking voice.
Kraft (Ger.) (kräft.) Power, strength, energy.
Kräftig (Ger.) (*krāf*-tĭg.) }
Kräftiglich (Ger.) (*krāf*-tĭg-lĭkh.) } Powerful; vigorous; full of energy.
Krakoviak (krä-kō-vĭ-äk.) } The
Krakovienne (Fr.) (krä-kō-vĭ-ĕn.) } *Cracovienne*, a Polish dance in ¾ time.
Kreuz (Ger.) (kroits.) A *sharp*.
Kreuz-doppeltes (Ger.) (kroits *dop*-pĕl-tĕs.) A *double sharp* × or 𝄪.
Kriegerisch (Ger.) (*krē*-ghĕr-ĭsh.) Warlike, martial.
Kriegs-gesang (Ger.)(*krēgs*-ghĕ-*sāng*.)
Kriegs-lied (Ger.) (*krēgs*-lēd.) A war-song; a soldier's song.
Krome. See *Croma*.
Krumm (Ger.) (kroom.) Crooked, curved, bent.
Krummhorn (Ger.) (*kroom*-hōrn.) *Crooked horn.* The name of a portable wind-instrument formerly much in use resembling a small cornet. Organ-builders corrupt this word into *cremona* and apply it to one of their organ-stops.

ă as in *ah* ; ā as in *hate* ; ă as in *at* ; ē as in *tree* ; ĕ as in *eh* ; ī as in *pine* ; ĭ as in *pin*;

Kuh-horn (Ger.) (*koo*-hōrn.) Cow horn; Swiss horn; Alpine horn.
Kühn (Ger.) (kün.) Dashing, audacious.
Kuhreihen (Ger.) (*koo*-rī-h'n.) Ranz des Vaches.
Kunst (Ger.) (koonst.) Art, skill.
Künstler (Ger.) (künst-ler.) An artist.
Kunstlied (Ger.) (*koonst*-leed.) An artsong. The opposite of the folksong. See *Strophe*.
Kuppel (Ger.) (*koop*-p'l.) See *Koppel*.
Kurz (Ger.) (koorts.) Short, detached staccato.
Kürzen (Ger.) (*kür*-tsen.) To abridge.
Kürzung (Ger.) (*kür*-tsoong.) Abbreviation.
Kürzungszeichen (Ger.) (*kür*-tsoongs-*tsī*-kh'n.) Sign of abbreviation.
Kussir (Fr.) (küs-sēr.) A Turkish musical instrument.
Kützial-flöte (Ger.) (küt-sĭ-*äl-flö*-tĕ.) An organ-stop of the flute species.
Kynnor (Heb.) (kĭn-nŏr.) The harp of David.
Kyrie eleison (Gr.) (kē-rē ā-lē-zŏn.) *Lord have mercy upon us.* The first movement in a Mass.
Kyrielle (Fr.) (kē-rē-ĕl.) Litany.

L

L. Left hand. Notes to be played with the left hand are sometimes written with an L over them. (Ger., *Links*; Eng., *Left*.)
La. A syllable applied in *solfa-ing*; to the note A; the sixth sound in the scale of Guido. In Italy and France, the note A is always called *La*-
La (It.) (lä.) } The.
La (Fr.) (lä.) }
La bémol (Fr.) (lä bā-mōl.) The note A flat.
La bémol majeur (Fr.) (lä bā-mōl mä-zhŭr.) The key of A flat major.
La bémol mineur (Fr.) (lä bā-mōl mē-nŭr.) The key of A flat minor.
Labial. Organ-pipes with *lips*, called also *flue* pipes.
Labial-stimmen (Ger.) (lä-bĭ-*äl-stĭm*-m'n.) Stops belonging to the *flue* work, not *reed*-stops.
Labium (Lat.) (*lä*-bĭ-ŭm.) The *lip* of an organ-pipe.

Lacrimándo (It.)(lä-crē-män-dō.) } Sadly;
Lacrimóso (lä-crē-mō-zō.) } in a mournful, pathetic style.
Lacrimosa (Lat.) A division of the Requiem Mass.
Lage (Ger.) (*lä*-ghĕ.) Position of a chord, or of the hand.
Lagnoso (It.) (län-*yō*-zō.) Plaintive, doleful.
Lagrimándo (It.) (lä-grē-*män*-dō.) }
Lagrimóso (It.) (lä-grē-*mō*-zō.) }
Weeping; tearful; in a sad and mournful style.
Lai (Fr.) (lā.) Lay; ditty; short, plaintive song.
La majeur (Fr.) (lä mä-zhŭr.) The key of A major.
L'âme (Fr.) (l'äm.) Sound-post of a violin, viola, etc.
Lament. An old name for harp music of the pathetic kind; applied also to the pathetic tunes of the Scotch.
Lamentábile (It.) (lä-měn-*tä*-bē-lĕ.) Lamentable, mournful.
Lamentabilménte (It.) (lä-měn-tä-běl-*men*-tĕ.) Lamentably, mournfully.
Lamentabondo (It.) (lä-měn-tä-*bōn*-dō.) Mournful, doleful.
Lamentándo (It.) (lä-měn-*tän*-dō.) Lamenting, mourning.
Lamentations. The funeral music of the ancient Jews was called by this name.
Lamentazione (It.) (lä-měn-tä-tsē-*ō*-nĕ.) A lamentation.
Lamentévole (It.) (lä-měn-*te*-vō-lĕ.) Lamentable, mournful, plaintive.
Lamentevolménte (It.) (lä-měn-te-vŏ*-men*-tĕ.) Mournfully, plaintively.
Lamentóso (It.) (lä-měn-*tō*-zō.) Lamentable, mournful.
La mineur (Fr.) (lä mĭ-nŭr.) The key of A minor.
Lampons (Fr.) (länh-pŏnh.) Drinking songs.
Länderer (Ger.) (*län*-dĕ-rĕr.) } A country
Ländler (Ger.) (*länd*-lĕr.) } dance, or air in a rustic and popular style, in ¾ time. It is like the *Tyrolienne*.
Länderisch (Ger.) (*län*-dĕr-ĭsh.) In the manner or measure of a country dance.
Ländlich (Ger.) (*länd*-lĭkh.) Rural.

ŏ as in *tone* · ŏ as in *dove*; ŏ as in *not*; ŭ as in *up*; ü the French sound of *u*.

155

LAND–LIED — LAUTENBALKEN

Land-lied (Ger.) (*länd*-lēd.) Rural song; rustic song.

Lang (Ger.) (läng.) Long.

Langsam (Ger.) (*läng*-säm.) Slowly; equivalent to *Lárgo*.

Langsamer (Ger.) (*läng*-sä-měr.) Slower.

Language. } In an organ flue-pipe, this is
Languid. } the flat piece of metal or wood placed horizontally just inside of the mouth.

Langueménte (It.) (län-guĕ-*men*-tĕ.) Languishingly

Languéndo (It.) (län-*guen*-dō.) } Lan-
Languénte (It.) (län-*guen*-tĕ.) } guish-
Lánguido (It.) (*län*-guē-dō.) } ing;
feeble; with languor.

Languettes (Fr.) (länh-*gätt*.) The brass tongues, belonging to the reed-pipes in an organ.

Largaménte (It.) (lär-gä-*men*-tĕ.) } Large-
Largaménto (It.) (lär-gä-*men*-tō.) } -y ;
fully; in a full, free, broad style of performance.

Large. The longest note formerly in use in ancient music. It is equal to eight whole notes or four breves.

Largement (Fr.) (lärzh-mänh.) Full; free in style. See *Largaménte*.

Larghetto (It.) (lär-*get*-tō.) A word specifying a time not quite so slow as that denoted by *largo*, of which word it is the diminutive.

Larghezza (It.) (lär-*get*-tsä.) Breadth, largeness, freedom.

Larghissimo (It.) (lār-*ghis*-sē-mō.) Extremely slow; the superlative of *largo*.

Lárgo (It.) (*lär*-gō.) A slow and solemn degree of movement.

Lárgo andante (It.) (*lär*-gō än-*dän*-tĕ.) Slow, distinct, exact.

Lárgo assai (It.) (*lär*-gō äs-*sä*-ē.) }
Lárgo di mólto (It.) (lär-gō dē *mōl*-tō.) }
Very slow.

Lárgo ma non tróppo (It.) (lär-gō mä nōn trŏp-pō.) Slow, but not too much so.

Lárgo un póco (It.) (lär-gō oon pō-kō.) Rather slow.

Larigot (Fr.) (*lär*-I-gō.) Shepherd's flageolet or pipe; an organ-stop tuned an octave above the twelfth.

Laringe (It.) (lä-*rĕn*-jĕ.) Larynx.

Larmoyant (Fr.) (lär-mwä-yänh.) Weeping; with a tearful expression.

Larynx. The upper part of the *trachea*. It is composed of five annular cartilages, placed above one another and united by elastic ligaments, by which it is so dilated and contracted as to be capable of varying the tones of the voice.

Laryngoscope, an instrument for examining the larynx. In 1854, M. Manuel Garcia, the well-known singing-master, thought of employing mirrors for studying the interior of the larynx during singing. He made his observations on himself and succeeded admirably. He used a small mirror on a long stem suitably bent, and introduced this into the pharynx. He directed the person experimented on to turn to the sun, so that the rays might be reflected into the larynx. To-day an electric light is used by experimenters with the laryngoscope, one of the most important inventions in vocal physiology.

Laud. To praise with words alone, or with words and music.

Laúd (Spa.) (läood.) A lute.

Láuda (It.) (lä-oo-dä.) Laud; praise; hymn of praise.

Laudamus te (Lat.) (law-*dä*-mŭs tā.) *We praise Thee;* part of the Gloria.

Laudes (Lat.) (law-dēs.) } Canticles, or
Láudi (It. pl.) (lä-oo-dēe.) } hymns of praise, that follow the early Mass.

Laudi spirituali (Lat.) (*law*-dē spĭr-ĭt-ū-ä-lē.) Sacred songs and dialogues sung by the priests in the oratory.

Lauf (Ger.) (louf.) That part of a violin, etc., into which the pegs are inserted; also, a rapid succession of notes; a trill.

Läufe (Ger. pl.) (*loi*-fĕ.) } Rapid divis-
Läufer (Ger.) (*loi*-fĕr.) } ions of notes; a flight or run of rapid notes; a roulade.

Launig (Ger.) (*lou*-nĭg.) Humorous, capricious.

Laut (Ger.) (lout.) Loud; also, sound.

Laute (Ger.) (*lou*-tĕ.) The lute.

Läuten (Ger.) (*loi*-t'n.) To ring; to toll; to sound.

Lautenbalken (Ger.) (*lou*-t'n-*bäl*-k'n.) The bridge of a lute.

ă as in *ah*; ā as in *hate*; ă as in *at*; ē as in *tree*; ĕ as in *eh*; ī as in *pine*; ĭ as in *pin*;

Lautenblatt (Ger.) (*lou*-t'n-blätt.) The table of a lute.
Lauten-futter (Ger.) (*lou*-t'n-*foot*-tĕr.) } Lute case.
Lauten-kasten (Ger.) (*lou*-t'n-*käs*-t'n.)
Lautenist (Ger.) (lou-t'n-*ĭst*.) Lute-player, lutenist.
Lauten-schläger (Ger.) (lou-t'n-*shlä*-ghĕr.)
Lauten-spieler (Ger.) (lou-t'n-*spē*-lĕr.) Lute-player, lutenist.
Lautlos (Ger.) (*lout*-lōs.) Soundless, mute.
La volta (It.) (lä *vōl*-tä.) } A lively, ani-
La volte (It.) (lä *vōl*-tĕ.) } mated tune performed to an old dance, the action of which consisted chiefly of quick turns and high leaps. It was in ¾ or ⅜ time.
Lay. A song; a species of narrative poetry among the ancient minstrels.
Lay clerk. A vocal officiate in a cathedral, who takes part in the services and anthems, but is not of the priesthood.
Laymen. Those vocal officiates in a cathedral who are not of the priesthood; the laity or people in distinction from the clergy.
Le (Fr.) (lŭh.) } The.
Le (It. pl.) (lĕ.) }
Leader. The first or principal violin in an orchestra; a director of a choir, or of a military band, generally the first cornet.
Leading chord. The dominant chord.
Leading melody. The principal melody in a composition of several parts.
Leading-note. The major seventh of any scale; the semi-tone below the key-note; the major third of the dominant.
Leaning-note. See *Appoggiatura*.
Leben (Ger.) (*lā*-b'n.) Life, vivacity.
Lebhaft (Ger.) (*lāb*-häft.) Lively, vivacious, quick.
Lebhaftigkeit (Ger.) (*lāb*-häf-tĭg-kīt.) Liveliness, vivacity.
Leçon (Fr.) (lā-sŏnh.) A lesson; an exercise.
Ledger lines. } The short extra, or addi-
Leger lines. } tional lines drawn above or below the staff, for the reception of

such notes as are too high or too low to be placed on or within the staff.
Left beat. A movement to the left in beating time.
Legábile (It.) (lĕ-*gä*-bē-lĕ.) } See *Legáto*.
Legándo (It.) (lĕ-*gän*-dō.) }
Legáre (It.) (lĕ-*gä*-rĕ.) To slur, or bind.
Legatíssimo (It.) (lĕ-gä-*tēs*-sē-mō.) Exceedingly smooth and connected.
Legáto (It.) (lĕ-*gä*-tō.) In a close, smooth, graceful manner; the opposite to *staccato*. It is often indicated by a sign called a slur ⌒.
Legato assai (It.) (lĕ-*gä*-tō äs-*sä*-ē.) Very close and connected.
Legato touch. A sliding of the fingers on and off the keys, holding down one key until the finger is fairly on another. It is indicated by the word *legato*, or by a curved line ⌒.
Legatúra (It.) (lĕ-gä-*too*-rä.) A slur; a ligature.
Legende (Fr.) (Le-*zhänd*.) A legend; a piece written in a romantic, narrative style.
Léger (Fr.) (lā-zhā.) Light, nimble.
Légèrement (Fr.) (lā-zhār-mänh.) Lightly, nimbly, gaily.
Léger et animé (Fr.) (lā-zhār ĕt än-ē-mā.) Light and animated.
Légereté (Fr.) (lā-*zhā*-rĕ-tā.) Lightness, agility.
Leggénda (It.) (lĕd-*jen*-dä.) A legend; a tale.
Leggeraménte (It.) (lĕd-jĕr-ä-*men*-tĕ.) Lightly, easily.
Leggeranza (It.) (lĕd-jĕr-*än*-tsä.) } Light-
Leggerezza (It.) (lĕd-jĕr-*et*-tsä.) } ness and agility.
Leggerissimamente (It.) (lĕd-jĕr-ēs-sē-mä-*mĕn*-tĕ.) Very light and sprightly.
Leggerissimo (It.) (lĕd-jĕr-*ēs*-sē-mō.) Very light and sprightly.
Leggermente (It.) (lĕd-jĕr-*men*-tĕ.) A light and easy movement.
Leggiadra (It.) (lĕd-jĕ-*ä*-drä.) Graceful, elegant.
Leggiadraménte (It.) (lĕd-jē-ä-drä-*men*-tĕ.) Gracefully, elegantly.
Leggiárdo (It.) (lĕd-jē-*är*-dō.) Lightly, delicately.

ŏ as in *tone*; ȯ as in *dove*; ŏ as in *not*; ŭ as in *up*; ü the French sound of *u*.

157

Leggieraménte (It.) (led-jē-ār-ä-*men*-te.)
Leggiére (It.) (lĕd-jē-*ā*-rĕ.)
Leggierménte (It.) (lĕd-jē-ĕr-*men*-tĕ.) Easily, lightly, delicately.
Leggierézza (It.) (led-jē-e-*ret*-tsä.) Lightness, delicacy; in a light, elastic style.
Leggiéro (It.) (lĕd-jē-*ā*-rō.) Light, swift, delicate.
Leggío (It.) (lĕd-jē-ō.) A chorister's desk, in a church-choir.
Légno (It.) (*lān*-yō.) *Wood.* See *Col Légno.*
Lehrer (Ger.) (*lā*-rer.) Teacher, master.
Lehrerin (Ger.) (*lā*-rĕr-ĭn.) Instructress, mistress.
Leichen-gedicht (Ger.) (*lī*-kh'n-ghĕ-dĭkht.) Funeral; poem elegy.
Leichen-gesang (Ger.) (*lī*-kh'n ghĕ-säng.) Dirge; funeral song.
Leichen-musik (Ger.) (*lī*-kh'n-moo-*zĭk.*) Funeral music.
Leicht (Ger.) (līkht.) Light, easy, facile.
Leichtfertig (Ger.)(*līkht*-fār-tĭg.) Lightly, carelessly.
Leichtheit (Ger.) (*līkht*-hīt.) } Lightness,
Leichtigkeit (Ger.) (*līkh*-tĭg-kīt.) } facility.
Leidenschaft (Ger.) (*lī*-d'n-shäft.) Passion.
Leidenschaftlich (Ger.) (*līd*-ĕn-shäftlĭkh.) Impassioned, passionate.
Leier (Ger.) (*lī*-ĕr.) A lyre; a hurdy-gurdy.
Leiermann (Ger.) (*lī*-ĕr-män.) A player on a hurdy-gurdy.
Leise (Ger.) (*lī*-ze.) Low, soft, gentle.
Leit-accord (Ger.) (*līt*-äk-*kōrd*.) A chord or harmony leading instinctively to another, as the chord of the dominant leading to the tonic.
Leiter (Ger.) (*lī*-ter.) Leader; also the scale of any key.
Leitereigen (Ger.) (*lī*-tĕr-*ī*-g'n.) Such tones as belong to the scale of any key; the notes forming the scale.
Leiter-fremd (Ger.) (*lī*-tĕr-frĕmd.) Accidental sharps or flats which do not belong to the key.
Leitmotif (Ger.) (*Lit*-mo-*teef.*) In modern music a new style of figure-treatment has been introduced. This is the use of the *leit-motif*, or guiding figure, a musical figure to which some definite meaning is attached. It represents some person, thing, or dramatic event. This idea is found in Mozart's "Don Giovanni," composed more than a century ago, but it is used by Wagner so prominently and so constantly that it assumes a new significance, causing the orchestra to speak an intelligible language. The *leitmotif* must be characteristic of the person or thing it is intended to represent, and must always remain very clearly recognizable. It is, therefore, not so freely developed as the ordinary musical figure. It is most frequently treated by transposition, with constant changes of harmony and modulation.
Leit-ton (Ger.) (*lī*-ton.) The leading tone.
Léno (It.) (*lāy*-nō.) Weak, feeble, faint.
Lent (Fr.) (lanh.) Slow.
Lentaménte (It.) (lĕn-tä-*men*-tĕ.) Slowly.
Lentándo (It.) (lĕn-tän-dō.) With increased slowness.
Lentement (Fr.) (*länht*-mänh.) } Slowly,
Lenteménte (It.) (len-tĕ-*men*-tĕ.) } leisurely.
Lentement, tres. (Fr.) (länht-mänh trā.) Very slow.
Lenteur (Fr.) (länh-tŭr.) Slowness, delay.
Lenteur, avec (Fr.) (länh-tŭr ä-vĕk.) }
Lentézza, con (It.) (lĕn-*tĕt*-tsa kŏn.) } With slowness and delay.
Lentissimaménte (It.) (lĕn-tis-sē-mä-*men*-tĕ.
Lentíssimo (It.) (lĕn-*tis*-sē-mō.) Extremely slow.
Lénto (It.) (*len*-tō.) Slow.
Lénto assái (It.) (len-to äs-sä-ē.) }
Lénto di mólto (It.) (len-tō dē mōl-tō.) } Very slowly.
Lesser appoggiatura. The short appoggiatura.
Lesser sixth. A minor sixth.
Lesser third. A minor third.
Lesson. Formerly applied to exercises or pieces consisting of two or three movements for the harpsichord, or pianoforte, forming a short suite.

Lestaménte (It.) (lĕs-tä-*men*-tĕ.) Quickly, lively.
Lestézza (It.) (lĕs-*tet*-tsä.) Agility, quickness.
Lestissimaménte (It.) (lĕs-tes-sē-mä-*men*-tĕ.) Very quickly.
Lestissimo (It.) (lĕs-*tis*-sē-mō.) Very quick.
Lésto (It.) (lĕs-tō.) Lively, nimble, quick.
Letter-names. The first seven letters of the alphabet, A, B,C,D, E, F,G, are used to form the letters of the scale, and are repeated in every octave. These letters serve to distinguish the notes and determine their pitch.
Letters, doubled. Capital letters doubled indicating that the tone is an octave lower than when the letters stand single.
Lettúra di música (It.) (lĕt-*too*-rä dē moo-zē-kä.) A musical lecture.
Leúto (It.) (loo-tō.) A lute.
Levé (Fr.) (lĕ-vä.) The up-stroke of the bâton.
Levézza (It.) (lĕ-*vāt*-tsä.) Lightness.
Levier pneumatique (Fr.) (lĕv-ĭ-ā noo-mä-*tēk*.) The pneumatic lever; a series of small bellows, or levers, placed on the wind-chest of an organ, containing air at a high pressure; by means of this the touch of a large organ may be made very light.
Lezzioni (It. pl.) (lĕt-tsē-*ō*-nĕ.) Lessons.
L. H. Initials indicating the use of the left hand in pianoforte music. *Linke Hand.*
Liaison (Fr.) (lē-ā-zŏnh.) Smoothness of connection ; also a *bind* or *tie.*
Liaison de chant (Fr.) (lē-ā-zŏnh dŭh shanht.) The *sostenuto* style of singing.
Liberaménte (It.)(lē-bĕ-rä-*men*-tĕ.) } Free-
Librement (Fr.) (läbr-mänh.) } ly, easily, plainly.
Libero (It.) (*lē*-bĕ-rō.) Free, unrestrained.
Librétto (It.) (lē-*brĕt*-tō.) The text of an opera or other extended piece of music. Literally *a little book.* It generally means the book or words of an opera or oratorio. The *librettist* is the author of such a book.
Lié (Fr.) (lĭ-*ā*.) Smoothly ; the same as *Legáto.*

Liebes-lied (Ger.) (*lē*-bĕs-lēd.) Love-song.
Liebhaber (Ger.) (*lēb*-hä-bĕr.) Amateur ; a lover of music.
Lieblich (Ger.) (*lēb*-līkh.) Lovely, charming.
Lieblich-gedacht (Ger.) (*lēb*-līkh ghĕ-däkht.) A stopped diapason organ-register of sweet tone.
Lié, coulant (Fr.) (lĭ-ā koo-länh.) Slurred, flowing.
Lied (Ger.) (lēed.) A song ; a ballad ; a lay.
Liedchen (Ger.) (*lēed*-kh'n.) A short song or melody.
Lieder (Ger.) (*lēe*-dĕr.) Songs.
Lieder-buch (Ger.) (*lē*-dĕr-bookh.) A song-book.
Lieder-bund (Ger.) (*lēe*-dĕr-boond.) A society of song-singers.
Lieder-dichter (Ger.) (*lēe*-dĕr-*dĭkh*-tĕr.) A lyrical poet ; a song-writer.
Lieder ohne Worte (Ger.) (*lēe*-dĕr ō-nĕ *vōr*-tĕ.) Songs without words.
Lieder-sammlung (Ger.) (*lēe*-dĕr-*säm*-loong.) Collection of songs.
Lieder-sänger (Ger.) (*lēe*-dĕr säng-ĕr.) A song-singer, a ballad-singer.
Lieder-spiel (Ger.) (*lēe*-dĕr-spēel.) An operetta, consisting of dialogue and music of a light, lively character.
Lieder-tafel (Ger.) (*lēe*-dĕr-tä-f'l.) *Song-table;* German glee club, generally consisting of male voices alone.
Lieder-tanz (Ger.) (*lēe*-dĕr-tänts.) A dance intermingled with songs.
Lied ohne Worte (Ger.) (lēed ō-nĕ *vōr*-tĕ.) See *Lieder ohne Worte.*
Lied singen (Ger.) (lēed-*sĭng*-'n.) To sing a song.
Ligare (It.) (li-*gä*-rĕ.) To bind ; to tie ; to join together.
Ligato (It.) (lē-*gä*-tō.) See *Legáto.*
Ligatur (Ger.) (li-gä-*toor*.) } A slur ; an
Ligatura (It.) (li-gä-*too*-rä.) } old name
Ligature. } for a *tie* or *bind.*
Ligne (Fr.) (līyn.) A line of the staff.
Lignes additionnelles (Fr.) (līyns ăd-dĕ-sĭ-ōn-*näl*.) Leger lines.
Lilt (Scotch.) (lĭlt.) To sing or play merrily.

ŏ as in *tone ;* ô as in *dove ;* ŏ as in *not ;* ŭ as in *up ;* ü the French sound of *u.*

159

LIMMA   LONG

Limma (Gr.) (*lĭm*-mä.) An interval used in the ancient Greek music, less by a comma than a major semi-tone.

Linea (It.) (*lē*-nĕ-ä.) A line of the staff.

Lines, added. Leger lines; lines added above and below the staff.

Lines, bar. Lines drawn perpendicularly across the staff, dividing it into measures.

Lines, horizontal. Lines placed after figures to signify that the same harmony is to be continued.

Lines, ledger. ⎱ Lines added above or
Lines, leger. ⎰ below the staff for the reception of such notes as are too high or too low to be placed upon or within it.

Língua (It.) (*lēn*-guä.) The tongue in organ-stop reeds.

Lingual. Pertaining to the tongue; a letter or sound pronounced chiefly by the tongue.

Linie (Ger.) (lĭn-ē.) A line of the staff.

Linien (Ger. pl.) (*lĭn*-ī-ĕn.) Lines of the staff.

Linien-system (Ger.) (*lĭn*-ī-ĕn sĭs-*tăm*.) A scale; the lines of the staff.

Lining. A term applied to a practice of reading one or two lines of a hymn before singing them, alternating reading and singing. Also called *lining-out*.

Link (Ger.) (lĭnk.) ⎱ Left.
Links (lĭnks.) ⎰

Linke Hand (Ger.) (*lĭn*-kĕ händ.) The left hand.

Lip. 1. The lips of a flue-pipe are the flat surfaces above and below the mouth, called the *upper* and *lower* lip. 2. (Ger., *Ansatz;* Fr., *embouchure;* It., *imboccatura*.) The art or faculty of so adjusting the lips to the mouth-piece of a wind-instrument as to produce artistic effects of tone. Also *lipping*.

Líra (It.) (*lēe*-rä.) A lyre.

Líra doppia (It.) (*lēe* rä *dōp*-pē-ä.) Double lyre.

Líra grande (It.) (*lēe*-rä grän-dĕ.) The *viol di gamba*, a viol with six strings formerly much used in Germany.

Líra rústica (It.) (*lēe*-rä roos-tē-kä.) A species of lyre, formerly in use among the Italian peasants.

Líra tedesca (It.) (*lēe*-rä tā-dĕs-kä.) The German lyre.

Lire (Fr.) (lēer.) To read.

Lírica (It.) (*lēe*-rē-kä.) ⎱ Lyric; lyric
Lírico (It.) (*lēe*-rē-kō.) ⎰ poetry; poetry adapted for music.

Liróne (It.) (lēe-*rō*-nĕ.) A large lyre, or harp.

Líscio (It.) (*lēe*-shē-ō.) Simple, unadorned, smooth.

Lispelnd (Ger.) (*lĭs*-pĕlnd.) Lisping, whispering.

L'istésso (It.) (l'ēs-*tes*-sō.) The same.

L'istésso movimento (It.) (l'ēs-*tes*-sō mō-vē-*men*-tō.) ⎫
L'istésso tempo (It.) (l'ĭs-*tes*-sō *tem*-pō.) ⎭ In the same time as the previous movement.

Litania (Lat.) (lĭ-*tä*-nĭ-a.) ⎫
Litanie (Fr.) (lĭ-tä-*nēe*.) ⎬ A litany.
Litanei (Ger.) (lĭt-ä-*nī*.) ⎭

Litany. A solemn form of supplication used in public worship.

Liturgía (It.) (lē-toor-jē-ä.) Liturgy.

Liturgy. The ritual for public worship in those churches which use written forms.

Lituus (Lat.) (*lĭt*-ū-ŭs.) An instrument of martial music; a kind of trumpet making a shrill sound.

Liúto (It.) (lē-*oo*-tō.) A lute.

Livre (Fr.) (lēvr.) A book.

Lob-gesang (Ger.) (*lōb*-ghĕ-*zäng*.) ⎱ A
Lob-lied (Ger.) (*lōb*-lēd.) ⎰ hymn, or song of praise.

Lobpsalm (Ger.) (*lōb*-psälm.) A psalm of praise.

Lobsingen (Ger.) (*lōb*-sĭng-'n.) To sing praises.

Lobsinger (Ger.) (*lōb*-sĭng-ĕr.) One who sings praises.

Lóco (It.) (*lō*-kō.) *Place;* a word used in opposition to 8*va-alta*, signifying that the notes over which it is placed are not to be played an octave higher, but just as they are written. It is little used at present, the end of the dotted line signifying the end of the octave transposition.

Lombárda (It.) (Lŏm-*bär*-dä.) A species of dance used in Lombardy.

Long. A note formerly in use equal to

ă as in *ah*; ā as in *hate*; ă as in *at*; ē as in *tree*; ĕ as in *eh*; ī as in *pine*; ĭ as in *pin*;

160

LONGA — LUTE

four semibreves, or half the length of the large.

Longa (Lat.) (*lŏn*-gä.) A long.

Long appoggiatura. An appoggiatura consisting of a single note forming a part of the melody. It borrows half the length of the next note, or more, and is accented. See *Appoggiatura*.

Long, double. An old character equal in duration to four breves.

Long drum. The large drum used in military bands, carried horizontally before the performer; the bass drum.

Long metre. A stanza of four lines in iambic measure, each line containing eight syllables.   Written.   Played.

Long mordent. A mordent formed of four notes.

Long particular meter. A stanza of six lines in iambic measure, each line containing eight syllables.

Long roll. A drum-beat calling the soldiers to arms.

Long spiel. An ancient Icelandic instrument, long and narrow, and played upon with a bow.

Longue pause (Fr.) (lŏnh pōz.) Make a long rest, or pause.

Lontanissimo (It.) (lon-ta-*niss*-see-mo.) Very far away; equivalent to *piano possibile*.

Lontáno (It.) (lŏn-*tä*-nō.) Distant; remote; a great way off.

Lontáno, da (It.) (lŏn-*tä*-nō dä.) At a distance.

Lorgnette (Fr.) (lŏrn-*yĕt*.) An opera-glass.

Lo stesso (It.) (lō *stĕs*-sō.) The same.

Loure (Fr.) (loor.) A dance of slow time and dignified character. It has sometimes three and sometimes four quarters in a bar, with the peculiarity of the second quarter of every bar being dotted.

Low. A word of relative signification and applied to any part, passage, or note, situated beneath, or lower in pitch than some other part, passage, or note; depressed in the scale of sounds; grave.

Low bass. Second bass.

Lugúbre (It.) (loo-*goo*-brĕ.) Lugubrious. sad, mournful.

Lullaby. A song to quiet infants; a soft, gentle song.

Lúnga páusa (It.) (loon-gä pä-oo-zä.) A *long pause*, or rest. Sometimes written *Lunga* alone.

Luógó (It.) (loo-ō-gō.) See *Lóco*.

Lusing. An abbreviation of *Lusingáto*.

Lusingándo (It.) (loo-zēn-*gän*-do.)

Lusingánte (It.) (loo-zēn-*gän*-tĕ.)

Lusingáto (It.) (loo-zēn-*gä*-tō.)

Lusinghévole (It.) (loo-zēn-*ge*-vō-lĕ.)

Soothing; coaxing; persuasively; insinuatingly; in a playful, persuasive style.

Lusinghevolménte (It.) (loo-zēn-gĕ-vōl-*men*-tĕ.) Soothingly, persuasively.

Lusinghiére (It.) (loo-zēn-ghē-*ā*-rĕ.)
Lusinghiéro (It.) (loo-zēn-ghē-*ā*-rŏ.)
Flattering, fawning, coaxing.

Lustig (Ger.) (*loos*-tĭg.) Merrily, cheerfully, gayly.

Lutenist. A performer upon the lute.

L'ut de poitrine (Fr.) (l'oot duh pwä-trēn.) High C with chest tone.

Lute. A very ancient stringed instrument, formerly much used, and containing at first, only five strings, but to which more were afterward added. The *lute* consists of four parts, viz., the table; the body which has nine or ten sides and is pear-shaped; the neck which has as many stops, or divisions; and the head or cross, in which the screws for tuning it are inserted. In playing this instrument, the performer strikes the strings with the fingers of the right hand, and regulates the sounds with those of the left. The strings, attached to a bridge fixed on the face of the instrument, and passing over or beside the fretted finger-board, were plucked by the fingers, and varied in number from six to thirteen, the highest or melody-string being single, and the others in pairs of unisons. Bass strings *off* the finger-board, similar to the bass strings of a zither, each yielding but one tone, were generally attached to a second neck. These bass strings were introduced in the sixteenth century, and led

ō as in *tone*; ŏ as in *dove*; ȯ as in *not*; ŭ as in *up*; ü the French sound of *u*.

161

to diverse modifications in the build of the instrument; the various forms of large double-necked lutes then evolved (*theorbo, archiliuto, chitarrone*) being general favorites. The lute came from the Orient, and its name is derived from an Arabic word *Elood* or *L'Eudo*, meaning *The Wood*.

Luth (Fr.) (loot.) A lute.

Luthier (Fr.) (lü-tĭ-ā.) Formerly a maker of lutes; at present a maker of stringed instruments.

Lutherie (Fr.) (lü-the-*ree*.) The making of lutes, violins, etc.

Luttuosaménte (It.) (loot-too-ō-zä-*men*-tĕ.) Sadly, sorrowfully.

Luttuóso (It.) (loot-too-*ō*-zō.) Sorrowful, mournful.

Lydian. See *Greek modes*.

Lydian chant. A chant of a sorrowful, melancholy style.

Lyra (It.) (*lēe*-rä.) }
Lyra (Ger.) (*lĭr*-ä.) } The lyre.

Lyra barbarina (It.) (*lē*-rä bär-bä-*rēe*-nä. An old instrument, resembling in shape the Spanish guitar, having three double niches.

Lyra doppia (It.) (*lēe*-rä *dōp*-pē-ä.) Double lyre, not at present used, but supposed to be a kind of *viol da gamba*.

Lyra hexachordis (Gr.) (*lĭr*-ä *hĕx*-ä-*kŏr*-dĭs.) A lyre with six strings.

Lyra mendicorum (Lat.) (*lĭr*-ä mĕn-dĭ-*kō*-rŭm.) A hurdy-gurdy.

Lyrasänger (Ger.) (*lĭr*-ä-*sāng*-ĕr.) } A
Lyraspieler (Ger.) (*lĭr*-ä-*spē*-lĕr.) } performer on the lyre.

Lyra-viol. An old instrument of the lyre or harp species; it had six strings and seven frets.

Lyre. One of the most ancient of stringed instruments said to have been invented by Mercury, about the year 2000 B. C., and formed of a tortoise shell; a species of harp.

Lyre Æolian. The Æolian harp.

Lyre, double. The *lyra doppia;* an instrument of the viol kind.

Lyre, Grecian. A lyre of the ancient Greeks, quite small, and having but seven strings, and held in the hand while being played upon.

Lyric. } Poetry adapted for singing.
Lyrical. } The word is borrowed from the lyre, and was originally confined to poetry meant to be accompanied by that instrument.

Lyric comedy. A comedy in which vocal music forms a principal part; comic opera.

Lyric drama. Opera; acting accompanied by singing.

Lyric tragedy. Tragic opera.

Lyricus (Lat.) (*lĭr*-ĭ-kŭs.) Pertaining to the lyre.

Lyriker (Ger.) (*lĭr*-ĭ-kĕr.) } Lyric, lyrical.
Lyrisch (Ger.) (*lĭr*-ĭsh.) } cal.

M

M. This letter is used as an abbreviation of mezzo, also of various other words, as *metronome, mano, main*, and also in connection with other letters; as M. F. for *mezzo forte;* M. P., *mezzo piano;* M. V., *mezzo voce*, etc.

M. M. The abbreviation for *Maëlzel's Metronome*. It is often misinterpreted as "metronome mark."

Ma (It.) (mä.) But, as *Allégro ma non tróppo*, quick, but not too much so.

Machalath (Heb.) (mä-kä-läth.) A kind of lute or guitar used by the Hebrews.

Machine-head. A mechanical device substituted for the ordinary tuning-pegs of the double-bass, the guitar, and of the melody-strings of the zither.

Mach-werk (Ger.) (mäkh-värk.) *Made work;* music made up; merely the result of labor and study without any musical inspiration.

Madriále (It.) (mä-drē-*ä*-lĕ.) A madrigal; the name formerly given by the Italians to the *intermezzi*, or pieces performed between the acts of a play or an opera.

Madrialétto (It.) (mä-drē-ä-*let*-tō.) A short madrigal.

Madrigal. An elaborate vocal composition, in three, four, five, or six parts, without accompaniment, in the strict or ancient style, with imitation; the parts or melodies moving in that conversational manner peculiar to the music of the sixteenth and seventeenth centuries. The madrigal is generally sung in chorus. The origin of the word is doubtful. The form probably had its beginning in the Netherlands. It was the earliest form of skilful secular composition, spite of one or two canons which bear earlier date. One characteristic of the madrigal was that the melody never appeared entire in any one voice. It was generally unaccompanied. See Grove's Dictionary.

Madrigal, accompanied. A madrigal in which the voices are sustained by a pianoforte, or organ.

Madrigále (It.) (mä-drē-*gä*-lĕ.) A madrigal.

Madrigalésco (It.) (mä-drē-gä-*lā*-skō.) Of, or belonging to, a madrigal

Maesta (It.) (mä-ĕs-*tä*.) ⎫ Majesty,
Maestáde (It.) (mä-ĕs-*tä*-dĕ.) ⎬ dignity,
Maestáte (It.) (mä-ĕs-*tä*-tĕ.) ⎭ grandeur.

Maestévole (It.) (mä-ĕs-*te*-vŏ-lĕ.) Majestic, majestical.

Maestevolíssimo (It.) (mä-ĕs-tā-vō-*lēs*-sē-mō.) Most majestically.

Maestevolménte (It.) (mä-ĕs-tā-vōl-*men*-tĕ.)

Maestosaménte (It.) (mä-ĕs-tō-zä-*men*-tĕ.) Majestically, nobly.

Maestosíssimo (It.) (mä-ĕs-tō-*zēs*-sē-mō.) Exceedingly majestic.

Maestóso (It.) (mä-ĕs-*tō*-zō.) Majestic, stately, dignified.

Maestrale (It.) (mä-ĕs-*trah*-lĕ.) The term for the stretto of a fugue, when in canon-form.

Maestrévole (It.) (mä-ās-*tre*-vŏ-lĕ.) Masterly; highly finished.

Maestri (It.) (mä-*es*-trē.) Masters.

Maestría (It.) (mä-ĕs-*trē*-ä.) Mastery, skill, art, ability.

Maéstro (It.) (mä-*es*-trō.) Master, composer; an experienced, skilful artist.

Maéstro di camera (It.) (mä-*es*-trŏ dē *kä*-mĕ-rä.) Leader or conductor of chamber-music.

Maéstro di canto (It.) (mä-*es*-trō dē *kän*-tō.) A singing-master.

Maéstro di cappélla (It.) (mä-*es*-trō dē käp-*pel*-lä.) Chapel-master; composer; director of the musical performances in a church or chapel. See *Kapellmeister*.

Magadis (Gr.) (mă-*gă*-dĭs.) The name of an ancient Greek treble instrument, furnished with double strings tuned in octaves, like those of a three-stop harpsichord.

Maggioláta (It.) (mäd-jē-ō-*lä*-tä.) A hymn or song in praise of the month of May.

Maggióre (It.) (mäd-jē-*ō*-rĕ.) The major key.

Magiscóro (It.) (mä-jēs-*kō*-rō.) The chief of a choir.

Magnificat (Lat.) (măg-*nĭf*-ĭ-kăt.) A part of the vespers, or evening service of the Roman Catholic Church.

Maidmarian. The lady of the May games in a morris dance; an old dance.

Main (Fr.) (mănh.) The hand.

Main droite (Fr.) (mănh drwät.) Right hand.

Main gauche (mănh gōsh.) The left hand.

Maître (Fr.) (mātr.) A master; a director.

Maître de chapelle (Fr.) (mātr dŭh shä-pĕll.) Chapel-master; director of the choir.

Maître de musique (Fr.) (mātr dŭh mü-zēk.) Musical director; a music teacher.

Maître des ménétriers (Fr.) (mātr dĕ mänh-ā-trĭ-ār.) Master of the minstrels.

Majesta (It.) (mä-yĕs-tä.) ⎫ Majesty,
Majesté (Fr.) (mä-zhĕs-tā.) ⎭ dignity.

Majestueux (Fr.) (mä-zhĕs-tü-ay.) Majestic.

Majeur (Fr.) (mä-zhŭr.) Major; major key.

Major. *Greater*, in respect to intervals, scales, etc.

Major, bob. A full peal upon eight bells.

Major diatonic scale. The scale in which the semi-tones fall between the third and fourth, and seventh and eighth tones, both in ascending and descending.

Major, drum. The chief drummer of a regiment.

Major fourth. Properly a *perfect* fourth; an interval containing two whole tones, and one semi-tone.

Major intervals. Those intervals containing the greatest number of semitones under the same denomination

ŏ as in *tone*; ô as in *dove*; ŏ as in *not*; ŭ as in *up*; ü the French sound of *u*.

Major key. } That mode or scale in
Major mode. } which the third from the tonic is major.

Major-modus (Lat.) (mä-jŏr-*mō*-dŭs.) Major mode.

Major seventh. An interval consisting of five tones and a semi-tone.

Major sixth. A sixth composed of four tones and a semi-tone.

Major third. An interval containing two whole tones or steps.

Major tonic. A major scale.

Major triad. A union of any sound with its major third and perfect fifth.

Malanconía (It.) (mä-län-kō-nē-ä.) }
Malencónico (It.) (mä-lĕn-*kō*-nē-kō.) }
Melancholy, sadness.

Malincólico(It.)(mä-lēn-*kō*-lē-kō.) } Mel-
Malinconia (It.) (mä-lēn-*kō*-nī-ä.) } ancholy.

Malinconicaménte (It.) (mä-lēn-kō-nē-kä-*men*-tĕ.) In a melancholy style.

Malincónico (It.) (mä-lēn-*kō*-nē-kō.) }
Malinconióso (It.)(mä-lēn-kō-nē-*ō*-zō.) }
Malinconóso (It.) (mä-lēn-kō-*nō*-zō.) }
In a melancholy style.

Mancándo (It.) (män-*kän*-dō.) Decreasing; dying away.

Manche (Fr.) (mänh-sh.) The neck of a violin or other instrument.

Mandola (It.) (män-dō-lä.) A mandoline or cithern, of the size of a large lute.

Mandoline. A Spanish instrument of guitar species,with frets like a guitar and four pairs of strings, tuned like the violin, and put in vibration with a *pick*, or plectrum. There is a difference in stringing and tuning, between the Neapolitan and the Milanese. Compass about three octaves.

Mandolíno (It.) (män-dŏ-*lee*-nō.) A mandolin.

Mandora. } A small kind of lute or gui-
Mandore. } tar, with frets and seven gut-strings, three of which are duplicates.

Mánico (It.) (*mä*-nē-kō.) The neck of the violin, guitar, etc.

Manichord. } Originally, an instru-
Manichordon. } ment with but one string; subsequently a stringed instrument resembling a spinet or harpsichord.

Maniéra (It.) (mä-nē-*ä*-rä.) } Manner,
Manière (Fr.) (mǎn-ē-*är*.) } style.

Manieren (Ger. pl.) (mä-nē-r'n.) Graces, embellishments, ornaments.

Manifold fugue. A fugue in which more than one theme is elaborated.

Männerchor (Ger.) (*men*-nĕr-chor.) } Men's
Männergesangs-verein (Ger.) } vocal
(*men*-nĕr-ghĕ-*zängs* fē-*rīn*.) } society.

Männliche Stimme (Ger.) (*mǎn*-lĭkh-ĕ *stĭm*-mĕ.) A male voice.

Máno (It.) (mä-nō.) The hand.

Máno destra (It.) (mä-nō *des*-trä.) }
Máno diritta (It.) (mä-nō dē-*rēt*-tä.) } The right hand.
Máno dritta (It.) (mä-nō *drit*-tä.) }

Máno sinistra (It.) (mä-nō sē-*nis*-trä.) The left hand.

Manual. The key-board; in organ music it means that the passage is to be played by the hands alone without using the pedals.

Manual (Ger.) (mä-noo-*äl*.) }
Manuale (Lat.) (mä-nū-*ä*-lĕ.) } Manual.
Manuále (It.) (mă-noo-*ä*-lĕ.) }

Manualiter (Ger.) (mä-noo-*ä*-lĭ-tĕr.) Organ pieces to be played by the fingers alone without the pedals.

Manual-untersatz (Ger.) (mä-noo-*äl* oon-tĕr-sätz.) An organ-stop of 32-foot tone, with stopped pipes; the *sub bourdon*.

Manúbrio (It.) (mä-*noo*-brē-ō.) } The
Manubrium (Lat.) (mă-*nū*-brĭ-ŭm.) } handle or knob by which a stop is drawn in an organ.

Manuscriptum (Lat.) (mǎn-ŭ-*skrĭp*-tŭm.) Manuscript.

Marcándo (It.) (mär-*kän*-dō.) } Marked;
Marcáto (It.) (mär-*kä*-tō.) } accented;
well-pronounced.

Marcatíssimo (It.) (mär-kä-*tĭs*-sē-mō.) Very strongly marked.

ä as in *ah*; ā as in *hate*; ă as in *at*; ē as in *tree*; ĕ as in *eh*; ī as in *pine*; ĭ as in *pin*;

MARCÁTA LA MELODIA　　　　　　　　　　　　　　　　MASS

Marcáta la melodia (It.) (mär-*kä*-ta lä měl-*ō*-dē-ä.) Accent the melody.

March. A military air or movement especially adapted to martial instruments; it is generally written in ¼ rhythm.

March, dead. A funeral march.

Marche (Fr.) (märsh.) A march.

Marche harmonique (Fr.) (märsh härmō-*něk*.) Harmonic progression.

Marche redoublée (Fr.) (märsh rē-doob-*lä*.) A double quick march.

Marche triomphale (Fr.) (märsh trē-ŏnh-fäl.) A triumphal march.

March, funeral. A slow, mournful march, adapted to the movement of a funeral procession. Also called "Dead March."

Márcia (It.) (*mär*-tshē-ä.) A march.

Márcia, con móto (It.) (*mär*-tshē-ä kŏn *mō*-tō.) A spirited martial movement.

Márcia funebre (It.) (*mär*-tshē-ä fōo-*nä*-brě.) Funeral march.

Marciále (It.) (mär-tshē-*ä*-lě.) See *Marziále*.

Marciáta (It.) (mär-tshē-*ä*-tä.) A march.

Marine band. A band employed on vessels of war.

Marked. Accented.

Mark, harmonic. A sign (○) used in music for the violin, violoncello, and harp, to indicate that the notes over which it is placed are to be produced on such parts of the open strings as will give the harmonic sounds.

Markiren (Ger.) (mär-*kē*-r'n.) } To mark;
Markirt. } to em-
Marquer (Fr.) (mär-kā.) } phasize.

Marks, abbreviation. Signs of abbreviation.

Marks, cadence. Short perpendicular lines which indicate the cadence notes in chanting.

Marks, division. Figures with a curved line above them showing the number of equal parts into which the notes are divided, when instead of 2, 4, or 8, they are divided into 3, 5, 7, 9, etc., 3̄, 5̄, 7̄, etc. See *Notation*.

Marks, metronomic. Figures appended to music, referring to M.M.♩ = 120 corresponding, figures M.M.♩ = 80 on a metronome. See *M.M.*

Marks, staccato. Dots or small dashes placed over notes to indicate that they are to be played short and detached.

Marsch (Ger.) (märsh.) A march.

Marschartig (Ger.) (*märsh*-är-tĭg.) In the style of a march.

Märsche (Ger. pl.) (*mǎr*-shě.) Marches.

Marseillaise (Fr.) (mär-sāl-yāz.) The Marseilles hymn; a French national air. See Elson's "Our National Music."

Martellándo (It.) (mär-těl-*län*-dō.) *Hammering*; strongly marking the tones as if hammered.

Martelláre (It.) (mär-těl-*lä*-rě.) To hammer, to strike the notes forcibly like a hammer.

Martelláto (It.) (mär-těl-*lä*-tō.) *Hammered*, strongly marked.

Martráza (It.) (mär-*trä*-tsa.) A Spanish dance.

Marziále (It.) (mär-tsē-*ä* lě.) Martial; in the style of a march.

Mascharada (It.) (mä-skä-*rä*-dä.) } Music
Mascheráta (It.) (mä-skě-*rä*-tä.) } composed for grotesque characters; masquerade music.

Maschera (It.) (*mä*-skě-rä.) A mask.

Mask. } A species of
Maske (Ger.) (*mäs*-kě.) } musical
Masque (Fr.) (mäsk.) } drama, or operetta, including singing and dancing, performed by characters in masks. The masque was the predecessor of the opera.

Mass. A vocal composition performed during the celebration of High Mass, in the Roman Catholic Church, and generally accompanied by instruments. The Mass contains the following numbers: "Kyrie," "Gloria" (containing also the "Qui Tollis," "Gratias," "Quoniam," and "Cum Sancto Spirito"), "Credo" (with "Et Incarnatus," "Et Resurrexit," and "Amen," as subdivisions), "Sanctus," "Benedictus," "Agnus Dei," and "Dona Nobis." These are in beautiful contrast in the emotions they express, and, therefore, the Mass has always been a favorite form of composition. The Requiem Mass, generally shorter, omits

ŏ as in *tone*; ô as in *dove*; ŏ as in *not*; ŭ as in *up*; ü the French sound of *u*.

the "Gloria," and contains a "Requiem Aeternam," "Lux Aeterna," and "Dies Iræ" (a mediæval poem picturing the Day of Judgment) as well as the other numbers. As the "Day of Wrath" is a most dramatic subject, the Requiem Mass is sometimes the most fiery of sacred compositions. See Dickinson's "Music in the History of the Western Church."

Mass (Ger.) (mäss.) Measure, time.

Mass bell. A small bell used in the service of the Roman Catholic Church to direct attention to the more solemn parts of the Mass.

Mass book. The missal, or Roman Catholic service-book.

Mass, canonical. A Mass in which the various parts of the musical service of the church are followed in their regular course, or in strict canonical order.

Mass, high. The Mass celebrated in the Catholic churches by the singing of the choristers; distinguished from the low Mass, in which prayers are read without singing.

Mässig (Ger.) (mäs-sĭg.) Moderate, moderately.

Mässig geschwind (Ger.) (mäs-sĭg ghĕ-shvĭnd.) Moderately quick.

Mässig langsam (Ger.) (mäs-sĭg längsäm.) Moderately slow.

Mässig schnell (Ger.) (mäs-sĭg schnĕll.) Moderately fast and animated.

Mássima (It.) (mäs-sē-mä.) A whole note.

Master, ballet. One who superintends the rehearsals and performances of the ballet.

Master, choir. A chorister; a choir-leader.

Master of music. A musical degree. See article "Degrees" in Grove's Dictionary.

Mastersingers. A class of poet-musicians who succeeded the minnesingers in Germany. The minnesingers were generally of the nobility, the mastersingers of the burgher class. They began in the fifteenth century. See Elson's "History of German Song."

Masure (Ger.) (mä-zoo-rĕ.) ⎫
Masureck (Ger.) (mä-zoo-rĕk.) ⎪ A lively
Masurek (Ger.) (mä-zoo-rĕk.) ⎬ Polish
Masurka (Ger.) (mä-zoor-kä.) ⎭ dance, in ⅜ or ¾

time, quicker than the Polonaise, and has an emphasis on one of the unaccented parts of the bar; the *Mazurka*.

Matelotte (Fr.) (*mä*-tĕ-lŏt.) A French sailor's dance in ⅔ time.

Matinare (It.) (mä-tē-*nä*-rĕ.) To sing matins.

Matinata (It.) (mä-tē-*nä*-tä.) A song for the morning. See *Aubade*.

Matinée (Fr.) (mä-tĭ-*nā*.) An entertainment given in the daytime.

Matinée musicale (Fr.) (mä-tĭ-*nā* müzē-*käl*.) A musical performance given in the daytime.

Matines (Fr.) (mä-tēn.) Matins; morning worship.

Matins. The name of the first morning service in the Roman Catholic Church.

Mattutino delle tenebre (It.) (mät-tootē-nō däl-lĕ tĕ-*nä*-brĕ.) The service of the Tenebræ.

Maul-trommel (Ger.) (moul-trŏm-mĕl.) A Jews'-harp.

Maxima (Lat.) (*mă*x-ĭ-mä.) The name of the longest note used in the fourteenth and fifteenth centuries; equal to eight whole notes.

Maximus bob. A full peal upon twelve bells.

Mazourk (Ger.) (mä-*tsoork*.) ⎫
Mazourka (Ger.) (mä-*tsoor*-kä.) ⎪ A lively
Mazur (Ger.) (mä-*tsoor*.) ⎬ Polish
Mazurca (Ger.) (mä-*tsoor*-kä.) ⎪ dance
Mazurka (Ger.) (mä-*tsoor*-kä.) ⎪ of a
Mazurke (Ger.) (mä-*tsoor*-kĕ.) ⎭ skipping
character in ⅜ or ¾ time, of a peculiar rhythmic construction, quicker than the Polonaise or Polácca. See *Masurka*.

M. D. The initals of Main Droite, the right hand.

Mean. A term formerly applied to the tenor or medium part in compositions for several parts, male and female.

Mean clef. Tenor clef.

Mean, harmonical The third in the harmonic triad.

Mean parts. Middle parts.

Measure. That division of time by which the air and movement of music are regulated; the space between two bar

The Child Handel Practicing in the Attic

Mellophone

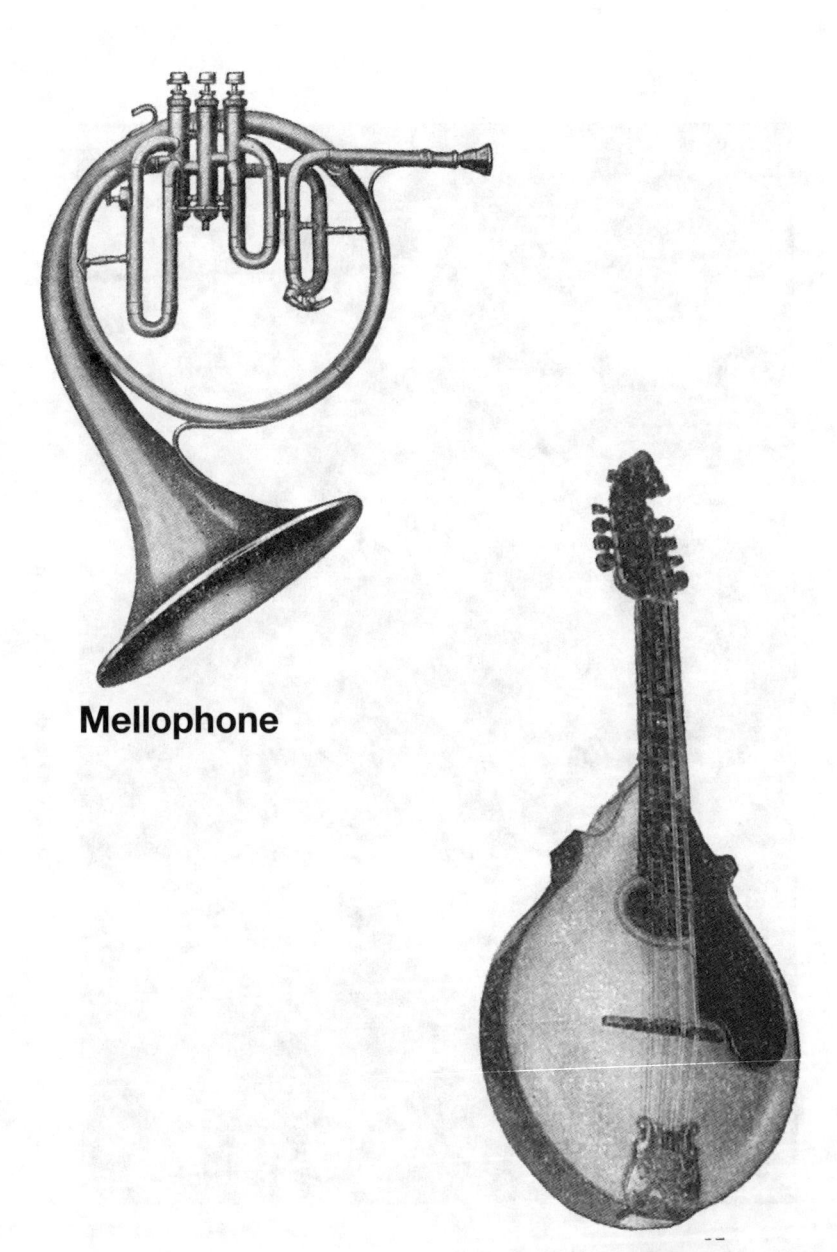

Mandolin

lines on the staff. The measure is often miscalled a *bar*, but the terms should not be confused. See *Time*.

Measure accent. The regular alternation of strong and weak part in a measure.

Measure, common. A measure having an even number of parts in a bar.

Medésimo (It.) (mĕ-*dā*-zē-mō.) ⎱ The
Medésmo (It.) (mĕ-*dās*-mō.) ⎰ same.

Medésmo móto (It.) (mĕ-*des*-mō *mō*-tō.) ⎱
Medésmo témpo (It.) (mĕ-*des*-mō *tĕm*-pō.) ⎰
In the same time or movement as before.

Mediant (Lat.) (*mā*-dĭ-ănt.) ⎱ The third
Médiante (Fr.) (mā-dĭ-*änht*.) ⎰ note of the scale; the *middle note* between the tonic and the dominant.

Meditatio (Lat.) (mĕd-ĭ-*tä*-shĭ-ō.) A word formerly used to signify the middle of a chant, or the sound which terminates the first part of the verse in the psalms.

Medius harmonicus (Lat.) (mā-dĭ-ŭs här-*mŏn*-ĭ-kŭs.) The third or middle note of the fundamental common chord.

Medley. A mixture; an assemblage of detached parts or passages of well-known songs or pieces so arranged that the end of one connects with the beginning of another. A *Potpourri*.

Meer-trompete (Ger.) (mār-trōm-*pā*-tĕ.) ⎱
Meer-horn (Ger.) (mār-hōrn.) ⎰
Sea-trumpet.

Mehr (Ger.) (mār.) More.

Mehrstimmig (Ger.) (mār-*stĭm*-mig.) For several voices.

Mehrstimmiger Gesang (Ger.) (mār-*stĭm*-mĭ-ghĕr ghĕ-*zäng*.) A glee or part song.

Meister (Ger.) (*mīs*-tĕr.) Master, teacher.

Meister-gesang (Ger.) (*mīs*-tĕr ghĕ-*zäng*.) Master's song; minstrel's song.

Meister-sänger (Ger.) (*mīs*-tĕr-*säng*-ĕr.) Mastersinger; minstrel. See *Master-singer*.

Meister-stück (Ger.) (*mīs*-tĕr-stük.) Masterpiece.

Mélancolie (Fr.) (*mā*-länh-kō-lē.) Melancholy; in a mournful style.

Mélange (Fr.) (mā-*länzh*.) A medley; a composition founded upon several popular airs.

Melisma (Gr.) (mĕ-*līs*-mä.) A vocal grace or embellishment; several notes sung to one syllable.

Melismatik (Ger.) (mĕl-ĭs-*mä*-tĭk.) ⎱
Melismatisch (Ger.) (mĕl-ĭs-*mä*-tĭsh.) ⎰
Florid vocalization. See *Melisma*.

Mellifluous (mĕl-*lĭf*-lū-ous.) Smoothly flowing; very melodious.

Melóde (It.) (mā-*lō*-dĕ.) Melody, tune.

Melodeon. A reed-instrument having a key board like the pianoforte. It is supplied with wind by a bellows worked with the feet of the performer.

Melodeon, double reed. A melodeon with two sets of reeds.

Melodeon, organ. A melodeon having a register of stops similar to those of an organ.

Melodía (It.) (mā-lō-dē-ä.) Melody, tune.

Melodic (mĕ-*lŏd*-ĭk.) Relating to melody.

Melodic language. The language of melody or song; ideas expressed by a melodious combination of sounds.

Melodic modulation. A change from one key into another.

Melodics. That department of vocal elementary instruction which relates to the *pitch* of tones.

Melodic step. The movement of a voice or part from one tone to the following one.

Melódico (It.) (mā-lō-dē-kō.) Melodious, tuneful.

Melodicon. An instrument invented by Riffel, in Copenhagen, the tones of which are produced from bent metal bars.

Mélodie (Fr.) (mā-lō-dēe.) Melody, tune.

Mélodieuse (Fr.) (mā-lō-dĭ-üz.) Melodious, smooth.

Mélodieusement (Fr.) (mā-lō-dĭ-üs-mänh.) ⎱
Melodiosaménte (It.) (mā-lō-dē-ō-zä-men-tĕ.) ⎰
Melodiously, sweetly.

Mélodieux (Fr.) (mā-lō-dĭ-ür.) ⎱ Melodi-
Melodik (Ger.) (mĕ-*lō*-dĭk.) ⎰ ous, tuneful.

Melodióso (It.) (mā-lō-dē-*ō*-zō.) ⎱ Melodi-
Melodisch (Ger.) (mĕ-*lō*-dĭsh.) ⎰ ous, musical, tuneful.

Melodious. Having melody, musical; a

ō as in *tone*; ô as in *dove*; ŏ as in *not*; ŭ as in *up*; ü the French sound of *u*.

term applied to a succession of pleasing sounds.

Melodious, bass. The *bass chantante;* the singing bass.

Melodrama. ⎱ A modern species of
Melodrame. ⎰ drama with music interspersed, both vocal and instrumental, the latter of a descriptive kind, serving to elucidate the action and heighten the passion of the piece. It is generally of a highly romantic or sensational character. In modern music the term is applied to a declamation, recited (not sung) to a musical accompaniment. Schumann's *Manfred* affords some good examples of such melodrame. It is sometimes called *Cantillation.*

Melodram (Ger.) (mĕ-lō-*dräm*.)
Mélodrame (Fr.) (mĕ-lō-*dräm*.)
Melodrámma (It.) (mä-lō-*drä*-mä.)
Melodrama.

Melodrammático (It.) (mä-lō-drä-*mä*-tē-kō.) Melodramatic.

Melody. A succession of simple sounds so arranged as to produce a pleasing effect upon the ear; distinguished from *harmony* by not necessarily including a combination of parts. By *the melody* the leading part in a harmonized composition is meant.

Melody, chromatic. A melody consisting of a series of tones moving by chromatic intervals.

Melody, diatonic. A melody whose tones move by diatonic intervals.

Melody, leading. The principal part of a composition containing several parts.

Melograph. A piano first invented in 1827, connected with which was machinery which recorded in notes whatever was improvised on the piano. The invention was not a complete success, but since that time many efforts have been made to achieve the same result more practically, and an electric melograph by an Englishman, named Fenby, promises success.

Melologue. A combination of recitative and music. See *Melodrama.*

Meloman (Ger.) (*mā*-lō-măn.) ⎱ A pas-
Mélomane (Fr.) (*mā*-lō-măn.) ⎰ sionate lover of music.

Mélomanie (Fr.) (mä-lō-mä-nē.) ⎱ Exces-
Melomany (mĕ-*lŏm*-ă-ny.) ⎰ sive love of music; music mania.

Melopéa (It.) (mā-lō-pā-ä.) ⎱ Poetical or
Mélopée (Fr.) (mā-lō-pā.) ⎰ rhetorical melody; words and music combined; the vocal declamation, or chant of the drama.

Melopiano. A pianoforte invented by Caldera, of Turin, in 1870, in which the tone is sustained by rapidly repeated blows of small hammers attached to a bar passing over and at right angles to the strings.

Melopœa (Gr.) (mĕ-lō-*pē*-ä.) A term in ancient music signifying the art of rules of composition in melody; melody.

Melopomenos (Gr.) (mĕl-ō-*pŏm*-ĕ-nŏs.) Vocal melody.

Melos (Gr.) (*mā*-lŏs.) Song. *Melos* is the name which Wagner applies to the vocal progressions of his later operas, which have not the form or symmetry of regular tunes.

Melpomene (Lat.) (mĕl-*pŏm*-ĕ-nĕ.) One of the nine muses. The muse of tragedy.

Même (Fr.) (mām.) The same.

Même mouvement (Fr.) (mām moov-mänh.) In the same movement.

Même mouvement que précédement (Fr.) (mām moov-mänh küh prĕ-*sād*-mänh.) In the same movement as the preceding.

Mén (It.) (mān.) Less; an abbreviation of *méno.*

Mén allégro (It.) (men äl-*lā*-grō.) Less quick.

Menéstrels (Fr.) (mĕ-nās-trĕl.) Minstrels.

Ménétrier (Fr.) (mĕ-nä-trī-*ā*.) A minstrel; a rustic musician.

Méno (It.) (*mā*-nō.) Less.

Méno allégro (It.) (*meh*-nō äl-*leh*-grō.) Less quick.

Méno fórte (It.) (*meh*-nō *fōr*-tĕ.) Less loud.

Méno mósso (It.) (*meh*-nō *mōs*-sō.) Less movement, slower.

Méno piáno (It.) (*meh*-nō pē-ä-nō.) Not so softly.

Méno presto (It.) (*meh*-nō *präs*-tō.) Less rapid.

ă as in *ah*; ā as in *hate*; ă as in *at*; ē as in *tree*; ĕ as in *eh*; ī as in *pine*; ĭ as in *pin*;

Méno vívo (It.) (*meh*-nō vē̆-vō.) Not so fast.

Menschen-stimme (Ger.) (*měn*-sh'n-*stĭm*-mě.) Human voice.

Mensur (Ger.) (měn-*soor*.) Time; tune; measurement of intervals; also, the diameter or scale of organ-pipes.

Mensural-gesang (Ger.) (měn-soo-*räl* ghě-*zäng*.) Measured music.

Mensural-noten (Ger.) (měn-soo-*räl-nō*-t'n.) Musical notation; measured notes; notes of a definite length.

Mensural signature. Fractions placed at the beginning of a composition, indicating the time, rhythm, or measure.

Menuet (Fr.) (mā-noo-ě.) ⎫ A min-
Menuetto (It.) (mě-noo-*ĕt*-tō.) ⎬ uet; a slow dance in ¾ time. See *Minuet*.

Mén vivo (It.) (mān vē̆-vō.) Less spirit.

Méssa (It.) (*mes*-sä.) A Mass.

Méssa bássa (It.) (*mes*-sä bäs-sä.) A silent Mass whispered by the priest during a musical performance.

Méssa concertáta (It.) (*mes*-sä kŏn-tshěr-*tä*-tä.) A Mass consisting of concerted music.

Méssa di vóce (It.) The gradual swelling and diminishing of the voice generally written thus: The *Méssa di Voce* appears in some vocal exercises (Concone's, etc.) in the first lesson, but most vocal teachers reserve its study for a much later period, as it requires thorough control of the breath.

Messe (Fr.) (māss.) ⎫ A Mass.
Messe (Ger.) (*měs*-sě.) ⎭

Messe brevi (It.) (*mes*-sě breh-vē.) A short Mass.

Messe concertati (It.) (*mes*-sě kŏn-tshěr-*tä*-tē.) Masses in which the recitation is intermixed with choruses.

Messa di cappella (It.) (*mes*-sä dē käp-*pel*-lä.) Masses sung by the grand chorus.

Messe, haute (Fr.) (mās-s'ō.) Grand Mass; high Mass.

Mésto (It.) (mes-tō.) Sad, mournful, melancholy.

Mestóso (It.) (mes-*tō*-zō.) Sadly, mournfully.

Mesure (Fr.) (mā-*zür*.) The bar, or measure; the species of time.

Mesure à deux temps (Fr.) (mā-*zür* ä dŭh tänh.) Common time of *two* beats in a measure.

Mesure à trois temps (Fr.) (mā-*zür* ä trwä tänh.) Triple time of *three* beats in a measure.

Mesure demi (Fr.) (mā-*zür* dě-*mē*.) Half measure.

Met. An abbreviation of *Metronome.*

Metal, organ. The material of which some organ-pipes are made, composed of a mixture of tin and lead in certain proportions.

Metállico (It.) (mā-*täl*-lē-kō.) ⎫ Metallic;
Metállo (It.) (mā *täl*-lō.) ⎭ clear in tone; *bel metállo di voce* means a voice clear, full, and brilliant.

Meter. See *Metre*.

Method. A course of instruction; classification; system.

Méthode (Fr.) (mā-tōd.) ⎫ A method;
Método (It.) (me-*tō*-dō.) ⎭ system; style; a treatise, or book of instruction.

Metre. Measure; verse; arrangement of poetical feet, or of long and short syllables in verse. The succession of accents in music. Metre is the rhythm of the *phrase*, not of the *measure*.

Metre, common. A stanza of four lines in iambic measure, the syllables of each being in number and order as follows: 8, 6, 8, 6.

Metre, common hallelujah. A stanza of six lines in iambic measure, the syllables in each being in number and order as follows: 8, 8, 6, 8, 8, 6.

Metre, eights. A stanza of four lines in anapestic measure, each line containing eight syllables and marked thus, 8s.

Metre, eights and sevens. Consists of four lines in trochaic measure, designated thus, 8s and 7s, the syllables as follows: 8, 7, 8, 7.

Metre, elevens. Designated thus, 11s, and consisting of a stanza of four lines in anapestic or dactyllic measure, each line containing eleven syllables.

Metre, hallelujah. A stanza of six lines in iambic measure, the syllables of each being in number and order as follows: 6, 6, 6, 6, 8, 8.

Metre, long. Four lines in iambic measure, each line containing eight syllables.

ō as in *tone*; ô as in *dove*; ŏ as in *not*; ŭ as in *up*; ü the French sound of *u*.

Metre, long particular. Six lines in iambic measure, each line containing eight syllables.

Metre, particular. This means that the poem has peculiarities or irregularities which prevent its being classified. Such poems generally require their own especial tunes.

Metre, sevens. Consists of four lines in trochaic measure, each line containing seven syllables.

Metre, short. Consists of four lines in iambic measure, the syllables in number and order as follows: 6, 6, 8, 6.

Metre, short particular. Consists of six lines in iambic measure, the syllables in number and order as follows: 6, 6, 8, 6, 6, 8.

Metre, tens and elevens. A metre designated thus, 10s and 11s, generally consisting of a stanza of four lines in anapestic measure, the syllables in number and order thus: 10, 10, 11, 11; or of six lines in iambic measure, as follows: 10, 10, 10, 10, 11, 11.

Metre, twelves. A metre designated thus, 12s, consisting of a stanza of four lines in anapestic measure, each line containing twelve syllables.

Metrical. Pertaining to measure, or due arrangement and combination of long and short syllables.

Metrically. In a metrical manner; according to poetic measure.

Metrik (Ger.) (*mĕt*-rĭk.) Metrical art.

Metrisch (Ger.) (*mĕt*-rĭsh.) Metrical.

Metro (It.) (mā-trō.) Metre, verse.

Metrometer (Ger.) (mĕ-*trŏm*-ĕ-tĕr.) }
Metrometro (It.) (mā-trŏ-mā-trō.) }
A metronome.

Metronom (Ger.) (mĕt-rō-*nŏm*.) } A
Metronome (Gr.) (*mĕt*-rō-*nō*-mĕ.) } machine invented by John Maelzel (in 1815), for measuring the time or duration of notes by means of a graduated scale and pendulum, which may be shortened or lengthened at pleasure. It is a pendulum with a movable counterweight which can be set at any designated figure and which will then swing to and fro that number of times per minute, an audible click accompanying each oscillation. When made with a bell, the sound of this appliance denotes the beginning of each measure. The words of *tempo* on the metronome, such as *Andante, Largo*, etc., are entirely misleading; the teacher must be guided by the numerals only. Beethoven and Czerny were the first composers to use the metronome.

Metronome, bell. A metronome with the addition of a small bell, which strikes at the commencement of each bar.

Metronomic marks. Figures appended to pieces of music, referring to corresponding figures on a metronome: The " M. M." employed in this connection means " Maelzel's Metronome," *not* " Metronome Mark." The following are examples of metronome marks: 1. M. M. ♩ = 112. 2. M. M. ♩· = 60. These would mean: 1. That the counterweight of the metronome is to be set at 112, and that each click is to represent the speed of a quarter-note, or in other words, that the speed is to be at the rate of 112 quarter-notes a minute. 2. This signifies that the metronome is to be set at sixty, and each click is to represent a dotted quarter.

Mette (Ger.) (*mĕt*-tĕ.) Matins.

Mettez (Fr.) (*met*-te.) Draw, add (referring to organ-stops.)

Mettere in musica (It.) (mĕt-te-rĕ ēn moo-zē-kä.) To set to music.

Mettre d'accord (Fr.) (mātr d'ăk-kōr.) To tune.

Mettre en musique (Fr.) (mātr änh mü-zĕk.) To set to music.

Mettre en répétition (Fr.) (mātr änh rā-pĕ-*tē*-sĭ-ŏnh.) To put in rehearsal.

Mez. An abbreviation of *Mezzo*.

Mez. F. An abbreviation of *Mezzo Forte*.

Mez. Pia. An abbreviation of *Mezzo Piano*.

Mézza (It.) (*met*-tsä.) }
Mézzo (It.) (*met*-tsō.) } Medium, half.

Mézza bravúra (It.) (*met*-tsä brä-*voo*-rä.) A moderately embellished song.

Mézza forza (It.) (*met*-tsä *fŏr*-tsä.) Moderately loud.

Mézza mánica (It.) (*met*-tsä *mä*-nē-kä.) The *half-shift*, in playing the violin, etc.

ă as in *ah*; ā as in *hate*; ă as in *at*; ē as in *tree*; ĕ as in *eh*; ī as in *pine*; ĭ as in *pin*;

Mezzána (It.) (met-*tsä*-nä.) The middle string of a lute.

Mézza orchéstra (It.) (met-tsä ŏr-käs-trä.) Half the orchestra.

Mézza vóce (It.) (met-tsä vō-tshĕ.) Half the power of the voice; softly.

Mézzo caráttere (It.) (met-tsō kä-*rät*-tä-rĕ.) A moderate degree of expression and execution; music of a medium character.

Mézzo fórte (It.) (met-tsō *fŏr*-tĕ.) Moderately loud.

Mézzo piáno (It.) (met-tsō pē-*ä*-nō.) Rather soft.

Mézzo sopráno (It.) (met-tsō sō-*prä*-nō.) A female voice of lower pitch than the soprano, or treble, but higher than the contralto. The general compass is See *Voice*.

Mézzo-sopráno clef. The C clef when placed on the second line of the staff, occurring in old church music or madrigals. The treble or soprano clef now supplies its place.

Mézzo staccáto (It.) (met-tsō stäk-*kä*-tō.) A little detached.

Mézzo tenore (It.) (met-tsō tĕ-*nō*-rĕ.) A half-tenor voice, nearly the same as a *baritone*.

Mézzo tuóno (It.) (met-tsō *twō*-nō.) A semi-tone; a half-tone.

Mézzo vóce (It.) (met-tsō *vō*-tshĕ.) In a subdued voice.

M. F. The initials of *Mezzo Forte*.

M.G. The initials of *Main Gauche*.

Mi (It.) (mē.) A syllable used in solfaing to designate E, or the third note of the major scale.

Mi bémol (Fr.) (mē bā-mōl.) The note E flat.

Mi bémol majeur (Fr.) (mē *bä*-mōl mä-zhŭr.) The key of E flat major.

Mi bémol mineur (Fr.) (mē *bä*-mōl mĭ-nŭr.) The key of E flat minor.

Microphone. (*mī*-krō-fōn.) Instrument for the augmentation of small sounds.

Microphonics. The science, or art of increasing the intensity of sounds.

Middle C. That C which is between the bass and treble staves.

Middle part. Any parts that lie between the outside voices.

Middle voices. Tenor and alto voices.

Mi diese (Fr.) (mē dĭ-*äz*.) The note E sharp.

Mignon (Fr.) (mēn-yŏnh.) Dainty, charming.

Militairement (Fr.) (mĭl-ē-*tär*-mänh.)
Milítáre (It.) (mē-lē-*tä*-rĕ.)
Militarménte (It.) (mē-lē-tär-*men*-tĕ.)
Military; in a warlike, martial style.

Military Music Music intended for military bands, marches, quicksteps, etc. A typical military band might have the following composition:

2 piccolos	1 contrafagotto
2 flutes	1 E♭ cornetto
2 oboes	2 1st B♭ cornets
1 A♭ piccolo clarinet	2 2nd " "
3 E♭ clarinets	2 trumpets
8 1st B♭ clarinets	2 flügelhorns
4 2nd " "	4 French horns
4 3rd " "	2 E♭ alto horns
1 alto "	2 B♭ tenor horns
1 bass "	2 euphoniums
1 sopr. saxophone	3 trombones
1 alto "	5 bombardoni
1 tenor "	3 drums
1 bass "	1 pair cymbals
2 bassoons	

The military band is composed, therefore, of the orchestral wind-instruments plus saxophones, cornets, and drums. The oboe is often omitted. The clarinets are made very prominent, taking the place of the strings. There are instruments of high pitch used, such as the E flat clarinet, the A flat clarinet, the tierce flute, and others, that would be too shrill for orchestral use. A military band has sometimes as many performers as a full orchestra.

Mi majeur (Fr.) (mēe mä-*zhŭr*.) The key of E major.

Mi mineur (Fr.) (mēe mĭ-*nŭr*.) The key of E minor.

Minaccevolménte (It.) (mē-nät-tshĕ-vōl-*men*-tĕ.) In a threatening, menacing manner.

ō as in *tone*; ŏ as in *dove*; ŏ as in *not*; ŭ as in *up*; ü the French sound of *u*.

Minacciándo (It.) (mē-nät-tshē-*än*-dō.)
Minacciévole (It.) (mē-nät-tshē-*ek*-vō-lĕ.)
Threatening, menacing.
Minacciosaménte (It.) (mē-nät-tshē-ō-zä-*men*-tĕ.) Threatening; menacing; in a menacing manner.
Minaccióso (It.) (mē-nät-tshē-*ō*-zō.) Threatening; menacing; in a menacing manner.
Minder (Ger.) (*min*-dĕr.) Less; not so much.
Mineur (Fr.) (mĭ-*nŭr*.) Minor.
Minim. A half-note; a note equal to one-half of a semibreve.
Miníma (It.) (*mē*-nē-mä.)
Minima (Spa.) (*mē*-nē-mä.) } A minim; literally,
Minima (Lat.) (*mĭn*-ĭ-mä.) } the *least*, because formerly the minim was the shortest note.
Minime (Fr.) (min-*ēm*.) A minim.
Minim rest. A mark of silence equal in duration to a half-rest, made thus, ▬.
Minnedichter (Ger.) (*mĭn*-nĕ-*dĭkh*-tĕr.)
Minnesänger (Ger.) (*mĭn*-nĕ-*sāng*-ĕr.)
Minnesinger (Ger.) (*mĭn*-nĕ-*sĭng*-ĕr.)
Minstrels of the twelfth and thirteenth centuries, who wandered from place to place singing a great variety of songs and melodies. They were *love-singers* (the word *Minne* meaning homage to woman) and generally of high rank. Wagner's opera *Tannhäuser* is founded upon the epoch of the minnesingers. The minnesingers were the troubadours of Germany.
Minor. Less; smaller; in speaking of intervals, etc.
Minor canons. Those clergymen of a cathedral or chapel, who occasionally assist at the performance of the service and anthem.
Minor diatonic scale. There are two kinds; one where the semi-tones fall between the second and third and seventh and eighth, both in ascending and descending; in the other the semitone falls between the second and third and seventh and eighth ascending, and descending, between the fifth and sixth and second and third. The former is the *harmonic*, the latter the *melodic* form.

Minor Scales; Pure (or Historic).

Harmonic.

Melodic, or Combination Minor Scales:

The last is most generally called the *melodic* minor scale.
Minóre (It.) (me-*no*-re.) Minor.
Minor key. } One of the modern
Minor mode. } modes, or scales, in which the third note is a minor third from the tonic.
Minor second. The smallest interval in practicable use, consisting of five commas, a semi-tone.
Minor semi-tone. A semi-tone which *retains* its place, or *letter* on the staff; thus C, C♯; A A♯, etc.
Minor seventh. An interval consisting of four tones and two semi-tones.
Minor sixth. An interval composed of three tones and two semi-tones.
Minor third. A diatonic interval containing three semi-tones.
Minor triad. A union of any tone with its minor third and perfect fifth.
Minstrels. The wandering poets or musicians of the tenth and following centuries.
Minstrel, squire. A title formerly given to a professional minstrel, a character combining the offices of poet, singer, and musician.
Minstrelsy. The art, or profession of a minstrel.
Minue (*Spa.*) (*mē*-nooä.) A minuet.
Minuet. The minuet is always in triple rhythm, and of slow tempo as a dance, but it has been so freely treated by the classical composers that its tempo is very often rapid. *Tempo di Minuetto* has come to mean an *allegretto*, or

even a quicker speed. The name comes from the Latin *minimus* (the smallest), since it was danced with dainty steps. The minuet is the most important of the dance forms, since it was the only dance regularly admitted into the modern sonata and symphony, and was also frequently used in the suite, while from its contrasts is derived a musical form used almost constantly in modern music, and called the minuet-form or *Song form with Trio*, in which a great deal of drawing-room, as well as some classical, music is written. See *Form.*

Minuétto (It.) (mē-noo-*et*-tō.) A minuet.

Minuétto, alternativo (It.) (mē-noo-*et*-tō äl-tĕr-nä-*tē*-vō.) Alternately perform the minuet and trio.

Minuge (It.) (mē-*noo*-jĕ.) Strings of instruments; catgut.

Mirliton (Fr.) (mēr-lĭ-tŏnh.) A small pan reed.

Mise de voix (Fr.) (mēz dŭh vwä.) See *Mézza Vóce.*

Mise en scène (Fr. meez-anh-sayn; It. *missa in scena;* Ger. *Inszenierung.*) Setting of a play on the stage; stage-setting; mounting.

Miserere (Lat.) (mi-sĕ-*rā*-rĕ.) *Have mercy;* a psalm of supplication, especially used during Holy Week.

Misericordia (Lat.) (*mi*-sĕ-rĭ-*kŏr*-dĭ-ä.) A miserere.

Missa (Lat.) (*mis*-sä.) A Mass.

Missa brevis (Lat.) (*mis*-sä brā-vĭs.) A short Mass.

Missa canonica (Lat.) (*mis*-sä kä-*nōn*-ĭ-kä) A canonical Mass.

Missal. The Mass-book.

Missa pro defunctis (Lat.) (*mis*-sä prō dĕ *fŭnk*-tĭs.) A Requiem; a Mass for departed souls.

Missa, solennis (Lat.) (*mīs*-sä sō-*lĕn*-nĭs.) A solemn Mass, for high festivals.

Míssel (Fr.) (mĭs-s'l.) Missal; the Mass-book.

Misshällig (Ger.) (*mĭss*-hāl-lĭg.) Dissonant, discordant.

Misshälligkeit (Ger.) (*mĭss*-hāl-lĭg-kīt.) Dissonance, discordance.

Missklang (Ger.) (*mĭss*-klāng.) Dissonance, discordance.

Misteriosamente (It.) (mēs-tĕr-ē-ō-zä-*men*-tĕ.)

Misterióso (It.) (mis-tĕr-ē-*ō*-zō.) Mysteriously; in a mysterious manner.

Mistero, con (It.) (mis-tā-rō.) With mystery.

Misúra (It.) (mi-*soo*-rä.) A bar; a measure; time.

Misuráto (It.) (mi-soo-*rä*-tō.) Measured · in strict, measured time.

Mit (Ger.) (mĭt.) With, by.

Mit Begleitung (Ger.) (mĭt bĕ-*glī*-toong.) With an accompaniment.

Mit Bewegung (Ger.) (mĭt bĕ-*vā* goong.) Synonymous with *con móto.*

Mitlaut (Ger.) (*mĭt*-lout.) Consonance.

Mitlauter (Ger.) (*mĭt*-lou-tĕr.) cord,

Mitlauten (Ger.) (*mĭt*-lou-t'n.) To sound at the same time, or in common with.

Mitleidsvoll (Ger.) (*mĭt*-līds-fōl.) Compassionate.

Mittel-mässig (Ger.) (*mĭt*-t'l-mās-sig.) Middling, moderately.

Mittel-stimme (Gēr.) (*mĭt*-t'l-stĭm-mĕ.) The *mean*, or middle voice, or part; the tenor.

Mittel-stimmen (Ger. *pl.*) (*mĭt*-t'l-stĭm-m'n.) The middle voices, or parts.

Mittel-ton (Ger.) (*mĭt*-t'l-tōn.) The *mediant.* See that word.

Mit voller Orgel (Ger.) (mĭt fōl-lĕr ōr-g'l.) With full organ.

Mixed canon. A canon of many parts, in which the parts begin at diffeient intervals.

Mixolydian. See *Greek modes.*

Mixture stop. An organ-stop consisting of three or more ranks of pipes. These are not intended to sound alone. They are voiced an octave, a fifth, a twelfth, etc., above the regular stops and they add the harmonics to the diapasons. See *Acoustics* and *Harmonics.*

M. M. The initials of Maelzel's Metronome. See *Metronomic marks.*

Móbile (It.) (*mō*-bĕ-lĕ.) Moveable, changeable.

Mode. A particular system or constitu-

ō as in *tone;* ŏ as in *dove;* ŏ as in *not;* ŭ as in *up;* ü the French sound of *u.*

tion of sounds, by which the octave is divided into certain intervals, according to the genus. The arrangement of notes in a scale, —major, minor, doric, etc. Consult *Greek Music* in Stainer & Barrett.

Mode, doric. The first of the authentic modes in the system of the ancient Greeks employed on martial and religious occasions.

Mode, major. That in which the third from the key-note is major.

Mode, minor. That which is the third degree from the tonic forms the interval of a minor third.

Mode, orthian. One of the ancient Greek modes.

Moderatamente (It.) (mŏd-ĕ-rä-tä-men-tĕ.)

Moderáto (It.) (mŏd-ĕ-rä-tō.) Moderately; in moderate time.

Moderazióne (It.) (mŏd-ĕ-rä-tsē-ō-nĕ.) Moderation.

Modéré (Fr.) (mō-dā-rā.) Moderate.

Mode, relative. A relative key.

Moderna, alla (It.) (mō-där-nä äl-lä.) In the modern style.

Modes, ancient. The modes or scales of the ancient Greeks and Romans.

Modes, authentic. Church modes, the melody of which was confined within the tonic and its octave.

Modes, church. The ancient modes called by the following names: *Dorian, Phrygian, Lydian, Mixo-Lydian, Æolian, Ionian,* or *Iastian.* The Gregorian tones. See Ritter's "History of Music," William's "Story of Notation," and the "Oxford History of Music."

Modes, ecclesiastical. The ancient church modes. The Gregorian tones.

Modes, plagal. Those modes in the Greek system whose tones lay between the dominant, and octave and twelfth.

Modestamente (It.) (mō-dĕs-tä-men-tĕ.)
Modésto (It.) (mō-dās-tō.) Modestly, quietly, moderately.

Modification. A term applied to the temperament of the sounds of those instruments whose tones are fixed, which gives a greater degree of perfection to one key than to another; as in organs, pianofortes, and the like.

Modificazióni (It. pl.) (mō-dē-fē-kä-tsē-ō-nē.) Modifications, light and shade of intonation; slight alterations.

Módo (It.) (*mō*-dō.) A mode; a scale.

Módo maggióre (It.) (*mō*-dō mäd-jē-*ō*-rĕ.) The major mode.

Módo minóre (It.) (*mō*-dō mē-*nō*-rĕ.) The minor mode.

Mod'to. An abbreviation of *Moderato.*

Modoláre (It.) (mō-dō-*lä*-rĕ.) To modulate; to accommodate the voice or instrument to a certain intonation.

Moduláre (It.) (mō-doo-*lä*-rĕ.)

Modulánte (It.) (mō-doo-*län*-tĕ.) Modulating.

Modulate. To move from one key to another in a manner agreeable to the ear.

Modulation. A transition of key; going from one key to another, by a certain succession of chords, either in a natural and flowing manner, or sometimes in a sudden and unexpected manner. As applied to the voice, modulation means to accommodate the tone to a certain degree of intensity, or light and shade.

Modulation, abrupt. Sudden modulation into keys which are not closely related to the original key.

Modulation, deceptive. Any modulation by which the ear is deceived and led to an unexpected harmony.

Modulation, enharmonic. A modulation effected by altering the *notation* of one or more intervals belonging to some *characteristic* chord, and thus changing the key and the harmony into which it would naturally have resolved. The chords which best admit of these alterations are, first, the diminished seventh and its inversions; secondly, the dominant seventh not inverted, and the chord of the superfluous sixth and perfect fifth.

Modulation, extraneous. A modulation into some other than the original key and its relatives.

Modulation, note of. A note introducing a new key; usually the leading-note or major seventh of the key introduced.

Modulation, passing.
Modulation, transient. A form of modulation which leaves a key nearly as soon as entered upon.

ă as in *ah*; ā as in *hate*; ă as in *at*; ē as in *tree*; ĕ as in *eh*; ī as in *pine*; ĭ as in *pin*;

Modulazióne (It.) (mō-doo-lä-tsē-ō-nĕ.) Modulation.

Moduliren (Ger.) (mō-doo-*lē*-r'n.) To modulate.

Modulo (Lat.) (*mō*-dŭ-lō.) To modulate; to compose.

Modus (Lat.) (*mō*-dŭs.) A key; mode; scale.

Mohrentanz (Ger.) (mō-r'n-tänts.) Morisco; morris dance.

Moins (Fr.) (mwänh.) Less.

Moll (Ger.) (mŏll.) Minor.

Molle (Fr.) (mōl.) Soft, mellow, delicate.

Molleménte (It.) (mōl-lĕ-*mĕn*-tĕ.) Softly, gently, delicately.

Mollis (Lat.) (*mŏl*-lĭs.) Soft.

Moll-tonart (Ger.) (*mol*-tōn-ärt.) Minor key, or scale.

Molossus (Gr.) (mō-*lŏs*-sŭs.) In Greek and Latin verse, a foot of three long syllables.

Mólta (It.) (*mōl*-tä.) } Much; very
Mólto (It.) (*mol*-to.) } much; extremely; a great deal.

Moltisonánte (It.) (mōl-tē-zō-*nän*-tĕ.) Resounding; very sonorous.

Monacórdo (It.)(mŏn-ä-*kor*-dō.) } An
Monochord (*mŏn*-ō-kŏrd.) } instrument with one string for measuring musical intervals, or sounds. The ancient monochord (before 1000) had a movable bridge which shortened or lengthened the string (wire did not exist) and thus gave different tones; afterwards other strings were added, and the monochord became the predecessor of the clavichord.

Monocorde (Fr.) (mŏn-ō-*kŏrd*.) } On
Monocórdo (It.) (mŏn-ō-*kŏr*-dō.) } one string only. See also *Monochord*.

Monodía (It.) (mō-nō-dē-ä.) } A com-
Monodie (Fr.) (mŏn-ō-*dēe*.) } position
Monody (Eng.) (*mŏn*-ō-dy.) } for a single voice. The term originally applied to those solos which were used in the earliest operas and oratorios, A.D. 1600 (*circa*.); for before that time solos did not exist in any large work. Monody, was homophony, as opposed to counterpoint or polyphony.

Monodic. For *one* voice; a solo.

Monodist. One who writes a monody.

Monodram (Ger.) (mōn-ō-*dräm*.) } A
Monodrama (It.) mŏn-ō-*drä*-mä) } musical drama in which only one actor appears; a monodrame.

Monodrame (Fr.) (mŏn-ō-*dräm*.) A drama performed by a single individual.

Monologue. A soliloquy; a poem, song, or scene written and composed for a single performer.

Monorhyme (Gr.) (*mŏn*-ō-*rē*-mĕ.) Where all the lines of a verse end in the same rhyme.

Monostich (Gr.) (mŏn-ō-stĭk.) A composition consisting of one verse only.

Monostrophe (Gr.) (*mŏn*-ŏ-*strō*-fĕ.) Having one strophe only; not varied in measure.

Monotone. Uniformity of sound; one and the same sound.

Monotonia (Spa.) (mŏn-ō-*tō*-nĭ-ä.) } Mo-
Monotonie (Fr.) (mŏn-ō-tō-nē.) } not-
Monotonie (Ger.) (mōn-ō-tō-nēe.) } ony; sameness of sound.

Montant (Fr.) (mŏnh-tänh.) Ascending.

Montant de cloche (Fr.) (mŏnh-tänh dŭh klōsh.) A belfry.

Montré (Fr.) (mŏnh-*trāy*.) Shown or mounted; in *front*; a term applied to pipes which are placed in front of the case.

Montré d'orgue (Fr.) (mŏnh-trāy d'ŏrg.) The range of pipes in the front of an organ.

Moorish drum. A tambourine.

Morbidezza con (It.) (mŏr-bē-*det*-sä.) Morbidly.

Morceau (Fr.) (mŏr-*sō*.) A choice and select musical piece, or composition; a fine phrase, or passage.

Morceau d'ensemble (Fr.) (mŏr-*sō* d'änh-sänhbl.) A piece harmonized for several voices.

Mordante (It.) (mŏr-*dän*-tĕ.) See *Mordént*.

Mordént (It.) (mŏr-*dänt*.) Transient shake or beat; an embellishment formed by two or more notes, preceding the principal note. An embellishment consisting of the note over which the sign is placed and the note below it: thus

ō as in *tone*; ŏ as in *dove*; ŏ as in *not*; ŭ as in *up*; ü the French sound of *u*.

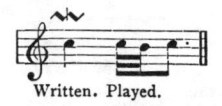

There is, unfortunately, considerable confusion in the nomenclature of the mordent. Some apply the word to an embellishment with the *upper* note as auxiliary, while others call this the *inverted* mordent, and others again the *Praller*, or *Prall-trill*. The most-used system of nomenclature is as follows:

Praller or Inverted Mordent.

If there should be any accompanying note to that over which the praller is written, it is to be struck simultaneously with the first note of the praller.

The accent is sometimes upon the first note of the group, and sometimes upon the last or principal note. The Germans sometimes distinguish these two kinds by different names, calling the first *Praller*, the second *Schneller*. Mordents, or prallers, over short notes, and in rapid passages, are generally accented upon the first note of the group.

Single Mordent.   Double Mordent.

The rule regarding chord-playing (given above) is also applied to the mordent and double mordente.

The word *mordent* is derived from the French verb *mordre* (to bite) and the mordent is really a fragment bitten out of a trill. The sign itself shows this, for in ancient days the trill was written thus ∿∿∿∿, while the mordent, written thus ∿, represents a single beat of it.

The intervals of the praller, unless altered by accidentals, are according to the scale, that is, a praller on the third or seventh degree would have a semi-tone interval, and all others would have whole tones, unless accidentals were combined with the sign. The interval of the mordent ∿ is generally a semi-tone. The great haziness of nomenclature in this subject, the fact that the mordent is very rarely met with in modern music, and the additional fact that the vertical line drawn through any sign is usually an indication of *inversion*, leads one to hope that the following simple nomenclature may yet be adopted by teachers:

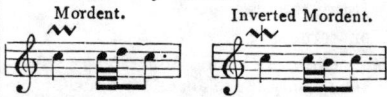

Mordent.   Inverted Mordent.

or that the former may be called an "upward mordent" and the latter a "downward mordent."

Mordente (It.) (mor-*den*-teh.) See *Mordent*.

Moréndo (It.) (mō-*ren*-dō.) ⎫
Moriénte (It.) (mō-rē-*en*-tĕ.) ⎬ Dying away; expiring; gradually diminishing the tone and the time.

Morésca (It.) (mō-*rēs*-kä.) ⎫ Moorish;
Moresque (It.) (mō-*rĕsk*.) ⎬ morris

ă as in *ah* ; ā as in *hate* ; ă as in *at* ; ē as in *tree* ; ĕ as in *eh* ; ī as in *pine* ; ĭ as in *pin* ;

dance, in which bells are jingled at the ankles, and swords clashed.

Morgen-gesang (Ger.) (*mōr*-g'n ghĕ-*zäng*.)

Morgen-lied (Ger.) (*mōr*-g'n-lēd.) Morning song, or hymn.

Morgen-ständchen (Ger.) (*mōr*-g'n-*ständ*-kh'n.) Morning serenade, or *Aubade*.

Morísco (It.) (mō-*rēs*-kō.) In the Moorish style. See *Morésca*.

Morisk (mō-rĭsk.) The morris dance.

Mormoramente (It.) (mŏr-mō-rä-*men*-tō.) A murmur, warbling, buzzing, purling.

Mormorándo (It.) (mŏr-mō-*rän*-dō.)
Mormorévole (It.) (mŏr-mō-*re*-vō-lĕ.)
Mormoróso (It.) (mŏr-mō-*rō*-zō.)
With a gentle, murmuring sound.

Morrice dance.
Morris dance. A peculiar kind of dance practised in the
Morriske dance. middle ages. It is supposed to have been introduced into England by Edward III. In the morris dance bells were fastened to the feet of the performer. It is in ¾ time. See Elson's "Shakespeare in Music."

Mort. A tune sounded at the death of game.

Mósso (It.) (*mōs*-sō.) Moved, movement, motion. *Meno Mosso*, less movement, slower. *Piu Mosso*, more movement; quicker.

Mósso, molto (It,)(*mōs*-sō *mōl*-tō.) Quick; with much motion.

Móstra (It.) (*mōs*-trä.) A direct ∿

Mot (Fr.) (mō.) Literally, a *word;* a note or brief strain on a bugle.

Motet.
Motett. A sacred composition of the anthem style, for several voices. The words are taken from the Scriptures. The motet is generally contrapuntal, and it is possible that the word is derived from *moto* (motion), because of the constant motion of all the parts.

Motette (Ger.) (mō-*tĕt*.)
Motet (Fr.) (mō-*tā*.) A motet.
Motétto (It.) (mō-*tāt*-tō.)

Motetten (Ger.) (mō-*tĕt*-t'n.)
Motetti (It.) (mō-*tĕt*-tē.) Motets.

Motetus (Lat.) (mō-*tĕt*-ŭs.) A motet.

Motif (Fr.) (mo-*teef*.) A motive, or figure. The term *Leit-motif* (which see) was used by Wagner for his guiding-figures.

Motion. The progression of a melody or part.

Motion, contrary. The movement of one part in an opposite direction to another.

Motion, direct. The movement of two or more parts in the same direction.

Motion, oblique. When one part ascends, or descends, while the other remains stationary, it is called oblique motion.

Motion, similar. When two or more parts ascend or descend at the same time.

Motive. The characteristic and predominant passage of an air ; the theme or subject of a composition ; a figure. See *Motif*.

Motivi (It.) (mō-*tēe*-vē.) Motives, or figures.

Motívo (It.) (mō-*tēe*-vō.) Motive; the theme or subject of a musical composition.

Móto (It) (*mō*-tō.) Motion, movement; *con mōto;* with motion ; rather quick.

Móto accelerato (It.) (*mō*-tō ät-tshä-lè-*rä*-tō.) Accelerated motion.

Móto contrário (It.) (*mō*-tō kŏn-*trä*-rē-ō.) Contrary motion.

Móto obliquo (It.) (*mō*-tō ŏb-*lē*-quō.) Oblique motion.

Móto perpetuo (It.) (*mo*-tō per-*pet*-oo-oh.) Perpetual motion ; a study in rapidity of execution.

Móto prímo (It.) The same time as the first.

Móto rétto (It.) (*mō*-tō *ret*-tō.) Direct, or similar motion.

Motteggiándo (It.) (mŏt-ted-jē-*än*-dō.) Jeeringly, mockingly, jocosely.

Mottétto (It.) (mŏt-*tet*-tō.) A motet.

Motus (Lat.) (*mō*-tŭs.) Motion, movement.

Motus contrarius (Lat.) (*mō*-tŭs kŏn-*trä*-rĭ-ŭs.) Contrary motion.

Motus obliquus (Lat.) (*mō*-tŭs ōb-*lē*-quŭs.) Oblique motion.

Motus rectus (Lat.) (*mō*-tŭs *rĕk*-tŭs.) Direct, or similar motion.

Mounted cornet. An organ-stop, usually consisting of five ranks of pipes, of large scale, and loudly voiced, placed upon a raised soundboard of their own (hence the name.) It is only to be met with in old organs.

Mouth. The opening on the front of an organ-pipe.

ō as in *tone*; ŏ as in *dove*; ŏ as in *not*; ŭ as in *up*; ü the French sound of *u*.

177

Mouth-harmonica. A set of graduated metal reeds mounted in a narrow frame, blown by the mouth, and producing different tones on expiration and inspiration.

Mouth-piece. That part of a trumpet, horn, etc. which is applied to the lips.

Mouvement (Fr.) (moov-mänh.) }
Movimento (It.) (mō-vē-*men*-tō.) }
Motion; movement; impulse; the time of a piece.

Mouvement de l'archet (Fr.) (moovmänh dŭh l'är-shā.) Bowing; the movement of the bow.

Movement. The name given to any portion of a composition comprehended under the same measure or time; a composition consists of as many *movements* as there are positive changes in time.

Movement, organ. A system of levers with their appendages, called trackers, rollers, etc., in an organ, which serves to transmit the action of the keys to the wind-chest, pallets, and soundboard.

Moviménto contrario (It.) (mō-vē-*men*-tō kŏn-*trä*-rē-ō.) Contrary movement.

M. P. The initials of *Mézzo Piáno.*

M. S. The initials of *Máno Sinistra.* Left hand.

Muance (Fr.) (mü-*änhs*.) A change, or variation of notes; a division.

Muet (Fr.) (mü-*ā*.) Mute.

Multisonous (Lat.) (*mŭl*-tĭ-*sō*-nŭs.) Many sounding, loud-sounding.

Mund (Ger.) (moond.) The mouth.

Mund-harmonica (Ger.) (moond-här-*mō*-nĭ-kä.) The Jews'-harp, or, a mouth-harmonica.

Mund-stück (Ger.) (moond stük.) Mouthpiece.

Münster (Ger.) (*mün*-stĕr.) Minster, cathedral.

Munter (Ger.) (*moon*-tĕr.) Lively, sprightly.

Munterkeit (Ger.) (*moon*-tĕr kīt.) Liveliness, briskness, vivacity.

Murmeln (Ger.) (*moor*-mĕln.) To murmer.

Murmelnd (Ger.) (*moor*-mĕlnd.) Murmuring.

Musa (Lat.) (*mū*-sä.) A song.

Mus Bac. An abbreviation of *Bachelor of Music.* (Little used.)

Mus. Doc. An abbreviation of *Doctor of Music.*

Muse. Name originally given to the muzzle or tube of the bagpipe.

Muses. In mythology, the nine sister goddesses who presided over the fine arts.

Musetta (It.) (moo-zĕt-tä.) } A species of
Musette (Fr.) (mü-*sĕt*.) } small bagpipes inflated by means of bellows placed under the arm of the performer; an air or dance composed for the musette. A primitive oboe. A composition, or movement in a composition, with a drone-bass. The *trios*, of many gavottes and other old dances having such a drone-bass, are called *Musettes.*

Música (It.) (*moo*-zē-kä.) Music.

Música antíqua (Lat.) (mū-sĭ-kä ăn-tĭ-quä.) Ancient music.

Música arrabbiáta (It.) (mū-sĭ-kä är-räb-bē-*ä*-tä.) Burlesque music.

Música di gátti (It.) (mū-sē-kä dē *gät*-tē.) Burlesque music; caterwauling.

Música choralis (Lat.) (mū-sĭ-kä kō-*rä*-lĭs.) The music of a chorus, or chant.

Música chromatica (Lat.) (mū-sĭ-kä krō-*mät*-ĭ-kä.) Music in which there are many chromatic signs.

Música colorata (Lat.) (mū-sĭ-kä kō-lō-*rä*-tä.) }
Música ficta (Lat.) (mū-sĭ-kä *jĕk*-tä.) } An old name for music which deviated from the church modes by means of accidentals.

Música da cámera (It.) (moo-zē-kä dä *kä*-mā-rä.) Music for the chamber.

Música da chiésa (It.) (moo-zē-kä dä kē-*äy*-zä.) Church music.

Música da teátro (It.) (moo-zē-kä dä tĕ-*ä*-trō.) Theatrical music.

Música dramatica (Lat.) (mū-sĭ-kä drä-*mä*-tĭ-kä.) Dramatic music.

Música ecclesiastica (Lat.) (mū-sĭ-kä ĕk-klā-zĭ-*ăs*-tĕ-kä.) Church music.

ä as in *ah*; ā as in *hate*; ă as in *at*; ē as in *tree*; ĕ as in *eh*; ī as in *pine*; ĭ as in *pin*;

Musicalement (Fr.) (mü-zē-kăl-mänh.)
Musicalménte (It.) (moo-zē-käl-mān-tĕ.)
Musically, harmoniously.

Musical glasses. Drinking glasses so tuned in regard to each other, that a wet finger being passed round their brims, they produce the notes of the diatonic scale, and are capable of giving the successive sounds of regular tunes, or melodies.

Musical grammar. The rules of musical composition.

Musical nomenclature. The vocabulary of names and technical terms in music.

Musical pantomine. A dramatic performance, the ideas and sentiments of which are expressed by music and gestures.

Musical science. The *theory* of music, in contradistinction from the *practice*, which is an *art;* the general principles and laws of harmonic relations.

Musical soirée. An evening musical entertainment, public or private.

Musical terms. Words and phrases appended to passages of music, indicating the manner in which they should be performed.

Music, Bachelor of. The first music degree conferred at the universities.

Music, Doctor of. A degree conferred by the universities. See Grove's Dictionary, article " Degrees in Music."

Musiker (Ger.) (*moo*-zĭ-kĕr.) A musician.

Musikfest (Ger.) (moo-*zĭk*-fĕst.) A musical festival.

Musikino (Ger.) (moo-zĭ-*kē*-nō.) A little musician.

Musik-lehrer (Ger.) (moo-zĭk-*lā*-rĕr.) Teacher of music.

Musikkenner (Ger.) (moo-zĭk-*kĕn*-ner.)
Musikliebhaber (Ger.) (moo-zĭk-*lēeb*-hä-bĕr.)
A lover of music ; an amateur.

Musikmeister (Ger.) (moo–zĭk-*mys*-tĕr.) A music-master.

Musik-saal (Ger.) (moo-zĭk-säl.)
Musik-zimmer (Ger.) (moo-zĭk-*tsĭm*-mer.)
Music-hall, music-room.

Musik-stunde (Ger.) (moo-zĭk *stoon*-dĕ.) A music-lesson.

Musikunterricht (Ger.) (moo-zĭk-*oon*-t'r-rĭkht.) Instruction in music.

Musik-verein (Ger.) (moo-zĭk fĕ-*rīn*.) A musical society.

Musik-zeitung (Ger.) (moo-zĭk-*tsī*-toong.) A musical journal.

Musique (Fr.) (mü-zēk.) Music.

Musique d'église (Fr.) (mü-zēk d'ā-glēz.) Church music.

Mutation. Change, transition ; the transformation of the voice occurring at the age of puberty.

Mutation (Fr.) (mü-*tä*-sĭ-ŏnh.)
Mutazióne (It.) (moo-tä-tsē-*ō*-nĕ.)
Mutation.

Mutation, or *filling up stops,* are those which do not give a tone corresponding to the key pressed down ; such as the quint, tierce, twelfth, etc.

Mute. A small clamp of brass, ivory, or wood, sometimes placed on the bridge of a violin, viola, or violoncello, to diminish the tone of the instrument by damping or checking its vibrations. The direction for using it is *Con Sordino*, for removing it *Senza Sordino*. In brass instruments the mute is a pear-shaped, leather-covered pad introduced into the bell of the horn or trumpet to modify the tone.

Muthig (Ger.) (*moo*-tĭg.) Courageous, spirited.

Muthwillig (Ger.) (*moot*-vĭl-lĭg.) Mischievous, lively.

Mutiren (Ger.) (moo-*tē*-r'n.) The change of voice from soprano to tenor, baritone, or bass.

Mystères (Fr.) (mĭs-tār.)
Mysteries.
A species of sacred drama with music, which was practiced in many of the European churches before the Reformation. Still presented, at intervals, in Oberammergau, in Bavaria, Germany. The mysteries were the predecessors of the oratorio.

N

Nabla (Heb.) (nä-blä.) The *nebel,* a ten-stringed instrument of the ancient Hebrews ; the harp of the Jews, sometimes written *Nebel Nasar.*

ŏ as in *tone* ; ô as in *dove* ; ŏ as in *not* ; ŭ as in *up* ; ü the French sound of *u.*

Nacaire (Fr.) (nä-*kār*.) ⎫
Nacara (It.) (nä-*kä*-rä.) ⎬ A brass drum with
Nacarre (It. pl.) (nä-*kä*-rĕ.) ⎭ a loud metallic tone, formerly much used in France and Italy.

Nácchera (It.) (näk-kā-rä.) Kettledrums.

Naccherétta (It.) (näk-kĕ-*rāt*-tä.) A small kettledrum.

Naccheríno (It.) (näk-kā-*rē*-nō.) A kettle-drummer.

Naccheróne (It.) (näk-kā-*rō*-nĕ.) A large pair of kettledrums.

Nachahmung (Ger.) (nä-kä-moong.) Imitation.

Nach der Reihe (Ger.) (näkh dĕr *rī*-ĕ.) In succession.

Nachdruck (Ger.) (*näkh*-drook.) Emphasis, accent.

Nachdrücklich (Ger.) (*näkh*-drük-līkh.) ⎫
Nachdrucksvoll (Ger.) (*näkh*-drooks-fōl.) ⎭
Energetic, emphatic, forcible.

Nachfolge (Ger.) (*näkh*-fōl-ghĕ.) Imitation.

Nachklang (Ger.) (*näkh*-kläng.) Resonance, echo.

Nachklingen (Ger.) (*näkh*-klĭng-ĕn.)
Nachschallen (Ger.) (*näkh*-shäl-l'n.)
To ring; to echo; to resound.

Nachschlag (Ger.) (*näkh*-shläg.) Additional, or after-note.

Nachsingen (Ger.) (*näkh*-sĭng-ĕn.) To repeat a song; to sing after.

Nachspiel (Ger.) (*näkh*-spēl.) *Afterplay*; a postlude, or concluding piece.

Nacht-glocke (Ger.) (näkht-*glō*-kĕ.) Night-bell; curfew.

Nacht-horn (Ger.) (*näkht*-'hōrn.) *Nighthorn*; an organ-stop of 8-foot tone, nearly identical with the *Quintaton* but of larger scale and more horn-like tone.

Nacht-musik (Ger.) (*näkht-moo*-zīk.) *Night-music*; serenade.

Nacht-sänger (Ger.) (*näkht-sāng*-ĕr.) A *night-singer*; a serenader.

Nacht-schläger (Ger.) (*näkht-shlā*-gĕr.) ⎫
Nachtigall (Ger.) (*näkh*-tĭ-gäll.) ⎭ Nightingale.

Nachtständchen (Ger.) (*näkht*-standkh'n.) A serenade.

Nachtstück (Ger). (näkht-stück.) A serenade; a nocturne.

Nach und nach (Ger.) (näkh oond näkh.) little by little; by degrees.

Naïf (Fr.) (nä-ēf.) ⎫
Naiv (Ger.) (nä-*ēf*.) ⎬ Simple, artless, natural.
Naïve (Fr.) (nä-ēv.) ⎭

Naïvement (Fr.) (nä-ēv-mänh.) Simply, naturally.

Naked. A term significantly applied by modern theorists to *fifths* when unaccompanied, and without their thirds, also called *bare* and *empty*.

Nänien (Ger.) (*nā*-nĭ-ĕn.) Dirges; an elegy.

Narránte (It.) (när-*rän*-tĕ.) In a narrative style.

Narrator. A name given to the character which gives Scriptural story, generally in recitative, in an oratorio, or Passion-music.

Nasard. ⎫
Nasat. ⎬ An old name for an organ-stop, tuned a twelfth above the diapasons.
Nassat. ⎪
Nazard. ⎭

Nason. A very quiet, and sweet-toned flute-stop, of 4-foot scale, sometimes found in old organs.

National-lied (Ger.) (nä-tsĭ-ō-*näl*-lēd.) National song

National music. ⎫ Music identified with
National song. ⎭ the history of a nation, or the manners and customs of its people, either by means of the sentiment it expresses, or by long use.

Natural. A character marked ♮ used to contradict a sharp, or flat. See *Flat*.

Natural Horn. The old horn, called also *Waldhorn*, without any keys. Such an instrument could produce only the *natural tones*. See *Harmonics*. A tube of wide bore will give the low and medium tones of the series, including the fundamental; a tube comparatively narrow, the medium and higher tones, omitting the fundamental.

Natural keys. Those which have no sharp or flat at the signature as C major, and A minor.

Naturalménte (It.) (nä-too-räl-*men*-tĕ.) Naturally.

ä as in *ah*; ā as in *hate*; ă as in *at*; ē as in *tree*; ĕ as in *eh*; ī as in *pine*; ĭ as in *pin*;

Neapolitan sixth. A chord composed of a minor third and minor sixth, and occurring on the sub-dominant, or fourth degree of the scale. In the key of C (major or minor) this chord is really the same as the first inversion of the triad of D♭.

Neben-gedanken (Ger.) (*nāy*-b'n-ghĕ-dänk-'n.) Accessory and subordinate ideas.

Neben-note (Ger.) (*nāy*-b'n-*nō*-tĕ.) Auxiliary note.

Neben-register (Ger.) (*nav*-b'n-rĕ-*ghĭs*-tĕr.)

Neben-züge (Ger.) (*nāy* b'n-*tsü*-ghĕ.) Secondary, or accessory stops in an organ, such as *couplers, tremulant, bells,* etc.

Neben-stimmen (Ger.) (*nāy*-b'n *stĭm*-měn.) Subordinate harmonic parts; also, secondary or mutation stops, such as the *quint, twelfths,* etc.

Necessario (It.) (ne-tshĕs-*sä*-rē-ō.) A term indicating that the passage referred to must not be omitted. *Obbligato.*

Neck. That part of a violin, guitar, or similar instrument, extending from the head to the body, and on which the fingerboard is fixed.

Negligénte (It.) (nāl-yē-*jen*-tĕ.) Negligent, unconstrained.

Negligenteménte (It.) (nāl-yē-jĕn-tĕ-*men*-tĕ.) Negligently.

Negligénza (It.) (nāl-yē-*jen*-tsä.) Negligence, carelessness.

Negli (It. pl.) (*nāl*-yē.)
Nei (It. pl.) (nā-ē.) } In the, at the.

Nel (It.) (nĕl.)
Nella (It.) (nĕl-lä.)
Nelle (It. pl.) (nĕl-lĕ.) } In the; at the.
Nello (It.) (nĕl-lō.)
Nell' (It.) (nĕl'l.)

Nenia (Lat.) (*nēn*-ĭ-ä.) } A funeral
Nenien (Ger.) (*nĕn*-ĭ-ĕn.) } song; an elegy.

Net (Fr.) (nā.)
Nett (Ger.) (nĕt.)
Nettaménte (It.) (nĕt-tä-*men*-tĕ.) } Neatly, clearly, plainly.
Nette (Fr.) (*nāt*.)

Netteté (Fr.) (nāt-tā-tā.) } Neatness,
Nettheit (Ger.) (*nĕt*-hīt.)
Nettigkeit (Ger.) (*nĕt*-tĭg-kīt.) } clearness, plainness.

Nétto (It.) (*net*-tō.) Neat, clear, quick, nimble.

Neu (Ger.) (noi.) New.

Neumæ (Lat.) (nū-mē.) The earliest attempts at notation in the dark ages. They merely indicated the inflections of the voice but had no definite pitch. See *Notation.*

Neun (Ger.) (noin.) Nine.

Neunte (Ger.) (*noin*-tĕ.) A ninth.

Neutralizing sign. The sign of a natural, ♮.

Neuvième (Fr.) (nūh-vĭ-*ǟm*.) The interval of a ninth.

Nicht (Ger.) (nĭkht.) Not.

Nicht zu geschwind (Ger.) (nĭkht tsoo ghĕsh-*vĭnd*.) Not too quick.

Nieder-schlag (Ger.) (*nē*-dĕr-shläg.) The down beat or accented part of the bar.

Niedrig (Ger.) (*nē*-drĭg.) Low, or deep in voice.

Nineteenth. An interval comprising two octaves and a fifth; also, an organ-stop tuned a nineteenth above the diapasons. See *Larigot.*

Ninnare (It.) (nēn-*nä*-rĕ.) To sing children to sleep.

Ninth. An interval consisting of an octave and a second.

Nóbile (It.) (*nō*-bē-lĕ.) Noble, grand, impressive.

Nobilita, con (It.) (nō-*bē*-lē-tä kŏn.) With nobility; dignified.

Nobilménte (It.) (nō-bēl-*men*-tĕ.) } Nobly, grandly.
Noblement (Fr.) (nō-bl-mänh.)

Nocturn. } A composition of a dreamy
Nocturne. } and romantic character suitable for evening recreation; also, a piece resembling a serenade to be played at night in the open air.

Nocturne (Fr.) (nŏk-türn.) } A
Nocturno (It.) (nŏk-toor-nō.) } nocturne.

Nodal points. } In *music*, the fixed
Nodes. } points of a sonorous chord, at which it divides itself, when it vibrates, by aliquot parts, and produces

ŏ as in *tone;* ô as in *dove;* ŏ as in *not;* ŭ as in *up;* ü the French sound of *u.*

181

the harmonic sounds. See *Acoustics* and *Harmonics*.

Noël (Fr.) (nō-ĕl.) A Christmas carol, or hymn. The word had its origin in *Nouvelles* or *News* — *i.e.* good tidings.

Noire (Fr.) (nwär.) *Black note;* a crotchet, or quarter-note.

Nomenclature, musical. A vocabulary of names and technical terms employed in music.

Nomes (Gr.) (nō-mēs.) Certain airs in the ancient music sung to Cybele, the mother of the gods, to Bacchus, to Pan, and other divinities. The name *nome* was also given to every air, the composition of which was regulated by certain determined and inviolable rules.

Nomo (It.) (nō-mō.) Nome. See *Nomes*.

Nomos (Gr.) (nō-mŏs.) } A tune; a melody; melodic sequence.
Nomus (Lat.) (nō-mŭs.) }

Non (It.) (nŏn.) Not, no.

Nona (It.) (nō-nä.) The interval of a ninth.

Nonétto (It.) (nō-*net*-tō.) A composition for nine voices or instruments.

Non mólto (It.) (nŏn mōl-tō.) Not much.

Non mólto allégro (It.) (nŏn mōl-tō äl-*lāy*-grō.) Not very quick.

Non tánto (It.) (nŏn *tän*-tō.) Not so much, not too much.

Non tánto allégro (It.) (nŏn *tän*-tō äl-*lāy*-grō.) Not so quick; not too quick.

Non troppó (It.) (nŏn trŏp-pō.) Not too much; moderately.

Non troppo allégro (It.) (nŏn trŏp-pō äl-*lāy*-grō.) }
Non troppo présto (It.) (nŏn trŏp-pō *pres*-tō.) Not too quick. }

Normal-ton (Ger.) (nōr-*mäl*-tōn.) The normal tone, the note A, the sound to which instruments are tuned in an orchestra.

Normal-tonleiter (Ger.) (nōr-mäl-*tōn*-lī-tĕr.) The natural scale; the scale of C; the open key.

Nóta (It.) (nō-tä.) } A note.
Nota (Lat.) (nō-tä.) }

Notation. The art of representing tones by written or printed characters. The earliest fixed system was that of the Greeks (600 B. C.), which used the letters of the alphabet, both complete and fragmentary, to indicate different pitches and intervals. This system, with various changes, existed well into the middle ages. In the earliest part of the dark ages another system existed contemporaneously with the employment of letters — the *neume* notation. In the *neumes*, we find the beginnings of an effort to appeal to the eye as well as to the thought. The chief elements of this mode of notation were the vertical line | (called *virga*), the dot . , and the horizontal line — (called *jacens*); and after these, came the upward loop ᴗ, called (*plica ascendens*), and the downward loop ᴖ (called *plica descendens*), besides a host of other similar characters. These marks were placed directly over each syllable; and while they could not give the exact pitch to the singer, they served very well to show the direction in which the voice should go, and also indicated roughly the length of the note. They were, in short, merely a reminder to the singer of the progressions of a melody which he had learned orally; a species of musical mnemonics. The letters now underwent a modification. A major scale, corresponding to the diatonic scale, which we begin on C, was represented by the letters *A B C D E F G A*. This was afterwards changed to represent a minor scale, in an effort to bring it more in consonance with the old Greek theory. Odo, of Cluny, is credited with making this reform during the tenth century — our present letter system. The next improvement was an endeavor to give actual and definite pitch to the neumes, by drawing a red line across the manuscript. This line which, represented F, was the very beginning of modern staff notation. Another line, this time of yellow color, was soon added above the red one; and this later line was to represent C. Soon, the colors of the two lines were omitted, and the letters *F* and *C* were placed at the beginning of each of them. From this arose our F and C clefs, which preceded the G clef by some centuries. Hucbald, a monk of St. Amand, in Flanders, is said to have

ă as in *ah;* ā as in *hate;* ă as in *at;* ē as in *tree;* ĕ as in *eh;* ī as in *pine;* ĭ as in *pin;*

182

been the inventor of the foundation of modern notation, the line system. He died about 932. Without digressing to a description of the many experiments which followed, we can state that the next important step forward was the establishment of the vocal syllable system (see *Aretinian Syllables*), by Guido, of Arezzo. In addition to this great invention (which was practically the beginning of reading at sight), Guido threw his power against the vagueness of the *neumæ*, and worked with might and main for the line (or staff) system. Taking the yellow, *c* line, and red, *f* line, he drew a black line between, to represent *a*. The staff was now represented thus:

c———————————————Yellow.
a———————————————Black.
f——————————————— Red.

And, most important improvement of all, Guido used the spaces to represent notes as well. It was practically the beginning of the modern staff. Besides this, there is evidence that Guido did not always confine himself to the three lines, but sometimes added a line above the yellow one to represent *e*, or below the red one to represent *d*. Guido's notes were still borrowed from the neumes, but he altered their shape somewhat, so that, even in these, we perceive the predecessors of modern notes. The next forward movement was in the establishment of notes of *definite length*. The honor of this improvement is claimed by Walter Odington, an Englishman, and Franco, of Cologne, probably a Netherlander. Both of these monks existed in the thirteenth century. Franco seems not to have invented much, but to have practically applied the invention of others. In the *Ars Cantus Mensurabilis* of this writer (the first practical treatise on notes of definite length), we come upon the true system of modern notation, although in a crude state. He presents to us these notes:

▐   ▐   ■   ♦
Large. Longa. Brevis. Semibrevis.

The semibrevis was the shortest note in Franco's system. Rests began at this time also, and were not vastly different from the longest rests of the present time. Early in the fifteenth century the above notes were written open (in outline) somewhat as at present. The change to the round shape, from the diamond and square, came about in the seventeenth century, for greater ease in manuscript work. Meanwhile, the accidental marks had come into existence. See *Sharp, Flat, Natural, Accidentals*. The time-signs, or rhythm-marks, of this epoch, before the invention of the bar and the division of music into measures, were fearfully complicated and vague. It is beyond the province of this book to explain this obsolete system. Only one vestige of it is left in modern music. The sign ₵ comes to us from the middle ages when the triple pulsation of music was held to be the only perfect rhythm, as the monks held that it represented the *Trinity*. It was written with the following sign O, and was called *Perfectum*: when the monks admitted an even rhythm, they called it *Imperfectum* and broke the circle in writing the sign thus: ₵, which we still use to represent ¾ rhythm. With the beginning of opera (about 1600) the signs of tempo and expression begin to appear, and music was *divided into measures!* Peri (in 1600) is said to have been the first practically to use the bar line in the modern style.

Grouping of notes together, a great aid in the representation of rhythm, was not adopted until near the beginning of the eighteenth century. Until that time, a passage like the following

would have been written thus:

The gradual introduction of changes in the system of notation, and the addition of various signs can be traced by consulting the following, rather rare musical dictionaries: Tinctor's "Terminorum Musicæ Diffinitorium" (first printed in 1475), Brossard's "Musical Dictionary" (1702), Grassineau's "Musical Dictionary" (1740), Callcott's "Explanation of Musical Terms, etc." (1792), Zarlino's Theoretical Works

ŏ as in *tone;* ȏ as in *dove;* ŏ as in *not;* ŭ as in *up;* ü the French sound of *u*.

NOTATION NOTES

(1562), Playford's "Skill of Musick" (1662), etc. At the beginning of the eighteenth century, the notation of the best printed works in England was not very different from that of the present.

Notes. Ger., *Note* (*no*-teh); Fr., *Note* (*noht*); It. *Nota* (*no*-tah). The notes which are in general use to-day to express the duration of tone are as follows:

AMERICAN	ENGLISH	GERMAN	FRENCH	ITALIAN
Double note	Breve	Brevis	Brève, or Carrée	Breve
Whole note	Semibreve	Ganzenote	Semi-brève, or Ronde	Semibreve
Half-note	Minim	Halbnote, or halbe note	Blanche	Minima, or Bianca
Quarter-note	Crochet	Viertel, or Viertelnote	Noire	Nera
Eighth-note	Quaver	Achtel, or Achtelnote	Croche	Croma
Sixteenth-note	Semiquaver	Sechzehntel, or Sehzechntel note	Double-croche	Semicroma
Thirty-second-note	Demisemiquaver	Zweiund-dreis-sigstel (note)	Triple-croche	Semibiscroma
Sixty-fourth-note	Hemidemi-semiquaver, or Semidemisemi-quaver	Vierundsech-zigstel (note)	Quadruple-croche	Quattricroma

Occasionally, in old editions of Palestrina or Di Lasso, one may find the *longa*, equalling four whole notes. In Beethoven's "Sonata Pathetique" (introduction), and in many other works, one hundred and twenty-eighth notes are to be found, and there are very rare instances of the use of even two hundred and fifty-sixth notes, but these are generally altered into cadenza notation (small notes) in recent editions. *Artificial grouping* of notes can produce notes of *any* length, such, for example as three five, six, seven, nine, etc., to a whole note. These are produced by grouping several notes together (by flags, or slurs, or both) and adding a numeral. The following rules are observed in such groupings: 1. Never add a numeral to a group which is to consist of normal notes. The numeral always gives the notes an abnormal value. 2. Any artificial group which is divided in half by the rhythm or the accompaniment, is incorrectly numbered. Thus:

the sextolet is incorrect, and should be written as two triplets. 3. The artificial group generally occupies a regular rhythmic division of the music; a single beat, a half measure, etc. The mode of writing such groups can be thus stated: In compound rhythm ($\frac{6}{8}$, $\frac{9}{8}$, $\frac{12}{8}$, etc.), and in triple rhythms, two or four artificial notes equal three normal ones of the same denomination

seven equal six

more rarely seven may equal four. Eight equal six

and in these rhythms, five may sometimes equal three. 13, 14, 16, or 17 are frequently written to take the value of 12.

In *all* rhythms three artificial notes equal two normal ones of the same denomination.

ă as in *ah*; ā as in *hate*; ă as in *at*; ē as in *tree*; ĕ as in *eh*; ī as in *pine*; ĭ as in *bin*;

NOTE, CHARACTERISTIC   NOTE, RADDOPPIATE

Five or six equal four

In even rhythms seven also equal four, and from 9 to 15 equal eight of their own denomination. When small notes are written, the time values are not necessarily adhered to, the group being played with the freedom of a cadenza.

Many errors of notation have been made, even by Mozart and Beethoven, in writing sextolets, groups of six, where double triplets were intended. An artificial group of two notes is called a *doublet*, of three a *triplet*, four a *quattrolet*, five a *quintolet*, six a *sextolet*, etc. The triplet is the artificial group most used, and its three notes have the value of two normal notes of their own denomination. Triplets of two notes can sometimes be used, one of the notes having two-thirds, the other one-third, of the total value.

For further study of origin of notation consult Grove's Dictionary, article "Notation," Elson's "Realm of Music," article, "The Rise of Notation," and Williams' "Story of Notation." See also *Rests*, *Signs*, *Time*, *Rhythm*, *Flat*, etc.

Note, characteristic. A leading-note.

Note, clef. The note upon which the clef is placed.

Note, connecting. A note held in common by two chords.

Note, crowned. A note marked with a hold.

Note d'agrément (Fr.) (not-d'ä-grämänh.) An ornamental note.

Note de passage (Fr.) (nŏt dŭh pässäzh.) A passing-note; a note of regular transition.

Note diésée (Fr.) (nŏt dĭ-ā-zā.) Note marked with a sharp.

Note, double. The ancient breve.

Note, double dotted. A note whose length is increased three-fourths of its original value, by two dots placed after it.

Note, double stemmed. A note having two stems, one upward and the other downward, the one showing the length of its duration and the other its relative value towards other notes in the measure, or indicating that two parts, or voices, unite in giving the note.

Note, eighth. A quaver.

Note, fundamental. The lowest note of a chord.

Note, grace. A note of embellishment.

Note, half. A minim.

Note, key. A note to which all the other notes of a piece bear a distinct and subordinate relation, and with which it generally closes.

Note, leading. The major seventh of any scale; the semi-tone below the key-note; the major third of the dominant.

Noten-pult (Ger.) (*nō*-t'n poolt.) A music-desk.

Noten-schreiber (Ger.) (*nō*-t'n-*shrī*-bĕr.) Music-copyist.

Noten-schwanz (Ger.) (*nō*-t'n-shvänts.) The stem of a note.

Noten-stecher (Ger.) (*nō*-t'n-*stĕkh*-ĕr.) An engraver of music.

Noten-system (Ger.) (*nō*-t'n-sĭs-*tām*.) The staff.

Note of modulation. A note which introduces a new key, usually applied to the leading-note, or sharp seventh.

Note of prolation. A note, the original and nominal duration of which is extended by the addition of a dot, or hold.

Note, open. A note produced on strings of a violin, guitar, etc., when not pressed by the finger.

Note, pedal. A note held by the pedal, or in the bass part, while the harmony forming the remaining parts is allowed to proceed.

Note, quarter. A crotchet.

Noter (Fr.) (nō-tā.) To write out a tune, or air.

Note raddoppiate (It.) (*no*-tĕ räd-dōp-pē-*ä*-tĕ.) Repeated notes.

ō as in *tone*; ŏ as in *dove*; ŏ as in *not*; ŭ as in *up*; ü the French sound of *u*.

185

Note, reciting. The note in a chord upon which the voice dwells in chanting until it comes to a cadence. See Dickinson's "Music in the History of the Western Church."

Notes, accented. Notes upon which emphasis is placed; in common time the first and third notes, and in triple time the first note.

Notes, accessory. Notes situated one degree above and one degree below the principal note of a turn.

Notes, accidental. Chromatic tones that do not belong to the harmony; passing-tones.

Notes, added. Notes written upon ledger, or added lines.

Note, scolte (It.) (nō-tē skōl-tĕ.) Staccato note.

Notes coulées (Fr.) (nōt koo-lā.) Slurred notes.

Notes de goût (Fr.) (nōt dŭh goo.) Notes of embellishment.

Notes, essential. The notes of a chord which constitutes its real component parts in distinction from accidental and ornamental notes.

Notes, passing. When one or more notes of a harmonic chord move to a tone foreign to the harmony, the chord otherwise remaining unchanged, these notes are called *passing-notes*.

Note sensible (Fr.) (nōt sänh-sēbl.) The leading-note of the scale; the seventh of the scale.

Note, sixteenth. A semi-quaver.

Note sixty-fourth. A hemidemisemiquaver.

Notes liées (Fr.) (nōt lē-ā.) Tied notes.

Notes, ornamental. Appoggiaturas, grace-notes, all notes of embellishment, not forming an essential part of the harmony.

Notes, stopped. In music for the violin, violoncello, and similar instruments, those notes that are sounded while the string is pressed.

Notes, subsidiary. Accessory notes.

Notes, tied. Notes having a tie over them denoting they are to be bound together. If on the same degree of the staff the tone must be sustained throughout.

Note, thirty-second. A demisemiquaver.

Note, tonic. The first note of any scale, the key-note.

Noteur (Fr.) (nō-tŭr.) Music-copyist.

Note, whole. A semibreve.

Notturni (It.) (nŏt-*toor*-nĕ.) Nocturnes.

Notturno (It.) (nŏt-*toor*-nō.) A nocturne; a composition suitable for an evening performance; a serenade.

Novellette. A name bestowed by Schumann (Op. 21) on instrumental compositions free in form, romantic in character, and characterized by a variety of contrasting themes.

Nowel (Fr.) (*No-ël*.) A Christmas carol. See *Noel*.

Nuances (Fr. pl.) (nü-änh-*s*.) Lights and shades of expression; variety of intonation.

Numerical notation. A system of notation first introduced by Rousseau, in which the first eight of the numerals are substituted for the eight notes, and points, ciphers, etc., for such other characters as represent pauses, time, etc.

Numero (It.) (noo-mā-rō.) } *Number*,
Numerus (Lat.) (*nū*-mĕ-rŭs.) } used to denote musical time, rhythm, harmony.

Nuóvo (It.) (noo-ō-vō.) New; *di nuóvo*, newly, again.

Nuptial songs. Wedding-songs; marriage-songs.

Nut. The small bridge at the upper end of the fingerboard of a guitar or violin, over which the strings pass to the pegs, or screws.

O

O. This letter, forming a circle or double C, was used by the mediæval monks as the sign of triple time from the idea that the *ternary*, or number *three*, being the most perfect of all numbers, and representing the *Trinity*, would be best expressed by a circle the most perfect of all figures. The imperfect, or common time, was designated by a C, or semi-circle — a broken circle.

O, before a consonant (It.) (ō.) } **Or, as,**
Od, before a vowel (It.) (ōd.) } **either.**

ă as in *ah*; ā as in *hate*; ă as in *at*; ē as in *tree*; ĕ as in *eh*; ī as in *pine*; ĭ as in *pin*;

Haydn Crossing the English Channel

Piccolo

Organ

Oboe

OBBLIGATO

Obbligáto (It.) (ōb-blē-*gä*-tō.) ⎫ *Indis-*
Obbligáti (It. pl.) (ōb-blē-*gä*-tē.) ⎪ *pen-*
Obligé (Fr.) (ŏb-lĭ-*zhä*.) ⎬ *sable,*
Obligat (Ger.) (ōb-lĭ-*gät.*) ⎪ *neces-*
⎭ *sary;*
a part, or parts which cannot be omitted, being indispensably necessary to a proper performance; a temporary solo in a concerted work, often misspelled *Obligato*.

Obbligato accompaniment. An accompaniment that must be used.

Ober. (Ger.) (*ō*-bĕr.) Upper, higher.

Ober-manual (Ger.) (*ō*-bĕr ma-noo-*äl*.) The upper manual.

Ober-stimme (Ger.) (*ō*-bĕr-*stĭm*-mĕ.) Treble, upper voice part.

Ober-tasten (Ger.) (*ō*-bĕr-*täs*-t'n.) The black keys.

Ober-theil (Ger.) (*ō*-bĕr-*tīl*.) The upper part.

Ober-werk (Ger.) (*ō*-bĕr-värk.) Upper work; highest row of keys.

Oblique motion. When one part ascends, or descends, whilst the others remain stationary.

Oblíquo (It.) (ōb-*lē*-quō.) Oblique.

Oboe (Ger.) (*ō*-bō-ĕ.) ⎫ A hautboy; also,
Oboé (It.) (*ō*-bō-ā.) ⎭ the name of an organ-stop; a double reed-instrument of much antiquity. It was a prominent instrument in the earliest orchestras. The double reed used gives to the tone a number of the higher harmonics with considerable prominence, the tone-color becoming thin, penetrating, and somewhat nasal. The oboe can depict direct pathos, as in the funeral march of the *Heroic* symphony; innocence and simplicity; and above all, rustic gayety, it being the pastoral instrument of the orchestra, and used in this manner in Beethoven's sixth symphony, and numerous other works. The compass of the instrument is about, but the lower notes are somewhat hoarse and the highest ones a trifle forced and screaming in quality, the best effects being attained in the middle register. The nearer we keep to the key of C, the easier and the more natural the oboe part will be. Because of its very characteristic color the oboe should not

OCTAVE, DOUBLE

be too freely used in prominent passages. The orchestra usually receives its pitch from the oboe, that instrument giving "A" at the beginning of each concert or composition The oboe requires great steadiness of blowing, the player becoming exhausted by *holding in*, not by exhaling, his breath. Consult A. Elson's "Orchestral Instruments," and Prout's "Orchestra."

Oboé da caccia (It.) (*ō*-bō-ā dä *kät*-tshē-ä.) A larger species of *oboe* with the music written in the alto clef. Its place is taken, in the modern orchestra, by the English horn. Bach calls for this oboe and the oboe d'amore in his *Passion music* and his *Christmas oratorio*. The oboe d'amore, which was also called *oboe lungo*, produced a delicate and sweet tone, while the *oboe da caccia* corresponded to the tenoroon oboe, or corno inglese. The latter though not in common use, is occasionally introduced into the scores of modern operas, as in Halévy's "Jewess" Meyerbeer's "Huguenots," etc.

Oboe d'amore (It.) (*ō*-bō-ā d' a-*mo*-re.) ⎫
Oboé lúngo (It.) (*ō*-bō-ā *loon*-gō.) ⎭
A species of *oboe*, longer than the ordinary *oboe*, with a thinner bore and lower pitch.

Octava (Lat.) (ŏk-*tä*-vä.) Octave; applied to 4-foot organ-stops.

Octava acuta (Lat.) (ŏk-*tä*-vä ă-*kū*-tä.) The octave raised by transposition.

Octava alta (It.) (ŏk-*tä*-vä *äl*-tä.) Play the passage an octave higher.

Octava gravis. (Lat.) (ŏk-*tä*-vä *grä*-vĭs.) The octave lowered by transposition.

Octave. An interval of eight diatonic sounds, or degrees; also the name of an organ-stop.

Octave, augmented. An interval consisting of thirteen half-steps or semitones.

Octave clarion. A 2-foot reed-stop in an organ.

Octave, Contra. See *Tablature*.

Octave, diminished. An interval consisting of eleven half-steps or semitones.

Octave, double. An interval of two octaves, or fifteen notes in diatonic progression.

ō as in *tone*; ǫ as in *dove*; ŏ as in *not*; ŭ as in *up*; ü the French sound of *u*.

Octave fifteenth. An organ-stop of bright, sharp tone, sounding an octave above the fifteenth.

Octave flute. A small flute an octave higher than the German, or ordinary flute; a piccolo.

Octave hautboy. A 4-foot organ reed-stop; the pipes are of the hautboy species.

Octave, large. The third octave, indicated in the German tablature by capital letters. See *Tablature.*

Octaves, short. Those lower octaves of old organs the extreme keys of which, on account of the omission of some of the intermediate notes, lie nearer to each other than those of the full octave.

Octave-stop. An organ-stop an octave above corresponding stops.

Octave trumpet-stop. An organ-stop an octave higher than the ordinary trumpet stop.

Octave twelfth-stop. An organ-stop the scale of which is an octave above the twelfth.

Octavflötchen (Ger.) (ōk-täf-flôt-kh'n.) An octave flute; a flageolet.

Octavflöte (Ger.) (*ōk*-täf-*flö*-tĕ.) Octave flute, flageolet; also an organ-stop of 4-foot scale.

Octavflötlein (Ger.) (*ōk*-täf-*flôt*-līn.) An octave flute.

Octavina (Lat.) (*ŏk*-tä-*vēe*-nä.) An old stringed instrument resembling a spinet, about three octaves in compass, and tuned an octave higher than the spinet and harpsichord.

Octavine (Fr.) (ŏk-tä-*vēen*.) The small spinet.

Octet. } A composition for eight parts,
Octett. } or for eight voices.

Octo-bass. A stringed instrument invented by M. Vuillaume, of Paris — the low octave of the violoncello. It is of colossal size, with three strings, and for the left hand there are movable keys, by which the string is pressed on the frets placed on the finger-board, with seven other pedal keys for the foot of the player. The sounds are full and strong, of great power without roughness.

Octochord (Lat.) (*ŏk*-tō-kŏrd.) An instrument like a lute, with eight strings.

Octuor (Fr.) (ŏk-*twōr*.) A piece in eight parts, or for eight voices, or instruments. An *Octette.*

Ode. A Greek word signifying an air, or song; a lyrical composition, of greater length and variety than a song; resembling the cantata.

Odelet. A short ode.

Odéon (Ger.) (ō-dā-ŏn.) } A circular
Odeum (Lat.) (*ō*-dĕ-ŭm.) } building in which the ancient Greeks and Romans held their festivals; a concert-room or hall for musical performance.

Oder (Ger.) (*ō*-dĕr.) Or, or else; *für ein oder zwei claviere,* for one or two manuals.

Odische Musik (Ger.) (*ō*-dĭ-shĕ moo-*zĭk*.) Vocal music.

Œuvre (Fr.) (üvr.) Work, composition, piece — a term used in numbering a composer's published works in the order of their publication.

Œuvre chef (Fr.) (üvr sheh.) A principal work; a masterpiece.

Œuvre premier (Fr.) (üvr prĕ-mĭ-*ā*.) The first work.

Off. In organ music, a direction to push in a stop, or coupler; as *choir to Gt. off.*

Offen-flöte (Ger.) (*ŏf*-f'n *flö*-tĕ.) An open flute; organ stop. See also *Clarabella.*

Offértoire (Fr.) (ŏf-fĕr-*twär*.) }
Offertório (It.) (ŏf-fĕr-*tō*-rĭ-ō.) }
Offertorium (Lat.) (ŏf-fĕr-*tō*-rĭ-ŭm.) }
Offertory (Eng.) (*ŏf*-fĕr-tō-ry.) }
A hymn, prayer, anthem, or instrumental piece sung or played during the collection of the offertory. It follows the *Credo* in the Mass.

Officium (Lat.) (ŏf-*fē*-shĭ-um.) The Mass.

Officium defunctorum (Lat.) (ŏf-*fē*-shĭ-um dĕ-fŭnk-*tō*-rŭm.) A requiem or Mass for the dead.

Officium diurnum (Lat.) (ŏf-*fē*-shĭ-um dĭ-*ŭr*-nŭm.) The *horæ,* the day service in the Catholic Church.

Officium divinum (Lat.) (ŏf-*fē*-shĭ-um dĭ-*vē*-nŭm.) High Mass.

Officium matutinum (Lat.) (ŏf-*fē*-shĭ-um mă-*tū*-tĭ-nŭm.) Early Mass.

Officium nocturnum (Lat.) (ŏf-*f ē*-shĭ-um nŏk-*tŭr*-nŭm.) The *hora* sung at night.

Officium vespertinum (Lat.) (ŏf-*f ē*-shĭ-ŭm vĕs-pĕr-*tē*-num.) Vespers; evening service.

Oficleida (It.) (ō-fē-klä-dä.) ⎱ The
Oficleide (It.) (ō-fē-klä-dĕ). ⎰ ophicleide.

Ohne (Ger.) (*ō*-nĕ.) Without.

Ohne Begleitung (Ger.) (*ō*-nĕ bĕ-*glī*-toong.) Without accompaniment.

Ohne Pedale (Ger.) (*ō*-nĕ pĕ-*dä*-lĕ.) Without the pedals.

Oktave (Ger.) (ōk-*tä*-fĕ.) Octave, eighth.

Olio. A miscellaneous collection of musical pieces.

Olivettes (Fr.) (ōlĭ-*vĕt*.) The dances of the peasants after the olives are gathered.

Ollapodrida (Spa.) (ōl-lä-pō-*drē*-dä.) An olio; a medley.

Omnes (Lat.) (*ŏm*-nēs.) ⎱ All. See
Omnia (Lat.) (*ŏm*-nĭ-ä.) ⎰ *Tutti.*

Ondeggiaménto (It.) (ōn-ded-jē-ä-*men*-tō.) *Waving;* an undulating, or tremulous motion of the sound; also a *close shake* on the violin.

Ondeggiánte (It.) (ōn-ded-jē-*än*-tĕ.) Waving, undulating, trembling.

Ondeggiare (It.) (ōn-dēd-jē-*ä*-rĕ.) Wave the voice.

Ondulé (Fr.) (ŏnh-dü-*lā*.) Waving, trembling.

Onduliren (Ger.) (ōn-doo-*lēe*-r'n.) A tremulous tone in singing, or in playing the violin, etc.

One-lined octave. See *Tablature.*

Ongarese (It.) (ōn-gä-*rā*-zē.) ⎱ Hun-
Ongherese (It.) (ōn-ghĕ-*rā*-zĕ.) ⎰ garian.

Onzième (Fr.) (ŏnh zhĭ-*ām*.) Eleventh.

Open diapason. An organ-stop, generally made of metal, and thus called because the pipes are open at the top. It commands the whole scale, and is the most important stop of the instrument.

Open harmony. See *Dispersed Harmony.*

Open note. A note on the open string of a violin, etc.

Open pedal. The right-hand pedal of a pianoforte; that which raises the dampers and allows the vibrations of the strings to continue.

Open stop. That which regulates the open pipes.

Open string. The string of a violin, etc., when not pressed by the finger.

Open tone. A tone produced on an open string.

Open unison stop. The open diapason stop.

Oper (Ger.) (*ō*-pĕr.) ⎱ A drama set to
Opera (It.) (*ō*-pĕ-rä.) ⎰ music, for voices and instruments, and with scenery, decorations, and action. The term is also applied to any *work*, or publication of a composer. (See also *Opus.*) *Opera*, more fully *opera di musica*, was a form of musical composition evolved shortly before 1600, by some enthusiastic Florentine amateurs who sought to bring back the Greek plays to the modern stage. But they achieved much more than this, for they led the way from polyphony to homophony, from counterpoint to monody. The chief parts of the opera, apart from the overture, are the recitative, aria, chorus, and the various kinds of *ensemble* — duet, trio, quartet, quintet, sextet, etc. — of which the *finale* is the most important. The finale is generally of a complex form; duets, trios, etc., are mostly, and choruses sometimes, modelled on the aria form, or, rather, forms. (See *Aria, Recitative.*) In France operas are classified as follows: GRAND OPERA, in which the plot is throughout earnest, and there are no spoken passages. OPÉRA BOUFFE. A comic opera, but one of a much lighter character than an *opéra comique.* OPÉRA COMIQUE. An opera with spoken dialogue, as distinguished from the *grand opera*, which has no spoken dialogue. OPÉRA LYRIQUE. A lyric opera. Thus "Carmen" would be classed as an *Opéra Comique.* In America the term *comic opera* has a much lower application and is applied to the *opéra bouffe.* Consult A. Elson's "Critical History of Opera," and Grove's Dictionary.

Operetta. A little opera, generally in a light and playful vein.

Ophicleide (*ŏf*-ĭ-klīd.) A large bass wind-

ō as in *tone*; ǫ as in *dove*; ŏ as in *not*; ŭ as in *up*; ü the French sound of *u.*

instrument of brass, sometimes used in large orchestras, but chiefly in military music. It has a compass of three octaves, and the tone is loud and of deep pitch. This instrument is now obsolete in Germany and America, although still employed in France and England. It has about the compass of the bass-tuba, but has a more rasping and rough tone. Mendelssohn used the ophicleide very successfully in his "Elijah," and in his overture to "Midsummer Night's Dream" comically expresses the snoring of the drunken weaver, Bottom, by means of it. The bass-tuba takes the place of the ophicleide in almost all modern works, but does not reproduce its peculiarly raucous tone.

Ophicleide stop. The most powerful manual reed-stop known, in an organ, of 8 or 4-foot scale, and is usually placed upon a separate sound-board, with a great pressure of wind.

Ophicleidist. A performer on the ophicleide.

Opus (Lat.) (ō-pŭs.) } Work, composition; as, Op.
Opus (Ger.) (ō-poos.) }
1, the first work, or publication of a composer. The numeration of musical works by *opus* numbers began in the last part of the eighteenth century. Mozart was the first great composer whose works have an occasional *opus* number, but Beethoven was the first to use this mode of numeration regularly. Properly, the number of an *opus* refers to the order of publication, *not* of composition. An *opus* may include several numbers or may consist of a single piece.

Orage (Fr.) (ō-razh.) A *storm;* the name of an organ-stop intended to imitate the noise of a storm.

Oratoire (Fr.) (ŏr-ä-twär.) Oratorio.

Oratório (It.) (ŏr-ä-tō-rĭ-ō.)
Oratorium (Lat.) (ŏr-ä-tō-rĭ-oom.) } Oratorio.
Oratorium (Ger.) (ŏr-ä-tō-rĭ-oom.) } A species of musical drama consisting of airs, recitatives, trios, choruses, etc. It is founded upon some Scriptural narrative, and performed without the aid of scenery and action. The oratorio received its name from the *oratory* of the church where it was at first performed. It was originally given with costumes and scenery, like an opera. It was founded by St. Philip Neri (d. 1595), and Emilio del Cavaliere whose first great oratorio was performed in 1600. The opera and oratorio went hand in hand for some decades, until Carissimi abolished dramatic action and made oratorio a concert, without operatic adjuncts. The oratorio gradually became the contrapuntal form that called forth the highest efforts of Bach and Handel. Consult Naumann's "History of Music," Ritter's "Students History of Music," Dickinson's "Music in the History of the Western Church," and Upton's "Standard Oratorios."

Orchestra. That portion of a theatre or concert-room where the musicians play; the term is also applied to the performers themselves, collectively.

Orchester (Ger.) (ōr-khĕs-tĕr.) } The orchestra.
Orchéstra (It.) (ōr-käs-trä.) }
Orchestre (Fr.) (ŏr-kĕstr.) } The orchestras of Bach or Handel were small compared with the modern Grand Orchestra. The first composers who had some semblance of the modern orchestra in their works, were Haydn and Mozart. Beethoven was, however, the true founder of the orchestra. The different parts of the orchestra can be classified as follows: The string band, or the *Strings* — first violins (soprano), second violins (alto), violas (tenor), and 'cellos and contra-basses (bass). The harp, which has become a member of most modern orchestras, is not to be classed with the strings, but stands by itself. The wooden wind-instruments, or the *wood-wind,*— flutes, oboes, clarinets, and bassoons, being respectively soprano, alto, tenor, and bass, of the quartette (for four-part writing is the foundation of almost all orchestral work), and an English horn, a piccolo, a contra-bassoon, and a bass-clarinet, are admitted to the ranks of this division. In the brass band we find the French horns, trumpets (generally replaced in American orchestras by cornets — a poor substitution), tubas, and trombones. The percussion is counted with the brasses, and consists of kettledrums, and occa-

sionally bass drum, side-drum, cymbals, triangle, gong, and other less important instruments. In the large modern works, by Wagner, the orchestra has numbered 116 men; and other composers, such as Richard Strauss, who may be called the chief orchestral colorist of his time, used instruments not numerated, in the above list. Consult Prout's "The Orchestra," or A. Elson's "Orchestral Instruments and their Use."

Orchestration. The performance of an orchestra; the arranging of music for an orchestra; scoring; instrumentation.

Orchestrer (Fr.) (ŏr-kĕs-trā.) To score.

Orchestrina (ŏr-kĕs-trē-nä.) } An instrument combining the power and variety of a full orchestra.
Orchestrion. (ŏr-kĕs-trĭ-ŏn.)

Organ. The largest and most harmonious of wind-instruments of music, of very ancient origin, used in churches and large concert halls. It contains numerous pipes of various kinds and dimensions and of multifarious tones and powers; in solemnity, grandeur, and rich volume of tone it stands preeminent over every other instrument. The pipes are made to sound by means of compressed air provided by bellows; it contains several sets (ranks), several or many pipes to each key on a *sound-board* above the *wind-chest*, whither the air is conveyed from the *bellows* through a *wind-trunk*. Two obstacles have to be removed before the air in the wind-chest can reach the *pipes*. *Pallets* closing *grooves* have to be pulled down, and *slides* below the mouths of the pipes have to be shifted. Each key is, by a complex mechanism (*sticker, roller, tracker*, etc.), in communication with a pallet. As soon as a key is pressed down the corresponding pallet gives the air access to a groove, above which are placed all the pipes belonging to the key. Still, no sound is produced, as the air is intercepted by the slides, each of which runs below the mouths of a whole rank of pipes (a complete rank of pipes being equal in number to the keys of the keyboard). Now, by pulling out a *stop*, one of the slides — which are flat boards with holes in them — is shifted in such a way as to bring the holes just below the mouths of the pipes. On drawing out one stop we can, by playing on the keyboard, make one of the ranks of pipes speak; on drawing out two stops, two ranks of pipes; and so on. The organ may vary greatly in size. A small organ may have but a single manual, while a very large one may have four or even five manuals, in addition to the pedals. These manuals are thus named:

ENGLISH	GERMAN	FRENCH	ITALIAN
Gt. org. manual	Hauptwerk (Man. I.)	Grand orgue (1er clavier)	Principales
Choir manual	Unterwerk (Man. II.)	Positif (2e clavier)	Organo di coro.
Swell manual	Schwellwerk (Man. III.)	Clav. de recit (3e clavier)	Organo d'espressione
Solo manual	Soloklavier (Man. IV.)	Clav. des bombardes (4e clav.)	Organo d'assolo
Echo manual	Echoklavier (Man. V.)	Clav. d'echo (5e clavier)	Organo d'eco

There are numerous *stops* on the manuals, as, for example — open diapason, double-diapason, stopped diapason, principal, fifteenth, flute, dulciana, gamba, bassoon. Mixture, sesquialtera, and some others are stops consisting of several ranks of pipes, sounding the fifth, third, etc., of the fundamental note in a higher octave, these last being intended to add the harmonics which are deficient in some of the pipes, especially in the stopped diapasons (see *Harmonies* and *Acoustics*). The pipes can be either of wood or metal. There are two distinct kinds of pipes: *flue-pipes* or *reed-pipes*. In flue-pipes the air is set in vibration by striking a sharp edge, in reed-pipes by a free reed of metal. See Zahm's "Sound and Music" for a full explanation of vibration of air in pipes. There are also stopped pipes and open pipes, the stopped ones sounding an octave lower than open ones of the same length, and having a much hollower tone. We use the term 8-foot, 4-foot, 16-foot, etc., in connection with organ-stops. 8-foot pipes give the pitch that we would get from a piano key; 4-foot, an octave higher, 2-foot, two octaves higher, 16-

ō as in *tone*; ŏ as in *dove*; ŏ as in *not*; ŭ as in *up*; ü the French sound of *u*.

191

foot an octave lower, etc. Thus, if we play the following note on different stops it would sound the following different pitches:

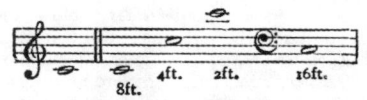

(musical notation: 8ft., 4ft., 2ft., 16ft.)

The pedals have also various stops and present a keyboard for the feet. By *couplers* the different manuals and the pedals can be combined with one another. Consult Gates' "Pipe and Strings," Hopkins and Rimbault's "The Organ," Wm. H. Clarke's "An Outline of the Structure of the Pipe-organ." See also *Stops* and *Pipes*.

Organ, barrel. A hand-organ.

Organ-bellows. A machine for supplying the pipes of an organ with wind.

Organ-blower. Person or machine providing air for sounding organ pipes.

Organ-buffet. A very small organ.

Organ, cabinet An improvement on the reed-organ, designed for the parlor and for small churches.

Organ, choir. In an organ with three rows of keys, the first or lower row used to accompany the choir, solos, duets, etc.

Organe (Fr.) (ŏr-*gän*.) An organ.

Organ, full. An organ performance with all the registers or stops in use.

Organ, great. In an organ with three rows of keys, usually the middle row so-called, because it contains the greatest number of stops, and the most important ones, and the pipes are voiced louder than those in the swell, or choir organ.

Organ, hand. A common wind-instrument carried about the street, consisting of a cylinder, turned by hand, the revolution of which causing the machinery to act upon the keys, produces a number of well-known airs and tunes.

Organ-harmonium. A reed-instrument, the reeds of which are voiced to imitate organ-stops.

Organical. Relating to the organ.

Organique (Fr) (ŏr-gän-*ēk*.) Relating to the organ.

Organist. A player on the organ.

Organísta (It.) (ŏr-gän-*ēs*-tä.) } An or-
Organista (Spa.) (ŏr-gän-*ēs*-tä.) } ganist.

Organo piéno (It.) (ŏr-*gä*-nō pē-*ăy*-nō.) }
Organo pléno (Lat.) (ŏr-*gä*-nō *plā*-nō.) }
The full organ with all the stops drawn.

Organ-point. A long pedal note, or stationary bass, upon which is formed a series of chords, or harmonic progressions.

Organ-reed. An organ of small size, the keys of which open valves that allow the wind from the bellows to act upon reeds.

Organ-stop. A collection of pipes of like tone and quality, passing through the whole or a part of the compass of an organ or a register

Organ. swell In an organ with three rows of keys, usually the upper row controlling one or more sets of pipes enclosed by a set of sliding shutters, the opening or closing of which by the swell pedal increases or diminishes the tone by degrees. at the pleasure of the performer.

Organum. A word used in various senses by the ancient composers. Sometimes it meant the organ itself; at other times it meant that kind of choral accompaniment which comprehended the whole harmony then known, a constant succession of fourths and fifths. It probably existed even in the sixth or seventh century, but it was first arranged as a system by Hucbald, a monk of St. Amands, about A.D. 900. Examples:

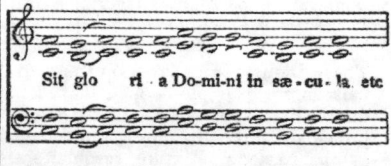

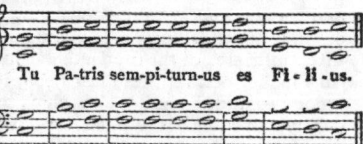

(musical notation: Sit glo ri a Do-mi-ni in sæ-cu-la, etc)

(musical notation: Tu Pa-tris sem-pi-turn-us es Fi-li-us.)

There were also examples of *Organum* in which the lowest voice gave a drone-bass.

ă as in *ah*; ā as in *hate*; ă as in *at*; ē as in *tree*; ĕ as in *eh*; ī as in *pine*; ĭ as in *pin*;

ORGEL   OVERTURE

Orgel (Ger.) (ōr-ghĕl.) An organ.

Orgel-bälge (Ger.) (ōr-ghĕl-bāl-ghĕ.) Organ-bellows.

Orgel-bank (Ger.) (ōr-ghĕl-bänk.) Organist's seat.

Orgel-kunst (Ger.) (ōr-ghĕl-koonst.) The art of organ-playing; art of constructing an organ.

Orgel-musik (Ger.) (ōr-gh'l moo-zĭk.) Organ-music.

Orgeln (Ger.) (ōr-gĕln.) To play on the organ.

Orgel-pfeife (Ger.) (ōr-gĕl-pfī-fĕ.) Organ-pipe.

Orgel-platz (Ger.) (ōr-ghel-pläts.) Organ-loft.

Orgel-punkt (Ger.) (ōr-g'l-poonkt.) Organ-point.

Orgel-schule (Ger.) (ōr-g'l-shoo-lĕ.) School, or method for the organ.

Orgue de salon (Fr.) (ōrg dŭh sä-lŏnh.)

Orgue expressif (Fr.) (ōrg-ĕgz-prā-sef.) The harmonium.

Orgue hydraulique (Fr.) (ōrg hĭ-drō-lēk.) Hydraulic-organ; water-organ.

Orgue plein (Fr.) (ōrg plănh.) Full organ; all the stops drawn.

Ornamental counterpoint. A kind of counterpoint admitting the use and mixture of every kind of note.

Ornamental notes. Appoggiaturas, grace-notes; all notes not forming an essential part of the harmony, but introduced as embellishments. See *Trill*, *Turn*, *Grace-notes*, *Appoggiatúra*, *Acciaccatúra*.

Ornaménti (It. pl.) (ōr-nä-men-tĕ.) Ornaments, graces, embellishments, as the *appoggiatúra*, *turn*, *tril* etc.

Ornaménte (It.) (ōr-nä-tä-men-tĕ.)
Ornáto (It.) (ōr-nä-tō.)
Ornamented, adorned embellished.

Orphéon (Fr.) (ōr-fay-on.) In France, a singing-society composed of men. *Orphéoniste*, a member of such a society.

Osánna (It.) (ō-zän-nä.) Hosanna.

Osannare (It.) (ō-zän-nä-rĕ.) To sing hosannas.

Oscillation. The vibration of tones in organ-tuning, etc.

Oscuro (It.) (ōs-koo-rō.) Obscure.

Osservánza (It.) (ōs-sĕr-vän-tsä.) Observation; attention; strictness in keeping time.

Ossía (It.) (ōs-sē-ä.) Or; otherwise; or else. Indicating another way of playing a passage.

Ossía più fácile (It.) (ōs-sē-ä pē-oo fä-tshē-lĕ.) Or else in this more easy manner.

Ostinato (It.) (ōs-tēe-nah-tō.) Obstinate, continuous, unceasing; adhering to some peculiar melodial figure, or group of notes.

Otez les anches (Fr.) (ō-tā lĕ sänhsh.) Remove, or push in the reeds.

Otium (Lat.) (ō-shĭ-ŭm.) Adagio; slowly; with grace and ease.

Ottáva (It.) (ŏt-tä-vä.) An octave; an eighth.

Ottáva álta (It.) (ŏt-tä-vä äl-tä.) The octave above, an octave higher; marked thus, 8va.

Ottáva bássa (It.) (ŏt-tä-vä bäs-sä.) The octave below, marked thus, 8va bássa.

Ottava supra (It.) (ŏt-tä-vä soo-prä.) The octave above.

Ottavína (It.) (ŏt-tä-vē-nä.) The higher octave.

Ottavíno (It.) (ŏt-tä-vē-nō.) The *fláuto piccolo*, or small octave flute.

Ottemole. A group of eight notes, marked with the figure 8.

Ottétto (It.) (ŏt-tet-tō.) A composition in eight parts, or for eight voices or instruments.

Ou (Fr.) (oo.) Or.

Outer voices. The highest and lowest voices.

Ouvert (Fr.) (oo-vār.) Open.

Ouverture (Fr.) (oo-vār-tür.) ⎫
Overtúra (It.) (ō-vĕr-too-rä.) ⎬ An introductory
Ouvertüre (Ger.) (ō-fĕr-too-rĕ.) ⎨ part to an
Overture (Eng.) (ō-vĕr-tshūr.) ⎭ oratorio, opera, etc.; also an independent piece for a full band or orchestra, in which case it is called a *concert overture*. Lulli first gave shape to the overture in the seventeenth century. The overtures of Bach and Handel follow his style. These had a short and simple slow movement and then a quicker and longer fugal or contrapuntal one. Mozart founded the classical overture

ȯ as in *tone*; ô as in *dove*; o͝o as in *not*; ŭ as in *up*; ü the French sound of *u*.

193

in the *sonata-allegro* form (which see). Mendelssohn was the chief founder of the concert overture, while Beethoven established the freer *dramatic* style. The medley overture, which began in England, is a succession of tunes from an opera, placed in contrast. Most light operas, and many of the operas of Rossini have the medley form. See also *Prelude, Vorspiel.*

P

P. Abbr. of *Pedal* (P. or Ped.); *piano* (*p*); *pp, pianissimo*; *ppp, pianississimo*; Verdi and Tschaikowsky have employed *ppppp* several times. P. F., *pianoforte*; *più forte* (louder); *poco forte* (rather loud); *fp, fortepiano* (*i.e.* loud, instantly diminishing to soft); *mp, mezzo-piano* (half-soft); and in Fr. organ-music, *P* stands for *Positif* (choir-organ).

Padiglione (It.) (pa-dil-*yo*-neh.) Bell of horn, etc.

Pacataménte (It.) (pä-kä-tä-*men*-te.) Placidly, quietly, calmly.

Pæan. } Among the *ancients* a song of
Pean. } rejoicing in honor of Apollo; a loud and joyous song; a song of triumph.

Pagina (It.) (*pä*-jē-nä.) A page or folio; *Pagina d'Album.* See *Album-leaf.*

Palco (It.) (päl-kō.) The stage of a theatre.

Pallet. A spring-valve in the wind-chest of an organ covering a channel leading to a pipe, or pipes.

Pan. One of the deities in Grecian mythology, so-called because he exhilarated the minds of all the gods with the music of his *pipe* which he invented, and with the *cithern*, which he played skilfully as soon as he was born.

Pandean. An epithet formed from the name of *Pan*, and applied to any music adapted to the *Fistulæ Panis*, or pipes of Pan.

Pandean pipes. } One of the most an-
Pan's pipes. } cient and simple of musical instruments; it was made of reeds or tubes of different lengths fastened together and tuned to each other, stopped at the bottom and blown into by the mouth at the top.

Pantalonnade (Fr.) (pänh-tä-lŏnh-*näd*.) A pantaloon dance; a merry dance of buffoons.

Pantomima (It.) (*pän*-tō-mē-mä.) Pantomime.

Pantomime. An entertainment in which not a word is spoken or sung, but the sentiments are expressed by mimicry and gesticulation accompanied by instrumental music.

Parallel intervals. In intervals passing in two parallel parts in the same direction; consecutive intervals.

Parallel motion. When the parts continue on the same degree, and only repeat the same sounds; also, two parts continuing their course and still remaining at exactly the same distance from each other.

Paraphrase. A transcription or rearrangement of a vocal or instrumental composition, for some other instrument or instruments, with more or less brilliant variations.

Parfait (Fr.) (*pahr*-fay.) Perfect (as to intervals), complete (as to cadences), pure (as to intonation).

Parlándo (It.) (pär-*län*-dō.) } Accented;
Parlánte (It.) (pär-*län*-tĕ.) } in a declamatory style; in a recitative, or speaking style.

Parlor-organ. A small organ suited to a private dwelling.

Parodía (It.) (pä-rō-*di*-ä.) A parody; music, or words comically altered, and adapted to some new purpose.

Parodiare (It.) (pä-rō-de-*ä*-rĕ.) To parody; to burlesque.

Paroles (Fr.) (pah-*roll*.) The words.

Part. The music for each separate voice or instrument.

Part, complementary. That part of a fugue additional to the subject and counter-subject.

Párte (It.) (pär-tĕ.) A part, or portion of a composition; a part or rôle in an opera.

Párte cantánte (It.) (pär-tĕ kän-tän-tĕ.) The singing, or vocal part; the principal vocal part, having the melody.

Parte clarino (It.) (klä-*ree*-nō.) The highest, or first trumpet part.

Partie (Fr.) (pär-*tē*.) See *Párte.*

ă as in *ah*; ā as in *hate*; ă as in *at*; ē as in *tree*; ĕ as in *eh*; ī as in *pine*; ĭ as in *pin*

Partial turn. A turn consisting of the chief note and three small notes, the leading note of which may be either a large or small second above the principal.

Participating tones. Accessory tones.

Parti d'accompagnamento (It.) (pär-tē d'ak-kŏm-pän-yä-*men*-tō.) Accompanying voices.

Parti di ripieno (It.) (pär-tē dē rē-pē-*āy*-nō.) Parts not obbligato; supplementary parts.

Partie du violon (Fr.) (pär-tē dü vē-ō-lŏnh.) A violin part.

Parties de remplissage (Fr.) (pär-tē düh ränh-plē-säzh.) Parts which fill up the middle harmony between the bass and upper part.

Partiménti (It. pl.) (pär-tē-*men*-tē.) Exercises for the study of harmony and accompaniment.

Partiménto (It.) (pär-tē-*men*-tō.) An exercise, figured bass. See *Partimenti*.

Partita (It.) (par-*tee*-ta.) The earliest form of the instrumental suite. The *partita* had often fewer movements than the suite and was treated in a freer manner.

Partition (Fr.) (pär-tē-sĭ-ŏnh.) ⎫
Partitur (Ger.) (pär-tĭ-*toor*.) ⎪ A
Partitúra (It.) (pär-tē-*too*-rä.) ⎬ *score;*
Partizióne (It.) (pär-tē-tsē-*ō*-ne.) ⎭ a *full score,*
or entire draft of a composition for voices, or instruments, or both.

Partíto (It.) (pär-*tē*-tō.) Scored, divided into parts.

Partitur-spiel (Ger.) (pär-tē-toor-spēl.) Playing from the score.

Part-songs. Songs for voices in parts, an unaccompanied choral composition for at least three parts; a melody harmonized by other parts more or less freely, but from which counterpoint is for the most part excluded. The part-song owes its origin to the habit prevalent among the Germans of adding simple harmonies to their folk-songs. The part-song is always simpler in construction than the glee, and is intended for chorus.

Pas (Fr.) (*pah.*) A step, or a dance in a ballet. *Pas de deux*, a dance performed by two dancers. *Pas seul*, a solo dance. Also, not; as *pas trop lent.* not too slow.

Pas redoublé (Fr.) (pä rĕ-doo-blā.) A quick-step; an increased, redoubled step.

Passacáglia (It.) (päs-sä-*käl*-yē-a.) ⎫ A
Passacaille (Fr.) (päs-sä-käl.) ⎬ species
of chaconne, a slow dance with divisions on a ground-bass in triple rhythm. Rather bombastic in character. It very closely resembles the chaconne, but is more generally minor than the latter. The word is generally derived from *Pasar Calle* (Spa.), going along the streets, but its inflated character and slow tempo lead us to imagine that the Passacaglia came from *Passo Gallo* — the rooster-step! Brahms has used the Passacaglia as finale in his fourth symphony.

Passage. Any phrase, or short portion of an air, or other composition. Every member of a strain, or movement, is a *passage.*

Passages, pedal. Those parts of a composition in which the pedals are used.

Passággio (It.) (päs-*säd*-jē-ō.) A passage, or series of notes.

Passamézzo (It.) (päs sä-*met*-sō.) An old slow dance, little differing from the *Pavane,* but somewhat more rapid. Generally in ¾ rhythm.

Passepied (Fr.) (pass-pi-*ay*.) A sort of jig; a lively old French dance in ¾, ⅜, or ⅙ time; a kind of quick minuet, with three or more strains, or reprises. A *Paspy.*

Pas seul (Fr.) (pä sŭl.) A dance by one performer.

Passing modulation. A transient modulation.

Passing-notes. Notes which do not belong to the harmony, but which serve to connect those which are essential, and carry the ear more smoothly from one harmony to another.

Passionáta (It.) (päs-sē-ō-*nä*-tä.) ⎫
Passionataménte (It.) (päs-sē-ō-nä-tä-*men*-tĕ.) ⎪
Passionáte (It.) (päs-sē-ō-*nä*-tĕ.) ⎬
Passionáto (It.) (päs-sē-ō-*nä*-tō.) ⎭
Passionate; impassioned; with fervor and pathos.

ŏ as in *tone;* ô as in *dove;* ŏ as in *not;* ŭ as in *up;* ü the French sound of *u.*

Passióne (It.) (päs-sē-ō-ně.) Passion, feeling.

Passióne (It.) (päs-sē-ō-ně.) The Passion, or seven last words of the Saviour on the cross, set to solemn and devotional music.

Passiones (Lat.) (păs-sĭ-ō-nēs.) Passion music.

Passion music.
Passions-musik (Ger.) (päs-sĭ-ōnsmoo-zĭk.) } Music picturing the sufferings of the Saviour, and his death. Although originally used in the Catholic Church, the subject became a favorite one with the Protestant German composers. Bach set the subject several times, and his "Passion Music, according to St. Matthew," is one of the great masterpieces of music.

Passo (It.) A step. See *Pas*.

Pasticcio (It.) (päs-*tit*-tshe-ō.) } A medley; an
Pastiche (Fr.) (păs-*tish*.) } opera made up of songs, etc., by various composers; the poetry being written to the music, instead of the music to the poetry.

Pastoral. A musical drama, the personages and scenery of which are chiefly rural. A *pastoral* is also any lyrical production, the subject of which is taken from rural life; and the Italians give the same name to an instrumental composition written in the pastoral style.

Pastorále (It.) (päs-tō-*rä*-lĕ.) } Pastoral;
Pastorelle (Fr.) (päs-tō-*rĕl*.) } rural; belonging to a shepherd; a soft movement in a pastoral and rural style.

Pastorello (It.) (päs-tō-*rĕl*-lō.) A pastoral.

Pastourelle (Fr.) (päs-too-*rĕll*.) One of the movements of a quadrille.

Patética (It.) (pä-*tä*-tē-kä.) Pathetic.

Pateticaménte (It.) (pä-tä-tē-kä-*men*-tĕ.) Pathetically.

Patético (It.) (pä-*te*-tē-kō.) }
Pathétique (Fr.) (pä-te-tēek.) } Pathetic.
Pathetisch (Ger.) (pä-*tāt*-ish.) }

Pathetic. Applied to music when it excites emotions of sorrow, pity, sympathy, etc.

Pathetica (Lat.) (pä-*thĕt*-ĭ-kä.) Pathetic.

Patiménto (pä-tē-*men*-tō.) Affliction. grief, suffering.

Patriotic. Songs having for their theme love of country.

Pauke (Ger.) (*pou*-kĕ.) A kettledrum.

Pauken (Ger. pl.) (*pou*-k'n.) Kettledrums; also, to thump.

Pauken-fell (Ger.) (*pou*-k'n-fĕll.) The leather, or skin of the kettledrum.

Pauken-klang (Ger.) (*pou*-k'n-*kläng*.) The clang of kettledrums.

Pauken-klöpfel (Ger.) (*pou*-k'n-*klŏp*-fĕl.) }
Pauken-schlägel (Ger.) (*pou*-k'n-*shläy*-g'l.) }

Pauken-stock (Ger.) (*pou*-k'n-*stŏk*.) Kettledrum-stick.

Pauken-schläger (Ger.) (*pou*-k'n-*shläy*-gĕr.) }
Pauker (Ger.) (pou-kĕr.) Kettle drummer.

Paulatinaménte (It.) (pou-lä-*tē*-nä-*men*-tĕ.) Gently, slowly.

Pausa (It.) (pou-zä.) }
Pausa (Spa.) (pou-zä.) } A pause.
Pausa (Lat.) (paw-zä.) }

Páusa generále (It.) (pou-zä jā-nē-*rä*-lĕ.) }
Pause générale (Fr.) (pōz zhä-nä-rä-lĕ.) } A pause, or rest for *all* the performers.

Pause (Fr.) (pōz.) A semibreve rest; also a whole bar's rest in any species of time.

Pause (Ger.) (*pou*-zĕ.) A rest.

Pause (Eng.) A character (⌒) which lengthens the duration of a note or rest over which it is placed, beyond its natural value, or at the pleasure of the performer. When placed over a double bar, it shows the termination of the movement or piece. See *Hold, Fermata*.

Pause, demi (Fr.) (pōz dĕ-*mē*.) A half-rest.

Pausen (Ger.) (*pou*-z'n.) } To
Pauser (Fr.) (pō-zā.) } pause;
Pausiren (Ger.) (pou-*zē*-rĕn.) } to rest; to keep silence.

Pause, general. A general cessation or silence of all the parts.

ă as in *ah*; ā as in *hate*; ă as in *at*; ē as in *tree*; ĕ as in *eh*; ī as in *pine*; ĭ as in *pin*;

Pavan (Eng.) ⎫ A grave,
Pavána (It.) (pä-*vä*-nä.) ⎬ stately dance,
Pavane (Fr.) (pä-*vänh*.) ⎭ which took its
name from *pavano*, a peacock. It was danced by princes in their mantles and ladies in gowns with long trains, whose motions resembled those of a peacock's tail. It is in quadruple rhythm, and is among the even rhythms what the Saraband is among the triple.

Paventáto (It.) (pä-věn-*tä*-tō.) ⎫ Fear-
Paventóso (It.) (pä-věn-*tō*-zō.) ⎬ ful;
timorous; with anxiety and embarrassment.

Pavillon (Fr.) (pä-vē-yŏnh.) The bell of a horn or other wind-instrument.

Pavillon chinois (Fr.) (*pä*-vē-yŏnh shē-nwä.) An instrument with numerous little bells, which impart brilliancy to lively pieces, and pompous military marches.

Peal. A set of bells tuned to each other; the changes rung upon a set of bells.

Pean. A pæan; a song of praise.

Peanna (It.) (pě-*ä*-nä.) A pæan; a hymn, or song of praise.

Ped. An abbreviation of pedal.

Pedal. This word is used in many different ways in music, but always has reference to some mechanism moved by the foot. The most general usage of the word applies to the *piano pedals*. The object of the right-hand piano-pedal is to raise the dampers from the wires, so that the sound may be prolonged after the finger of the player has left the key. This device existed upon the old harpsichords in the shape of a knee-stop. John Broadwood, in London, first introduced the pedal on his pianos in 1783. The marking of this pedal is generally *Ped.* for its application and ✱ or ⊕ for its discontinuance. *Con pedale*, or *con ped.*, indicates the employment of the damper-pedal, without explicit directions as to when to apply and to release it. The German terms *senza sordine* (without dampers), also means to *employ* the damper-pedal, and *con sordine* to *cease* using it. Another system which has found vogue in America is the following mark ⌐┘ indicating exactly when to put down and when to release the damper pedal.

As it is the bass notes which are generally sustained in piano-playing, it was desirable to have a damper-pedal which should sustain the lower tones without blurring the upper ones. This has been introduced in the *bass damper-pedal* (often the centre pedal when there are three upon the piano) which lifts the dampers from the *lowest* strings only. A still greater improvement has been made in the *sostenuto pedal*, which, on being pressed down, raises only those dampers which belong to the notes which are being held down by the player at the time of its application. By this means we can sustain any note, or notes, at will. The damper-pedal has no effect upon the highest notes of the piano since these are not provided with dampers. This is done that the high tones may furnish overtones (see *Acoustics* and *Harmonics*) when the lower tones are sounded. The pedal at the left hand is called the soft pedal. It is to decrease the tone of the strings. The majority of the notes on a modern piano have three strings to each key or tone. On the grand piano, and on some uprights, the soft pedal pushes the entire action, keys, hammers, etc., to one side, so that the hammer, when the soft pedal is depressed, strikes but *one* of these three wires. Therefore, the soft pedal is marked *una corda* (one string), and the sign for releasing it is *tre corde* (three strings). (See also *a due corde*.) The Germans also use the words *mit Verschiebung* (pushing aside) for the soft pedal, and *ohne Verschiebung* for its release. The soft-pedal mechanism on the majority of upright pianos simply brings the hammer nearer the wire, so that it cannot deliver as strong a blow. On the old square pianos the soft pedal placed a piece of felt between the hammer and the wire, thus muting the sound, but also altering its quality. This device is still applied to some pianos as a *practice-pedal*, so that the pianist need not disturb the neighborhood with her exercises. Sometimes this practice-pedal is set permanently by a stop, which is drawn out when it is desired to mute the instrument, and pushed back when the normal tone is desired. On the *organ* the pedals are a set of keys played with the feet, and present-

ō as in *tone* : â as in *dove* ; ŏ as in *not*; ŭ as in *up*; ü the French sound of *u*.

ing different tone-qualities according to the stops used, exactly as with the manuals. Sometimes these pedals are built in a fan-like radiation from the player, for greater convenience. Pianos are sometimes built with a pedal-keyboard to assist organists in practising their feet without the necessity of going to the organ. There are also mechanical pedals upon the organ, such as the *swell pedal*, which automatically opens the blinds which surround the swell organ and thus increases the volume of its tone. There are also pedals which draw all the stops, pedals which act as couplers, etc. The piano *damper-pedal* is often miscalled the *loud pedal*, but it should be used for its sustaining effect and not for loudness. Pianos are generally provided with three pedals, the right-hand one being the *damper-pedal*; the middle one the *bass damper-pedal*, or the *sostenuto pedal* (sometimes also the *practice-pedal*), and the left-hand pedal always the *soft pedal*. There is generally no distinguishing sign for the *bass damper* or the *sostenuto*, the sign of the *damper-pedal* being used for all three. The soft pedal is sometimes called *harp pedal*, and in France, *petite pedale*.

Pedal, damper. See *Pedal*.

Pedal-claves (Ger.) (pĕd-*äl-klä-*fĕs.)

Pedal-claviatur (Ger.) (pĕd-*äl-klä-*vĭ-ä-*toor*.)
The pedal keyboard, in an organ.

Pedále (It.) (pē-*dä*-lĕ.) A pedal bass, or a stationary bass. See *Pedal point*.

Pedale (Ger. pl.) (pĕ-*dä*-lĕ.) The pedals are that set of keys in an organ which are played by the feet; in organ-music, it means that the notes or passage must be played by the feet.

Pedale doppelt (Ger.) (pē-*dä*-lĕ *dōp*-pĕlt.)

Pedále dóppio (It.) (pä-*dä*-lĕ *dōp*-pē-ō.)
Double pedals, in organ-playing; playing the pedals with both feet at once.

Pedále d'organo (It.) (pä-*dä*-lĕ *d'ōr*-gä-nō.) The pedals in an organ.

Pédales (Fr. pl.) (pä-*däl*.) The pedals.

Pédales de combinaison (Fr.) Combination pedals.

Pedal, extension. The loud pedal of a pianoforte; that by which the sound is increased and extended.

Pedal-harfe (Ger.) (pĕd-*äl-här*-fĕ.) ⎱ A
Pedal-harp (Eng.) (*pĕd*-äl-härp.) ⎰ harp with pedals, to produce the semi-tones. See *Harp*.

Pedáli (It. pl.) (pĕ-*dä*-lē.) The pedals.

Pedaliéra (It.) (pĕ-dä-lē-*ä*-rä.) The pedal keys of an organ.

Pedal keys. That set of keys belonging to an organ or similar instrument, which is played by the feet.

Pedal note. A note held by the pedal while the harmony formed by the other parts proceeds independently.

Pedal, open or loud pedal. That which raises the dampers and allows the full vibration of the strings to continue.

Pedal pianoforte. A pianoforte having pedals suitable for organ-practice.

Pedal pipes. Pipes in an organ which sound only when the pedals are pressed.

Pedal point. A sustained bass, or pedal note, held on or sustained for several bars, while a variety of chords are introduced.

Peg (Ger., *Wirbel*; Fr., *cheville*; It., *bischero*.) In the violin, etc., one of the movable wooden pins set in the head, and used to tighten or loosen the tension of the strings; a tuning-pin.

Pentameter. In poetry, a verse of five feet, the first two of which may be either dactyls, or spondees, the third always a spondee, and the last two anapests.

Pentametro (It.) (pĕn-tä-mä-trō.) Pentameter; verse of five feet.

Pentatonic scale. A scale of five notes, sometimes called the *Scotch scale*, and similar to the modern diatonic major scales, with the fourth and seventh degrees omitted. The Chinese also use this scale. See *Scales*.

Per (It.) (*pair*.) For, by, from, in, through; *per l'organo*, for the organ; *per il flauto solo*, for solo flute.

Percussion (Eng.) (pĕr-*kŭsh*-ŏn.) ⎱
Percussióne (It.) (pär-koos-sē-*ō*-nĕ.) ⎰

ă as in *ah*; ā as in *hate*; ă as in *at*; ē as in *tree*; ĕ as in *eh*; ī as in *pine*; ĭ as in *pin*;

Striking, as applied to instruments, notes, or chords; or the *touch* on the pianoforte. A general name for all instruments that are struck, as a gong, drum, bell, cymbals, triangle, tambourine, all of which are used in the orchestra.

Perdéndo (It.) (pār-*den*-dō.) } Gradually decreasing the tone and the time; dying away, becoming extinct.
Perdendósi (It.) (pār-*den*-dō-zē.)

Perfect. A term applied to certain intervals and chords.

Perfect cadence. Dominant harmony followed by that of the tonic; a close upon the key-note preceded by the dominant.

Perfect close. A perfect cadence.

Perfect concords. } These are the unison, the perfect fourth, perfect fifth, and the octave.
Perfect consonances.

Perfect fifth. An interval containing three whole tones and one semi-tone.

Perfect fourth. An interval containing two whole tones and one semi-tone.

Perfect octave. An interval containing five whole tones and two semi-tones.

Perfect period. A complete termination satisfactory and agreeable to the ear.

Perfect time. Among the ancients a measure consisting of three beats in a measure and designated by the circle O.

Perfect triad. A fundamental note with its major third and perfect fifth.

Perfétto (It.) (pĕr-*fāt*-tō.) Perfect, complete.

Pergolo (It.) (pĕr-gō-lō.) A box in a theatre; a stage for operatic performance.

Perigourdine (pĕr-ĭ-goor-dēn.) A French dance in ⅜ rhythm.

Period (Eng.) } A complete and perfect musical sentence, containing at least two phrases and bringing the ear to a perfect conclusion or state of rest. See *Form*.
Période (Fr.) (pā-rĭ-ōd.)
Periode (It.) (pā-rē-ō-dĕ.)

Période musicale (Fr.) (pā-rĭ-ōd mü-zē-kăl.) A musical period.

Periodenbau (Ger.) (pĕ-rĭ-ōd'n-bou.) Composition; the construction of musical periods.

Period, imperfect. A close not satisfactory to the ear.

Period, perfect. A termination agreeable to the ear.

Perlé (Fr.) (pĕr-lā.) Pearled, brilliant; *cadence perlée*, brilliant cadence.

Per ogni tempi (It.) (pār ōn-yē *tem*-pē.) A term sometimes introduced in a motet, signifying that it is suited to any time and occasion.

Perpetual canon. A canon so constructed that its termination leads to its beginning, and hence may be perpetually repeated.

Per recte et retro (Lat.) (pĕr *rĕk*-tĕ ĕt *rā*-trō.) Forward, then backward; the melody or subject reversed, note for note.

Personæ dramatis (Lat.)(*pĕr*-sō-nē *drăm*-ă-tĭs.) The characters of an opera or play.

Personaggio (It.) (pĕr-sōn-*äd*-jē-ō.) One of the characters of a play.

Pes (Lat.) (pēs.) Foot, measure, species of verse; rhythm, time; also a kind of ground, or burden, the basis for the harmony in old English music.

Pesánte (It.) (pĕ-*zän*-tĕ.) Heavy, ponderous; with importance and weight, impressively.

Pesanteménte (It.) (pē-zän-tĕ-*men*-tĕ.) Heavily, forcibly, impressively.

Pestalozzian system. A system of *induction*, presenting the rudiments of study in their natural progressive order. It was first applied to music by a wealthy Swiss gentleman by the name of Pestalozzi.

Petit (Fr.) (pĕ-*tē*.) Little, small.

Petit chœur (Fr.) (pĕ-*tē* kür.) Little choir.

Petite flûte-a-bec (Fr.) (pĕ-*tēt* flüt-ä-bĕk.) A flageolet.

Petite flûte (Fr.) (pĕ-*tēt* flüt.) The small flute; the octave or piccolo flute.

Petits morceaux (Fr.) (pĕ-*tē* mŏr-*sō*.) Short pieces.

Petits pièces (Fr.) (pĕ-*tē* pĭ-*ās*.) Little pieces, short and easy compositions.

Petits riens (Fr.) (pĕ-*tē* rĭ-ănh.) Light, trifling compositions.

Petits violons (Fr.) (pĕ-*tē* vē-ō-lônh.) Small violins. The kit.

Pétto (It.) The chest, the breast; *vóce di petto*, the chest voice.
Peu (Fr.) (pŭh.) Little, a little.
Peu à peu (Fr.) (pŭh ä pŭh.) Little by little, by degrees.
Pézzi (It. pl.) (*pet*-si.) Fragments, scraps; select, detached pieces.
Pézzi concertanti (It. pl.) (pet-si kŏn-tshĕr-*tän*-tē.) Concerted pieces, in which each instrument has occasional solos.
Pézzi di bravura (It.) (pĕt-si di brä-*voo*-rä.) Compositions for the display of dexterity or rapid execution.
Pezzo (It.) (*pet*-sō.) A fragment; a detached piece of music.
Pfeife (Ger.) (*pfī*-fĕ.) Pipe, fife, flute.
Pfeifen (Ger.) (*pfī*-f'n.) To play on a fife or flute.
Pfeifen-deckel (Ger.) (*pfī*-f'n-*dĕk*-ĕl.) The stopper, or covering of an organ pipe.
Pfeifer (Ger.) (*pfī*-fĕr.) A fifer, a piper.
Phantasie (Ger.) (fän-tä-*zē*.) See *Fantasía*.
Phantasiren (Ger.) (fän-tä-*zē*-r'n.) Improvising.
Phantasirte (Ger.) (fän-tä-*zīr*-tē.) Improvised.
Phantasy. A fantasia.
Philharmonic (Ger.) (fĭl-här-*mŏn*-ĭk.) Music-loving.
Phone (Ger.) (fō-nĕ.) A sound or tone.
Phonetic. Vocal, representing sounds.
Phonetik (Ger.) (fŏ-*nĕt*-ĭk.) System of singing, or of notation and harmony.
Phonetics. } The doctrine or science of
Phonics. } sounds, especially those of the human voice.
Phonograph. An instrument invented in 1877, by Thomas A. Edison, by means of which sounds, either vocal or instrumental, the tones of the speaking voice, and even noises, can be recorded and reproduced. The records are made by a steel point working on soft material. In the improved phonograph (1895), wax was first substituted for tin-foil, which had been employed in the earlier phonographs. Still further improvements led to the employment of gutta percha. There were countless improvements made upon the device, leading to sound recordings of greater and greater fidelity. Other improvements in phonographic technology involved revolving the record at different speeds or RPMs (revolutions per minute). This allowed a longer section of music to be contained on each side of a record. Entire symphonies, operas and long jazz and popular works could be put on record with a minimum of disc changes. In subsequent decades, phonograph records have been mostly displaced by cassettes and permanent compact discs. However, the phonograph record still has its devotees.

Phrase. A short musical sentence; a musical thought or idea.
Phrase, extended. } Any variation of
Phrase, irregular. } a melody by which an unequal number of measures are used. The phrase in music may be regarded as a dependent division, like a single line in a poem. In simple music the phrases balance each other.
Phraser (Fr.) (frä-*zä*.) } Dividing the
Phrasing. } musical sentences into rhythmical sections. The punctuation of music.
Physharmonica (Gr.) (fĭs-här-*mŏn*-ĭ-kä.) An instrument, the tone of which resembles that of the reed-pipes in an organ, and is produced by the vibration of thin metal tongues, of a similar construction to those of the harmonium; the name is also applied to a stop in the organ with *free reeds*, and with tubes of half the usual length.
Piacére (It.) (pē-ä-*tshāi*-rĕ.) Pleasure, inclination, fancy; *a piacére*, at pleasure.
Piacévole (It.) (pē-ä-*tshe*-vō-lĕ.) Pleasing, graceful, agreeable.
Piacevolézza (It.) (pē-ä-tshe-vō-*let*-zä.) Gracefulness, sweetness.
Piacevolménte (It.) (pē-ä-tshĕ-vŏl-*men*-tĕ.) Gracefully, delicately.
Piaciménto (It.) (pē-ä-tshē-*men*-tō.) See *Piacére*.
Piagnévole (It.) (pē-än-*ye*-vō-lĕ.) Mournful, doleful, lamentable.

ä as in *ah*; ā as in *hate*; ă as in *at*; ē as in *tree*; ĕ as in *eh*; ī as in *pine*; ĭ as in *pin*;

Pianaménte (It.) (pē-ä-nä-*men*-tĕ.) Softly, gently, quietly.

Pianétto (It.) (pē-ä-*net*-tō.) Very low, very soft.

Piangéndo (It.) (pē-än-*gen*-dō.) Plaintively, sorrowfully.

Piangévole (It.) (pē-än-*ge*-vō-lĕ.) Lamentable, doleful.

Piangevolménte (It.) (pē-än-ge-vŏl-*men*-tĕ.) Lamenting, dolefully.

Pianíno (It.) (pē-ä-*nē*-nō.) A small pianoforte.

Pianíssimo (It.) (pē-än-*is*-sē-mō.) Extremely soft.

Piano (It.) (pee-*a*-no.) Soft.

Pianoforte or Piano. The piano comes from the combination of the two instruments of antiquity, the *Dulcimer*, and the *Monochord*. The immediate predecessors of the piano were the *Clavichord*, the *Harpsichord*, and the *Spinet* (see these words). The principle of striking the wires of the instrument with hammers was invented by Cristofori, a native of Padua, Italy, about 1710. The invention seems to have sprung up simultaneously in various countries, for very soon after (without knowing of the Cristofori invention) a Frenchman named Marius, a German named Schroeter, and an English monk at Rome, Father Wood, all brought forth the hammer action, but Cristofori was probably the first inventor of it, and his instruments, of which two still exist, were much the best. The name of the instrument came from the fact that the Harpsichord, called in Italy *Clavicembalo*, could not shade. Therefore Cristofori's instrument, which could alter the power of the tones, was called *Clavicembalo con piano e forte*, i.e., a harpsichord which could play soft and loud. The name has been shortened since that time. There are some extreme purists who attack the use of the word *Piano* and insist upon the full term *Pianoforte*, forgetting that if the former term is incorrect the word *pianist* is equally so, and the artist must be called a *pianofortist*. The piano at first made but slow headway. Bach thought it only fit for playing rondos and light music. It was only when Beethoven threw his influence on the side of the piano that the instrument began to outstrip its weak-toned or monotonous predecessors. (See *Technique*.) Great improvements were made in the piano in Germany, Silbermann manufacturing very sweet-toned instruments, and Stein inventing the soft pedal. But the best pianos at the beginning of the nineteenth century were made in England, where an Alsatian, named Erhardt, afterwards changed into Erard, and a Scotchman named Broadwood, made many improvements in the instrument, the latter inventing the damper-pedal. (See *Pedal*.) Cramer, Clementi, and Czerny developed the technique of the instrument, and the invention of the full grand piano caused Beethoven to produce his greatest sonata, in B flat, Op. 106. To describe the mechanism of the piano, its various shapes, etc., would scarcely be within the scope of a volume of this kind, but the student will find the following useful works of reference for details, Weitzmann's "History of Pianoforte Playing," Rimbault's "The Pianoforte," Hopkins' "Description and History of the Pianoforte," Bie's "Pianoforte" and Gates' "Pipe and Strings" (a short description of Piano, Violin and Organ). America soon began to outstrip the European countries in the manufacture of pianos. Probably the first piano made in this country was manufactured by John Behrent, in Philadelphia, in 1774. Boston at one time achieved preëminence in this branch of manufacture, through the invention of the iron bed-plate, by Jonas Chickering in 1843. In 1853, the house of Steinway was founded in New York, and since that time America has made as many and as good pianos as any country in the world. For details of the early stages of the piano industry in the United States, see Elson's "History of Music in America." The piano is given the following names in foreign countries: Germany, *Klavier*; France, *Piano*; Italy, *Piano*, or *Pianoforte*. The frame of the piano is now generally cast in a single piece, with cross-bars and bracings made to resist an enormous tension, for the total strain upon a concert-grand piano (called *Flügel* in Germany, and *Piano a queue* in France) is not far from thirty tons. Below this frame is the soundboard, of almost the entire length and breadth of the instrument. Upon the soundboard is a bridge which supports the strings, and transmits their vibrations to the soundboard. The strings of the upper five octaves of the piano are three to each single tone (called a *unison*), the lowest octaves having two strings or one to a unison. The lowest strings are woven around with copper or soft iron to cause them to vibrate more slowly. The *action* of the piano consists of its mechanism for striking, and consists of the key, the hopper or escapement (which throws the hammer against the wire), and the hammer.

Piano assai (It.) (pē-*ä*-nō *ȧs-sä-ē*.) As soft as possible.

Piano carré (Fr.) (pē-*ä*-nō kär-rā.) A square pianoforte.

Piano droit (Fr.) (pē-*ä*-nō drwä.) An upright pianoforte.

Pianoforte action. The mechanism of a pianoforte.

Pianoforte, Æolian. A pianoforte so united with a reed instrument that the same set of keys serve for both, or for either singly at the pleasure of the player.

Pianoforte, concert grand. The largest sized grand pianoforte.

Pianoforte, cottage. An upright pianoforte.

Pianoforte, dumb. A keyboard arranged for the practice of pupils without producing sound.

Pianoforte, electric. A pianoforte, the wires of which are vibrated by electromagnetism.

Pianoforte, grand. A wing-shaped pianoforte in which most of the octaves have for each note, three strings tuned in unison and struck at once by the same hammer.

Pianoforte hammer. That part of the mechanism of a pianoforte which strikes the wires.

Pianoforte melographic. A piano connected with which was an automatic movement, by which the improvisation of a composer was recorded.

Pianoforte, overstrung. An arrangement by which the strings of at least two of the lowest octaves are raised, running in respect to the other strings, diagonally above them. Almost all pianos are now overstrung.

Pianoforte, parlor grand. A grand pianoforte of the second size.

Pianoforte, piccolo. A small upright pianoforte.

Pianoforte school. A book of instruction for the pianoforte.

Pianoforte score. A score in which every part has been so arranged that it may be played on a pianoforte.

Pianoforte, upright. A pianoforte whose strings run obliquely or vertically upward.

Piano-player. An invention for playing the piano mechanically, which was first perfected in 1897. There are many devices for such playing which have been made and sold. The principle of almost all of them is a motive power of two pedals, like those of a cabinetorgan, which revolve a roll of heavy paper on which there are perforations which give the value of the notes and their pitch. There are also stops which regulate the expression, speed, and dynamic force of the strokes. There are more than sixty automatic fingers which are moved by the mechanism. The apparatus is not generally attached to the piano, but is quite separate, and set in front of it, with its fingers in proper position. Some pianos have been built to contain the piano-player as part of the mechanism of the instrument These pianos may be played by the fingers in the usual way or automatically as desired. In addition to the numerous automatic piano-players there are similar devices made for the organ, by which it can be played automatically, although it is also furnished with a keyboard for manual playing. For the several inventions of this character, there was made an overwhelming repertoire of perforated rolls representing every branch of music, even to the most classical. By means of these inventions a person without any technical knowledge of the instruments can become familiar with their chief master pieces, playing them himself.

Piano, mezzo (It.) (pē-ä-nō mĕt-zō.) Moderately soft.

Piano-piano (pē-ä-nō-pē-ä-nō.) Very soft.

ä as in *ah*; ā as in *hate*; ă as in *at*; ē as in *tree*; ĕ as in *eh*; ī as in *pine*; ĭ as in *pin*;

202

Mozart in Vienna

Piano

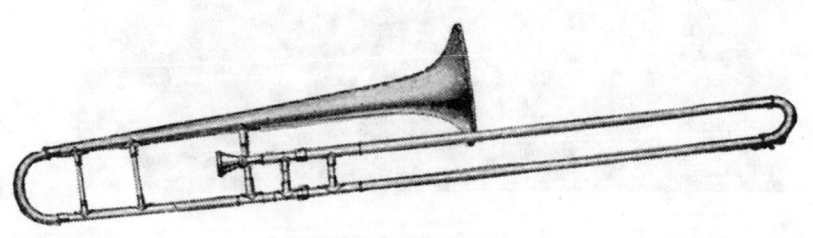

Slide Trombone

Piano solo. For the pianoforte only.

Piano-violino (It.) (pe-ä-nō-vē-ō-*lē*-nō.) A curious instrument invented in 1837. It is a common piano containing a violin arrangement inside of it, which is set in motion by a pedal. When this instrument is played upon it gives the sound of both violin and piano.

Pián-piáno (It.) (pē-än-pĕ-*ä*-nō.) Very softly; with a low voice. (See *Piano-piano.*)

Pian-pianissimo (It.) (pē-än-pē-än-*ēs*-sē-mō.) Exceedingly soft and gentle.

Piátti (It. pl.) (pē-ät-tē.) Cymbals.

Pibroch. (*pē*-brŏk.) A wild, irregular species of music peculiar to the Highlands of Scotland, performed on the bagpipe.

Picchiettáto (It.) (pē-kē-ĕt-*tä*-tō.) Scattered, detached; in violin-playing, it means that sort of staccáto indicated by dots under a slur.

Pícciolo (It.) (pēt-tshē-*ō*-lō.) ⎫
Piccolíno (It.) (pē-kō-*lē*-nō.) ⎬ Small; little.
Píccolo (It.) (*pē*-kō-lō.) ⎭

Piccolo. A 2-foot organ-stop, of wood pipes, producing a bright and clear tone in unison with the fifteenth.

Píccolo flute. A small flute. See *Flute.*

Picchettáto (It.) (pē-kĕt-*tä*-tō.) See *Picchiettáto.*

Pièce (Fr.) (pĭ-*ās*.) A composition or piece of music; an opera or drama.

Pieces, fugitive. Short compositions of no permanent value.

Pieds (Fr. pl.) (pĭ-*ā*.) The foot; *avec les pieds*, with the feet, in organ-playing.

Piéna (It.) (pē-ā-nä.) ⎫
Piéno (It.) (pē-ä-nō.) ⎬ Full.

Pienaménte (It.) (pē-ā-nä-*men*-tĕ.) Fully.

Piéno córo (It.) (pē-*ä*-nō *kō*-rō.) A full chorus.

Piéno organo (It.) (pē-*ä*-nō ŏr-*gä*-nō.) With the full organ.

Pierced gamba. An organ-stop of the gamba species.

Pieta (It.) (pē-*ä*-tä.)
Pietosaménte (It.) (pē-ā-tō-zä-*men*-tĕ.) ⎬
Pietóso (It.) (pē-ā-*tō*-zō.) ⎭
Compassionately; tenderly; implying also a rather slow and sustained movement.

Pifferáre (It.) (pēf-fĕ-*rä*-rĕ.) To play upon the fife; also a piper, such as in Italy play pastoral airs in the streets at Christmas.

Pifferári (It. pl.) (pēf-fĕ-*rä*-rē.) Pipers. See *Pifferáre.*

Pífferina (It.) (pēf-fĕ-*rē*-nä.) A little fife.

Píffero (It.) (*pĕf*-fĕ-rō.) A fife, or small flute; also an organ-stop of 4-foot tone.

Pifferóne (It.) (pef-fĕ-*rō*-nĕ.) A large fife.

Pincé (Fr.) (*pănh*-sā.) *Pinched.* See *Pizzicáto.*

Pincer (Fr.) (*pănh*-sā.) To pluck a stringed instrument.

Pincés (Fr.) (*pănh*-sā.) A general name for stringed instruments which are played by plucking.

Pipe. Any tube formed of a reed, or of metal, or of wood, which, being inflated at one end, produces a musical sound. The *pipe*, which was originally no more than a simple oaten straw, was one of the earliest instruments by which musical sounds were attempted. (See *Horn, Stop,* and *Organ.*) Organ-pipes divide into two classes, the *reed* and the *flue-pipe.* The reed-pipe has its column of air set in vibration by means of a reed which is set in a box or reservoir. The air being forced into this box can only enter the pipe by pushing aside the reed, which is called the *tongue.* When this is lifted up, the air passes through the fissure; when the tongue springs back by its own elasticity, it closes the passage. The vibration of the tongue induces a rapid opening and closing of this fissure; the air penetrates at intervals, in regular puffs, and thus a sound is obtained. The *flue-pipe* is caused to sound by directing the wind against a thin edge in the mouth of the pipe, only a slight portion of the current of air entering the pipe, but this causes the column of air within to vibrate. Flue-pipes may be stopped or open (see *Organ*). For description of the method or vibration of various kinds of pipes, see Blaserna's "Sound and Music," Zahm's "Sound and Music," and Pole's " Phi-

---

ō as in *tone;* ô as in *dove;* ŏ as in *not;* ŭ as in *up;* ü the French sound of *u.*

losophy of Music." A single pipe can, if desired, produce not only a single tone, but an entire series of tones.

Pipeau (Fr.) (pēe-pō.) A pipe.

Piper. A performer on the pipe; pipers were formerly one of the class of itinerant musicians, and performed on a variety of wind-instruments, as the bagpipe, musette, etc.

Pipes of pan. A wind-instrument consisting of a range of pipes bound together, side by side, and gradually lessening with respect to each other in length and diameter; Pandean pipes.

Pipes, pandean. Pan's pipes.

Piqué (Fr.) (pĭ-*kā*.) ⎱ To play on a vio-
Piquer (Fr.) (pĭ-*kā*.) ⎰ lin, etc., a series of notes a little staccáto, and with a light pressure of the bow to each note.

Pitch. The acuteness or gravity of any particular sound, or of the tuning of any instrument. Pitch can most scientifically be defined as the *rate of vibration*. Rapid vibrations mean a high tone, slow vibrations a deep one. It seems strange that one cannot represent a fixed tone, as, for example, middle C, to the mind by a set number of vibrations, but the standard of pitch has always been a variable one and the note in question might consist of more or less vibrations according as it belonged to a higher or lower standard of pitch. Thus the note A, which now commonly has 440 vibrations, in 1858 was given 448, and in 1699 had only 404, while Handel's tuning-fork, dated 1740, gives the same note 416 vibrations. The standard of pitch has been gradually rising since the days of Bach and Handel, in whose time it was about two-thirds of a tone deeper than at present. Concert-pitch does not mean any definite pitch, but merely the pitch which this or that manufacturer chose as best suited to his instruments. It was, however, always a high pitch. In 1859, the French government reformed the matter of the varying and acute *concert-pitches* by establishing the pitch of one-lined A (the scientists' A [3]) at 435 vibrations per second. Prof. Charles R. Cross, in his "Historical Notes Relating to Musical Pitch in the United States," says: "In 1889, the National Music Teachers' Association at its Philadelphia meeting adopted the French pitch, and the National League of Musicians, at Milwaukee, in March, 1891, also urgently recommended the adoption of this standard. For several years prior to this date, the question of bringing the standard pitch used for pianos and organs into unison with the low pitch which had come to be the generally accepted pitch for orchestral use, had been agitated by a number of persons engaged in the manufacture of pianos and organs, and especially by the late Gov. Levi K. Fuller, of the Estey Organ Co., of Brattleboro, and Mr. William T. Miller, of Boston. Finally, at a meeting of the Piano Manufacturers' Association, held in New York, March 31, 1891, it was unanimously decided that it was desirable that a uniform pitch should be adopted in the United States, and a committee was appointed, of which Mr. William Steinway was chairman, and Gov. Levi K. Fuller, secretary, to consider what standard should be adopted. This committee collected much evidence relating to the subject, and in response to a request therefor, received expressions of opinion from a large number of manufacturers and others interested in the determination of a standard together with sample tuning-forks giving the pitch then in use by those sending them. The committee reported in favor of the adoption of the A of 435 double vibrations per second as a standard of pitch, and their recommendation was adopted by the association. It was also decided to call the newly adopted standard the *International Pitch*." However, the pitch which became common in America soon later was "A=440". Germany kept a pitch slightly higher than this. The relative pitch of two tones in proportion to each other has been determined, even in ancient times, by the measurement of the segments of a vibrating string, or of a tube, the proportion of length agreeing with the proportion of vibrations. The proportions of pitch in true intervals, according to scientific law, would be as follows:

Octave.	Major seventh.	Minor seventh.
2	15/8	16/9
Major sixth.	Minor sixth.	Perfect fifth.
5/3	8/5	3/2
Diminished fifth.	Perfect fourth.	Major third.
36/25	4/3	5/4
Minor third.	Major second.	Minor second.
6/5	9/8	16/15

The logarithms of these ratios would be as follows :

Octave.	Major seventh.	Minor seventh.
301	273	250
Major sixth.	Minor sixth.	Perfect fifth.
222	204	176
Diminished fifth.	Augmented fourth.	Perfect fourth.
158	143	125
Major third.		Major second.
97	Minor third.	51
	79	
	Minor second.	
	28.	

Thus, if middle, or one-lined C has 260 vibrations per second, this note being a perfect fifth above it would have the proportion of three to two, *i.e.*, three-halves of $260 = 390$; this note an octave above the last would have twice its vibrations, *i. e.*, 780; this note a major third above middle C would have five-fourths of $260 = 325$; and in the table of logarithms a fifth added to a fourth, a minor third to a major sixth, a minor second to a major seventh, etc., will give the logarithm of the octave. The above would be the proportion if any musical interval were given in true intonation, but in our system, only the octave intervals are thus given. See *Tempered Scale*. Consult Pole's " Philosophy of Music " for full tables of relative pitch of intervals. For names of notes on different pitches (octaves) see *Tablature*.

Più (It.) (pēe-*oo*.) More.

Più allégro (It.) (pēe-oo äl-*lāy*-grō.) A little quicker, more lively.

Più fórte (It.) (pēe-oo *fŏr*-tĕ.) Louder.

Più lénto (It.) (pēe-oo *len*-tō.) More slowly.

Più mósso (It.) (pēe-oo *mōs*-sō.) ⎫
Più móto (It.) (pēe-oo *mō*-to.) ⎬ motion, quicker.

Più piáno (It.) (pēe-oo pē-*ä*-nō.) Softer.

Più più (It.) (pēe-oo pēe-oo.) Somewhat more.

Più présto (It.) (pēe-oo *pres*-tō.) Quicker, more rapidly.

Più vívo (It.) (pēe-oo *vē*-vō.) More lively, more animated.

Píva (It.) (*pēe*-vä.) A pipe, a bagpipe.

Pizzicándo (It.) (pit-sē-*kän*-dō.) ⎫
Pizzicáto (It.) (pit-sē-*kä*-tō.) ⎬
Pinched; meaning that the strings of the violin, violoncello, etc., are not to be played with the bow, but pinched, or snapped with the fingers, producing a *staccáto* effect.

Placebo (Lat.) (*plä*-sĕ-bō.) In the Roman Catholic church, the vesper hymn for the dead, commencing " Placebo Domino."

Placenteraménte (It.) (plä-tshĕn-tĕr-ä-men-tĕ.) Joyfully.

Placidaménte (It.) (plä-*tshée*-dä-men-tĕ.) Calmly, placidly, quietly.

Plácido (It.) (*plä*-tshēe-dō.) Placid, tranquil, calm.

Plagal. Those ancient modes, in which the melody was confined within the limits of the dominant and its octave.

Plagal cadence. A cadence in which the final chord on the tonic is preceded by the harmony of the sub-dominant.

Plagalisch (Ger.) (plä-*gä* lĭsh.) Plagal.

Plain chant (Fr.) (plănh-shänh.) The plain-song. See *Cánto Férmo*.

Plain counterpoint. ⎫ Simple counterpoint.
Plain descant. ⎬

Plain trill. A trill ending without a turn, also called incomplete trill. Written. Played.

Plain-song. The name given to the old ecclesiastical chant when in its most simple state and without those harmonic appendages with which it has since been enriched. See Stainer & Barrett, Dickinson's " Music in the History of the Western Church," or Helmore's " Plain-Song."

Plainte (Fr.) (plănht.) A complaint, a lament.

Plaintif (Fr.) (plănh-tēf.) Plaintive, doleful.

Plaisant (Fr.) (plā-zänh.) Pleasing.

ō as in *tone ;* ŏ as in *dove ;* ŏ as in *not ;* ŭ as in *up ;* ü the French sound of *u.*

Plaisanteries (Fr.) (plā-zänh-t'rē.) Amusing, light compositions.

Planxty. Old harp music of a lively, tuneful kind.

Plaqué (Fr.) (plä-*kā*.) *Struck at once*, without any arpéggio, or embellishment.

Plaquer (Fr.) (plä-kā.) To strike at once, speaking of chords.

Plectrum (Lat.) (*plĕk*-trŭm.) A quill, or piece of ivory or hard wood used to twitch the strings of the mandolin, lyre, etc. (It.) *Penna*.

Plein jeu (Fr.) (plănh zhü.) Full organ; the term is also applied to a mixture-stop of several ranks of pipes.

Plein jeu harmonique (Fr.) (plănh zhü här-mŏnhn-*ĕk*.) A mixture-stop in an organ.

Pleno organo (Lat.) (*plā*-nō ŏr-*gä*-nō.) Full organ.

Plus (Fr.) (plü.) More.

Plus animé (Fr.) (plü sä-nē-mā.) With more animation.

Plus lentement (Fr.) (plü *länht*-mänh.) Slower, more slowly.

Pneumatic (nū-*măt*-ĭk.) Relating to the air or wind.

Pneumatic action. } Mechanism
Pneumatic lever. } intended to lighten the touch, etc., in large organs.

Pneumatic organ. An organ moved by wind, so named by the ancients to distinguish it from the hydraulic organ, moved by water.

Pocetta (It.) (pō-tshāt-tä.) } A kit, a
Poche (Fr.) (pōsh.) } small violin used
Pochette (Fr.) (pō-shĕt.) } by dancing masters.

Pochettíno (It.) (pō-kĕt-*tē*-nō.) } A
Pochétto (It.) (pō-*ket*-tō.) } very
Pochíno (It.) (pō-*kē*-nō.) } little

Pochissimo (It.) (pō-*kēs*-sē-mō.) A very little, as little as possible.

Póco (It.) (*pō*-kō.) Little.

Póco adágio (It.) (*pō*-kō ä-dä-jē-ō.) A little slower.

Póco allégro (It.) (*pō*-kō äl-lāy-grō.) A little faster.

Póco animáto (It.) (*pō*-kō än-ē-mä-tō.) A little more animated.

Póco a póco (It.) (pō-kō ä pō-kō.) By degrees, little by little.

Póco a póco crescéndo (It.) (pō-kō ä pō-kō krĕ-*shen*-dō.) Gradually louder and louder.

Póco a póco diminuéndo (It.) (pō-kō ä pō-kō dē-mē-noo-*en*-dō.) Gradually diminishing.

Póco fórte (It.) (*pō* kō *fŏr*-tĕ.) Moderately loud, a little loud.

Póco lárgo (It.) (*pō*-kō *lär*-gō.) } Moderately
Póco lénto (It.) (*pō*-kō *len*-tō.) } slow.

Póco méno (It.) (*pō*-kō *may*-nō.) A little less, somewhat less.

Póco piáno (It.) (*pō*-kō pē-ä-nō.) Somewhat soft.

Póco più (It.) (*pō*-kō *pēe*-oo.) A little more, somewhat more.

Póco più allégro (It.) (*pō*-kō *pēe*-oo äl-*lā*-grō.) A little quicker.

Póco più forte (It.) (pō-kō pēe-oo *fŏr*-tĕ.) A little louder.

Póco più lárgo (It.) (pō-kō pēe-oo *lär*-gō.) }
Póco più lénto (It.) (pō-kō pēe-oo *len*-tō.) } A little slower.

Póco più mósso (It.) (pō-kō pēe-oo mōs-sō.) A little faster.

Póco più piáno (It.) (pō-kō pēe-oo pē-ä-nō.) A little softer.

Póco présto (It.) (*pō*-kō *pres*-tō.) Rather quick.

Poggiáto (It.) (pŏd-jē-*ä*-tō.) Dwelt upon, leaned upon.

Pói (It.) (*pō*-ē.) Then, after, afterwards: *piáno pói fórte*, soft, then loud.

Pói a pói (It.) (pō ē ä pō-ē.) By degrees.

Pói a pói tútte le córde (It.) (pō-ē ä pō-ē *too*-tĕ lĕ *kŏr*-dĕ.) All the strings one after another. Lift the soft pedal gradually. See *Pedal*.

Point (Fr.) (pwanh.) A dot.

Point de repos (Fr.) (pwänh dŭh rĕ-*pō*.) A pause.

Point d'orgue (Fr.) (pwänh d'ŏrg.) See *Organ point*. Also a Cadenza.

Pointée (Fr.) (pwänh-tā.) Dotted: *blanche pointée*, a dotted half-note.

Point final (Fr.) (pwänh fī-*näl*.) A final or concluding cadence.

ä as in *ah* ; ā as in *hate* ; ă as in *at* ; ē as in *tree* ; ĕ as in *eh* ; ī as in *pine* ; ĭ as in *pin*

206

Point of repose. A pause; a cadence.

Point, organ. A long or stationary bass note, upon which various passages of melody and harmony are introduced.

Pói ségue (It.) (pō-ē sā́-gwĕ.)
Pói seguénte (It.) (pō-ē sā-guĕ́n-tĕ.) Then follows, here follows.

Polácca (It.) (pō-*läk*-kä.) A Polish national dance in ¾ time. See *Polonaise*.

Polácca, alla (It.) (pō-*läk*-kä äl-lä.) In the style of a Polácca.

Polka. A lively Bohemian dance in ²⁄₄ time.

Polka mazurka (*pōl*-kä mă-zŭr-kä.) A dance in triple time, played slow, and having its accent on the last part of the measure.

Polka redowa (*pōl*-kä rĕ́d-ō-ä.) A dance tune in triple time, played faster than the polka mazurka, and having its accent on the first part of the measure.

Póllice (It.) (*pōl*-li-tshĕ.) The thumb.

Polonaise (pŏl-ō-*nāz*.)
Polonese.
Polonoise.
A Polish dance written in ¾ rhythm, and containing every contrast possible. The melody contains runs, skips, and many artificial groupings, and syncopation occurs freely both in the melody and the accompaniment. The accompaniment has many rhythmic changes in its construction, but this rhythm predominates:

The melody is often completed with the third beat of the measure. The polonaise, as its name indicates, is a Polish dance, and was as much of a processional as a dance, the former characteristic being clearly perceptible in some of the polonaises of Chopin and Liszt. The bolero is similar to the polonaise, but has not its dignity and loftiness. The bolero is of Spanish origin.

Polyphonic. *Polyphonic music* is *many voiced* or *plural-voiced* music, and is where the music is formed of two or more different melodies going on simultaneously. This is contrapuntal music, which had its origin about the year 1200, and was developed into a science by the early Flemish composers, in the fourteenth, fifteenth, and sixteenth centuries. It preceded homophonic music by many centuries, for the first attempt at a method of harmonic construction was printed in 1722, (by Rameau), and the first practical method of Harmony, by Catel, was published as late as 1790. *Homophonic music* is *united sounding*, that is, music of different parts, which, however, are blended into a single mass. Such music, represented by the modern harmonic progressions, is not three-hundred years old. Some writers make no distinction between the words *monophonic* and *homophonic*, but the definition above given will nevertheless be clearly grasped by the student, and the necessity of a distinction between the two schools understood. *Monophonic music* is *single sounding*, that is, melody, or passages given in unison. For countless ages the world was satisfied with this species of music, the division of music into parts being scarcely more than eight hundred years old. It is probable that all the music of the ancient world was monophonic, although there are some indications that the ancient Greeks employed a *drone bass* occasionally, and called it *Sumphonia*.

Pompös (Ger.) (pōm-*pŏs*.) Pompous, majestic.

Pomposaménte (It.) (pŏm-pō-zä-*men*-tĕ.) Pompously, stately.

Pompóso (It.) (pŏm-*pō*-zō.) Pompous, stately, grand.

Ponderóso (It.) (pŏn-dĕ-*rō*-zō.) Ponderously, massively, heavily.

Ponticéllo (It.) (pŏn-tē-*tshel*-lō.) The bridge of a violin, guitar, etc. The direction to bow near the bridge is *sull ponticello*, and the result is a thin, squeaky, but incisive tone.

Pont-neuf (Fr.) (pŏnh-nŭf.) A street ballad; a vulgar song.

Portaménto (It.) (pōr-tä-*men*-tō.) A term applied by the Italians to the manner or habit of sustaining and conducting the voice. It is also used to connect two notes separated by an in-

PORTAMÉNTO DI VOCE   POUR

terval, by gliding the voice from one note to the other, and by this means anticipating the latter in regard to intonation. Unfortunately there is another, totally different use of the term, in piano music; in this latter *portamento* is applied to a pressing accent, with some degree of separation, written thus:

The word *portamento* is decidedly misapplied in this case, for it means *carried over*, which is by no means the effect desired when the above sign is written. The fact that the singer uses the word in another, and its true sense, would seem to make a change desirable, and we suggest that the term *Demi-marcato* be applied to this mode of execution.

Portaménto di voce (It.) (pŏr-tä-*men*-tō dē *vō*-tshĕ.) Carrying the voice; the blending of one tone into another.

Portándo la vóce (It.) (pŏr-*tän*-dō lä *vō*-tshĕ.) Carrying the voice from one note to another.

Portár la battúta (It.) (pŏr-tär lä bät-too-tä.) To beat the time.

Portáre la vóce (It.) (pŏr-tä-rĕ lä vō-tshĕ.) To carry the voice.

Portative A portable organ.

Portáto (It.) (pŏr-*tä*-tō.) Sustained; drawn out.

Porte de voix (Fr.) (pŏrt důh vwä.) An appoggiatura, or beat.

Portée (Fr.) (pŏr-tä.) The staff.

Porter la voix (Fr.) (pŏr-tä lä vwä.) To carry the voice.

Porte-vent (Fr.) (pŏrt-vänh.) The pipe which conveys the wind from the bellows into the soundboard of an organ.

Porte-voix (Fr.) (pŏr-vwä.) A speaking-trumpet.

Portez la voix (Fr.) (pŏr-tä lä vwä.) See *Portándo la Voce*.

Portunal-flaut (Ger.) (pŏr-too-näl.) An organ-stop of the clarabella species, the pipes of which are larger at the top than at the bottom, and produce a tone of clarionet quality

Posáto (It.) (pō-*zä*-tō.) Quietly, steadily.

Posaune (Ger.) (pō-*zou*-nĕ.) A trombone: also, an organ-stop. See *Trombone*.

Posaunen (Ger.) (pō-*zou*-nĕn.) To sound on the trombone.

Posaunen-bläser (Ger.) (pō-*zou*-nĕn-*blä*-zär.)

Posauner (Ger.) (pō-*zou*-nĕr.) A trombone-player.

Posément (Fr.) (pō-*zä*-mänh.) Without hurry; moderately; gravely; slowly.

Positif (Fr.) (pō-zē-*tēf*.) } The choir-
Positiv (Ger.) (pō-zĭ-*tĭf*.) } organ, or lowest row of keys with soft-toned stops in a large organ; also, a small *fixed* organ, thus named in opposition to a *portative* organ.

Position. A shift on the violin, viola, or violoncello; the arrangement, or order, of the several members of a chord.

Position, close. A term given to a chord when its tones are near together.

Position, dispersed. A term given to a chord when its tones are remote from each other.

Position, fundamental. A term applied to an uninverted chord, its root forming the lowest note of the chord.

Positive. An appellation formerly given to the little organ placed in front of the full, or great organ.

Possíbile (It.) (pŏs-*si*-bē-lĕ.) Possible; *il piu forte possibile*, as loud as possible.

Post-horn (Ger.) (pŏst-hŏrn.) A species of bugle, but in straight form. It has no keys.

Postlude (Lat.) (*pōst*-lūde.)
Postludium (Lat.) (pŏst-*lū*-dĭ-ŭm.)
After-piece, concluding voluntary.

Post, sound. A small post within a violin, nearly under the bridge.

Pot-pourri (pŏt-poor-rē.) A medley; a *capriccio*, or *fantásia* in which favorite airs and fragments of musical pieces are strung together and contrasted.

Pouce (Fr.) (pooss.) The thumb; a term used in guitar-music, indicating that the thumb of the right hand must be passed lightly over all the strings.

Pour (Fr.) (poor.) For.

Pour finir (Fr.) (poor fĭ-nĕr.) To finish; indicating a chord or bar which is to terminate the piece.

Pour la première fois (Fr.) (poor lä prĕm-ĭ-ār fwä.) For the first time, meaning that on the repetition of the strain this passage is to be omitted.

Poussé (Fr.) (poos-sā.) *Pushed;* meaning the *up-bow*.

Præambulam (Lat.) (prē-ăm-bū-lăm.)
Præcentio (Lat.) (prē-sĕn-shĭ-ō.)
A prelude.

Præcentor (Lat.) (prē-sĕn-tŏr.) Precentor; leader of the choir.

Præfectus chori (Lat.) (prē-fĕk-tŭs kō-rē.) Master of the choristers.

Prall-triller (Ger.) (*präl-tril*-lĕr.) See *Mordent*.

Präludien (Ger. pl.) (prä-*loo*-dĭ-ĕn.) Preludes.

Präludiren (Ger.) (prä-loo-*dē*-r'n.) To prelude; to play a prelude.

Präludium (Ger.) (prä-*loo*-dĭ-oom.) A prelude; an introduction.

Preambule (Ger.) (pre-am-*bool*-ē.) A preamble; a prelude.

Précenteur (Fr.) (prĕ-sänh-tŭr.) A precentor.

Precentor. The appellation given to the master of the choir.

Precentore (It.) (prā-tshĕn-tō-rĕ.) A precentor.

Precipitaménte (It.) (prā-tshē-pē-tä-men-tĕ.)
Precipitáto (It.) (prāy-tshē-pē-*tä*-tō.)
In a precipitate manner; hurriedly.

Precipitándo (It.) (prāy-tshē-pē-*tän*-dō.) Hurrying.

Precipitazióne (It.) (prāy-tshĕ-pē-tät-sē-ō-nĕ.) Precipitation, haste, hurry.

Précipité (Fr.) (prāy-sē-pĭ-tā.) Hurried, accelerated.

Precipitóso (It.) (prāy-tshē-pē-*tō*-sō.) Hurrying, precipitous.

Precisióne (It.) (prāy-tshē-zē-ō-nĕ.) Precision, exactness.

Precíso (It.) (prāy-*tshē*-zō.) Precise, exact, exactly.

Prefazióne (It.) (prāy-fä-tsē-*ō*-nĕ.) Préface, introduction.

Preghiéra (It.) (prāy-ghē-*ä*-rä.) Prayer, supplication.

Prelude. A short introductory composition, or *extempore* performance, to prepare the ear for the succeeding movements. The word *prelude* has been applied to compositions of a free and improvised character. Chopin's preludes are not introductory to any other movements. Bach's forty-eight preludes, in the "Well-tempered Clavichord," are introductions to the fugues which follow them, yet they are also quite independent pieces. In opera the distinction between *prelude* (or *vorspiel*) and *overture* lies in the fact that the overture is an independent piece while the vorspiel leads directly into the opera. Gluck was the first to use the prelude before the opera in this manner. His preludes lead into the first scene of the opera, and in some degree prepare for it. Wagner, when he promulgated his views regarding the continuity of the music in an opera, was bound to sacrifice the overture (a distinct and separate number), and substitute the *prelude*. Therefore, while Wagner's early operas, "Rienzi," "The Flying Dutchman," and "Tannhäuser" have overtures, all the later ones, beginning with "Lohengrin" have preludes. Even "Tannhäuser" finally had its overture discarded by the composer, and a long prelude substituted. The Wagner *vorspiel* has no definite shape, but always presents some clear guiding motives (see *guiding-figure*) and develops them with much beauty. Thus the "Lohengrin" prelude is founded chiefly upon the *Monsalvat* figure, and the "Parsifal" prelude presents the *Communion, Holy Grail,* and *Faith,* figures in remarkable development. The *vorspiel* to "The Mastersingers of Nuremberg" is one of the finest examples of the modern operatic prelude. The prelude to the suite appears under many different names in the old compositions, and *intrada; preambule, fantasia, overture, toccata,* and *sinfonia,* are among the names used.

Preludiare (It.) (prē-loo-dē-*ä*-rĕ.) To perform a prelude.

Preludío (Spa.) (prĕ-*loo*-dē-ō.)
Preludium (Lat.) (prĕ-*lū*-dĭ-ŭm.)
Preludío (It.) (prĕ-loo-dē-ō.)
A prelude, or introduction.

ō as in *tone;* ŏ as in *dove;* ŏ as in *not;* ŭ as in *up;* ü the French sound of *u.*

Premier (Fr.) (prĕm-ĭ-ā.) } First.
Première (Fr.) (prĕm-ĭ-ār.) }
Première dessus (Fr.) (prĕm-ĭ-ār dās-sü.) First treble; first soprano.
Première fois (Fr.) (prĕm-ĭ-ār fwä.) First time.
Première partie (Fr.) (prĕm-ĭ-ār pär-tē.) First part.
Preparation. That disposition of the harmony by which discords are lawfully introduced. A discord is said to be prepared, when the discordant note is heard in the preceding chord, and in the same part as a consonance.
Preparative notes. Appoggiaturas, or leaning-notes.
Preparazione (It.) (prĕ-pä-rä-tsē-ō-nĕ.) Preparation.
Prepared discord. That discord, the discordant notes of which have been heard in concord.
Prepared intervals. Intervals changed from large to small, and from small to large, by the aid of intermediate tones.
Prepared trill. A trill preceded by two or more introductory notes.
Pressante (Fr.) (prĕs-sänht.) Pressing on; hurrying.
Pressure-tone. An accented tone.

Prestaménte (It.) (prĕs-tä-men-tĕ.) Hurriedly, rapidly.
Prestant (Fr.) (prĕs-tänh.) The open diapason stop in an organ, of 4-foot scale.
Prestézza (It.) (prĕs-tet-sä.) Quickness, rapidity.
Prestissimaménte (It.) (prĕs-tis-sē-mä-men-tĕ.) }
Prestíssimo (It.) (prĕs-tis-sē-mō.) } Very quickly; as fast as possible.
Présto (It.) (pres-tō.) Quickly, rapidly.
Présto assái (It.) (pres-tō äs-sä-ē.) Very quick; with the utmost rapidity.
Présto, ma non tróppo (It.) (pres-tō mä nŏn trŏp-pō.) Quick, but not too much so.
Prière (Fr.) (prē-ār.) A prayer; supplication.

Priests, chantry. Stipendiary priests whose particular object it is to sing Mass in the chantries.
Príma (It.) (prēe-mä.) First, chief, principal.
Príma búffa (It.) (prēe-mä boof-fä.) The principal female singer in a comic opera.
Príma dónna (It.) (prēe-mä dŏn-nä.) Principal female singer in a serious opera.
Príma dónna assolúta (It.) First female singer in an operatic establishment; the only one who can claim that title.
Príma opera (It.) (prēe-mä ōp-ĕ-rä.) First work.
Príma párte (It.) (prēe-mä pär-tĕ.) First part.
Prima párte repetita (prēe-mä pär-tĕ rä-pĕ-tē-tä.) Repeat the first part.
Primary chord. The common chord; the first chord.
Prima vísta (It.) (prēe-mä vēs-tä.) At first sight.
Príma vólta (It.) (prēe-mä vōl-tä.) The first time.
Prime (Ger.) (prēem.) First note, or tone of a scale.
Prime donne (It. pl.) (prēe-mĕ dŏn-nĕ.) The plural of prima donna.
Primes. Two notes placed on the same degree of the staff, and having the same pitch of sound.
Primes, perfect. Primes uninfluenced in their tones by sharps, or flats.
Prime, superfluous. An interval arising from the flatting or sharping of one of the two notes denominated primes.
Prímo (It.) (prēe-mō.) Principal, first.
Prímo búffo (It.) (prēe-mō boof-fō.) First male singer in a comic opera.
Prímo témpo (It.) (prēe-mō tem-pō.) The first, or original time.
Prímo tenóre (It.) (prēe-mō tĕ-nŏ-rĕ.) }
Prímo uómo (It.) (prēe-mō wō-mō.) } The first tenor singer.
Prímo violíno (It.) (prēe-mō vē-ō-lēe-nō.) The first violin.
Prim-töne (Ger. pl.) (prĭm-tŏ-nĕ.) Fundamental tones, or notes.
Principal, or octave. An important organ-stop, tuned an octave above the

diapasons, and therefore of 4-foot pitch on the manual, and 8-foot on the pedals. In German organs the term *principal* is also applied to all the open diapasons.

Principal bass. An organ-stop of the open diapason species on the pedals.

Principal close. The usual cadence in the principal key, so-called because generally occurring at the close of a piece.

Principále (It.) (prēn-tshē-*pä*-lĕ.) Principal, chief: *violino principále,* the principal violin.

Principalménte (It.) (prēn-tshē-päl-*men*-tĕ.) Principally, chiefly.

Principal octave. An organ-stop. See *Principal.*

Procélla (It.) (prō-*tshel*-lä.) A storm; musical delineation of a storm.

Professeur de chant (Fr.) (prō-fĕs-sŭr dŭh shänh.) A professor of vocal music; a singing-master.

Professeur de musique (Fr.) (prō-fĕs-sŭr dŭh mü-*zēk*.)
Professóre di música (It.) (prō-fĕs-*sō*-rĕ dē *moo*-zē-kä.)
Professor of music. In the universities, the professor of music enjoys academical rank, confers musical degrees, lectures on harmonic science, etc. In America, Harvard University and the University of Pennsylvania were the first to establish professional chairs of music. At present, Yale, Columbia, Michigan, and many other great colleges have such chairs.

Prográmme (It.) (prō-*gräm*-mĕ.) A program.

Program. An order of exercises for musical, or other entertainments.

Program-music. Instrumental music which either by its title, or by description printed upon the composition, gives a definite picture of events or objects. Although Bach, Rameau, and other old composers wrote a few small works of this description, Beethoven was really the founder of the school with his "Pastoral Symphony." Berlioz in his "Symphonie Fantastique" and "Childe Harold," and Richard Strauss in his "Heldenleben" have given the largest examples of program music. Instrumental music which attempts no such definite effects, as Beethoven's "Sonata, Op. 106," or Brahm's "C Minor Symphony," are called *Pure Music* or *Absolute Music.* See Hadow's "Studies in Modern Music," Weingartner's "Symphony Since Beethoven," and Hanslick's "Beautiful in Music."

Progression. *Melodic* progression is the advance from one tone to another. *Harmonic* progression is the advance from chord to chord.

Prolatio (Lat.) (prō-*lä*-shī-ō.) Adding a dot, to increase, or lengthen, the value of a note.

Prolation. A method used in old music of determining the value of semibreves and minims.

Prolazióne (It.) (prō-lä-tsē-*ō*-nĕ.) Prolation.

Prologhétto (It.) (prō-lō-*get*-tō.) A short prologue.

Prologue, musical. The preface, or introduction to a musical composition, or performance; a prelude.

Promenade concert. A vocal, or instrumental concert, during which the audience promenade the hall instead of being seated.

Promptement (Fr.) (prŏnht-mänh.)
Prontaménte (It.) (prŏn-tä-*men*-tĕ.)
Readily, quickly, promptly.

Prónto (It.) (*prōn*-tō.) Ready, quick.

Pronunziáre (It.) (prō-noon-tsē-*ä*-rĕ.) To pronounce; to enunciate.

Pronunziato (It.) (prō-noon-tsē-*ä*-tō.) Pronounced.

Propósta (It.) (prō-*pōs*-tä.) Subject, or theme of a fugue.

Proscenio (It.) (prōs-*shä*-nē-ō.)
Proscenio (Spa.) (prōs-*thä*-nī-ō.)
Proscenium.

Proscenium (prŏs-*sĕn*-ĭ-ŭm.) The front part of the stage where the drop scene separates the stage from the audience.

Proslambanomenos (Gr.) (prŏs-lăm-bă-*nŏm*-ĕ-nŏs.) The lowest note in the Greek system, equivalent to A on the first space in the bass of modern music.

Prosodia (Gr.) (prŏ-*sō*-dĭ-ä.) A sacred song, or hymn, sung by the ancients in honor of the gods.

ō as in *tone;* ô as in *dove;* ŏ as in *not;* ŭ as in *up;* ü the French sound of **u.**

Prosody. A term, partly grammatical and partly musical, relating to the accent and metrical quantity of syllables, in lyrical composition.

Protagonista (It.) (prō-tä-gō-*nēs*-tä.) The principal character of a drama, or opera.

Prothalamion (Gr.) (prō-thă-*lā*-mĭ-ŏn.) A nuptial song.

Próva (It.) (*prō*-vä.) Rehearsal.

Próva generale (It.) (*prō*-vä jĕn-ĕ-*rä*-lĕ.) The last rehearsal previous to a public performance.

Psalm. A sacred song or hymn.

Psalm-buch (Ger.) (*psälm* bookh.) A psalter, a book of psalms.

Psalmen (Ger.) (*psäl*-měn.) To sing, to chant psalms.

Psalm-gesang (Ger.) (psälm ghĕ-zäng.) Psalmody.

Psalmist. A composer, writer, or singer of psalms or sacred songs. "The Psalmist" — King David.

Psalm-lied (Ger.) (psälm lēd.) Psalm, sacred song or hymn.

Psalmodie (Fr.) (psăl-mŏ-dēe.) Psalmody.

Psalmodier (Fr.) (psăl-mō-dĭ-ā.) To chant psalms.

Psalmody. The practice or art of singing psalms; a style or collection of music designed for church service.

Psalmsammlung (Ger.) (sälm-säm-loong.) Collection of psalms.

Psalm-sänger (Ger.) (psälm säng-ĕr.) Psalmodist, psalm singer.

Psalm-singen (Ger.) (psälm sĭng-ĕn.) Psalmody.

Psalter. The book of Psalms.

Psalter (Ger.) (*psäl*-tĕr.) Psaltery.

Psalterion (Fr.) (psäl-tā-rĭ-ŏnh.)
Psalterium (Lat.) (säl-*tā*-rĭ-ŭm.)
Psaltery (Eng.) A stringed instrument much used by the Hebrews, supposed to be a species of lyre, harp, or dulcimer.

Psaume (Fr.) (psōm.) A psalm.

Psaume des morts (Fr.) (psōm dĕ mŏr.) Death psalm, funeral hymn.

Punctum contra punctum (Lat.) (*pŭnk*-tŭm *kŏn*-trä *pŭnk*-tŭm.) Point against point; see *Counterpoint.*

Punctus (Lat.) (*pŭnk*-tŭs.) A dot, a point. Originally a note.

Punkt (Ger.) (poonkt.) A dot.

Punkte (Ger.) (*poonk*-tĕ.) Dots.

Punktirt (Ger.) (poonk-*teert*.) Dotted.

Punktirte Noten (Ger.) (poonk-*teer*-tĕ *nō*-t'n.) Dotted notes.

Púnta (It.) (*poon*-tä.) The point, the top; also, a thrust, or push.

Púnta d'arco (It.) (*poon*-tä d'är-kō.)
Púnta del'arco (It.) (*poon*-tä dĕl är-kō.) The point or tip of the bow.

Puntáto (It.) (poon-*tä*-tō.) Pointed, detached, marked.

Púnto (It.) (poon-tō.) A dot, a point.

Púnto d'organo (It.) (poon-tō d'ōr-gä-nō.) Organ point.

Púnto per púnto (It.) (poon-to pĕr-poon-tō.) Note for note.

Pupitre (Fr.) (pü-pētr.) A music desk.

Pyramidal flute. An 8-foot organ-stop of wood.

Pyramidon (Gr.) (pĭ-*răm*-ĭ-dŏn.) An organ-stop of 16- or 32-foot tone, on the pedals, invented by the Rev. F. A. G. Ouseley. The pipes are four times larger at the top than at the mouth, and the tone of remarkable gravity, resembling that of a stopped pipe in quality.

Q

Quadrat (Ger.) (quäd-*rät*.) The mark called a natural, ♮. See *Flat.*

Quadráto (It.) (quäd-*rä*-tō.) The note B in the natural or diatonic scale.

Quadricinium (Lat.) (quäd-rĭ-*sĭn*-ĭ-ŭm.)
Quadripartite (Fr.) (kad-rĭ-pär-*tĕt*.)
A quartet; a composition in four parts.

Quadriglio (It.) (quäd-*rēl*-yē-ō.) Quadrille.

Quadrille (Fr.) (kä-*drĕl*.) A French dance, or set of five consecutive dance movements, called La Pantalon, La Poule, L'Ete, La Trenise (or La Pastourelle), and La Finale. Generally in ⅜ or ¾ rhythm.

Quádro (It.) (quä-drō.) The mark called a natural, ♮.

Quadruple. Fourfold.

ă as in *ah;* ā as in *hate;* ă as in *at;* ē as in *tree;* ĕ as in *eh;* ī as in *pine;* ĭ as in *pin:*

212

Quadruple counterpoint. Counterpoint in four parts, all of which may be inverted, and each of them taken as a bass, middle, or high part.

Quadruple croche (Fr.) (käd-rüpl krōsh.)

Quadruple quaver (Eng.) (kwäd-rū-pl-quā-vĕr.) *Four-hooked;* a sixty-fourth note.

Quádruplo (It.) (*quäa-roo-plō.*) In four parts.

Quadruplo (Lat.) (*quäa-roo-plō.*)

Quantity. The relative duration of notes or syllables.

Quárta (It.) (*quär-*tä.) A fourth; also the fourth voice, or instrumental part.

Quárto (It.) (*quär-*tō.)

Quárta módi (It.) (*quär-*tä mō-dē.)

Quárta tóni (It.) (*quär-*tä tō-nē.) The subdominant, or fourth note of the scale.

Quart de son (Fr.) (kär dŭh sōnh.) A quarter tone.

Quart de ton (Fr.) (kär dŭh tōnh.)

Quart de soupir (Fr.) (kär dŭh soo-pēr.) A sixteenth rest.

Quarte (Fr.) (kärt.) A fourth.

Quarté (Fr.) (*quär-*tĕ.)

Quarte augmentée (Fr.) (kärt ōg-mänh-tā.) Sharp fourth.

Quarte diminuée (Fr.) (kärt dĭ-mē-noo-ā.) Minor fourth.

Quarte de nazard (Fr.) (kärt dŭh nä-zärd.) *Fourth above* the *nazard,* an organ-stop identical with the fifteenth.

Quarte du ton (Fr.) (kärt dü tōnh.) The fourth note of the scale.

Quarter note. A crotchet.

Quarter rest. A pause equal in duration to a quarter note. See *Rests.*

Quarter tone. A small interval, or deviation in pitch, which, in the mathematical theory of music is found to exist, approximately, between D♯ and E♭, G♯ and A♭, etc.

Quartes (Fr.) (kärt.) Fourths.

Quartet, string. A quartet, or composition arranged for four stringed instruments, consisting of first and second violins, viola, and violoncello.

Quartet (Eng.) (quär-*tĕt.*) A composition for four voices or instruments.

Quartett (Ger.) (quär-*tĕtt.*)

Quartétto (It.) (quär tĕt-tō.)

Quartettíno (It.) (quär-tĕt-*tē*-nō.) A short quartet.

Quartet, wood. A quartet consisting of the flute, oboe, clarinet, and bassoon.

Quart-fagott (Ger.) (*quärt* fä-*gōt.*)

Quart-fagótto (It.) quärt fä-*gōt*-tō.) An old sort of bassoon, formerly used as a tenor to the oboe; called also, *Dulcíno* and *Dulzain.*

Quart-flöte (Ger.) (*quärt flö*-tĕ.) A flute sounding a fourth above.

Quárto (It.) (quär-tō.) The fourth; the quarter-note.

Quárto d'aspétto (It.) (quár-tō d'äs-*pet*-tō.) A sixteenth rest.

Quárto di tuono. (It.) (quär-tō dē *twō*-nō.) Quarter tone.

Quárto violino (It.) (quär-tō vē-ō-*lē*-nō.) The fourth violin.

Quási (It.) (*quä-*zi.) In the manner of, in the style of, or somewhat

Quási allegrétto (It.) (*quä-*zi äl-lĕ-*gret* tō.) Like an *Allegrétto.*

Quási andánte (It.) (*quä-*zi än-*dän*-tĕ.) In the style of an *Andánte.*

Quási présto (It.) (*quä-*zi *près*-tō.) Like a *Présto.*

Quási recitativo (It.) (*quä-*zi rā-tshē-tä-*tē*-vō.) Resembling a recitative.

Quási una fantasía (It.) (*quä-*zi oo-nä fän-ta-zē-ä.) As if it were a fantasia.

Quatrain. A stanza of four lines rhyming alternately.

Quatre (Fr.) (kätr.) Four; a

Quáttro (It.) (quät-trō.) *quatre mains,* or, *a quáttro máni,* for four hands; a pianoforte duet.

Quattricóma (It.) (quät-trē-*kō*-mä.) A thirty-second note.

Quátuor (Lat.) (*quä-*tŭ-ŏr.) A quartet.

Quaver. An eighth-note.

Quaver rest. A mark of silence equal in value to a quaver.

Querstriche (Ger.) (*quär-strĭ*-khĕ.) Ledger lines.

Quer-flöte (Ger.) (*quär flö*-tĕ.) German flute. See *Fláuto Travérso.*

ŏ as in *tone;* ô as in *dove;* ŏ as in *not;* ŭ as in *up;* ü the French sound of *u.*

213

QUER-PFEIFE   RADICAL BASS

Quer-pfeife (Ger.) (*quär pfī*-fĕ.) A fife.

Quer-stand (Ger.) (*quär* ständ.) False relation; in harmony.

Quésta (It.) (*ques*-tä.) } This, or that.
Quésto (It.) (*ques*-tō.) }

Queue (Fr.) (küh.) The tail, or stem, of a note; also, the tail-piece of a violin, etc.

Quickstep. A lively march, generally in ⁶⁄₈ time.

Quiéto (It.) (quē-ā-tō.) Quiet, calm, serene.

Quint (Lat.) (quĭnt.) } A fifth; also
Quínta (It.) (quēn-tä.) } the name of
Quinte (Fr.) (kănht.) } an organ-stop
Quinte (Ger.) (quĭn-tĕ.) } sounding a fifth (or twelfth) above the foundation stops.

Quínta acuta (Lat.) (*quĭn*-tä ä-*kū*-tä.) Fifth above.

Quínta décima (It.) (quēn-tä dā-tshē-mä.)
Quintus decimus (Lat.) (*quĭn*-tŭs *děs*-ĭ-mŭs.)
The *fifth above the tenth*, an organ-stop identical with the fifteenth; also *Quindecima* (It.), and *Quindezime* (Ger.).

Quintadena. } An organ-stop. See
Quinta-ed-una. } *Quintaton.*

Quinta módi (It.) (*quēn*-tä *mō*-dē.) } The
Quínta tóni (It.) (*quēn*-tä *tō*-nē.) } dominant or fifth from the tonic.

Quintaton (Ger.) (quĭn-tä-*tōn*.) A manual organ-stop of eight-foot tone; a stopped diapason of rather small scale producing the twelfth, as well as the ground tone; it also occurs as a pedal-stop of thirty-two and sixteen-foot tone.

Quint-bass. An organ pedal-stop. See *Quint.*

Quinte (Fr.) (kănht.) Interval of a fifth.

Quinte cachée (Fr.) (kănht kä-shā.) Hidden fifths.

Quinte de viole (Fr.) (kănht dŭh vē-*ōl.*) The viola.

Quinte octaviante (Fr.) (kănht ŏk-tä-vĭ-änht.) Octave quint; the twelfth.

Quintes (Fr.) (kănht.) Fifths.

Quintet. A composition for five voices or instruments.

Quintétto (It.) (quēn-tāt-tō.) } A quin-
Quintette (Fr.) (kănh-tĕt.) } tet.

Quint-fágott (It.) (quēnt-fägōt.) The small bassoon, or *fagottína*, sounding a fifth higher than the common bassoon.

Quint-gedacht (Ger.) (quĭnt ghĕ-däkht.) An organ-stop of the stopped diapason species, sounding the fifth above.

Quínto (It.) (quēn-tō.) A fifth.

Quintoire (Fr.) (kănh-twär.) An old French term applied to a species of descant consisting chiefly of fifths.

Quintole (Lat.) (*quĭn*-tō-lĕ) A group of five notes, having the same value as four of the same species; quintolet. See *Notes.*

Quint-saite (Ger.) (quĭnt sī-tĕ.) Treble string.

Quire. A choir, a body of singers; that part of a church where the choristers sit. See *Choir.*

Qui tollis (Lat.) (quē *tŏl*-lĭs.) A part of the *Gloria* in the Mass.

Quodlibet (Lat.) (*quŏd*-lĭ-bĕt.) A medley of airs, etc., out of different works, or by various composers; a musical pot-pourri.

Quoniam tu solus (Lat.) (quō-nĭ-äm tū *sō*-lŭs.) Part of the *Gloria* in the Mass.

R

R for *right* (Ger. *rechte*); *r. h.* = right hand (*Rechte Hand*); for *ripieno;* stands in Catholic church music for *Responsorium;* R in French organ-music, stands for *clavier de récit* (swell manual).

Rábbia (It.) (*räb*-bē-ä.) Rage, fury, madness.

Raccourcir (Fr.) (rä-coor-sēr.) To abridge.

Raddolcéndo (It.) (räd-dōl-*tshen*-dō.) }
Raddolcénte (It.) (räd-dōl-*ishen*-tĕ.) }
With increasing softness; becoming softer by degrees; gentler and calmer.

Raddoppiaménto (It.) (räd-dōp-pē-ä-men-tō.) Augmentation; reduplication; the doubling of an interval.

Raddoppiáte nóte (It.) (räd-dōp-pē-*ä*-tĕ nō-tĕ.) Repeated, or reiterated notes.

Raddoppiáto (It.) (räd-dōp-pē-*ä*-tō.) Doubled, increased, augmented.

Radical bass. The fundamental bass, the roots of the various chords.

ä as in *ah* ; ā as in *hate* ; ă as in *at* ; ē as in *tree* ; ĕ as in *eh* ; ī as in *pine* ; ĭ as in *pin* ;

214

Raggióne (It.) (räd-jĕ-ō-nĕ.) Ratio; proportion.

Rallentaménto (It.) (räl-lĕn-tä-*men*-tō.) }
Rallentándo (It.) (räl-lēn-*tän*-dō.) }
Rallentáto (It.) (räl-lēn-*tā*-tō.) }
The time gradually slower.

Rallentándo assai (It.) (räl-lēn-*tän*-dō äs-*sä*-ē.) Much slackening of the time.

Ranz des vaches (Fr.) (ränh dĕ väsh.) Pastoral airs played by the Swiss herdsmen, to assemble their cattle together for the return home.

Rapidaménte (It.) (rä-pē-dä-*men*-tĕ.) Rapidly.

Rapidaménte e brillante (It.) (rä-pē-dä-*men*-tĕ ā brēl-*län*-tē.) Rapidly and brilliantly.

Rapidita (It.) (rä-pē-dē-*tä*.) Rapidity.

Rápido (It.) (*rä*-pē-dō.) Rapid.

Rapsodie (Fr.) (răp-sō-*dēe*.) A *capríccio*, a fragmentary piece; a wild, unconnected composition.

Rasch (Ger.) (räsh.) Swift, spirited.

Rase-gesang (Ger.) (*rä*-zĕ ghĕ-*zäng*.) }
Rase-lied (Ger.) (*rä*-zĕ-*lēed*.) }
A wild song; a dithyrambic.

Rattenéndo (It.) (rät-tĕ-*nen*-dō.) } Holding
Rattenúto (It.) (rät-tĕ-*noo*-tō.) } back; restraining the time.

Rauco (It.) (rä-oo-kō.) Hoarse, harsh.

Rauh (Ger.) (*rä*-ooh.) } Rough.
Rauque (Fr.) (rōk.) }

Rausch-pfeife (Ger.) (roush-pfī-fĕ.) }
Rausch-quint (Ger.) (roush-quĭnt.) }
A mixture-stop in German organs, the twelfth and fifteenth on one slide.

Ravanastron. A very simple form of bow instrument among the Hindus of ancient origin. Possibly the progenitor of the violin.

Ravvivándo (It.) (räv-vē-*vän*-dō.) Reviving, quickening, accelerating.

Ravvivándo il témpo (It.) (räv-vē-*vän*-dō ēl *tem*-pō.) Accelerating the time.

Re (rā.) A syllable applied in solfaing, to the note D. In France and Italy D is called *Re*.

Rebec. } A Moorish word signifying
Rebecca. } an instrument with two strings played on with a bow. The Moors brought the rebec into Spain, whence it passed into Italy, and after the addition of a third string obtained the name of *rebecca*, whence the old English rebec, or fiddle with three strings.

Rebecchíno (It.) (re-bĕ-*kē*-nō.) Small rebec guitar.

Re bémol (Fr.) (rā-bā-mōl.) The note D ♭.

Re bémol majeur (Fr.) (rā bā-mōl mă-zhŭr.) The key of D ♭ major.

Rechanter (Fr.) (rĕ-shänh-*tā*.) To sing again.

Recherche (Fr.) (rĕ-*shārsh*.) Research; name formerly given by the French to an extemporaneous prelude introducing a piece.

Recherché (Fr.) (rĕ-shĕr-*shā*.) Rare, affected, formal.

Recht (Ger.) (rĕkht.) Right.

Rechte Hand (Ger.) (rĕkht *händ*.) Right hand.

Recitándo (It.) (re-tshē-*tän*-dō.) } Declamatory,
Recitánte (It.) (re-tshē-*tän*-tĕ.) } in the style of a recitative.

Recitative. (rĕ-sĭ-tä-*tēev*.) A species of musical declamation in which the performer rejects the rigorous rules of time and endeavors to imitate the inflections, accent, and emphasis of natural speech. There are two chief kinds of recitative, the free (*secco*) and the measured (*misurato* or *stromentato*). The free is without tempo mark and with only a few chords for accompaniment to sustain the intonation. The modulations are always very bold and free. Even in orchestral works the free recitative is often accompanied merely by piano. The measured recitative has tempo, and full accompaniment, and is like a fragment of a song.

Recitatif (Fr.) (rĕ-sē-tä-*tēf*.) }
Recitativ (Ger.) (rĕt-sĭ-tä-tĭf.) }
Recitatívo (It.) (rĕ-tshē-tä-*tēe*-vō.) }
Recitative.

Recitative, accompanied. A recitative is said to be accompanied when, be-

ŏ as in *tone*; ô as in *dove*; ŏ as in *not*; ŭ as in *up*; ü the French sound of *u*.

RECITATIVO INSTROMENTATO — REED-PIPE

sides the bass, there are *parts* for other instruments, as violins, flutes, etc.

Recitatívo instromentáto (It.) (rĕ-tshĭ-ta-*tēe*-vō ēn-strō-mĕn-tä-tō.) Accompanied recitative.

Recitatívo parlánte (It.) (rĕ-tshĭ-tä-tēe-vō pär-*län*-tĕ.)

Recitativo sécco (It.) (rĕ-tshĭ-tä-tēe-vō *sek*-kō.)
Unaccompanied recitative; also when accompanied only by the violoncello and double bass, or the pianoforte or organ.

Recitativo stromentáto (rĕ-tshĭ-tä-tēe-vō strō-mĕn-*tä*-tō.) Recitative accompanied by the orchestra. See *Recitatívo instromentáto*.

Réciter (Fr.) (re-sĭ-*tāy*.) To recite.

Reciting-note. The note in a chant upon which the voice dwells until it comes to a cadence.

Recorders. An old wind-instrument somewhat resembling a flageolet, but of smaller bore and shriller tone. Shakespeare alludes to the *Recorders* in "Hamlet."

Recreation. A composition of attractive style, designed to relieve the tediousness of practice; an amusement.

Recréations musicales (Fr.) (rĕk-rā-*ä*-sĭ-ŏnh mü-zĭ-*käl*.) Musical recreations.

Recte (Lat.) (*rĕk*-tĕ.) Right, straightforward.

Recte et retro (Lat.) (rĕk-tĕ ĕt *re*-trō.) Forward, then backward; the subject, or melody, reversed, note for note.

Rector chori (Lat.) (*rĕk*-tŏr *kō*-rĭ.) The leader of choral performances.

Recueil d'hymnes (Fr.) (rĕ-kü-ē d'ēmn.) Hymn-book.

Reddíta (It.) (rĕd-*dēe*-tä.)
Redita (It.) (rĕ-*dēe*-tä.) } Return to the subject; repetition of a melody.

Redoublement (Fr.) (rĕ-*doobl*-mänh.) See *Raddoppiamento*.

Redowa (*rĕd* ŏ-wä.)
Rédowak (*rĕd*-ŏ-wäk.)
Redowazka (*rĕd*-ŏ-wäts-kä.) } A Bohemian dance in ¾ and ¾ time alternately.

Redublicánte (It.) (rĕ-doob-lē-*kän*-tĕ.) Redoubling.

Redublicáto (It.) (rĕ-doob-lē-*kä*-tō.) Redoubled.

Reduciren (Ger.) (*rĕ*-doo-*tseer*-ĕn.) To reduce, or arrange, a full instrumental score, for a smaller band, or for the pianoforte, or organ.

Reductio (Lat.) (rĕ-*dŭk*-shĭ-ō.) Reducing, or bringing back augmented intervals to their original value. See, also, *Reducíren*.

Redundant chord. A chord which contains a greater number of tones or half-tones than it has in its natural state, as from C to sharp G.

Redundant fourth. An augmented fourth.

Redundant intervals. See *Augmented Intervals*.

Reed. The flat piece of cane placed on the beak or mouth-piece of the clarinet or saxophone. This is called a *single reed*. The *double reed* is the mouthpiece of the oboe, English horn and bassoon, formed of two pieces of cane bound together. A reed, in musical instruments, is a thin tongue of wood, or metal, against which a current of air is directed; the reed, swaying rapidly to and fro, breaks this current into intermittent puffs, which form the tone. Reed-vibrations generally produce many overtones, and therefore a rather thin and penetrating quality of sound. Cabinet-organs, oboes, clarinets, bassoons, etc., are examples of reed vibrations.

Reed fifth.
Reed-nasat. } A *stopped-quint* register in an organ, the stopper of which has a hole or tube in it.

Reed, free. When, in an organ reed-pipe, the tongue vibrates in the middle of the tube, without striking against its sides, it is called a *free reed*.

Reed-instruments. Instruments whose sounds are produced by the action of air upon reeds formed of metal, or wood.

Reed-organ. An organ of small size in which the keys open valves and allow the wind from the bellows to act upon reeds.

Reed-pipe. A pipe formed of reed, used singly or in numbers, as the pipes of Pan, in ancient times, or in connection with other kinds of pipes, as in the organ.

ä as in *ah* ; ā as in *hate* ; ă as in *at* ; ē as in *tree* ; ĕ as in *eh* ; ī as in *pine* ; ĭ as in *pin*;

216

REED-STOPS   REPEAT

Reed-stops. Those stops in an organ, the peculiar tone of which is produced by the wind having to pass against a reed placed at the bottom of the pipe and putting the *tongue* into vibration.

Reed, striking. When in an organ reed-pipe, the wind passing through causes the tongue to strike against the tube, it is called a *striking reed*.

Reel. A lively Scotch dance. Originally the term *Rhay*, or *Reel*, was applied to a very ancient English dance, called *the Hay*. The reel is usually in $\frac{1}{4}$ or $\frac{6}{8}$ time.

Refrain. The *burden* of a song; a ritornel; a repeat. See *Burden*.

Regal. A portable organ, used in former times in religious processions.

Regens chori (Lat.) (*rā-*jĕns *kō-*rī.) The choir-master in German churches.

Regimental band. A company of musicians attached to a regiment; a military band.

Regina cœli (Lat.) (rā-jē-nä *sē-*lī.) *Queen of Heaven;* a hymn to the Virgin.

Register. The stops, or rows of pipes in an organ; also applied to the high, low, or middle parts, or divisions, of the voice; also the compass of a voice, or instrument.

Registering. } The proper management
Registration. } of the stops in an organ.

Registerstimme (Ger.) (rĕ-*ghĭs-*tĕr-*stĭm-*mĕ.) Tone produced by a register or stop on the organ.

Registre (Fr.) (rĕg-*ēstr.*) } Register;
Registro (It.) (rĕ-jĕs-trō.) } draw stop.

Règle (Fr.) (rāgl.) } Rule, or pre-
Régola (It.) (*rā-*gō-lä.) } cept, for composition, or performance.

Regula (Lat.) (*rĕg-*ū-la.) A rule.

Rein (Ger.) (rīn.) Pure, clear, perfect; *kurz und rein*, distinct and clear.

Reine Stimme (Ger.) (*ry-*nĕ *stĭm-*mĕ.) Clear voice.

Reiselied (Ger.) (*rī-*zĕ-*lēd.*) A travelling song; a pilgrim's hymn, or song.

Related. A term applied to those chords, modes or keys, which, by reason of their affinity and close relation of some of their component sounds, admit of an easy and natural transition from one to the other.

Relation. That connection which any two sounds have with one another in respect of the interval which they form.

Relatio non harmonica (Lat.) (rĕ-*iā-*shĭ-ō nŏn här-*mŏn-*ĭ-kä.) False relation.

Relation, false. That connection which any two sounds have with one another when the interval which they form is either superfluous or diminished. See *False Relation*.

Relative keys. Keys which only differ by one sharp or flat, or which have the same signatures.

Religiosaménte (It.) (rĕ-lē-jē-ō-zä-*men-*tĕ.) }
Religióso (It.) (rĕ-lē-jē-*ō-*zō.) }
Religiously; solemnly; in a devout manner.

Relish, double. One of the old harpsichord graces.

Re majeur (Fr.) (rā mä-zhŭr.) D major.

Re mineur (Fr.) (rā mē-nŭr.) D minor.

Reminiscenz (Ger.) (rĕ-mĭ-nĭs-*tsĕnts.*) Reminiscence.

Remote keys. Those keys whose scales have few tones in common, as the key of C and the key of D♭.

Remplissage (Fr.) (ränh-plĭ-säzh.) Filling up; the middle parts; also, a term applied to the decorative flourishes introduced in *concertos* and *bravura* airs.

Rentrée (Fr.) (ränh-trā.) *Return;* re-entry of the subject, or theme.

Renverdie (Fr.) (ränh-vĕr-dē.) Songs celebrating the return of verdure and springtime.

Renversement (Fr.) (ränh-*vērs-*mänh.) An inversion.

Renverser (Fr.) (ränh-*vēr-*sā.) To invert.

Renvoi (Fr.) (ränh-vwä.) A repeat; the mark of repetition.

Reol (Dan.) (rā-ōl.) A Danish peasant dance very similar to the reel.

Repeat. A character indicating that certain measures or passages are to be sung, or played twice. (Ger., *Wiederholungszeichen;* Fr., *bâton de reprise;* It., *replica.*) Written

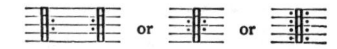

‖:⋮‖ or ‖⋮:‖ or ‖:⋮:‖

ŏ as in *tone* · ŏ as in *dove;* ŏ as in *not;* ŭ as in *up;* ü the French sound of *u*.

213

See also *Da Capo*, and *Dal Segno*. It is not imperative to observe every repeat-mark. In the older composers there is much more repetition than is necessary, and the teacher may be permitted to disregard some of the repeats marked by Bach, Handel, Haydn, Mozart and Schubert. The repeat-marks of Beethoven, however, are generally respected. In the first movement of many of the older sonatas, there is a repeat at the end which is almost always disregarded. *Per contra*, the *first* repeat in such a movement (sonata-allegro) is generally observed. Sometimes the repeat-sign is made clearer by the addition of side-lines thus

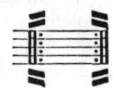

Repeat 8va. Repeat an octave higher.

Repercotiménto (It.) (rĕ-pār-kō-tē-*men*-tō.)

Repercussio (Lat.) (rĕp-ĕr-*kŭs*-sĭ-ō.) Repercussion.

Repercussion. A frequent repetition of the same sound. The regular reëntrance, in a fugue, of the subject and answer after the episodes immediately following the exposition, when these do not overlap each other. When they overlap, the word *stretto* is applied.

Répertoire. (Fr.) (rā-per-twäh.) Those pieces which can readily be performed by an operatic company, or by a solo performer, because of their familiarity with them, or their constant practice of them. A repertory.

Répéter (Fr.) (rā-pā-tā.) To repeat.

Repetiménto (It.) (rĕ-pā-tē-*men*-tō.)
Repetizióne (It.) (rĕ-pā-tē-tsē-*ō*-nĕ.)
Repetition.

Répétition (Fr.) (rā-pā-tē-sĭ-ŏnh.) Rehearsal, repetition.

Repetitóre (It.) (rĕp-ā-tē-*tō*-rĕ.) The director of an opera chorus.

Repitatore (It.) (rĕp-ē-tä-*tō*-rĕ.) A private teacher; the director of a rehearsal.

Réplica (It.) (*re*-plē-kä.) Reply, repetition. See also, *Repercussio*.

Replicáto (It.) (rĕp-lē-*kä*-tō.) Repeated.

Replicazióne (It.) (rĕp-lē-kä-tsē-*ō*-nĕ.) Repetition.

Répondre (Fr.) (rā-pŏnhdr.) To respond; to answer.

Réponse (Fr.) (rā-pŏnhs.) The answer, in a fugue.

Repos (Fr.) (rā-pō.) A pause.

Reprise (Fr.) (rā-*prēz*.) The burden of a song; a repetition, or return, to some previous part; in old music, when a strain was repeated, it was called a *reprise*.

Requiem (Lat.) (*rā*-quĭ-ĕm.) A Mass, or musical service for the dead. Its divisions are as follows: (1) Requiem, Kyrie; (2) Dies iræ, Requiem; (3) Domine Jesu Christe; (4) Sanctus, Benedictus; (5) Agnus Dei, Lux æterna.

Resolutio (Lat.) (rĕz-ō-*lū*-shĭ-ō.) Resolution.

Resolution. Resolving a discord into a concord according to the rules of harmony.

Resoluzione (It.) (rĕs-ō-loo-tsē-*ō*-nĕ.) Resolution, decision, firmness; also, the progression from a discord to a concord.

Resolving a discord. Passing a dissonance into a concord, usually after it has been heard in the preceding harmony.

Resonance. Sound, reverberation, echo.

Resonant. Resounding.

Resonanz-boden (Ger.) (rĕ-sō-*nänts-bō*-d'n.) The sounding-board of a pianoforte, etc.

Résonnement (Fr.) (*rā*-sŏnh-mänh.) Resonance.

Résonner (Fr.) (rā-sŏnh-nā.) To resound; to echo.

Respiration (Eng.) (rĕs-pĭ-*rā*-shŭn.)
Respirazióne (It.) (rĕs-pē-rä-tsē-*ō*-nĕ.)
Respiro (It.) (rĕs-*pē*-rō.)
Taking breath in singing.

Respiro (It.) (rĕs-*pē*-rō.) A semi-quaver rest.

Response.
Responsióne (It.) (rĕ-spŏn-sē-*ō*-nĕ.)
Respónso (rĕ-*spōn*-sō.)
Response, or answer of the choir. The name of a kind of anthem sung in the Roman Catholic Church after the morning lesson. In a fugue the *response* is

ă as in *ah*; ā as in *hate*; ă as in *at*; ē as in *tree*; ĕ as in *eh*; ī as in *pine*; ĭ as in *pin*;

218

| RESPONSORIEN | | | RHYTHMUS |

the repetition of the given subject by another part.

Responsorien (Lat.) (rĕ-spŏn-*sō*-rĭ-ĕn.)
Responsorium (Lat.) (rĕ-spŏn-*sō*-rĭ-ŭm.)
Responsum (Lat.) (rĕ-*spŏn*-sŭm.) See *Response*.

Responsivo (It.) (rĕ-spŏn-*sēe*-vō.) Responsive.
Resserrement (Fr.) (rĕs-*sār*-mänh.) See *Strétto*.
Rest. A character indicating silence. The following are the signs and names of the various rests:

	AMERICAN	GERMAN	FRENCH	ITALIAN
	1. Whole rest.	Taktpause.	Pause.	Pausa della semibreve.
	2. Half-rest.	Halbe.	Demi-pause.	" " minima.
	3. Quarter-rest.	Viertelpause.	Soupir.	" " semiminima (*or* Quarto).
	4. Eighth-rest.	Achtelpause.	Demi-soupir.	" " croma (*or* Mezzo-quarto).
	5. 16th-rest.	Sechzehntelpause.	Quart de soupir.	" " semicroma (*or* Respiro).
	6. 32nd-rest.	Zweiunddreissigstelp.	Demi-quart de soupir.	" " biscroma.
	7. 64th-rest.	Vierundsechzigstelp.	Seizième de soupir.	" " semibiscroma.

The *English* names are similar to those given to notes. See NOTES.

In some music the quarter-rest is written ↾ but as this is apt to produce confusion with the eighth rest— ↽ — it has been altered into ≿. The *whole* rest is not a definite value, as the others are. It means *a whole measure rest*, in *every* rhythm except ¾ or ¼. In these two rhythms it is the exact equivalent of a whole note, in value. All smaller rests have a definite and unchanging value. In ¾ rhythm a dotted whole rest would fill the measure, and in ¼ a ▭ double whole rest would be ▭ required.

Retardation. Slackening, or retarding the time; also, a suspension, in harmony, prolonging some note of a previous chord into the succeeding one.

Retentir (Fr.) (rā-tänh-tēr.) To resound.
Retentissement (Fr.) (rā-tänh-tĕss-mänh.) Peal; loud sound; re-echoing.
Retraite (Fr.) (rĕ-*trāt*.) Retreat; tattoo; in military music.
Retro (Lat.) (*rā*-trō.) Backward; the melody reversed, note for note.
Retrograde (*rĕt*-rō-grāde.) Going backward.
Retrograde imitation. Where the answer, or imitating part, takes the subject backward.
Retrograde inversion. An inversion made by commencing on the last note of the subject, and writing it backward to the first note.
Retrográdo (It.) (rā-trō-*grā*-dō.) Retrograde; going backward.

Rétto (It.) (*rāt*-tō.) Right, straight, direct.
Réveille (Fr.) (rĕ-*vā*-yĕ.) Awakening, a military morning-signal; also horn-music played early in the morning, to awake the hunter.
Reverberiren (Ger.) (rĕf-ĕr-bĕ-*rē*-r'n.) To reverberate.
Reversed retrograde imitation. A form of imitation in which the subject is commenced backward in the answer, and in contrary motion.
Reversed-motion. Imitation by contrary motion, in which the ascending intervals are changed into descending, and *vice versa*.
Revoice. To repair an organ-pipe so as to restore its proper quality of tone.
R. H. In pianoforte music used to indicate the right hand.
Rhapsode (Gr.) (răp-sō-dē.) Persons among the ancients whose profession it was to sing or recite the verses of Homer and other celebrated poets.
Rhapsodie (Ger.) (räp-sō-*dē*.) } See *Rapsodie*.
Rhapsody (Eng.)(*răp*-sō-dy.) }
Rhay. An old Anglo-Saxon name for the dance called the *Hay*. See *Reel*.
Rhythm (Eng.) (rĭthm.) } The division
Rhythmus (Gr.) (*rĭth*-mŭs.) } of musical
Rhythmus (Lat.) (*rĭth*-mŭs.) } ideas or
Rhythmus (Ger.) (*rĭth*-moos.) } sentences into regular metrical portions; musical accent and cadence as applied to melody. Rhythm represents the regular pulsation of music. The

ŏ as in *tone*; ô as in *dove*; ŏ as in *not*; ŭ as in *up*; ü the French sound of *u*.

219

word *time* is constantly applied where *rhythm* is meant. Thus we have *common time, two-quarter time*, etc., which have nothing to do with the *tempo* of the music. In this book we have most frequently replaced the misuse of the word *time* by the more correct name *rhythm*. It is possible that the word *measure* might also replace the more faulty expression. *Three-quarter measure* would express much more than *three-quarter time*. While we deem it impossible to change every misnomer in music, we believe that a beneficial change is possible in this instance. See *Time*.

Rhythme (Fr.) (rĭthm.) Rhythm.

Rhythmique (Fr.) (rĭth-*měk*.) } Rhyth-
Rhythmisch (Ger.) (rĭt-mĭsh.) } mical.

Ribattere (It.) (rē-*bät*-tā-rĕ.) To reverberate.

Ribattiménto (It.) (rē-bät-tē-*men*-tō.) Repercussion, reverberation.

Ribattúta (It.) (rē-bät-*too*-tä.) A beat; a passing-note.

Ribéba (It.) (rē-*bā*-bä.) A Jew's-harp.

Ribéca (It.) (rē-*bā*-kä.) See *Rebec*.

Ribecchíno (It.) (rē-běk-*kē*-nō.) A small rebec.

Ricantare (It.) (rē-kän-*tä*-rĕ.) To sing again.

Ricercáre (It.) (rē-tshěr-*kà*-rĕ.)
Ricercari (It. pl.) (re-tshěr-*kä*-rē.)
Ricercáta (It.) (rē-tshěr *kä*-tä.)
Ricercáto (It.) (rē-tshěr-*kä*-tō.)
Sought after; this term is applied to every kind of composition wherein researches of musical design are employed. It is suitable to certain figures replete with contrapuntal artifices, also to madrigals, and the term was formerly applied to complex fugues, and also to instrumental exercises, when of considerable difficulty.

Ricordánza (It.) (rē-kŏr-*dän*-tsä.) Remembrance, recollection.

Riddone (It.) (rēd-*dō*-ně.) A roundelay; a village dance.

Rideau (Fr.) (rē-dō.) Curtain, in opera.

Ridevolménte (It.) (rē-dĕ-vōl-*men*-tĕ.) Ludicrously, pleasantly.

Ridiciménto (It.) (rē-dē-tshē-*men*-tō.) Repetition, repeating.

Ridicolosaménte (It.) (rē-dē-kō-lō-zä-*men*-tĕ.) Ridiculously.

Ridótto (It.) (rē-*dōt*-tō.) *Reduced; arranged* or *adapted* from a full score; also, an entertainment consisting of singing and dancing; a species of opera.

Rifaciménto (It.) (rē-fä-tshē-*men*-tō.) Reconstruction of a work in order to improve it.

Rifiormenti (It. pl.) (rē-fē-ŏr-*men*-tĕ.) Ornaments, embellishments.

Rigaudon (Fr.) (*rig*-o-don.) } A lively
Rigodon. } French
dance in $\frac{4}{4}$, sometimes in $\frac{2}{4}$ rhythm. The name is spelled in many different ways, but the first is the correct spelling, as it was first brought out in the court of Louis XIII by a dancing-master named Rigaud. It begins on the third, or fourth beat, has a lively character, and was sometimes sung as well as danced. It is sometimes called the *Rigadoon* or *Rigadoons*.

Rigóre (It.) (ri-*go*-rĕ.) Rigor, strictness; *al rigóre di témpo*, with strictness as to time.

Rigoróso (It.) (ri-gō-*rō*-zō.) Rigorous, exact, strict.

Rilasciándo (It.) (ri-lä-shē-*än*-dō.) Relaxing the time; giving way a little.

Rima (It.) (*ree*-mä.) Verse, poem, song.

Rimbombamento (It.) (rēm-bŏm-bä-*men*-tō.) Resounding, booming.

Rinforzándo (It.) (rin-fŏr-*tsän*-dō.)
Rinforzáre (It.) (rin-fŏr-*tsä*-rĕ.)
Rinforzáto (It.) (rin-fŏr-*tsä*-tō.)
Rinfórzo (It.) (rin-*fōr*-tsō.)
Strengthened; reinforced; a reinforcement of tone, or expression; indicating that either a single note or chord, or *several* notes, are to be played with emphasis, although not with the suddenness of a *sforzando*.

Ringelstück (Ger.) (*rĭn*-g'l-*stük*.) Rondeau, roundelay.

Ringen (Ger.) (*rĭng*-ĕn.) To ring, or sound.

Rintoccáre (It.) (rin-tōk-*kä*-rĕ.) To toll a bell.

Rintócco (It.) (rin-*tōk*-kō.) Tolling; a knell.

ă as in *ah* ; ā as in *hate* ; ă as in *at* ; ē as in *tree* ; ĕ as in *eh* ; ī as in *pine* ; ĭ as in *pin*;

RINTRONÁTO   RIVOLTARE

Rintronáto (It.) (rin-tro-*na* tō.) Resounded, reëchoed.

Ripetitura (It.) (ri-pĕ-tē-*too*-rä.) }
Ripetizióne (It.) (ri-pĕ-tē-tsē-*ō*-nĕ.) }
Repetition; the burden of a song; a refrain.

Ripienist. A player of the *ripiéno* or *tútti* parts, in an orchestera.

Ripiéni (It. pl.) (ri-pē-*ä*-nē.) } The
Ripiéno (It.) (ri-pē-*ä*-nō.) } *tútti*, or full parts which fill up and augment the effect of the chorus of voices and instruments. In a large orchestra all the violins, violas, and basses, except the principals, are sometimes called *ripiéni*. The word means literally, *filling-up*, and is the opposite of *solo*, or *obbligato; i.e.* a *supplementary* part.

Ripiéno di cínque (It.) (ri-pē-*ä*-nō dē tshēn-quĕ.)
Ripieur de cinque (Fr.) (rĭp-ǐ-*ŭhr* dŭh sănhk.) Mixture stop of five ranks in Italian organs.

Ripiéno di due (It.) (ri-pē-*ä*-nō dē doo-ĕ.) Mixture stop of two ranks.

Ripiéno di quáttro (It.) (ri-pē-*ä*-nō dē quät-trō.) Mixture stop of four ranks.

Ripiéno di tre (It.) (ri-pē-*ä*-nō dēträy.) Mixture stop of three ranks.

Riposta (It.) (ri-*pōs*-tä.) Repeat.

Riprésa (It.) (ri-*prä*-zĕ.) } Repetition,
Riprése (It.) (ri-*prä*-sĕ.) } reiteration; also the sign 𝄋 used with *D.S.*

Risentitaménte (It.) (ri-sĕn-tē-tä-*men*-tĕ.) }
Risentíto (It.) (ri-sĕn-*tē*-tō.) }
Marked, distinct, forcibly, firmly.

Risolutaménte (It.) (ri-zō-loo-tä-*men*-tĕ.) Resolutely, boldly.

Risolutézza (It.) (ri-zō-loo-*tet*-sä.) Resolution, boldness.

Risolutíssimo (It.) (ri-zō-loo-*tis*-sē-mō.) Very resolutely; as boldly as possible.

Risolúto (It.) (ri-zō-*loo*-tō.) Resolved, resolute, bold.

Risoluzióne (It.) (ri-zō-loo-tsē-*ō*-nĕ.) Resolution, determination; also, the resolution of a discord.

Risonánte (It.) (ri-zō-*nän*-tĕ.) Resounding, ringing, sounding.

Risonánza (It.) (ri-zō-*nän*-tsä.) Resonance.

Risonáre (It.) (ri-zō-*nà*-rĕ.) To resound to ring, or echo.

Rispósta (It.) (ris-*pōs*-tä.) The answer, in a fugue.

Ristrétto (It.) (ri-*stret*-tō.) The *strétto*, the restriction, or contraction, of the subject, in a fugue.

Risvegliáre (It.) (ris-vāl-yē-*ä*-rĕ.) To wake up; to revive; to reanimate.

Risvegliáto (It.) (ris-vāl-yē-ä-tō.) Awakened, reanimated.

Rit. } Abbreviations of *Ritardando*.
Ritard. }

Ritardándo (It.) (ri-tär-*dän*-dō.) Retarding; delaying the time gradually.

Ritardáto (It.) (ri-tär-dä-tō.) Retarded, delayed.

Ritárdo (It.) (ri-tär-dō.) Retardation, gradual delay; in harmony, prolonging some note of a previous chord into the succeeding one.

Ritárdo un pochettíno (It.) (ri-*tär*-dō oon pō-kĕt-*tē*-nō.) Slacken the time a very little.

Riten. An abbreviation of *Ritenuto*.

Ritenéndo (It.) (rē-tĕ-*nen*-dō.) } Detain-
Ritenénte (It.) (rē-tĕ-*nen*-tĕ.) } ing: holding back the time.

Ritenénto (It.) (rē-tĕ-*nen*-tō.) } *Detained*;
Ritenúto (It.) (rē-tĕ-*noo*-tō.) } slower; kept back.

Ritmo (It.) (*rit*-mō.) Rhythm, cadence, measure.

Ritmo a tre battute (It.) (rit-mō ä träy bät-*too*-tĕ.) Rhythm in three beats.

Ritornél (It.) (ri-tōr-*nel*.) } The
Ritornéllo (It.) (ri-tōr-*nel*-lō.) } burden
Ritournelle (Fr.) (ri-toor-*nel*.) } of a song; also, a short prelude or introduction to an air; and the postlude which follows an air; it is also applied to *tútti* parts, introductory to, and between, or after, the solo passages in a concerto.

Riverberaménto (It.) (ri-vĕr-bĕ-rä-*men*-tō.) Reverberation.

Rivérso (It.) (ri-*vär*-sō.) } See
Rivérscio (It.) (ri-*vär*-shē-ō.) } *Rovéscio*.

Rivolgiménto (It.) (ri-vōl-yē-*men*-tō.) Inversion of the parts, in double counterpoint.

Rivoltáre (It.) (ri-vōl-*tä*-rĕ.) To change.

ŏ as in *tone*; ô as in *dove*; ŏ as in *not*; ŭ as in *up*; ü the French sound of *u*.

221

Rivoltáto (It.) (ri-vōl-*tä*-tō.) Inverted;
Rivólto (It.) (ri-*vōl*-tō.) in counterpoint.

Roccoco (rō-kō-kō.) Old-fashioned;
Rococo (rō-kō-kō.) odd; quaint.

Roehr-quint (Ger.) (rôh'r-quĭnt.) Reed-
Rohr-quint (Ger.) (rōr-quĭnt.) fifth; an organ-stop, sounding the fifth above the diapasons.

Rohr (Ger.) (rōr.) Reed, pipe.

Röhre (Ger. pl.) (rô-rĕ.) Reeds.

Rohr-flöte (Ger.) (*rōr-flŏ*-tĕ.) Reed-flute; a stopped diapason in an organ.

Rohr-nasat (Ger.) (*rōr*-nä-*sät*.) See Reed-nasat.

Rohr-pfeife (Ger.)(*rōr-pfī*-fĕ.) Reed-pipe.

Rohr-werk (Ger.) (*rōr*-värk.) Reed-work; the reed-stops in an organ.

Rôle (Fr.) (rōll.) A part, or character, performed by an actor in a play, or opera.

Rolling. A term applied to that rapid pulsation of the drum by which the sounds so closely succeed each other as to beat upon the ear with a rumbling continuity of effect.

Roll, long. A prolonged roll of drums signalizing an attack by the enemy, and for the troops to place themselves in line of battle.

Romaika. A dance-tune of the modern Greeks to accompany a dance of the same name.

Romance (Fr.) (rō-*mänhs*.) Formerly
Románza (It.) (rō-*män*-tsä.) the name
Romanze (Ger.) (rō-*män*-tsĕ.) given to the long lyric tales sung by the minstrels; now a term applied to an irregular, though delicate and romantic composition.

Romanésca (It.) (rō-mä-*nes*-kä.) A
Romanesque (Fr.) (rō-män-ĕsk.) favorite Roman, or Italian, dance of the sixteenth century, resembling the *Galliard.*

Romantique (Fr.) (rō-mănh-tēek.)
Romanzesco (It.) (rō-män-tsĕs-kō.) Romantic, imaginative, fairy-like.

Römischer Gesang (Ger.) (rô-mĭ-shĕr ghĕ-*säng*.) Gregorian plain-chant.

Ronde (Fr.) (rōnd.) A whole note.

Rondeau (Fr.) (rŏnh-*dō*.) A composi-
Róndo (It.) (*rōn*-dō.) tion, vocal or instrumental, consisting of one prominent theme which reappears again and again in alternation with other contrasted themes. There are various forms of the *rondo*, but the above is the underlying principle of them all. Ph. Em. Bach first brought the *rondo* into a useful and practical form.

Rondeau mignon (Fr.) (rŏnh-*dō* mēn-yŏnh.) A favorite rondo.

Rondeaux (Fr.) (rŏnh-*dō*.) Rondos.

Ronde pointée (Fr.) (rŏnhd *pwänh*-tä.) Dotted whole note.

Rondilétta (It.) (rōn-dĕ-*let*-tä.) A
Rondinétto (It.) (rōn-dĕ-*net*-tō.) short
Rondíno (It.) (rōn-*de*-nō.) and
Rondolétto (It.) (rōn-dō-*let*-tō.) easy rondo.

Rondo form. In the style of a rondo.

Ronzaménto (It.) (rōn-tsä-*men*-tō.) Humming, buzzing.

Root. The fundamental note of any chord.

Rosalia (Lat.) (rō-*sāl*-yä.) The repetition of a passage several times over, each time on a different degree of the staff.

Rossignoler (Fr.) (rō-sēn-yō-lä.) To imitate the song of the nightingale.

Róta (It.) (*rō*-tä.) A wheel; applied to a canon, or a round. The name formerly applied to the hurdy-gurdy.

Rotóndo (It.) (rō-*tōn*-do.) Round, full.

Rótte (It.) (*rōt*-tĕ.) Broken, interrupted.

Rotulæ (Lat.) (*rō*-tū-lē.) Christmas roundelays.

Roulade (Fr.) (roo-*läd*.) A florid vocal passage; a division, or rapid series of notes, using only one syllable.

Roulement (Fr.) (*rool*-mänh.) A roll, or shake, upon the drum or tambourine; prolonged reiterations of one note upon the guitar, etc.

Round. A species of canon in the unison, or octave; also a vocal composition in three or more parts, all written in the same clef, the performers singing each part in succession. They are called *rounds* because the performers follow one another in a circulatory motion, and as they generally have no cadence they move around without cessation, like an infinite canon.

Roundel. From the French word
Roundelay. *rondelet* ; a species of antique rustic song, or ballad, common in the fourteenth century, and so-called on account of form, by which it constantly returned to the first verse and thus went *round;* also a circular dance. See Shakespeare's "Midsummer Night's Dream."

Rovesciamento (It.) (rō-vé-shē-ä-*men*-tō.)
Rovéscio (It.) (rō-*ve*-shē-ō.)
Reverse motion; the subject backward and often in double counterpoint.

Rubáto (It.) (roo-*bäh*-tō.) *Robbed, stolen ;* taking a portion of the duration from one note and giving it to another. See *Témpo Rubáto.*

Rückung (Ger.) (*rük*-oong.) Syncopation.

Ruf (Ger.) (roof.) Call, cry, voice; to wind a horn; to sound a trumpet-call.

Ruhepunct (Ger.) (*roo*-hĕ-*poonkt.*)
Ruhepunkt (Ger.) (*roo*-hĕ-*poonkt.*)
Pause; point of rest, or repose; a cadence.

Ruhestelle (Ger.) (*roo*-hĕ-*stĕl*-lĕ.)
Ruhezeichen (Ger.) (*roo*-hĕ-*tsī*-k'n.)
A pause; a rest.

Rule of the octave. The art of accompanying the scale, either ascending or descending, when taken in the bass, with the proper chords, or harmony.

Rullándo (It.) (rool-*län*-dŏ.) Rolling
Rullánte (It.) (rool-*län*-tĕ.) on the drum, or tambourine.

Run. A rapid flight of notes introduced as an embellishment; a roulade.

Rundgedicht (Ger.) (*roond*-ghĕ-dĭkht.)
Rundgesang (Ger.) (*rond*-ghĕ-säng.)
Rondeau; roundelay; a convivial song.

Russe (Fr.) (rüss.) Russian ; *à la Russe,* in the Russian style.

Rústico (It.) (roos-tē-kō.) Rural, rustic.

S

S. As an abbreviation " S " means *Segno, Sinistra,* or *Subito.*

Saccade (Fr.) (săk-*käd.*) A firm pressure of the violin-bow against the strings, enabling the player to produce two, three, or four notes at one stroke.

Sackbut. An old bass wind-instrument, resembling a trombone.

Sack-geige (Ger.) (*säk-ghī*-ghĕ.) A pocket-fiddle ; a *kit.*

Sack-pfeife (Ger.) (*säk pfī*-fĕ.) A bagpipe. See *Cornamúsa.*

Sack-pfeifer (Ger.) (*säk-pfī*-fĕr.) Player on the bagpipe.

Sacrist. A person employed in a cathedral, whose office it is to copy out the music for the use of the choir and take care of the books.

Saengerfest (Ger.) (*sāng*-ĕr-*fĕst.*) A festival among the Germans of a musical and social character in which the *Maennerchor* plays an important part.

Saison (Fr.) (*sā*-sŏhh.) The musical season.

Saite (Ger.) (*sy*-tĕ.) A string of a musical instrument.

Saiten (Ger.) (*sy*-t'n.) Strings of a violin, guitar, etc.

Saiten-draht (Ger.) (*sy*-t'n-*drät.*) Wire-string.

Saiten-halter (Ger.) (*sy*-t'n-*häl*-tĕr.) The tail-piece of a violin, etc.

Saiten-instrument (Ger.) (*sy*-t'n-ĭn-stroo-mĕnt.*) A stringed instrument.

Saiten-klang (Ger.) (*sy*-t'n-*kläng.*) The sound, or vibration of a string.

Saiten-spiel (Ger.) (*sy*-t'n spēel.) Stringed instrument; music of a stringed instrument.

Saiten-spieler (Ger.) (*sy*-t'n *spēe*-lĕr.) Player on a stringed instrument.

Saiten-ton (Ger.) (*sy*-t'n *tōn.*) The tone of a stringed instrument.

Saitig (Ger.) (*sy*-tĭg.) Stringed.

Salcional (Fr.) (săl-sĭ-ō-*näl.*)
Salicet (Fr.) (sä-lĭ-*sā.*)
Salicional (Fr.) (sä-lē-sĭ-ō-*näl.*)
An 8 or 16-foot organ-stop of small scale and reedy tone.

Salle de concert (Fr.) (säll düh kŏnh-*sārt.*) A concert-room.

Salle de musique (Fr.) (säll düh mü-zĕk.) A music-room.

ō as in *tone ;* ô as in *dove ;* ŏ as in *not ;* ŭ as in *up ;* ü the French sound of *u.*

Salm (Ger.) (sälm.) } A psalm.
Sálmo (It.) (säl-mō.)

Saltándo (It.) (säl-*tän*-dō.) Leaping, proceeding by skips, or jumps ; *arco saltando* in violin music, means skipping the bow upon the strings.

Saltarélla (It.) (säl-tä-*rel*-lä.) } A Roman, or
Salterélla (It.) (säl-tĕ-*rel*-lä.) Italian dance, very quick, skipping in character, and in $\frac{2}{4}$ or $\frac{6}{8}$ time.

Saltatóri (It. pl.) (säl-tä-*tō*-rē.) *Jumpers*, or dancers of very great agility.

Salter (Ger.) (*säl*-tĕr.) Psalter; book of psalms.

Salterétto (It) (säl-tĕ-*ret*-tō.) A musical figure in $\frac{6}{8}$ time, the first and fourth quavers being dotted ; very usual in movements *alla Siciliana*.

Salterio (It.) (säl-*tā*-rē-ō.) } Psalter,
Saltéro (It.) (säl-*tā*-rō.) book of psalms.

Sálto (It.) (*säl*-tō.) A leap, or skip, from one note to a distant one ; also a dance.

Salve Regina (Lat.) (*săl*-vĕ rā-*jē*-nä.) *Hail Queen!* a hymn to the Virgin Mary.

Sambuque (Heb.) (säm-book.) An old Hebrew instrument of the harp-kind.

Sammlung (Ger.) (*säm*-loong.) A collection.

Sampógna (It.) (säm-*pōn*-yä.) A species of pipe. See *Zampógna*.

Sanctus (Lat.) (*sănk*-tŭs.) Holy; a principal movement of the Mass.

Sanft (Ger.) (sänft.) Soft, mild, smooth ; *mit sanften stimmen ;* with soft stops.

Sanft-flöte (Ger.) (sänft flô-tĕ.) Soft-toned flute.

Sanftheit (Ger.) (*sänft*-hīt.) Softness, smoothness. gentleness.

Sänftig (Ger.) (*sănf*-tĭg.) Soft, gentle.

Sanftmuth (Ger.) (*sänft*-moot.) }
Sanftmüthigkeit (Ger.) (*sänft*-mü-tĭg-kīt.)
Softness, gentleness.

Sanftmüthig (Ger.) (*sänft*-mü-tĭg.) Softly, gently.

Sang (Ger.) (säng.) Song.

Sänger (Ger.) (*săng*-ĕr.) A singer.

Sängerbund (Ger.) (*săng*-ĕr-*boond*.) A league, or brotherhood of singers ; a convention of singing societies.

Sängerinn (Ger.) (*săng*-ĕr-inn.) A female singer ; a songstress.

Sängerverein (Ger.) (*săng*-ĕr-fĕ-*rīn*.) Singers' union.

Sang-meister (Ger.) (*săng*-mīs-tĕr.) Singing-master.

Sans (Fr.) (sänh.) Without.

Sans frapper (Fr.) (sänh frăp-*pā*.) *Without striking;* play the notes without striking them hard, or forcibly.

Sans pédales (Fr.) (sänh pā-däl.) Without the pedals.

Saraband (Eng.) (*săr*-ă-bănd.) } A
Sarabánda (It.) (sär-ä-*bän*-dä.) dance
Sarabande (Fr) (săr-ä-bănd.) said
Sarabande (Ger.) (sär-ä-bän-dĕ.) to be originally derived from the Saracens, and danced with castanets ; it is in slow $\frac{3}{4}$ or $\frac{3}{2}$ time, and characterized by the second note of the measure being lengthened, which gives gravity and majesty to the movement. It is the stateliest of the dances in the suite, and became the central movement, following the *courante*, and preceding the *intermezzi*. See *Suite*.

Sarrusophone. A brass wind-instrument named after the band-master Sarrus, of Paris, with a *double reed* like the oboe and bassoon. In its keying it resembles the saxophone, the latter, however, having a *single reed.* The sarrusophone is made in various pitches,— soprano, alto, tenor, bass, and contra-bass, the last-named making an excellent substitute for the contra-bassoon.

Sattel (Ger.) (*sät*-t'l.) The nut of the finger-board of the violin, etc.

Satz (Ger.) (sätz.) Musical passage ; theme, or movement. The word *sazt* is very freely applied to any division of a composition, especially in sonatas.

Saut (Fr.) (so.) A skip, or leap. See *Salto*.

Sax-horns. Cylinder horns invented by Antoine (usually called Adolph) Sax. They have 3, 4, or 5 cylinders, so that each horn is capable of playing all the notes of its scale without difficulty. A sax-horn band comprises seven instruments,— a small high horn (*sopranino*), a soprano, an alto, a tenor, a baritone, a

ă as in *ah ;* ā as in *hate ;* ă as in *at ;* ē as in *tree ;* ĕ as in *eh ;* ī as in *pine ;* ĭ as in *pin ;*

Wolfgang Amadeus Mozart

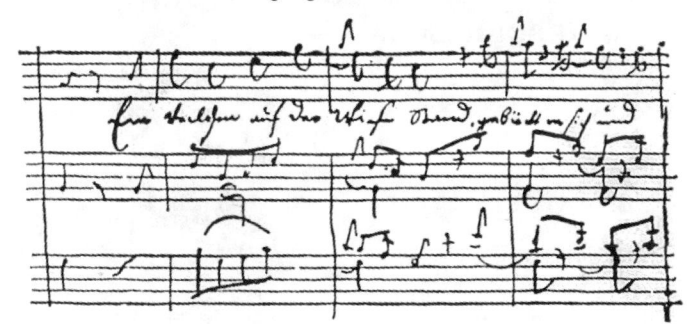

Helicon Bass

Saxophone

bass, and a double-bass. They are not adapted for additional crooks.

Saxophones. A family of brass wind instruments invented by M. Sax about 1840. The body of these instruments is a parabolic cone of brass, provided with a set of keys; their tones are soft and penetrating in the higher part, and full and rich in the lower part of their compass. The saxophones are six in number,—the *sopranina*, the soprano, the alto, the tenor, the baritone, and the bass; they are played with a single reed and a clarinet mouth-piece. The fingering is like the clarinet. Bizet used the alto saxophone in the orchestra in his *Suite Arlesienne*, but the instrument's more common home is in a jazz band.

Saxotromba. A brass instrument introduced by M. Sax, with a wide mouthpiece and 3, 4, or 5, cylinders; the tone is of a shrill character, partaking of the quality both of the trumpet and the bugle. It is made in various pitches.

Sax-tuba. A brass instrument introduced by M. Sax, with a wide mouthpiece and three cylinders; the tone is very sonorous.

Sbálzo (It.) (*sbäl*-tsō.) Skip, or leap, in melody.

Sbárra dóppia (It.) (*sbär*-rä *dŏp*-pē-ä.) A double-bar.

Scagnéllo (It.) (skän-*yel*-lō.) The bridge of the violin, etc.

Scála (It.) (*skä*-lä.) A scale, or gamut.

Scála cromática (It.) (*skä*-lä krō-*mä*-tē-kä.) The chromatic scale.

Scald. The name given by the ancient Scandinavians to their bards, whose employment it was to compose odes and songs which were chanted at their public festivals.

Scale (Lat., *Scala;* Ger., *Tonleiter;* Fr., *Echelle;* It., *Scala.*) The succession of tones upon which any music is built. The scales of different epochs and nations differ quite as much as their languages. It is impossible to demonstrate scientifically (by any laws yet discovered) the *reason* of the subdivisions made in some scales. The scale seems to have been, like the art of music itself, an invention of man, which did not always seek a foundation in scientific laws. We cannot *prove* that the scales which we employ are better than those used by other races or at other epochs. Our musical system makes use of the following scales:

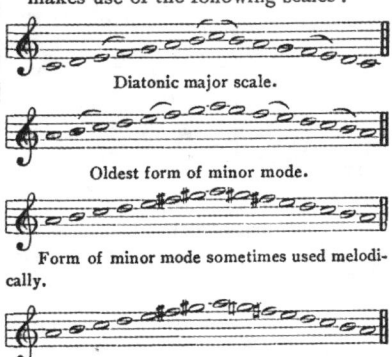

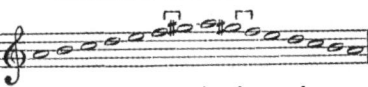

Diatonic major scale.

Oldest form of minor mode.

Form of minor mode sometimes used melodically.

Transition form of minor mode.

Modern or Harmonic minor mode.

Chromatic scale.

(Enharmonic Scale, merely theoretical, not used in practice.)

The Old Greeks had other scales which have caused much dispute among theorists. (For full essays upon these, see Stainer and Barrett's and Baker's Dictionaries of musical terms.) These led finally to the Gregorian tones or modes as follows:

AUTHENTIC MODE.
Mode I.

ŏ as in *tone;* ô as in *dove;* ŏ as in *not;* ŭ as in *up;* ü the French sound of *u.*

SCALE

[Musical notation: Mode III, Mode V, Mode VII]

PLAGAL MODES.

[Musical notation: Mode II, Mode IV, Mode VI, Mode VIII]

Greek names are attached to these Gregorian modes, but, because of the re-arrangements of Glareanus (in the 16th century) we are not certain that these names are applied as they were in ancient Hellenic days. The Hindoo scale divides into third-tones and quarter-tones, in a manner that defies notation by our system, or performance upon our keyed instruments. The chief scale of China runs thus:

[Musical notation]

This is probably the most primitive scale now extant. Many Scottish melodies are written in this scale, as, for example, "Bonnie Doon," "Auld Lang Syne," and "The Campbells are Comin'." There is a scale much used in old folksongs running thus:

[Musical notation]

The melody of the favorite song of "Loch Lomond" is in this mode. The chief scale of the Byzantine music is as follows:

SCANNETTO

[Musical notation]

Leading to signatures (not comprehensible to those who understand only our own system) such as In Hungary the gypsies use the following scale:

[Musical notation]

and Paderewski used this very prominently in his opera of "Manru." Modern composers are beginning to enrich the *Materi Musica* by the use of many of these scales or modes For fuller study of this subject, see Parry's "Evolution of the Art of Music," Hatherly's "Byzantine Music," Elson's "Folksongs of Many Nations," Pole's "Philosophy of Music," and Grove's Dictionary.

Scale, accompaniment of the. The harmony assigned to the series of notes forming the diatonic scale, ascending and descending.

Scale, German. A scale of the natural notes formed of A, H, C, D, E. F, G, the B being reserved to express B ♭.

Scale, Guido's. The syllables *ut, re, mi, fa, sol, la,* used by Guido d'Arezzo, called also the *Aretinian scale;* the syllable *si* was introduced afterwards. See *Aretinian.*

Scale, major diatonic. A scale in which the semi-tones fall between the third and fourth, and seventh and eighth notes, both in ascending and descending.

Scale, natural. The scale of C, called *natural* because it does not require the aid of flats, or sharps.

Scalen-schule (Ger.) (*skä-l'n-shoo*-lĕ.) School for scale-playing; exercises on the scales.

Scales, relative. A major and minor scale having the same signature; as C major and A minor.

Scampanare (It.) (skäm-pä-*nä*-rĕ.) To chime bells.

Scampanio (It.) (skăm-*pä*-nē-ō.) Chimes.

Scannello (It.) (skăn-*nĕl*-lō.) } The
Scannetto (It.) (skăn-*nĕt*-to.) } bridge of a violin, violoncello, etc., also *Scagnello.*

ā as in *ah*, ă as in *hat*; ă as in *at;* ē as in *tree;* ĕ as in *eh ;* ī as in *pine ;* ĭ as in *pin ;*

Scemándo (It.) (shĕ-*män*-dō.) Diminishing; decreasing in force.

Scéna (It.) (*shāy*-nă.) A scene, or portion of an opera, or play. The *scena* is the largest and most brilliant vocal solo form. It generally consists of *recitative*, *cavatina* and *aria* (see these) displaying the vocalist in three schools of work; the recitative for dramatic, declamatory style, the cavatina for smooth and expressive work (*Bel Canto*), and the aria, generally an *aria di bravura*, for *coloratur* singing. The *scena* is sometimes called *scena ed aria*, *recitative ed aria*, *cavatina ed aria*, etc. It generally forms part of an opera, but it may be an independent composition, as Mendelssohn's "Infelice," Beethoven's "Ah Perfido," etc.

Scéna da camera (It.) (*shāy*-nä dä *kä*-mĕ-rä.) Chamber-music; a scena not designed for the church, or theatre.

Scenario (It.) (shĕ-*nä*-rē-ō.) Actor's guide-book; a program; scenes; decorations. The plot of a dramatic work. A skeleton libretto of such a work, sketching the plot, and giving entrances and exits of leading personages.

Scene. Part of an act; portion of an opera; an act generally comprises several scenes. See *Scena*.

Scenic music. Music adapted to dramatic performances.

Schäfer-gedicht (Ger.) (*shā*-fĕr-ghĕ-*dĭkht*.) Idyl, eclogue, pastoral.

Schäfer-lied (Ger.) (*shā*-fĕr-*lēd*.) Pastoral song; shepherd song.

Schäfer-pfeife (Ger.) (*shā fĕr-p fī*-fĕ.) Shepherd's pipe.

Schalkhaft (Ger.) (*shällk*-häft.) Roguish, playful.

Schall (Ger.) (shäll.) Sound.

Schallen (Ger.) (*shäl*-l'n.) To sound; to echo.

Schall-becken (Ger.) (*shäll bĕk*-ĕn.) Cymbal.

Schall-bret (Ger.) (*shäll*-brĕt.) Sound-board.

Schall-loch (Ger.) (*shäll*-lōkh.) Sound-hole.

Schall-rohr (Ger.) (*shäll*-rōr.) Speaking-trumpet.

Schall-stück (Ger.) (*shäll*-stük.) The bell of a trumpet, bugle, horn, etc.

Schalmay (Ger.) (shäl-*mī*.) } A shawm;
Schalmei (Ger.) (shäll-*mī*.) } also, an 8-foot reed organ-stop; the tone resembles that of the cremona. or clarinet.

Scharf (Ger.) (shärf.) *Sharp, acute;* a shrill mixture stop, of several ranks of pipes.

Schauspiel (Ger.) (*shou*-spēl.) Drama dramatic piece.

Schauspielhaus (Ger.) (shou-spēl-hous.) A theatre.

Schelle (Ger.) (*shĕl*-lĕ.) A bell; a jingle.

Schellen (Ger.) (*shĕl*-l'n.) To ring.

Schellentrommel (Ger.) (*shĕl*-l'n-*trŏm*-mĕl.) A tambourine; a timbrel.

Scheme. A term used in ancient music to express the varieties arising from the different positions of tones and semi-tones in a consonance.

Scherzandíssimo (It.) (skĕr-tsän-*dis*-sē-mō.) Exceedingly playful and lively.

Scherzándo (It.) (skĕr-*tsän*-dō.) ⎫ Play-
Scherzánte (It.) (skĕr-*tsän*-tĕ.) ⎪ ful,
Scherzévole (It.) (skĕr-*tse*-vō-lĕ.) ⎬ lively,
Scherzhaft (Ger.) (shĕrts-häft.) ⎭ sportive, merry.

Scherzevolménte (It.) (skĕr-tsĕ-vŏl-*men*-tĕ.) Playfully, merrily.

Scherzhaftigkeit (Ger.) (shĕrts-häf-tĭg-kīt.) Playfulness, sportiveness.

Scherz (Ger.) (shĕrts.) } Play, sport, a
Scherzo (It.) (*skĕr*-tsō.) } jest; a piece of a lively, sportive character, and marked, animated rhythm; also one of the movements in a symphony. The *scherzo* was established by Beethoven, as a symphonic movement to take the place of the minuet which Haydn and Mozart had worn threadbare. The influence of the minuet upon the scherzo form is not difficult to trace, for, although a scherzo may be written in any rhythm and in almost any form, yet the great majority of scherzo movements are in ¾ rhythm, and possess a *trio*. (See *Minuet*.) All of Beethoven's symphonic scherzos are in triple rhythm, but in some of his other works ²⁄₄ rhythms appear in the scherzo movement. The scherzo was very much

ŏ as in *tone*; ŏ as in *dove*; ŏ as in *not*; ŭ as in *up*; ü the French sound of *u*.

like the minuet; but the dance-like character of the minuet-themes was absent, the treatment was freer, and development was possible. The contrast between the scherzo and its trio is often more marked than would be the case in a minuet, and the form is often much more developed than the minuet. It has become customary, with modern composers, to introduce folk-music, and especially folk-dances, into the scherzo. Chopin first made the scherzo an independent movement apart from the sonata or symphony.

Scherzóso (It.) (skĕr-*tsō*-zō.) Merry, playful, jocose.

Schiettaménte (It.) (skē-ĕt-tä-*men*-tĕ.) Simply, unadorned. Also written *Con Schiettezza*.

Schiêtto (It.) (skē-*ĕt*-tō.) Simple, plain, neat.

Schisma (Ger.) (shĭs-mä.) A very minute difference between the sound of intervals. In ancient music, a small interval equal to the eighteenth part of a tone.

Schlacht-gesang (Ger.) (*shläkht*-ghĕ-säng.)

Schlacht-lied (Ger.) (*shläkht*-lēd.) War-song.

Schlag (Ger.) (shläg.) Stroke, blow; a beat, as regards time.

Schlagen (Ger.) (*shlä*-g'n.) To strike; to beat; to warble, or trill.

Schleifen (Ger.) (*shlī*-f'n.) To slide; to glide.

Schleifer (Ger.) (*shlī*-fĕr.) Slurred note; gliding-note.

Schleife-zeichen (Ger.) (*shlī*-fĕ-*tsī*-khĕn.) A slur; a mark of the *legato* style.

Schleppend (Ger.) (*shlĕp*-pĕnd.) Dragging, drawling.

Schluss (Ger.) (shlooss.) The end; conclusion.

Schlüssel (Ger.) (*shlüs*-s'l.) A clef.

Schluss-fall (Ger.) (*shloos*-fäll.) A cadence.

Schluss-reim (Ger.) (*shloos*-rīm.) The *burden*, or refrain of a song.

Schluss-stück (Ger.) (*shloos*-stük.) Concluding piece; finale.

Schmachtend (Ger.) (*shmäkh*-tĕnd.) Languishing.

Schmelzend (Ger.) (*shmĕl*-tsĕnd.) Diminishing; melting away.

Schmerz (Ger.) (shmĕrts.) Grief, sorrow.

Schmerzhaft (Ger.) (*shmĕrts*-häft.) Dolorous, sorrowful.

Schmerzhaftigkeit (Ger.) (*shmĕrts*-häf-tĭg-kīt.)

Schmerzlich (Ger.) (*shmerts*-līkh.) In a dolorous style.

Schnabel (Ger.) (schnä-b'l.) Mouthpiece of the clarinet, flûte à béc, and other similar instruments.

Schnarr-bass (Ger.) (*shnärr*-bäss.) The drone-bass.

Schnarr-pfeifen (Ger.) (*shnärr*-*pfī*-f'n.)

Schnarr-werk (Ger.) (*shnarr*-värk.) Reed-pipes, reed-work, or stops in an organ.

Schnell (Ger.) (shnĕll.) Quickly, rapidly.

Schnelle (Ger.) (*shnĕl*-lĕ.)

Schnelligkeit (Ger.) (*shnĕl*-līg-kīt.) Quickness, swiftness, rapidity.

Schneller (Ger.) (*shnĕl*-lĕr.) Quicker, faster.

Schnell-waltzer (Ger.) (*shnĕl*-*vält*-tsĕr.) Quick waltzes.

Schottisch (Ger.) (*shŏt*-tĭsh.) A modern dance, rather slow, in ¾ time.

Schreibart (Ger.) (*shrīb*-ärt.) Style; manner of composing.

Schreiend (Ger.) (*shrī*-ĕnd.) Acute, shrill, screaming.

Schreiwerk (Ger.) (*shrī*-värk.) *Shrill-work;* acute, or mixture stops.

Schrittmässig (Ger.) (*shrĭt*-*mäs*-sĭg.) Slow time; *andante*.

Schule (Ger.) (*shoo*-lĕ.) A school, or method for learning any instrument; also, a peculiar style of composition, the manner or method, of an eminent composer, performer, or teacher.

Schulgerecht (Ger.) (*shool*-ghĕ-*rĕkht*.) Regular; in due form; written correctly in accordance with the rules and principles of musical art.

Schusterfleck (Ger.) (*shoos*-tĕr-*flĕk*.) See *Rosália*.

Schwach (Ger.) (shväkh.) *Piáno,* soft, weak.

ă as in *ah*; ā as in *hate*; ă as in *at*; ē as in *tree*; ĕ as in *eh*; ī as in *pine*; ĭ as in *pin*;

SCHWÄCHER   SDRUCCIOLATO

Schwächer (Ger.) (shvä-kĕr.) Fainter; softer; more *piáno*.

Schwebung (Ger.) (*shvĕ*-boong.) *Waving;* a lighter species of *tremulant*, for the more delicate stops, such as the *vox humana*, etc.

Schweige (Ger.) (*shvī*-ghĕ.) A rest.

Schweigen (Ger.) (*shvī*-ghĕn.) Silence; being silent.

Schweizer-flöte (Ger.) (*shvī*-tsĕr*flŏ̄*-tĕ.)

Schweizer-pfeife (Ger.) (*shvī*-tsĕr-*pf ī*-fĕ.)
Swiss flute, or pipe; an organ-stop.

Schwer (Ger.) (shvār.) Heavily, ponderously.

Schwermüthig (Ger.) (shvār-*mü*-tig.) In a pensive, melancholy style.

Schwiegel (Ger.) (*shvēe*-g'l.) An organstop of the flute species, of metal, pointed at the top.

Schwingung (Ger.) (*shvĭng*-oong.) Vibration of a string, etc.

Scialumo (Fr.) (sē-ä-*lü*-mō.) A word employed in clarinet music, signifying that the notes are to be played an octave lower than written. Chalumeau.

Scioltaménte (It.) (shē-ōl-tä-*men*-tĕ.) With freedom, agility; easily; the notes being rather detached than *legáto*.

Scioltézza (It.) (shē-ōl-*tet*-sä.) Freedom, ease, lightness.

Sciólto (It.) (shē-*ōl*-tō.) Free, light. See *Scioltaménte*.

Scordáre (It.) (skŏr-*dä*-rĕ.) To be out of tune; to grate upon the ear with discordant notes.

Scordáto (It.) (skŏr-*dä*-tō.) Out of tune; false; untuned.

Scordatúra (It.) (skŏr-dä-*too*-rä.) Tuning a violin differently, for the more easily performing of certain peculiar passages.

Score. The whole instrumental and vocal parts of a composition, written on separate staves, placed under each other. (Ger., *Partitur;* Fr., *Partition;* It., *Partitura*.)

Score, full. A complete score of all the parts of a composition, either vocal or instrumental, or both.

Score, instrumental. A score in which the instrumental parts are given in full.

Score, piano. A score in which the orchestral accompaniments are compressed into a pianoforte part; an arrangement of music for the piano.

Score, short. An abbreviated, or a skeleton score.

Score, vocal. The notes of all the voiceparts placed in their proper order under each other for the use of the conductor.

Scoring. The forming of a score, by collecting and properly arranging the different parts of a composition.

Scorréndo (It.) (skŏr-*ren*-dō.) Gliding from one sound into another.

Scotch scale. A scale differing from that of the other nations of Europe by its omission of the fourth and seventh. See *Scale*.

Scotch snap. A peculiarity in Scotch tunes, and those written in imitation of the Scotch character; it is the lengthening the time of a second-note at the expense of the one before it; placing a sixteenth before a dotted eighth it gives emphasis and spirit to dance-tunes, and, when well applied, has a lively effect.

Scozzése (It.) (skŏt-*sā*-zĕ.) In the Scotch style.

Scríva (It.) (skrē-vä.) *Written; st scríva*, as it is written, without any alteration or embellishment.

Scuóla (It.) (skoo-*ō*-lä.) A school; a course of study.

Sdegnánte (It.) (sden-*yän*-tĕ.) Angry, passionate.

Sdégno (It.) (*sden*-yō.) Anger, wrath, passion.

Sdegnosaménte (It.) (sden-yō-zä-*men*-tĕ.) Scornfully, disdainfully.

Sdegnóso (It.) (sden-*yō*-zō.) Furious, passionate, fiery.

Sdrucciolándo (It.) (sdroot-tshē-ō-*län*-dō.) Sliding, slipping.

Sdrucciolare (It.) (sdroot-tshē-ō-*lä*-rĕ.) To slide the hand, by turning the finger nails toward the keys of the pianoforte, and drawing the hand lightly and rapidly, up or down.

Sdrucciolaménto (It.) (sdroot-tshē-ō-lä-*men*-tō.)

Sdrucciolato (It.) (sdroot-tshē-ō-*lä*-tō.)

ō as in *tone;* ŏ as in *dove;* ŏ as in *not;* ŭ as in *up;* ü the French sound of *u*.

Sliding the fingers along the strings or the keys of an instrument.

Se (It.) (sā.) If; in case; provided; as.

Sea-trumpet. A marine-trumpet formerly much used on ship-board.

Se bisógna (It.) (sā be-*sōn*-yä.) If necessary, if required.

Sec (Fr.) (sĕk.) } Dry, unornamented, coldly;
Sécco (It.) (sāk-kō.) } the note, or chord, to be struck plainly, without ornament, or *arpéggio*. See *Recitative*.

Sechs (Ger.) (sĕkhs.) Six.

Sechs-achteltact (Ger.) (sĕkhs-äkh-t'l-*täkt*.) Measure in $\frac{6}{8}$ time.

Sechs-saitig (Ger.) (sĕkhs-*sī*-tĭg.) Instrument with six strings.

Sechs-theilig (Ger.) (*sĕkhs-ti*-līg.) In six parts.

Sechste (Ger.) (*sĕkhs*-tĕ.) A sixth.

Sechzehn (Ger.) (sĕkh-tsĕn.) Sixteen.

Sechzehnte (Ger.) (sĕkh-tsĕn-tĕ.) Sixteenth.

Sechzehntel (Ger.) (sĕkh-tsĕn-t'l.) Sixteenth notes.

Sechzehntelpause (Ger.) (sĕkh-tsĕn-t'l-pou-zĕ.) A sixteenth rest.

Second. An interval of one degree, as from A to B, B to C, etc.

Secónda (It.) (sā-*kōn*-dä.) Second; a second.

Secónda dónna (It.) (sā-*kōn*-dä don-nä.) Second female singer.

Second, augmented. An interval containing three half-steps.

Secónda vólta (It.) (sĕ-*kōn*-dä *vōl*-tä.) The second time.

Second-dessus (Fr.) (sā-kŏnhd dĕs-sü.) The second treble.

Seconde (Fr.) (sā-kŏnhd.) Second.

Seconde fois (Fr.) (sā-kŏnhd fwä.) Second time.

Second inversion. A term applied to a chord when its fifth is the lowest tone.

Second, major. An interval consisting of two half-steps.

Second, minor. An interval measured by one half-step.

Secóndo (It) (sā-kōn-dō.) Second, a second.

Secóndo partíto (It.) (sā-kōn-dō pär-tē-tō.) The second part, or voice.

Second soprano. The low soprano.

Section. A complete, but not an independent musical idea; a part of a musical period. The word is very vaguely used in music, differently by various teachers. It is often applied to a semi-phrase.

Secular music. Music which is composed for the theatre, or chamber; an expression used in opposition to *sacred* music, which is for the church, or worship.

Seculars. Unordained officiates of any cathedral, or chapel, whose functions are confined to the vocal department of the choir.

Secunde (Ger.) (sĕ-*koon*-dĕ.) Second.

Secundiren (Ger.) (sĕ-koon-*dīr*-ĕn.) To play the second part.

Seelen-amt (Ger.) (*sā*-l'n-*ämt*.) }
Seelen-messe (Ger.) (*sā*-l'n *mĕs*-sĕ.) }
Requiem, or Mass for departed souls.

Ségno (It.) (*sen*-yō.) A *sign*, 𝄋: *al ségno*, return to the sign; *dal ségno*, repeat from the sign.

Segue (It.) (*sā*-gwĕ.) } Follows;
Seguíto (It.) (sĕ-*gwē*-tō.) } now follows; as follows; it also means, go on, *in a similar, or like manner*, showing that a passage is to be played like that which precedes it.

Segue córo (It.) (sā-guĕ *kō*-rō.) }
Segue il córo (It.) (sā-guē el *kō*-rō.) }
The chorus follows; go on to the chorus.

Segue la finále (It.) (sā-guē lä fē-*nä*-lĕ.) The finale now follows.

Seguéndo (It.) (sĕ-guän-dō.) } Following
Seguénte (sĕ-*guen*-tĕ.) } next.

Seguénza (It.) (sĕ-*guen*-tsä.) A sequence.

Seguidilla (Spa.) (sā-guē-*dēl*-yä.) A favorite Spanish dance in ¾ time.

Seguíto (It.) (sā-*guē*-tō.) Followed imitated.

Sehnsucht (Ger.) (*sān*-sookht.) Desire, longing, ardor, fervor.

Sehnsüchtig (Ger.) (*sān*-sükh-tĭg.) Longingly.

Sehr (Ger.) (sāir.) Very, much, extremely.

ă as in *ah*; ā as in *hate*; ă as in *at*; ē as in *tree*; ĕ as in *eh*; ī as in *pine*; ĭ as in *pin*;

Sehr lebhaft (Ger.) (sāir *lĕb*-häft.) Very lively; extremely animated and vivacious.

Séi (It.) (sā-ē.) Six.

Seiten-bewegung (Ger.) (*sy*-t'n-bĕ-*vay*-goong.) Oblique motion.

Seizième de soupir (Fr.) (sē-zē-*ăm* dŭh *soo*-pēr.) Semidemisemiquaver rest. A sixty-fourth rest.

Sekunde (Ger.) (sĕ-*koon*-dĕ.) Second.

Semi (Lat.) (sĕm-ĭ.) Half.

Semibreve (Eng.) (*sĕm*-ĭ-brēv.)
Semibréve (It.) (sĕm-ē-brā-vĕ.)
Semibrevis (Lat.) (sĕm-ĭ-*brā*-vĭs.)
Half a breve; whole note.

Semibreve rest. A rest usually filling an entire measure, except in 3/2 or 4/2 rhythms.

Semicadenza (It.) (sĕmē-kä-*den*-tsā.) Semi-cadence.

Semi-chorus. A chorus to be sung by half or only a few of the voices.

Semicroma (Gr.) (sĕm-ĭ-*krō*-mä.)
Semicróma (It.) (sĕm-ē-*krō*-mä.)
A semiquaver.

Semidemisemiquaver. A half demisemiquaver; a sixty-fourth note.

Semidemisemiquaver rest. A rest equal in duration to a semidemisemiquaver.

Semi-diapente (Lat.) (sĕm-ĭ-dĭ-ă-*pen*-tĕ.) Diminished, or imperfect fifth.

Semi-diatessaron (Lat.) (sĕm-ĭ-dĭ-ä-*tes*-să-rŏn.) Diminished fourth.

Semi-ditone (Lat.) (sĕm-ĭ-dĭ-*tō*-nĕ.)
Semi-ditóno (sĕm-ē-dē-*tō*-nō.)
A minor third.

Semi-fredon (Fr.) (sĕm-ĭ-frā-dŏnh.) A sixteenth note.

Semi-fusa (Lat.) (sĕm-ĭ-*fū*-sä.) A sixteenth note.

Semi-minim (Lat.) (sĕm-ĭ-*mĭn*-ĭm.)
Semi-mínima (It.) (sĕm-ē *mē*-nē-mä.)
A *half-minim;* a crotchet; a quarter-note.

Semiquaver. A note equal to half a quaver; a sixteenth note.

Semiquaver rest. A rest equal in duration to a semiquaver.

Semitone (Eng.) (*sĕm*-ĭ-tōn.)
Semitonium (Lat.) (sĕm-ĭ-*tō*-nĭ-ŭm.)
A half-tone.

Semi-tone major. A semi-tone produced by ascending a degree, as from G to A flat. (This distinction of major and minor semi-tones is uncalled for, and not usually accepted.)

Semi-tone minor. A semi-tone produced by passing from a note to its sharp, or flat.

Semitonium modi (Lat.) (sĕm-ĭ-*tō*-nĭ-ŭm *mō*-dĭ.) The leading-note, or major seventh.

Semituóno (It.) (*se*-mē-*twō*-nō.) A semitone.

Sémplice (It.) (*sem*-plē-tshĕ.) Simple, pure, plain.

Sempliceménte (It.) (sĕm-plē-tshĕ-*men*-tō.) Simply; plainly; without ornament.

Semplicissimo (It.) (sĕm-plē-*tshee*-sē-mō.) With the utmost simplicity.

Semplicita (It.) (sĕm-plē-tshē-tä.) Simplicity, plainness.

Sémpre (It.) (*sem*-prĕ.) Always, evermore, continually.

Sémpre forte (It.) (*sem*-prĕ *fŏr*-tĕ.) Always loud.

Sémpre legáto (It.) (*sem*-prĕ lĕ-*gä*-tō.) Always smooth.

Sémpre piáno (It.) (*sem*-prĕ pē-*ä*-nō.) Always soft.

Sémpre più fórte (It.) Continually increasing in power.

Sémpre più présto (It.) (*sem*-prĕ pē-oo *pres*-tō.) Continually quicker.

Sémpre ritardándo (It.) (*sem*-prĕ rē-tär-*dän*-dō.) Always slower; slower and slower.

Sémpre staccáto (It.) (*sem*-prĕ stäk-*kä*-tō.) Always detached; *staccáto* throughout.

Sensíbile (It.) (sĕn-*see*-bē-lĕ.) Expressive; with feeling.

Sensibilita (It.) (sĕn-sē-bē-lē-*tä*.) Sensibility, expression, feeling.

Sensibilménte (It.) (sĕn-sē-bēl-*men*-te.) Expressively; in a feeling manner.

Sensible (Fr.) (sänh-*sēbl*.) The leading-note, or major seventh of the scale.

ŏ as in *tone* : ŏ as in *dove* : ŏ as in *not;* ŭ as in *up;* ü the French sound of *u*.

231

Sentences. Certain interlude strains sometimes introduced into the service of the established church, especially of particular chapels; short anthems.

Sentié (Fr.) (sänh-*tēe*.) Felt, expressed; *mélodie bien sentié*, the melody well-expressed, or accented.

Sentito (It.) (sĕn-*tee*-tō.) See *Sentie*.

Sentimentále (It.) (sĕn-tē-mĕn-*tä*-lĕ.)
Sentiménto (It.) (sĕn-tē-*men*-tō.)
Feeling; sentiment; delicate expression.

Sénza (It.) (sen-tsä.) Without.

Sénza accompagnaménto (It.) (sen-tsä äk-kōm-pän-yä-men-tō.) Without accompaniment.

Sénza battúta (It.) (sĕn-tsä bä-*too*-tä.) At the pleasure of the performer as regards the beat, or time.

Sénza fióri (It.) (sen-tsä fē-*ō*-rē.)
Sénza ornaménti (It.) (sen-tsa ōr-nä-*men*-tē.)
Without embellishments; without ornament.

Sénza interruzione (It.) (sen-tsä ēn-tĕr-roo-tsē-ō-nĕ.) Without interruption.

Sénza órgano (It.) (sen-tsä ōr-*gä*-nō.) Without the organ.

Sénza pedále (It.) (sen-tsä pĕ-*dä*-lĕ.) Without the pedals.

Sénza repetizióne (It.) (sen-tsä re-pĕ-tē-tsē-*ō*-nĕ.)
Sénza réplica (It.) (sen-tsä *re*-plē-kä.)
Without repetition.

Sénza rigóre (It.) (sen-tsä ri-*gō*-rĕ.) Without regard to exact time.

Sénza sordíni (It. pl.) (sen-tsä sŏr-*dēe*-nē.) Without the dampers, in pianoforte playing, meaning that the dampers are to be raised from the strings, that is, the damper-pedal *is to be used*.

Sénza sordíno (It.) (sen-tsä sŏr-*dēe*-nō.) Without the mute, in violin-playing, etc.

Sénza stroménti (It. pl.) (sen-tsä strō-*men*-tē.) Without instruments.

Sénza témpo (It.) (sen-tsä *tem*-pō.) Without regard to the time; in no definite time.

Se piáce (It.) (se pē-*ä*-tshĕ.) At will; at pleasure.

Septet (Eng.) (sĕp-*tĕt*.)
Septétto (It.) (sĕp-*tet*-tō.)
A composition for seven voices, or instruments.

Septième (Fr.) (sĕt-ĭ-*ām*.)
Septime (Ger.) (sĕp-*ti*-mĕ.)
The interval of a seventh.

Septimen-accord (Ger.) (sĕp-*tĭ*-mĕn-äk-kōrd.) The chord of the seventh, comprising the root, the third, fifth, and seventh.

Septimole (Lat.) (*sĕp*-tĭ-*mō*-le.)
Septiole (Lat.) (*sĕp*-tĭ-*ō*-lĕ.)
A group of seven notes, having the value, and to be played in the time of four, or six, of the same species. See *Notes*.

Séquence (Eng.) (*sē*-quĕns.)
Séquence (Fr.) (sā-*känhss*.)
Sequenz (Ger.) (sĕ *quĕnts*.)
Sequénza (It.) (sĕ-*quen*-tsä.)
A series, or progression, of similar chords, or intervals, in succession.

Serbáno (It.) (sĕr-*bä*-nō.) The serpent, a bass wind-instrument.

Sérénade (Fr.) (sĕr-ĕ-*näd*.)
Serenáta (It.) (sĕr-ĕ-*nä*-tä.)
Night music; an evening concert in the open air and under the window of the person to be entertained. This word is used in different senses in instrumental music. In the eighteenth century, it was used to denote a rather free suite of pieces, often orchestral, and forming a short program of music for an evening performance; such serenades generally began with a march-like movement, contained a slow movement and a minuet among their intermezzi, and concluded with a brilliant movement, but the form was not a fixed one. In another sense the serenade denoted a nocturnal love-song of soothing and tranquil character. There is also a contrast to the serenade, intended for morning performance, which *properly* is called an *aubade*. Schubert's song "Hark, Hark, the Lark," is a vocal specimen of an *aubade*, but there are instrumental works in this spirit also.

Seréno (It.) (sĕ-*rā*-nō.) Serene, calm, tranquil, cheerful.

Séria (It.) (*sā*-rē-ä.)
Serióso (It.) (sā-rē-*ō*-zō.)
Serious, grave; in a serious, sedate style.

Séria, opera (It.) (*sā*-rē-ä ō-pĕ-rä.) Serious, or tragic opera.

Sérieusement (Fr.) (sā-rĭ-üs-mănh.) Seriously, gravely.

Sério (It.) (*sā*-rē-ō.) Serious, grave.

ă as in *ah*; ā as in *hate*; ă as in *at*; ē as in *tree*; ĕ as in *eh*; ī as in *pine*; ĭ as in *pin*;

SERIO-COMIC   SFORZÁTO

Serio-comic. A song combining the grave with the ludicrous, or humorous.

Serpeggiándo (It.) (sĕr-pĕd-jē-*än*-dō.) Gently winding; sliding; creeping.

Serpent (Eng.) (*sĕr*-pĕnt.)
Serpénte (It.) (sĕr-*pen*-tĕ.)
Serpentóno (It.) (sĕr-pĕn-*tō*-nō.) } A bass wind-instrument, of deep, coarse tone, resembling a serpent in form. It was chiefly used in military bands. The serpent is replaced in the modern band by the bass tuba. The name is sometimes given to a reed-stop in an organ.

Service. A musical composition adapted to the services of religious worship.

Service-book. A missal; a book containing the musical service of the church.

Service, choral. A form of religious service in which the priest sings in response to the choir.

Sesqui (Lat.) (*sĕs*-quĭ.) A Latin particle, signifying a whole and a half, and which, when joined with *altera, terza, quarta*, etc., expresses a kind of ratio.

Sesquialtera (Lat.) (sĕs-quĭ-*ăl*-tĕ-rä.) The name given by the ancients to that ratio which includes one and a half to one. An organ-stop, comprising two or more ranks of pipes, of acute pitch.

Sesquitone (Lat.) (sĕs-quē-*tō*-nĕ.) A minor third, or interval consisting of three semi-tones.

Sésta (It.) (*săs*-tă.) } The interval of a
Sésto (It.) (*săs*-tō.) } sixth. See also *Sexte*.

Sestet (Eng.) (sĕs-*tĕt*.) } A composi-
Sestétto (It.) (sĕs-tāt-tō.) } tion for six voices or instruments.

Sestína (It.) (sĕs-tē-nä.) } A sextole, or
Sestóla (It.) (sĕs-*tō*-iä.) } sextolet. See *Notes*.

Sétte (It.) (*seï*-tĕ.) Seven.

Séttima (It.) (*set*-tē-mä.) } The interval
Séttimo (It.) (*set*-tē-mō.) } of a seventh.

Séttima maggióre (It.) (*set*-tē-mä mäd-jē-*ō*-rĕ.) Major seventh.

Séttima minóre (It.) (*set*-tē-mä mē-*nō*-rĕ.) Minor seventh.

Settimóla (It.) (set-ti-*mō*-lä.) A septimole. See *Notes*.

Setz-art (Ger.) (*sets*-ärt.) Style, or manner of composition.

Setzen (Ger.) (*set*-tsĕn.) To compose.

Seventeenth. An organ-stop. See *Tierce*.

Seventh. An interval containing six diatonic degrees.

Sevens and fives metre. Consists of a stanza of four lines in trochaic measure and designated, 7s and 5s.

Sevens and sixes metre. A metre designated thus: 7s and 6s, consisting of a stanza of four lines, iambic.

Sevens metre. A stanza of four lines in trochaic measure, each line containing seven syllables.

Seventh, diminished. An interval measured by nine half-steps.

Seventh, major. An interval measured by eleven half-steps.

Seventh, minor. An interval measured by ten half-steps.

Severaménte (It.) (sĕ-vĕr-ä-*men*-tĕ.) Severely, strictly, rigorously.

Severita (It.) (sĕ-vĕ-rē-*tä*.) Severity, strictness.

Sexta (Lat.) (*sĕx*-tä.) Sixth.

Sexte (Ger.) (*sĕx*-tĕ.) A sixth; also, the name of an organ-stop with two ranks of pipes, sounding the interval of a major sixth, a twelfth, and tierce on one slide.

Sextetto. See *Sestetto*.

Sextole (Lat.) (*sĕx*-tō-lĕ.) } A group
Sextuplet (Lat.) (*sĕx*-tū-*plĕt*.) } of six notes, having the value, and to be played in the time of four. See *Notes*.

Sextuple measure. The name formerly given to measures of two parts, composed of six equal notes, three for each part. This is more generally called *compound even* rhythm.

Sfogato (It.) (sfō-*gä*-tō.) A very high soprano.

Sfórza (It.) (*sför*-tsä.) Forced; with force and energy.

Sforzándo (It.) (sfōr-*tsän*-dō.) } *Forced;*
Sforzáto (It.) (sfōr-*tsä*-tō.) } one particular chord, or note, is to be played with force and emphasis.

ō as in *tone*; ô as in *dove*; ŏ as in *not*; ŭ as in *up*; ü the French sound of *u*.

233

SFORZATAMÉNTE　　　　　　　　　　　　　　　SIGNATURE

Sforzataménte (It.) (sfŏr-tsä-tä-*men*-tĕ.) Impetuously, energetically.

Sfumato (It.) (sfoo-*mäh*-tō.) Very lightly, like a vanishing smoke-wreath. *Sfumatura*, "Smoke-wreath" (title of a light, airy composition).

Shake. An ornament produced by the rapid alternation of two successive notes, comprehending an interval not greater than a whole tone, nor less than a semi-tone. Plain shake, or trill. See *Trill*.

Written.　　Played.

Sharp (Ger., *Kreuz*; Fr., *Dièse*; It., *Diesis*.) The sign ♯, which occurring either before a note or in the signature, raises the pitch of a tone one chromatic semitone. The sign had its origin in a St. Andrew's cross × which was used in the notation of the middle ages. See *Accidentals* and *Chromatics*.

Sharp, accidental. An occasional sharp placed before a note in the course of a piece, but not the same letter found sharp in the signature.

Sharp, double. A double sharp is equivalent to two sharps, raising a note a whole tone instead of a semi-tone; expressed thus: ♯♯ ×.

Sharp sixth. In the first inversion of the minor chord of the seventh; by sharpening the fundamental tone we obtain the chord of the *Sharp Sixth*, or as some writers call it, the *German Sixth*.

Shawm. A wind-instrument of the ancient Hebrews, supposed to be of the reed, or hautboy species.

Shift. A change of position of the left hand, in playing the violin, etc. See *Violin Shifts*.

Shift, double. A shift on the violin, to D in alt.

Shift, first. A violin shift on the fifth line, also called the *half-shift*.

Shift, half. See *First Shift*.

Shift, last. In violin-playing, the shift nearest the bridge.

Short metre (abb. *S. M.*) Four lines to each stanza; iambic verse, with the following arrangement of syllables — 6, 6, 8, 6. The pulsations being

◡ — ◡ — ◡ —
◡ — ◡ — ◡ —
◡ — ◡ — ◡ — ◡ —
◡ — ◡ — ◡ —

Short octaves. A term applied to the lower notes in old organs, where some of the notes were omitted.

Si (Fr.) (sē.) Applied in *solfáing* to the note B.

Si bémol (Fr.) (sēe bā-mōl.) ⎫
Si bemolle (It.) (sēe bā-mōl-lĕ.) ⎬ The note B♭.

Si bémol majeur (Fr.) (sēe bā-mōl mäzhür.) The key of B♭ major.

Si bémol mineur (Fr.) (sēe bā-mōl menür.) The key of B♭ minor.

Sibilate (*sĭb*-ĭ-lāte.) To sing with a hissing sound.

Siciliána (It.) (sē-tshē-lē-*ä*-nä.) ⎫ A
Siciliáno (It.) (sē-tshē-lē-*ä*-nō.) ⎬ dance of the Sicilian peasants, a graceful movement of a slow, soothing, pastoral character, in 6/8 or 12/8 time.

Side-drum. The common military drum so-called from its hanging at the side of the drummer when played upon.

Si dièse (Fr.) (sē dī-āz.) The note B♯.

Sieben (Ger.) (*sē*-b'n.) Seven.

Sieben-klang (Ger.) (*sĕ*-b'n-*kläng*.) Heptachord, a scale of seven notes.

Siebente (Ger.) (*sēe*-bĕn-tĕ.) Seventh.

Siebenzehnte (Ger.) (*sēe*-bĕn-tsĕn-tĕ.) Seventeenth.

Siegesgesang (Ger.) (*sēe*-ghĕs-ghĕ-säng.) ⎫
Siegeslied (Ger.) (*sēe*-ghĕs-*lēd*.) ⎬
A triumphal song.

Siegesmarsch (Ger.) (*sēe*-ghĕs-*märsh*.) A triumphal march.

Siffler (Fr.) (sĭf-flā.) To whistle.

Signature (Eng.) (*sĭg*-nă-tshūr.) ⎫ Name
Signatura (Spa.) (sēn-yä-*too*-rä.) ⎬ given
Signatur (Ger.) (*sĭg*-nä-*toor*.) ⎭ to the sharps, or flats, placed at the beginning of a piece, and at the commencement of each staff, to indicate the key in which it is written. See *Key*.

ă as in *ah*; ā as in *hate*; ă as in *at*; ē as in *tree*; ĕ as in *eh*; ī as in *pine*; ĭ as in *pin*;

234

Beethoven's House in Vienna

Sarrusophone

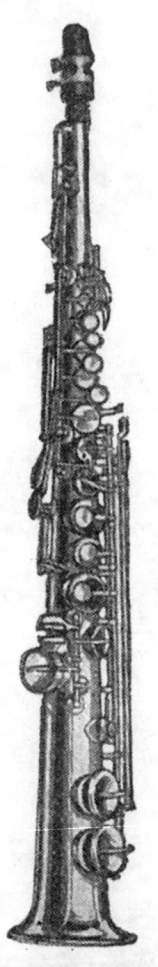

Straight Soprano Saxophone

Signature, time. Figures, in the form of a fraction, placed at the beginning of a piece to indicate the time. See *Time.*

Sign, cancelling. ♮ natural.

Sign, da capo. A mark placed before a bar, indicating that the piece, or movement, is to be repeated from that point.

Signe (Fr.) (sēn.) The sign, :𝄋: See *Segno.*

Signes accidentels (Fr.) (sēn ăk-sĭ-*dänh*-t'l.) Accidental sharps, flats, and naturals.

Signes de silences (Fr.)(sēen dĕ sĭ-*länhs.*) Rests.

Sign, neutralizing. A cancelling sign; a natural.

Signs. The following are the chief signs used in music:

. (1) A dot above or below a note signifies *staccato.* (2) After a note, or rest, it is a sign of length.

ı A dash above or below a note signifies *staccatissimo* (becoming obsolete at present).

⌢ A slur, bind, tie.

⌢⋯ A slur and dots above or below two or more notes (one dot to each note) indicate that the latter have to be played somewhat detached. See *Portamento.*

— Sustained. Horizontal dashes above or below a series of notes indicate that they have to be sustained but not slurred.

⁻ Accented and sustained, *ben pronunziato* or *marcato.*

▭ With a weighty and well-sustained touch, *pesante,* or *martellato.*

< *Crescendo.*

> *Diminuendo.*

> and < *Rinforzando,* accented.

∧ *Forzando,* or *sforzato,* accented. ∧ and > mean practically the same, unless used together, when the first has the stronger accent.

<> In vocal music would mean *Missa di Voce* (which see). In instrumental music it would also mean *crescendo* and *diminuendo* (a swell mark), but it is sometimes used over a single note, or chord, in piano music, in which case it means resonance without suddenness.

V Up-bow. Λ Down-bow in violoncello music.

⊔ or ⊓ down-bow in violin-music.

⌒ Hold, or *Fermata.*

⤳ Repeat preceding measure.

𝄋: :𝄋: Segno. Repeat from this sign.

✳ ✵ ⋕ Double sharp.

𝄇 𝄆 𝄇 𝄆 Repeat.

:‖: Repeat.

× or + Thumb (pfte-music.) *American Fingering.*

ʼ Breathing-mark.

≡ Added lines to call attention to repetition dots. *Bis* is also sometimes used as a repeat-mark.

⋀ ⋀ᐟ Mordent and Praller.

∼ ∼ᐟ 𝆗 Turns.

／ Repeat preceding figure of eighth notes.

⫽ Repeat preceding figure of sixteenth notes.

⫻ Repeat preceding figure of thirty-second notes.

∼∼∼∼ Indicates the continuation of a trill, or an octave mark.

{ *Arpeggio.*

⌈ Signifies sometimes in pianoforte ⌊ music that two notes on different staves have to be played with one hand.

≡ A stave. ≣ A bar.

𝄁 A double bar.

⊕ The coda mark. First time of playing disregard the sign. Second time (after D. C.) skip from this sign to the coda. Sometimes the sign is also placed at the coda.

Iᵐᵒ Iᵐᵃ : Primo, Prima (*prima volta*).

IIᵈᵒ IIᵈᵃ : Secondo, Seconda (*seconda volta*).

M. M. ♩ 120. Refers to Mäelzel's metronome. This or any other figure indicates to which part of the pendulum the regulator is to be moved,

ŏ as in *tone;* ô as in *dove;* ŏ as in *not;* ŭ as in *up;* ü the French sound of *u.*

235

and this or any other note indicates whether it beats halves, quarter-notes, or eighths, so many to the minute.

≡ or ≡ A direct.

✱ ⊕ These signs refer to the pianoforte-pedal. The first is the only one now in use, and indicates where the foot is to be raised after the pedal has been pressed down. The second is sometimes found in German editions.

⌐⌐ An American pedal-mark, showing exactly how long to use the damper-pedal.

Clefs.

Time signatures.

○ ♩ ♪ ♫ Notes.

Rests.

∪ A breathing-mark in some *vocalises*.

Organ-music, pedal; notes so connected are to be played with alternate toe and heel of same foot. Heel and toe are also sometimes marked ∧ ∨ and also o, ∧ over the note meaning right foot, and under left foot.

o Thumb positions (violoncello-playing).

∧ – ∨ Change toes on organ-pedal.

⌢⌢ Slide same toe to next note.

a′ b″ c‴
a¹ b² c³
- ⁼ ≡
a b c
A₁ B₁ C₂

} etc. See *Pitch* and *Tablature*.

{ Brace.

Tr. ∿∿ Trill.

♪ Short grace-note or acciaccatura.

♪ ♫ Long grace-note or appoggiatura. See also *Abbreviations, Notation, Notes, Accidentals, Turns, Trills, Flat, Sharp, Mordent, Direct, Rests*, etc.

Si majeur (Fr.) (see mä-zhür.) The key of B major.

Similar motion. Where two or more parts ascend, or descend, at the same time.

Simile (It.) (sĕ-mē-lĕ.) Similarly; in like manner.

Si mineur (Fr.) (see mĭ-*nür*.) The key of B mineur.

Simple counterpoint. That counterpoint in which note is set against note, and which is called *simple*, in opposition to more elaborate counterpoint which is known as *figurative*. Also sometimes called *harmonic counterpoint*.

Simple intervals. Those which do not exceed an octave.

Simple inversion. An inversion made by reversing the notes of fugal, or other subject in its answer, so that the ascending notes of the original passage descend in the answer, and *vice versa*.

Simple recitative. A recitative with the accompaniment of a bass part only; a plain recitative. See *Recitative*.

Sin 'al fine (It.) (sin äl fee-nĕ.) To the end; as far as the end.

Síncopa (It.) (sin-kō-pä.)
Síncope (It.) (sin-kō-pĕ.) } See *Syncopation*.

Sinfonía (It.) (sin-fō-*nĕ*-ä.)
Sinfonie (Fr.) (sănh-fō-*nĕ*.) } An orchestral composition in many parts; used by Bach and others for *prelude*. See *Symphony*.

Singen (Ger.) (sĭng-ĕn.) To sing; to chant; singing; chanting.

Singend (Ger.) (sĭng-ĕnd.) See *Cantábile*.

Sing-gedicht (Ger.) (sĭng-ghĕ-dĭkht.) Hymn; poem intended to be sung.

Singhiozzándo (It.) (sēn-ghēe-ōt-sän-dō.) Sobbingly.

Sing-kunst (Ger.) (sĭng-koonst.) The art of singing.

Single-action harp. A harp with pedals, by which each string can be raised one semi-tone. For *double-action harp*, see *Harp*.

ä as in *ah* · ā as in *hate;* ă as in *at;* ē as in *tree;* ĕ as in *eh;* ī as in *pine;* ĭ as in *pin;*

236

Single chant. A simple harmonized melody, extending only to one verse of a psalm, as sung in cathedrals, etc.

Sing-mährchen (Ger.) (*sĭng-mär*-kh'n.) A ballad.

Sing-meister (Ger.) (*sĭng-mīs*-tĕr.) Singing-master.

Sing-pult (Ger.) (sĭng-poolt.) Singing-desk.

Sing-schauspiel (Ger.) (*sĭng*-shous-pēl.) Singing-drama; a drama with songs, etc., interspersed.

Sing-schule (Ger.) (*sĭng-shoo*-lĕ.) Singing-school; a school, or method, for the voice.

Sing-spiel (Ger.) (sĭng-spēl.) An opera; melodrama; a piece interspersed with songs.

Sing-stimme (Ger.) (*sĭng-stĭm*-mĕ.) Singing-voice; a vocal part.

Sing-stimmen (Ger. pl.) (*sĭng-stĭm*-mĕn.) The voices; the vocal parts.

Sing-stück (Ger.) (sĭng-stük.) Air, melody.

Sing-stunde (Ger.) (*sĭng-stoon*-dĕ.) Singing-lesson.

Sing-tanz (Ger.) (sĭng-tänts.) Dance, accompanied by singing.

Sing-verein (Ger.) (*sĭng*-vĕ-*rīn*.) A choral society.

Sing-weise (Ger.) (*sĭng-vī*-sĕ.) Melody, tune.

Siniestra (Spa.) (sē-nĭ-*äs*-trä.) } The left
Sinistra (Lat.) (sĭn-ĭs-trä.) } hand.

Sinístra máno (It.) (si-*nēs*-trä *mä*-nō.) }
Sinistra manu (Lat.) (sĭn-ĭs-trä *mä*-nū.) } The left hand.

Síno (It.) (si-nō.) } To; as far as; until;
Sín (It.) (sin.) } *con fuòco sín 'al fíne*, with spirit to the end.

Síno al ségno (It.) (*si*-nō äl *sen*-yō.) As far as the sign.

Si piáce (It.) (sē pē-*ä*-tshĕ.) At pleasure; as you please.

Siren. } An instrument used for ascertain-
Sirene. } ing the rapidity of aërial vibration, corresponding to the different pitches of musical sounds.

Sirenen-gesang (Ger.) (sĭr-*ĕ*-nĕn-ghĕ-*säng*.) Siren-song; a soft, luscious, seductive melody.

Si réplica (It.) (sē *re*-plē-kä.) A repeat; to be repeated.

Si réplica una vólta (It.) (sē *re*-plē-kä oo-nä vōl-tä.) Play the part over again.

Si segue (It.) (sē sä-guĕ.) Go on.

Sistema (It.) (sēs-tĕ-mä.) System.

Sistrum (Lat.) (*sĭs*-trŭm.) An instrument of percussion of very great antiquity, supposed to have been invented by the Egyptians, and was much used by the priests of Isis and Osiris in sacrifice. It consisted of a rod of iron, bent into an oval, or oblong shape, or square at two corners, and curved at the others, and furnished with a number of movable rings, so that, when shaken, or struck with another rod of iron, it emitted the sound desired.

Si táce (It.) (sē *tä*-tshĕ.) Be silent.

Si vólga (It.) (sē *vōl*-gä.) Turn over the leaf.

Sixain (Fr.) (sēz-ănh.) Stanza; strophe of six verses.

Six-eighth measure. A measure having the value of six eighth-notes, marked $\frac{6}{8}$.

Sixes and fives metre. A metre consisting of a stanza of four lines alternating in length, of 6 and 5 syllables. Generally trochaic verse, as follows:

— ︶ — ︶ — ︶
— ︶ — ︶ —
— ︶ — ︶ — ︶
— ︶ — ︶ —

marked 6s and 5s.

Sixième (Fr.) (sēz-ĭ-*ām*.) A sixth.

Six pour quatre (Fr.) (sēz poor kätr.) A double triplet, or sextuplet; six notes to be played in the time of four.

Six-quarter measure. A measure having the amount of six quarter-notes, marked $\frac{6}{4}$.

Sixte (Fr.) (sĕkst.) A sixth.

Sixteenth note. A semiquaver, ♬.

Sixteenth rest. A pause equal in duration to a sixteenth note.

Sixtes (Fr.) (sĕkst.) Sixths.

Sixth. An interval comprising six sounds, or five diatonic degrees.

Sixth, augmented. An interval measured by ten half-steps.

Sixth, German. See *Extreme*.

ŏ as in *tone;* ô as in *dove;* ŏ as in *not;* ŭ as in *up;* ü the French sound of *u.*

Sixth, Italian. An interval obtained by suppressing the original seventh in the chord of the sharp sixth.

Sixth, major. An interval measured by nine half-steps.

Sixth minor. An interval measured by eight half-steps.

Sixth, sharp. An interval obtained from the first inversion of the minor chord of the seventh, by sharping the fundamental tone.

Sixty-fourth note. A hemidemisemiquaver.

Sixty-fourth rest. A pause equal in point of duration to a sixty-fourth note.

Skip. A term applied to any transition exceeding that of a whole tone step.

Skizzen (Ger. pl.) (*skĭts*-tsĕn.) *Sketches;* short pieces.

Skolien (Sweden) (skō-*lēn*.) Drinking-song.

Slancio, con (It.) (kon *slan*-shee-oh.) With vehemence; impetuously. (Sometimes written *islancio* for the sake of euphony.)

Slargándo (It.) (slär-*gän*-dō.)
Slargandósi (It.) (slär-gän-*dō*-zēe.)
Extending, enlarging, widening; the time to become gradually slower.

Slentándo (It.) (slĕn-*tän*-dō.) Relaxing the time; becoming gradually slower.

Slide. A movable tube in the trombone (formerly in the trumpet), which is pushed in and out to alter the pitch of the tones while playing. It is more perfect than the valve, because it changes only the length of the air-column, not its direction and form; and also because every interval of pitch is obtainable; but it is more difficult of manipulation than the keys, or valves. A rapid run of two or more notes as, for example, the following:

is called a Slide.

Slur (Ger., *Legatobogen;* Fr., *liaison;* It., *legatura*.) A curve drawn over or under two or more notes, signifying that they are to be executed *legato.* The slur over two notes is called the short slur. The slur first appeared in notation in connection with violin-music, and was used to show how many notes were to be executed with a single stroke of the bow. Soon after this it was also admitted into vocal notation to indicate the number of notes to be sung in a single breath. It is almost impossible to give absolute rules for the execution of the slur, there are so many exceptions. Yet the following rules may apply in general cases: 1. When two notes of small denomination (quarter-notes or less) are connected by a slur, the first note is generally accented, the second played lightly; the tone of the first is to overlap into that of the second note; and the second note is frequently shortened. This example,

would often be played thus:

2. When the slurred notes are of a longer denomination, the second is not generally shortened. 3. When the second note is longer than the first, the effect of the slur is often nothing more than a *legato* mark. 4. In vocal music, both long and short slurs are often used merely to show how many notes are to be sung to a single syllable. The *long slur* (over more than two notes) is frequently a very indefinite sign. It is one of the most vague signs in piano-music, often merely indicating a legato execution, and not the phrasing. In vocal-music it is used properly as a phrasing and breathing-mark, but it is impossible to formulate any rules that will cover the contradictory uses of the long slur in piano-music. See Elson's "Theory of Music."

Slurred. Notes, or passages, performed in a smooth and gliding manner, are said to be *slurred.*

Slurring. Performing in a smooth, gliding style.

ä as in *ah*; ā as in *hate*; ă as in *at*; ē as in *tree*; ĕ as in *eh*; ī as in *pine*; ĭ as in *pin;*

SMALL OCTAVE

Small octave. The name given in Germany to the notes included between C on the second space of the bass staff and the B above, these notes being expressed by small letters, as *a, b, c, d,* etc.

Smanicáre (It.) (smän-ē-*kä*-rĕ.) To shift, or change the position of the hand in playing the violin, guitar, etc.

Smaniánte (It.) (smän-ē-*än*-tĕ.) ⎫
Smaniáto (It.) (smä-nē-*ä*-tō.) ⎬ Furious; vehe-
Smanióso (It.) (smä-nē-*ō*-zō.) ⎭ ment; frantic with rage.

Sminuéndo (It.) (smē-noo-*en*-dō.) ⎫
Sminuíto (It.) (smē-noo-*ē*-tō.) ⎬
Smoréndo (It.) (smō-*ren*-dō.) ⎭
Diminishing; decreasing; gradually softer.

Smorfióso (It.) (smōr-fē-*ō*-zō.) Affected; coquettish; full of grimaces.

Smorz. An abbreviation of *Smorzándo.*

Smorzándo (It.) (smŏr-*tsän*-dō.) ⎫ Ex-
Smorzáto (It.) (smŏr-*tsä*-tō.) ⎭ tinguished; put out; suddenly dying away.

Snare-drum. The commonly used small drum, so named on account of strings of raw-hide drawn over its lower head, and to distinguish it from the large, or bass drum.

Soáve (It.) (sō-ä-vĕ.) A word implying that a movement is to be played in a gentle, soft, and engaging style.

Soaveménte (It.) (sō-ä-vĕ-*men*-tĕ.) Sweetly, agreeably, delicately.

Société chantante (Fr.) (sō-sĭ-ā-*tā* shänh-tänht.) Singing-society.

Soggétto (It.) (sōd-*jet*-tō.) Subject, theme, motive.

Soggétto di fúga (It.) (sōd-*jet*-tō dē *foo*-gä.) Subject of the fugue.

Soggétto invariato (It.) (sōd-*jet*-tō in-vä-rē-ä-tō.) The invariable subject — a term applied to the subject of counterpoint when it does not change the figure, or situation of the notes.

Soggétto variato (It.) (sōd-*jet*-tō vä-rē-ä-tō.) Variable subject — a term applied to the subject of a counterpoint when it changes the figure, or situation of the notes.

Soirée musicale (Fr.) (swä-rā mü-zē-*käl.*) A musical evening.

SOLFAING

Sol (sōl.) A syllable applied by the Italians and French to G, the fifth sound of the diatonic scale, or octave of C.

Sóla (It.) (*sō*-lä.) Alone. See *Sólo.*

Sol bémol (Lat.) (sōl bā-mōl.) The note G flat.

Sol bémol majeur (Fr.) (sōl bā-mōl mä-zhür.) The key of G flat major.

Sol bémol mineur (Fr.) (sōl bā-mōl mē-nür.) The key of G flat minor. (Not in use.)

Sol dièse (Fr.) (sōl dĭ-āz.) The note G sharp.

Sol dièse mineur (Fr.) (sōl dĭ-āz mē-nür.) The key of G sharp minor.

Solénne (It.) (sō-*len*-nĕ.) Solemn.

Solenneménte (It.) (sō-lĕn-nĕ-*men*-tĕ.) Solemnly.

Solfaing. Singing the notes of the scale to the monosyllables applied to them by Guido. Guido was a Benedictine monk (b. Arezzo, about A.D. 1000) and taught music in the monastery at Pomposa, about 1032. He found great difficulty in his work because of the vagueness of notation, particularly in the matter of pitch. He observed that each line of a certain hymn which the students sang daily to St. John began with a different syllable, and also rose one degree at each phrase. The music was as follows:

UT que-ant la - xis, RE-so - na-re

fi - bris, MI - ra ge-sto-rum FA-mu-li-tu-

o-rum, SOL-ve pol - lu - ti, LA-bi - i re-

a - tum, San - cte Jo - han - nes.

Here was Guido's opportunity. He caused these syllables to be used to represent the notes by the students, who had already learned to associate them together in their minds, and the greater part of the modern scale was formed. It may be mentioned that

ô as in *tone;* ô as in *dove;* ŏ as in *not;* ŭ as in *up;* ü the French sound of *u.*

the French today use *ut* as the first note of the scale although other nations have changed it to *do*. Guido's scale was hexachordal, and contained no *leading-tone*. The seventh note was added in the sixteenth or seventeenth century, and received the name of *si*. The change of *ut* to *do* is attributed to Buononcini, about 1700.

Solfège (Fr.) (sōl-*fezh*.) } Exercises for the voice according to the rules of solmization.
Solféggi (It. pl.) (sōl-*fed*-ji.)
Solféggio (It.) (sōl-*fed*-jē-ō.)

Solfeggiaménti (It.) (sōl-fed-jē-ä-*men*-tē.) Solféggi.

Solfeggiáre (It.) (sōl-fed-jē-*ä*-rĕ.) To practice Solféggi.

Solfeggiren (Ger.) (sōl-fĕg-ghĭ-r'n.) }
Solfier (Fr.) (sōl-fē-ā.) To solfa.

Sóli (It.) (*sō*-lē.) A particular passage played by principals only, one performer to each part.

Sólito (It.) (*sō*-lē-tō.) *Accustomed;* in the usual manner.

Sollécito (It.) (sō-*le*-tshē-tō.) *Careful, solicitous;* meaning an attentive and careful style of execution.

Sol majeur (Fr.) (sōl mä-zhür.) The key of G major.

Sol mineur (Fr.) (sōl mē-nür.) The key of G minor.

Solmisáre (It.) (sōl-mē-zä-rĕ.) } The practice
Solmizáre (It.) (sōl-mē-*tsä*-rĕ.)
Solmisiren (Ger.) (*sōl*-mĭ-*sĭr*-ĕn.)
of the scales, applying to the different tones their respective syllables, *do, re, mi, fa, sol, la, si;* to this kind of vocal exercise the practice of Solféggi is added.

Solmization. See *Solféggi* and *Solmisáre*.

Sólo (It.) (*sō*-lō.) } A composition for a single voice, or instrument.
Solo (Fr.) (*sō*-lō.)
Solo (Ger.) (*sō*-lō.)

Soloist. One who sings, or performs alone, with or without the aid of accompaniment.

Solo pitch. The tuning of an instrument a little higher than the ordinary pitch in order to obtain brilliancy of tone with a certain amount of ease to the player.

Solospieler (Ger.) A solo player.
Solostimme (Ger) A solo part.
Sómma espressióne (It.) (sōm-mä ĕs-prĕs-sē-*ō*-nĕ.) Very great expression.

Sommeils (sŏm-māl.) The name by which the French distinguished the airs in their old serious operas, because they were calculated to tranquillize the feelings and induce drowsiness.

Sommerlied (Ger.) (sōm-mĕr-lēd.) A song in praise of summer.

Sommier (Fr.) (sō-mĭ-ā.) The wind-chest.

Sommier d'orgue (Fr.) (sō-mĭ-ā d'ōrg.) Wind-chest of an organ.

Son (Fr.) (sŏnh.) } Sound.
Son (Spa.) (sōn.)

Sonábile (It.) (sō-*nä*-bē-lĕ.) } Sonorous, resonant.
Sonable (Spa.) (sō-*nä*-blĕ.)

Sonagliáre (It.) (sō-näl-yē-*ä*-rē.) To jingle; to ring a small bell.

Sonáglio (It.) (sō-*näl*-yē-ō.) A small bell.

Sonaménto (It.) (sō-nä-*men*-tō.) Sounding, ringing, playing.

Sonáre (It.) (sō-*nä*-rĕ.) To sound; to have a sound; to ring; to play upon.

Sonáre álla ménte (It.) (sō-*nä*-rĕ *äl*-lä *men*-tĕ.) To play extempore; to improvise.

Sonáre il violíno (It.) (sō-*nä*-rĕ ēl vē-ō-*lē*-nō.) To play upon the violin.

Sonáta (It.) (sō-*nä*-tä.) } An instrumental composition, usually of three or four distinct movements, each with a unity of its own, yet all related so as to form a perfect whole. It commonly begins with an allegro, sometimes preceded by a slow introduction. Then come the andante, adagio, or largo; then the minuet and trio, or scherzo; and lastly the finale in quick time. This form is applied not only to large piano sonatas, but to symphonies, string quartet, etc. The form of the sonata grew slowly from the first vague shapes used in the seventeenth century, which often resembled the suite. The sonatas of Domenico Scarlatti, Ph. Em. Bach, and Corelli, show the old form gradually crystallizing into two movements. Of
Sonate (Fr.) (sō-*nät*.)
Sonate (Ger.) (sō-*nä*-tĕ.)

ä as in *ah*; ā as in *hate*; ă as in *at*; ē as in *tree*; ĕ as in *eh*; ī as in *pine*; ĭ as in *pin*;

240

these, the first movement was very important, for it led to the *sònata allegro*, the most important single movement form of sonata and one which is even now constantly used for the first movement (and sometimes other movements) of the sonata, and symphony. Briefly stated, this form is follows:

EXPOSITION.	MIDDLE PART OR DEVELOPMENT.	RECAPITULATION.
Chief Theme. Subordinate Theme in related key. Closing Theme. (Repetition.)	often Followed by Returning Passage	Chief Theme. Subordinate Theme (generally in Tonic key). Closing Theme.

Haydn first established the classical sonata form, although Ph. Em. Bach, Dittersdorf, Kozeluch, and others, produced sporadic works in very nearly the same shape. Mozart improved and Beethoven culminated the form. In the full sonata form the second movement would be in slow *tempo*. In a three-movement sonata the slow movement becomes the central movement of the work. The slow movement is the emotional or romantic part of the sonata, and is more free than the first movement. Some composers who are not successful in the sonata-movement or sonata-allegro form, are yet very expressive in the slow movement. Chopin is an example of this. The slow movement is generally in a related key to that of the first movement. Beethoven frequently used the key of the submediant for this part of the sonata. The *tempo* of the slow movement varies from *largo* (used by Haydn and others) to *allegretto* (used by Beethoven in his seventh symphony and elsewhere), but is most frequently either *andante*, or *adagio*. The slow movement has no fixed form, but is often in *song form*, *variation form sonata-allegro*, or *rondo*. The third movement (if the four-movement form is used) is a *minuet*, or *scherzo* (see these nouns, and also *Form*), but in the three-movement form this movement is omitted. Concertos omit this part. The forms chiefly employed in the finale are: 1. The *sonata-rondo*. 2. The *sonata-allegro*, but with less development than is used in the opening movement, as development should be the chief feature of the first movement, at least, in a large work. 3. *Grand variations*, which are certainly the best offset to the development of the first movement, since variation differs from development in keeping the harmonic shape unchanged. Examples of these modes of ending may be found in Beethoven's works, as follows: 1st mode, Sonatas Op. 2, and Op. 13. 2d mode, Sonata Op. 2, No. 1. 3d mode, Sonatas Op. 109 and 111. For further study of the sonata see Prout's "Musical Form," Pauer's "Musical Forms," Goetschius' "Lessons in Music Form," Elson's "Theory of Music."

Sonata da cámera (It.) (sō-nä-tä dä kä-mĕ-rä.) A sonata designed for the chamber, or parlor.

Sonata da chiésa (It.) (sō-*nä*-tä dä kē-*ā*-zä.) A church-sonata, an organ-sonata.

Sonata di bravúra (It.) (sō-*nä*-tä dē brä-*voo*-rä.) A brilliant, bold style of sonata.

Sonata form. In the style of a sonata. Sonata form is also synonymous with *sonata-allegro*.

Sonata, grand. A massive and extended sonata, consisting usually of four movements.

Sonatína (It.) (sō-nä-*tē*-nä.) } A short,
Sonatine (Fr.) (sō-nä-*tēn*.) } easy sonata, generally two or three movements. The *sonatina movement* differs from the *sonata-allegro* in having no development, or middle section, being merely an exposition, followed by a recapitulation.

Sonatójo (It.) (sō-nä-*tō*-hō.) A sounding-board.

Sonatóre (It.) (sō-nä-*tō*-rĕ.) An instrumental performer.

Son doux (Fr.) (sŏhn doo.) Soft sound.

Song. 1. (Ger., *Gesang;* Fr., *chant;* It., *canto*.) Vocal musical expression or utterance. 2. (Ger., *Lied;* Fr., *chanson;* It., *canzone*.) A lyrical poem set to music. The *song* deals with emotions; the *ballad* tells a story. *Song form* is a musical form originally derived from vocal music. (See *Form*.)

Folk-song is a simple song (frequently a ballad) which is popular with the common people. *Songs* are chiefly of two styles of composition. 1st. The *strophe form* in which the music is set to the first stanza and then repeated to each succeeding stanza. 2d. The *art-song* (or *through-composed — Durch componiert* style) in which each stanza receives separate musical treatment according to its contents. Among Schubert's songs " The Miller's Flowers" and "Impatience" are strophe forms, and the " Erl-King" and " The Wanderer " are *art-songs*. The *strophe form* can only be artistically employed when there are very few stanzas in a poem and all of the same general purport, as in Schubert's " Impatience."

Song, Bacchanalian. A song which either in sentiment, or style, relates to scenes of revelry.

Song, boat. A song sung by the rowers; gondolier-song.

Song, erotic. A love-song.

Song, florid. A term applied by musicians of the fourteenth century to figured descant, in order to distinguish it from the old chant, or plain song.

Song-form. See *Form*.

Song, four-part. A song arranged for four voices.

Song, gondolier. A song sung by the Venetian gondoliers; a barcarolle.

Song, hunting. A melody set to words in praise of the chase.

Song, martial. A song, the subject and style of which are war-like.

Song, national. A song identified with the history of a nation, on account of the sentiments it expresses, or from long use.

Song, nautical. A song relating to the sea.

Song, nuptial. A song celebrating marriage.

Song, patriotic. A song intended to inspire a love of country.

Song, plain. The old ecclesiastical chant, without any of the harmony which now enriches it.

Songs without Words (Ger., *Lieder ohne Worte*; Fr., *Chants sans Paroles*.) Pianoforte-pieces of a short, undeveloped and vocal character, consisting of a melody and accompaniment.

Sonnerie (Fr.) A *Carillon* (peal, or chime of bells).

Sóno (It.) (soh-no.) Sound, tone.

Sonnet. A short poem of fourteen lines, two stanzas of four verses each and two of three each, the rhymes being adjusted by a particular rule.

Sonnettier (Fr.) (sŏnh-nĕt-tĭ-ā.) Bellmaker, or seller.

Sorneur (Fr.) (sŏnh-nür.) A bellringer.

Sonometer (sō-*nŏm*-ĕ-tĕr.) An instrument for measuring intervals, or the vibrations of sounds.

Sonoraménte (It.) (sō-nō-rä-*men*-tĕ.) Sonorously, harmoniously.

Sonore (Fr.) (sŏ-*nōr*.) } Sonorous, harmonious, resonant.
Sonóro (It.) (sō-*nō*-rō.) }

Sonorific (sō-nō-*rĭf*-ĭk.) Producing sound.

Sonorita (It.) (sō-nō-rē-*tä*.) } Harmony,
Sonorité (Fr.) (sō-nō-rē-*tā*.) } resonance, sonorousness.

Sonorous (sō-*nō*-rous.) An epithet applied to whatever is capable of yielding sound; full, or loud in sound; rich-toned, musical.

Son perçant (Fr.) (sŏnh pär-sänh.) A shrill, piercing sound.

Sons étouffés (Fr. pl.) (sŏnhs'ā-toof-fā.) Stifled, or muffled tones.

Sons harmoniques (Fr. pl.) (sŏnh' härmŏnh-*ēk*.) Harmonic sounds.

Sons pleins (Fr. pl.) (sŏnhs' plănh.) In flute music, this means that the notes must be blown with a very full, round tone.

Sonus (Lat.) (*sō*-nŭs.) Sound, tone.

Sópra (It.) (*sō*-prä.) Above, upon, over, before. See *Super*.

Sópra dominánte (It.) (*sō*-prä dō-mē-*nän*-tĕ.) The fifth, or upper dominant.

Sopráni (It. pl.) (sō-*prä*-nē.) Treble voices.

Sopran (Ger.) (sō-*prän*.) } The treble;
Sopráno (It.) (sō-*prä*-nō.) } the highest kind of female voice; a treble, or soprano singer. Normal compass about

SOPRANO

The soprano is the highest part in concerted vocal music, and carries the air, or melody, in any modern composition that presents harmony, or counterpoint. But this was not always the case. In the early days of counterpoint it gave support to the melody, which always lay in the *tenor*. See *Tenor*. It was then called "*Discantus*," which indicated that it was "against the melody," and not the melody itself. We give an example of this old kind of counterpoint with the melody in the *tenor* part, the *discant* giving counterpoint against it: it is "Old Hundred," in Dowland's setting of about three centuries ago:

[musical notation: "All people that on earth do dwell, Sing to the Lord with cheerful voice, Him serve with fear, His praise forth tell, Come ye before Him and rejoice."]

It was about three hundred years ago also, that the change in part-writing took place. Lucas Osiander and Hans Leo Hassler should be mentioned as reformers in music. The innovation which they made may seem a very slight one, but it was none the less of great importance. It was the giving of the melody, in part-music, to the highest voice, changing its name from *discant* to *soprano* (meaning *above*). To us it seems self-evident that this voice should carry the tune, but, as the above selection shows, it was not so with the early composers. They desired to make the most of their discant, and the melody, given in the tenor, in a part-song, served only as a peg whereon to hang the counterpoint. See *Voice, Tenor, Descant.*

Sopráno acúto (It.) (sō-*prä*-nō ä-*koo*-tō.) High soprano.

Soprano clef. The C clef on the first line of the staff for soprano, instead of using the G clef on the second line for that part.

Soprano clef, mezzo. The C clef when placed on the second line of the staff, formerly used for the second treble voice, and for which the soprano clef is now substituted.

Sopráno concertáto (It.) (sō-*prä*-nō kŏn-tshĕr-*tä*-tō.) The soprano solo part, the part for a solo treble voice in a chorus.

Sopránā córda (It.) (sō-*prä*-nō *kŏr*-dä.) The E string of a violin.

Sopráno mézzo (It.) (sō-*prä*-nō *met*-sō.) A species of female voice between soprano and alto.

Soprano, second. Low soprano.

Sopráno secúndo od álto (It.) (sō-*prä*-nō sā-*koon*-dō ōd *äl*-tō.) The second soprano, or alto.

Sopran-stimme (Ger.) (sō-*prän stĭm*-mĕ) A soprano voice.

ō as in *tone*; ô as in *dove*; ŏ as in *not*; ŭ as in *up*; ü the French sound of *u*.

Sópra quinta (It.) (*sō*-prä *quēen*-tä.) Upper dominant.

Sópra úna córda (It.) (*sō*-prä *oo*-nä *kŏr*-dä.) On one string.

Sórda (It.) (sōr-dä.) Muffled; veiled tone.

Sordaménte (It.) (sōr-dä-*men*-tĕ.) Softly, gently; also, damped, muffled.

Sordellína (It.) (sōr-dĕl-*lēe*-nä.) A species of bag-pipe.

Sordína (It.) (sōr-*dēe*-nä.) } A sordine,
Sordina (Spa.) (sōr-*dēe*-nä.) } or mute.

Sordet. } A small instrument, or
Sordine. } damper, in the mouth of a trumpet, or on the bridge of a violin, or violoncello, to make the sound more faint and subdued; a mute.

Sordíni (It. pl.) (sōr-*dēe*-nē.) *Mutes* in violin-playing; and the *dampers* in pianoforte music. See *Con Sordíni*, and *Sénza Sordíni*.

Sordíni levati (It.) (sŏr-*dēe*-nē lĕ-*vä*-tĕ.) The dampers removed.

Sordíno (It.) (sōr-*dēe*-nō.) A sordine; a mute.

Sórdo (It.) (*sōr*-dō.) Muffled; veiled tone.

Sorgfältig (Ger.) (*sōrg*-fäl-tĭgh.) Carefully.

Sortíta (It.) (sŏr-*tēe*-tä.) The opening air in an operatic part, the entrance *ária*; also a closing voluntary.

Sospensióne (It.) (sōs-pĕn-sē-*ō*-nĕ.) A suspension.

Sospensivaménte (It.) (sōs-pĕn-sē-vä-*men*-tĕ.) Irresolutely, waveringly.

Sospirándo (It.) (sōs-pē-*rän*-dō.) ⎫
Sospiránte (It.) (sōs-pē-*rän*-tĕ.) ⎪
Sospirévole (It.) (sōs-pē-*reh*-vo-lĕ.) ⎬
Sospiróso (It.) (sōs-pē-*rō*-zō.) ⎪
Sighing; very subdued; doleful. ⎭

Sospíro (It.) (sōs-*pēe*-rō.) A quarter-rest.

Sostenéndo (It.) (sōs-tĕ-*nän*-dō.) }
Sostenúto (It.) (sōs-tĕ-*noo*-tō.) }
Sustaining the tone; keeping the notes down their full duration.

Sostenúto mólto (It.) (sōs-tĕ-*noo*-tŏ mōl-tō.) In a highly sustained manner.

Sotto (It.) (sōt-tō.) Under, below.

Sótto vóce (It.) (sōt-tō *vō*-tshĕ.) Softly; in a low voice; in an undertone.

Soubrette (Fr.) (soo-*brĕtt*.) A female singer for a subordinate and playful part in a comic opera.

Sou-chantre (Fr.) (soo-shäntr.) A sub-chanter.

Soufflerie (Fr.) (soof-flĕ-rē.) The machinery belonging to the bellows in an organ.

Souffleur (Fr.) (soof-flŭr. } Bellows-
Souffleuse (Fr.) (soof-flüs.) } blower; also a prompter in a theatre.

Souffleur d'orgues (Fr.) (soof-flŭr d'ōrgh.) Bellows-blower of an organ.

Sound-board. } The thin board over
Sounding-board. } which the strings of the pianoforte and similar instruments are distended.

Sound-post. A small post, or prop, within a violin, nearly under the bridge; it is not only to sustain the tension but to carry the vibrations from the front-board, or *belly* to the back, thus making the whole sound-box vibratory.

Soupir (Fr.) (soo-pēer.) A quarter-rest.

Soupir de croche (Fr.) (soo-pēer dŭh krōsh.) See *Demi-soupir*.

Soupir de double croche (Fr.) (soo-pēer dŭh doobl krōsh.) See *Quart de soupir*.

Soupir de triple croche (Fr.) (soo-pēer-dŭh trēpl krōsh.) See *Demi-quart de soupir*.

Sourdeline (Fr.) (*soor*-dĭ-lēen.) An Italian bag-pipe, or *musette*.

Sourdement (Fr.) (*soord*-mänh.) In a subdued manner.

Sourdet (Fr.) (soor-*dĕ*.) The little pipe of a trumpet; a sordine, or mute.

Sourdine (Fr.) (soor-dēen.) The name of a harmonium stop. See also *Sordino*.

Sous (Fr.) (soo.) Under, below.

Sous-chantre (Fr.) (soo-*shänhtr*.) A sub-chanter.

Sous-dominante (Fr.) (soo-dō-mĭ-*nänh*.) The subdominant, or fourth of the scale.

Sous-médiante (Fr.) (soo-mā-dĭ-*änht*.) The submediant, or sixth of the scale.

Sous-tonique (Fr.) (soo-tōn-*ēk*.) The seventh of the scale, or subtonic.

ă as in *ah*; ā as in *hate*; ă as in *at*; ē as in *tree*; ĕ as in *eh*; ī as in *pine*; ĭ as in *pin*;

The soprano is the highest part in concerted vocal music, and carries the air, or melody, in any modern composition that presents harmony, or counterpoint. But this was not always the case. In the early days of counterpoint it gave support to the melody, which always lay in the *tenor*. See *Tenor*. It was then called "*Discantus*," which indicated that it was "against the melody," and not the melody itself. We give an example of this old kind of counterpoint with the melody in the *tenor* part, the *discant* giving counterpoint against it: it is "Old Hundred," in Dowland's setting of about four centuries ago:

on .
All peo - ple that on .
. . . . earth do
earth do dwell, Sing
cheer - ful
to the Lord with cheer - ful
voice, Him serve with fear, His
Come
praise . . forth tell, Come

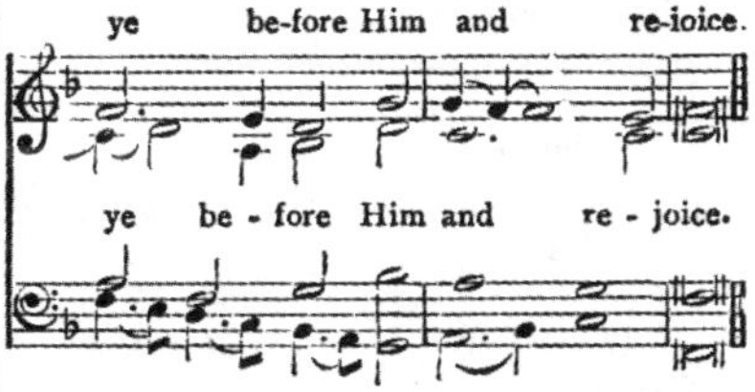
ye be-fore Him and re-joice.
ye be - fore Him and re - joice.

It was about four hundred years ago also, that the change in part-writing took place. Lucas Osiander and Hans Leo Hassler should be mentioned as reformers in music. The innovation which they made may seem a very slight one, but it was none the less of great importance. It was the giving of the melody, in part-music, to the highest voice, changing its name from *discant* to *soprano* (meaning *above*). To us it seems self-evident that this voice should carry the tune, but, as the above selection shows, it was not so with the early composers. They desired to make the most of their discant, and the melody, given in the tenor, in a part-song, served only as a peg whereon to hang the counterpoint. See *Voice*, *Tenor*, *Descant*.

Sopráno acúto (It.) (sō-*prä*-nō ä-*koo*-tō.) High soprano.

Soprano clef. The C clef on the first line of the staff for soprano, instead of using the G clef on the second line for that part.

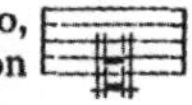

Soprano clef, mezzo. The C clef when placed on the second line of the staff, formerly used for the second treble voice, and for which the soprano clef is now substituted.

Sopráno concertáto (It.) (sō-*prä*-nō kŏn-tshĕr-*tä*-tō.) The soprano solo part, the part for a solo treble voice in a chorus.

Sopràna córda (It.) (sō-*prä*-nō *kŏr*-dä.) The E string of a violin.

Sopráno mézzo (It.) (sō-*prä*-nō *met*-sō.) A species of female voice between soprano and alto.

Soprano, second. Low soprano.

Sopráno secúndo od álto (It.) (sō-*prä*-nō sā-*koon*-dō ōd *äl*-tō.) The second soprano, or alto.

Sopran-stimme (Ger.) (sō-*prän stĭm*-mĕ.) A soprano voice.

ō as in *tone;* ô as in *dove;* ŏ as in *not;* ŭ as in *up;* ü the French sound of *u*.

Squillanteménte (It.) (squil-län-tĕ-*men*-tĕ.) Clearly, loudly, shrilly.

Squilláre (It.) (squil-*lä*-rĕ.) To sound loud and shrill.

Sta (It.) (stä.) This, as it stands; to be played as written.

Stabat mater (Lat.) (*stä*-băt *mä*-tĕr.) The Mother stood — a hymn on the crucifixion.

Stábile (It.) (*stä*-bē-lĕ.) Firm.

Stac. An abbreviation of *Staccáto*.

Staccatíssimo (It.) (stäk-kä-*tēs*-sē-mō.) Very much detached; as *staccáto* as possible.

Staccáto (It.) (stäk-*kä*-tō.) Detached; distinct; separated from each other.

Staccato marks. Small dots or dashes placed over or under the notes, thus: The wedge-shaped marks are shorter than the dots, but are little used by modern composers. See *Touch*.

Staccato touch. A sudden lifting up of the fingers from the keys, giving to the music a light, detached, airy effect.

Staccáre (It.) (stäk-*kä*-rĕ.) To detach; to separate each note.

Stadt-musikus (Ger.)(*städt-moo*-sĭ-kŭs.)
Stadt-pfeifer (Ger.) (*städt-pfī*-fĕr.) Town-musician.

Staff. The five horizontal and parallel lines on and between which the notes are written. See *Notation*.

Staff of four lines. In the earlier ages of the Christian Church, the monks frequently used music written on four lines with bass clefs. See *Notation*.

Staff, bass. The staff marked with the bass clef.

Staff, tenor. The staff marked with the tenor clef.

Staff, treble. The staff marked with the treble clef.

Stagióne (It.) (stä-jē-*ō*-nĕ.) The season; the musical season.

Stagióne di cartéllo (It.) (stä-jē-*ō*-nĕ dē kär-*täl*-lō.) The operatic season.

Stambuzáre (It.) (stäm-boo-*tsä*-rĕ.) To beat the drum.

Stamm-accord (Ger.) (stäm-äk-kōrd.) A radical, or fundamental chord from which others are derived.

Stampita (It.) (stäm-*pē*-tä.) An air; a tune; a song.

Stance (Fr.) (stänhts.) A stanza.

Stanchezza (It.) (stan-*ket*-za.) Weariness; *con st.*, wearily; very dragging.

Ständchen (Ger.) (*stend*-khĕn.) A serenade.

Standhaft (Ger.) (*ständ*-häft.) Steadily, firmly, resolutely.

Standhaftigkeit (Ger.) (*ständ*-häft-tĭg-kīt.) Firmness, resolution.

Stand, music. A light frame designed for holding sheets, or books, for the convenience of performers.

Stanghétta (It.) (stän-*get*-tä.) A bar line. The fine line drawn across and perpendicular to the staff.

Stánza (It.) (*stän*-tsä.) A verse of a song, or hymn.

Stark (Ger.) (stärk.) Strong, loud, vigorous.

Stärke (Ger.) (*stär*-kĕ.) Vigor, force, energy.

Starke Stimmen (Ger.) (*stär*-ke *stĭm*-mĕn.) Loud stops; *Mit starken Stimmen*, with loud stops.

Stat (Lat.) (stăt.) This; as it stands.

Stave. Name formerly given to the staff.

Steg (Ger.) (stĕgh.) The bridge of a violin, etc.

Stem. The thin stroke which is drawn from the head of a note.

Stem, double. A stem drawn both upward and downward from a note, indicating that the note belongs to two parts.

Stentándo (It.) (stĕn-*tän*-dō.) Heavy, and retarding.

Stentáto (It.) (stĕn-*tä*-tō.) Hard, forced, loud.

Stentor. A herald, in Homer, having a very loud voice — hence, any person having a powerful voice.

Stentorian. Extremely loud.

Step. A degree upon the staff. Some teachers use the terms *step* and *half-step* in place of *tone* and *semi-tone*.

Step, half. A semi-tone.

ă as in *ah* ; ā as in *hate* ; ă as in *at* ; ē as in *tree* ; ĕ as in *eh* ; ī as in *pine* ; ĭ as in *pin* ;

246

Sterbe-gesang (Ger.) (*stĕr*-bĕ-ghĕ-säng.)
Sterbe-lied (Ger.) (*stĕr*-bĕ-*lēd*.) Funeral hymn.
Sterbe-ton (Ger.) (*stĕr*-bĕ *tōn*.) A tone diminishing, dying away insensibly. *Sterbend* is similar to *morendo*.
Stéso (It.) (*stā*-zō.) Extended, diffused, larger.
Stéso móto (It.) (*stā*-zō *mō*-tō.) A slow movement.
Stésso (It.) The same; *l'istésso témpo*, in the same time.
Stibacchiáto (It.) (stē-bäk-kē-*ä*-tō.) Relaxing; retarding the time.
Sticcádo (It.) (stēk-*kä*-dō.) }
Sticcáto (It.) (stēk-*kä*-tō.) } An instrument consisting of little bars of wood rounded at the top and resting on the edges of a kind of open box. They gradually increase in length and thickness, are tuned to the notes of the diatonic scale and are struck with a little ball at the end of a stick. A *Xylophone*.
Stich (Gr.) (stīkh.) A dot, or point.
Sticker. A portion of the connection, in an organ, between the keys, or pedals, and the valve; a short link attached to a key or pedal, and acting on the backfall.
Stíle (It.) (stē-lĕ.) Style.
Stíle a cappélla (It.) (stē-lĕ ä käp-*pel*-lä.) In the chapel style. A *Cappella*.
Stíle grandióse (It.) (stē-lĕ grän-dē-*ō*-zō.) In a grand style of composition, or performance.
Stíle rigoróso (It.) (stē-lĕ rē-gō-*rō*-zö.) In a rigid, strict style.
Still (Ger.) (stĭll.) Calmly; quietly.
Still-gedacht (Ger.) (stĭll-ghĕ-*däkt*.) A stopped diapason; of a quiet tone.
Stilo (It.) (stēe-lō.) Style; manner of composition, or performance.
Stimm-deckel (Ger.) (*stĭm dĕk*-ĕl.) Sound-board.
Stimme (Ger.) (*stĭm*-mĕ.) The voice; sound; also, the sound-post in a violin, etc.; also a part in vocal, or instrumental music; also an organ-stop, or register.
Stimmen (Ger. pl.) (*stĭm*-m'n.) Parts, or voices; also organ-stops.

Stimmer (Ger.) (*stĭm*-mĕr.) Tuner; also a tuning-hammer.
Stimm-gabel (Ger.) (*stĭm-gä*-b'l.) Tuning-fork.
Stimm-hammer (Ger.) (*stĭm-häm*-mĕr.) Tuning-key, tuning-hammer.
Stimmig (Ger.) (*stĭm*-mĭg.) Having a sound.
Stimm-pfeife (Ger.) (*stĭm-pfī*-fé.) Wooden-fife; pitch-pipe.
Stimm-stock (Ger.) (stĭm-stōk.) The sound-post of a violin, etc.
Stimmung (Ger.) (*stĭm*-moong.) Tuning, tune, tone.
Stinguéndo (It.) (sten-*guen*-dō.) Dying away; becoming extinct.
Stiracchiáto (It.) (stē-räk-kēe-*ä*-tō.) }
Stiráto (It.) (stē-*rä*-tō.) } Stretched, forced, retarded. See *Allargándo*.
Stonánte (It.) (stō-*nän*-tĕ.) Discordant; out of tune.
Stop. A register, or row of pipes in an organ; on the violin, etc., it means the pressure of the finger upon the string. DOUBLE STOP, pressing two strings at once. ORGAN-STOPS are of two kinds, *flue*, and *reed-stops*. (See *Organ*.) The *flue-stops* are subdivided into, 1st, *principal*, or cylindrical pipes of diapason style; 2d, *gedackt* (or covered) pipes, which are stopped at the end, and give a hollow tone; 3d, *flute-work*, which includes pipes which are too narrow to sound their fundamental tones, stopped pipes, with chimneys, and three-sided or four-sided pipes. MECHANICAL-STOPS are those which do not give a tone, but work some mechanism, as the couplers, etc. MIXTURE-STOPS are those sounding more than one note to a single key. They are to add the harmonics to the *principals*. See *Harmonics, Acoustics, Organ, Pipe*.
Stop, bassoon. A reed-stop in an organ resembling the bassoon in quality of tone.
Stop, claribel. A stop similar to the clarinet-stop.
Stop, clarion, or octave trumpet. A stop resembling the tone of a trumpet, but an octave higher than the trumpet-stop.

ō as in *tone*; ŏ as in *dove*; ŏ as in *not*; ŭ as in *up*; ü the French sound of *u*.

247

Stop, cornet. A stop consisting of five pipes to each key.

Stop, cremona. A reed-stop in unison with the diapasons.

Stop, double diapason. An open set of pipes tuned an octave below the diapasons.

Stop, double trumpet. The most powerful reed-stop in the organ, the pipes being of the same length as the double diapason, to which it is tuned in unison.

Stop, dulciana. A stop of peculiar sweetness of tone, which it chiefly derives from the bodies of its pipes, being longer and smaller than those of the pipes of other stops.

Stop, fagotto. The bassoon-stop.

Stop, fifteenth. A stop which derives its name from its pitch, or scale, being fifteen notes (two octaves) above that of the diapason.

Stop, flute. An organ-stop, resembling in tone a flute, or flageolet.

Stops, foundation. The diapasons and principal, to which the other stops, be they few or many, are tuned.

Stop, hautboy. A reed-stop having a tone in imitation of the oboe.

Stop, larigot, or octave twelfth. A stop, the scale of which is an octave above the twelfth. It is only used in the *full organ*.

Stop, mixture, or furniture. A stop comprising two or more ranks of pipes, shriller than those of the *sesquialtera*, and only calculated to be used together with that and other pipes.

Stop, nazard. Twelfth stop.

Stop, open diapason. A metallic stop which commands the whole scale of the organ, and which is called *open* in contradistinction to the *stop* diapason, the pipes of which are closed at the top.

Stop, organ. A collection of pipes similar in tone and quality, running through the whole, or a great part, of the compass of the organ; a register.

Stopped diapason. A stop, the pipes of which are generally made of wood, and its bass, up to middle C, *always* of wood. They are only half as long as those of the open diapason, and are stopped at the upper end with wooden *stoppers*, or plugs, which render the tone more soft and mellow than that of the open diapason, and lower it an octave.

Stop, salcional. The dulcima-stop.

Stops, compound. An assemblage of several pipes in an organ, three, four, five, or more to each key, all answering at once to the touch of the performer. *Mixture-stops*.

Stops, draw. Stops in an organ placed on each side of the rows of keys in front of the instrument, by moving which the player opens, or closes, the stops within the organ.

Stop, sesquialtera. A stop resembling the mixture, running through the scale of the instrument, and consisting of three, four, and sometimes five, ranks of pipes, tuned in thirds, fifths, and eighths.

Stops, mutation. In an organ, the twelfth, tierce, and their octaves.

Stop, solo. A stop which may be drawn alone, or with one of the diapasons.

Stops, reed. Stops consisting of pipes upon the end of which are fixed thin, narrow plates of brass, which, being vibrated by the wind from the bellows, produce a reedy thickness of tone. See *Pipes*.

Stop, stopped unison. The stopped diapason stop.

Stop, tierce. A stop tuned a major third higher than the fifteenth, and only employed in the full organ.

Stop, treble forte. A stop applied to a melodeon, or reed-organ, by means of which the treble part of the instrument may be increased in power, while the bass remains subdued.

Stop, tremolo. A contrivance, by means of which a tremulous effect is given to some of the registers of an organ.

Stop, trumpet. A stop, so-called, because its tone is imitative of a trumpet. In large organs it generally extends through the whole compass.

Stop, twelfth. A metallic stop, so denominated from its being tuned twelve notes above the diapason. This stop, on account of its pitch, or tuning, can never be used alone; the open diapason, stopped diapason, principal and fifteenth, are the best qualified to accommodate it to the ear.

Stop, vox-humana. A stop, the tone of which resembles the human voice.

Stórta (It.) (stōr-tä.) A *serpent*. See that word.

Stortína (It.) (stōr-*tē*-nä.) A small serpent.

Straccináto (It.) (strä-tshē-*nä*-tō.) See *Strascináto*.

Stradivari. The name of a very superior make of violin, so-called from their maker, Stradivarius, who made them at Cremona, Italy, in the first part of the eighteenth century. See article "Stradivari," in Grove's Dictionary, and also Stoeving's "The Violin."

Strain. A portion of music divided off by a double bar. A period. See *Form*.

Strascicándo (It.) (strä-shē-*kän*-dō.) Dragging the time; trailing; playing slowly.

Strascicáto (It.) (strä-shē-*kä*-tō.) Dragged; trailed; played slowly.

Strascinándo (It.) (strä-shē-*nän*-dō.) Dragging the time; playing slowly.

Strascinándo l'árco (strä-shē-*nän*-dō l'är-kō.) Keeping the bow of the violin close to the strings, as in executing the tremolándo, so as to slur, or bind the notes closely.

Strascináto (It.) (strä-shē-*nä*-tō.) Dragged along; played slowly.

Strascinío (It.) (strä-*shē*-nē-ō.) Dragging; playing slowly.

Strathspey. A lively Scotch dance, somewhat slower than the reel, and like it in ¾ time, but in dotted eighth notes alternating with sixteenths, producing the peculiar jerky rhythm of the Scotch snap. See *Scotch Snap*.

Stravagánte (It.) (strä-vä-*gän*-tĕ.) Extravagant, odd, fantastic.

Stravagánza (It.) (strä-vä-*gän*-tsä.) Extravagance, eccentricity.

Street-organ. Hand-organ.

Streichinstrument (Ger.) (strīk-ĭn-stroo-mĕnt.) A stringed instrument played by the stroke of a bow.

Streng (Ger.) (strĕng.) Strict severe, rigid.

Strenge gebunden (Ger.) (*strĕn*-ghĕ ghĕ-*boon*-d'n.) Strictly legáto; exceedingly smooth.

Streng im Tempo (Ger.) (strĕng ĭm *tĕm*-pō.) Strictly in time.

Strépito (It.) (*stre*-pē-tō.) Noise.

Strepitosaménte (It.) (strĕ-pē-tō-sä-*men*-tĕ.) With a great noise.

Strepitóso (It.) (strĕ-pē-*tō*-zō.) Noisy, boisterous.

Strétta (It.) (*stret*-tä.) A concluding passage, coda, or finale, taken in quicker time to enhance the effect.

Strétto (It.) (*strĕt*-tō.) *Pressed, close,* contracted; formerly used to denote that the movement indicated was to be performed in a quick, concise style. In fugue-writing, that part where the subject and answer overlap one another.

Stricciándo (It.) (strit-tshē-*än*-dō.) See *Strascicándo*.

Strich (Ger.) (strīkh.) *Stroke;* the manner of bowing.

Strich-arten (Ger.) (strīkh-är-t'n.) Different ways of bowing.

Strict inversion. The same as simple inversion, but requiring that whole tones should be answered by whole tones, and semi-tones by semi-tones.

Strictly inverted imitation. A form of imitation in which half and whole tones must be precisely answered in contrary motion.

Strident (Fr.) (stre-dänh.) ⎫ Sharp,
Stridente (It.) (strē-*den*-tĕ.) ⎬ shrill,
Stridevole (It.) (strē-*de*-vo-lĕ.) ⎭ acute.

Striking reed. That kind of reed-pipe in an organ, in which the tongue strikes against the tube in producing the tone.

Strillare (It.) (strēl-*lä*-rē.) To scream; shriek; screech.

Strillo (It.) (*strēl*-lō.) A loud scream; shrill cry; shriek.

String band. A band of stringed instruments only.

Stringed instruments. Instruments whose sounds are produced by striking, or plucking strings, or by the friction of a bow drawn across them.

Stringéndo (It.) (strēn-*gen*-dō.) Pressing, accelerating the time.

ō as in *tone*; ô as in *dove*; ŏ as in *not*; ŭ as in *up*; ü the French sound of *u*.

String quartet. A composition of four instruments of the violin species, as, two violins, a viola, and violoncello.

Strings. Wires or chords used in musical instruments, which, upon being struck, or drawn upon, produce tones; the stringed instruments in a band, or orchestra.

Strings, open. The strings of an instrument when not pressed.

Strisciándo (It.) (strē-shē-*än*-dō.) Gliding; slurring; sliding smoothly from one note to another.

Strófa (It.) (*strō*-fä.) ⎫
Strófe (It.) (*strō*-fĕ.) ⎭ A strophe; stanza.

Strombazzáta (It.) (strōm-bät-*tsä*-tä.) ⎫
Strombettáta (It.) (strōm-bĕt-*tä*-tä.) ⎭ The sound of a trumpet.

Strombettáre (It.) (strōm-bĕt-*tä*-rĕ.) To sound, or play on the trumpet.

Strombettiére (It.) (strōm-bĕt-tē-*ā*-rĕ.) A trumpeter.

Stromentáto (It.) (strō mĕn-*tä*-tō.) Instrumented; scored for an orchestra.

Stroménti (It. pl.) (strō-*men*-tē.) Musical instruments.

Stroménti d'arco (It. pl.) (strō-*men*-tē d'ar-kō.) Instruments played with the bow.

Stroménti da fiáto (It. pl.) (strō-*men*-tē dä fē-*ä*-tō.)
Stroménts di vénto (It. pl.) (strō-*men*-tē dē *ven*-tō.)
Wind-instruments.

Stroménti di rinfórzo (It. pl.) (strō-*men*-tē dē rēn-*fōr*-tsō.) Instruments employed to support, or strengthen, a performance.

Stroménto (It.) (strō-men-tō.) An instrument.

Strophe. In the ancient theatre, that part of a song, or dance, around the altar which was performed by turning from the right to the left. It was succeeded by the antistrophe, in a contrary direction. Hence, in ancient lyric poetry, the former of two stanzas was called the *strophe* and the latter the *antistrophe*.

Stück (Ger.) (stük.) Piece, air, tune.

Stücken (Ger.) (*stük*-ĕn.) Pieces.

Studien (Ger. pl.) (*stov*-dĭ-ĕn.) Studies.

Stúdio (It.) (*stoo*-dē-ō.) ⎫ A study;
Studium (Ger.) (*stoō*-dĭ-ŭm.) ⎭ an exercise intended for the practice of some particular difficulty.

Stufe (Ger.) (*stoo*-fĕ.) Step, degree.

Stufe der Tonleiter (Ger.) (*stōo*-fĕ dĕr *tōn*-ly-tĕr.) A degree of the scale.

Stufen (Ger. pl.) (*stoo*-f'n.) Steps, or degrees.

Stufenweise (Ger.) (*stoo*-f'n-*vī*-sĕ.) By degrees.

Stuonánte (It.) (stoo-ō-*nän*-tĕ.) ⎫ Dissonant;
Stuonáto (It.) (stoo-ō-*nä*-tō.) ⎭ out of tune.

Stuonáre (It.) (stoo-ō-*nä*-rĕ.) To sing out of tune.

Sturm-drommete (Ger.) (stoorm-drŏm-mĕ-tĕ.) The alarm-trumpet.

Sturm-glocke (Ger.) (*stoorm-glo*-kĕ.) The tocsin; the alarm-bell.

Stürmisch (Ger.) (*stürm*-ĭsh.) Impetuously, boisterously, furiously.

Style. The manner of composition, or performance, on which the effect chiefly if not wholly depends.

Stylo (It.) (stēe-lō.) Style.

Stylo choraico (It.) (stēe-lō kō-*rä*-ē-kō.) A style suitable for dances.

Stylo dramatico (It.) (stēe-lō drä-*mä*-tē-kō.) In dramatic style.

Stylo ecclesiastico (It.) (stēe-lō ĕk-klä-zē-*äs*-tē-kō.) In church style.

Stylo fantastico (It.) (stēe-lō fän-*täs*-tē-kō.) An easy, fantastic style; free from all restraint.

Stylo rappresentativo (It.) (stēe-lō räp-rä-zĕn-tä-tē-vō.) A term applied to recitative music, because almost exclusively adapted to the drama.

Stylo recitatívo (It.) (stēe-lō rä-tshē-rä-*tē*-vō.) In the style of a recitative.

Styrienne. An air in slow movement and ¾ time, often in minor, with *Jodler* after each verse.

Su (It.) (soo.) Above, upon.

Suabe-flute. An organ-stop of clear, liquid tone, not so loud as the *wald-flute;* it was invented by William Hill, of London.

Suáve (It.) (*swä*-vĕ.) ⎫ Sweet, mild,
Suave (Spa.) (*swä*-vĕ.) ⎬ agreeable,
Suave (Fr.) (swäv.) ⎭ pleasant.

ă as in *ah*; ā as in *hate*; ă as in *at*; ē as in *tree*; ĕ as in *eh*; ī as in *pine*; ĭ as in *pin*;

Ludwig Van Beethoven

From Sonata. Op. 26

Sousaphone

String Bass

Suavemente (Spa.) (swä-vĕ-*men*-tĕ.)
Suaveménte (It.) (swä-vĕ-*men*-tĕ.)
Suavita (It.) (swä-vē-*tä*.)
Suavity, sweetness, delicacy.
Sub (Lat.) (sŭb.) Under, below, beneath.
Sub-bass (Ger.) (soob-bäss.) *Underbass;* an organ-register in the pedals, usually a double-stopped bass of 32 or 16-foot tone, though sometimes open wood-pipes of 16-foot, as at Haarlem; the ground bass.
Subbourdon. An organ-stop of 32-foot tone, with stopped pipes.
Subcantor (Spa.) (soob-kän-*tōr*.) Subchanter.
Subchanter. The precentor's deputy in a cathedral choir.
Subdominant. The fourth note of any scale, or key.
Subitaménte (It.) (soo-bē-tä-*men*-tĕ.)
Súbito (It.) (*soo*-bē-tō.)
Suddenly; immediately; at once.
Subject. A melody, or theme; a leading-text, or *motívo.*
Subject, counter. See *Fugue.*
Submediant. The sixth tone of the scale.
Suboctave. An organ-coupler producing the octave below.
Subprincipal. *Under principal,* that is, below the pedal-diapason pitch; in German organs this is a double open bass-stop of 32-foot scale.
Subsemitone. The semi-tone below the key-note; the subtonic.
Subsemitonium modi (Lat.) (sŭb-sĕm-ĭ-tō-nĭ-ŭm mō-dī.) The leading-note.
Subsidiary notes. Notes situated one degree above and one degree below the principal note of a turn.
Subtonic. Under the tonic; the semitone immediately below the tonic.
Succession. A word applied to the notes of a melody, in contradistinction to those of harmony, which are given in *combination.*
Succession, conjunct. A succession of sounds proceeding regularly upward or downward, through the several intervening degrees.
Succession, disjunct. Where the sounds pass from one degree to another without touching the intermediate degrees.

Suffolamento (It.) (soof-fō-lä-*men*-tō.) Hiss, whistle, murmur.
Suggeritore di teatro (It.) (sood-jä-rē-tō-rĕ dē tä-*ä*-trō.) The prompter of a theatre.
Suggetto (It.) (sood-*jet*-tō.) The subject, or theme of a composition. See *Soggetto.*
Suite (Fr.) (swēet.) A series, a succession; *une suite de pièces,* a series of lessons, or pieces.
Suite de danses. A set of dances. It was generally known as the *suite,* and probably began not far from the year 1600 in the freer *Partita.* Both had their origin in dances. Dances were composed of marked and attractive rhythm, differing essentially from each other in character, and capable of very contrasted effects. In Spain were the stately *Sarabande,* the dignified *Pavane,* and the more rapid *Loure;* in Italy, the gay *Courante,* the sedate *Chaconne,* and the quiet *Passa Mezzo;* in England, the *Hornpipe,* the *Country Dance,* and others embraced in the general Continental appellation of *Anglaise;* in Germany the cheerful dance known in the works of Mozart and others as the *Danza Tedesca;* in France the noble *Minuet,* and half-playful *Gavotte,* the merry *Branle,* the dashing *Passe-pieds,* and the pleasing *Rigaudon;* and, in all of these countries, the hearty *Gigue,* or *Jig.* The essence of form is contrast, and it is not surprising that the composers soon invented a simple form by combining two or three dance-rhythms of contrasted style and tempo into a single cycle form. The contrasts of the suite were well-established by Bach, and the movements gradually assumed the following order in his suites: A prelude or not, as the composer desired, after which came the *allemande,* the *courante,* the *sarabande,* the *intermezzi,* and finally the *gigue.* The *intermezzi* were from two to four dances, or other movements, left to the choice of the composer, as *minuets, gavottes,* etc. They were generally of moderate tempo, in order that they might not destroy the effect of the *sarabande* and the *gigue,* between which they came. The suite, in the eighteenth century, had all of its movements in the same key;

SUIVEZ

a uniformity which tended to monotony. Handel left the precise order of movements prescribed by Bach, and his suites are very free — even the dance names being discarded in some of them. Sometimes in the old suites, a movement could be duplicated, and two *courantes*, two *minuets*, or two *bourrées* appear. The modern orchestral suite is of a much freer character and is practically a small symphony. Franz Lachner wrote many orchestral suites, and suites by Bizet, Massenet, Tschaikowsky and Moszkowski have become well-known. These are less ambitious than the symphony, generally beginning with a march, or variations, having a slow movement near the centre, and ending with a lively finale. They have generally four movements.

Suivez (Fr.) (swē-vā.) Follow, attend, pursue; the accompaniment must be accommodated to the singer, or solo player.

Sujet (Fr.) (sü-zhā.) A subject, melody, or theme.

Súl (It.) (sool.)
Súll' (It.) (sool.) } On, upon the.
Súlla (It.) (*sool*-lä.)

Súl A. On the A string.

Súl D. On the D string.

Súlla mézza córda (It.) (*sool*-lä *met*-sä *kŏr*-dä.) On the middle of the string.

Súlla tástiéra (It.) (*sool*-lä täs-tē-*ā*-rä.) Upon the keys; upon the finger-board.

Súl ponticello (It.) (sool pŏn-tē-*tshĕl*-lō.) On or near the bridge.

Sumsen (Ger.) (soom-s'n.) To hum.

Súo lóco (It.) (soo-ō lō-kō.) In its own, or usual place.

Suonáre (It.) (swō-*nä*-re.) To play upon an instrument.

Suóno (It.) (swō-nō.) Sound; tone; music; a song.

Suóno délle campáne (It.) (swō-nō *dāl*-lĕ käm-*pä*-nĕ.) The sound of bells.

Super (Lat.) (*sü*-pĕr.) Above, over.

Superdominant. The note in the scale next above the dominant.

Superfluous intervals. Those which are one semi-tone more than the *perfect*, or *major*, intervals. See *Augmented Intervals.*

SUSPENSION, SINGLE

Superoctave. An organ-stop tuned two octaves, or a fifteenth, above the diapasons; also a coupler producing the octave above.

Supertonic. }
Supertonique (Fr.) (sü-pĕr-tŏnh-*ēk*.) } The note next above the tonic, or keynote; the second note of the scale.

Supplichévole (It.) (soo-plē-*keh*-vō-lĕ.) }
Supplichevolménte (It.) (soop-plē-*keh*-vŏl-*men*-tĕ.) }
In a supplicatory manner.

Súr (It.) (soor.) } On, upon, over.
Sur (Fr.) (sür.) }

Surdeline. The old Italian bagpipe, a large and rather complicated instrument, consisting of many pipes and conduits for the conveyance of the wind, with keys for the opening of the holes by the pressure of the fingers, and inflated by means of bellows which the performer blows with his arm, at the same time that he fingers the pipe. Also called *Sourdeline* and *Sordellino.*

Suspended cadence. See *Interrupted Cadence.*

Suspension. A theoretical expression applied to the retaining in any chord some note, or notes, of the preceding chord. A dissonant note which finally sinks into the harmony of the chord. If the dissonant note does not appear in the preceding chord as a harmonic note it is said to be *unprepared*, or *free.* Suspensions, which may occur in any part, are said to be double when two, and triple when three, notes are suspended.

Prepared. Unprepared.

Suspension, double. A suspension retaining two notes and requiring a double preparation and resolution.

Suspension, single. A suspension retaining but one note and requiring only a single preparation and resolution.

Suspension, triple. A suspension formed by suspending a dominant, or diminished seventh, on the tonic, mediant, or dominant of the key.

Süss (Ger.) (süss.) Sweetly.

Süssflöte (Ger.) (*süss-flö*-tĕ.) In organs, the soft flute.

Sussurándo (It.) (soos-soo-*rän*-dō.)
Sussuránte (It.) (soos-soo-*rän*-tĕ.) Whispering, murmuring.

Sutonique (Fr.) (sü-tŏnh-*ēk*.) Supertonic.

Svegliáto (It.) (sväl-yē-*ä*-tō.) Brisk, lively, sprightly.

Svélto (It.) (*svel*-tō.) Free, light, easy.

Swell. A gradual increase of sound.

Swell-organ. In organs having three rows of keys, the third, or upper row, controlling a number of pipes enclosed in a box, which may be gradually opened, or shut, and thus the tone increased, or diminished, by degrees. See *Organ*.

Swell-pedal. That which opens the blinds of the swell-organ, increasing the tone.

Swiss flute. An organ-stop, of agreeable tone, something like that of the *gámba*.

Syllables, fixed. Syllables which do not change with change of key.

Syllables Guidonian. The syllables *ut, re, mi, fa, sol, la*, used by Guido for his system of tetrachords. See *Aretinian Syllables* and *Solfaing*.

Sympathetic strings. Strings which were formerly fastened under the fingerboard of the *viola d'amore*, beneath the bridge, and, being tuned to the strings above, vibrated with them and strengthened the tone. Blüthner, in Germany, has added sympathetic octave-strings to his *aliquot grand* pianos.

Symphonie (Fr.) (sănh-fō-nē.)
Symphonie (Ger.) (sĭm-fō-nēe.) In the first
Symphony (Eng.)
half of the eighteenth century *symphony* meant any instrumental prelude, or interlude, or postlude. In this sense Handel uses it in "The Messiah," and Bach thus called his three-part inventions *symphonies*. It now means a grand composition of several movements, for a full orchestra. The symphony in its present form was introduced by Haydn, and generally consists of an allegro movement (sometimes with a slow introduction), a slow movement, a *minuet*, or *scherzo*, and a *finale*. It is a *sonata for orchestra*. (See *Sonata*.) Beethoven introduced the *scherzo* to take the place of the threadbare *minuet*. (See *Minuet* and *Scherzo*.) The greatest symphonists are Beethoven and Brahms, although the pioneer work by Haydn and Mozart must always receive due acknowledgments. Beethoven's nine symphonies remain . the purest models of the symphonic form, although the G minor symphony, and particularly the *Jupiter* symphony, by Mozart, show that the form had become great even in the eighteenth century. The four movements of the symphony are intended to be in the best contrast with each other. Thus, the first movement, which is in the *sonata-allegro* form, may be called the most intellectual movement of the work. The second (which is generally *andante* or *adagio*) is the romantic, or emotional movement. The third (usually the *scherzo*, or *minuet*) is the dainty, playful or popular movement, and the *finale* is the brilliant, and climax movement. In the early symphonies the finale was always jovial, copying the jollity of the *gigue*, which ended the *suite*. Beethoven reformed this defect and gave to the finale a broader and more ambitious character.

The chief symphonies of Haydn were those that he wrote for London during his two visits to England. These twelve are called the *English* symphonies. The symphony did not stand revealed in all its grand proportions until 1804, when Beethoven brought forth his *Heroic* symphony, the greatest of the world up to that time. In modern times the symphony has been growing more free than formerly. Brahms in his four symphonies still held to the classical path and proved that there was much to say in this form yet; but Bruckner, Mahler, St. Saëns, D'Indy, Tschaikowsky, and many others, have deserted the strict form — sometimes to advantage, but more generally the reverse. The logical outcome of the attempts at

ō as in *tone*; ô as in *dove*; ŏ as in *not*; ŭ as in *up*; ü the French sound of *u*.

freer expression came in the *symphonic poem*, which has found its broadest expression in the works of Richard Strauss. The *poème symphonique*, which Liszt established, did not signify a *symphonic poem*, for the word *symphonique* in French merely meant *orchestral*. But many of Liszt's successors embodied the effects of the symphony in the symphonic poem, so that it has, in some degree, become the modern representative of the classical form. The *symphonic poem* has no fixed shape, but relies for its effects chiefly upon figure development, and very powerful orchestration. Some of the symphonic poems of Richard Strauss are the broadest orchestral works at present existing. For further information regarding symphony see Grove's "Beethoven's Nine Symphonies," Weingartner's " Symphony since Beethoven," Elson's " Famous Composers and their Works" (new series), article " Some Orchestral Masterpieces," and Arthur Elson's " Modern Composers of Europe."

Symphonion. An instrument invented by Fr. Kaufmann, resembling the orchestrion, and combining the tone of a pianoforte with that of the flute, clarinet, etc.

Symphonious. Harmonious; agreeing in sound.

Symphonische Dichtung (Ger.) (sĭm-*fō*-nĭ-shĕ dĭkh-toong.) Symphonic poem.

Symposia. An epithet generally applicable to cheerful and convivial compositions, as catches, glees, rounds, etc.

Syncopáta (It.) (sin-kō-*pä*-tä.)
Syncopáte (It.) (sin-kō-*pä*-tĕ.)
Syncopáto (It.) (sin-kō-*pä*-tō.)
Contracted, bound together;
Syncopated (Eng.)
contraction of a note by cutting off part of its value and giving it to the following note. See *Syncopation*.

Syncopation (Eng.)
Syncopatio (Lat.) (sĭn-kō-*pä*-shĭ-ō.)
Syncope (Fr.) (sănh-kōp.)
An unequal division of the time, or notes; irregular accent; binding the last note of one bar to the first note of the next; accented notes occurring on the unaccented part of a bar. Syncopation is an artificial accent, an interruption of the natural pulsation of the music. It can be produced by giving an accent where none is expected, by taking away the accent from a point where it is expected, or by both methods combined. The natural rhythm must be restored after the syncopation has been used for a short time, otherwise the ear will accept the artificial accent as a natural one and the effect of syncopation be lost. Syncopations in accompaniments must be strong to be effective.

T

T. An abbreviation of *Talon, Tasto* (*t. s.* = tasto solo), *Tempo* (*a t.* = a tempo), *Toe* (in organ-music), *Tre* (T. C. = tre corde), and *Tutti*.

Tablatúra (It.) (täb-lä-*too*-rä.)
Tablature (Fr.) (tä-blä-*tür*.)
Tablature (Eng.) (*tăb*-lä-tshūr.)
Tabulatur (Ger.) (tä-boo-lä-toor.)
A term formerly applied to the totality, or general assemblage of the signs used in music; so that to understand the notes, clefs, and other necessary marks, and to be able to sing at sight, was to be skilled in the *tablature*. The method of notation for the lute, and other similar instruments, was also distinguished by this appellation. The musical rules of the master-singers were also called the *tablatur*. But the chief use of the word is to designate the *pitch* of different notes in different octaves by letters with numerals, accents, or adjectives attached. The principle of the tablature of pitches dates back to the time of Guido of Arezzo, about A. D. 1000. The chief system used by musicians is the following:

Sub-contra Octave.   Contra Octave.
C,, D,,E,,F,,G,,A,,B,,   C,D,E,F,G,A,B,

8va............

Great Octave.   Small Octave.
C D E F G A B   c d e f g a b

ä as in *ah* ; ā as in *hate* ; ă as in *at* ; ē as in *tree* ; ĕ as in *eh* ; ī as in *pine* ; ĭ as in *pin*;

254

One-lined Octave. Two-lined Octave.
c' d' e' f' g' a' b'
c'' d'' e'' f'' g'' a''b''
Three-lined Octave.
c''' d''' e''' f''' g''' a''' b'''
Four-lined Octave.
8va........
c'''' d'''' e'''' f'''' g'''' a''''b''''

In many cases, however, the lines are made horizontal instead of vertical, thus, c̄, ē, etc., and sometimes the subcontra-notes are written with three capitals (CCC, DDD, etc.), and the contra notes with two (CC, DD, etc.), instead of having lines attached. Another method is to count the octave by the length of an open pipe required to produce its fundamental tone. As it would take a pipe 32 feet long to produce subcontra C (the lowest tone audible to the human ear), that note is called "32-foot C" and the same adjective is applied to all other notes in the "32-foot" octave. The contra octave is called the "16-foot" octave, the great octave the "8-foot," the small octave the "4-foot," the one-lined octave the "2-foot," etc. Still another method of tablature is used by scientists and acousticians. In this the subcontra notes are marked thus, C₂, D₂, etc.; the contra notes C₁, D₁, etc.; the notes of the great octave c¹, d¹, etc.; the small octave c², d², etc.; the one-lined octave c³, d³, etc.; the two-lined octave c⁴, d⁴, etc.; and thus up the scale. It will be well, therefore, not to use numerals in any other system; c'' for example (or c̄) must not be written c², but c⁴; and the tuning note of the orchestra, one-lined A, is not a¹, but a³. A lack of knowledge of this system has led to some confusion in otherwise valuable books of reference. It may also be stated that the English call the small octave the *tenor octave*, and the one-lined octave the *middle octave*. There is also a vocal nomenclature in the higher octaves, as follows: alt octave and altissimo octave. Thus three-lined C would be called *C in alt*, and three-lined G would be *G in altissimo*. See *Alt*.

Table d'harmonie (Fr.) (tä́bl d'är-mō-nḗ.)
Table d'instrument (Fr.) (tä́bl d'änh-strü-mä́nh.)
The belly of an instrument. The sounding-board.

Table-songs. Songs for male voices formerly much in vogue in German glee clubs.

Tabor. A small drum, generally used to accompany the pipe, or fife, in dances.

Taboret. A small tabor.

Tabourin (Fr.) (tä-boo-rănh.) A tabor, or tambourine — a shallow drum with but one head.

Tabret. A kind of drum used by the ancient Hebrews.

Tacet (Lat.) (tä-sĕt.) ⎫ *Be silent;*
Táce (It.) (tä-tshḗ.) ⎪ meaning
Táci (It.) (tä-tshḗ.) ⎬ that certain instruments
Taciási (It.) (tä-tshē-ä-zē.) ⎭ are not to play; as *violíno tacet*, the violin is not to play; *óboe tacet*, let the oboe be silent.

Tact (Ger.) (täkt.) Time, measure; also *Takt*.

Tact-art (Ger.) (täkt-ärt.) Species of time; common, or triple.

Tact-führer (Ger.) (täkt-füh-rĕr.) A conductor; leader.

Tact-linie (Ger.) (täkt-lǐn-ē-ĕ.) ⎫ A bar
Tact-strich (Ger.) (täkt-strǐkh.) ⎬ line; the lines which mark the bars.

Tactmässig (Ger.) (täkt-mä-sǐg.) Conformable to the time.

Tactmesser (Ger.) (täkt-mĕs-sĕr.) A metronome.

Tact-pause (Ger.) (täkt-pou-zĕ.) Bar rest.

Tact-schläger (Ger.) (täkt-shlä-ghĕr.) Time-beater.

ŏ as in *tone*; ô as in *dove*; ŏ as in *not*; ŭ as in *up*; ü the French sound of *u*.

TACT-STOCK TELL-TALE

Tact-stock (täkt-stŏck.) A *bâton* for beating time.

Tactus (Lat.) (tăk-tŭs.) In the ancient music, the stroke of the hand by which the time was measured, or beaten.

Tact-zeichen (Ger.) (*täkt tsī*-kh'n.) The figures, or signs, at the beginning of a piece, to show the time.

Tafel-musik (Ger.) (*tä*-f'l-*moo*-zĭk.) Table-music; music sung at the table; as, part-songs, glees, etc.

Tagliáto (It.) (täl-yē-*ä*-tō.) Clef.

Taille (Fr.) (*tā*-ŭh.) The tenor part; the viola.

Taille de violon (Fr.) (*tā*-ŭh dŭh vē-ō-lŏnh.) The viola, or tenor violin.

Tail-piece. That piece of ebony to which the strings of the violin, viola, etc., are fastened.

Takt (Ger.) (täkt.) See *Tact*.

Talking machine. See *Phonograph*.

Talon (Fr.) (tä-lŏnh.) The *heel* of the bow; that part nearest the nut.

Tambour (Fr.) (tänh-boor.) Drum; the great drum; also, a drummer.

Tambour de basque (Fr.) (tänh-boor dŭh bäsk.) A tabour, or tabor; a tambourine.

Tambouret (Fr.) (tänh-boo-rā.)) A tim-
Tambourine (Eng.) { brel; a small instrument of percussion, like the head of a drum, with little bells placed round its rim to increase the noise.

Tambourin (Fr.) (tänh-boo-rĕn.) A species of dance accompanied by the tambourine; also a tambourine.

Tam-tam. The gong.

Tändelnd (Ger.) (*tän*-dĕlnd.) In a playful manner.

Tangent (Ger.) (*tän*-ghĕnt.) The *jack* of a harpsichord.

Tánto (It.) (*tän*-tō.) So much, as much; *allégro non tánto*, not so quick; not too quick.

Tantum ergo (Lat.) (*tăn*-tüm *ār*-gō.) A hymn sung at the benediction in the Roman Catholic service.

Tanz (Ger.) (tänts.) A dance.

Tanz-kunst (Ger.) (tänts-koonst.) The art of dancing.

Tanz-stück (Ger.) (tänts-stük.) A dance tune.

Tap. A drum-beat of a single note.

Tarantélla (It.) (tär-rän-*tel*-lä.) A swift delirious Italian dance in ⅜ time. The form has been adopted by many of the finest composers, as Liszt, Chopin, etc.

Tardaménte (It.)(tär-dä-*men*-tĕ.) Slowly.

Tardándo (It.) (tär-*dän*-dō.) Lingering; retarding the time.

Tárdo (It.) (*tär*-dō.) Tardy, slow.

Tastáme (It.) (täs-tä-mĕ.)
Tastatur (Ger.) (*täs*-tä-toor)
Tastatúra (Ger.) (täs-tä-*too*-rä.)
Tastiéra (It.) (täs-tē-*ā*-rä.)
The keys, or key-board, of a piano, organ, etc.

Taste (Ger.) (*täs*-tĕ.) } The touch of any
Tásto (It.) (*täs*-tō.) { instrument; hence also, a key, or thing touched.

Tasten-brett (Ger.) (*täs*-t'n brĕt.) Keyboard of a pianoforte, etc.

Tásto sólo (It.) (*täs*-tō *sō*-lō.) *One key alone;* in organ, or pianoforte music, this means a note without harmony; the bass notes over or under which it is written are not to be accompanied with chords.

Tattoo. The beat of a drum at night calling the soldiers to their quarters.

Teatrino (It.) (tā-ä-*trĕ*-nō.) A little theatre.

Teátro (It.) (tā-*ä*-trō.) A theatre, playhouse.

Technik (Ger.) (*tĕkh*-nĭk.) Technique.

Technisch (Ger.) (*tĕkh*-nĭsh.) Technical; this word is also used to indicate mechanical proficiency, as regards execution.

Technique. The mechanical skill of playing or of singing.

Teddéo (It.) (tĕd-dā-ō.) *Te Deum.*

Tedésca (It.) (tĕ-*des*-kä.) } German: *álla*
Tedésco (It.) (tĕ-*des*-kō) { *tedésca*, in the German style.

Te Deum laudamus (Lat.) (tĕ dā-ŭm law-dä-mŭs.) *We praise Thee, O God;* a canticle, or hymn of praise.

Tell-tale. A movable piece of metal, bone, or ivory, attached to an organ, indicating by its position the amount of wind supplied by the bellows.

ă as in *ah*; ā as in *hate*; ă as in *at*; ē as in *tree*; ĕ as in *eh*; ī as in *pine*; ĭ as in *pin*;

Téma (It.) (*tāy*-mä.) A theme, or subject; a melody.

Temperament. The adjustment of the imperfect sounds of the scale, by transferring a part of the defects to the more perfect ones, in order to remedy, in some degree, the false intervals of the organ, pianoforte, and similar instruments, whose sounds are fixed; that equalization of the intervals, in tuning, which brings their whole system as near as possible to that of the diatonic scale. That equalization, or tempering of the twelve sounds included in an octave, which renders all the scales equally in tune; the imperfection being divided equally amongst the whole. The division of the octave into twelve *equal* semi-tones, in defiance of the law of nature, which demands a different proportion. The introduction of equal temperament was a modification of the scale of nature that alone made music on keyed instruments practicable. The scale of true intonation, with its varying intervals, beautiful in progressions and harmonies, and eminently fitted for the vocalist, or violinist, could only be employed on the organ when modulation was absent, and the work remained entirely (or nearly so) in one key. By the simple device of dividing the octave into twelve equal semi-tones, Willaert (about 1550) solved a problem that, although not of vast importance in his day, when modulations were but sparingly used, became each century of greater dimensions. This reform, because of the reason stated, was but slowly adopted by the world. As the field of music began to enlarge, a system of partial temperament was adopted which allowed the organist to play in a few keys closely related to F and C, without getting discordantly out of tune, but such keys as F ♯ major, D ♭ major, etc., were deemed altogether unnecessary, and were not used until a much later epoch. The tuning which is at present employed by all civilized nations is a compromise. The octave which must always be taken as a true interval, its upper note vibrating twice as fast as its lower, is divided into twelve equal semi-tones, all a trifle out of tune but none distressingly so, and this *tempered scale* as it is called, admits of the use of all the twenty-four major and minor keys with equal facility. This system of *equal temperament* was advocated as early as the sixteenth century by Willaert, Zarlino, and others; but it was not thoroughly adopted until J. S. Bach, in his noble collections of preludes and fugues entitled "The Well-tempered Clavichord," proved the practicability of the system, by writing compositions in all of the different keys, where before only a very limited number had been employed. The "Well-tempered Clavichord," Part I, was given to the world in 1722, and Part II, in 1742, and settled the matter of the division of the scale forever, for from this epoch dates the beginning of *freedom of modulation*. Regarding the effect of the tempered scale as compared with the scale of true intonation, the following facts not generally known to amateurs, may be stated. The tempered scale is close enough to just intonation not to shock the ear of any musician (especially on the pianoforte) and admits of modulations freely into all keys. The interval of the major third is, however, an exception to this, and causes the major triad to sound somewhat harsh. On the organ the tempered major triad is especially disagreeable. The tempered scale is, after all, only a compromise, an escape from a difficulty, and while it is necessary upon keyed instruments, is adhered to far too faithfully by violinists and vocalists, who, when unaccompanied, could obtain a far richer, mellower, and finer effect by keeping to the scale of true intonation. The deflections from true pitch in the different intervals of the tempered scale may be thus summarized: The perfect fifth is one-fiftieth of a semi-tone flat. The perfect fourth is one-fiftieth of a semi-tone sharp. The major third, one-seventh of a semi-tone sharp. The minor third, one-sixth of a semi-tone flat. The major sixth, one-sixth of a semi-tone sharp. The minor sixth, one-seventh of a semi-tone flat. The minor seventh, one-sixth of a semi-tone flat. The major seventh, one-eighth of a semi-tone sharp. In the scale of true intonation, or the enharmonic scale, there would be a distinct differ-

TABLE OF VIBRATIONS OF ALL TONES USED IN MUSIC.
For comparison of true and tempered intervals (Orchestral tuning to A^3) International Pitch 435.

Octaves		C	C sharp, or D flat	D	D sharp, or E flat	E	F
Subcontra, or 32-foot	Pure	16.313	.....	18.352	.....	20.391	21.750
	Tempered	16.166	17.127	18.146	19.225	20.368	21.579
Contra, or 16-foot	Pure	32.625	.....	36.703	.....	40.781	43.500
	Tempered	32.332	34.254	36.291	38.449	40.735	43.158
Great, or 8-foot	Pure	65.250	.....	73.406	.....	81.563	87.000
	Tempered	64.663	68.508	72.582	76.898	81.470	86.315
Small, or 4-foot	Pure	130.500	.....	146.813	.....	163.125	174.000
	Tempered	129.326	137.016	145.164	153.795	162.941	172.630
One-lined, or 2-foot	Pure	261.000	.....	293.625	.....	326.250	348.000
	Tempered	258.652	274.032	290.327	307.591	325.881	345.259
Two-lined, or 1-foot	Pure	522.000	.....	587.250	.....	652.500	696.000
	Tempered	517.304	548.064	580.654	615.181	651.762	690.518
Three-lined, or 6-inch	Pure	1,044.000	.....	1,174.500	.....	1,305.000	1,392.000
	Tempered	1,034.608	1,096.128	1,161.308	1,230.362	1,303.524	1,381.036
Four-lined, or 3-inch	Pure	2,088.000	.....	2,349.000	.....	2,610.000	2,784.000
	Tempered	2,069.216	2,192.256	2,322.616	2,460.724	2,607.048	2,762.072
Five-lined, or 1½-inch	Pure	4,176.000	.....	4,698.000	.....	5,220.000	5,568.000
	Tempered	4,138.432	4,384.512	4,645.232	4,921.448	5,214.096	5,524.144

Octaves		F sharp, or G flat	G	G sharp, or A flat	A	A sharp, or B flat	B
Subcontra, or 32-foot.	Pure	.....	24.469	.....	27.188	.....	30.586
	Tempered	22.862	24.221	25.662	27.188	28.804	30.517
Contra, or 16-foot	Pure	.....	48.937	.....	54.375	.....	61.172
	Tempered	45.724	48.443	51.323	54.375	57.608	61.034
Great, or 8-foot	Pure	.....	97.875	.....	108.750	.....	122.344
	Tempered	91.448	96.885	102.646	108.750	115.217	122.068
Small, or 4-foot	Pure	.....	195.750	.....	217.500	.....	244.688
	Tempered	182.895	193.770	205.292	217.500	230.433	244.135
One-lined, or 2-foot	Pure	.....	391.500	.....	435.000	.....	489.375
	Tempered	365.789	387.540	410.585	435.000	460.866	488.270
Two-lined, or 1-foot	Pure	.....	783.000	.....	870.000	.....	978.750
	Tempered	731.578	775.080	821.169	870.000	921.732	976.540
Three-lined, or 6 inch	Pure	.....	1,566.000	.....	1,740.000	.....	1,957.500
	Tempered	1,463.156	1,550.160	1,642.338	1,740.000	1,843.464	1,953.080
Four-lined, or 3-inch	Pure	.....	3,132.000	.....	3,480.000	.....	3,915.000
	Tempered	2,926.312	3,100.320	3,284.676	3,480.000	3,686.928	3 906.160
Five-lined, or 1½ inch	Pure	.....	6,264.000	.....	6,960.000	.....	7,830.000
	Tempered	5,852.624	6,200.640	6,569.352	6,960.000	7,373.856	7,812.320

ence between such notes as A♯ and B♭, or C♭ B♮, but in the tempered scale these distinctions disappear.

The last three figures in the above table are decimals in each case. The pitch of the sharps and flats according to the *enharmonic* scale is not given, as they are not used in practical music, but the table will readily show the exact amount of deflection from true pitch of any note used in our system. See *Pitch*. Consult Pole's "Philosophy of Music" and Zahm's "Sound and Music" for details of temperament.

Temperament, unequal. That method of tuning the twelve sounds included in an octave, which renders some of the scales more in tune than the others. Also called *Mean Temperament*.

Temperatur (Ger.) (tĕm-pĕ-rä-*toor*.) Temperament.

Tempered. Having a perfect adjustment of sounds; tuned.

Tempestosaménte (It.) (tĕm-pĕs-tō-zä-*men*-tĕ.) Furiously, impetuously.

Tempestóso (It.) (tĕm-pĕs-*tō*-zō.) Tempestuous, stormy, boisterous.

Tempête (Fr.) (tänh-*pāt*.) A boisterous dance in 2/4 time.

Tempo (It.)(*tem*-pō.) The Italian word for *time*. Tempo is rather loosely defined as the speed of the music, but it ought rather to be regarded as the speed of the rhythm, the rapidity with which the natural accents follow each other. In the mediæval music the *tempo* marks were very few. Jean de Muris, about 1350, wrote that there were three speeds in music — quick, slow, and medium. At about this time one might find an occasional *C* marked in the music, meaning *celeriter*, to accelerate the *tempo*; or a *T* for *teneatur*, similar to the modern *ritenuto*. The marks of *tempo* began (practically) with the beginning of opera. When emotional and expressive composition began, about A. D. 1600, the marks of *tempo* at once commenced to appear. So far as we have traced the matter, the word *adagio* (misspelt *adazio*) in one of Frescobaldi's works was the beginning of proper tempo-marking. It should be remembered by the teacher that up to the beginning of the nineteenth century the tempo-marks were less extreme than at present; the slow movements were less slow, and the quick movements less quick than they are in the modern works. The chief terms used for speed are (from slowest to quickest) *grave, largo, larghetto, adagio, lento, andante, andantino, moderato, allegretto, allegro, presto*, and *prestissimo*. These Italian words have been given in this order by custom rather than by their literal meaning. *Andantino*, for example, literally means slower than *andante*, yet, by a misunderstanding, it is frequently used in exactly the opposite sense. (See *Anaantino*.) The slow tempo-marks are not so fixed in their succession as the others, and *larghetto, adagio*, and *lento* are used interchangeably by some composers. There are many other Italian words used for tempo-marks which will be found under their own headings. The words for *tempo* and expression are usually in Italian, although Schumann and Wagner used German, and Berlioz, French. It is best that Italian should be used for: 1st. It has been employed for three hundred years. 2d. It would be impossible to allow every composer (Russian, Hungarian, Norwegian, Polish etc.), the use of his own language in music of world-wide importance. 3d. A universal language such as *notation* has become, must not have a language of terms less universal than itself.

Témpo alla breve (It.) (*tem*-pō *al*-lä *brā*-vĕ.) In a quick species of common time.

Témpo a piacére (It.) (*tem*-pō ä pē-ä-*tshā*-rĕ.) The time at pleasure.

Témpo cómodo (It.) (*tem*-pō *kō*-mō-dō.) Convenient time; an easy, moderate degree of movement.

Témpo di bállo (It.) (*tem*-pō dē *bāl*-lō.) In dance time; rather quick.

Témpo di cappélla (It.) (*tem*-pō dē käp-*pel*-lä.) In the church-time. See *Alla Brève*.

Témpo di gavótta (It.) (*tem*-pō dē gä-*vōt*-tä.) In the time of a gavot.

Témpo di menuétto (It.) (*tem*-pō dē mĕ-noo-*et*-tō.) In the time of a minuet.

Témpo di polácca (It.) (*tem*-pō dē pō-*läk*-kä.) In the time of a polacca.

Témpo di valse (It.) (*tem*-pō dē *väl*-sĕ.) In waltz time.

Témpo frettévole (It.) (*tem*-pō frĕt-*teh*-vō-lĕ.)
Témpo frettolóso (It.) (*tem*-pō frĕt-tō-*lo*-zō.)
In quicker time; hurrying; hastily.

Témpo giústo (It.) (*tem*-pō jē-*oos*-tō.) In just, exact strict time.

Témpo ordinário (It.) (*tem*-pō ōr-dē-*nä*-rē-ō.) Ordinary, or moderate time.

Témpo perdúto (It.) (*tem*-pō pär-*doo*-tō.) Lost; interrupted, irregular time.

Témpo prímo (It.) (*tem*-pō *prē*-mō.) First, or original time.

Témpo reggiáto (It.) (tem-pō rĕd-jē-*ä*-tō.) The time is to be accommodated to the solo singer, or player.

Témpo rubáto (It.) (tem-pō roo-*bä*-tō.) *Robbed* or *stolen* time; irregular time; meaning a slight deviation to give more expression by retarding one note, and quickening another, but so that the time of each measure is not altered as a whole.

Témpo wie vorher (Ger.) (tĕm-pō vē *fō*-rär.) The time as before.

ō as in *tone*; ô as in *dove*; ŏ as in *not*; ŭ as in *up*; ü the French sound of *u*.

Temps (Fr.) (tänh.) } Time; also the various parts or divisions of a bar.
Tems (Fr.) (tänh.) }
Temps frappé (Fr.) (tänh fräp-pā.) The down-beats, or accented parts.
Temps levé (Fr.) (tänh lĕ-vā.) The up-beats, or unaccented parts.
Tendre (Fr.) (tänhdr.) Tender.
Tendrement (Fr.) (tänhdr-mänh.) Tenderly, affectionately.
Tenebrae (Lat.) (*těn*-ĕ-brā.) *Darkness;* a name given to the Roman Catholic service during Holy Week, in commemoration of the darkness which attended the crucifixion.
Tenéndo il cánto (It.) (tĕ-nen-dō il *kän*-tō.) Sustain the melody.
Teneraménte (It.) (tĕn-ĕ-rä-*men*-tĕ.) Tenderly, delicately.
Tenerézza (It.) (tĕn-ĕ-*ret*-tsä.) Tenderness, softness, delicacy.
Ténero (It.) (*te*-nĕ-rō.) Tenderly, softly, delicately.
Tenir (Fr.) (tĕ-*nēer*.) To hold a violin bow, etc.
Tenor. That species of male voice next above the baritone, and extending from the C upon the second space in bass, to G on the second line in the treble. So-called from *teneo* (I hold), since it held the *melody* in old times. See *Soprano* and *Voice.*
Tenor C. The lowest C in the tenor voice; the lowest string of the viola, or tenor violin.
Tenor clef. The C clef, when placed upon the fourth line.
Tenóre (It.) (tĕ-*nō*-rĕ.) Tenor voice; a tenor singer. See, also *Vióla.*
Tenóre búffo (It.) (tĕ-*nō*-rĕ *boof*-fō.) The second tenor singer of an opera company for comic parts.
Tenóre di grázia (It.) (tĕ-*nō*-rĕ di *grä*-tsē-ä.) A delicate and graceful tenor.
Tenóre leggiéro (It.) (tĕ-*nō*-rĕ lĕd-jĕ-*āi*-rō.) A tenor voice of a light quality of tone.
Tenóre prímo (It.) (tĕ-*nō*-rĕ *prēe*-mō.) First tenor.
Tenóre ripiéno (It.) (tĕ-*nō*-rĕ rē-pē-*āy*nō.) Tenor of a grand chorus.

Tenóre robústo (It.) (tĕ-*nō*-rĕ rō-*boos*-tō.) A strong tenor voice.
Tenóre secóndo (It.) (tĕ-*nō*-rĕ sĕ-*kōn*-dō.) Second tenor.
Tenóre vióla (It.) (tĕ-*nō*-rĕ vē-*ō*-lä.) Tenor viol. A viola.
Tenorist (Ger.) (tĕn-ō-rĭst.) } A tenor singer
Tenorista (It.) (tĕn-ō-*rēs*-tä.) }
Tenoroon. The old tenor *oboe da caccia,* the compass of which extended downward to tenor C. The name is sometimes applied to an organ-stop.
Tenor-posaune (Ger.) (tĕn-*ōr*-pō-*zou*-nĕ.) The tenor trombone.
Tenor-schlüssel (Ger.) (tĕn-*ōr*-*shlüs*-s'l.) The tenor clef.
Tenor, second. Low tenor.
Tenor-stimme (Ger.) (tĕn-*ōr*-*stĭm*-mĕ.) Tenor voice; a tenor.
Tenor trombone. A trombone having a compass from the great B flat to the one-lined g, and noted in the tenor clef.
Tenor-viole (Ger.) (tĕn-*ōr*-vĭ-*ō*-lĕ.) } The viola.
Tenor-violin (Eng.) }
Tenor voice, counter. The male voice next above the tenor voice; the lowest of the female voices.
Tenor-zeichen (Ger.) (tĕn-*ōr* *tsy*-kh'n.) The tenor clef.
Tentellare (It.) (tĕn-tĕl-*lä*-rĕ.) To jingle.
Tenth. An interval comprising an octave and a third; also, an organ-stop tuned a tenth above the diapasons, called, also, decima and double tierce.
Tenue (Fr.) (tā-nü.) See *Tenúto.*
Tenúte (It.) (tā-*noo*-tĕ.) } Held on; sustained; or kept down the full time.
Tenúto (It.) (tā-*noo*-tō.) }
Téorbe (Fr.) (tā-ōrb.) See *Theorbo.*
Teorético (It.) (tā-ō-*re*-tĕ-kō.) Theoretical.
Teoría (It.) (tā-ō-*rēe*-ä.) Theory.
Teoría del cánto (It.) (tā-ō-*rē*-ä dĕi *kän*-tō.) The theory, or art, of singing.
Tepidaménte (It.) (tĕ-pē-dä-*men*-tĕ. Coldly; with indifference.
Tepidita (It.) Coldness, indifference.
Ter (Lat.) (tĕr.) Thrice; three times.
Tercet (Fr.) (tĕr-sä.) A triplet.

𝔄 as in *ah*; ā as in *hate*; ă as in *at*; ē as in *tree*; ĕ as in *eh*; ī as in *pine*; ĭ as in *pin;*

260

Terceto (Spa.) (tĕr-*thā*-tō.) A triplet.

Terms, musical. Words and sentences applied to passages of music for the purpose of indicating the style in which they should be performed. See *Tempo.*

Ternario témpo (It.) (tĕr-*nä*-rē-ō tempō.) Triple time.

Ternary measure. Threefold measure; triple time.

Terpsichore. In classical mythology, the muse of choral dance and song.

Terpsichorean. Relating to Terpsichore, the muse who presided over dancing.

Tertia (Lat.) (*tĕr*-shĭ-ä.) ⎱ Third, tierce;
Tertzia (Ger.) (*tĕr*-tsĭ-ä.) ⎰ also an organ-stop sounding a third, or tenth, above the foundation stops.

Tertian (Lat.) (*tĕr*-shĭ-ăn.) An organ-stop composed of two pipes, tierce and larigot, on one slide, sounding the interval of a minor third.

Terz (Ger.) (tairts.) ⎫
Térza (It.) (*tāir*-tsä.) ⎪ A third; the interval of a
Terze (Ger.) (*tāir*-tsĕ.) ⎬ third; also an organ-stop
Terzie (Ger.) (*tāir*-tsĭ-ĕ.) ⎪ sounding a
Térzo (It.) (*tāir*-tsō.) ⎭ third above the fifteenth See *Tierce.*

Terz decimole (Ger.) (*tāirts* dā-tsĭ-*mō*-lĕ.) A group of thirteen notes having the value of eight, or twelve similar ones.

Térza maggióre (It.) (*tāir*-tsä mäd-jĕ-*ō*-rĕ.) Major third.

Térza minóre (It.) (*tāir*-tsä mē-*nō*-rĕ.) Minor third.

Terzen (Ger.) (*tāir*-ts'n.) Thirds.

Terzétto (It.) (tāir-*tset*-tō.) A short piece, or trio, for three voices.

Terz-flöte (Ger.) (*tāirts-flö*-tĕ.) A flute sounding a minor third above; also, an organ-stop.

Terzína (It.) (tāir-*tsē*-nä.) A triplet.

Tessitura (It.) (*tĕs*-sē-*too*-rä.) The general position, as to pitch, of the tones of a composition. A work with many high tones is said to have a "high tessitura."

Tetrachord (Gr.) (*tĕt*-rä-kŏrd.) ⎱ A
Tetracorde (Fr.) (*tät*-rä-kŏrd.) ⎬ fourth;
Tetracórdo (It.) (tät-rä-*kŏr*-dō.) ⎭ also, a system of four sounds among the ancients, the extremes of which were fixed, but the middle sounds were varied according to the *mode.*

Tetrachords, conjoint. Two tetrachords, or fourths, where the same note is the highest of one and the lowest of the other.

Theile (Ger. pl.) (*ty*-lĕ.) Parts, divisions of the bar; also, strains, or component parts of a movement, or piece.

Theme. 1. A subject, in the development of sonata-form. 2. The *cantus firmus* on which counterpoint is built. 3. The subject of a fugue. 4. A simple tune on which variations are made.

Thema (Gr.) (tha-ma.) ⎫
Thema (Lat.) (thā-mä.) ⎬ A theme, or
Thema (Ger.) (*tāy*-mä.) ⎪ subject.
Thème (Fr.) (tāym.) ⎭

Theorbe (Ger.) (tĕ-*ōr*-bĕ.) ⎱ An old
Theorbo (Eng.) (thĕ-*ŏr*-bō.) ⎰ stringed instrument resembling the lute in form, or tone. It had two necks, to the longest of which the bass strings were attached. It was employed for accompanying voices, and was in great favor during the seventeenth century.

Theory of music. The science of music. The speculations arising from a knowledge of the principles of sound. The rules for composition and arrangement of music for voices and instruments in rhythm, melody, harmony, counterpoint, and instrumentation.

Thesis (Gr.) (thā-sĭs.) Down-beat, the accented part of the bar. See *Arsis.*

Theurgic hymns. Songs of incantation, such as those ascribed to Orpheus, performed in the mysteries upon the most solemn occasions. These hymns were the first of which we have any account in Greece.

Third. An interval comprising three diatonic degrees.

Third, diminished. An interval measured by two half-steps.

Third inversion. A name given to an inverted chord of the seventh when its seventh is the lowest.

Third, major. An interval measured by four half-steps.

THIRD, MINOR   TIERCE DE PICARDIE

Third, minor. An interval measured by three half-steps.

Third shift. The double shift in violin-playing.

Thirteenth. An interval comprising an octave and a sixth. It contains twelve diatonic degrees, *i.e.*, thirteen sounds.

Thirty-second note. A demisemiquaver.

Thirty-second rest. A rest, or pause, equal to the length of a thirty-second note.

Thorough bass. Figured bass; a system of harmony which is indicated by a figured bass. When there is no figure, it is understood that the common chord of such a note is to be used as its harmony. The following table will show the manner in which figures are used:

The figure 2 implies a 4th and 6th,
   "   "   3   "   a 5th perfect, or diminished, according to the position of the note in the key.
The figure 4 implies a 5th, or 5th and 8th.
   "   "   5   "   3d and 8th.
   "   "   6   "   3d.
   "   "   7   "   5th and 3d.
   "   "   8   "   3d and 5th.
   "   "   9   "   3d and 5th.

A stroke through a figure directs the raising of the interval by a natural, or sharp, as the case may be. An accidental standing alone implies a corresponding alteration of the 3d of the chord. Horizontal lines direct the continuance of the harmony of the previous chord. If there are no figures under the previous chord, the line or lines direct the continuance of the common chord of the first note under which they were placed.

Three-eighth measure. A measure having the value of three eighth notes, marked ⅜.

Three fold. A chord consisting of three tones, comprising a tone combined with its third and fifth.

Threnodia (Lat.) (thrĕ-*nō*-dĭ-ä.) ⎫
Threnodie (Gr.) (thrĕ-*nō*-dē.) ⎬ An elegy;
a funeral song.

Threnody. Lamentation; a song of lamentation.

Thrice-marked octave. The name given in Germany to the notes between the C on the second added line above the treble staff and the next B above, inclusive; these notes are expressed by small letters, with three short strokes, also *thrice-accented octave*, or *three-lined octave*. See *Tablature* and *Temperament*.

Thumb-string. Melody-string of the banjo.

Tie. A curved line placed over two or more notes in the same position on the stave:

The tie is also called a *bind*, and the curved line, when used over notes representing different sounds, is called a *slur*. (See *Slur*.) These notes need not be written on the same degree of the staff, (although they generally are) for in the tempered scale (which see) the flat and the sharp of two contiguous notes can mean the same sound, and the following would therefore be an enharmonic tie:

If the two notes under the curved line have dots above them, the curved line is not a tie, but becomes a *portamento* (*demi-marcato*) mark. This is an example of such a mark:

If the second note only, in such an example, has a dot over it, the effect would be that of a short slur. The following, therefore, would be played as two notes,

the first receiving some degree of accent, and the second being played with lightness, and a little shorter than its written value.

Tief (Ger.) (tēf.) Deep, low, profound.

Tiefer (Ger.) (*tē*-fĕr.) Deeper; lower; 8va *tiefer*, octave below.

Tieftönend (Ger.) (*tēf-tŏ*-nĕnd.) Deep toned.

Tierce (Fr.) (tērs.) A third; also, the name of an organ-stop tuned a major third higher than the fifteenth.

Tierce de Picardie (Fr.) (tērs dŭh pĭ-*kär* dē.) *Tierce of Picardy;* a term applied to a *major third*, when introduced in the last chord of a composition in a *minor* mode; the custom was supposed to have originated in Picardy, and formerly was quite common. It will be found in the final cadence of very many of Bach's compositions in minor.

Tierce maxime (Fr.) (tērs măx-ēm.) *Augmented third*, containing five semitones; as, from F to A ♯.

Tiercet (Gr.) (tēr-sĕt.) A triplet.

Timbal (Spa.) (tim-*bäl*.) ⎫
Timbale (Fr.) (tănh-*bäl*.) ⎬ A kettle-
Timbállo (It.) (tēm-*bäl*-lō.) ⎭ drum.

Timballes (Fr. pl.) (tănh-băl.) Kettledrums.

Timbre (Fr.) (tănhbr.) *Quality* of tone, or sound.

Timbrel. An ancient Hebrew instrument, supposed to have been like a tambourine.

Time. The measure of sounds in regard to their continuance, or duration. The speed of the rhythm. The rapidity with which the natural accents follow each other. This is the correct meaning of *time*. (See *Tempo*.) Nevertheless, an almost universal custom prevails of using the word *time* to express the *division* of the measure as well as the speed. Such division should properly be called either *rhythm*, or *measure*. There could be no possibility of being misunderstood if a composition marked [notation] were described as being in ¼ *rhythm* or in ¼ *measure*, instead of *common time*. An eminent American teacher has suggested *meter* as a fitting word, but this would lead to confusion with hymns and poetical meters. As the word *time* is almost always used to denote the divisions of the measure, we present the divisions under this head. They are classified as even, triple, and peculiar. Even times are those where the measure divides naturally into halves. $\frac{2}{1}, \frac{2}{2}, \frac{2}{4}, \frac{2}{8}, \frac{4}{1}, \frac{4}{2}, \frac{4}{4}, \frac{4}{8}$, and $\frac{4}{8}$ are examples of such rhythms. The following signs are also employed: [symbol] or [symbol] for $\frac{4}{4}$, [symbol] for $\frac{2}{2}$, and [symbol] for $\frac{2}{4}$. When the measure divides naturally into halves or quarters and each of these subdivisions into thirds, the result is compound even time, as follows: $\frac{6}{8}, \frac{6}{4}, \frac{6}{8}, \frac{6}{16}, \frac{12}{4}, \frac{12}{8}, \frac{12}{16}$, and even $\frac{24}{16}$. Triple times occur when the measure divides itself naturally into thirds, as, $\frac{3}{1}, \frac{3}{2}, \frac{3}{4}, \frac{3}{8}, \frac{3}{16}$, and compound triple rhythms are those where the measure divides into thirds, and each of these thirds again subdivides into thirds, as $\frac{9}{4}, \frac{9}{8}, \frac{9}{16}$; even $\frac{18}{8}$ has been used. Septuple or quintuple times are where the measure divides into fifths, or sevenths, as, $\frac{5}{2}, \frac{5}{4}, \frac{5}{8}, \frac{5}{16}, \frac{7}{2}, \frac{7}{4}, \frac{7}{8}, \frac{7}{16}$. Sometimes when these rhythms are employed they are only an alternation of even and triple times. There are also compound derivations from these, and Scriabine has written on etude in $\frac{15}{8}$ time, being merely a $\frac{5}{4}$ time subdivided into triplets. Instead of the words *even* and *triple*, the English often use *duple*, or *binary* and *ternary*. We hope yet to see the whole of the misleading nomenclature

TABLE OF PRINCIPAL RHYTHMS.

English	German	French
Two-two (alla breve)	Zweizweiteltakt	Deux-deux
Two-four	Zweivierteltakt	Deux-quatre
Four-two	Vierzweiteltakt	Quatre-deux
Four-four (common)	Viervierteltakt	Quatre-quatre
Six-four	Sechsvierteltakt	Six-quatre
Six-eight	Sechsachteltakt	Six-huit
Six-sixteen	Sechssechzehnteltakt	Six-seize
Twelve-eight	Zwolfachteltak	Douze-huit
Three-two	Dreizweiteltakt	Mesure à trois deux
Three-four	Dreivierteltakt	Mesure à trois quatre
Three-eight	Dreiachteltak	Mesure à trois huit
Nine-eight	Neunachteltakt	Mesure à neuf huit
Five-four	Fünfvierteltakt	Mesure à cinq quatre
Five-eigth	Fünfachteltakt	Mesure à cinq huit

ŏ as in *tone*; ŏ as in *dove*; ŏ as in *not*; ŭ as in *up*; ü the French sound of *u*.

abolished and *even rhythm* and *triple rhythm*, come into use. There is also a comical error frequently made in imagining the sign for ¼ rhythm — C — to be a letter *C* used as an abbreviation for *common time*. The sign comes to us from the middle ages when the triple pulsation of music was held to be the only perfect rhythm, as the monks held that it represented the *Trinity*. It was written with the following sign, ◯, and was called *perfectum*: when the monks admitted an even rhythm, they called it *imperfectum* and broke the circle writing it thus — C.

Timidezza, con (It.) (tē-mē-*det*-sä.) With timidity.

Timorosaménte (It.) (tē-mō-rō-zä-*men*-tĕ.) Timidly; with fear.

Timoróso (It.) (tē-mō-*rō*-zo.) Timorous; with hesitation.

Timpanétto (It.) (tēm-pä-*net*-tō.) A small drum, or timbrel.

Tímpani (It. pl.) (tēm-*pä*-nē.) } The
Timpani (Spa. pl.) (tēm-*pä*-nē.) } kettledrums.

Tímpani sordi (It.) (tēm-*pä*-nē *sōr*-dē.) Drums having mutes.

Timpanísta (It.) (tēm-pä-*nēs*-tä.) A performer on the kettledrums.

Tímpano (It.) (*tēm*-pä-nō.) } Drum,
Timpano (Spa.) (tēm-pä-nō.) } timbrel, tabor.

Tintement (Fr.) (tănh-t-mänh.) Tingling of a bell; vibration, or ringing sound.

Tinter (Fr.) (tănh-tā.) To toll a bell; to jingle.

Tintinnabulum (Lat.) (*tĭn*-tĭn-*năb*-ū-lŭm.) }
Tintinnábolo (It.) (tēn-tēn-*nä*-bō-lō.) }
Tintinnábulo (It.) (tēn-tēn-*nä*-boo-lō.) } A little bell.

Tintinnaménto (It.) (tēn-tēn-nä-*men*-tō.) Tinkling of small bells.

Tintinnire (It.) (tēn-tēn-*nē*-rĕ.) To tinkle; to resound.

Tintínno (It.) (tēn-*tēn*-nō.) Vibration; ringing of a bell.

Tióṛba (It.) (tē-*ōr*-bä.) } Theorbo.
Tiorba (Spa.) (tē-*ōr*-bä.) }

Tipping. A distinct articulation given to the tones of a flute by placing the end of the tongue on the roof of the mouth. See *Double-tonguing.*

Tirant (Fr.) (tē-ränh.) } Brace of a
Tirante (Spa.) (tē-*rän*-tĕ.) } drum.

Tirasse (Fr.) (tĭ-*räss*.) The pedals of a small organ which act on the manual keys, by pulling, or drawing them down.

Tiráto (It.) (tē-*rä*-tō.) Drawn, pulled, stretched out; a down-bow. See, also, *Tirasse.*

Tíra tútto (It.) (*tē*-rä *toot*-tō.) A pedal, or mechanism, in an organ, which, acting upon all the stops, enables the performer to obtain at once the full power of the instrument.

Tiré (Fr.) (tē-rā.) *Drawn, pulled;* a down-bow.

Tirolese (It.) (tē-rō-*lā*-zĕ.) A kind of dance. See *Tyrolienne.*

Tobend (Ger.) (*tō*-bĕnd.) Blusteringly, violently.

Toccáta (It.) (tō-*kä*-tä.) An old form of composition for the organ, or pianoforte, something like our capriccio, or fantasia; a piece requiring brilliant execution, the *toccata* was a technical work (from the word *toccare, to touch*), a study in which some difficulties of execution were always present, and it generally preceded a fugue. In modern times it is still a study, but is more generally founded on the treatment of a single figure.

Toccatina (It.) (tŏk-kä-*tē*-nä.) A short *toccáta.*

Tocsin. An alarm-bell; ringing of a bell for the purpose of alarm.

Todesgesang (Ger.) (*tō*-dĕs-ghĕ-*säng*.) }
Todeslied (Ger.) (*tō*-dĕs-*lēd*.) }
A dirge; a funeral song.

Todtenglöckchen (Ger.) (*tōd*-t'n-*glŏk*-kh'n.) Funeral bell.

Todtenlied (Ger.) (*tōd*-t'n-*lēd*.) Funeral song, or anthem.

Todten-marsch (Ger.) (*tōd*-t'n-*märsh*.) Funeral march.

Todten-musik (Ger.) (*tōd*-t'n-*moo*-zĭk.) Funeral music.

Tolling. The act of ringing a church-bell in a slow, measured manner.

Tome (Fr.) (tōm.) Volume, book.

Ton (Fr.) (tŏnh.) } Tone, sound,
Ton (Ger.) (tōn.) } voice, melody;
Töne (Ger. pl.)(*tŏ*-nĕ.) } also, accent,
Tono (Spa.) (tō-nō.) } stress; also the
Tons (Fr. pl.) (tŏnh.) } pitch of any note as to its

ä as in *ah*; ā as in *hate*; ă as in *at*; ē as in *tree*; ĕ as in *eh*; ī as in *pine*; ĭ as in *pin*;

acuteness, or gravity; also, the key, or mode; *le ton d'ut*, the key of C. See also *Tone*.

Ton-abstand (Ger.) (*tōn-äb*-ständ.) An interval.

Tonart (Ger.) (tō-närt.) Mode, scale, key.

Ton-ausweichung (Ger.) (*tōn*-ous-vī-khoong.) Modulation.

Ton, bas (Fr.) (tŏnh bä.) A low, deep, tone.

Ton, demi (Fr.) (tŏnh dĕ-*mē*.) A semitone.

Ton de voix (Fr.) (tŏnh dŭh vwä.) Tone of voice.

Ton-dichter (Ger.) (*tōn-dĭkh*-tĕr.) Poet *of sound;* a composer of music.

Ton-dichtung (Ger.) (*tōn-dĭkh*-toong.) Musical composition of a poetic character.

Tóndo (It.) (*tōn*-dō.) Round, or full, as regards tone.

Ton doux (Fr.) (tŏnh doo.) Soft, sweet tone.

Tone. A given, fixed sound of certain pitch; it is used to signify a certain degree of distance, or interval, between two sounds, as in the major tone and minor tone; also the particular quality of the sound of any voice, or instrument.

Tone, explosive. A tone produced by striking a note suddenly and with great force, and as suddenly causing it to cease, > ∨

Tönen (Ger.) (*tŏ*-nĕn.) To sound; to resound.

Tönend (Ger.) (*tŏ*-nĕnd.) Sounding.

Tone, open. A tone produced on an open string.

Tone, quarter. A small interval, which, in the mathematical theory of music, is found to exist between D♯ and E♭, G♯ and A♭, etc.

Tones, accessory. Harmonics; tones faintly heard in the higher octaves, as the principal tone dies away. See *Harmonics*.

Tones, chest. The lowest register of the human voice.

Tones, Gregorian. The chants used for the psalms in the Roman Catholic service; the ancient modes or tones on which the Gregorian chants are based.

Tones, passing. Whenever one or more of the parts constituting an harmonic chord moves to a tone foreign to the harmony, the chord otherwise remaining unchanged, such movements are called *passing tones*.

Tone, whole. An interval consisting of two half-tones.

Ton-fall (Ger.) (tōn-fäll.) A cadence.

Ton-farbe (Ger.) (*tōn-fär*-bĕ.) Tone-color.

Ton-folge (Ger.) (*tōn-fōl*-ghĕ.) A succession of tones.

Ton-führung (Ger.) (*tōn-fü*-roong.) Modulation; also succession of melody, or harmony.

Ton-fuss (Ger.) (*tōn*-foos.) Meter.

Ton-gang (Ger.) (*tōn*-gäng.) Tune, melody.

Ton-gattung (Ger.) (*tōn-gät*-toong.)
Ton-geschlecht (Ger.) (*tōn*-ghĕ-shlĕkht.)
The individuality of the two modes, the major and minor; *Ton-geschlech* is the more correct term.

Ton-générateur (Fr.) (tŏnh-zhā-nā-rä-tür.) The ruling, or principal key in which a piece is written.

Tongue. In the reed-pipe of an organ, a thin elastic slip of metal.

Tonguing. A mode of articulating quick notes, used by flutists and cornetists.

Tonic. The key-note of any scale; the chief, fundamental ground-tone, or first note, of the scale.

Tónica (It.) (*tō*-nē-kä.)
Tonica (Ger.) (*tō*-nĕ-kä.) } Tonic.
Tonique (Fr.) (tŏnh-*ēk*.)

Tonic-pedal. A continued bass note on which chords foreign to its harmony are given.

Tonic Sol-fa. A method of teaching vocal music, invented by Miss Sarah Ann Glover, of Norwich, England, about 1812 (called by her the *tetrachordal* system), and afterwards perfected by the Rev. John Curwen, who became acquainted with the method in 1841. Its formal basis is the *movable-do* system; the seven usual solmisation syllables are employed, as follows; *doh, ray, me, fah, soh, lah, te.* The rea-

ŏ as in *tone*; ô as in *dove*; ŏ as in *not*; ŭ as in *up*; ü the French sound of *u*.

son for this departure from the ordinary spelling is, that the above is considered easier for English people to pronounce. In printing music, the initial letter of the syllable indicates the scale note. *Si* and *soh* having the same initial, the former is altered to *te*. Higher or lower octaves are shown by figures placed by the side of the notes, d^1, d^2, m^3, and s_1, m_2, d_3. The particular pitch of the key-sound is shown by the statement at the beginning of the piece, key G, key E♭, key A, etc. The minor mode is regarded as derived from the relative major, its tonic being called *lah*. Great use is made, in this system, of a *modulator*, a chart of the musical sounds. It presents succinctly the relative places of the notes of the scale, the relative minor modes, the chromatics, related keys, etc.

r¹	s	d¹		f¹			
		t —	m¹	—	l	r¹	s
t¹	f						
t	m	l =	r¹	—	s	d¹	f
						t	m
l	r	s —**DOH**¹—		f			
			TE	— m	l	r	
s	d	f	ta	le			
	t₁	m —	LAH =	r	s	d	
f		la	se				t₁
m	l₁	r —	**SOH** —	d	f		
			ba	fe	t₁	m	l₁
r	s₁	d —	FAH				
		t₁ —	**ME**	—	l₁	r	s₁
d	f₁	ma	re				
t₁	m₁	l₁ =	RAY —	s₁	d	f₁	
			de		t₁	m₁	
l₁	r₁	s₁ —**DOH**—		f₁			
			t₁	— m₁	l	r₁	
s₁	d₁	f₁					
	t₂	m₁ —	l₁ =	r₁	s₁	d₁	
f₁						t₂	
m₁	l₂	r₁ —	s₁	— d₁	f		
				t₂	m₁	l₂	
r₁	s₂	d₁ —	f₁				
	t₂	—	m₁	— l₂	r₁	s₂	

The advantage of the system is that it teaches sight singing much more rapidly and easily than can be done by notation. It has been applied to very large works with considerable success. See Grove's Dictionary, for fuller details of this important system.

Ton-kunst (Ger.) (tōn-koonst.) Music; the art and science of music.

Ton-künstler (Ger.) (*tōn-künst*-lĕr.) Musician.

Ton-künstlich (Ger.) (*tōn künst*-līkh.) Musical.

Ton-leiter (Ger.) (*tōn-lī*-tĕr.) Scale, gamut.

Ton-majeur (Fr.) (tŏnh-mä-zhur.) Major key.

Ton-mass (Ger.) (tōn-mäss.) Measure, time.

Ton-messer (Ger.) (*tōn-mĕs*-sĕr.) A monochord.

Ton-mineur (Fr.) (tŏnh-mē-*nŭr*.) Minor key.

Ton-satz (Ger.) (*tōn-sätz*). A musical composition.

Ton-schluss (Ger.) (tōn-shloos.) A cadence.

Ton-schlüssel (Ger.) (*tōn-shlüs*-s'l.) The key; key-note.

Ton-schrift (Ger.) (tōn shrift.) Musical notes.

Tons de l'église (Fr.) (tŏnh dŭh l'ā-glēz.) Church modes, or tones.

Ton-setzer (Ger.) (*tōn-set*-tsĕr.) A composer; a less flattering term than *ton-dichter*.

Ton-setzung (Ger.) (*tōn-sĕt*-tsoong.)
Ton-stück (Ger.) (tōn-stük.)
A musical piece, or composition.

Ton-stufe (Ger.) (*tōn-stoo*-fĕ.) A degree of the staff.

Ton-system (Ger.) (*tōn-sĭs*-tĕm.) System of tones, or sounds; the science of harmony, the systematic arrangement to musical tones, or sounds, in their regular order.

Ton-veränderung (Ger.) (*tōn*-fĕ-*rān*-dĕ roong.) Modulation.

ä as in *ah*; ā as in *hate*; ă as in *at*; ē as in *tree*; ĕ as in *eh*; ī as in *pine*; ĭ as in *pin*;

TON-WERK

Ton-werk (Ger.) (tōn-värk.) A musical composition.

Ton-wissenschaft (Ger.) (*tōn-vĭs*-s'n-shäft.) The science of music.

Tostaménte (It.) (tōs-tä-*men*-tĕ.) Quickly, rapidly.

Tostíssimaménte (It.) (tōs-tēs-sē-mä-*men*-tĕ.)

Tostíssimo (It.) (tōs-*tēs*-sē-mō.) Extremely quick; with great rapidity.

Tósto (It.) (*tōs*-tō.) Quick, swift, rapid.

Touch. Style of striking, or pressing the keys of an organ, pianoforte, or similar instrument; the resistance made to the fingers, by the keys of any instrument, as when the keys are put down with difficulty, an instrument is said to have a *hard*, or *heavy touch*; when there is little resistance the *touch* is said to be *soft*, or *light*.

Touch, demi-legato. A touch indicated by dots under a slur, and played by gently raising the hand, with a motion from the wrist, and pressing the keys, carefully detaching the notes. See *Portamento*.

Touch, demi-staccato. The striking the key and raising the hand quickly, retaining the note not more than half its full value. At present, however, the dots are employed for all kinds of staccato.

Touche (Fr.) (toosh.) The *touch*; also a key of the pianoforte, etc.

Touche d'orgue (Fr.) (toosh d'org.) Key of an organ.

Toucher (Fr.) (too-shā.) To play upon an instrument.

Touch, legato. A sliding of the fingers on and off the keys; holding down one key until the finger is fairly on to another. It is indicated by a curved line over or under the note.

Touch, piano. The manner of striking the keys of the pianoforte.

Touch, staccato. A short and sudden striking of the keys, making the notes very detached.

Toujours (Fr.) Always; used in the same sense as *Sempre*.

Tours de force (Fr.) (toor dŭh fŏrs.) *Bravúra* passages, roulades, divisions, etc.

Tout ensemble (Fr.) (too t'änh-sänhbl.) The whole together; the general effect.

Trabattere (It.) (trä-bät-tā-rĕ.) To beat.

Trachea (Lat.) (*trä*-kē-ä.) The windpipe.

Tracto (Spa.) (träk-tō.) Versicles sung at Mass between the Epistle and the Gospel.

Tradolce (It.) (trä-*dōl*-tshĕ.) Very soft; sweet.

Tradótto (It.) (trä-*dō*-tō.) Translated; arranged; adapted; fitted to.

Tragedy, lyric. A tragedy accompanied by singing; tragic opera.

Trainé (Fr.) (trā-nā.) Slurred; bound; lingering; drawn along.

Trait (Fr.) (trā.) Passage; run; a phrase.

Trait de chant (Fr.) (trā dŭh shänh.) A melodic passage, or phrase.

Trait d'harmonie (Fr.) (trā d'är-mō-nē.) Succession of chords; a sequence.

Trait d'octave (Fr.) (trā d'ŏk-täv.) See *Rule of the Octave*.

Traité (Fr.) (trā-*tā*.) A treatise on the practice, or the theory of music.

Trällern (Ger.) (*trāl*-lĕrn.) To trill; to hum a tune.

Tramoya (Spa.) (trä-*moi*-ä.) Scene; operatic decoration.

Tranquillaménte (It.) (trän-quil-lä-*men*-tĕ.) Quietly, calmly, tranquilly.

Tranquillézza (It.) (trän-quil-*let*-sä.)

Tranquillita (It.) (trän-quil-lē-*tä*.)

Tranquíllo (It.) (trän *queel*-lō.) Tranquillity, calmness, quietness.

Transcription. An arrangement for any instrument, of a song or other composition, not originally designed for that instrument; an adaptation.

ō as in *tone*; ŏ as in *dove*; ŏ as in *not*; ŭ as in *up*; ü the French sound of *u*.

Transient. An epithet applied to those chords of whose harmony no account is meant to be taken, but which are used as passing chords.

Transitio (Lat.) (trăn-sē-shǐ-o.) } Passing
Transition (Eng.) suddenly out of one key into another, also a passage leading from one theme to another.

Transposed. Removed, or changed into another key.

Transposer (Fr.) (tranhs-pō-zā.)
Transponiren (Ger.)(träns-pō-nee-rĕn.) Change of key; removing a piece into another key.

Transposing Instruments. Instruments which have their natural scale written as the *C* scale, while actually sounding a different pitch; the contra-bass sounds an octave lower, and the piccolo an octave higher than written, and it is natural and correct to speak of such instruments as transposing: but these transpose only to avoid leger lines; there are other instruments which transpose to other degrees than the octave, instruments which, therefore, give forth a different note from that which is written. The reason of this practice is found in the fact that wind-instrument players frequently perform on two or more different instruments of the same family, and, in order to secure uniformity of fingering and blowing, the system applied to one is applied to others; for example, the English-horn, which is a larger oboe, is notated as that instrument, and the performer who is accustomed to the oboe will play the English-horn in a similar manner, but it will actually sound a perfect fifth below the notes which are written. The clarinets, in the same way, are all written alike, but the C clarinet only, sounds the notes as they are written, the B flat clarinet sounding a tone below, and the A clarinet a minor third below. The horns (except C alto) the trumpets, and cornets (except those in C), the B flat bass clarinet, and other instruments, are treated in this manner, sounding notes of a different pitch from those written.

Transverse flute. The German flute the *flauto traverso.*

Traquenard (Fr.) (trä-kĕ-närd.) A brisk sort of dance.

Trascinándo (It.) (trä-shi-*nän*-dō ; Dragging the time.

Trascrítto (It.) (trä-*skrēt*-tō.) Copied, transcribed.

Trasognata (It.)(trä-sōn-*yä*-tä.) Dreamily.

Trattáto (It.) (trät-*tä*-tō.) See *Traité.*

Trattenuto (It.) (trät-tĕn-*noo*-tō.) Holding back.

Trauer-gesang (Ger.) (*trou*-ĕr-ghĕ-*zäng.*) Mourning song; dirge.

Trauer-marsch (Ger.) (*trou*-ĕr-*märsh.*) Funeral march.

Trauer-musik (Ger.) (*trou*-ĕr-*mbo*-zĭk.) Funeral music.

Traurig (Ger.) (*trou*-rĭg.) Heavily, sadly, mournfully.

Traversiere (Fr.) (trä-vĕr-sē-*är*.)
Travérso (It.) (trä-*vär*-sō.) Cross, across; applied to the *transverse*, or German flute, to distinguish it from the *flûte à bec.*

Travestie (Ger.) (*trä*-fĕs-*tē*.) Parody.

Travestiren (Ger.) (*trä*-fĕs-*teer*-ĕn.) To parody.

Tre (It.) (träy.) Three; *à tre*, for three voices, or instruments.

Treble. The upper part; the highest voice; the soprano; that which generally contains the melody.

Treble clef. The G clef, the soprano clef.

Treble, first. The highest treble, or soprano.

Treble forte stop. A stop applied to cabinet-organs, by means of which the treble part of the instrument may be increased in power, while the base remains subdued.

Treble second. Low soprano.

Treble staff. The staff upon which the treble clef is placed.

Treble viol. An instrument invented before the modern viol, furnished with six strings tuned chiefly by *fourths.*

Treble voice. The highest species of the female, or boy's voice.

Tre córde (It.) (träy *kŏr*-dĕ.) *Three strings;* in pianoforte music this means that the pedal which moves the keys, or

TREMANDO

action, the soft pedal, must no longer be pressed down.

Tremándo (It.) (trā-*män*-dō.) See *Tremolándo*.

Tremblant (Fr.) (tränh-blänh.) *Shaking*. See *Tremulant*.

Tremblement (Fr.) (tränhbl-mänh.) A trill, or shake.

Trembler (Fr.) (tränh-blā.) To tremble; to shake.

Tremblotant (Fr.) (tränh-blō-tänh.) Quivering.

Trembloter (Fr.) (tränh-blō-tā.) To quiver; to shake.

Treméndo (It.) (trĕ-*men*-dō.) Terrible, dreadful.

Tremolándo (It.) (trĕm-ō-*län*-dō.)
Tremoláte (It.) (trĕm-ō-*lä*-tĕ.)
Trémolo (It.) (*trā*-mō-lō.)
Trémulo (It.) (*trā*-moo-lō.)
Trembling, quivering; a note, or chord, reiterated with great rapidity, producing a tremulous effect.

Tremolant. } An organ-stop which gives
Tremulant. } to the tone a waving, trembling, or undulating effect, resembling the *vibráto* in singing, and the *tremolándo* in violin-playing; also, a harmonium-stop of the same kind.

Tremóre (It.) (trā-*mō*-rĕ.) } Tremor;
Tremoróso (It.) (trā-mō-*rō*-zō.) } trembling; see also *Tremolándo*.

Trenchmore. An old English dance, of a lively species.

Trenodia (It.) (trā-*nō*-dē-ä.) A funeral dirge.

Trental. An office for the dead in the Roman Catholic Church, consisting of thirty Masses.

Très (Fr.) (trāy.) Very, most.

Très-animé (Fr.) (trā sän-ē-māy.) Very animated; very lively.

Trésca (It.) (*tres*-kä.) A country dance.

Très fort (Fr.) (trāy fōr.) Very loud.

Très lentement (Fr.) (trāy länht-mänh.) Very slow.

Très piano (Fr.) (trāy pē-ä-nō.) Very soft.

Très vif (Fr.) (tray veef.) Very lively; very brisk.

Très vite (Fr.) (tray veet.) Very quick.

TRILL

Treter (Ger.) (trā-tĕr.) *Treader*, of the bellows, in German organs.

Tre vólte (It. pl.) (träy vōl-tĕ.) Three times.

Triad. The common chord, consisting of a note sounded together with its third and fifth.

Triad, extreme. A triad consisting of a fundamental tone, a major third, and an augmented fifth.

Triad, imperfect. The chord taken on the seventh of the key, consisting of two minor thirds.

Triad, major. A union of any sound with its major third and perfect fifth.

Triad, minor. A union of any sound with its minor third and perfect fifth.

Triad of the dominant. A triad on the dominant, or major fifth.

Triad, perfect. The harmonic division of the fifth into two thirds, of which the greater third is lowest.

Triad, tonic. A triad on the tonic, in major, or minor.

Triangle. A small three-sided steel frame, which is played upon by being struck with a rod. It gives no definite pitch.

Triangolo (It.) (trē-än-gō-lō.) } A
Triangulo (Spa.) (trē-än-goo-lō.) } tri-
Triangulus (Lat.) (tre-*än*-gū-lŭs.) } angle.

Trill (Ger., *Triller;* Fr., *Trille;* It., *Trillo;* in England, *The Shake.*) Its sign is *tr* or *tr*〰〰, and it consists of a rapid alteration of the printed note and the next note above, to the value of the printed note:

Written.   Played.   Or thus.

In the eighteenth century the trill always began on the *upper* note, as in the second example, but early in the nineteenth century Hummel established the rule of beginning with the principal note. Bülow returns to the older method in most of his editions of the masterworks. Yet we think the Hummel method, to begin the trill upon the principal note, the better one. The interval is according to the scale, unless otherwise indicated by accidentals, therefore, it can be either a tone, or a

ŏ as in *tone*; ô as in *dove*; ŏ as in *not*; ŭ as in *up*; ü the French sound of *u*.

269

semi-tone. The wavy line indicating the trill is as old as the time of the *Neumes* (see *Notation*). *Grace-notes* before or after a trill form part of it and are played in the same speed as the trill itself. A trill generally ends with a turn, especially if it has the rhythmic value of a half-note or more, and if it occurs in an ascending passage (in descending passages the final turn is sometimes omitted) and this turn is indicated by two *grace-notes*, the note below and the principal note, written after the trill; these two notes, added to the last beat of the trill, form a turn, naturally. The concluding *grace-notes* are often omitted in careless notation, therefore it is important to remember this rule. If the trill is begun on the auxiliary note (the upper note) the unequal group at the close disappears. See also, Dannreuther's "Musical Ornamentation," and Fay's "Ornaments in Music."

Trillándo (It.) (trēl-*län*-dō.) Trilling.

Trilláre (It.) (trēl-*lä*-rĕ.) To shake; to trill.

Trille (Fr.) (trēll.) }
Triller (Ger.) (*trĭl*-lĕr.) } A shake; a trill.
Tríllo (It.) (trēl-lō.) }

Triller-kette (Ger.) (*trĭl*-lĕr-*kĕt*-tĕ.) A chain, or succession of shakes. It., *Catena di Trilli*.

Trillern (Ger.) (*trĭl*-lĕrn.) To trill; to shake.

Trillette (Fr.) (trīl-lĕtt.) }
Trillétta (It.) (trēl-*le*-tä.) } A short trill, or shake.
Trillétto (It.) (trēl-*let*-tō.) }

Trill, imperfect. A trill, or shake without a turn at the close.

Trilli (It.) (trēl-lē.) Trills, shakes.

Trill, perfect. A quick alteration of two notes ending with a turn.

Trink-gesang (Ger.) (*trĭnk*-ghĕ-*zäng*.) }
Trink-lied (Ger.) (trĭnk-lēed.) } A Bacchanalian, or drinking-song.

Trino (Spa.) (trēe-nō.) A trill.

Trinona. An organ-stop, of open 8-foot small scale, and pleasant, gamba-like tone.

Trio (It.) (trēe-ō.) A piece for three instruments, or voices. The word *trio* is also applied to a contrasted song-form in the minuet form of composition. (See *Form*.) This arose from the custom (in the seventeenth and eighteenth centuries) of placing two *minuets* in contrast in a single form. This second *minuet* being generally played by the wood-wind in three-part harmony, soon received the name of *the trio*, a name which is applied to it still, although it is no longer necessarily in three-part harmony. The trio is generally *cantabile* in character. The trio appears in *marches, walzes, gavots, minuets,* and much other light music in the *minuet* (or *song form with trio*) form.

Triole (Ger.) (trĭ-ō-lĕ.) }
Triolet (Fr.) (trĭ-ō-lā.) } A triplet; a group of three notes to be played in the time of two.

Triomphale (Fr.) (trē-ŏnh-fäl.) }
Trionfále (It.) (trē-ōn-*fä*-lĕ.) } Triumphal.

Triomphant (Fr.) (trē-ŏnh-fänh.) }
Trionfánte (It.) (trē-ōn-*fän*-tĕ.) } Triumphant.

Tripartite. Divided into three parts; scores in three parts are said to be *tripartite*.

Triphony. Three sounds heard together.

Triple. Threefold, treble.

Triple counterpoint. Counterpoint in three parts, invertible; that is, so contrived that each part will serve for either bass, middle or upper part.

Triple croche (Fr.) (krō-shā.) A 32nd note, a demisemiquaver.

Triple dotted note. A note whose length is increased seven-eighths of its original value by three dots placed after it.

Triple dotted rest. A rest whose value is increased seven-eighths by three dots placed after it.

Triple octave. See *Tridiapason*.

Triplet. A group of three notes, played in the usual time of two similar ones.

Triple time. Such as has an odd, or uneven number of parts in a bar, as *three*, or *nine*.

Triplice (It.) (trē-plē-tshĕ.) Triple, treble, threefold.

Triplum (Lat.) (*trĭp*-lŭm.) Formerly the name of the treble, or highest part.

Trisagion (Ger.) (trĭ-*sä*-ghĕ-ŏn.) } A **Trisagium** (Lat.) (trĭ-sä-ghē-ūm.) } hymn in which the word *Holy* is repeated three times in succession.

Trisemitonium (Lat.)(*trĕ*-sĕm-ĭ-*tō*-nĭ-ŭm.) The lesser, or minor third.

Tristézza (It.) (trĭs-*tet*-sä.) Sadness, heaviness, pensiveness.

Triton (Fr.) (trē-tŏhn.)
Tritone (Eng.) (trī-tōn.) } A superfluous, or augmented fourth,
Tritóno (It.) (trē-*tō*-nō.)
Tritonus (Lat.) (trē-*tō*-nŭs.) containing three whole tones, once held to be the worst possible interval in music.

Triumphirend (Ger.) (*trĭ*-oom-*fee*-rĕnd.) Triumphant.

Triumphlied (Ger.) (*trĭ*-oomf-*leed*.) Song of triumph.

Trochäisch (Ger.) (trō-*kā*-ĭsh.) Trochaic.

Trochäus (Ger.) (trō-kā-ŭs.) Trochee.

Trochee (Lat.) (trō-kā.) A dissyllabic musical foot, containing one long and one short syllable, — ⌣.

Trómba (It.) (*trŏm*-bä.) A trumpet; also an 8-foot reed organ-stop.

Trómba di básso (It.) (trŏm-bä dē *bäs*-sō.) The bass trumpet.

Trómba príma (It.) (trŏm-bä *prē*-mä.) First trumpet.

Trombare (It.) (trŏm-*bä*-rĕ.) To sound the trumpet.

Trómba secónda (It.) (*trŏm*-bä sä-*kōn*-dä.) Second trumpet.

Trómbe sórde (It. pl.) (*trŏm*-bĕ *sŏr*-dĕ.) Trumpets having dampers.

Trombétta (It.) (trŏm-*bet*-tä.) A small trumpet.

Trombone. (Ger., *Posaune*, It. and Fr., *Trombono*.) This brass instrument is made on two different systems. The valve-trombone lengthens its tube by means of keys which open extra crooks of the tube and thus lengthen it, the slide-trombone has no keys, but is made in two sections, the tubes of which are caused to overlap, so that the player, by drawing them out, can elongate the instrument, and cause it to give different series of tones. The natural tones are those produced with closed slides, but in the slide-trombones there is little difference in quality between these and the tones produced with open slides, since the shape of the tube remains unchanged. The trombone with keys is the easier to play, but the slide-trombone has the better tone. The slides are drawn into six positions, each one being a semi-tone lower than the one preceding, thus lowering the pitch of the instrument a diminished fifth. The trombone is at present made in three pitches, alto, tenor, and bass. The trombones are generally written in three-part harmony, and are treated as non-transposing. The alto trombone is called the E flat trombone, as, with closed slides, it gives the harmonic series of E flat, beginning not with the fundamental, but with the first overtone. The general compass of the trombone is a little more than two octaves, the pitch of the instrument varying with the length of the tube. Thus an alto trombone, the part for which is written in the alto clef, can play all notes between

a tenor trombone all between

and a bass trombone all between

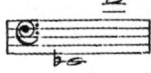

including every intermediate semi-tone, and six semi-tones deeper than the lowest natural tone (given above) by drawing the slides, or using the ventils. Each instrument can also sound the note an octave deeper than the one given as the lowest in the above schedule. This is however very difficult to do, yet good players can attain this fundamental, by protruding the lips well into the mouthpiece, and can then lower the tone by means of the slides. These deep tones are called the *pedal tones* and must be sparingly used. The following would be the practicable pedal tones on a tenor-trombone:

The pedal tones have a growling, unpleasant quality. See Prout's "Orchestra," or A. Elson's "Orchestral Instruments."

Tromboni (It.) (trŏm-bō-nēe.) Trombones.

Trommel (Ger.) (*trŏm*-m'l.) The military drum.

Trommel-boden (Ger.) (*trŏm*-m'l-*bō*-d'n.) Bottom of a drum.

Trommler (Ger.) (*trŏm*-lĕr.) A drummer.

Trommel-kasten (Ger.) (*trŏm*-m'l-*käs*-t'n.) The body of a drum.

Trommel-klöpfel (Ger.) (*trŏm*-m'l-*klŏp*-fĕl.)

Trommel-schlägel (Ger.) (*trŏm*-m'l-*shlä*-g'l.) Drumstick.

Trommel-schläger (Ger.) (*trŏm*-m'l-*shlä*-gher.) Drummer.

Trommeln (Ger.) (*trŏm*-mĕln.) To drum; drumming; beating the drum.

Trompa (Lat.) (trŏm-pä.) } A trumpet.
Trompe (Fr.) (trŏnhp.)

Trompe de béarn (Fr.) (trŏmhp dŭh-bā-ärn.) The Jews'-harp.

Trompete (Ger.) (trŏm-*pā*-tĕ.) A trumpet; also, a reed-stop in an organ.

Trompeten (Ger.) (trŏm-*pā*-t'n.) To play upon the trumpet.

Trompeten-register (Ger.) (trŏm-*pā*-t'n-rĕ-*ghĭs*-tĕr.)

Trompeten-zug (Ger.) (trŏm-*pā*-t'n-*tsüg*.) Trumpet-stop, or register in an organ.

Trompeter (Ger.) (trŏm-*pā*-tĕr.)
Trompeteur (Fr.) (trŏnh-pā-tŭr.) A trumpeter.

Trompette (Fr.) (trŏnh-pāt.) A trumpet; also, a trumpeter; also, a reed-stop in an organ.

Trompette à pistons (Fr.) (trŏnh-pāt ä-pēs-tŏnh.) The valve-trumpet.

Trompette harmonique (Fr.) (tronh-pāt här-mŏnh-ēk.) Harmonic-trumpet, a reed-stop in an organ of 8 or 16-foot tone. See *Harmonic Flute*.

Trompette marine (Fr.) (trŏnh-pāt mä-rēn.) See *Trumpet-marine*.

Trompette parlante (Fr.) (trŏnh-pāt pärlänht.) A speaking-trumpet.

Tronco (It.) (trŏn-kō.) An intimation that the sounds are to be cut short.

Troop. A quick march; a march in quick time.

Troper. A book formerly used in the church, containing the sequences, or chants, sung after the recital of the Epistle.

Tróppo (It.) (trŏp-pō.) Too much; *non tróppo*, not too much.

Troubadours (Fr. pl.) (troo-bä-door.)
Trouvères (Fr. pl.) (troo-vāir.)
Trouveurs (Fr. pl.) (troo-vŭr.)
The bards, and poet-musicians of Provence, and of North France, about the twelfth century. See Rowbotham's "Troubadours and Courts of Love."

Troupe, opera. A company of musicians associated for the purpose of giving operas, generally traveling from place to place.

Trovatóre (It.) (trō-vä-tō-rĕ.) A minstrel; a troubadour.

Trug-schluss (Ger.) (troog-shloos.) Interrupted, or deceptive cadence; an unexpected, or interrupted resolution of a discord.

Trump. A trumpet; to blow a trumpet.

Trüb (Ger.) (treeb.) Sad, mournful, gloomy.

Trumpet (It. *Tromba*, Fr., *Trompette*, Ger., *Trompete*.) A brass instrument with long and narrow tube and a rather shallow mouthpiece. The trumpet was once neglected in favor of the cornet in America. The substitution was a poor one, since the cornet has a shorter, wider tube and a different tone quality. The trumpet's natural tones are a harmonic series

ă as in *ah*; ā as in *hate*; ă as in *at*; ē as in *tree*; ĕ as in *eh*; ī as in *pine*; ĭ as in *pin*;

Timpani

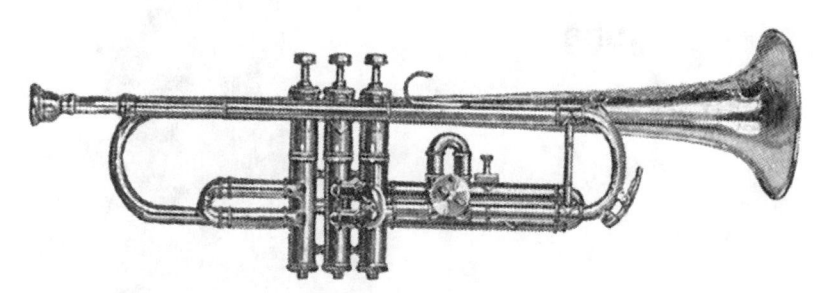

Trumpet

Tuba

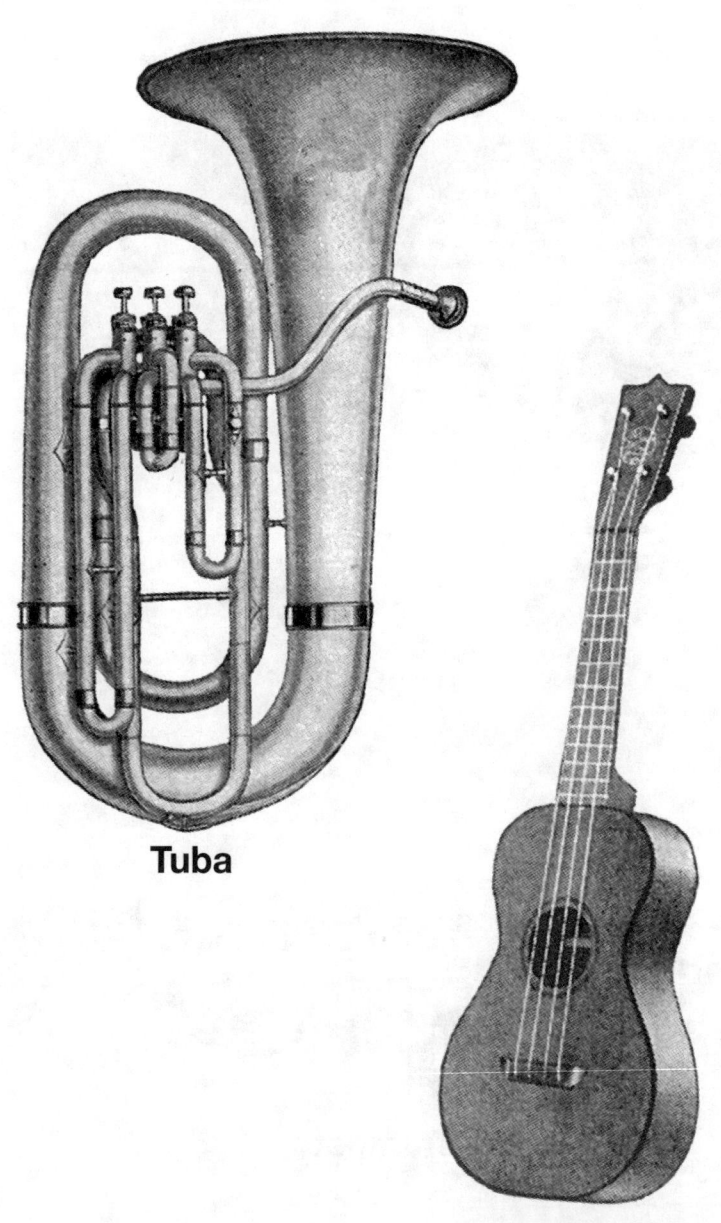

Ukelele

beginning on the second overtone of a deep series, while those of the cornet begin on the first overtone of a high series. The following is the natural series of a trumpet in C:

The trumpet is generally used in open tones, most of the muted tones sounding almost comical and very much like a child's toy, a fact which was taken advantage of by Wagner, in his "Mastersingers of Nuremburg," in the procession of the guilds, to usher in the toymakers. The C trumpets are non-transposing, and like the horns, the trumpets are scored in the key of C. There are trumpets in B, B-flat, A, A-flat, and G, transposing downwards, and others in D, E-flat, E, and F, transposing upwards. There is also another trumpet in F, sounding a fifth lower than written, and bass-trumpets are used by Wagner and others, in various keys, transposing even to a ninth downward. The B-flat trumpet is the most used. See Prout's "Orchestra," or A. Elson's "Orchestral Instruments." See also *Ventil*.

Trumpet harmonical. An instrument, the sounds of which resemble those of a trumpet, differing from that instrument only in being longer and having more branches; the sackbut.

Trumpet-marine. An ancient species of monochord, played with a bow, and producing a sound resembling that of a trumpet. It is also called *Trummscheidt* and *Tromba marina*, but is not a trumpet.

Trumpet-stop. A stop in an organ having a tone similar to that of a trumpet.

Trumpet-stop, octave. A stop in an organ sounding an octave higher than the trumpet-stop.

Trumpet-valve. A trumpet the tones of which are changed by the use of valves. See *Ventil*.

T. S. The initials of *Tasto Solo*.

Tuba (Lat.) (*too*-ba.) The name applied to the deepest saxhorns. The tuba is made in different pitches, the deepest being called the *contra-bass* (not to be confounded with the string instrument). The tuba is non-transposing, and is played with keys. It was the invention of a German bandmaster named Wieprecht. Sometimes a fine effect is attained by using a quartet of tubas, in which case the euphonium and the baritone, both saxhorns of a higher pitch, are employed, together with bass-tubas. Wagner, in the barbaric *Hunding motive* in "Die Walküre," makes masterly use of the tubas. Tubas are made with three, four and even five, keys; also the name of a powerful reed-stop in an organ. See *Ventil*.

Tuba clarion (Lat.) (*tū*-bä *klä*-rĭ-ŏn.) A 4-foot reed-stop of the *tuba* species.

Tuba mirabilis (Lat.) (*tū*-bä mĭ-*rä*-bĭ-lĭs.) An 8-foot reed-stop, on a high pressure of wind, first introduced into the Birmingham Town Hall organ, and invented by William Hill.

Tubular instruments. Instruments formed of tubes, straight, or curved, of wood, or metal.

Tuiau d'orgue (Fr.) (twē-ō d'ōrg.) See *Tuyau d'orgue*.

Tumultuóso (It.) (too-mool-too-*ō*-zō.) Tumultuous, agitated.

Tune. An air; a melody; a succession of measured sounds, agreeable to the ear, and possessing a distinct and striking character; to bring into harmony.

Tuning-fork. A small steel instrument, having two prongs, which upon being struck, gives a certain fixed tone, used for tuning instruments, and for ascertaining or indicating the pitch of tunes. Tuning-forks were invented in England in 1711, by John Shore, a sergeant-trumpeter in the army. Shore *dated* his forks, a proceeding that has aided much in ascertaining the old pitches. Tuning-forks are generally made in two pitches — A^3 (or one-lined A) for orchestra, and C^4 (or two-lined C) for pianos and organs.

Tuning-hammer. A steel, or iron utensil used by harpsichord and pianoforte, tuners.

Tuning-key. A *tuning hammer*.

Tuning-slide. An English instrument for pitching the key-note, producing thirteen semi-tones from C to C. Also

ŏ as in *tone*; ô as in *dove*; ŏ as in *not*; ŭ as in *up*; ü the French sound of *u*.

a crook on some brass instruments which by lowering the tone as it is drawn out, puts the instrument in pitch with the orchestra.

Tuóni ecclesiástici (It. pl.) (two̅-ne̅ ĕk-klä̆-ze̅-äs-te̅-tshe̅.) Ecclesiastical modes, or tones.

Tuóno (It.) (two̅-no̅.) A tone; a sound; a tune.

Tuóno mézzo (It.) (two̅-no̅ mĕt-so̅.) A semi-tone.

Turbae (Lat.) The chorus part of voice of the multitude in a Passion music.

Túrca (It.) (*toor*-kä.) ⎫ Turkish;
Turchésco (It.) (toor-*kes*-ko̅.) ⎬ *álla*
Túrco (It.) (*toor*-ko̅.) ⎭ *Túrca*,
in the style of Turkish music.

Türkisch (Ger.) (*tür*-kĭsh.) See *Túrca*.

Turkish-music. See *Janitscharenmusik*.

Turn. An embellishment of four, five, or three notes, being made of the note above and the note below the principal note. It is called *Gruppetto* in Italian, *Doppelschlag* in German, and *Groupe* in French. Its sign, ∾, came from the neume notation of the dark ages, and showed the direction of the progression of the music. Draw a line through the following group, from note to note, and the origin of the sign of the turn will be at once perceived:

A line drawn through any sign of embellishment, ∾, is to denote its inversion. The turn is generally played rapidly, but some deviation is made at times, in very slow and expressive passages. The turn takes its rhythmic value from the note over or after which it stands. The intervals of the turn are most frequently a tone for the upper, a semi-tone for the lower, interval,

but on the third and seventh degrees in a major scale they are a semi-tone above and a tone below unless otherwise indicated, while in a minor scale a turn on the fifth degree is generally made of semi-tones both above and below. Occasionally there are turns of a tone above and a tone below, but these intervals should *never* be played, or sung, unless clearly indicated. Such a turn is sometimes found on the second degree of the major scale (see Schumann's "Der Dichter Spricht," or "Novellette," in F.) The following general rules for turns may be given. If a turn follows a note and the next note is of a different pitch, play *four* notes in the last part of the rhythmic value of the principal note:

Written.   Played.

Written.   Played.

But if the next note is of the same pitch play but three notes in the same manner:

Written.   Played.

Written.   Played.

Let it be clearly understood that a turn *over* or *under* a note means something *entirely different* from the turn *after* a note, as illustrated above. A turn over (or under) a note takes its time value from the *beginning* of the note, and is played in two ways. If the note is of any length (even of moderate duration) *always* play three quick notes before the principal note, and accent the latter thus:

Written.   N. B. Played.

But if the note is quite short (and the tempo-mark must guide us somewhat here) let it dissolve entirely in a turn thus:

ă as in *ah* ; ā as in *hate* ; ă as in *at* ; ē as in *tree* ; ĕ as in *eh* ; ī as in *pine* ; ĭ as in *pin*;

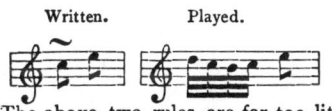

The above two rules are far too little understood by young teachers, yet they are very simple, and almost invariable. If, however, the next note is of the same pitch, and the principal note is very short, let it dissolve into a turn, but now beginning with the principal note:

If it is over a long note follow the preceding rule, which is practically invariable: *A turn over a note of some length, is played as three quick notes before the principal note*, as in the example marked *N. B.* When a turn follows a dotted note and the next note is a single, short, unaccented note, filling out a rhythmical division of the measure, the value of the dotted note is divided into thirds; on the first third comes the principal note, on the second third, three notes of the turn are played, and on the last third comes the last note of the turn. This forms a group beginning and ending with the same note, and with a note of the same rhythmic value. Example:

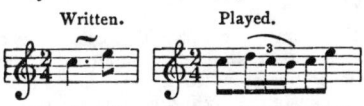

Occasionally some very slight deviation is made, and the first note played a little longer and the triplet a little shorter than above. If the dotted note be very short we can still follow the above rule, or we can play a group beginning with the principal note to the value of the simple note (without the dot) and then play the principal note to the value of the dot:

Turns after long dotted notes, or after such dotted notes as constitute a regular rhythmic division of the measure, do not follow these rules, but are played as when the turn follows an ordinary note, as in the first example given:

It will be observed that in the last example the turn takes the value of the dot. Accidentals in turns can be written to affect either note. When it is intended to affect the upper note the accidental is written above the turn; when the lower note is to be affected, the sign is written below the turn. Accidentals can be written simultaneously both above and below, affecting both auxiliary notes. The inverted turn, written ∫ or ∿, follows the above rules but begins on the *lower*, not on the *upper* note. Sometimes, when a note is dissolved into a turn (as in the example next following the one marked *N. B.*), particularly if the tempo is slow, it may be dissolved into *five* notes:

Tusch (Ger.) (toosh.) A flourish of trumpets and kettledrums.

Tuthorn (Ger.) (toot-hōrn.) The horn of a cowherd.

Tútta (It.) (too-tä.) } All; the whole;
Tútto (It.) (too-tō.) } entirely; quite.

Tútta fórza (It.) (*too*-tä-*fōr*-tsä.) }
Tútta la fórza (It.) (*too*-tä lä *fōr*-tsä.) }
The whole power, as loud as possible, with the utmost force and vehemence.

Tútte (It.) (too-tĕ.) } All, the entire
Tútti (It.) (too-tē.) } band, or chorus; in a solo, or concerto, it means that the full orchestra is to come in.

Tútte córde (It.) (*too*-tĕ *kŏr*-dĕ.) *All the strings;* in pianoforte-music this means that the soft pedal which shifts the action, must no longer be pressed down

Tútti unísoni (It. pl.) (toot-tē oo-nē-*zō*-nē.) All in unison.

Tútto árco (It.) (toot-tō *är*-kō.) With the whole length of the bow.

Tuyau d'orgue (Fr.) (tü-yō d'ōrg.) An organ-pipe.

Twelfth. An interval comprising eleven conjunct degrees, or twelve sounds, also, an organ-stop tuned twelve notes above the diapasons.

Twelfth-stop, octave. A stop of an organ sounding an octave higher than the twelfth stop.

Twenty-second. See *Octave-fifteenth*.

Tymbale. See *Timbale*.

Tympani (It. pl.) (*tĕm*-pä-nē.) Kettle-drums.

Tympano (It.) See *Timpano*.

Tympanon (Fr.) (tănh-pä-nŏnh.) Dulcimer.

Tympanum (Lat.) (*tĭm*-pă-nŭm.) Timbrel, tabor; old name for the drum.

Tyrolienne (Fr.) (tĭ-rō-lĭ-ĕn.) Songs, or dances, peculiar to the Tyrolese.

U

Udíta (It.) (oo-*dē*-tä.) } Heard; the sense
Udíto (It.) (oo-*dē*-tō.) } of hearing.

Uditóre (It.) (oo-dē-*tō*-rĕ.) An auditor, listener; hearer.

Uebereinstimmung (Ger.) (*ü*-bĕr-īn-*stĭm*-moong.) Consonance, harmony, accordance.

Uebergang (Ger.) (*ü*-bĕr-*gäng*.) Transition; change of key.

Uebermässig (Ger.) (*ü*-bĕr-*mās*-sĭg.) Augmented, superfluous.

Uebung (Ger.) (*ü*-boong.) An exercise; a study for the practice of some peculiar difficulty. *Uebungsstück*: an exercise.

Uebungen (Ger. pl.) (*ü*-boon-ghĕn.) Exercises.

Uguále (It.) (oo-*gwä*-lĕ.) Equal, like, similar.

Ugualménte (It.) (oo-gwäl-*men*-tĕ.) Equally, alike.

Umána (It.) (oo-*mä*-nä.) } Human; *vóce*
Umáno (It.) (oo-*mä*-nō.) } *umána*, the human voice.

Umfang (Ger.) (*oom*-fäng.) Compass, extent.

Umfang der Stimme (Ger.) (oom-fäng dĕr stĭm-mĕ.) Compass of the voice.

Umkehrung (Ger.) (*oom*-kā-roong.) Inversion.

Umore (It.) (oo-*mor*-e.) Humor, playfulness.

Umschreibung (Ger.) (*oom*-shrī-boong.) Circumscription, limitation.

Un (It.) (oon.)
Una (It.) (*oo*-nä.) } A, an, one.
Uno (It.) (*oo*-no.)

Unaccompanied. A song, or other vocal composition without instrumental accompaniment.

Una córda (It.) (oò-nä *kŏr*-dä.) *One string*, on one string only; in pianoforte-music it means that the soft pedal is to be used. See *Pedal*.

Unbezogen (Ger.) (*oon*-bĕ-*tsō*-ghĕn.) Unstrung; not furnished with strings.

Und (Ger.) (oond.) And; *Aria und Chor*, air and chorus.

Unda maris (Lat.) (*ŭn*-dä *mä*-rĭs.) *Wave of the sea;* an organ-stop tuned rather flatter than the others, and producing an undulating, or waving effect, when drawn in conjunction with another stop; this effect is sometimes produced by means of a pipe with two mouths, the one a little higher than the other.

Undecima (Lat.) (ŭn-*dĕs*-ĭ-mä.) The eleventh.

Under song. In very old English music this was a kind of ground, or drone accompaniment to a song, and which was sustained by another singer; called also *burden* and *foot*.

Undulazióne (It.) (oon-doo-lä-tsē-*ō*-nĕ.) Undulation; the expressive, tremulous tone produced by a peculiar pressure of the finger upon the strings of the violin. *Vibrato*.

Unequal counterpoint. Parts moving in notes of unequal duration.

Unequal temperament. That method of tuning the twelve sounds included in an octave, which renders some of the scales more in tune than the others. See *Temperament*.

Ungar (Ger.) (oon-gär.) } Hun-
Ungarisch (Ger.) (*oon*-gä-rĭsh.) } garian; in the Hungarian style.

ă as in *ah*; ā as in *hate*; ă as in *at*; ē as in *tree*; ĕ as in *eh*; ī as in *pine*; ĭ as in *pin*;

UNGERADE TAKT-ART   VALVE HORN

Ungerade Takt-art (Ger.) (*oon*-ghĕ-*rä*-dĕ täkt-ärt.) Triple time; uneven time.

Ungestüm (Ger.) (oon-ghĕs-tŭm.) Impetuous.

Ungezwungen (Ger.) (*oon*-ghĕts-*voon*-g'n.) Easy, natural, unstrained.

Unharmonious. Dissonant, discordant.

Unharmonischer Querstand (Ger.) (oon-här-mō-nĭsh-ĕr quĕr-ständ.)

Unharmonischer Umstand (Ger.) (oon-här-mō-nĭsh-ĕr oom-ständ.) A false relation.

Unison. An accordance or coincidence of sounds proceeding from an equality in the number of vibrations made in a given time by a sonorous body; a tone that has the same pitch with another.

Unisonance. Accordance of sounds.

Unisonant. } Being in unison; having
Unisonous. } the same degree of gravity, or acuteness.

Unison, augmented. A semi-tone on same degree of staff.

Unísoni (It. pl.) (oo-nē-zō-nē.) *Unisons;* two, three, or more parts are to play, or sing, in unison with each other; or if this be not practicable, in octaves.

Unísono (It.) (oo-nē-zō-nō.) } A uni-
Unisonus (Lat.) (ū-nĭ-*sō*-nŭs.) } son; in unison; two or more sounds having the same pitch.

Unitaménte (It.) (oo-nē-tä-*men*-tĕ.) Together, jointly, unitedly.

Unsingbar (Ger.) (oon-*sĭng*-bär.) Impossible to be sung.

Unstrung. Relaxed in tension; an instrument from which the strings have been taken.

Unter (Ger.) (*oon*-tĕr.) Under, below.

Unter-bass (Ger.) (*oon*-tĕr-*bäss*.) The double-bass.

Unterbrechung (Ger.) (*oon*-tĕr-*brĕ*-khoong.) Interruption.

Unterhaltungs-stück (Ger.) (oon-tĕr-*häl*-toongs-*stük*.) Entertainment; an amusing, bright piece of music.

Untertasten (Ger.) (*oon*-tĕr-*täs*-t'n.) The white keys.

Unterricht (Ger.) (*oon*-tĕr-*rĭkht*.) Instruction, information.

Untersatz (Ger.) (*oon*-tĕr-*sätz*.) Supporter; stay; a pedal-register; double-stopped bass of 32-foot tone in German organs. See *Subbourdon*.

Up-bow. The sign ∧ or V.

Ut (Fr.) (oot.) The note C; the syllable originally applied by Guido to the note C, or *do*.

Ut bémol (Fr.) (oot bā-mōl.) The note C flat.

Ut dièse (Fr.) (oot dĭ-āz.) The note C sharp.

Ut dièse mineur (Fr.) (oot dĭ-āz mē-nŭr.) The key of C sharp minor.

Ut mineur (Fr.) (oot mē-nŭr.) C minor.

Ut queant laxis (Lat.) (ŭt *quā*-änt *lăx*-ĭs.) The commencing words of the hymn to St. John the Baptist, from which Guido is said to have taken the syllables, *ut, re, mi, fa, sol, la,* for his solmisation. See *Aretinian syllables.*

Ut supra (Lat.) (ŭt sū-prä.) As above; as before. See *Come Sopra.*

V

V. An abbreviation for *Violin, Vólti,* (V. S. = *volti subito*), *Voce* (m. v. = *mezza voce.*) Vc, or Vcello, *Violoncello;* Vla, *Viola;* Vv., *violini.*

Va (It.) (vä.) Go on.

Vaceto (vä-tshā-tō.) Quick.

Vacilándo (It.) (vät-tshē-*län*-dō.) Wavering; uncertain; irregular in the time.

Vágo (It.) (*vä*-gō.) Vague; rambling; uncertain, as to the time of expression.

Valeur (Fr.) (vä-lŭr.) } The value,
Valóre (It.) (vä-*lō*-rĕ.) } length, or duration of a note.

Valse (Fr.) (väls.) A waltz; a dance in ¾ time.

Valse à deux temps (Fr.) (väls ä dü tänh.) A quick waltz, in which the dancers make two steps in each measure.

Valve. A close lid or other contrivance designed to retard or modify the sound of an organ-pipe, or any wind-instrument. See *Ventil.*

Valve horn. A horn in which a portion of the tube is opened or closed by the use of valves, whereby a higher or lower pitch is obtained. The opening of the valve always lowering the tone. See *Horn* and *Ventil.*

ŏ as in *tone ;* ô as in *dove ;* ŏ as in *not ;* ŭ as in *up ;* ü the French sound of *u.*

Valve trumpets, whose tones are varied by the use of valves.

Vamp. To improvise an accompaniment.

Variaménte (It.) (vä-rē-ä-*men*-tĕ.) }
Variaménto (It.) (vä-rē-ä-*men*-tō.) } In a varied, free style of performance, or execution.

Variations. Repetitions of a theme, or subject, in new and varied aspects, the form or outline of the composition being preserved while the different passages are ornamented and amplified. With Bach and Handel they were often called *Doubles.*

Variationen (Ger. pl.) (fä-rē-ä-tē-ō-nĕn.)

Variazióni (It. pl.) (vä-rē-ä-tsē-*ō*-nē.) Variations.

Variazióne (It.) (vä-rē-ä-tsē-*ō*-nĕ.) Variation.

Variáto (It.) (vä-rē-*ä*-tō.) }
Varié (Fr.) (vä-rē-*ā*.) } Varied; diversified; with variations.

Varsovienne. A dance in moderate tempo, and ¾ time.

Vaudevil. A ballad; a song; a vaudeville.

Vaudeville (Fr.) (vō-dĕ-*vĕl*.) A street ballad, or song; a roundelay; also, a simple form of operètta; a comedy, or short drama, interspersed with songs.

Veeménte (It.) (vā-*men*-tĕ.) Vehement, forcible.

Veeménza (It.) (vā-*men*-tsä.) Vehemence, force.

Veláta (It.) (vā-*lä*-tä.) }
Veláto (It.) (vā-*lä*-tō.) } *Veiled;* a voice sounding as if it were covered with a veil.

Vellutáta (vĕl-loo-*tä*-tä.) }
Vellutáto (vĕl-loo-*tä*-tō.) } In a velvety manner; in a soft, smooth, and velvety style.

Velóce (It.) (vĕ-*lō*-tshĕ.) }
Velocem é́nte (vĕ-lō-tshĕ-*men*-tĕ.) } Swiftly; quickly; in a rapid time.

Velocissimaménte (It.) (vĕ-lō-tshēs-sē-mä-*men*-tĕ.)

Velocíssimo (It.) (vĕ-lō-*tshēs*-sē-mō.) Very swiftly; with extreme rapidity.

Velocita (It.) (vĕ-lō-tshē-tä.) Swiftness, rapidity.

Veneziána (It.) (vĕ-nā-tsē-*ä*-nä.) Venetian; the Venetian style.

Ventil (Ger.) (*fĕn*-tĭl.) }
Ventíle (It.) (vĕn-*tē*-lĕ.) } Valve in modern wind-instruments for producing the semitones; also, a valve for shutting off the wind in an organ. The keys and valves upon modern brass instruments enable such instruments as the horn or the trumpet, which formerly gave only the broken scale of harmonics, to give an entire chromatic series of tones. The invention dates from the early days of the nineteenth century, and is claimed by several musicians and manufacturers. It is probably not entirely due to any one discoverer. The method of using the ventils, valves, or keys, is the same on *trombone, tuba, trumpet, horn,* or *cornet.* It is based upon the principle that the longer the tube the deeper is the tone. The keys open certain bends, or crooks, in the tube, which are shut off when the keys are not touched. The key nearest the mouthpiece opens a short bend; the middle key one still shorter, the third key (there are generally but three) one longer than either of the other two. These added lengths can be combined together if desired. Thus the natural tube would sound, not one tone, but a series. (See *Harmonics.*) The middle key would add a short length to the tube, and cause it to sound all these harmonics a semi-tone lower. The first key would give the series a tone lower; the third a minor third lower; the third and second keys combined a major third lower; the first and third combined a perfect fourth lower; and all three, a diminished fifth lower. See Elson's "Famous Composers and their Works," new series, article "Orchestral Instruments," for a full table of these changes. Those tones, which do not require the use of any key, sound somewhat clearer than those produced with one or more keys down.

Venústo (It.) (vĕ-*noos*-tō.) Beautiful, gracefully.

Vêpres (Fr.) (vāpr.) Vespers; evening prayers.

Veränderungen (Gr. pl.) (fĕ-*rän*-dĕ-roong-ĕn.) Variations.

Verbindung (Ger.) (fĕr-*bĭn*-doong.) Combination, union, connection.

Vergellen (Ger.) (fĕr-*ghĕl*-l'n) To diminish gradually.

ă as in *ch*; ā as in *hate;* ă as in *at;* ē as in *tree;* ĕ as in *eh*; ī, as in *pine;* ĭ as in *pin;*

Verger. The chief officer of a cathedral; a pew opener, or attendant at a church.

Vergette (It.) (vĕr-*get*-tĕ.) } The tail, or stem of a note.
Verghetta (It.) (vĕr-*get*-tä.) }

Vergliedern (Ger.) (fĕr-*glē*-dĕrn.) To articulate.

Verhallen (Ger.) (fĕr-*häl*-l'n.) To diminish gradually.

Verhallend (Ger.) (fĕr-*häl*-lĕnd.) Dying away.

Verilay. Street ballad; a roundelay. See *Vaudeville*.

Verlagsrecht (Ger.) (fĕr-*lägs-rĕkht*.) Copyright.

Verlöschend (Ger.) (fĕr-*lŏ*-shĕnd.) Extinguishing.

Vermindert (Ger.) (fĕr-*mĭn*-dĕrt.) Diminished; diminished interval.

Vers (Ger.) (fĕrs.) Verse, strophe, stanza.

Verschiebung (Ger.) (fĕr-*shēe*-boong.) The soft pedal; *Mit Verschiebung*, with the soft pedal. See *Pedal*.

Verschwindend (Ger.) (fer-*schwind*-ĕnt.) Vanishing; dying away.

Verse. That portion of an anthem, or service, intended to be sung by one singer to each part, and not by the full choir in chorus. In secular music, as a song, or ballad, each stanza of the words is a verse.

Verse and chorus anthem. An anthem composed of verse and chorus, but commencing with chorus.

Verse anthem. An anthem which contains a solo, duet, etc., or one or more *verses*. See *Verse* and *Full Anthem*.

Versette (Ger.) (fĕr-*sĕt*-tĕ.) } Short pieces for the organ, intended as preludes, interludes, or postludes.
Versetten (Ger.) (fĕr-*sĕt*-t'n.) }

Versetzen (Ger.) (fĕr-*sĕt*-tsĕn.) To transpose.

Versetzung (Ger.)(fĕr-*sĕt*-tsoong.) Transposition.

Versetzungs-zeichen (Ger.) (fĕr-*sĕt*-tsoongs-*tsī*-kh'n.) The marks of transposition, the *sharp*, the *flat*, the *natural*.

Versicle. A little verse.

Versikel (Ger.) (fĕr-*sĭk*'l.) } A versicle.
Versillo (Spa.) (vĕr-*sĕl*-yō.) }

Versmass (Ger.) (fĕrs-mäss.) The measure of the verse; the meter.

Vérso (It.) (*vār*-sō.) Verse.

Vérso eróico (It.) (*vār*-sō ā-rō-ē-kō.) Heroic verse.

Vérso sciólto (It.) (*vār*-sō shē-*ŏl*-tō.) Blank verse.

Verspätung (Ger.) (fĕr-*spä*-toong.) Retardation, delay.

Verstimmt (Ger.) (fĕr-*stĭmt*.) Out of tune; also moody, depressed; out of humor.

Vertatur (Lat.) (vĕr-*tä*-tŭr.) } Turn ovt.
Verte (Lat.) (*vĕr*-tĕ.) }

Verte subito (Lat.) (*vĕr*-tĕ *sŭb*-ĭ-tō.) Turn the leaf quickly. See *Volti*.

Vertical slur. A perpendicular slur, or curved line, denoting that the chord before which it stands is to be performed in imitation of harp-music, or in arpeggio style. This mark is now found only in old music. In modern editions it is written:

Vertönen (Ger.) (fĕr-*tŏ*-nĕn.) To cease sounding; to die away.

Verwandt (Ger.) (fĕr-*vändt*.) Related, relative keys, etc.

Verwechselung (Ger.) (fĕr-*vĕkh*-sĕl-oong.) Changing, mutation, as to key, tone, etc.

Verweilend (Ger.) (fĕr-*vī*-lĕnd.) Delaying; retarding the time.

Verwerfung (Ger.) (fĕr-*vĕrf*-oong.) Transposing.

Verziert (Ger.) (fĕr-*tsērt*.) Embellished, decorated.

Verzierung (Ger.) (fĕr-*tsē*-roong.) Embellishment, ornament.

Verzögerung (Ger.) (fĕr-*tsŏ*-ghē-roong.) Retardation.

Verzweiflungsvoll (Ger.)(fĕr-*zwi*-floongs-fŏll.) Despairing; with desperation.

Vesperæ (Lat.) (vĕs-pĕ-rē.) Vespers, or the evening service in the Roman Catholic Church.

Vesper (Ger.) (*fĕs*-pĕr.)

Véspero (It.) (*ves*-pĕ-rō.) } Vespers.
Véspro (It.) (*ves*-prō.) }

Vespers. Name of the evening service in the Roman Catholic Church, consisting chiefly of singing.

ĕ as in *tone*; ŏ as in *dove*; ŏ as in *not*; ŭ as in *up*; ü the French sound of *u*.

Vesper bell. The sounding of a bell about sunset in Roman Catholic countries, calling to vespers.

Vesper hymn. A hymn sung in the evening service of the Roman Catholic Church.

Vespertini psalmi (It. pl.) (vĕs-pĕr-tḗ-nē psäl-mḗ.) Evening psalms, or hymns.

Vezzosaménte (It.) (vet-tsō-zä-*men*-tĕ.) Tenderly, softly, gracefully.

Vezzóso (It.) (vet-*tsō*-zō.) Graceful, sweet, tender.

Vibránte (It.) (vi-*brän*-tĕ.) Vibrating; a tremulous, quivering touch; full resonance of tone.

Vibráte (It.) (vi-*brä*-tĕ.) } A strong, vi-
Vibráto (It.) (vi-*brä*-tō.) } brating, full quality of tone : resonant.

Vibration. The tremulous or undulatory motion of any sonorous body (or of the air) by which the sound is produced, the sound being grave or acute, as the vibrations are fewer or more numerous in a given time. See *Acoustics*.

Vibratíssimo (It.) (vi-brä-*tēs*-sē-mō.) Extremely vibrating and tremulous.

Vibráto mólto (It.) (vi-*brä*-tō *mōl*-tō.) Extremely rapid.

Vibrazióne (It.) (vi-brä-tsē-ō-nĕ.) Vibration, tremulousness.

Vicénda (It.) (vi-*tshen*-dä.) Alteration, change.

Vicendévole (It.) (vi-tshĕn-*de*-vō-lĕ.) }
Vicendeveloménte (It.) (vi-tshĕn-de-vō-lä-*men*-tĕ.) }
Alternately ; by turns.

Vide (Fr.) (veed.) } Open ; as *open*
Vído (It.) (*vēe*-dō.) } strings.

Viel. An old name for instruments of the violin species.

Viel (Ger.) (fēel.) Much ; a great deal ; *mit vielem tone*, with much tone.

Vielle (Fr.) The hurdy-gurdy.

Vielleur (Fr.) (vē-yŭr.) The hurdy-gurdy-player.

Viel-stimmig (Ger.) (*fēel-stĭm*-mĭg.) For many voices.

Viel-tönig (Ger.) (*fēel-tō*-nĭg.) Multisonous ; many-sounding.

Vier (Ger.) (fēer.) Four.

Vier-fach (Ger.) (fēer-fäkh.) Fourfold of four ranks of pipes, etc.

Vier-gesang (Ger.)(*fēer*-ghĕ-*säng*.) Song for four voices.

Vier-händig (Ger.) (*fēer-hän*-dĭg.) For four hands.

Vier-saitig (Ger.) (*fēer-sī*-tĭg.) Four stringed.

Vier-spiel (Ger.) (fēer-spēl.) Quartet ; for four performers.

Vier-stimmig (Ger.) (*fēer-stĭm*-mĭg.) Four-voiced ; in four parts ; for four voices, or instruments.

Vierte (Ger.) (*fēer*-tĕ.) Fourth.

Viertel-note (Ger.) (*fēer*-t'l-*nō*-tĕ.) *Quarter-note*, a crochet.

Viertel-ton (Ger.) (fēer-t'l-*tōn*.) A quarter-tone.

Vierundsechzigstel (Ger.) (*fēer*-oond-*sĕkh*-tsĭg-stĕl.) Sixty-fourth notes.

Vier-viertel-tact (Ger.) (*fēer-fēer*-t'l-*täkt*.) Common time of four quarters.

Vier-zweitel-tact (Ger.) (*fēer-tsvī*-t'l *täkt*.) Time of four halves.

Vierzehn (Ger.) (fēer-tsän.) Fourteen.

Vierzehnte (Ger.) (*fēer-tsän*-tĕ.) Fourteenth.

Vietáto (It.) (vē-ä-*tä*-tō.) Forbidden ; prohibited ; a term applied to such intervals and modulations as are not allowed by the laws of harmony.

Vif (Fr.) (vēef.) Lively, brisk, quick, sprightly.

Vigorosaménte (It.) (vi-gō-rō-zä-*men* tĕ.) Vigorously ; with energy.

Vigoróso (It.) (vi-gō-*rō*-zō.) Vigorous, bold, energetic.

Villageois (Fr.) (vēl-lä-zhwá.) Rustic ; *à la villageoise*, in a rustic style.

Villáncico (Spa.)(vēl-lä-*thē*-kō.) } A
Villáncio (Spa.)(vēl-*yän*-thĭ-ō.) } species of pastoral poem, or song.

Villanélla (It.) (vēl-lä-*nel*-lä.) } An old
Villanelle (Fr.) (vē-yá-*nel*.) } rustic Italian dance, accompanied with singing.

Vináte (It.) (vē-*nä*-tĕ.) Drinking-songs.
Vinettes. See *Vináte*.

Viol. An old instrument somewhat resembling the violin, of which it was the origin ; it had six strings with frets, and was played with a bow.

ä as in *ah ;* ā as in *hote ;* ă as in *at ;* ē as in *tree ;* ĕ as in *eh ;* ī as in *pine ;* ĭ as in *pin ;*

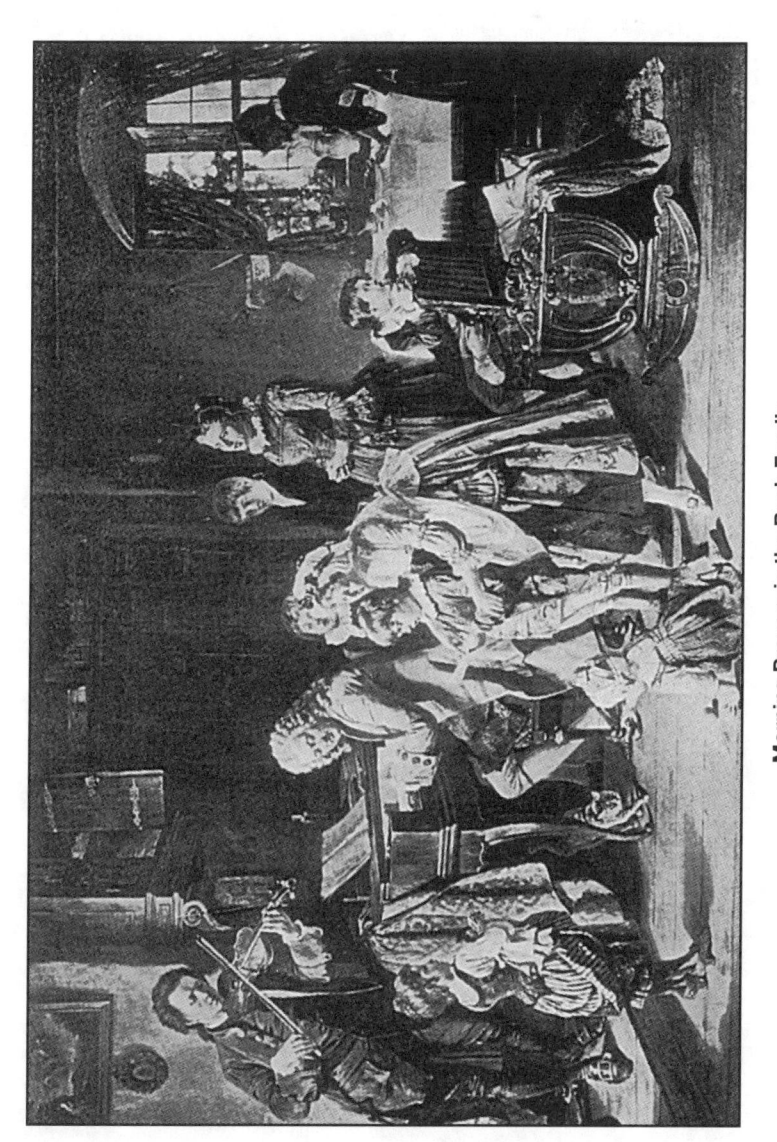

Morning Prayers in the Bach Family

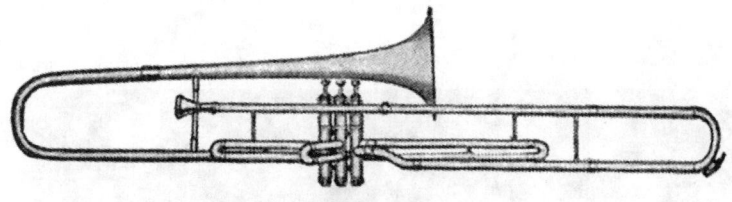

Valve Trombone

Violin

Vióla. A tenor-violin; an instrument similar in tone and formation to the violin, but larger in size and having a compass a fifth lower. It is played in the same manner as a violin, and all points of violin execution are possible upon it, but its tone-color is more sombre. It suits best to the expression of a tender melancholy, or gloom. It has four strings, the two lowest of which are wired. It must be borne in mind that it plays the tenor part in the string quartet, and the English call it the tenor-viol, although the French give it the misleading name of *Viola Alto*. It is notated in the alto clef, and its four strings are tuned thus:
Its compass in orchestral use is about as follows:

Viol, bass. The violoncello; a stringed instrument in the form of a violin, but much larger, having four strings, and is performed on with a bow. See *Violoncello*.

Vióla da bráccio (It.) (vē-*o*-la da *brät*-tshē-ō.) The *vióla;* thus named because it rested on the arm. From *Braccio* (arm) comes its German name *Bratsche*.

Vióla d'amore (It.) (vē-*ō*-lä d'ä-*mō*-rĕ.)
Viole d'amour (Fr.) (vē-*ōl* d'ä-*moor*.)
An instrument a little larger than the *viola*, furnished with frets, and a greater number of strings, seven above the finger-board, and seven below. The name is also given to an organ-stop of similar quality to the *gamba*, or *salcional*.

Vióla pompósa (It.) (vē-*ō*-lä pŏm-*pō*-zä.) An enlarged viol, or *vióla*, of the same compass as the *violoncéllo*, but with the addition of a fifth string. It is said to have been invented by J. S. Bach. It is no longer used.

Viol da bráccio (It.) (vē-ōl dä *brät*-tshē-ō.) See *Vióla da Bráccio*.

Viol da gámba (It.) (vē-ōl dä *gäm*-bä.)
Viol di gámba (It.) (vē-ōl dē *gäm*-bä.)
Legviol; an instrument formerly much used in Germany, but now nearly obsolete. It was a little smaller than the violoncello, furnished with frets and six strings and held between the legs in playing, hence its name.

Viol, double-bass. The largest and deepest-toned of stringed instruments. The contra bass.

Viole (Ger.) (fĕ-*ō*-lĕ.) } The *vióla*.
Viole (Fr.) (vē-*ōl*.) }

Viole alt (Ger.) (fĭ-*ō*-lĕ ält.) The tenor violin. The viola.

Violeteménte (It.) (vē-ō-lĕn-tĕ-*men*-tĕ.) Violently; with force.

Violénto (It.) (vē-ō-*len*-tō.) Violent, vehement, boisterous.

Violénza (It.) (vē-ō-*len*-tsä.) Violence, force, vehemence.

Violet. A species of *viole d'ámŏur*, with only six strings; the name is also applied to a gamba-stop of 4-foot tone.

Violetta (It.) (vē-ō-*lĕt*-tä.) Small alto viol.

Violicembalo. A pianoforte played with a bow, invented in 1823.

Violin. A well-known stringed instrument. It is the most perfect musical instrument known, of brilliant tone and capable of every variety of expression. The violin has four strings, which were formerly made of "catgut" but which are now usually of wire. The G string is wired. The four strings are tuned as follows:

The ordinary orchestral compass of the violin is about although Wagner and other composers have demanded a greater compass from orchestral players. The soloist can play nearly an octave higher. The violin is always notated in the G clef, whence that clef is often called the *violin clef*. At times the quality of the tone is altered and its power much diminished by an appliance called the *mute*, or *sordino*. This is a clamp which being placed upon the bridge, prevents that conductor from freely transmitting the vibrations of the strings to the sounding-board. When this is used it is marked *con sordino;* when removed from the bridge the music is marked *senza sordino*. The

ŏ as in *tone;* ŏ as in *dove;* ŏ as in *not;* ŭ as in *up;* ü the French sound of *u.*

violin can produce all embellishments and also all possible emotions from the deepest pathos to the wildest jollity. It is as varied in its expression as the human voice. Like the human voice, too, it is rather a melodic than a harmonic instrument. One can produce two tones simultaneously from the violin, and this is called *double-stopping*, but *single-stopping* or producing a single note at a time, is the real character of the instrument, which, therefore, like the solo voice, needs the support of other instruments. At times the bow of the violin is discarded altogether and the instrument plucked like a guitar; this mode of playing is called *pizzicato*, and is most effective on the open strings, or in the middle register, since it sounds woodeny and dry in the higher register. High tones of a peculiar, piping quality can be produced from the instrument by placing the finger very lightly on the vibrating string at a regular proportion of its length, thus causing it to vibrate in ventral segments and give forth one of its overtones instead of its fundamental. These tones, which require considerable skill on the part of the performer, are very properly called *harmonics*, but the Germans call them *flageolet tones* because their quality resembles that instrument. Double harmonics, that is double-stopping in harmonics, is one of the most difficult points of virtuosity upon the violin. For a full account of the technique of the instrument, its history and its repertoire see Stoeving's "The Violin."

Violinbogen (Ger.) (fee-ō-leen-bō-g'n.) A violin-bow.

Violine (Ger.) (fee-ō-leen-ĕ.) The violin; also, an organ-stop of 8, 4, or 2-foot tone.

Violinier (Fr.) (vē-ō-lĭ-nēr.) A violinist.

Violinist. A performer on the violin.

Violinista (It.) (vē-ō-lēn-*ēs*-tä.) }
Violinista (Spa.) (vē-ō-lēn-*ēs*-tä.) } A violinist.

Violini unisoni (It.) (vē-ō-*lēe*-nē oo-ne-zō-nē.) The violins in unison.

Violíno (It.) (vĕ-ō-*lēe*-nō.) The violin; it attained its present shape, with four strings, in the sixteenth century.

Violíno píccolo (It.) (ve-ō-*lēe*-nō *pĕk*-kō-lō.)
Violíno pochétto (It.) (ve-ō-*lēe*-nō pō-*khet*-tō.)
A small violin; a kit.

Violíno prímo (It.) (vē-ō-*lēe*-nō *prēe*-mō.)
Violíno princípále (It.) (vē-ō-*lēe*-nō prēn-tshē-*pä*-lĕ.)
The first, or principal violin part; the leading violin-player, or *chef d'attaque*.

Violin-principal. An 8 or 4-foot organ-stop, with an agreeable and violin-like tone.

Violin-saite (Ger.) (fee-ō-*leen-sī*-tĕ.) Violin-string.

Violin-schlüssel (Ger.) (fee-ō-*lēen-shlüs*-s'l.)
Violin-zeichen (Ger.) (fee-ō-*leen-tsī*-k'hn.)
The treble clef used for the violin.

Violin-schule (Ger.) fee-ō-*leen-shoo*-lĕ.) School for the violin.

Violin-spieler (Ger.) (fee-ō-*leen-spē*-lĕr.) A violin-player.

Violin-steg (Ger.) (fee-ō-*leen*-stĕgh.) Violin-bridge.

Violin-stimme (Ger.) (fee-ō-*leen-stĭm*-mĕ.) Part for the violin.

Violon (Fr.) (vĭ-ō-lŏnh.) The French name for the violin.

Violon (Ger.) (fĭ-ō-*lōn*.) The double-bass; see also *Violóne*.

Violoncell (Ger.) (fĭ-ō-lon-*tsĕll*.)
Violoncelle (Fr.) (vi-ō-lŏnh-*sāl*.)
Violoncéllo (It.) (vē-ō-lŏn-*tchel*-lō.)
The large, or bass violin; the name is also applied to an organ-stop of small scale, and crisp tone. The instrument took its name from the *Violone*, the contra-bass viol, and *Violoncello* means "little Violone." Of course to spell the word, as is sometimes done — *Violincellō*, makes nonsense of its etymology. The violoncello is as expressive as the violin but is masculine where the latter is feminine, having a broader, richer tone. It has four strings, the two lower ones being wired. These strings are tuned as follows and the compass of the

---

ă as in *ah* ; ā as in *hate* ; ă as in *at* ; ē as in *tree* ; ĕ as in *eh* ; ī as in *pine* ; ĭ as in *pin* ;

VIOLONE | VOCE DI CAMERA

instrument is about [musical notation] All the violin points of technique (see *Violin*) are possible upon the violoncello. It is often abbreviated into *Cello*.

Violóne (It.) (vē-ō-*lō*-nĕ.) } The name
Violóno (It.) (vē-ō-*lō*-nō.) } originally given to the double-bass. Its pitch is an octave below that of the violoncello and its true use is to sustain the harmony; the name is also applied to an open wood-stop, of much smaller scale than the diapason, on the pedals of an organ.

Viols, chest of. An expression formerly applied to a set of viols, consisting of six, the particular use of which was to play fantasias in six parts, generally two each of bass, tenor, and treble. See Elson's "Shakespeare in Music."

Virelay. A rustic song, or ballad, in the fourteenth century; nearly the same as the roundel, but with this difference, the roundel begins and ends with the same sentence, or strain, but the virelay is under no such restriction.

Virgil Practice-Clavier. A dumb keyboard instrument for mechanical piano practice invented by A. K. Virgil, of New York in 1883. It differs from the old dumb piano in giving a click at the depression and release of the key, and in allowing a gradation of the touch so that one may produce a light or heavy touch upon the keys at will.

Virginal. A small keyed instrument, much used about the time of Queen Elizabeth, and placed upon a table when played upon. It is supposed to have been the origin of the spinet, as the latter was of the harpsichord. See Elson's "Shakespeare in Music," and Naylor's "An Elizabethan Virginal Book."

Virtuose (Ger.) (fĭr-too-*ō*-zĕ.) } A skillful
Virtuóso (It.) (vēr-too-*ō*-zō.) } performer upon some instrument.

Virtuosität (Ger.) (fĭr-too-*ō*-zĭ-tāt.) Remarkable proficiency; fine execution; applied both to singers and players.

Vista (It.) (*vēs*-tä.) Sight; *à prima vista*, at first sight.

Vistaménte (It.) (vēs-tä-*men*-tĕ.) }
Vitaménte (It.) (vē-tä-*men*-tĕ.) } Quickly, swiftly, briskly, immediately.

Vite (Fr.) (vēt.) } Quickly,
Vitement (Fr.) (*vēt*-mänh.) } swiftly ; *un peu plus vite*, a little more quickly.

Vitesse (Fr.) (vē-tĕss.) Swiftness, quickness.

Viváce (It.) (vē-*vä*-tshĕ.) }
Vivaceménte (It.) (vē-vä-tshĕ-*men*-tĕ.) } Lively, briskly, quickly.

Vivacézza (It.) (vē-vä-*tshet*-sä.) }
Vivacita (It.) (vē-vä-tshē-tä.) } Vivacity, liveliness.

Vivacíssimo (It.) (vē-vä-*tshēs*-sē-mō.) Very lively; extreme vivacity.

Vivaménte (It.) (vi-vä-*men*-tĕ.) In a lively, brisk manner.

Vive (Fr.) (vēev.) Lively, brisk, quick, sprightly.

Vivénte (It.) (vē-*ven*-tĕ.) Animated, lively.

Vivézza (It.) (vē-*vet*-tsä.) Vivacity, liveliness.

Vívido (It.) (*vi*-vi-dō.) Lively, brisk.

Vívo (It.) (*vēe*-vō.) Animated, lively, brisk.

Vocal. Belonging, or relating to the human voice.

Vocále (It.) (vō-*kä*-lĕ.) Vocal; belonging to the voice.

Vocalézzo (It.) (vō-kä-*let*-tsō.) A vocal exercise.

Vocalization. Command of the voice; vocal execution; also, vocal writing, or composition.

Vocalize. To practice vocal exercises using the vowels and the letter A, sounded in the Italian manner, for the purpose of developing the voice, and of acquiring skill and flexibility.

Vocalizes (Fr.) (vō-kä-leez.) Solfeggios exercises for the voice, also *Vocalises*.

Vocalizzare (It.) (vō-kä-lit-*tsä*-rĕ.) To vocalize; to sing exercises for the voice.

Vocalízzi (It. pl.) (vō-kä-*lit*-tsi.) Vocal exercises, to be sung on the vowels.

Vocal score. An arrangement of all the separate voice parts, placed in their proper order under each other, and used by the conductor of a vocal performance.

Vóce (It.) (vō-tshĕ.) The voice.

Vóce di cámera (It.) (vō-tshĕ dē *kä*-mä-

ŏ as in *tone*; ŏ as in *dove*; ŏ as in *not*; ŭ as in *up*; ü the French sound of *u*.

283

rä.) Voice for the chamber; one suited for private, rather than public, singing.

Vóce di góla (It.) (vō-tshĕ dē *gō*-lä.) The throat voice; also, a gutteral voice.

Vóce di pétto (It.) (vō-tshĕ dē *pet*-tō.) The chest-voice, the lowest register of the voice.

Vóce di tésta (It.) (vō-tshĕ dē *tes*-tä.) The head-voice, the *falsétto*, or feigned voice; the upper register of the voice.

Vóce, mézza (It.) (vō-tshĕ *met*-tsä.) Half the power of the voice; a moderate, subdued tone, rather soft than loud.

Vogel-flöte (Ger.) (fō-g'l-flô-tĕ.) Bird-flute.

Vogel-pfeife (Ger.) (*fō*-g'l-*pfi*-fĕ.) Bird-call, flageolet.

Vogel-gesang (Ger.) (*fō*-g'l-ghĕ-*säng*.) Singing of birds; an accessory stop in some very old German organs, producing a chirping effect, by some little pipes standing in a vessel with water, through which the wind passes to them.

Vóglia (It.) (*vōl*-yē-ä.) Desire, longing, ardor, fervor.

Voice. The sound, or sounds, produced by the vocal organs in singing; applied also to the tuning, and quality of tone, of organ-pipes, the *voicing* being a most important part of the organ-builder's work. The human voices are classified, from lowest to highest, as follows: bass, baritone, tenor, alto, mezzo-soprano, and soprano, or treble. The bass has an average compass from great F, or E, to one-lined e. (See *Tablature*.) The baritone from great A to one-lined f; the tenor from small c to one-lined a or b; the alto from small g to two-lined d or e; the mezzo-soprano from small a or b to two-lined g or a; the soprano from middle c (one-lined) to c in alt (three-lined c) or even higher. Sybil Sanderson was easily able to take g *in altissimo* (three-lined g) and in the eighteenth century there lived a singer, Agujari by name, who could go much higher. The above voices are sub-divided, especially in operatic work. The deep slow-moving bass is called *Basso Profundo*, and, a little higher are the *Basso Seriō*, and the *Basso Cantante*. The light, playful bass is called *Basso Buffo*. The baritones are sometimes called *bass-baritone*, or *tenor-baritone* according to the tone-color of their voices. Tenor voices are divided into *Tenòre Eroico* or *Tenore Robusto* who sing broad and dramatic works, and *Tenore Lirico*, who sing light and graceful rôles, and possess flexibility rather than majesty. *Alto* and *contralto* have no longer any different meaning; they are identical; but when one finds an alto voice of smooth and graceful, rather than of broad, character, it is sometimes called a *mezzo-contralto*. It leans toward the *mezzo-soprano* voice in its characteristics. See *Tenor, Soprano, Descant*.

Voice, chest. The register of the chest-tones.

Voice, falsetto. *Head voice; feigned voice;* certain tones in a man's voice which are above its natural compass, and which can only be produced in an artificial, or feigned tone.

Voice, fourth. The bass.

Voice, first. The soprano.

Voice, guttural. A voice produced by a contracted pharynx.

Voice, head. The highest register of the female voice; the falsetto in male voices.

Voice parts. The vocal parts; chorus parts.

Voice, treble. The soprano.

Voicing. The adjustment of the parts of an organ-pipe for the purpose of giving it its proper pitch and its peculiar character of sound.

Voix (Fr.) (vwä.) The voice.

Voix aigre (Fr.) (vwäsägr.) Harsh voice.

Voix argentine (Fr.)(vwä-sär-zhänh-tēn.) A clear-toned voice; a silvery voice.

Voix célestes (Fr.) (vwä sā-lĕst.) *Celestial voices;* an organ-stop of French invention, formed of two dulcianas, one of which has the pitch slightly raised, which gives to the stop a waving, undulating character; also, a soft stop on the harmonium.

Voix de poitrine (Fr.) (vwä dŭh pwä-trēen.) Chest-voice; natural voice.

Voix de tête (Fr.) (vwä dŭh tāt.) Head-voice; falsetto voice.

Voix éclatante (Fr.) (*vwä'sä-klä-tänht.*) Loud, piercing voice.

Volánte (It.) (vō-län-tĕ.) *Flying;* a light and rapid series of notes.

Voláta (It.) (vō-*lä*-tä.) A flight; run; rapid series of notes; a *roulade*, or *division*.

Voláte (It. pl.) (vō-*lä*-tĕ.) See *Voláta*.

Volatína (It.) (vō-lä-*tē*-nä.) A little flight, etc. See *Voláta*.

Volatíne (It. pl.) (vō-lä-*tē*-nĕ.) Short runs. See *Voláta*.

Volée (Fr.) (vō-*lā*:) A rapid flight of notes.

Volks-gesang (Ger.) (*fōlks*-ghĕ-*säng.*)
Volks-lied (Ger.) (fōlks-lēd.) National song; popular air; tune, or ballad.

Voll (Ger.) (fōll.) Full; *mit vollem werke*, with the full organ.

Volle-orgel (Ger.) (*fōl*-lĕ-*or*-g'l.) Full organ.

Völler (Ger.) (*fŏl*-lĕr.) Fuller, louder.

Volles-werk (Ger.) (*fōl*-lĕs-värk.) The full organ.

Voll-gesang (Ger.) (*fōll*-ghĕ-*säng.*) Chorus.

Vollkommen (Ger.) (*fōll-kōm*-mĕn.) Perfect, complete.

Voll-stimmig (Ger.) (*foll-stĭm*-mĭg.) Full-toned, full-voiced.

Voll-stimmigkeit (Ger.) (*fōll-stĭm*-mĭg-kīt.) Fullness of tone.

Voll-tönend (Ger.) (*fōll-tō*-nĕnd.) Full-sounding, sonorous.

Volonté (Fr.) (vō-lŏnh-tā.) Will, pleasure; *à volonté*, at will.

Vólta (It.) (*vōl*-tä.) Time; also, an old air in ¾ time, peculiar to an Italian dance of the same name, and forming a kind of galliard. See *Volte*.

Vólta príma (It.) (vōl-tä-*prēe*-mṳ) First time.

Voltáre (It.) (vōl-*tä*-rĕ.) To turn; te turn over.

Vólta secónda (It.) (*vōl*-tä se-*kon*-dä.) The second time.

Vólte (It.) (*vōl*-tĕ.)
Volte (Fr.) (vōlt.) An obsolete dance in ¾ time, resembling the *galliard*, and with a rising and leaping kind of motion. See *Volta*.

Volteggiándo (It.) (vōl-tĕd-jē-*än*-dō.) Crossing the hands, on the piano.

Volteggiáre (It.) (vōl-tĕd-jē-*ä*-rĕ.) Tc cross the hands, in playing.

Vólti (It.) (*vōl*-tē.) Turn over.

Vólti súbito (It.) (*vōl*-ti *soo*-bi-tō.) Turn over quickly.

Volubilita (It.) (vō-loo-bi-li-tä.)
Volubilménte (It.) (vō-loo-bel-*men*-tĕ.) Volubility; freedom of performance; fluency in delivery.

Volume. The quantity of fullness of the tone of a voice, or instrument.

Voluntary. An introductory performance upon the organ, either extemporaneous, or otherwise; also, a species of *toccáta*, generally in two or three movements, calculated to display the capabilities of the instrument, and the skill of the performer.

Von (Ger.) (fōn.) By, of, from, on.

Vorausnahme (Ger.) (fō-*rous*-nä-mĕ.) Anticipation.

Vorbereitung (Ger.) (*fōr*-bĕ-*rī*-toong.) Preparation of discords, etc.

Vorbereitungsunterricht (Ger.) (*for*-bĕ-rī-toongs-*oon*-tĕr-rĭkht.) Preparatory lesson; elementary instruction.

Vorgreifung (Ger.) (fōr-*grī*-foong.)
Vorgriff (Ger.) (fōr-*grĭff*.) Anticipation.

Vorhalt (Ger.) (fōr-*hält*.) A suspension, or syncopation.

Vorher (Ger.) (fōr-*hār*.) Before; *tempo wie vorher*, the time as before.

Vorsang (Ger.) (fōr-*säng*.) Leading off in the song; act of beginning the tune.

Vorsänger (Ger.) (fōr-*säng*-ĕr.) The leading singer in a choir; a precentor.

Vorschlag (Ger.) (fōr-*shläg*.) Appoggiatúra, beat.

Vorspiel (Ger.) (fōr-*spēl*.) Prelude, introductory movement. Wagner employed the *Vorspiel* in his later operas to replace the overture. See *Overture*.

Vorspieler (Ger.) (fōr-*spē*-lĕr.) Leader of the band; the principal, *primo*, performer upon any orchestral instrument.

Vorsteller (Ger.) (fōr-*stĕl*-ler.) Performer, player.

Vortrag (Ger.) (fōr-*träg*.) Execution, mode of executing a piece; delivery,

---

ō as in *tone*; ō as in *dove*; ŏ as in *not*; ŭ as in *up*; ü the French sound of *u*.

elocution, diction; the act of uttering or pronouncing.

Vortragsstück (Ger.) A piece for performance before an audience; a concert-piece.

Vorzeichnung (Ger.) (fōr-*tsīkh*-noong.) The signature. See *Signature* and *Key.*

Vox (Lat.) (vŏx.) Voice.

Vox acuta (Lat.) (vŏx ă-*kū*-tä.) A shrill, or high voice. In the ancient music, the highest note in the bisdiapason, or double octave.

Vox angelica (Lat.) (vŏx ăn-*jĕl*-ĭ-kä.) Angelic voice. See *Voix Célestes.*

Vox humana (Lat.) (vŏx hū-*mä*-nä.) *Human voice;* an organ reed-stop of 8-foot tone, intended to imitate the human voice which it sometimes does, though very imperfectly.

Vue (Fr.) (vü.) Sight, as, for example, *à première vue;* at sight, *a prima vista.*

Vuide (Fr.) (vwēd.) Open; on the open string.

W

Waits. An old word meaning oboes; also, players on the oboes; persons who play hymn tunes, etc., in the streets during the night, about Christmas. See Elson's "Realm of Music," article "Old English Ballads."

Wald-flöte (Ger.) (väld-flō-tĕ.) *Forest-flute,* shepherd's-flute; an organ-stop with a full and powerful tone.

Waldhorn (Ger.) (väld-hōrn.) *Forest-horn;* also, the French horn in its natural form, without valves.

Waltz. The name of a modern dance originally used in Suabia. The measure of its music is triple, usually, in ¾ time, and performed moderately slow, or, at the quickest, in allegretto. The waltz was derived from the minuet. In the waltz, as in all the dance forms, the phrases are of eight, sixteen, or thirty-two measures, generally. The rhythm of the waltz is marked ¾, but it will be found that each alternate measure only, has a strong accent; therefore, almost all waltzes sound best if played as if they were written in 6/8 rhythm. In a set of waltzes each waltz is generally in first rondo or song form, but in an extended single waltz the second rondo form, or the minuet form, can be used Berlioz and Tschaikowsky have used the waltz as a symphonic movement.

Walzer (Ger.) (*väl*-tsĕr.) Waltz.

Wassail. An old term signifying a merry, or convivial song.

Wasserorgel (Ger.) (väs sĕr-*ōr* g'l.) Hydraulic organ.

Weber chronometer. An instrument similar to a metronome, but simpler in its construction. It consists of a piece of twine, about five feet in length, on which are fifty-five inch spaces, and a small weight at the lower end, the degree of motion being determined by the length of string swinging with the weight. Web. Chron ♩ = 38″ Rh. (39⅛ Eng.) G. Weber copied this from a much older invention, a divided pendulum which was advocated by a Frenchman, Etienne Loulié, in 1696. If Bach and Handel had only used the invention they would have spared the modern conductor much unnecessary trouble in the matter of *tempi.*

Wechsel-gesang (Ger.) (*vĕkh*-s'l-ghĕ-säng.) Alternative, or antiphonal song.

Wechsel-noten (Ger. pl.) (*vĕkh*-s'l-*nō*-t'n.) *Changing notes:* passing notes; notes of irregular transition; appoggiaturas.

Wehmuth (Ger.) (*vā*-moot.) Sadness.

Wehmüthig (Ger.) (vā-*mü*-tĭg.) Sad, sorrowful.

Weiber-stimme (Ger.) (*vī*-bĕr-*stĭm*-mĕ.) A female voice; a treble voice.

Weich (Ger.) (vīkh.) Soft, gentle.

Weihnachtslied (Ger.) (*vīn*-äkhts-lēd.) Canticle at Christmas; Christmas hymn, or carol.

Weise (Ger.) (*vī*-zĕ.) Melody, air, song.

Weite Harmonie (Ger.) (*wī*-tĕ här-mō-nē.) Dispersed, or open harmony.

Weltliche (Ger.) (*vĕlt*-līkh-ĕ.) Secular.

Weltliche Lieder (Ger.) (*vĕlt*-līkh-ĕ *lā*-dĕr.) Secular songs.

Wenig (Ger.) (*vā*-nĭg.) Little; *ein wenig stark,* a little strong; rather loud.

Werk (Ger.) (värk.) *Work,* movement, action. See *Hauptwerk* and *Oberwerk.*

Wesentlich (Ger.) (*vā*-sĕnt-līkh.) Essential.

Wesentliche septime (Ger.) (vā-sĕnt-līk-ĕ sĕp-*tē*-mĕ.) Dominant seventh.

ă as in *ah:* ā as in *hate;* ă as in *at;* ē as in *tree;* ĕ as in *eh;* ī as in *pine;* ĭ as in *pin;*

Wettgesang (Ger.) (*vĕt*-ghĕ-*säng.*) A singing-match.

Whiffle. Anciently, a fife, or small flute.

Whistle. A small, shrill wind-instrument, in tone resembling a fife, but blown at the end like an old English flute.

Whole note. A semibreve.

Whole rest. A pause equal in length to a whole *measure* in every modern rhythm except $\frac{2}{4}$.

Whole tone. A tone; a large second; a whole step.

Wieder anfangen (Ger.) (*vē*-dĕr-*än*-fäng'n.) To begin again; to recommence.

Wiederholung (Ger.) (*vē*-dĕr-*hō*-loong.) Repeating, repetition.

Wiederholungszeichen (Ger.) (*vē*-dĕr-*hō*-loongs-*tsī*-khĕn.) Signs of repetition.

Wiederklang (Ger.) (*vē*-dĕr-*kläng.*)
Wieder-schall (Ger.) (*vē*-dĕr-*shäll.*) Echo, resounding.

Wind. To give a prolonged and varied sound, as, to *wind* a horn.

Wind-chest. An air-tight box under the sound-board of an organ, into which the wind passes from the bellows, and from which it passes to the pipes.

Wind-coupler. A valve in the wind-trunk of an organ, to shut off, or on, the wind.

Wind-instruments. A general name for all instruments, the sounds of which are produced by the breath, or by the wind of bellows.

Wind-harfe (Ger.) (*vĭnd*-*här*-fĕ.) Æolian-harp.

Wind-lade (Ger.) (*vĭnd*-*lä*-dĕ.) Wind-chest in an organ.

Wind-messer (Ger.) (*vĭnd*-m*ĕs*-sĕr) Anemometer, wind-gauge.

Wind-stock (Ger.) (*vĭnd*-stŏk.) Cover of organ-pipes.

Wind-trunk. A large passage in an organ through which air is conveyed from the bellows to the wind-chest.

Windzunge (Ger.) (*vĭnd*-*tsoon*-ghĕ.) Tongue of an organ-pipe.

Winselig (Ger.) (*vĭn*-se-lĭg.) Plaintive.

Wirbel (Ger.) (*vĭr*-b'l.) Peg of a violin, viola, etc.; the stopper in an organ-pipe; a roll on a drum.

Wirbel-kasten (Ger.) (vĭr-b'l-*käs*-t'n.) That part of the neck of a violin, etc., which contains the pegs.

Wogend (Ger.) (*vō*-ghĕnd.) Waving.

Wolf. A name applied to an impure fifth, which occurs in pianofortes, or organs, tuned in unequal temperament. Any dissonance caused by imperfection in the tuning, or manufacture, of an instrument.

Wood wind. The orchestral wind-instruments which are made of wood. See *Orchestra*.

Wrest. An old name for a tuning-key.

Wrest-pins. Movable pins in a piano about which one end of the string is wound, and by turning which the instrument is tuned.

Wrist-guide. A part of the chiroplast, invented by Logier, to assist young pianoforte players in keeping the wrist in proper position.

Wuchtig (Ger.) (*vooch*-tig.) Weightily, ponderously.

Würde (Ger.) (*vür*-dĕ.) Dignity.

Würdig (Ger.) (*vür*-dĭg.) Dignified.

Wuth (Ger.) (voot.) Madness, rage.

X

Xylophone. An instrument composed of dry staves of wood arranged in rows and struck in the same manner as a dulcimer. It is given many different names as Ger., *Strohfiedel Holzharmonika;* Fr., *claquebois échelette, patouille, xylorganon;* It., *gigelira, sticcado.* It has a compass of a little more than two octaves and gives as much of a *click* as of a tone. It was used by St. Saëns in his *Danse Macabre*, to picture the bones of skeletons knocking against each other.

Y

Yodel or *Jodel.* The peculiar high warbling of the Swiss and Tyrolean mountaineers, in which falsetto tones are interspersed with chest-tones.

Z

Za. A syllable formerly applied by the French, in their church music, to B flat,

ŏ as in *tone ;* ô as in *dove ;* ŏ as in *not ;* ŭ as in *up ;* ü the French sound of *u*.

ZAMACUCA   ZÓPPA

to distinguish it from B natural, called *si*.

Zamacuca. The national dance of the Chilians.

Zambacucca. A favorite dance of the Peruvians.

Zampogino (It.) (tsäm-pō-jē-nō.) A small flageolet, or bagpipe.

Zampógna (It.) (tsäm-*pon*-yä.) } An
Zampúgna (It.) (tsäm-*poon*-ya.) } ancient pipe, or bagpipe, now nearly extinct, with a reedy tone, resembling, but much inferior, to the clarinet. See *Cornamusa* and *Chalumeau*.

Zampognare (It.) (tsäm-pōn-*yä*-rĕ.) To play on the pipes.

Zapateádo (Spa.) (thä-pä-tĕ-*ä*-dō.) A Spanish national dance in which a noise is made with the shoe.

Zapatear (Spa.) (thä-pä-tĕ-*är*.) To beat time with the foot.

Zapfen-streich (Ger.) (tsäp-f'n-*strīkh*.) The tattoo. In Germany the *grosser Zapfenstreich* is an impressive finale of a military review, commencing with a grand *crescendo* roll on the drums of all the regimental bands.

Zarge (Ger.) (tsär-ghĕ.) The *sides* of a violin, guitar, etc.

Zart (Ger.) (tsärt.) } Tenderly,
Zärtlich (Ger.) (*tsairt*-līkh.) } softly, delicately.

Zarte Stimmen (Ger. pl.) (tsär-tĕ *stĭm*-m'n.) Delicate stops.

Zart-flöte (Ger.) (tsärt-*flö*-tē.) *Soft-flute;* an organ-stop of the flute species.

Zarzuéla (Spa.) (thär-thoo-*ā*-lä.) A short drama, with incidental music, something similar to the *vaudeville*.

Zeffiroso (It.) tsĕf-fē-*rō*-zō.) Like a zephyr. Very light.

Zehn (Ger.) (tsān.) Ten.

Zehnte (Ger.) (*tsān*-tĕ.) Tenth.

Zeichen, alt (Ger.) (*tsī*-khĕn ält.) The C clef on the third line. [ure.

Zeit-mass (Ger.) (tsīt-mäss.) Time meas-

Zel. A moorish instrument of music, similar to the cymbals.

Zele (Fr.) (zhāl.) } Zeal, ardor, energy.
Zélo (It.) (tsā-lō.) }

Zelosaménte (It.) (tse-lō-zä-*men*-tĕ.) Zealously, ardently.

Zelóso (It.) (tse-*lō*-zō.) Zealous, ardent, earnest.

Zerstreut (Ger.) (tsĕr-*stroit*.) Dispersed, scattered, with respect to the notes of arpeggios, or chords, the situation of the different parts of a composition, etc.

Ziemlich (Ger.) (*tsēem*-līkh.) Tolerably, moderately

Ziemlich langsam (Ger.) (*tsēem*-līkh *läng*-säm.) Tolerably slow.

Zierlich (Ger.) (*tsēēr*-lich.) Neat, graceful.

Zingarésa (It.) (tsin-gä-*rā*-zä.) In the style of gypsy music.

Zingarésca (It.) (tsin-gä-*res*-kä.) A song, or dance, in the style of the gypsies.

Zingaro (It.) (*tsin*-gä-rō.) Gypsy ; in the gypsy style.

Zink-bläser (Ger.) (*tsĭnk-blā*-zĕr.) Cornet player.

Zinke (Ger.) (*tsĭnk*-ĕ.) } Small
Zinken (Ger. pl.) (*tsĭn*-k'n.) } cornet, species of horn, or trumpet of very ancient date, now almost obsolete. It was made either of wood, or the small branches on the head of the deer. Also, the name of a treble stop, in German organs, which is sometimes a reed, and at others, a mixture stop.

Zisch (Ger.) (tsĭsh.) A hiss.

Zischlaut (Ger.) (tsĭsh-lout.) A hissing sound.

Zither (Ger.) (*tsĭt*-ĕr.) An instrument which may be called a compound of the harp and guitar. The harmonies of the first-named instrument are produced from it, and it possesses the delicate notes pertaining to both, but not great compass. The zither is also like the lute in the quality of its tones. It is a sweet-toned instrument of about thirty strings (some have a less number), and is plucked by the fingers, and by a hook of iron which is worn on the thumb of the performer.

Zittern (Ger.) (*tsĭt*-tĕrn.) Trembling.

Zögernd (Ger.) (*tsö*-ghĕrnd.) A contin. ual retarding of the time ; hesitating.

Zólfa (It.) (*tsōl*-fä.) See *Sólfa*.

Zóppa (It.) (*tsōp*-pä.) } Lame, halting.
Zóppe (It.) (*tsōp*-pĕ.) } See *Syncopation*.
Zóppo (It.) (*tsōp*-pō.) }

ă as in *ah* ; ā as in *hate* ; ă as in *at* ; ē as in *tree* ; ĕ as in *eh* ; ī as in *pine* ; ĭ as in *pin* ;

288

Johann Sebastian Bach

Opening Measures of the First Prelude in Book 1,
Well-Tempered Clavichord

Xylophone

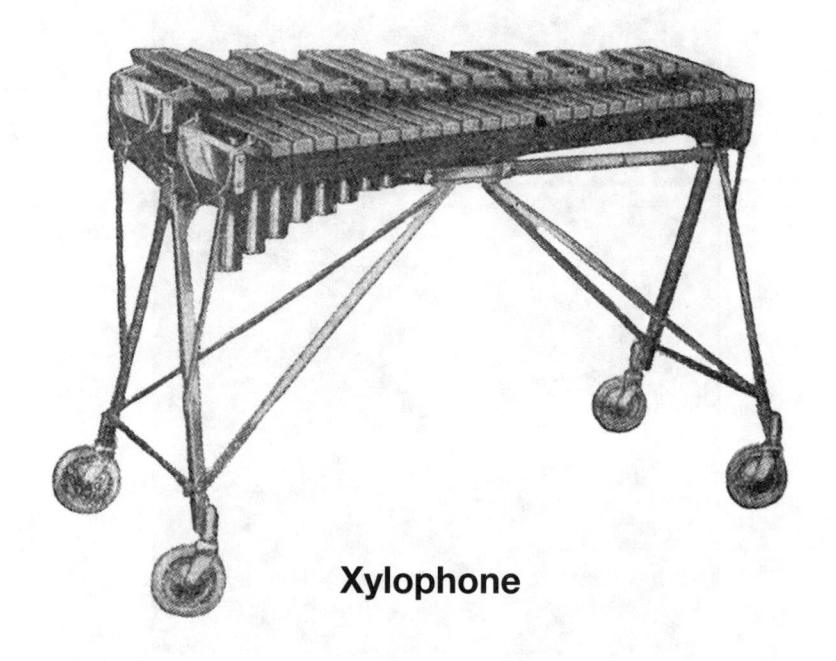

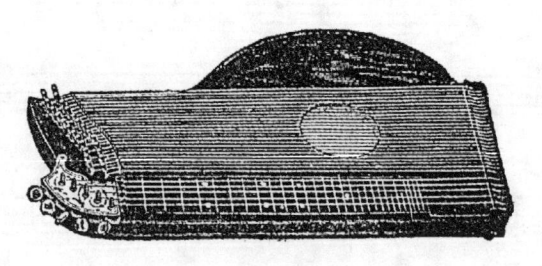

Zither

Zornig (Ger.) (*tsör*-nĭg.) Angry, wrathful.
Zu (Ger.) (tsoo.) At, by, in, to, unto.
Zug (Ger.) (tsoog.) Draw-stop, or register, in an organ.
Züge (Ger. pl.) (*tsü*-ghĕ.) See *Zug*.
Zügeglöckchen (Ger.) (*tsü*-ghĕ-*glôk*-khĕn.) The passing bell; a knell.
Zuklang (Ger.) (*tsōo*-klang.) Unison, harmony, concord.
Zunehmend (Ger.) (tsoo-*nā*-mĕnd.) Increasing.
Zunge (Ger.) (*tsoon*-ghĕ.) The tongue of a reed-pipe.
Zurückhaltung (Ger.) (tsoo-*rük-häl*-toong.) Retardation; keeping back.
Zusammen (Ger.) (tsoo-*zäm*-m'n.) Together.
Zusammen-blasen (Ger.) (tsoo-*zäm*-m'n-*blä*-z'n.) To play together on wind-instruments.
Zusammen-gesetzt (Ger.) (tsoo-*zäm*-m'n-ghĕ-*setst*.) Compound; condensed; compiled; put together.
Zusammen-klang (Ger.) (tsoo-*zäm*-m'n-*kläng*.) Harmony, consonance.
Zusammen-laut (Ger.) (tsoo-*zäm*-m'n-*lout*.) Harmony, consonance.
Zusammen-stimmig (Ger.) (tsoo-*zäm*-m'n-*stĭm*-mĭg.) Harmonious, concordant.
Zusammen-stimmung (Ger.) (tsoo-*zäm*-m'n-*stĭm*-moong.) Harmony, concord, consonance.
Zutraulich (Ger.) (tsoo-*trou*-lĭkh.) Confidently.
Zuversicht (Ger.) (tsoo-fĕr-*sĭkht*.) Confidence.
Zwanzig (Ger.) (*tsvän*-tsĭg.) Twenty.
Zwei (Ger.) (tsvī.) Two.
Zwei-fach (Ger.) (*tsvī*-fäkh.) ⎫ Two-
Zwei-fältig (Ger.) (tsvī-*fāl*-tĭg.) ⎭ *fold*, of two ranks, in organ-pipes; *compound*, speaking of intervals, such as exceed the octave; as the 9th, 16th, etc.
Zwei-gesang (Ger.) (*tsvī*-ghĕ-*säng*.) For two voices; a duet.
Zwei-gestrichen (Ger.) (*tsvī*-ghĕs-*trĭkh*-ĕn.) *With two strokes;* applied to C on the third space in the treble and the six notes above. See *Tablature*.

Zwei-händig (Ger.) (*tsvī*-hän-dĭgh.) For two hands.
Zwei-mal (Ger.) (*tsvī*-mäl.) Twice.
Zwei-sang (Ger.) (tsvī-säng.) ⎫
Zwei-stimmig (Ger.) (*tsvī-stĭm*-mĭg.) ⎭ For two voices, or parts; a duet.
Zwei-spiel (Ger.) (tsvī-spēel.) A duet.
Zweite (Ger.) (*tsvī*-tĕ.) Second.
Zweite mal (Ger.) (tsvī-tĕ-*mäl*.) Second time.
Zweites Manual (Ger.) (*tsvī*-tĕs mä-nooäl.) The second manual.
Zwei-und-dreissigstel-note (Ger.) (*tsvī*-oond-*drī*-sĭg-stĕl-*nō*-tĕ.) A thirty-second note.
Zwei-und-dreissigstelspause (Ger.)(tsvī-oond-*drī*-sīgs-tĕls-*pow*-zĕ.) A thirty-second rest.
Zwei-viertel-takt (Ger.) (tsvī-*fēer*-tĕl-täkt.) Time of two-quarters, $\frac{2}{4}$.
Zwei-zweitel-takt (Ger.) (tsvī-*tsvī*-t'l-täkt.) Time of two halves, $\frac{2}{2}$.
Zwerch-flöte (Ger.)(*tsvĕrkh-flō*-tĕ.) *Transverse flute*, the German flute.
Zwerch-pfeife (Ger.) (*tsvĕrkh pfī*-fĕ.) *Transverse pipe*, the fife.
Zwischen-gesang (Ger.) (*tsvĭ*-shĕn-ghĕ-*zäng*.) ⎫
Zwischen-handlung (Ger.) (*tsvĭ*-shĕn-*händ*-lōong.) ⎭ An episode.
Zwischen-harmonie (Ger.) (*tsvĭ*-shĕn-här-mō-nē.) Between harmony; the connecting harmony in a fugue.
Zwischen-räume (Ger. pl.) (*tsvĭ*-shĕn-*roy*-mĕ.) The spaces between the lines of the staff.
Zwischen-satz (Ger.) (*tsvĭ*-shĕn-sätz.) Intermezzo; intermediate theme; episode.
Zwischen-spiel (Ger.) (*tsvĭ*-shĕn-spēel.) Interlude played between the verses of a hymn.
Zwischen-ton (Ger.) (*tsvĭ*-shĕn-*tōn*.) Intermediate tone.
Zwölf (Ger.) (tsvôlf.) Twelve.
Zwölfachteltakt (Ger.) (tsvôlf-äkh-t'l-täkt.) Twelve-eight time.
Zymbel (Ger.) (*tsĭm*-b'l.) Cymbal.

ŏ as in *tone*; ô as in *dove*; ŏ as in *not*; ŭ as in u_4; ü the French sound of *u*.

A LIST OF PROMINENT FOREIGN COMPOSERS, ARTISTS, Etc.

Giving the pronunciation of their names and their *chief* works or claims to fame

Abt, Franz (Ahbt.) Eilenburg, 1810 — Wiesbaden, 1885. Songs "When the Swallows Homeward Fly."

Adam, Adolph Charles (Ah-dam.) Paris, 1803–1856. Light operas. "Postillon de Longjumeau."

Alard, J. Delphin (Ah-*lahr*.) Bayonne, 1815 — Paris, 1888. Violinist and composer of violin works.

Albani, Emma (Ahl-*bahn*-ee.) Canada, 1850. Singer.

Amati, Nicolo (Ah-*mah*-tee.) Italy, 1596–1684. Violin-maker.

Arditi, Luigi (Ahr-*dee*-tee Loo-*ee*-gee.) Conductor. Italy, 1822. — Brighton, Eng., 1903.

Arensky, Anton Stepanovitch (Ah-*ren*-schkee.) Novgorod, Russia, 1862 — Terioki, Finland, 1906. Composer. Orchestral and operatic works.

Arne, Dr. Thomas Augustine. London, 1710–1778. Much vocal music. Many celebrated songs.

Artchiboucheff, Nicolas V. (Ahr-*tschee*-boo-shef.) Tsarskoe-Sielo, Russia, 1868. Pianist and composer.

Auber, Daniel, F. E. (*Oh*-behr.) Caen, France, 1782 — Paris, 1871. Operas. "Masaniello."

Audran, Edmond (*Oh*-drahng.) Lyons, 1842 — Tierceville, 1901. Light operas. "La Mascotte."

Aus der Ohe, Adele (Ous-der-*oh*-eh.) Classical pianist and composer.

Bach, Johann Sebastian (Bahchh.) Eisenach, 1685 — Leipsic, 1750. "Passion Music," B minor Mass, "Well-tempered Clavichord," Two and three-part inventions. Organ works.

Bach, Karl Philipp Emanuel. Weimar, 1714 — Hamburg, 1788. Third son of above. One of the founders of piano-technique. First good piano method, 1753.

Backer-Gröndahl, Agathe (Bakker-*Gren*-dahl.) Norway, 1847–1907. Pianist and composer.

Baermann, Carl (*Bair*-mann.) Munich, 1839. Classical pianist.

Balakirew, Milly A. (Bah-*lah*-kee-reff.) Nijni-Novgorod, Russia, 1836. Composer in all large forms. Symphony, overture, etc. Very difficult piano piece — "Islamey."

Balfe, Michael Wm. Dublin, 1808 — England, 1870. Lyric operas. "The Bohemian Girl."

Bantock, Granville. London, 1868. Composer in large and small forms.

Bargiel, Woldemar (*Bahr*-geel.) Berlin, 1828–1897. Composer in large and small forms.

Barnby, Sir Joseph. York, England, 1838 — London, 1896. Organist, conductor, and composer of much sacred music, hymns, etc.

Bauer, Harold (*Bow*-er.) Pianist. London, 1873.

Beethoven, Ludwig van (*Bay*-toh-**ven**, not Bay-*toh*-ven, and *van* not *von*.) Bonn, 1770 — Vienna, 1827. Nine great symphonies, thirty-eight sonatas for the piano, ten for violin and piano, five piano concertos, one violin concerto, eleven overtures, sixteen string quartets, one opera — "Fidelio" — a great contrapuntal Mass, an oratorio, etc. The composer who best combined intellectual and emotional qualities in his music.

Behr, Franz (Bare.) Germany, 1837. Light piano pieces.

Bellini, Vincenzo (Bell-*leen*-ee.) Catania, Sicily, 1802 — Paris, 1835. Operatic composer. "La Somnambula," "Norma," "Puritani."

Bendel, Franz (*Bend*-dl.) Bohemia, 1833 — Berlin, 1874. Pianist and composer of salon-pieces.

Beriot, Charles Augustus de (De *Bair*-yoh.) Louvain, 1802 — Brussels, 1870. Violinist and violin composer.

Berlioz, Hector (*Bair*-lee-ohs, not Bairlee-oh.) Near Grenoble, France, 1803 — Paris, 1869. The earliest of the great orchestral colorists. Wrote the largest orchestral works in "Program-music" style. (See *Programme-music*.) "Symphonie Fantastique," "Childe Harold Symphony," "Romeo and Juliet Symphony," "Carnaval Romaine Overture," etc. Four large operas and large choral works. Great Requiem, "Damnation de Faust," "Les Troyens," etc.

Best, Wm. T. Carlisle, 1826 — Liverpool, 1897. Organist and composer. Important organ studies.

Bishop, Sir Henry R. London, 1786–1855. Operas, ballads, songs, etc. "My Pretty Jane." Believed to have composed "Home, Sweet Home."

Bizet, Georges (Bee-zay.) Paris, 1838 — Bougival, 1875. Great French composer. "Carmen," "Suites Arlesiennes," etc.

Boccherini, Luigi (Bock-er-*ee*-nee.) Lucca, 1743 — Madrid, 1805. Violoncellist and composer in all forms.

Bohm, Carl (Bōm.) Berlin, 1844. Many piano pieces.

Boieldieu, Francois Adrien (Bwahl-dyay.) Rouen, 1775 — Jarcy, 1834. Operatic composer. "La Dame-Blanche," chief work. Overtures to "Jean de Paris" and "Caliph of Bagdad" often performed.

Boito, Arrigo (Boh-*ee*-toh.) Padua, 1842. Composer and poet. Opera, "Mefistofele." Librettos to Verdi's "Otello" and "Falstaff." Pseudonym is "Tobio Gorria," an anagram.

Bordogni, Giulio Marco (Bor-*dohn*-yee.) Bergamo, 1788 — Paris, 1856. Tenor and vocal teacher. Many exercises for voice.

Borodin, Alexander P. (Bor-oh-*deen*.)

St. Petersburg, 1834 — 1887. Symphonies, opera, and other large forms.

Bortnianski, Dimitri (Bort-*niahn*-schki.) Russia, 1752 — 1825. The Russian Palestrina. Some great sacred music. Chiefly for the Greek Church service.

Brahms, Johannes (German "a" is sounded.) Hamburg, 1833 — Vienna, 1897.) Four great symphonies. German Requiem, powerful choral work. Violin concerto; sonatas, chamber-music, etc. The greatest recent classicist.

Brassin, Louis (*Brass*-sang.) Aix-la-Chapelle, 1840 — St. Petersburg, 1884. Pianist and composer.

Breitkopf & Härtel (*Bright*-kopf and *Hair*-tl.) Leipzig music-publishers, founded in 1719.

Bruch, Max (Broochh.) Cologne, 1838. Choral works, cantatas, etc. "Frithjof," "Fair Ellen," "Arminius," "Odysseus," etc. Violin concerto in G minor, and two others of less rank.

Bruckner, Anton (*Brook*-ner) Ausfelden, Austria, 1824 — Vienna, 1896. Composed in large forms. Nine symphonies. Very free in form. Enthusiastic Wagnerite, and endeavored to adapt his theories to symphonic forms.

Brüll, Ignaz (Brill.) Moravia. 1846 – Vienna, 1907. Operas. "Golden Cross."

Bruneau, Alfred (Brü-*noh*, acute French "u.") Paris, 1857. Operas. "L'Attaque du Moulin."

Bull, Ole (Bool, O-leh.) Norway, 1810–1880. Violinist and composer.

Buonamici, Giuseppe (Boo-oh-nah-*mee*-chee.) Florence, 1846. Pianist and conductor. Piano etudes, etc.

Bülow, Hans Guido von (*Bee*-loh, fon, the French "u" sound in first syllable.) Dresden, 1830 — Cairo, 1894. Pianist, conductor, and editor of many musical classics.

Bungert, August (*Bŏong*-gert.) Mühlheim, 1846. Great German operas in modern school.

Busoni, Feruccio (Boo-*zohn*-ee.) Near Florence, 1866. Pianist and composer in extreme modern instrumental school. Has edited Bach's piano works.

Calve, Emma (*Kahl*-veh.) Madrid, 1864. Celebrated operatic singer and actress.

CARREÑO, TERESA — DE RESZKÉ, JEAN

Carreño, Teresa (Cahr-*rain*-yo.) Venezuela, 1853. Pianist.

Chabrier, Alexis E. (*Shah*-bree-ay.) Puy-de-Dome, 1841 — Paris, 1894. French composer, operas, etc.

Chaminade, Cécile (Sha-mee-*nahd*.) Paris, 1861. Graceful songs, piano-pieces, etc.

Charpentier, Gustave (Shar-pahn-tiay.) Lorraine, 1860. Opera "Louise," Cantata, "Vie du Poete," etc. One of the leading French composers of his day.

Chausson, Ernest (*Shoh*-song.) France, 1855–1899. Orchestral works. Symphonic poem "Viviane;" opera "Le Roi Arthus," etc.

Cherubini, Luigi (Keh-roo-*bee*-nee.) Florence, 1760 — Paris, 1842. Pure classicist. Opera "Deux Journées" ("The Water-carrier"). Two great Requiems. Many compositions in a noble contrapuntal school.

Chopin, Frédéric (*Sho*-pang, last syllable nasal.) Poland, 1810 — Paris, 1849. Some doubts about date of birth. The poet of the piano. Reputation rests wholly upon piano compositions.

Clementi, Muzio (Kleh-*men*-tee.) Rome, 1752 — England, 1832. Piano-pedagogue. Piano studies, "Gradus ad Parnassum." One of the most important of early technical works.

Coleridge-Taylor, Samuel. London, 1875. The first eminent musical composer of African descent. Writer in large and small forms. Symphony, chamber-music, cantatas, etc. "Hiawatha," a large cantata, chief work.

Concone, G. (Kon-*kohn*-eh.) Turin, 1810–1861. Vocal-teacher. Wrote some very popular *vocalises*.

Corelli, Arcangelo (Koh-*rel*-lee.) Fusignano, Italy, 1653 — Rome, 1713. Great violinist and composer. Helped the "sonata-allegro" (see *Sonata*) greatly.

Cornelius, Peter (Kor-*nay*-lee-oos.) Mayence, 1824–1874. Follower of the Wagnerian school. Chief opera, "The Barber of Bagdad."

Couperin, François (*Koop*-e-rang, last syllable nasal.) Paris, 1668–1733. One of the greatest of the old harpsichord and spinet composers.

Cowen, Frederic H. Kingston, Jamaica, 1852. Excellent composer in all forms. "Scandinavian Symphony" best work.

Cramer, Johann Baptist (*Krah*-mer.) Mannheim, 1771 — London, 1858. One of the eminent piano-pedagogues. Important studies for the instrument.

Cristofori, Bart (Kris-to-*foh*-ree.) Padua, 1653 — Florence, 1731. Inventor of the pianoforte, 1709–11.

Cui, César A. (Quee.) Vilna, Russia, 1835. One of the prominent composers of the new Russian school. Operas, symphonies, etc.

Curwen, Rev. John. Yorkshire, 1816. — Manchester, 1880. Chief founder of tonic sol-fa system (which see).

Czerny, Carl (*Tschair*-nee.) Vienna, 1791–1857. One of the important workers in piano-technique. Numerous studies of all grades of difficulty.

D'Albert, Eugen (*Dahl*-bair.) Glasgow, 1864. Pianist and composer. Several operas.

Dancla, Charles (*Dahnk*-lah.) Bagnères-de-Bigorre, France, 1818—Tunis, 1907. Violinist and composer. Many violin works and studies.

Dargomyzsky, Alexander S. (Dahr-goh-*misch*-kee.) Russia, 1813–1869. Many operas.

David, Ferdinand (*Dah*-veed.) Hamburg, 1810—Switzerland, 1873. Violinist and composer.

David, Félicien C. Cadenet, 1810 — St. Germain, 1876. Composed in all forms. Great success in France and elsewhere. Ode-symphonie, "Le Desert."

Debussy, Achille Claude (Deh-*büs*-see.) St. Germain-en-Laye, 1862. Very characteristic French composer; one of the prominent figures of his time. Orchestral, vocal, and piano works. "L'Apres-midi d'un Faune," for orchestra. Very delicate sketches for piano.

Delibes, Léo (Deh-*leeb*.) St. Germain-du-Val, 1836 — Paris, 1891. Composer of operas and ballets of much delicacy and grace. Opera, "Lakme"; Ballet, "Coppelia."

De Reszké, Jean (Deh *Resch*-keh.) Warsaw, 1852. Prominent tenor

Dohnanyi, Ernest von (Doh-*nan*-yee). Pressburg, Hungary, 1877. Pianist and composer.

Donizetti, Gaetano (Doh-nee-*tset*-tee.) Bergamo, 1797–1848. Operatic composer. "Lucia di Lammermoor," "Fille du Regiment," "Linda," "Don Pasquale," "La Favorita," "Lucrezia Borgie," and many others.

Dubois, Théodore (Dü-*bwah*.) Rosnay, 1837. Operas, oratorios, etc. Chief oratorio, "Paradise Lost."

Dussek, Johann L. (*Doo*-scheck.) Bohemia, 1761 — St. Germain-en-Laye, 1812. Composer in all fields. Piano sonatas still important.

Dvořák, Antonin (*Dvor*-zhak.) Mühlhausen, Bohemia, 1841 — Prague, May 1, 1904. Composer in all fields of music. Bohemian operas; "Stabat Mater," "Spectres Bride," "St. Ludmilla." Requiem Mass, five symphonies including "From the New World," chamber-music, piano works, songs, etc.

Elgar, Sir Edward. Broadheath, Worcester, England, June 2d, 1857. Most prominent English composer. Oratorio, "Dream of Gerontius," "The Apostles"; songs with orchestra, "Sea Pictures," etc.; orchestral variations, overtures, etc.

Faure, J. (Fohr.) France, 1830. Singer. Composer of "Palm Branches."

Fauré, Gabriel (Fohr-*ay*.) (Often confounded with the above.) Pamiers, France, 1845. Prominent composer in all forms, from symphonies to songs.

Field, John. Dublin, 1782 — Moscow 1837. Piano composer. First writer of nocturnes.

Fielitz, Alex. von (*Feel*-its.) Leipsic, 1860. Excellent vocal composer. Vocal cycle "Eliland."

Flotow, Frederick von (*Floh*-toh.) Mecklenburg, 1812 — Darmstadt, 1883. Operatic composer. "Martha."

Franchetti, A. (Frahn-*ket*-tee.) Turin, 1850. Important Italian composer, chiefly operatic.

Franck, César Auguste (Frahnk.) Liége, 1822 — Paris, 1890. Most important composer and teacher. Founder of the most modern French school of choral and orchestral work. "Beatitudes," orchestral and chorus. "Chasseur Maudit," orchestra, a noble symphony, etc.

Franz, Robert (Frahnts.) Family name Knauth, changed by royal permission. Halle, 1815–1892. One of the greatest of "Lied" composers. His songs equal those of Schumann and Schubert.

Gabrilowitch, Ossip (Ga-bril-*oh*-vitsch. not Ga-*bril*-oh-vitsch.) St. Petersburg, 1878. Pianist.

Gade, Niels Wilhelm (*Gah*-deh.) Copenhagen, 1817–1890. Composer. His cantatas are most performed of his works.

Gadski, Johanna(*Gahd*-skee.) Anclam, Prussia, 1871. Celebrated soprano. Dramatic school.

Garcia (*Gar*-thee-a.) Noted family of singing-teachers and singers, of whom Manuel (Madrid, 1805—London, 1906) invented the laryngoscope.

Genée, Franz F. R. (Zhe-*nay*.) Dantzig, 1823 — Vienna, 1895. Comic operas.

Gerardy, Jean (Zhe-*rar*-dy.) Luttich, 1878. Violoncellist.

German, J. Edward, Shropshire, England, 1862. Composer in large forms. Symphonies, suites, etc.

Gericke, Wilhelm (*Geh*-rick-eh.) Graz, 1845. Orchestral-conductor.

Glazounow, Alexander (Glaz-oo-*noff*.) St. Petersburg, 1865. Important Russian composer in large orchestral forms. Symphonies and symphonic poems.

Glinka, Michail Ivanovitch (*Glin*-ka.) Novospaskoi, Russia, 1804 — Berlin, 1857. First great Russian composer in secular vein. First of new Russian, national school. Operas, etc. "Life for the Czar," "Russlan and Ludmilla."

Gluck, Christoph Willibald (Glook.) The name is sometimes misspelled Glück.) Weidenwang, 1714 — Vienna, 1787. Founder of true dramatic opera. "Orpheus."

Godard, Benjamin (Go-*dahr*.) Paris, 1849 — Cannes, 1895. Operas, orchestral works, chamber-music, charming songs, and piano pieces.

Goldmark, Karl (*Golt*-mark.) Hungary, 1830 (often misstated, 1832). Operatic and orchestral composer. "Queen of

Sheba," "Heimchen am Herd," "Rustic Wedding Symphony," etc.

Gounod, Charles (Goo-noh.) Paris, 1818–1893. Operatic and oratorio composer. "Faust," "Romeo and Juliet," "Mireille," "Redemption," "Mors et Vita," celebrated Mass, etc.

Grieg, Edvard Hagerup (Greeg) Bergen, 1843-1907. Greatest Norwegian composer in orchestral, piano, and vocal works. "Peer Gynt" suite; piano concerto; song-albums; piano sketches; violin sonatas; and chamber-music.

Guilmant, Alexandre (Geel-mang.) Boulogne, 1837. Great organist and composer for the instrument.

Handel, George Frideric (Handle.) Name properly spelled Händel, but custom sanctions the spelling given. Oratorios. "The Messiah" "Israel in Egypt," and "Judas Maccabaeus."

Haupt, K. August (Howpt.) Silesia, 1810—Berlin, 1891. Celebrated organist and teacher. Many prominent American organists and composers were his pupils.

Hauptmann, Moritz (*Howpt*-man.) Dresden, 1792—Leipsic, 1868. Theorist, composer and teacher. Many valuable instruction-books.

d'Hardelot, Guy (Ghee-*dard*-loh.) Real name Mrs. Rhodes. Born near Boulogne. Many popular and beautiful songs. Resided in London.

Haydn, Josef (*High*-dn.) Rohrau, 1732—Vienna, 1809. Composer in all the large forms. "The Creation," The English Symphonies, some charming string quartets, Austrian national hymn, piano (spinet) sonatas.

Heller, Stephen. Pesth, 1815—Paris, 1888. Piano studies.

Helmholtz, Hermann L. (*Helm*-holts.) Potsdam, 1821—Charlottenburg, 1894. Acoustician. Discoverer of the laws of the overtones. (See *Harmonics* and *Acoustics*.) Chief work, "The sensations of tone."

Henschel, Georg (*Hen*-shl.) Breslau, 1850. Composer, conductor, etc. Many songs, and a requiem.

Henselt, Adolf von (*Hen*-slt.) Bavaria, 1814—Silesia, 1889. Pianist and composer, a famous piano concerto, etudes, etc.

Holmés, Augusta Mary Ann (*Ol*-mes, but properly Augusta Holmes.) Paris, 1847–1903. Born of Irish parents. Composed in large forms. One of the chief woman composers.

Huber, Hans (*Hoo*-ber.) Switzerland, 1852. Excellent symphony inspired by Boecklin's paintings.

Hummel, Johann Nepomuk (*Hoom*-ml.) Pressburg, 1778—Weimer, 1837. Noble septet, fine sonatas, etc.

Humperdinck, Engelbert (*Hoom*-per-dink.) Near Bonn, 1854. Folk-song opera, "Hänsel and Gretel."

Indy, Vincent d' (*Dan*-dy, but with nasal touch on first syllable.) Paris, 1851. Greatest pupil of César Franck. Music not always pleasing, but very intellectual. Orchestral compositions and chamber-music the most important.

Jadassohn, Salomon (*Yah*-das-sohn.) Breslau, 1831—Leipsic, 1901. Best modern composer of canons. Nicknamed the *Musical Krupp*. Some fine chamber-music. Books on *harmony counterpoint, canon and fugue.*

Jankó, Paul von (*Yan*-koh.) Hungary, 1856. Inventor of a new keyboard for the piano. See *Janko Keyboard*.

Jensen, Adolf (*Yen*-sen.) Konigsberg, 1837—Baden-Baden, 1879. Excellent songs and some very expressive studies.

Joachim, Joseph (*Yoh*-a-chim.) Near Pressburg, 1831—Berlin, 1907. Was for a long time one of the greatest violinists. A violin-concerto (the "Hungarian") and other works.

Joseffy, Rafael (Yoh-*zeff*-fee.) Hungary, 1853. Famous pianist and teacher.

Karganov, Genari (Kahr-*gahn*-off.) Caucasus, 1852-1890. Pianist and composer.

Kirchner, Theodor (*Kirchh*-ner.) Saxony, 1824-1903. Organist, teacher, and composer.

Kjerulf, Halfdan (*Chhyair*-ulf.) Christiania, 1818-1868. Norwegian songs.

Klindworth, Carl (short *i* is sounded.) Hanover, 1830. Celebrated pianist and teacher. Has edited many classical works. His editions of Wagner, Chopin, etc., are celebrated.

Kneisel, Franz (*Knigh*-zl.) Roumania, 1865. Violinist. Founded a famous quartet.

Kocian, Jaroslav (*Kotsch-ee-an.*) Bohemia, 1884. Violinist.

Köhler, Louis (*Kay*-ler, the first syllable covered.) Brunswick, 1820 — Königsberg, 1886. Many pianoforte studies.

Kreutzer, Conradin (*Króytz*-er.) Baden, 1780 — Riga, 1849. Some excellent operas. "Das Nachtlager von Granada," his best work.

Kreutzer, Rodolphe. Versailles, 1766 — Geneva, 1831. Famous violinist. Beethoven dedicated the "Kreutzer Sonata" to him.

Kubelik, Johann (*Koo*-be-lick.) Near Prague, 1880. Violinist.

Kuhlau, Friedrich (*Koo*-lou, the last "ou" as in bough.) Hanover, 1786 — Copenhagen, 1832. Sonatinas.

Kullak, Theodor (*Kool*-lack.) Posen, 1818 — Berlin, 1882. Technical piano works. Octave studies.

Lachner (*Lachh*-ner.) A family of celebrated composers, brothers, of whom Franz Lachner is the greatest, and is chiefly remembered by his orchestral suites. But Ignaz and Vincenz Lachner have also left good compositions.

Lalo, Edouard (*Lah*-low.) Lille, 1823 — Paris, 1892. Violin concertos, and an opera, "Le Roi D'Ys." Also orchestral works, chamber-music and songs.

Lange, Gustav (*Lahng*-eh.) Schwerstedt, 1830 — Wernigerode, 1889. Popular piano compositions.

Lassen, Edward (*Lahs*-sn.) Copenhagen, 1830–1904. Songs.

Lebert and Stark (*Lay*-bert and Stahrk.) Editors of several educational editions of piano works.

Lecocq, Charles (Leh-*kok*.) Paris, 1832. Comic operas. "Fille de Mme. Angot," "Girofle-Girofla," etc.

Lehmann, Lilli (*Lay*-man.) Würzburg, 1848. Celebrated singer.

Lehmann, Liza (Mrs. Bedford.) London. Composer of many songs. A cycle "In a Persian Garden."

Leoncavallo Ruggiero (Lay-on-ka-*vahl*-loh.) Naples, 1858. Operas. "Pagliacci."

Leschetizky, Theodor (Lay-scheh-*titch*-ky.) Austria, 1830. Famous piano-teacher.

Liadow, Anatole (Lee-*ah*-doff.) St. Petersburg, 1855. Russian composer.

Lichner, Heinrich (*Lichh*-ner.) Silesia, 1829 — Breslau, 1898. Organist and composer. Popular works for piano.

Liszt, Franz (List.) Raiding, Hungary, 1811 — Bayreuth, 1886. For a long time the greatest pianist of the world. Great numbers of valuable piano works. Helped found the modern symphonic poem, for orchestra. Much national (Hungarian) music. Two powerful piano concertos, symphonies, sonatas, etc. A large number of compositions which are constantly performed. Exerted great influence on piano-playing by his teaching at Weimar and Rome.

Loeffler, Charles Martin Tornov (*Leff*-ler.) Mühlhausen, Alsatia, 1861. Violinist and composer of the most modern school.

Loeschhorn, Albert (*Lesh*-horn.) Berlin, 1819–1905. Piano teacher and composer. Many good studies.

Loewe, Karl (*Lay*-veh.) Near Halle, 1796 — Kiel, 1869. Large vocal forms. Superb ballads.

Lully, or Lulli, Jean Baptiste (*Lil*-lee, French "u" sound in first syllable.) Florence, 1633 — Paris, 1687. Ballets, songs, harpsichord works, etc.

Macfarren, Sir George Alexander, London, 1813–1887. Celebrated English composer. Wrote in all forms, oratorios, symphonies, overtures, etc.

Mackenzie, Sir Alexander Campbell, Edinburg, 1847. Composer and conductor. Operas, oratorios, concertos, etc.

Marchesi, Mathilde (Mahr-*kay*-zee.) Frankfort, 1826. Singing-teacher. Many useful vocalises.

Martucci, Giuseppe (Mahr-*tootch*-ee.) Capua, 1856–1909. Pianist, conductor, and composer in orchestral forms. Symphony, piano concerto, etc.

Mascagni, Pietro (Mahs-*kahn*-yee.) Leghorn, 1863. "Cavalleria Rusticana," his first and chief opera.

Massenet, Jules (*Mas*-seh-nay.) Montaud, 1842. Operas, "Manon," and others. Stage music, orchestral works and songs.

Melba, Nellie (properly Mitchell, "Melba" being stage-name taken from her birthplace.) Melbourne, 1865. Soprano-singer.

Mendelssohn, Felix (*Men*-del-sohn.) Hamburg, 1809 — Leipsic, 1847. Composer in all forms. Chief works, "Elijah," "St. Paul," "Hymn of Praise," "Scotch Symphony," overtures, "Midsummer Night's Dream," "Hebrides," octet, "Songs without Words," organ sonatas, etc.

Merkel, Gustav (*Mair*-kl.) Saxony, 1827 — Dresden, 1885. Organist and composer. Some popular organ and piano-music.

Meyerbeer, Giacomo (*My*-er-bair.) Berlin, 1791 — Paris, 1864. Operatic composer. "Huguenots," "Robert," "The Prophet," etc.

Meyer-Helmund, Erik (*My*-er-*hel*-moond.) St. Petersburg, 1861. Operas, and some very popular songs.

Milloecker, Karl (*Mill*-leck-er.) Vienna, 1842–1899. Many popular operas. "The Beggar Student."

Moscheles, Ignaz (*Mos*-shel-lez.) Prague, 1794 — Leipsic, 1870. Piano-teacher and composer of some good studies.

Moszkowski, Moritz (Mosh-*koff*-skee.) Breslau, 1854. Very graceful piano compositions.

Mottl, Felix. Near Vienna, 1856. Celebrated conductor. Wagnerian.

Mozart, Wolfgang A. (*Moh*-tsahrt.) Salzburg, 1756 — Vienna, 1791. Master of all musical forms. Symphonies, the G minor, and the Jupiter; Operas, "Don Giovanni," "Magic Flute," and "Marriage of Figaro"; Requiem Mass; piano sonatas, and string quartets, are among his best works.

Nicodé, Jean-Louis (*Nik*-o-day.) Near Posen, 1853. Pianist-conductor and composer in the large forms.

Nikisch, Arthur (*Neek*-ish.) Szent Mikloo, Hungary, 1855. Great orchestral conductor.

Offenbach, Jacques (*Of*-fen-bachh.) Cologne, 1819 — Paris, 1880. Comic operas. "Grande Duchesse," "Belle Helene," etc. One serious opera, "Les Contes d'Hoffman."

Pachmann, Valdimir de (*Pahch*-mahn.) Odessa, 1848. Noted pianist. Great Chopin interpreter.

Paderewski, Ignace Jan (Pah-der-*eff*-skee, not Pader-*oo*-ski, or Pader-*es*-ski.) Podolia, Poland, 1859. Eminent pianist and composer. Opera "Manru," and works for piano with orchestra and piano solos.

Paganini, Niccolò (Pah-gah-*nee*-nee.) Genoa, 1782 — Nice, 1840. The greatest virtuoso upon the violin. Many display works for that instrument.

Palestrina, Giovanni Pierluigi (Pah-les-*tree*-nah.) Palestrina, near Rome, about 1515 (uncertainty about date), — Rome, 1594. Greatest of the old Catholic Church composers. "Mass of Pope Marcellus," "Improperia," etc.

Parry, Sir Charles Hubert H. Bournemouth, 1848. Famous English composer in all forms. Also a musical author of merit.

Patti, Adelina (*Paht*-tee, not properly Pat-tee.) Madrid, 1843. Great coloratura singer.

Paur, Emil (Powr.) Czernowitz, 1855. Orchestral-conductor.

Pergolesi, Giovanni Baptiste (Pair-go-*lay*-zee.) Jesi, Italy, 1710 — near Naples, 1736. A great "Stabat Mater," and his opera, "La Serva Padrone," is a model of its kind. Comic opera.

Perosi, Don Lorenzo (Pay-*roh*-zee.) Tortona, Italy, 1872. Modern church-composer. Catholic music of all kinds.

Philipp, Isidor. Pesth, 1863. Teacher and composer. Chiefly piano works.

Pierné, Gabriel (*Pyair*-nay.) Metz, 1863. Pupil of César Franck, and prominent French composer in various forms.

Plançon, C. Pol (*Plahn*-song.) Celebrated French basso.

Planquette, Robert (Plahn-*kett*.) Paris, 1850–1903. Light operas. "The Bells of Corneville" ("Chimes of Normandy").

Ponchielli, Amilcare (Pohn-kee-*yell*-ee.) Cremona, 1834 — Milan, 1886. Operatic composer. Chief work, "La Gioconda."

Prout, Dr. Ebenezer. Northampton-shire, 1835—London, 1909. Prominent theorist, author and composer. Many valuable educational works.

Puccini, Giacomo (Poo-*tschee*-nee.) Lucca, 1858. Most prominent Italian operatic composer. "La Tosca," "La Bohême," "Madame Butterfly," etc.

Purcell, Henry. London, 1658-1695. The chief vocal composer of England. Many operas, cantatas, songs, etc.

Rachmaninoff, Sergei V. (Rachh-*mahn*-nee-noff.) Novgorod, 1873. One of the finest Russian composers. Best known by songs and piano works, but composed in the larger forms also.

Raff, Joachim (Rahf.) Lachen, Switzerland, 1822 — Frankfort, 1882. Composer. "Lenore" and "Im Walde" symphonies; "Cavatina" for piano; wrote in all forms of composition. Besides the above, his songs and piano pieces are much performed.

Rameau, Jean Philippe (Rah-moh.) Dijon, 1683 — Paris, 1764. French composer for harpsichord and spinet. Works still played. Wrote first method of harmony, 1722.

Reger, Max (*Ray*-gher.) Brand, Bavaria, 1873. Composer of aggressive temperament.

Reinecke, Carl (*Ry*-neck-eh.) Altona, 1824—Leipzig, 1910. Eminent composer, teacher, and conductor.

Reisenauer, Alfred (*Ry*-sen-au-er.) Königsberg, 1863-1907. Famous pianist.

Rheinberger, Joseph (*Rhine*-bair-ger.) Lichtenstein, 1837 — Munich, 1902. Composer in all forms. Taught many American composers.

Richter, Ernst Friedrich (*Richh*-ter.) Saxony, 1808 — Leipsic, 1879. Theorist and composer. "Method of Harmony," "Fugue," etc.

Richter, Hans. Raab, Hungary, 1843. Eminent orchestral conductor.

Riemann, Hugo (*Ree*-mann.) Near Sondershausen, 1849. Musical-writer and reviewer.

Rimsky-Korsakow, Nikolas A. (Rim-schkee-*kor*-sah-koff.) Novgorod, 1844— St. Petersburg, 1908. Great modern Russian composer. All musical forms. Best known in America by his brilliant orchestral works, symphonies, etc.

Rode, Pierre (Rohd.) Bordeaux, 1774 — Damazon, 1830. Violin method and solos.

Rosenthal, Moritz (*Roz*-en-tahl.) Lemberg, 1862. Pianist of great technique. Also wrote a piano method.

Rossini, Gioachino A. (Ros-*see*-nee.) Pesaro, 1792 — Ruelle, near Paris, 1868. Operatic composer. "Barbiere Di Seviglia" ("Barber of Seville"), "Semiramide," and "William Tell"; the last his best work. Very popular "Stabat Mater."

Rubinstein, Anton (*Roo*-bin-styne.) Wechwotynecz, 1830 — near St. Petersburg. 1894. Famous as pianist, conductor, and composer. All forms. Operas least successful. The "Ocean Symphony," piano concertos, sonatas, piano works, songs. Ballet-music, sacred operas, "Tower of Babel," etc.

Saint-Saëns, Camille (Sang-*sahng*, is as near as any English spelling can reproduce the name, which sounds like "Cinq Cents," a fact which led to many puns.) Paris, 1835. One of the leading French composers, although not of the "César Franck school." All musical forms. Eminent organist, and wrote some for that instrument. Orchestral works most prized. Chief operas, "Samson and Delilah," and "biblical opera"—"Le Deluge." Important symphonies and the most brilliant symphonic poems. "Danse Macabre," "Phæton," etc.

Sarasate, Pablo de (Sah-rah-*sah*-teh.) Pamplona, Spain, 1844—Biarritz, 1908. Celebrated violinist.

Scarlatti, Alessandro (Scahr-*laht*-tee.) Sicily, 1659 — Naples, 1725. Oratorio and opera composer.

Scarlatti, Domenico. Son of the above. Naples, 1683-1757. Great composer for harpsichord and spinet. Foreshadowed piano-technique. Invented cross-hand work. Charming old sonatas.

Scharwenka, Xaver (Schahr-*venk*-kah.) Samter, Posen, 1850. Composer and pianist. Piano concertos, opera, piano pieces. His brother Philipp is also a well-known composer.

Schubert, Franz P. (*Shoo*-bairt.) Lichtenthal, near Vienna, 1797 — Vienna, 1828. The most melodious of composers. Wrote in all forms. Greatest works are his songs, the C major symphony, the unfinished symphony, his quartets for strings, and his short piano works.

Schuett, Eduard. St. Petersburg, 1856. Composer chiefly of pianoforte music. Piano concerto, etc.

Schumann, Robert (*Shoo*-manh.) Zwickau, 1810 — Endenich, 1856. Most poetic and romantic composer. Chief works are "Manfred," and "Faust" (both cantatas). Songs of the noblest character, symphonies of which the first, in B flat, is the best, a piano quintet, the best of its class, most powerful piano pieces, such as "Carnaval-scenen," "Etudes Symphoniques," "Fantasie," and many others.

Schumann-Heink, Ernestine (*Shoo*-mahn-*highnk*.) Opera-singer, Lieben, near Prague, 1861.

Schytte, L. (Shee-tay.) Jutland, 1850. Many excellent piano works.

Scriabine, Alex. (Scree-*ah*-been.) Moscow, 1872. Chief success in piano works. Also piano studies.

Seidl, Anton (*Sigh*-dl.) Pesth, 1850 — New York, 1898. Great Wagnerian conductor.

Sembrich, Marcella (*Sem*-brichh.) Real name Praxede Kochanska. Galicia, 1858. Opera-singer and thorough musician.

Servais, Adrian F. (Sair-*vay*.) Brussels, 1807-1866. Great violoncellist. Three 'cello concertos. His son, Joseph, was also an eminent performer on the same instrument.

Sevčik, Pan. (*Save*-chick.) Bohemia, 1852. Celebrated Bohemian violin-teacher. Taught Kubelik, Kocian, etc.

Sgambati, Giovanni (Sgahm-*bah*-tee.) Rome, 1843. The chief Italian instrumental composer. Symphonies, chamber-music, piano concerto, etc.

Sibelius, Jean (See-*bay*-lee-oos.) Finland, 1865. Important northern composer. All forms. Symphony and remarkable orchestral works in the most modern vein.

Sinding, Christian (*Sind*-ing.) Norway, 1856. Orchestral composer. Symphonies, chamber-music, etc., in modern vein. Also some songs in true Norwegian moods.

Sitt, Hans. Prague, 1850, violinist and composer of many works for violin and violoncello.

Sjögren, Emil (*Schay*-gren.) Stockholm, 1853. Organist and composer in the classical forms; sonatas, some exquisite piano works in the smaller forms.

Smetana, Friedrich (*Smeh*-tah-na, not Sme-*ta*-na.) Bohemia, 1824-1884. Pioneer of modern Bohemian music. Fine opera, "The Bartered Bride," great symphonic poems on national subjects. Taught Dvořák.

Spindler, Fritz. Wurzbach, 1817-1905. Composed symphonies, concertos, and other large works, but is best known by his popular piano pieces.

Spohr, Louis. Brunswick, 1784 — Cassel, 1859. Composer in all forms. His violin and chamber-music is still much performed.

Stainer, Sir John (*Stay*-ner.) London, 1840 — Verona, 1901. Excellent English contrapuntist. Much Episcopal Church music, and a dictionary of musical terms.

Stanford, Sir Charles Villiers. Dublin, 1852. Most classical of Irish composers. Has composed in all forms. Opera, "The Canterbury Pilgrims," "Shamus O'Brien"; an "Irish Symphony"; some exquisite Irish folk-songs. His music is national in character, but highly developed.

Stcherbatcheff Nicolai de (Stchair-baht-*cheff*.) Russia, 1853. Prominent composer of the new Russian school. Orchestral and other works. His piano works are remarkably effective.

Strauss (Strouss.) A family of waltz composers in Vienna. The senior, Johann Strauss, was born in Vienna in 1804. Since then, Johann, Jr., Joseph, and Edward Strauss have written waltzes for Vienna.

Strauss, Richard. Munich, June 11, 1864. The chief orchestral composer of the present. Very radical and modern. First works are in the classical vein; a symphony, chamber-music, etc. His more advanced works are "In Italy" symphonic poem (transitional 1886), "Macbeth" (1887), "Don Juan" (1888), "Death and Transfiguration" (1889). After these came "Don

Quixote," "Till Eulenspiegel," "Heldenleben" ("Hero's Life") and "Sinfonia Domestica." All works of the utmost importance. Three operas are less significant than these great symphonic poems. The songs of Strauss are much more melodic and comprehensible than his vast orchestral utterances, although these too, have very highly developed accompaniments.

Sullivan, Sir Arthur. London, 1842–1900. Composed in almost all forms, but his chief successes were in light opera, which he (with his excellent librettist, W. S. Gilbert) placed in a newer and purer path. Long list of successes with "Trial by Jury," "Pinafore," "Patience," "Pirates of Penzance," "Mikado," etc.

Suppe, Franz von (*Soop*-peh.) Dalmatia, 1820 — Vienna, 1895. Light opera composer of much merit. "Fatinitza," "Poet and Peasant." Has composed in more ambitious forms also.

Svendsen, Johann (*Svent*-zen.) Christiania, 1840. Norwegian composer in large forms. Many orchestral successes.

Tartini, Giuseppe (tahr-*tee*-nee.) Pirano, 1692 — Padua, 1770. Eminent violinist. Many violin sonatas. The sonata called "The Devil's Trill," is his best known work.

Taneieff, Sergei (Tan-*yay*-eff.) Russia, 1856. All forms. A trilogy opera— "Oresteia"—with striking overture. A symphony, etc.

Tausig, Carl (*Tow*-sig.) Warsaw, 1841 — Leipsic, 1871. Very great pianist. Some useful etudes.

Tchaikovsky, Peter I. (Tchigh-*koff*-skee, with long "i" sound on first syllable.) Wotinsk, 1840 — St. Petersburg, 1893. One of the greatest of all the modern Russians. Has composed in all forms. His six symphonies are all of importance, the last, the "Pathétique," being his greatest success. Beautiful chamber-music, and many strong overtures. "Romeo and Juliet" overture the best of these.

Ternina, Milka (Turn-*nee*-nah.) Croatia, 1864. Noted dramatic soprano.

Thalberg, Sigismund (*Tahl*-bairg.) Geneva, 1812 — Naples 1871. Pianist.

Piano method "L'Art du Chant appliqué au Piano."

Thomas, Ambroise (*Toh*-mas.) Metz, 1811 — Paris, 1896. Operatic composer. "Mignon," "Hamlet."

Thomas, Theodore, Esens, E. Friesland, 1835 — Chicago, 1905. A most eminent conductor whose labors had an enormous influence on the development of American musical taste.

Thomson, César. Liege, 1857. Notable violin virtuoso.

Tinel, Edgar (Tee-*nel*.) Sinay, Belgium, 1854. Large sacred works. Great oratorio, "Franciscus."

Vaccai, Niccolò (Vack-*kah*-ee.) Tolentino, 1790 — Pesaro, 1848. Vocal teacher. Composed a well-known vocal method.

Verdi, Giuseppe (*Vair*-dee.) Le Roncole, 1813 — Milan, 1901. Great operatic composer. Many successes. "Trovatore," "Ernani," "Rigoletto," "La Traviata," "Ballo in Maschera," "Aïda," "Otello," and "Falstaff." Possibly "Aïda" may be considered as great as any of his works. Composed a very dramatic requiem. His instrumental works are inferior.

Vieuxtemps, Henri (*Vyay*-tangh.) Verviers, 1820 — Algiers, 1881. Belgian violinist. Many violin works and concertos.

Volkmann, Robert (*Folk*-mahn.) Saxony, 1815 — Pesth, 1883. Composer in all forms. Two fine symphonies and an excellent overture to "Richard III."

Viotti, Giovanni Baptiste (vee-*ot*-tee.) Vercelli, Italy, 1753 — London, 1824. Violin works and several violin concertos.

Wagner, Richard (*Vahg*-ner.) Leipsic, 1813 — Venice, 1883. The most important composer of the 1800s. Almost entirely operatic. Founder of the modern "Music-Drama." "Rienzi" does not belong to his reforms, but his new path begins with "Tannhäuser." After this, one can mention "Flying Dutchman," "Lohengrin," "Tristan and Isolde" (first opera in which all his new theories were represented), "Mastersingers of Nuremberg," the trilogy, consisting of "Rheingold," "Die Walküre," "Siegfried" and "Götterdämmerung," and finally, "Parsifal."

Wallace, Wm. Vincent. Waterford, Ireland, 1814 — Haute Garonne, 1865. Popular opera, "Maritana."

Weber, Carl Maria von (*Vay*-ber.), Eutin, 1786 — London, 1826. Wrote in many musical forms (no symphonies). Chief successes, "Der Freischütz," which opera is still performed; overtures to this and to "Oberon" and "Euryanthe"; "Invitation to the Dance," for piano; concert-stück for piano and orchestra; great sonatas in brilliant style, and a jubilee overture ending with "God Save the King."

Weingartner, Felix (*Vine*-gahrt-ner.) Dalmatia, 1863. Conductor and composer. Large forms. Symphony, opera, chamber-music, etc.

Widor, Charles Marie (*Vee*-dor.) Lyons 1845. Composer and organist. Has tried many large forms with success, but his chief claim to fame will be found in his organ sonatas, and other large compositions for this instrument.

Wieniawski, Henri (Veen-ni-*off*-ski.) Poland, 1835 — Moscow, 1880. Violinist and composer for that instrument.

Wolf, Hugo (Vohlf.) Vienna, 1860–1902. A modern genius who was only recognized after his death. Much of his music is bizarre, but his songs show him at his clearest and best. Successful comic opera, "Der Corregidor."

Wood, Henry J. London, 1869. Celebrated English conductor and composer. Many large vocal works.

Ysaye, Eugène (Ee-*zigh* the last syllable to rhyme with "sigh.") Liege, 1858. Prominent violinist.

Zichy, Count Geza (*Tschi*-shee.) Hungary, 1849. Noted one-armed pianist. Lost right arm in youth. Has composed some remarkable piano pieces and etudes for the left hand alone.

(Note. In the above pronunciation *chh* stands for the gutteral "**ch**" of Germany, and *igh* for the long sound of "i," as in "sigh.")

A SHORT VOCABULARY OF ENGLISH MUSICAL TERMS OF TEMPO OR EXPRESSION, WITH THEIR ITALIAN EQUIVALENTS

(In this table it has been deemed best to give Italian equivalents only. Although Schumann and Wagner use German terms in their works, and Berlioz and the César Franck school, French, Italian is the preferable tongue for musical terms, for the following reasons: 1st. It has priority. It was the first language used in this field, and has been in almost universal use for three centuries. 2d. It is impossible to allow each composer the use of his native language. If Liszt had used Hungarian, Tchaikowsky Russian, Dvořák Bohemian, Grieg Norwegian, etc., we should find many more difficulties in the matter than in the use of a single language. 3d Musical notation is a single, universal, written language. Such a language requires an equally universal set of tempo or expression-marks. Exactly as in affairs of state, diplomats have chosen the English language as the universal tongue, music has chosen Italian as her language of tempo and expression-marks; and we urge upon every composer to further this unity by discarding English, French, or German markings, and using Italian only.)

A

Abandonment. Abbandonamento.
Abrupt. Subito.
Accompaniment. Accompagnamento.
Affectionately. Affettuoso.
Afflicted. Con afflizione.
Against. Contro.
Agility. Agilita.
Agitated. Agitato.
Agreeable. Piacevole.
Air. Aria. Canto. Melodia.
All together. Tutti.
Almost. Quasi.
Always. Sempre.
And. E, before a consonant, Ed, before a vowel.
Anguished. Angosciamente.
Animated. Animato.
Artless. Semplice.
As. Come.

B

Begin. Attacca. Cominciare.
Bell. Campana. A Little Bell. Campanella.

Below. Sotto.
Boat-Song. Barcarolla; Gondoliera.
Boldly. Coraggioso; con abbandono, con bravura; intrepido.
Bound. Legato.
Bow. Arco (of a violin).
Breath. Fiato; respiro.
Bridge (of violin, etc.) Ponticello.
Brilliant. Brillante.
Broader Growing. Allargando.
Broadly. Largamente.
But. Ma.
By. Da; per.
By Degrees. Poco a poco.

C

Calm. Calmato; tranquillo; placido.
Canon. Canone.
Caprice. Capriccio.
Carried Over. Portamento.
Chorus. Coro.
Clear. Chiaro; distinto.
Coaxingly. Lusingando.
Coquettishly. Con civetteria.
Continually. Sempre.

Counterpoint. Contrappunto.
Crash. Fracasso; strepito.
Cradle-Song. Ninnarella.

D

Dance. Danza; ballo.
Dark. Oscuro.
Decisively. Deciso.
Declamatory. Declamando; parlando.
Decreasing in Force. Decrescendo; diminuendo; perdendosi.
Decreasing in Speed. Rallentando; ritardando; slentando.
Decreasing in Both the Above. Calando; morendo.
Delicately. Con Delicatezza.
Delight. Con diletto; con gioja.
Deliriously. Con Delirio.
Despairingly. Disperatamente.
Diminish. Diminuendo.
Distant. Lontano.
Distant (growing.) Allontandosi.
Distracted. Smaniosamente.
Disturbed. Inquieto.
Divided. Divisi.
Doleful. Dolente. Con Dolore.
Doubtingly. Dubbiosamente.
Dragging. Strascinamento; trascinando.
Dreaming. Sognante.
Drinking-Song. Brindisi.
Dying Away. Morendo.

E

Easier. Facilita.
Easy. Facile; commodo.
Echoing. Echeggiando.
Embellishments. Fioriture, coloratura.
Emphatic. Marcato sforzando; enfatico.
End. Fine.
Energetic. Energico; con energia; risoluto.
Entreating. Supplichevole.
Exalted. Con esaltamento; elevato.
Exact Time. Tempo Giusto. The opposite of this, irregular time, is *Tempo Rubato*.
Expiring. Morendo; espirando.

Expression. Espressivo; con Espressione.
Extravagantly. Stravagantemente.
Extremely. Molto. All words ending in *-issimo*.

F

Fancy. Fantasia.
Fast. Allegro; vivace; presto. **Very Fast.** Presto; prestissimo; velocissimo; vivacissimo. **Rather Fast.** Allegretto; allegro moderato; allegro giusto. **Not too Fast.** Non troppo allegro; non tanto allegro. **Twice as Fast.** Doppio movimento. There are many words which qualify an allegro, as *Vivace, con brio*, etc.
Faster. Più mosso; accelerando; stringendo.
Fearful. Timidamente.
Feebly. Debole.
Feeling. Espressione.
Festive. Festivo.
Fervently. Con fervore.
Fiery. Con fuoco; fuocoso; ardente; con calore.
Fierce. Feroce, furioso.
First Part. Primo.
Fluency. Volubilita.
Flying. Volante.
Following. Seguente; segue. **Go on to the Following.** Attacca il seguente.
Fondly. Teneramente.
For. Per.
Forcibly. Con forza. **As Forcibly as Possible.** Con tutta forza.
Forced. Sforzando; forzando; sforzato.
Free (in time.) Tempo Rubato.
From. Da; dal. **From the Beginning.** Da Capo. **From the Sign.** Dal segno.
Fugue. Fuga.
Furiously. Con rabbia; furioso; con furia.

G

Gay. Giojoso; gaiamente.
Gentle. Piacevole.
Gliding. Glissando; portamente
Gloomily. Tristamente.
Gondola-Song. Gondoliera.

Grace. Grazia; con Garbo.
Graceful. Grazioso.
Gradually. Poco a poco (little by little.)
Grand. Grandioso.
Grave. Grave.
Great. Nobile; grande.
Grieving. Affanosamente.
Gypsy Style. Alla zingara, or zingarese.

H
Half. Mezzo.
Hammered. Martellato.
Hastening. Accelerando; affrettando; stringendo.
Hand. Mano.
Heavily. Pesante.
Heroic. Eroico; *fem*, eroica.
Hold. Fermata.
Humorously. Con umore.
Hunting Piece. Alla caccia.
Hurried. See *Hastening*.

I
If. Se.
Impassioned. Appassionata.
Imperious. Imperioso.
Impetuously. Impetuoso.
Increasing Speed. Accellerando; affrettando; stringendo.
Increasing Loudness. Crescendo; rinforzando.
Innocently. Con Innocenza.
In the Same Manner. Simile.
Interlude (in a song.) Ritornella (also applied to prelude and postlude).
In the Same Time. L'Istesso tempo.
In Time. A tempo.
In the Preceding Time. Tempo Primo.
Irregular Time. Tempo rubato.

J
Jestingly. Scherzando.
Jocosely. Giocoso.
Joyously. Giojoso.

L
Lamenting. Lamentando; lamentoso; piangendo.
Languishing. Languente.

Languid. Languido.
Left Hand. Mano Sinistra.
Leisurely. Adagio.
Less. Meno.
Lightly. Leggiero. Con legerezza.
Little by Little. Poco a poco.
Lively. Vivace; vivo.
Lofty. Nobile; pomposo; elevato.
Longing. Con desiderio.
Loud. Forte.
Louder. Più forte.
Loud, Very. Fortissimo.
Loud, Continually. Sempre forte.
Loud as Possible. Con tutta forza forte possibile.
Lovingly. Amoroso; amabile.
Lullaby. Ninnerella (for an infant.)

M
Madrigal. Madrigale.
Majestic. Maestoso.
Major. Maggiore.
Marked. Marcato.
Martial. Marziale.
Master (in music.) Maestro.
Measured. Misurato.
March. Marcia.
Melancholy. Con malinconia.
Melody. La Melodia. Il Canto.
Menacingly. Minacciando.
Minor. Minore.
Moderately. Moderato.
More. Più.
Mournfully. Mesto; flebile; con dolore; dolente.
Movement. Movimento.
Movement, Twice The. Doppio movimento.
More Movement or Motion. Più mosso; più moto.
Movement, Less. Meno mosso.
Much. Molto.
Murmuring. Mormorando.
Muted. Con sordino.
Mysteriously. Misterioso.

N
Night-piece. Notturno.
Nobly. Nobile.

Noisily. Strepitoso. Con fracasso.
Not. Non.
Not so Fast. Meno mosso.
Not too Fast. Non troppo allegro.

O

Obligatory. Obbligato.
Of. Di.
One. Uno; una.
Or ; Otherwise. Ossia: oppure; ovvere; o; od.
Other. Altro.

P

Passionately. Con passione; appassionate; con calore.
Pastoral. Pastorale.
Pathetic. Patetico.
Pedal. Con Pedale. **Without pedal.** Senza Pedale. **With soft pedal.** Una corda. **Without soft pedal.** Tre corde.
Picked (on strings.) Pizzicato.
Piece. Pezzo.
Plaintively. Lamentando; dolente flebile; piangendo.
Playfully. Giocoso; scherzando.
Pleadingly. Supplichevole.
Pompously. Pomposo.
Ponderously. Pesante.
Possible, The Utmost. Possibile, as *presto possibile*, as rapidly as possible.
Prayer. Preghiera.
Precipitately. Precipitato.
Pressing (the tempo.) Stringendo.
Pronounced (accented.) Pronunziato
Proudly. Fiero.

Q

Quietly. Quieto; tranquillo.

R

Rapidly. Rapido; veloce; presto.
Rather. Quasi.
Recitative. Recitativo; (*accompanied.*) Recitativo Stromentato; (free.) Recitativo Secco; (measured.) Recitativo misurato.
Repeat. Repetition, Ripetizione; replica.

Reversing. Al Rovescio.
Right Hand. Mano Destra.
Rustic. Rustico; pastorale.

S

Sad. Tristo; flebile; mesto; malinconico.
Same. Stesso; l'istesso.
Score. Partitura.
Second. Secondo.
Sighing. Sospirando.
Simple. Semplice.
Singing. Cantando; cantabile.
Sliding. Sdrucciolando; glissando.
Slowly. Lento. See *Tempo-marks*.
Slower. Più lento; meno mosso; slentando.
Smoothly. Legato; piacevole.
Sobbing. Singhiozzando.
Softly. Piano.
Solemn. Solenne; con solennita.
Somewhat. Quasi.
Song. Canto; melodia; canzone. **A Little Song.** Canzonetta.
Song-like. Cantilena (an instrumental work in song-style.) Cantabile.
Sorrowful. Dolente; doloroso; flebile; con dolore.
Sparkling. Scintillante.
Spirited. Spiritoso; con spirito; con brio; brioso.
Still or Yet. Ancora; ancor.
Subject. Soggetto.
Suddenly. Subito.
Supplicating. Supplichevole.
Sustained. Sostenuto.
Sweetly. Dolce.
Swelling. Crescendo.
Swelling and Diminishing (the voice.) Missa di voce; messa di voce.
Symphony. Sinfonia.

T

Tearfully. Piangendo; lagrimoso.
Tenderly. Teneramente; con tenerezza.
Theme. Tema.
Then. Poi.
Threatening. Minacciando.

TIMIDLY   WITHOUT

Timidly. Timido.
To. A; ad.
Too Much. Troppo.
Tranquil. Tranquillo; placido
Translated. Tradotto.
Triumphal. Trionfale.
Troubled. Inquieto.
Turn Quickly. Volti suoito.
Two. Due.

U
Unaccompanied Voices. A cappella.
Under. Sotto.
Until, up to. Fino; sino.

V
Variations. Variazioni.
Velocity. Veloce.

Very. Assai; molto.
Very. All Italian words ending in *issimo* as *pianissimo*, very soft; *prestissimo*, very fast.
Voice. Voce.
Voice, Follow the. Colla voce; colla parte; col canto.

W
Warlike. Guerriero; marziale.
Warmly. Con calore.
Well. Ben; bene.
Whispered. Sotto voce; mezza voce.
With. Con; col; colle: colla.
Without. Senza.